P9-BZS-504

Lamppost Library & Resource Center
Christ United Methodist Church
4488 Poplar Avenue
Memphis, Tennessee 38117

This book just made my top ten list for congregations. It sets a new standard by which all church leaders will be measured.

Bill Easum
President, 21st Century Strategies, Inc.

Leonard Sweet gives hope in a world being shaken at its roots. Rather than running and hiding from it or yelling and raging against it, he shows us how to ride the wave of change to make the gospel relevant and powerful to a lost world. He challenges the church and its people to learn to breathe in a postmodern atmosphere—to stop grumbling about it and start living the life of Christ in it. *SoulTsunami* is refreshing and practical—not a "must read," but a "must do" to help us thrive in times of massive cultural and societal shifts. This book will make you uncomfortable, but it will also give you hope.

Dr. Jerry White
President, The Navigators

A mind awake! Sweet moves beyond prediction to creative intervention. Rather than cursing the darkness, he lights a candle in our pre-Christian culture. The "Hot" church is timeless and progressive. How? By worshiping Jesus. And by loving actual people in a "virtual" world. The Gospel is the most "real" reality, the truest truth, in the universe. Don't skip a page!

Kelly Monroe
Founder, Harvard Veritas Forum, and
chaplain for the Harvard-Radcliffe United Ministry

SoulTsunami is more than just another "trend" book that spoon-feeds Christian leaders so they can appear to be relevant and state-of-the-art. It has the same potential to transform the church as Joel Barker's *Paradigm Shift* changed the business world in the early '90s. *SoulTsunami* is the "Y2K" and "21-C" compliant manual for Christian leaders.

Frank Breeden, President
The Gospel Music Association

Like dust motes in sunlight, Leonard Sweet illumines the invisible obvious and asks us bluntly, "Do you see it?" and "What are you doing to do about it?" This is not a book to help the church *feel* good, but to *be* good—not a book to help folk *learn about* God, but to *experience* God.

Dan E. Solomon
Bishop, The United Methodist Church

This book will challenge every church to examine its past, take an honest look at its present, and change all its plans for the future—if it has any plans in the first place.

Louis Dorn, Editor, *Helps for Translators*
United Bible Societies

We live in a pluralistic age of sophistry. With a fine poetic pen, Leonard Sweet portrays the myriad confusions of our age and gives us some pointed insights into how the timeless gospel of Jesus Christ can speak to us anew.

Dr. Ted Baehr
Chairman, The Christian Film and Television Commission

It's been said that no church leader understands how to navigate the seas of the 21st century like Dr. Leonard Sweet. He's been called a modern-day prophet who "sees things the rest of us do not see, and dreams possibilities that are beyond most of our imagining." *Vital Ministry* magazine calls on Dr. Sweet twice each year to serve as a lookout from the crow's nest on the ship we call the church. His words are meant to warn us of potential disasters and to steer us toward bountiful ports of call. Listen here as he shouts down words of warning for the church, as well as for times when he calls, "All is well."

Vital Ministry magazine

soulTsunami

SINK OR SWIM IN NEW MILLENNIUM CULTURE

BOOKS BY LEONARD SWEET

11 Genetic Gateways to Spiritual Awakening
AquaChurch
Communication and Change in American Religious History
A Cup of Coffee at the SoulCafe
FaithQuakes
Health and Medicine in the Evangelical Tradition
The Jesus Prescription for a Healthy Life
Quantum Spirituality: A Postmodern Apologetic
SoulTsunami
Strong in the Broken Places: A Theological Reverie on
 the Ministry of George Everett Ross

Learn about these books at http://www.leonardsweet.com

LEONARD SWEET

10 Life Rings for You and Your Church

soulTsunami

SINK OR SWIM IN NEW MILLENNIUM CULTURE

"'SoulTsunami' shows us why these are the greatest days for evangelism since the first century." RICK WARREN

ZondervanPublishingHouse

Grand Rapids, Michigan

A Division of HarperCollinsPublishers

SoulTsunami
Copyright © 1999 by Leonard I. Sweet

See the Web site www.soultsunami.com

Requests for information should be addressed to:

 ZondervanPublishingHouse
Grand Rapids, Michigan 49530

Library of Congress Cataloging-in-Publication Data

Sweet, Leonard I.
    SoulTsunami : sink or swim in new millennium culture / Leonard Sweet.
       p.   cm.
    Includes bibliographical references.
    ISBN 0-310-22762-3 (hardcover : alk. paper)
      1. Christianity and culture—United States. 2. Twenty-first century—Forecasts.
  3. Christianity—Forecasting. 4. Church renewal. I. Title. II. Title: Soul tsunami.
  BR526.S943   1999
  261—dc21   98-32034
                                                                    CIP

This edition printed on acid-free paper and meets the American National Standards Institute
Z39.48 standard.

All Scripture quotations, unless otherwise indicated, are taken from the *New Revised
Standard Version Bible* Copyright © 1989 by the Division of Christian Education of the
National Council of the Churches of Christ in the United States of America. Used by
permission of Zondervan Publishing House.

All rights reserved. No part of this publication may be reproduced, stored in a retrieval
system, or transmitted in any form or by any means—electronic, mechanical, photocopy,
recording, or any other—except for brief quotations in printed reviews, without the prior
permission of the publisher.

Interior design by Sherri L. Hoffman

Printed in the United States of America

---

99 00 01 02 03 04 05 06 /❖ DC/ 10 9 8 7 6 5

269
SWE

To Elizabeth

My confederate in calling out an "educated third."

My life partner and companion in creating

mountain, sea, and desert "third places."

contents

acknowledgments

One of the greatest poets of the last century, Philip Larkin (1922–1985), wrote a poem on "Church Going"[1] in which he speaks of stepping inside a church and feeling

> a tense, musty, unignorable silence,
> brewed God knows how long.

He continues to go to church, but sees fewer and fewer like him who will endure the "brewed mustiness," which leads him

> wondering, too,
> When churches fall completely out of use
> What we shall turn them into, if we shall keep
> A few cathedrals chronically on show.

Larkin also confesses to speculating who

> Will be the last, the very last, to seek
> This place for what it was; one of the crew
> That tap and jot and know what rood-lofts were?

SoulTsunami was written to expunge the modern mustiness that has been "brewed God knows how long" in the church. More importantly, *SoulTsunami* was written to advocate the exciting new advantages for the body of Christ in postmodern culture.

Members of an online class at Drew and my first batch of "Dean's Fellows" (Steve Ayers, Bradley Bergfalk, John Calhoun, Rob Duncan, Scott McKay, John Newell, Bob Shettler, John Whitehurst, Patrick Wrisley, Ernie VanderKruik, with their team leader Dr. Younglae Kim) tutored me in seeing no such thing as a postmodern culture, only multiple postmodern cultures.

Author/biologist/environmental scientist Leonard Sweet Jr. (who used to be known as "Sweet's son," whereas now *I'm* increasingly known as "Sweet's father") continually instructs me in the art of being totally committed and completely unattached. His warnings about postmodernism as a conceptual bucket with a hole into which any number of definitions can be poured have been duly ignored by his father.

11

For two years I carted around a letter from John H. Brand of Austin, Texas. My stamina in seeing this project to its conclusion was partly his gift and that of Sally Morgenthaler, who believed in this book even when I lost confidence in it. My notes say "Thank Landrum Leavell III *big time*." I just did, big, big-time friend. You ensured this book's panoptic sweep more than you know. Steve Hudson, executive director of Mission USA for the Evangelical Free Church of America, first suggested a "killer app" section called "Now What?" that inspired a skeletal structure whereby this book is best read, not in one 448-page gout, but in snatches and snippets where you can give the ironies time to play and work themselves out. Carol Childress of Leadership Network rescued me from writing for those wearing a jersey that belongs to any camp. My colleague Professor Otto Maduro of Drew saved some stumbles in chapter 2.

Poet Ben Okri penned this tribute to Poet Laureate Ted Hughes after his death on 30 October 1998.[2]

You meet them once and it's electrifying,
Those Titans: they stand there outside
Their own time, strangers to us,
Like monoliths discovered in ancestral caves,
Charged with the scraggy godlike rawness
Of their great fame and hidden suffering.

As soon as I read these words, my words bowed in thanksgiving for two friends—both Presbyterians, both pastors of two of USAmerica's largest churches, both traditional, but both so immersed in God's mission in their cities that people wonder why they don't burn out. Frank Harrington (Atlanta) and John Buchanan (Chicago) don't burn out because they're fired up and so on fire for God that they keep lesser feet like mine to the fire.

Two critics almost derailed this book by their sharp queries. Joe Frye of Gatesville Texas, seared my soul after one of my lectures on "The Postmodern Reformation" when he casually mentioned his belief that "reformations" are human-induced and temporary, while "transformations" are God-made and eternal. Why shouldn't my theme have been "The Postmodern Transformation"? Timothy George, Dean of Beeson Divinity School at Samford University, provoked me in his office with the question "Who is willing to die for a postmodern paradigm?" Chicago Lutheran pastor Bruce Cole roused in me a response to that challenge sufficient enough to complete this study.

It is said that behind every successful author stands an amazed research assistant. Whatever this book's success, I want to thank an amazing cadre of RA's over the past four years (Kim Gray, Richard Lamborn, Sarita Marie Melkon, Elena Vishnevskaya, Tasha Whitton) who tracked my scent and trailed my tail on this safari through some rather strange sources. If Callimachus was right—"big book, big crime"—then Betty O'Brien belongs in the cell with me. Her bibliographic métier and moxie opened this book to lucky-dip pleasures and oxbow surprises without unloading lots of lumber. Because of my skilled and longsuffering editor at Zondervan, Jim Ruark, the reader can smile approvingly at the epigraph to Ovid's *Amores:*

I am the author's book. Much fatter
I was at first. He made me slighter.
Scant joy you may get from my chatter,
But think how your labours are lighter.

Donald Hoff, pastor of Riverside Church in Elmira, New York, had the original idea of sending out "Noah's Doves" to growing churches in the community with some standard questions to ask of the worship services they encountered. To get the full complement of material Dr. Hoff prepared for "the doves," contact him at donaldhoff@aol.com.

For 38 years Charles H. Parkhurst held forth at Madison Square Presbyterian Church in Manhattan (1880 to 1918). He devoted his life to bridging the gap, as he put it, "between the life of the church and the life of the times."[3] He devoted his every breath to making the church the public language of the Industrial Age. In my attempts to give the church a public language for postmodern culture, I have been blessed with a bar-none team at Drew. For their ideas in birthing the divine form in our new world and culture, I thank Heather Murray Elkins, Virginia Samuel Cetuk, Robert Duncan, Michael Christiansen, Kathi Brown, and John Kirk. Their leadership serves as a constant reminder that I am not saying things for the first time, nor am I saying them louder or with more passion than others.

For the past three years I am afraid I have harried more than hailed my chief administrative assistant Lyn Stuntebeck, who joins me among the heavily caffeinated postmodern believers. If greatness is not something you get as an award but something you earn as a reward, then great is her reward. The best spiritual fencer I have ever faced is Martha Talton of Naples, Florida. She can parry and thrust at my most vulnerable places. Her earned and learned wisdom keeps my spirit "right": The more I know God, the more I know a great deal and virtually nothing about who God is.

This book is not the product of a single mind. To every pastor who challenged me in a lecture, to every dinner companion who tested and taunted my ideas, to every cyberspace correspondent (phone, e-mail, chats) and MUD-flapper who reminded me that I had written more than I can chew, to every student who forced me to look a challenging fact in the eye, I thank you. I also leave you the task of doing the close reading and in-depth, close-focus analysis that this eagle-eyed book really requires.

SoulTsunami is no "get-out-of-jail-free" card from some future tidal wave or tornado. It is more of a "welcome-to-your-new-home" greeting card to the "educated third" invoked by my favorite postmodern writer, Michel Serres. A mariner/mathematician/poet/essayist/historian of sciences/Christian, French philosopher Michel Serres travels across disciplines like a sailor in search of new worlds (what he calls "third places") where an "educated third" can converge in a mélange (*mestizaje*) of historical, scientific, literary, cultural, genetic, and ecclesial endowments. As I write this "acknowledgment" on the tenth anniversary of my marriage to Elizabeth, I thank God for this utterly out-of-the-ordinary woman on whom I am more dependent than I have any right to be or anyone has a right to know. Her stake in my life and ministry is only partially conveyed by these words from Serres, which I invoke to dedicate this book to her:[4]

> I call [her] the Educated third; expert of cognizance, formal or experimental, versed in natural sciences of the living and nonliving. . . . She who prefers action to capitulation, direct human experience to interviews and dossiers, traveler of nature and society, lover of rivers, sand, wind, seas and mountains, walker of the entire earth, passionate for diverse gestures as for diverse landscapes, solitary sailor across the North-West Strait, latitudes where the positive mixed knowledge communicates in delicate and rare manner with humanities, she who is inversely versed in ancient languages, mythical traditions, and religions . . . hence, archaic and contemporary, traditional and futurist, humanist and wise . . . more distant from power than every possible legislator . . . capable of recognizing and understanding failures . . . and finally, and above all, burning with love for the earth and humanity.

Leonard Sweet
Madison, New Jersey

NOTES

1. Philip Larkin, *The Less Deceived and the Whitsun Weddings* (London: Marvell Press, 1977), 28–29.

2. Quoted in *TLS, Times Literary Supplement* (6 Nov 98): 20.

3. Charles H. Parkhurst, *My Forty Years in New York* (New York: Macmillan, 1923), 113.

4. Michel Serres, *The Natural Contract*, trans. Ciro A. Sandoval (Paris: Flammarion, 1992), 147–48.

Wake up, O sleeper, rise from the dead,
and Christ will shine on you.

Ephesians 5:13–14 NIV

Introduction
GET WITH IT

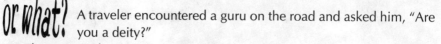

or what? A traveler encountered a guru on the road and asked him, "Are you a deity?"

The guru said no.

"Are you a saint?"

The guru said no.

"Are you a prophet?"

The guru said no.

Exasperated, the traveler asked, "Then what are you?"

The guru answered, "I'm awake."

This book is an early warning signal intended to wake us up and keep us awake.

Wake up and smell the future.

Wake up on the right side of history.

Wake up and breathe in the cold, arctic air of a moribund modernity.

Wake up and breathe out the fire of a postmodern future—with all its omens, amens, and amends.

Can the church tell a sleeping world what the best part of waking up is?

Can the church stop its puny, hack dreams of trying to "make a difference in the world" and start dreaming God-sized dreams of making the world different? Can the church help invent and prevent,

> **The best part of waking up is Folger's in your cup.**
>
> **Radio and TV commercial**

redeem and redream, this postmodern future? If the future ain't what it used to be, as the great philosopher Yogi Berra once said, can the church make the future what God wants it to be? Or will the church be more a surf rider of events than surf creator? Can the church reach postmodern culture in its quest for understanding the universe's unknowable beginnings and unforeseeable ends?

SoulTsunami is a successor book to *FaithQuakes*,[1] which tried to awaken a quake-illiterate culture and church. The book picked up on Pope John Paul II's missionary challenge to relate faith and culture: "I have considered the Church's dialogue with the cultures of our time to be a vital area, one in which the destiny of the world at the end of this twentieth century is at stake."[2] By the time my investigation was completed, *FaithQuakes* ended up being a survival guide for the seismic changes and storms that followed the Great Postmodern Earthquake—at least 9.0 on the cultural Richter scale.

> **The best way to make your dreams come true is to wake up.**
>
> **French poet/critic Paul Valery**

What I failed to appreciate in *FaithQuakes*, however, was just how seismically dangerous postmodern culture could be. Earthquakes, volcanoes, and asteroids sometimes kick up tsunamis—tidal waves. There have been 17 killer tsunamis since 1975. In fact, more people are killed and injured in tsunamis every year than in earthquakes. When a 9.2 quake hit Alaska on "Good Friday" in 1964, it released the power of 25,000 Hiroshima atomic bombs; tsunami waves more than 100 feet high killed people as far away as California.

TIDAL WAVES OF CHANGE ~ The seismic events that have happened in the aftermath of the postmodern earthquake have generated tidal waves that have created a whole new world out there. In your lifetime and mine, a tidal wave has hit. We are now in transition and in transit out of *terra firma* (if ever there were such a thing) and into *terra incognita*. A sea change of transitions and transformations is birthing a whole new world and a whole new set of ways of making our way in the world. We have moved from the solid ground of *terra firma* to the tossing seas of *terra aqua*.

> And Abraham . . . looked down toward Sodom and Gomorrah, and toward all the land of the Plain, and saw the smoke of the country going up like the smoke of a furnace.
>
> Genesis 19:27–28[3]

The Dick-and-Jane world of my '50s childhood is over, washed away by a tsunami of change. Some technologies function as deluges that sweep all before it; some technologies are most like winter storms that swell the rivers of change. Electronics is the former. It has created a sea change such as the world has never experienced before, including a huge shift in religious sensibility. While the world is rethinking its entire cultural formation, it is time to find new ways of being the church that are true to our postmodern context. It is time for a Postmodern Reformation.

I am not the first to use the metaphor of tidal wave. Back in the early '80s, Wilfred Cantwell Smith warned that the rising "current" of religious plurality would soon become a "flood" that would sweep away the church unless it could learn to swim in its thrashing waves. Smith's warning is even more timely now than the day he wrote it. More recently, in the distant past of December 1995, Bill Gates booted up his computer, logged on to the Internet he had bad-mouthed for so long, and for the first time realized its awesome implications for Microsoft. He announced in a repentant, panting, prophetic internal memo the coming "Internet tidal wave" as he launched the company into its chaotic waters. ("Embrace and Extend" is the company motto.)

> One of the best rules of making forecasts . . . is to remember that whatever is to happen is happening already.
>
> Economist Sylvia Porter

This book is based on the belief that a flood tide of a revolution is cutting its swath across our world and is gathering prodigious momentum. The term *postmodern* ("pomo" for short) is used to denote a 40-year transition from an Information Age to a Bionomic Age that will begin no later than 2020.[4] My generation (the Boomers) and our children (Gen-Xers and Net-Gens) are the transitional generations to this new world. The Net-Gens (those born after 1981) will be the first ones to really live the majority of their time in the new world. We Boomers will make it to the river, but we won't cross over. The crossover to a post-postmodern world will be made by the generations that follow ours.

SINK OR SWIM ~ There are three responses to a tidal wave. Each one has its defenders and manifestations in the church.

1. Denial. The first and by far most prevalent response to a tidal wave is denial, or the Not Noticing Syndrome.

> Denial ain't just a river in Egypt.
>
> Grateful Dead song

Ever wonder what is the most powerful force in the universe? Jesus taught what it should be: love. Albert Einstein conjured what it was: compound interest. Futurist Watts Wacker says what it is becoming: denial. Denial is the refusal to see the world from any other perspective than your limited one or the one in which you feel comfortable.

Denial comes in the form of a hissed "Biotechnology? Come on! There's nothing new here. What vanity to think otherwise when we've been doing biotechnology for thousands of years. How else did our ancestors make yogurt and cheese or ferment beer?"

Hello?! Biotechnology is no longer about yeast, but microbionics and DNA-based computers. It's a world of difference. Literally.

Or denial can go like this: "DNA-based computers? Come on! It'll never happen. Back in 1900 some predicted that by 2000 every person would have their own personal rockets, too!"

Hello?! We are now living in an anything-can-happen-and-probably-will world. The Nobel Prize-winner/Australian virologist Sir Frank Macfarlane Burnet wrote in 1971, "I should be willing to state in any company that the chance of doing this [gene therapy by virus] will remain infinitely small to the last syllable of recorded time." Twenty years later, Burnet's face is beet-red.[5]

Or denial can be expressed in the form of academic sniggerings: "'Postmodern?' Get serious! This is the biggest, softest conceptual marshmallow to appear in the mouth in years. Every generation claims that its pace of change is unprecedented. In fact, what historian can't introduce any century by saying 'This was an age of transition. Times were changing—they were changing from a past which was familiar to a future which was uncertain.'"

> There is a tendency to overestimate the impact of phenomena in the short run and underestimate it in the long run.
>
> Roy Amara of the Institute for the Future (IFTF)

Hello?! But it is really the case that more has changed in the past 50 years than in the past 500 years put together. It is really true that today we are sitting on a demolition site—the modern world—while a new world—the postmodern world—is being constructed all around us.

The only concession to a tidal wave by a culture in denial is to do what it has always done, except faster. So we microwave Minute Rice, or get faxes on our car phones, or buy the *59 Second Employee Book* to keep ahead of the *One Minute Manager*, or dish out double program offerings, or triple the same worship services.

> *"Status Quo"* is Latin for "the mess we're in."
>
> President Ronald Reagan

In spite of all the energy of denial, finally the tidal wave hits. Unprepared institutions in "persistent make-believe"[6] can tread water only so long before going under. We have a lot of drowning victims out there, churches a couple of funerals away from closing, because the denial response has taken them almost to the point of no return.[7] It is not easy to pull someone out of the water and bring her back to life. It is not easy to defibrillate a nearly comatose church. The amount of divine intervention required to bring back to life some of our churches ranks right up there with the parting of the Red Sea.

And we wonder: Where have all the pastors gone?

Unprepared leaders can tread water only so long before going under. One of the saddest commentaries on the church today is the number of veteran clergy who are opting for retirement at the earliest possible date. United Methodist clergy are aging and leaving the ministry faster than they are being replaced. The increase in women ministers hasn't reversed the trend. Our clergy ancestors clung to their saddles for as long as they could sit up and take nourishment. Today we clergy are halfway out the door, retiring posthaste, the spring having gone out of our step.[8] Despite our denial, we know deep inside we are not on top of our ministry; our ministry is on top of us. We are leading churches that have lost touch with the texts, texture, and tensions of our times.

2. Out of Here. The second response to a tidal wave is, "Yep, it's a tidal wave. It really is! I can smell the storm in the air. I can see the rain cloud coming. I can feel it in my bones. I'm out of here! Shields up!"

> Came in,
> Walked about,
> Didn't like it,
> Walked out.
>
> Suffolk tombstone[9]

This is the hunker-in-the-bunker response, the barricade-building, trench-digging, wall-bricking activity that comes from dreaming the past while demeaning the future. Much like Sir Thomas Beecham, who announced in a 1946 speech, "I have recently been all around the world and have formed a poor opinion of it," survivalists have "been around," seen the emergence of a new world out there, and want no part of it. The survivalist model of cultural encounter with the messy present (but not, note, the mythical past) is contamination.

Bunker mania is understandable. People want the world to hold still. The temptation to return to unmistakably premodern or modern ideals is strong. The way to do this is to disengage from society and live within the bounds of a recognizable reality. It is not just Christian survivalists in Montana who are pulling the shutters down on the outside world, insulating themselves, and refusing to move into the future. Much of the church has bought into a defensive, "survivalist" mentality based on confessional, apostolic, sectarian, or "let the church be the church" subculture stances.

Survivalism comes in a variety of both fundamentalisms and liberalisms, populisms and elitisms (especially the out-and-out theological elitists who believe that seekers must make the effort to understand, rather than the church make the effort to be understood). Political scientist Ashley Woodiwiss names the burgeoning genre of literature that promotes the church as a self-contained ("let-the-church-be-the-church") island immune to the culture and indifferent to the individual "ecclesiocentrism," which he defines as "the claim that the church, rightly understood, possesses the very resources for its own liberation." In the ecclesiocentric view, "the church is a total institution, possessing its own language, its own history, its own practices, its own way of eating, handling conflict, propagating, and, even, its own politics."[10]

> The world is full of people whose notion of a satisfactory future is, in fact, a return to an idealized past.
>
> Novelist/essayist
> Robertson Davies

An image I shall never forget is that of a farming family in the Dakotas during the summer flooding of 1997. They had so rallied the troops and summoned friends and relatives that their farmhouse was ringed to the roof by sandbags. As they worked around the clock to raise the height and thicken the leaking base of the sand fortress that was keeping back the waters, I watched their frenzy as cars, boats, and even other houses floated by while they saved their little island.

I don't know what ever happened to that Dakota family, for the waters were still rising when the cameras left them. But I do know that even if you manage to save yourself and what family members you can, you have lost your neighborhood, your city, your nation, and even your world. Furthermore, you spend all your time sandbagging and living in a trough. No matter how hard you try, or how many you enlist to hunker down with you, there is no way back to premodern bliss. There is no safe "bunker" where the church can "hunker."

In-*Not-Of-But-Not*-Out-Of-It *Either.* The truth of hunker-in-the-bunker survivalism is that we are called to live "in the world" without becoming "of the world" or removing ourselves "out of it" (John 17). Substitute the word "water" for "world" and "boat" for "church." The boat belongs "*in*" the water. If the boat takes on too much water, however, we become "*of*" the water and quickly sink. But the ship's airy abstractions can also raise her right up "*out of*" the water, the church is a hovercraft[11] haughtily perched above the realities in which we are to enact God's mission and with a respect for the realities of culture and history that is essentially Olympian.

One of the church's great roles is as the great dissenter of every age, the bearer of unwelcome truths, the rebuffer of the wisdoms of the world. Sentries must not abandon their posts to clamber aboard bandwagons. At times the church must be determined to go its own way; at times the church will be criticized for being foolish, wrong, out-of-date, and out-of-it. The church is a counterflow to the undertow.

Indeed, it is precisely to preserve dissidence as an essential quality of the Christian that the boat must move not against the tide, not with the tide, but ahead of the tide. If the church is to demythologize the culture's reigning myths instead of the culture always demythologizing the church; if the church is to say that the Emperor of Technism, the Emperor of Scientism, the Emperor of Miraculism has no clothes; if technologies are to be deflected so that they not degenerate into unspeakable evil—then the church must be prepared to anticipate change and get ahead of the culture, not always be in a reactive—whether catch-up or put-down—posture.

> The world is a severe Schoolmaster, for its frowns are less dang'rous than its smiles and flatteries, and it is a difficult task to keep in the path of Wisdom.
>
> Poet Phyllis Wheatley to philanthropist John Thornton, 30 October 1774[12]

The falsity of bunkering is that it makes Jesus into a Savior *from* the world, not the Savior *of* the world. Gated churches are designed to keep people in and reality out. Separation and engagement go together. The best way to defuse the principalities and powers of postmodern culture is not to escape from it, but to learn its language, master its media, and engage it on a higher level.

3. Hoist the Sails. The third response to a tidal wave is the focus of this book: Hoist the sails. Or in the language of Hawaii, "Surf's up!" It's sink-or-swim time.

The wind blows where it wills. Our job is to hoist the sail and catch God's wave. What would it mean for Christians to fully inhabit the new amphibious landscape we live in, even to the point of making some waves ourselves?

This does not mean we ride the waves for the sheer buzz of it. "Surf's up!" is not a form of vanguardism, a soulless hankering after the next big wave, the next big trend. The third response to a tidal wave is the belief that it is the church's task to catch God's wave and make some good waves ourselves in the wake of God's wave.[13] The church is now on the wrong side of history. Even if we have to be lashed to the mast like Odysseus—the only way he could resist the temptations that lured sailors to their doom—the church must be lashed to the mast of word and sacrament if we are to resist the siren songs of postmodern culture.

> When you pass through the waters, I will be with you.
>
> Isaiah 43:2 NIV

In other words, this book takes as its patron saint Noah, who built some new structures and adopted some new strategies in the midst of a sea change for his day.[14] Like Noah, this book gives little credit and no cheers to those who invest their time denying the coming flood or crying, "The sky is falling." A lot of Christians are doing the "cultural cringe"[15]—a hip rain dance of hand-wringing, tongue-whanging, nose-whining, hot-water-bottle-clutching, pill-popping, teeth-gnashing to the tune of wailings and railings against the evils of the postmodern world (if not the flesh and the devil). They simply cannot see how any of these revolutionary changes we are going through can be for the better.

To be sure, howls of protest by people who fear a *Waterworld* future get the best press. A large segment of the church is decrying the state of the world and denying we can do much about it. The sounds of griping, grumping, and nursed grievances against the hot mantle bubbling up through modernity's suboceanic ridges play the loudest in the church as well as in the club.

In this time of transition, with one modern continent after another submerged by the postmodern flood, information overload and overabundance can yield disorientation, incoherence, and despair. To those for whom a steady stream of public complaint against postmodern culture has become a cottage industry,[17] this book repeats these words: "God did not send his Son into the world to *condemn* the world, but to save the world through him" (John 3:17 NIV, emphasis added). Let's get this out in the open from the start: The sound you hear this book make is "croaking," not condemning. Early Methodism was so successful that some of the early circuit riders, fearful that nothing fails like success, invented a new genre of autobiographical literature warning against the church's slide into complacency and respectability. They were widely known by the name "croakers" (the sound of the raven). I croak. I don't condemn.

> There is no good in arguing with the inevitable. The only argument available with an east wind is to put on your overcoat.
>
> James Russell Lowell[16]

Praise God, I'm not the only one croaking. German theologian Jürgen Moltmann croaks that "The Christian faith is losing its mobilizing power in history" primarily because of its failure to realize that we are moving into the future at a high-speed rate of 60 seconds per minute, 60 minutes per hour, 24 hours per day, 365 days per year. "Many abandon Christianity because they can find in it no power of the future."[18]

You don't think the beliefs that human beings have about the future make a difference? Tell that to anyone on Wall Street. Tell that to Nick Leeson (the British trader who single-handedly brought Baring Bank into bankruptcy in the mid-'90s) or anyone else playing the futures market.[19]

NOAH'S DOVE CHURCHES ～ The arks of modern civilization list badly. Our sundered society, buckling morality, criminal depravity have done more than just threaten to submerge modern civilization and modern culture. Like the *Titanic*, the modern world has taken on water and is sinking fast.

It's time to build new arks—or as Jesus would say, create "fresh wine-skins" (Matt. 9:17).

Late in 1996 police in Wisconsin arrested a man in the ladies restroom at a mall. Asked what he was doing there, he said he thought it would be "a good place to meet women."

The church is almost as clueless about how this postmodern world works and where to encounter people for Jesus as that hapless man in the wrong restroom. Who in our 320,000 churches, synagogues, and mosques in USAmerica can say, "I have seen the past, and it works"? The wisdom of the past isn't working the way it worked in the past. Past analysis has little to offer in our attempts to understand the present and future. Church hierarchies and bureaucracies are catastrophically wrong about a remarkably high proportion of the most important issues with which they deal.

> The ratio of illiterates to literates is unchanged from a century ago, but now the illiterates can read and write.
>
> Italian novelist
> Alberto Moravia

For a church where the future has almost become a no-go zone; for a church increasingly (if not terminally) out of touch with postmodern culture; for a church trying to do "'American Bandstand' ministry in an MTV world," in the words of Presbyterian minister Patrick Wrisley, God is already raising up "Noah's Dove Churches."

Noah's Dove Churches are faith-communities that with boldness and courage are scouting this new world after the sea change. They are then bring-ing back to the rest of us evidences of what works and what doesn't. Noah's Dove Churches are slicing the sharpest leading edges of creative thinking and deep spirituality. They are the places to find out how to do ministry in the postmodern world.

LIFE RINGS ～ In a future book called *Tornado Touchdowns* I intend to detail more fully these Noah's Dove Church explorations of the wisdom of the future.[20] *SoulTsunami* is more a semiotic exercise in helping "Noah's Dove" churches and leaders come to terms with our sea-change future and in understanding what theosemioticians (get used to that word; I promise not to use it again; but it's the new word for theologian) call ecriture (theoretical-symbolical activity).

Lastopost Library & Resource Center
Christ United Methodist Church
4488 Poplar Avenue
Memphis, Tennessee 38117

The defining question for the church today is what to do about the future. Do we say, "Go there!" Or do we say, "Don't go there!" These two poles— "Go there" and "Don't go there"—are increasingly delineating the church's political, social, and theological and ecclesiastical landscape.

SoulTsunami is dedicated to helping the church "go there." It does this through an exercise called "futuring." Futuring is nothing more nor less than raising the bar, measuring the horizon, scanning alternative scenarios, studying images of the future, and then getting the church to do some prospective thinking. This book approaches the wisdom of the future through "life rings." Life rings are exercises in envisioning possibilities, even promises, by cultivating memories of the future.

Swedish researcher David Ingvar has discovered that the human brain creates time paths for future activity. As you are reading this page you are probably also thinking about something else you need to do today and what you will do if that something else doesn't work out. In other words, you are right now creating time paths, or action plans for the future. These time paths make up what Ingvar calls "memories of the future."

These life rings are what some others have called "futuribles"—a phrase not yet common in English, though it is in France, where the monthly journal *Futuribles* (futurible@pratique.fr) exegetes the "signs of the times." Whatever we call them, they are not predictions, or what the Jet Propulsion Laboratory in Pasadena, California, on one of its walls calls "precision guesswork." Again, in the wisdom-words of the philosopher Yogi Berra (who now rates eight entries in *Bartlett's Familiar Quotations*), "Prediction is very bad, especially when it's about the future." (This saying isn't one of the eight.)

Just how bad was revealed by the magazines *The Futurist* and *The Economist*. *The Futurist* did a study of the predictions made within its covers over the past 30 years and found that the best futurists in the country had an accuracy rate of just 68%—they scored 23 hits, and 11 misses.[21] In 1984 *The Economist* asked corporate heads, finance ministers, and London garbage collectors to predict economic prospects for the next 10 years; in 1994 the garbage men proved just as prescient as the CEOs, and both did better than the finance experts.

Some of history's most brilliant thinkers have made brilliantly wrong predictions. Abraham Lincoln had no way of knowing he was authoring one of history's greatest untruths in his revered "Gettysburg Address": "The world will little note nor long remember what we say here: but it cannot forget what they did here." Or remember Nick Leeson, that above-mentioned British trader? He was a genius at knowing the market and, because of that, a genius at predicting the market's future. But he had no way of knowing that a violent earthquake in Japan would tripwire a series of collapses in prices that would bring everything down. Retrodiction is as problematic as prediction.

Complexity theory teaches us that one has to know the initial conditions of a system with infinite precision to be able to predict its course. When you are living in an "anything-can-happen-and-probably-will" world, 10 years away is unthinkable—and therefore unpredictable.

The first rule of futuring is this: Beware of Predictions.

If life rings are not predictions, what are they? And why this book? This book is not an exercise in predicting, but in preparing for present-future potentials and promises. What's the difference? The Bible is a book of promises and potentials, not predictions. Promises are fulfilled and potentials are realized in ways that could not have been imagined at the time by those making the promise or seeing the potential. Biblical promises have a "transformable quality" that enables them to be fulfilled in ways that were very different from how they were originally understood.[22]

> Shallow men speak of the past; wise men of the present; and fools of the future.
>
> Marquise du Deffand

The same is true with life rings—improbably plausible scenarios and future hot spots that are more than extrapolations but less than speculations.

> He who lives by the crystal ball is bound to eat glass.
>
> Futurists' saying

> Nature abhors a forecast even more than a vacuum.
>
> James Lovelock

If we approach these life rings in the same spirit with which Peter Stearns approaches forecasts (which he calls a kind of "art form" that "must not be spoiled by too much academic nicety"),[23] then this book is a form of play, a game for individuals and groups to enjoy.

The 10 life rings around which *SoulTsunami* is built can help leaders make *informed* preparations, not predictions, as you claim your cultural moment. They provide a handbook for the new religious and theological literacy of our emerging postmodern world, and they challenge the church to stop making faces at those who face the future. They present new ways of thinking about what makes the postmodern world tick, and how to do ministry amid its ticking time bombs. They offer the church ways to think seriously and substantively about the long run, and help, as one of my professors used to say, "unscrew the inscrutable." They help create the historical and theological software—with passing suggestions of hardware—for the habitation of the third millennium.

> Never make forecasts, especially about the future.
>
> Film mogul Samuel Goldwyn

SAFE WITHOUT SAFETY-FIRST ~ So far, so good. But we are not very far . . . actually, so far, so old-hat. These 10 presentfutures I've selected are the tame, safe futuribles about which you can't be safety-first.[24] Know that you are not hearing from me anything all that revolutionary. Revolutionary would have been for someone to stand up in 1989 and announce that the Soviet Union would collapse from within without a drop of blood, or that Germany would be reunited and West Germany would pay for it, or that Nelson Mandela would go from being a prisoner to being a president elected in an open multiracial election, or that the Israelis and Palestinians would shake hands and sign a peace agreement, or that the newest status symbol is not a BMW, not a mountain retreat home, not a six-figure income, not a yacht for the ocean, but the ability of one spouse to stay home and take care of the kids.[25]

I haven't begun to press the envelope or get radical. Maybe another time. Or maybe never. After all, a writer needs to be on his best behavior towards the reader, to be gentle and give the reader the wherewithal to make up his own mind and see things for herself. My motivation has been more to prepare you than to scare you. Hence you will not find discussions here about how people in the future will be so much smarter, thanks to molecular genetics, that we will keep up with the intelligence of computers and look back on our ancient geniuses like Stephen Hawking as little smarter than simpletons. You will also not find here explorations of the ways in which computers are becoming a new species, like plants and animals, and may even evolve in similar fashion to plants and animals themselves. I have tried not to congratulate postmoderns on being the endpoint of a historical process that leads inevitably to us. I have tried to resist every inclination to indulge in sociological or technological or spiritual hyperbole. I have dealt sparingly with "trends," although the only church that can afford to be indifferent to trends is a church that is not on a mission.

Even so, some of my readers are likely to raise a ruckus at what they read here, or at least raise eyebrows, grind teeth, gnash gums, etc. You may at times feel that I am less mentor than tormentor, or as someone once said to me after a lecture where some of the above material was presented, "Sweet, you're a treat, but you're a treatment."

How welcome is any wake-up call, anyway? Unfortunately, the ticking sounds of the church's clocks tend to lull rather than alarm, partly because they have a dated ring, sounding the ring of a culture that is rapidly disappearing. This book's ringing can be upsetting, even make you start out the day less glad than sad, mad, or bad. So mad, in fact, that some may identify with those early skeptics who, "when they heard this, they were enraged and shouted, 'Great is Artemis of the Ephesians!'" (Acts 19:28).

> First they ignore it, then they laugh at it, then they say they knew it all along.
>
> 19th century German philosopher Alexander Humboldt

The unintended merit of this book may be that it's a matchbook for sparks that can light new torches and uncomfortable thoughts. Unlike Jeremiah, who loved telling people what they most hated to hear, I don't particularly relish this role of disturbing the equilibrium. My consolation is that, as a disturber of the peace, I'm only being polite. Miss Manners says that sometimes good etiquette is not saying what people want to hear, or not making people comfortable. To be polite, says Miss Manners, "There are times when you are going to have to upset people. There are times when you have to upset the whole society."[26] In fact, it may be that part of being a "Noah's Dove" leader in postmodern culture is making people feel slightly uncomfortable, making life difficult, getting those you love to do the difficult but right thing.

DOUBLE-RING MINISTRIES ~ You will quickly notice a "double ring" in each chapter. One of the characteristic features of postmodern culture is that opposite things happen at the same time without being contradictory.[27] Anyone who doesn't feel pulled in conflicting directions doesn't understand Heisenberg's uncertainty principle, Pauli's exclusion principle, and Schrödinger's wave equation. Where the modern age was predominantly either-or, the postmodern world is and/also. Or phrased more memorably, "the postmodernist always rings twice."

> I have two lasting impressions: the horror of what we are able to do to each other and almost exhilaration at the nobility of the human spirit that so many demonstrate.
>
> Archbishop Desmond Tutu[28]

This is an in-your-face society. This is a get-out-of-my-face society.

This is a culture where you want it to stop and you want it to go on.

This is a culture of outplacing and replacing, deployment and unemployment, high fat and low fat, no fat and fake fat.

This is a society where the nun Isabella in Hal Hartley's 1994 movie *Amateur* can confess that she is a nymphomaniac—and admit she has never had sex. This is a culture where the sexiest lingerie and negligees are marketed by a firm that promotes a Victorian ambiance.[29] This is a double-edged culture, a culture of paradox.[30] Philosopher Manuel Castell, the intellectual heir to Hegel, has written a three-volume magnum opus, *The Information Age*. He devotes his first volume to exploring how communications technologies are pulling us together. His second volume is dedicated to exploring the forces that are pulling us apart.[31]

> There is an eagle in me that wants to soar, and there is a hippopotamus in me that wants to wallow in the mud.
>
> Carl Sandburg

Four fundamental transitions in our perception of the world divide the modern from the postmodern era, creating the double-ring phenomenon.[32]

1. In the cosmic and quantum worlds, there are always two sides or parts to all the wholes.[33] Physicist Niels Bohr's principle of complementarity provides a scientific scaffolding to the double-ring phenomenon. Light is parti-

cles. Light is waves. Human existence is both then and there, particle and wave. Physicist Joseph J. Thomson received the Nobel Prize for showing that matter is made up of particles known as electrons. His son received the same prize for showing that electrons exhibit the properties of waves. Sound is both wave and particle; light is both wave and particle. You and I are both matter and energy; you and I are both clumps of particles and waves of energy. Given the oneness of matter and spirit, not to hit the double ring is to sound a half-truth.

2. There is no understanding without standing under. Life exists for each one of us in the same state as Schrödinger's cat, neither alive nor dead, except when one stands under and looks. And once one stands under, one alters the understanding; once one looks, one changes what is seen. If I set up my lab equipment to see if light is a wave, it will behave as a wave; if I alter my equipment to test if light is transmitted as particles, it will behave as particles. Truth is both objective and subjective. Also known as the participant-observer methodology, it is this methodology that has been followed throughout the writing of this book.

> Knowledge is both objective and particpatory.
>
> Chemist Ilya Prigogine

3. The Heisenberg Uncertainty Principle proves that indeterminacy is inherent in the very structures of the universe. Not one of us can boast immaculate perceptions. Yet at the same time Heisenberg's principle raises the level of human responsibility to a height perhaps only Calvin dreamed of in the history of the church.

4. The universe is an undivided whole and not a set of separate states. What goes on in the largest galaxy of the cosmos is not unconnected to a single-celled amoeba swimming merrily in the Bering Sea. What did Jesus say? "Just as you did it to one of the least . . ." (Matt. 25:40).

These four transitions, both together and singly, sound double rings. The church sounds the double ring, not to eliminate the polarities, but to sound both notes in a dynamic embrace. The double ring is not a melding of opposing sides into one middle-way, or a splitting of the difference between two poles, or a halfway compromise between two positions.

To survive in postmodern culture, one has to learn to speak out of both sides of the mouth. It should not be hard, since Christianity has always insisted on having things both ways. Isn't it based on the impossible possibility of Jesus being "beyond us, yet ourselves" (poet Wallace Stevens)? Biblical theological is not circular with a fixed center, but elliptical, revolving around the double foci of God's immanence and God's transcendence.

The double ring is more than a metaphor; it's a ministry strategy of triangulation where both extremes are brought together and become a *tertium quid*. The

> The moment two bubbles are united, they both vanish.
>
> Japanese saying

double-ring model yields a trinitarian strategy for dealing with times of immense change; it's a diagnostic that can help churches and individuals think about their attitudes, their directions, and their capacities. In a double-ring world, play both rings simultaneously.

My favorite double-ring analogy for what it's like to do ministry today, as one way of being in the world is giving way to another way of being, is the example of the new eight-billion-dollar Washington National Air-port, which opened in July 1997. For eight years, year after year, managers of the airport had to endure the experience of building a new one-million-square-foot main terminal for a state-of-the-art airport for the 21st century while keeping 16 million annual passengers happy and on time using the old, dilapidated 115,00-square-foot terminal.

> Be all that you can be ... in the Army.
>
> Recruiting commercial

TECHNOLOGICAL CODA ~ An intended feature of this book is an attempt to address the church's dysfunctional, love-hate relationship with technology. Yet there is no separate section given to technology. Unlike past technological innovations—agriculture, sailing ships, the printing press, gunpowder, industrialization, the automobile, atomic energy— it is now impossible to talk about anything without talking about technology. Technology is no longer a separate category. It does not exist on its own, but is intrinsic and implicit in all of life. Technology is now a part of everything—from sneakers to toothpaste, from genetics to religion, from you to me.

> Live with your century, but do not be its creature; render to your contemporaries what they need, not what they praise.
>
> Poet Frederich von Schiller

Technology is formed and altered by a host of factors. Because of the social construction of technology, we should really speak of *technoculture,* not culture. Technology is beyond even culture. It pervades who we are as people.

We are technology. We are no longer natural. We are now constructed, and we're constructing ourselves, which is the basis for Donna Haraway's famous declaration that we are all cyborgs. Our relationship with technology, from antibiotics to orthodontics to prosthetics to athletics, is so intimate that it is hard to tell where we begin and technology leaves off. "The great convergence" (where there are no specific industries anymore) is now taking place.

No one can escape technology, not even the Unabomber. The local woman who worked as the jailhouse barber described how she used to trim Ted Kazsyinski's mustache. One day he told her the story of an ancient Japanese tribe that used to grow their hair as long as possible. In loving detail the Unabomber described a special tool designed to lift the hairs of their mustaches off their lips so they could eat. "I'd love to see that tool," he lamented.[34]

Every technology, if it is circumscribed within normative boundaries,[35] can contribute to an enhanced and enriched life. What is more, God has a history of speaking through new media forms in the Christian tradition. Indeed, scholar Andrew Walls talks about Christianity's "infinite translatability."[36]

I take great comfort from the fact that this is not the first time Christians have had to face this challenge of "translatability." If we find the transition from page to screen difficult, it may help to reflect that this is nothing compared to the transition from oral to literate culture. French historian Roger Chartier argues that the so-called Gutenberg revolution was not really a revolution at all because a manuscript book was not structurally different from a printed book. Both had folded sheets, quires, pages, and leaves. Both reading practices were similar. The only thing that poor German jeweler Johannes Gutenberg changed—"He didn't know what he was starting, and he died broke"—was the method of producing and reproducing the text.

> A sufficiently advanced technology is indistinguishable from magic.
>
> Communication scientist/ university chancellor/ science-fiction writer Arthur C. Clarke's Third Law

The emergence of electronic culture is truly revolutionary, Chartier insists, because it is a "revolution in the technique of production and reproduction of the text, revolution in the structure of the vehicle, the support of the text, and revolution in the reading practices understood as gestures and categories." In the history of written culture, Chartier argues, the only legitimate comparison to the cultural transition we are now undergoing with electronic texts was the shift from the scroll to the codex.[37]

And when did this shift from scroll to codex occur? Much earlier than the second century after Christ, as historians have previously thought. Christianity itself arose in history during this sea change. God chose a transition century in which to incarnate the very being of God. The culture of Jesus' day underwent two cultural transitions—one in the field of communications, the other in the field of construction.

The first technological transition was in the area of construction. How did Jesus earn his living? Not as a "carpenter," but more accurately as a "builder," an "artisan," a "contractor." In Jesus' time it was discovered that one material could be mixed with another material to create a single and singular kind of material called . . . concrete. Concrete construction began in earnest during Jesus' time. See the octagonal domed fountain hall of Nero's Golden House (A.D. 64–68).[38] The technological advance of concrete dominated and drove civilization until the advent of steel in the early 1800s.

The second transition was in the movement from oral to literate culture, from scroll to codex. The culture of the first century was oral. Most of Jesus' disciples were illiterate. Levels of literacy in the population were very low. Yet Jesus himself was literate (he stood up in synagogue and read Scriptures).

Jesus was part of an elite group in Galilee who could read and write. Jesus was trilingual—he spoke Greek as well as Hebrew and Aramaic.[39]

Biblical scholar/storyteller Thomas Boomershine argues persuasively that Jesus was the oral precursor of a literacy movement, and that Jesus' teachings and actions actually established the new culture of literacy and written communication. The Jewish Scriptures were written revelation, but this written revelation was orally transmitted. Jesus and Paul changed all that.[40]

One of the most amazing features of the first Christians was their total preference for the paged book or codex over the more widespread scroll.[41] This helps explain why, according to Leslie Houlden, "unlike all other literature from the ancient world, the New Testament is extant in an abundance of sources—more than 2,000 manuscripts from the first 1,500 years of its existence."[42]

> Technology is today the mass, the motor, and the mark of nearly every cultural activity or field.
>
> Philosopher/author
> Egbert Schuurman[45]

The phrase "people of the Book" was actually coined by Muhammad, the Prophet of Islam, to distinguish the Islamic tradition, which handed down its revelation orally, from that of Judaism and Christianity, which hands down its tradition in writing.[43] By the time of Jerome's Latin Vulgate (late 4th century), the entire Scriptures were bound up as a single volume.

Both Jesus and Paul were part of a movement within Judaism that attempted to make the reality of God known through literacy and documents. Duke historian Elizabeth Clark has studied extensively how some early Christians objected to having the gospels written down instead of circulated word-of-mouth. To base Christianity on the distribution of documents contradicted the reigning orthodoxy of orality, which depended on memory and interpersonal communication through "the living and abiding voice."[44]

> Will the last person to leave please see that the perpetual light is extinguished.
>
> Sign in the vestry of a New England church

One only has to look at the history of the Christian church and the misuse of Scripture to see that some of our ancestors' concerns about how Scriptures could be hijacked were right on target. Literacy fossilized an author's telling of the story (or four authors' interpretations) to the exclusion of other tellings. It made one prone to worship the text itself rather than the message of the text. In Tom Troeger's words, these warnings "stand as a reminder to us that no strategy for presenting the word of God, even when inspired by the Holy Spirit, can communicate the full and perfect wholeness of the divine."[46]

The irony of the church's response to postmodern technology is this: Christians used to fear the codex and clung to the scroll. Then the church feared the printed page and clung to the codex. Now we are opposing the screen (an updated scroll—the unfurling text on screen) and clinging to the page (an updated codex). John W. Campbell Jr., the great science-fiction editor, "once noted that the dilemma of paper is that it doesn't stretch: 'You can only get in as much material as you physically have room for.'"[47] The screen does indeed scroll and stretch—close to forever in both directions, above and below to accommodate staggering amounts of information.

The issue for us today is not *whether* the gospel will be inculturated in this electronic age, but *how*; not *whether* our social context shapes the experience of the gospel, but *how*. The core technology of the Postmodern Reformation is the screen—or what Walter J. Ong calls "secondary orality,"[48] the subjection of literacy to the demands of orality. The modern world made us text-trained, with the book our chief icon. The postmodern world needs us to be light-trained, with the screen the chief icon.

Phyllis A. Tickle argues that "more theology is conveyed in, and probably retained from, one hour of popular television than from all the sermons that are also delivered on any given weekend in America's synagogues, churches, and mosques."[49] But the "screen" is less television than computer. If the technology that fueled the Protestant Reformation was the printing press, and the product was "The Book," the technology that is fueling the Postmodern Reformation is the microprocessor, and the product is "The Net," which has been defined as "an organic combination of hardware, software, and humans endlessly self-balancing."[50] When a church sets out to construct a Web site ministry, it is actually building a postmodern cathedral. If cathedrals connected heaven and earth, the postmodern cathedral is the Web.[51]

Katherine Amos, Director of Accreditation and Educational Technology for the Associations of Theological Schools in the United States and Canada, notes that "It is ironic—schools of different denominations are more split over whether and how to use technology in training their students than they are over the differences between their respective faith traditions."[52]

Digital technology is dividing Christians in ways not yet fully appreciated. The most basic social divisions are economic and technological: the have and have-nots in the world of economics, and the haves and the "want-nots" in the world of technology.[53] For the haves and the want-nots, the issue is not money. The issue is simply that older generations see no need for the technology, while younger generations—appropriately called the "Net-Gens"—can't imagine living without it.

In all of economic history, there is no technology that has grown faster than the World Wide Web. In 1969 only four primitive Web sites existed in the entire world. In 1990 there were 333,000. By the end of 1997 there were almost 20 million. It took 40 years for radio to reach 50 million domestic users; it took 14 years for television to do that; and for the Internet, four years.

It is soon becoming the case that if you had a calling card in the 20th century, you will have a Web site in the 21st.

> In the world you have tribulation; but be of good cheer, I have overcome the world.
>
> John 16:33 RSV

As the Protestant Reformation Church used the book, the Postmodern Reformation Church will use the hypertext of the Net, a nonlinear[54] form of communication ("text") that is brought to life on the screen, can be experienced ("read") in a multitude of ways, and is altered by the contribution of others at the site. The Internet has become the number one means of moving information worldwide, and it is attracting more economic and intellectual capital than any prior technology in history. It is exploding globally even more rapidly than it is expanding in the US. The number of online users throughout Europe grew in 1997 by double that in the US. The number of Internet hosts in Japan as of 1998 is growing twice as fast as anywhere else in the world. Moreover, Canada is now the most wired nation in the world.

LIVING THE PROMETHEAN HELL ~ My favorite image for what it means to live in a time of transition is that of the myth of Prometheus. I may like this myth so much because you will remember it was Prometheus who gave fire to mortals. The invention of the microprocessor will have a far greater impact on this planet than not just the invention of writing, when the Greeks first put stylus to clay tablet, but the discovery of fire or the invention of the wheel.

After Prometheus gave fire to mortals, an angry Zeus chained him to Mount Caucasus, where each day an eagle devoured his liver, and each night the liver grew back, to go through the pain of hell all over again.

Promethean hell is still being lived today in this new technological slavery, beeper bondage, and bionomic experimentation. I am deeply concerned with the way electronic technology can become a new form of enslavement. Anytime-anywhere work quickly becomes everytime-everywhere work. When it comes to bionomics, I feel like the supporting actor who said he was best known for three basic talents: "groveling, brooding, and mulling."

> A balance that does not tremble cannot weigh. A person who does not tremble cannot live.
>
> Chemist Erwin Chargraff[55]

I have tried not to be a hypist for the postmodern era, a mixed bag with innumerable tradeoffs and circularities. Postmodern culture is rife with content deficits and thought disorders. In many ways we lose as much as we gain. I sympathize with the woman paralyzed from the neck down who petitioned the Quebec courts to allow her respirator to be turned off. After two and a half years of doing nothing but watching television, she protested that she had had enough.

My hype and hope for this Postmodern Reformation is thoroughly mixed with fear and trembling. I have no doubt that God will be in this future, yet I

> You must never mistake a clear view for a short distance.
>
> Paul Saffo of the Institute for the Future (IFTF)

worry deeply about whether my own tribe will be there. The church can lead the move into the new intellectual and technological territory of the soon-to-be Bionomic Age. We are not condemned end-lessly to rework the ideas of the key thinkers of the old world. But first we must choose hope over despair.

Whether we like it or not, God has chosen you and me to live in inter-esting times. And interesting times, as the ancient curse has it, are unpre-dictable, chaotic, dangerous. This is not the time I would have picked. But the words of Jesus keep ringing in my ears: "Your time is now" (see John 7:6).

The doctrine of the incarnation is this: If our Savior joins us where we are, not where we ought to be, then what excuse do we have? If Jesus descended into hell, then where should we not be willing to go?

The future can no longer be an assumption. The future is now an achievement. There is a race to the future. Who will get there first? Will the Christian church? The time to save God's Dream is now. The people to save God's Dream are you.

This is an extraordinary moment in history. God wants you to do some extraordinary things. You can do some extraordinary things. Will you? The choice is yours.

> It's not only what we do, but also what we do not do for which we are accountable.
>
> Molière

God is birthing the greatest spiritual awakening in the history of the church. God is calling you to midwife that birth. Are you going to show up?

It's such an exciting time to be alive. So I repeat: Is this a great time, or what?

say what? 1. A true story:

On September 13, 1987, two unemployed young men in search of a fast buck entered a partly demolished radiation clinic in Goianaia, Brazil. They removed a derelict cancer therapy machine containing a stain-less steel cylinder, about the size of a gallon paint can, which they sold to a junk dealer for $25. Inside the cylinder was a cake of crumbly powder that emitted a mysterious blue light. The dealer took the seemingly magi-cal material home and distributed it to his family and friends. His six-year-old niece rubbed the glowing dust on her body. One might imagine that she danced, eerily glowing in the sultry darkness of the tropic night like an enchanted elfin sprite. The dust was cesium-137, a highly radioactive sub-stance. The lovely light was the result of the decay of the cesium atoms.

Another product of the decay was a flux of invisible particles with the power to damage living cells. The girl is dead. Others died or became grievously sick. More than two hundred people were contaminated.

A beautiful, refulgent dust, stolen from an instrument of healing had become an instrument of death. The junk dealer's niece was not the only child who rubbed the cesium on her body like carnival glitter, and the image of those luminous children will not go away. Their story is a moral fable for our times—a haunting story, touched with dreamlike beauty and ending in death.[56]

2. Create some scenarios for your church, both positive and negative, that can help you discuss and deal with change. "Scenarios" are imaginative stories about the future of your church. Let scenario building help you think the unthinkable.

3. Look into the heavens. The farther you look into space, and what seems to be peering into the future, the farther you are looking into the past. When you look at Cassiopeia in the night sky, you are seeing something that was there 500 million years ago. Cassiopeia may not even exist today. When scientists observe systems in space that are 5 billion light-years away, they are seeing things that God created even before Earth, the garden planet of the galaxy, was created.

Time and space are intimately related to one another. The past, present, and future can easily become spatial concepts. "Space" and "time" have lost their separate meanings in theoretical physics and mathematics.

From a spiritual standpoint, there is no such thing as past, present, and future. Time doesn't pass. It stays still. It remains "now." "A thousand years in your sight are like yesterday when it is past, or like a watch in the night" (Ps. 90:4). I don't wear a watch on my wrist partly for this reason.

What does it mean to your relationships that space and time are relative?

4. Have someone review the book *In the Blood: God, Genes and Destiny* by Steve Jones.[57] Or, since the book began as a television series, schedule some time to watch a video of the series before discussing the book.

5. The Church of the Next, the Church of the Now, the Church of the Past, and the Church of the Way Back There. What churches that you know of would you fit into each of these categories?

6. Discuss: "It isn't just the failure of so many predictions to come true that makes reasonable people doubt the whole futurist enterprise . . . but the fact that so many predictions have come true without changing the tenor of lived experience. . . . Maybe only the animators at Hanna-Barbera, back in the '60s, ever really grasped this truth in all its complexity, thereby producing what some bright student of cultural history has probably already called the Flintstones-Jetsons Theory: it is not just that the ancient past and the dim

future will resemble each other but that both will resemble the basic plot line of 'The Honeymooners.'"[58]

7. A church consultant out of the Southern Baptist tradition once asked me in desperation how I would address the two basic attitudes he finds in churches he works with: People feel *hope-less* about their situation and at the same time they are *fear-ful* about the future. How would you answer his question about the church's hopelessness and fearfulness?

8. One scholar of film history makes an analogy between verbal language and screen culture:

"Imagine that a new language form came into being at the turn of the twentieth century," and that "although public anxiety about the potentially corrupting influence of the new language was constant from its birth, it was *perceived* not as a language at all but as a medium of popular entertainment." As we begin the 21st century, suddenly we discover that "we have become massively illiterate in a primary language form" that has "become so pervasive in our daily lives" that it "surrounds us, sending us messages, taking positions, making statements, and constantly redefining our relationship to material reality." To make matters the worst, when it comes to understanding this new language we find ourselves "barely literate—able to assimilate the language form without fully comprehending it."[59]

To what extent is this a description of our current position?

9. Discuss the double-ring phenomenon of postmodern culture. Can you find the double ring in the Scriptures?

(Example 1: "If you want to *find* your life, *lose* it.")

(Example 2: "The *first* shall be *last*.")

In hymnody?

(Example 1: "Nobody knows the *trouble* I've seen: *Glory hallelujah!*")

(Example 2: "*Sorrow* and *love* flow mingled down.")

10. What's happened to our dreams, church? Novelist William S. Burroughs has said that a society without dreams is a dead society. Are we dreaming anymore, church? And if we are, do we remember our dreams? People leave anything, not because their work is completed, but because their dream is dead.

Institutions, friendships, marriages, corporations fall apart "at their dreams." You say: No, the metaphor is "at their seams." I say: No, the metaphor is "at their dreams" because their dreams *are* their seams. Dreams constitute the new grand narratives, which are in short supply in postmodern culture. Dreams are the visions and vibrations.

Is your church dreaming anymore? Not the American Dream, not the Dream Machine of Madison Avenue marketers, but God's dreams and God-sized dreams. What would it mean for your church to "Dream On"? Can your church dream in color? Is your church life more filled with little heroisms, little hypocrisies, or big dreams, big ambitions, big failures, big mistakes?

Is your church today more prone to breast-beat its doubts than to breast-beat your dreams? Hollywood has given birth to "DreamWorks." What would it be like for your church to be more than a pipe-dreaming, more than a fire-breathing "DreamChurch?"

11. Listen to my lecture "A Dream Church for 21-C" in "The Pastor's Update," Audio Series, Fuller Theological Seminary. To order call 1-800-999-9578.

12. Identify how many double rings you can hear in this early Christian document called the *Epistle to Diognetus*, an anonymous writing dated no later than the third century of the Christian era.

> The distinction between Christians and other men is neither in country nor language nor customs. For they do not dwell in cities in some place of their own, nor do they use any strange variety of dialect, nor practise an extraordinary kind of life. This teaching of theirs has not been discovered by the intellect or thought of busy men, nor are they the advocates of any human doctrine, as some men are. Yet while living in Greek and barbarian cities, according as each has obtained his lot, and following the local customs both in clothing and food and in the rest of life, they show forth the wonderful and confessedly strange (*paradoxos*) character of the constitution of their own citizenship. They dwell in their own fatherlands, but as if sojourners in them; they share all things as citizens, and suffer all things as strangers. Every foreign country is their fatherland, and every fatherland is a foreign country. They marry as all men, they bear children, but they do not expose their offspring. They offer free hospitality but guard their purity. [They have a common table but not a common bed.] Their lot is cast in the flesh, but they do not live according to the flesh. They pass their time on earth, but they have their citizenship in heaven.

The author concludes:

> To put it shortly, what the soul is in the body, that the Christians are in the world. The soul is spread through the members of the body, but is not of the body, and Christians dwell in the world but are not of the world. The soul is indivisible, and is guarded in a visible body, and Christians are recognized when they are in the world, but their religion remains invisible. The flesh hates the soul, and wages war upon it, though it has suffered no evil, because it is prevented from gratifying its pleasures, and the world

hates the Christians though it has suffered no evil, because they are opposed to its pleasures. The soul loves the flesh which hates it and Christians love those that hate them. The soul has been shut up in the body, but itself sustains the body; and Christians are confined in the world as in a prison, but themselves sustain the world. The soul dwells immortal in a mortal tabernacle, and Christians sojourn among corruptible things, waiting for the incorruptibility which is in heaven.[60]

13. What do we learn about God from Psalm 115:2–3 and 2 Chronicles 2:5–6 that needs the companion Psalm 119:151 and Deuteronomy 4:7?

In what way does Isaiah 57:15 bring both foci together?

14. Multiple Choice: "Shout louder! . . . Surely he is a god! Perhaps he is [a] deep in thought, or [b] busy, or [c] traveling. Maybe he is [d] sleeping and must be awakened" (1 Kings 18:27 NIV). Is it *a, b, c, d,* or *e*—none of the above?

15. Assign someone the task of looking up the biblical references to "revival" as "rain," "latter rain," "water," and so on. For example, Habakkuk 2:14 defines revival as the cascading of a people with "the knowledge of the glory of the LORD, as the waters cover the sea." Close your study session by singing the song "Send Your Rain" (Integrity's Hosanna! Music).

16. Phyllis A. Tickle is a contributing editor in religion to *Publishers Weekly* and editor-at-large for its Religion Bookline. In her book *God-Talk in America* (New York: Crossroad, 1997), which you may want to read and review as a group, she contends that "with few exceptions, Della Reese's theology [on TV's *Touched by an Angel*] is going to win out every time over that of any sermon that runs counter to it."[61] Do you agree with such an assessment of the power of electronic media?

> Traveler, there are no roads.
> Roads are made by walking.
>
> Spanish proverb

17. Why will you never find the phrase "postmodern church" in this book? Why is the distinction between a holy ambition to build a "postmodern church" or a church for postmodern culture such a big one?

18. Discuss the double-ring phenomenon while using a mirror to show how a page of writing when looked at in a mirror will make an E appear different but not an A. Why does a mirror reverse left-right but not up-down?[62] Does the gospel do just the opposite—turn the world upside down, or more accurately right-side up, while bringing the ends together?

now what? See the Net Notes in http://www.soultsunami.com

NOTES

1. Leonard I. Sweet, *FaithQuakes* (Nashville: Abingdon, 1994).

2. Letter to Agostino Cardinal Casaroli, on the occasion of the creation of the Pontifical Council for Culture, *Osservatore romano* (English ed., 28 June 1982): 7.

3. Scholars call this the oldest historical record of an earthquake. In southern California the dry ground also produces huge clouds of dust, "the smoke of the country," during earthquakes.

4. The term *postmodern* was first used in the 1870s by the British artist John Watkins Chapman. The next instance was in 1917 by Rudolf Pannwitz. Its dominant usage in the 1970s and '80s was a negative association with deconstruction and dialectics, with a more positive connotation in the '90s coming with "ecological postmodernism," "constructive postmodernism," "restructive postmodernism," etc. The best introductory guide to the labyrinthine genesis of this word *postmodern* is Margaret Rose's *The Postmodern and the Post-Industrial: A Critical Analysis* (New York: Cambridge Univ. Press, 1991).

5. For further examples of this short-sighted view, see Brunet's *Genes, Dreams and Realities* (New York: Basic Books, 1971).

6. This is the wonderful phrase of C. W. Previte-Orton, *The Shorter Cambridge Medieval History* (Cambridge: Cambridge Univ. Press, 1966), I:102.

7. Half of US Protestant churches have fewer than 75 congregants. See Charles Trueheart, "Welcome to the Next Church," *Atlantic Monthly* (Aug 1996): 37–58, esp. 38.

8. In the '70s the United Methodist Church was ordaining about 700 men each year; now it's down to 400. The number of women being ordained, though increasing until 1992, was not enough to offset the decline. In 1993 and 1994 the totals fell sharply for both men and women clergy. Since 1974, the average age of pastors has risen from 28 to 36 (for males) and 41 (for females): see *Religion Watch* (Oct 1996): 7. See also John E. Phelan Jr., "Where Have All the Pastors Gone?" *The Covenant Companion* (Dec 1997): 5. Phelan attributes the vanishing pastor syndrome at both the beginning and the end of ministry due to lack of support and encouragement from and for the pastor and his or her family.

9. Nicola Gillies, *The Last Word: Tombstone Wit and Wisdom* (Oxford: Past Times, 1997), 31.

10. Ashley Woodiwiss, "What Is the Church Good For?" *Books and Culture* (Nov-Dec 1997): 38–39.

11. I want to thank Episcopal priest Hank Dewire of New Jersey for this "hovercraft" image.

12. As quoted in William H. Robinson, *Phyllis Wheatley and Her Writings* (New York: Garland, 1984), 40.

13. If Christian scholars like Duns Scotus and William of Ockham helped to provide the intellectual scaffolding for the building of modern culture, what's preventing contemporary Christian scholars from helping to built the postmodern city?

14. One of the most important of these was the Noah's Ark Standard: Please Proceed in Pairs.

15. I am reappropriating this phrase from Australian critic Arthur Phillips.

16. James Russell Lowell, *Democracy and Other Addresses* (Boston: Houghton Mifflin, 1887), 16.

17. Those most hostile to postmodern culture include Gene Edward Veith, *Postmodern Times* (Wheaton, IL: Crossway, 1994), and Marva Dawn, *Reaching Out Without Dumbing Down: A Theology of Worship for the Turn-of-the-Century Culture* (Grand Rapids: Eerdmans, 1995). Evangelical and nonevangelical theologians most open to postmodern paradigms include Stanley Grenz, *A Primer on Postmodernism* (Grand Rapids: Eerdmans, 1996), Nancey Murphy, *Beyond Liberalism and Fundamentalism* (Valley Forge, PA: Trinity Press, 1996), Catherine Keller, *Apocalypse Now and Then: A Feminist Guide to the End of the World* (Boston: Beacon Press, 1996), Brian Walsh and Richard Middleton, *Truth Is Stranger Than It Used to Be* (Downers Grove, IL: InterVarsity Press, 1995).

18. Jürgen Moltmann, *Religion, Revolution, and the Future*, ed. and trans. Douglas Meeks (New York: Scribner's, 1969), 133.

19. See Bill Powell, Daniel Pederson et al., "Busted," *Newsweek* (13 Mar 1995): 36–42.

20. We instinctively know our need for this wisdom of the future. After all, at the century's end our culture's dominant orientation has been toward the future, not judging the past 100 years or 1000 years, which it very easily could have been.

21. Edward Cornish, "Forecasts 30 Years Later," *The Futurist* (Jan-Feb 1997): 48.

22. Christopher J. H. Wright, *Knowing Jesus Through the Old Testament* (Downers Grove, IL: InterVarsity Press, 1995).

23. Peter N. Stearns, *Millennium III, Century XXI: A Retrospective on the Future* (New York: Westview, 1996), 176–77.

24. For some other "safe" futuribles, see Joseph F. Coates, John B. Mahaffie, and Andy Hines, *2025: Scenarios of US and Global Society Reshaped by Science and Technology* (Akron: Oakhill Press, 1996).

25. David C. Korten, *When Corporations Rule the World* (West Hartford, CT: Kumarian Press, 1995), 303.

26. "She says: Miss Manners" (a.k.a. Judith Martin), interview by Sandy M. Fernandez, *Ms.* (Mar-Apr 1997): 52.

27. I am in obvious debt to Jacques Derrida at this point, who argues that the deconstructive methodology is "a double gesture, a double science, a double writing." See his *Positions*, trans. Alan Bass (Chicago: Univ. of Chicago Press, 1972), 41, 100. For help in how to come to terms with this phenomenon of doubleness, see Peter Elbow, *Embracing Contraries: Explorations in Learning and Teaching* (New York: Oxford Univ. Press, 1986), and Richard Tanner Pascale, *Managing on the Edge: How the Smartest Companies Use Conflict to Stay Ahead* (New York: Simon & Schuster, 1990), 110ff.

28. Colin Greer, "Without Memory, There Is No Healing; Without Forgiveness, There Is No Future," *Parade* (11 Jan 1998): 4.

29. The Victorian Era has been defined as a time when people found it better to be preoccupied than occupied with sex. See Nancy V. Workman, "From Victorian to Victoria's Secret: The Foundations of Modern Erotic Wear," *Journal of Popular Culture* (Fall 1996): 61–73.

30. Richard P. Hansen, "Preaching Paradox in a Give-It-to-Me-Straight World," *Preaching* (Jan-Feb 1998): 34–38.

31. Manuel Castells, *The Information Age: Economy, Society and Culture* (Malden, MA: Blackwell, 1996).

32. I am obviously indebted here to David Bohm's work in *Wholeness and the Implicate Order* (Boston: Routledge & Kegan Paul, 1980).

33. For the possibility in the philosophical world that "two statements which are incompatible at face value can sometimes both be true," see Hilary Putnam, *Realism with a Human Face* (Cambridge, MA: Harvard Univ. Press, 1991).

34. Mark Dery, "Nature," *21C* (Apr 1996): 52.

35. For an excellent listing of these normative boundaries, see the Dutch scholar Egbert Schuurman's *Perspectives on Technology and Culture*, trans. John H. Kok (Sioux Center, IA: Dordt College Press, 1995).

36. As quoted by Tom Troeger, *Ten Strategies for Preaching in a Multi-Media Culture* (Nashville: Abingdon Press, 1996), 17.

37. Sue Waterman, "Chartier Interview," *SHARP News* 6 (Spring 1997): 4–6, 5. This is the professional newsletter for the 1000-plus members of the Society for the History of Authorship, Reading & Publishing.

38. Mortar was initially a mixture of lime, sand, and water. But beginning in the 2nd century B.C., a new ingredient was introduced into the mix: called pozzolana (named by the Romans after the town of Pozzuoli where it was first found). When mixed with the mortar, pozzolana forms a natural cement that, when combined with stones and broken brick and water, formed the first true concrete. By contrast, ancient civilizations used mortar almost

from the dawn of social life; Egyptians used what today we would call "plaster of paris" (see Lev. 14:42–48).

39. We know this because (1) Jesus conversed with Pilate and the centurion, and in fact, Greek was the official common language in Galilee as well as the language of the home; (2) he had disciples with Greek names—Philip and Nathaniel; (3) as a builder, Jesus worked extensively with Gentiles; and (4) Jesus wrote in the sand.

40. Professor Boomershine asks pointedly: "Could a movement that was so radically literate and distinguished by documents have emerged out of someone who wrote nothing?"

41. D. C. Parker, *The Living Text of the Gospels* (Cambridge: Cambridge Univ. Press, 1998).

42. J. Leslie Houlden, "The Fluidity of the Gospels," *TLS, Times Literary Supplement* 2 (Jan 1998): 28.

43. See David Lyle Jeffrey, *People of the Book: Christian Identity and Literary Culture* (Grand Rapids: Eerdmans, 1996).

44. Elizabeth A. Clark, "Biblical Interpretation in the Early Church" in *The Oxford Study Bible* (New York: Oxford Univ. Press, 1992), 129. Tom Troeger uses Clark's work creatively in *Ten Strategies for Preaching in a Multi-Media Culture,* 16.

45. Schuurman, *Perspectives on Technology and Culture ,* 131.

46. Troeger, *Ten Strategies for Preaching in a Multi- Media Culture,* 16.

47. As quoted in Keith Ferrell, "Entering the New Frontier: The Omni Experience Goes Electronic and Interactive," *Omni* (16 Oct 1993): 24.

48. Walter J. Ong, *Interfaces of the Word: Studies in the Evaluation of Consciousness and Culture* (Ithaca, NY: Cornell Univ. Press, 1977), 298–99.

49. Phyllis A. Tickle, *God-Talk in America* (New York: Crossroad, 1997), 126.

50. The definition of the Net is that of Andrew Leonard in *Bots: The Origin of New Species* (San Francisco: Hardwired, 1997), 182.

51. I was brought to this point in my thinking by Steven Johnson, *Interface Culture: How New Technology Transforms the Way We Create and Communicate* (San Francisco: Harper-SanFrancisco, 1997).

52. As quoted in Jeremy Langford, "Working at a Distance," *In Trust* 9 (Spring, 1998): 8.

53. The phrase is that of Cheryl Russell in "The Haves and the Want-Nots," *American Demographics* 20 (Apr 1998): 10–12.

54. The linearity of print is overstated when one considers index, footnotes, cross-references, pagination, chapters, etc.

55. As quoted in Chet Raymo, *The Virgin and the Mousetrap* (New York: Viking, 1991), 191.

56. Raymo, *The Virgin and the Mousetrap,* 183–84.

57. Steve Jones, *In the Blood: God, Genes and Destiny* (New York: HarperCollins, 1996). The set of six videocassettes of *In the Blood* (Princeton, NJ: Films for the Humanities and Sciences, 1997) originally appeared as a BBC Production.

58. Adam Gopnik, "What Next?" *The New Yorker* (20 and 27 Oct 1997): 30.

59. David Cook, *A History of Narrative Film,* 2nd ed. (New York: W. W. Norton, 1990), xv-xvi: as quoted in William D. Romanowski, *Pop Culture Wars: Religion and the Role of Entertainment in American Life* (Downers Grove, IL: InterVarsity Press, 1996), 310.

60. *Epistle to Diognetus,* in *The Apostolic Fathers,* tr. Kirsopp Lake (Cambridge, MA: Harvard Univ. Press, 1976), 2:359–63.

61. Tickle, *God-Talk in America,* 126.

62. You can find the answer to this conundrum in Richard Gregory's *Mirrors in Mind* (New York: W. H. Freeman/Spektrum, 1997).

IS THIS A GREAT TIME, OR WHAT?

Get Into It

A PRE-CHRISTIAN SOCIETY

or what?

- In the original *Bartlett's Familiar Quotations* (1855), the Bible and Shakespeare both constituted one-third of the text. Today there are about 2,000 quotes from Shakespeare and about 1,500 from the Bible. Shakespeare has won over Jesus.
- In Bernadette Vallely's manual *The Young Person's Guide to Mind, Body and Spirit* (1994), an A-to-Z encyclopedia of spirituality, Jesus gets only a page, less than "Vampires" and "Sacred Stones."
- According to the co-founder of *Mondo 2000*, the thing to be feared in cyberculture is not weird Web sites or violence on the Internet but the book of Revelation. "I'm not implying that we should regulate the Book of Revelations. I'm just saying that we should have congressional hearings about the terrible dangers that this book presents."[1]
- *Spitfire Grill* is a movie about a young woman who brings spiritual redemption to a small town in Maine. Even though it cost only $6.1 million to make, Castle Rock liked it enough to buy it for $10 million. It premiered at the 1996 Sundance Film Festival, where it was early on the most popular movie at the festival, winning the Audience Award for drama.

  Then chaos erupted. Sundance attenders found out that the financing, production, and marketing of the movie came from Gregory Productions, a company owned by a Roman Catholic order of priests. Instead of raising money for their order by baking bread or making trinkets, the Priests of the Sacred Heart decided to venture-capital family-friendly movies that promote "Judeo-Christian values." The profits would go to their charitable works—including health care for children and AIDS counseling.

  Spitfire Grill, with its Catholic backers, Protestant characters, and Jewish director, has had a hard time of it. It has been attacked for its "hidden message," and its "outside agenda." Castle Rock has been castigated for buying the film, and Disney, which initially showed an interest in distributing *Spitfire Grill*, dropped it like a hot potato.
- In 1976 the Jimmy Carter candidacy for president sent political journalists into a research frenzy. They wanted to know, as presidential scholar James D. Barber wryly observed, about this curious religious creature, the orthodox Christian. What was this oddity?

  Twenty years later, at a cocktail party in South Carolina, the discussion turned to religion. Someone asked what "born again" meant. Another said, "Oh, that's something that Jimmy Carter started when he was in the White House."

The lone Christian in the crowd tried to explain, "No, 'born again' was something Jesus started when he said, 'You must be born again.'" But no one listened.

- Daphne Hampson, who writes about Christianity with a hatred that is matched by many others, admits in her introduction to her good riddance book that "there was a time when it took much courage to say publicly in the media that one was not a Christian. Now it takes none at all."[2]

  She underestimates the case.

POST-CHRISTIAN ~ The era of Christendom is over.[4] Postmodern culture is sometimes described as "post-Christian." What captures the postmodern imagination and inflames its spirits is not Christianity. Does the Christian church have any good news left?

WIWAK (When I Was A Kid) in the 1950s, people's minds were still naturalized in Christianity. If you breathed air, you knew who a "Pharisee" was, or what it meant to call a city "Sodom and Gomorrah." When Bob Dylan was on a tour of Britain in 1965, he was attacked by folk music purists for "selling out." With the first bars of "Ballad of a Thin Man," someone in the Manchester audience yelled "Judas" at the singer. The band stopped and refused to go on. They knew what it meant.

> The West appears to have said its definitive farewell to a Christian culture.... Our secular colleagues are happy to recognize the debt our civilization owes to the Christian faith to the extent that the faith, having been absorbed by culture itself, has become simply another cultural artifact. Christianity has become a historical factor subservient to a secular culture rather than functioning as the creative power it once was.
>
> Yale Professor Louis Dupré[3]

No longer. Christianity is now culturally as well as socially and religiously disestablished. Your computer's spell check proves it. Before I could write this book, I had to program the spell check of Windows 95 because it does not know the books of the Bible, or recognize biblical names.

The pastoral team at Trinity Church in Columbus, Ohio, "retreated" to Indianapolis for the NCAA "March Madness" basketball playoffs. The ubiquitous guy with orange hair and a homemade "John 3:16" sign was under the basket at the other end of the court. Seated directly behind the pastoral team were two well-dressed couples debating what the "John 3:16" sign meant. Reduced to guessing, one thought it must be an ad for a new restaurant in town. The others dissed that idea since "who would send someone out with orange hair and a hand-drawn sign to advertise anything?" Another thought the "John 3:16" sign might be a signal to someone to meet at the John on the third floor, stall 16. Talk about clueless. They were totally in the dark why anyone would be holding a sign with those words on it.

> Whenever, in a detective story, we are taken inside a church, candles underlighting spooky statues, there is sure to be a corpse in the clerestory.
>
> P. J. Kavanagh[5]

Within my lifebank of memory, the very thing that used to get pastors on community boards and other privileged positions in any town in the nation—their religious leadership, especially of once-dominant Protestant dominations—is now exactly the reason why they are kept off community boards and prevented from power positions.

Christian faith was never universal in USAmerica. But there was a broad consensus that our national culture should rest on a Christian worldview. It is this idea that is now suspect—partly because a new global context de-centers any single worldview; partly because secular rationality has advanced to the point where we have pensioned off from the imagination things like Satan, hell, guilt, and grace; partly because religious plurality is a dominant feature of life in the US, as Professor Diana Eck of Harvard University has shown through her "Pluralism Project."[6]

It is partly also because science has replaced religion as the basis of social morality. Pitrim Sorokin, founder of the Harvard University Department of Sociology, argued that when something other than religious faith underpins morality, which underpins society, the society begins to crumble. This was, said Sorokin, who died in 1968, "The Crisis of Our Age."[7] If Christianity no longer provides the dominant language of public discourse, what does? Hasn't the grammar of therapy now become the discourse language that expresses the obligations and expectations between the governed and the elected officials?

From a statistical standpoint, very few unbelievers are making first-time commitments to Christ as Lord and Savior.[8] The American church may be working harder than ever before, but it is getting fewer results than perhaps ever before. Attendance at places of worship in USAmerica will continue to decline, as it has since mid–'91, when Boomers stopped coming back to church. Under the arresting headline "All But Elderly Shun Church Services," the *Wall Street Journal* reported the findings of Roper Starch Worldwide that 28% of those attending religious services during the week preceding the 1994 survey were 60 or older.[9] The upsurge in religious observance among Boomers predicted by many sociologists simply hasn't happened. Among those aged 18 to 29, attendance has fallen to 27% from 35%.[10] Actually, church membership and church-related activities have been declining for 20 years, according to the General Social Survey. In 1984 more than 37% of people aged 30 to 39 attended religious services once a week; for their 1995 counterparts, that figure had dropped to 25%.[11]

What is more, some statistics reveal that the percentage of unchurched people in the South is nearly identical to that in the East and Midwest (41%, 45%, and 43% respectively).[12] This does not even factor in the fact that church attendance rates are about half what they are reported as being—i.e., 20% as opposed to 40%.[13] Americans may see themselves as churchgoers, but they aren't.

ANTI-CHRISTIAN ~ More accurately, postmodern culture can be described as "anti-Christian." P. J. Kavanagh estimates that 70% of the popular mention of Christianity in Great Britain is "either negative or derisive."[14] The biggest issue facing the World Council of the 30-million-member YMCA in 1998 is whether or not to keep the "C" in their name; the proclamation of Christ as Redeemer is seen as a sign of Western imperialism by many of the 114 countries.

We can expect increased hostility to Christianity in general and, even more so, to organized religion in particular. In the few weeks between the day kids leave high school and the day they respond to their college's entering freshman survey, one out of eight of them bolt from the church.[15] Why? The Dean of the Chapel at the University of Chicago gives a hint: "If the chapel at which I serve were to offer a program on 'Spirituality,' the room would be full. If the same program were to be entitled 'Religion,' the room would be empty."[16]

In interviews on the spirituality of their music, musicians are flattered by the question but most often deny any concrete denominational identity:

"I don't have any allegiance to an organized religion; I have an allegiance to the gifts that I find for myself in those religions."

Pop composer/singer Jeff Buckley[17]

"I'm a very religious person. I just don't worship at any particular shrine."

Singer/composer Robyn Hitchcock[18]

"I'm not gonna downplay organized religion because it makes a lot of sense for someone who doesn't know anything. . . . I pretty much like to make my own religion. I don't go to church, but I respect God."

Lead rapper for PM Dawn/hip-hop artist Prince Be/Reasons[19]

Pop singer Gloria Estafan says that "organized religion is detrimental to the spirit" and inhibits spirituality. But she prays daily and testifies that "we are all part of God."[20]

Skeptical of institutions, postmoderns are getting spiritual help from videos, books, radio, newsletters, and a host of do-it-yourself sources. People may be "high on God," but they are "low on the church."

How low? One only needs to look at the literary and scholarly worlds, where Christians bear the brunt of jokes, jabs, and judgment, to see how low. Playwright/novelist/critic Octave Mirbeau is celebrated for his creation of slimy priests that he called "ecclesiastical woodlice." In Sandra Loh's novel

Depth Takes a Holiday,[21] evangelism is equated with sexual abuse and body violation. A young women is on a date, and at dinner her date asks her if she knows Jesus. In the novel, the character says that he had assaulted her just as if he had grabbed her breasts.

A. D. Harvey, who has worked through the *Arts and Humanities Citation Index,* has published a list of the 23 most-footnoted thinkers of 1996. The writers most frequently cited in English academic journals in 1997 were Sigmund Freud and Michel Foucault, closely followed by Aristotle and Jacques Derrida, with Plato in fifth place.[22] Totally missing are religious thinkers other than Aquinas. The fourth-most-quoted scholar in the world today, academic superstar Jacques Derrida, has written a commentary on religion called *The Gift of Death* that begins sanely enough: "Religion is responsibility or it is nothing at all." But then Derrida goes on to argue that Christianity really exists and belongs "outside" the church and even the history of Christianity itself. He sees the "religiosity" of Christianity already existing "'in' our interhuman relations, in openness to mystery and vulnerability in society, and that these aspects may be repressed and incorporated by institutionalized Christianity."[23]

A recent Oxford publication puts the Christian dilemma in sharp relief. Ian S. Markham compiled for Oxford *A World Religions Reader.*[24] Claiming to present each tradition "in the best possible light," the author does so for every non-Christian tradition. But Christianity fares badly. His first chapter on Christianity is on "secular humanism," which rejects all religion. His testimonies about Christianity are from lapsed believers who have rejected the Christian faith. His treatment of Christianity's treatment of women stresses Thomas Aquinas' negativity, while Islam's attitude toward women is stressed positively (nothing about polygamy, wearing the veil, opposition to divorce, etc.).

Why is it that C. S. Lewis has such little standing in the intellectual community? Here is one of the most outstanding literary scholars, one of the most astute and authoritative philosophical voices, one of the most popular children's writers of all time. Yet, in academic circles Lewis is little more than a joke. Why? One scholar can only conclude the reason: "The most probable is his frank profession of Christianity."[25]

Harvard professor Henry Louis Gates Jr., in his *New Yorker* article on "Hating Hillary," admits that he is religious himself but tries to keep quiet about it because at Harvard spirituality is considered "one of those conditions that suggest some lapse of hygiene of those afflicted, as with worms or lice."[26] Christian novelist Reynolds Price, who lives in Durham, North Carolina, talks about people who are "religious" being seen as "kooky" in the publishing world and as even stranger in the academic world. People in the arts and media who were religious had secret meetings. Price said that "it's like being a member of a masturbation club."[27]

Princeton sociologist Robert Wuthnow has written about one of the "two dirty little secrets" in American higher education—the one being its "disdain for evangelical Christians. Few groups are as despised a minority." Christians in general, and evangelicals in particular, arouse the greatest passion and prejudice, according to Wuthnow.[28]

Postmodern society may be intrinsically hostile to the Christian faith. But it is extremely open to Jesus the Christ, even its truth claims that Jesus is The Way, The Truth, and The Life. If I want to witness to my faith and begin by saying "I am a Christian," chances are the other person leans away from me. If I begin my witness by saying "I am a disciple of Jesus," chances are the other person leans in and wants to hear more. For mission's sake, what if Christians were to renounce Christianity and become disciples of Jesus?

At best, that word *Christian* has a bittersweet guilt-by-association in postmodern culture. At worst, that word *Christian* is so greasy and slimy from everyone's fingerings that no one wants to pick it up. Ambient musician/ raver/deejay/vegan/Christian Moby tells of signing autographs at a rock festival in Detroit when someone came up to him and said, "'I think it's really cool that you're a Christian.' And the guy standing next to her said, 'You're a Christian? That's ———,' and walked away. They were both responding to that word *Christian*, and I wanted to say to them, 'Look, I like both of you, but neither one of you probably understands what that word means.'"[29]

There is something about the person of Jesus that fascinates postmoderns—partly because they sense instinctively that he was one of them. "Christ was extremely dynamic: he swore, and he drank, and he ran around, and he screamed at people. He loved his friends and was a very human, passionate figure," contends Moby.[30] One Gen-X church planter of a new African-American church in Chicago scheduled worship services, not when it was most convenient to his Gen-X constituency, but at a time when "worship" was least corrupted by church culture stereotypes—5 o'clock Sunday evening. As one of his young "members" admitted to him, "Shawn, I hope you know that if it weren't for Jesus, I wouldn't be a Christian."

To be sure, some of this hostility we have caused ourselves. Mark Twain, who announced that after having spent a lot of time with "good people" he could understand why Jesus preferred to spend his time with tax collectors and sinners, was not the first to observe the Christians' hard-earned

> Jesus
> Save Me
> From Some of
> Your Followers
>   T-shirt

reputation for being "mean spirited and uncompassionate."[31] The most "Christianized" nation in Africa (95%) was Rwanda, the nation where ethnic cleansing and genocide raised its ugly head and where clergy themselves participated in murderous rampages.[32]

so what? FROM CHRISTENDOM CULTURE TO PRE-CHRISTIAN MISSION FIELDS

~ We could say this, from churchbroken to the unchurched and the overchurched. Bill Easum and Thomas Bandy state in their pathbreaking book, "Christendom is dead, and with it the institutionalized distinctions of leadership. The pre-Christian era has begun, and with it a whole new understanding of leadership."[33]

Postmodern culture is most accurately described as "pre-Christian."[34] We are in many ways back in the first century in the midst of a culture that still has yet to hear about who we are and what we believe. Instead of the Christian church giving off nothing so much as the sour whiff of the rejected suitor, what if we were to look at USAmerica as a vast mission field—120 million pre-Christian people 14 or older? What if we were to stop picking on CEOs (Christmas-and-Easter Onlys) and ETCs (Easter-Thanksgiving-Christmas) and started treating them special?

The church's two largest mission constituencies are the unchurched and the overchurched. Only two countries have more nonbelievers than the US: India and China. The US is the third-largest mission field in the world. Unfortunately, our efforts at evangelizing the unchurched have all the pace of a southern summer. Few believers have relationships, much less friendships, with nonbelievers. And our bluntness of touch when handling the unchurched—how would *you* like to be a lion in a den of Daniels?—is made even more artless by our interior distractions, effortful compassion, and dependence on the sedimental sentiments of establishment religion.

The second mission of a pre-Christian church is the overchurched. Each month, according to George Barna, Christian churches come into contact with 100 million adults and more than 30 million children. Unfortunately, "most of them are involved in a religious ritual," Barna observes, "and have little connection with Christ." If by "Christian" one means that someone has had a life-transforming encounter with the gospel that has consequences for both earth and eternity, then Barna's studies reveal that one-half the church lacks both convictions and compulsion at best or is non-Christian at worst, with only 10–15% of the nation's 320,000 churches rated "highly effective."[35] Postmodern Christianity is chock-full of "religious" men and women with little faith in Christ—"Christian agnostics," if you will. One wonders if the church's new mission to one-and-the-same "Christians" and "agnostics" is like saying two people deserve each other. You don't know whether it is a beautiful compliment or a bitter insult.

It is tempting to lament the loss of a time when people were churchbroken—trained to know what to do in church and when to do it. Much of the church is still trying to wish and wash away its catacomb culture. But postmodern culture is indifferent at best to the squawks and squeals of our vested interests being displaced at the head of the table. The question of "How do we stop the collapse of church culture?" is a misplaced, fear-driven response to the decline of Christendom culture, according to Southern Baptist consultant Reggie McNeal. The proper question that addresses the missionary needs of both the unchurched and the overchurched is "How do we re-conceptualize a Christianity that is not tied to the church culture?"[36]

GET IT ~ We are not living in the world we grew up in, much less our parents grew up in. Churched culture is over. The church is dead! Long live the church!

In Oregon, April is now "Christian Heritage Month": Christians get a month alongside other religious traditions. In Berkeley, California, busloads of children are brought in for a 60-foot Christmas Tree (scratch that: "Holiday Tree") lighting ceremony that features rituals for Christ's birth, Hanukkah, Kwanza, Diwali (Hindu), and a pagan candle-lighting ceremony. At the Richman Gordman -1/2 Price Stores chain, there is now once a year a "Religion Day" in which 5% of every purchase (before tax) goes to your-choice place of worship. In the retail world, religion gets one day a year.

It is not that we haven't been here before. In John Weever's *Ancient Funeral Monuments* (1611),[37] there is the complaint that "tombs make good pissing-places in churches, a custom (to our shame) too commonly used of us in these days." But defacement of the sacred implied sacredness itself. This is the world that is no more. We early Boomers and Boosters must escape our toilet training in a world where the culture loved the Christians and thought we had something to contribute.[38] Kids today never even heard of "blue laws." Don't believe me? Ask them.

Have you heard the story of the Christian on a desert island who built two churches—one to go to, and one to stay away from? Denominations could start offering people Frequent Flier points to come to church, and they still wouldn't come. "We must accept that the traditional place of the institutional church in American society is dying," argues Mike Regele in his book *Death of the Church,* "and with it the institutional church itself."[39] Nobel Prize-winning novelist Toni Morrison, when asked, "Are your religious?" responds, "I have a problem with institutions, I don't have a problem with faith."[40]

Emil Brunner once was impressed in Japan by an organization that called itself the "No Church Church." I have heard nothing more about it, but that's the future of the church if it is to have one. There is even out now *A NonChurchgoer's Guide to the Bible*[41] for those who don't want their Bible tainted by any church or denominational tradition. In the words of one contributor to the *Newsweek* chat room after the cover article on "Living in the Holy Spirit": "The only denominations I like are 10's, 100's, etc."[42]

It is interesting that classical Hebrew has no word for *religion*. (Neither *emunah* nor the Aramaic-mediated loan-word *dath* conveys what we know today as "religion.") Perhaps that word *Torah*, which has a composite meaning of law, learning, and living (i.e., spiritual practice) is ripe for Christian rediscovery.

GET OVER IT ~ I don't like it that Christians are the brunt of new slams and slurs being slung left and right. I don't like it that publisher Adam Parfrey, founder of Feral House, was asked in an interview if there is one book he'd like everyone to read: "I know a book that I'd like everyone to *stop* reading, because it spreads strange and untenable ideas about life: the Bible."[43] I don't like it that one recent biographer commanded his readers to snatch "every Gideon Bible" from its hotel drawer and throw it in the trash.[44]

Guess what, Bible-toting Sweet? *Deal with it. Get over it. Or get help!*

I don't like it that a New York representative to Congress, Peter King, criticizing the House GOP leadership, said that "it's a southern, anti-union attitude that appeals to the mentality of hillbillies at revival meetings."

Guess what, hillbilly Sweet, who grew up going to revival meetings? *Deal with it. Get over it. Or get help!*

I don't like it that a new book on pool celebrates the game for being a sport not yet tainted or sanitized by what the author calls "the Fellowship of Christian Athletes types."[45]

Guess what, sports enthusiast Sweet, who played one year of college basketball? *Deal with it. Get over it. Or get help!*

I don't like it that at the Second Luddite Congress Christian writers David Kline and Art Gish, both of whom live in "plain" Christian communities, were maligned and attacked by other neo-Luddites because of their Christian lifestyles and beliefs.[46]

Guess what, Sweet, who came out of the "plain" holiness tradition of Pilgrim Holiness and Free Methodist movements? *Deal with it. Get over it. Or get help!*

I don't like it that the media (e.g., *US News & World Report, Time, Newsweek)* consistently choose the holiest Christian week of the year to present cover stories raising questions about what can be believed in the gospels and explore whether or not Jesus did what the Bible says he did.

Guess what, dangerously Christian Sweet? *Deal with it. Get over it. Or get help!*

I don't like it that at the January 1996 ComNet Convention in Washington a frame-relay switch vendor hired a gospel choir to sing "We Shall Overcome" to unveil its newest switch.[47]

Guess what, gospel-music-loving Sweet, who is convinced that the angels in heaven sing southern gospel music? *Deal with it. Get over it. Or get help!*

I don't like it that Nebraska native Chip Davis, founder of the group Mannheim Steamroller, wrote a new song for his school in Omaha that debuted on homecoming day in 1996. The response? One former Nebraska band director commented, "It's bad. It sounds like you're in church. Anybody can make up a tune like that."[48]

Guess what, former organist Sweet? *Deal with it. Get over it. Or get help!*

I don't like it that screen versions of novels like *Sense and Sensibility* and *Pride and Prejudice* filtered out much of Jane Austen's biblical vocabulary, since the language of Christianity is no longer a cultural signifier as it once was and because "we would have risked alienating an audience for whom such language is not the natural expression of moral conviction, but the private language of a sect."[49]

Guess what, Jane-Austen-fanatic Sweet? *Deal with it. Get over it. Or get help!*

I don't like it that for 50 years the Barrington, Rhode Island, town council volunteered to plow the snow from the parking lots of nine churches and one synagogue—until the Rhode Island branch of the American Civil Liberties Union (ACLU) sued the town, and Federal Judge Joseph DiClerico decreed in 1996 that the good deed was unconstitutional.

Guess what, small-town-lover Sweet? *Deal with it. Get over it. Or get help!*

I don't like it that my son Justin brought one of his old girlfriends to hear me preach. "Dad, you need to know that I didn't tell her we were going to church to hear you preach. I told her we were going somewhere to listen to you speak." I don't like it that sermons, even of those by Archbishop Desmond Tutu, are called "descents into vulgar oratory."[50] I don't like it that for the first time in its 75-year history, the atheists and witches conducted the 1996 sunrise service from San Diego's famous old rugged cross at Mount Soledad. They beat preachers from the Easter service organizers to City Hall for the requisite permits.

Guess what, preacher Sweet? *Deal with it. Get over it. Or get help!*

GET ON WITH IT! GET INTO IT! ~ Postmodern preachers don't populate the pews; they connect people to the living Christ. Postmodern evangelism doesn't say to the world, "Come to church." Rather, it says to the church, "Go to the world."

Evangelism in a culture that is transitioning from Christendom to post-Christendom is different. Postmodern evangelism is more John the Baptist than Peter and Paul. Postmodern evangelism is constructing new constituencies for Christ.

Postmodern evangelism is recognizing that God is already at work in people's lives before we arrived on the scene, and that our role is helping people to see how God is present and active in their lives, calling them home. Postmodern evangelism is not "I have Jesus, and you don't. How can I get you here so that I can give you my Jesus?" but "you already know Jesus, even if you don't think you know Jesus. How can I help you see and know what you already know, and how can I know and meet your Jesus?"

DEVELOP JOHN-THE-BAPTIST MINISTRIES ~ John the Baptist had a ministry that came before Christ, not after Christ. John the Baptist met people where they were, as Jesus did after him. He was second only to Jesus as the greatest communicator of his day. He knew what it took to get people's attention, even to the point of our knowing to this day how he dressed, what he ate, and how he sounded. He pioneered lifestyle branding.

The advertising world has discovered the power of "lifestyle marketing," wherein companies go beyond selling products to selling lifestyle—what to wear, drink, play, drive, and read. Inundated by a proliferation of choices, brands are providing buying reassurances for people who want to "get a life."

More John-the-Baptist ministries means more body evangelism and lifestyle evangelism that emphasizes the quality of living in Christ. Christians are people who show others how to "get a life," whose lifestyle evangelizes: what and how we wear, drink, play, drive, and read can communicate our values and faith. First-century Christians represented a whole new way of quality living in the world, a way of living that could be found nowhere else. First Peter tells what this distinctive quality of lifestyle of Christians was like:

1. Extend goodness toward Gentiles (2:12)
2. Confront evil with good (2:8–20)
3. Exercise patience, humility, and a good conscience (3:15, 16, 21)
4. Practice servanthood (3:21ff.)
5. Know that God cares for you (5:6ff.; 1:3ff.)[51]

Pre-Christian communities of faith must not retreat from the church or withdraw from the world, but stay where we are and resist the pagan ways of living. John-the-Baptist leaders engage in guerilla preaching/evangelism in which we poach the culture, "plunder the Egyptians," and rework popular culture to the gospel's advantage. This is the real "cross-over"—not from sacred to secular, but from secular to sacred.

Marriott's motto stretches over the doorways of its hotels: "Every guest leaves satisfied." The Postmodern Reformation Church's motto must stretch over its doorways: "Every worshiper leaves welcomed." Instead of so much talk about love, perhaps it's time the church helped people experience how the love of Christ plays in one's life. In fact, wasn't the name "Christian" given to the early believers in Antioch (Acts 11:26) because they lived out in their lives the Christ they followed?

At a university chapel in the Northeast, there is printed in the Sunday bulletin after the words "The Signs of Peace" these instructions: "Please make an effort to greet all newcomers."

John-the-Baptist worship makes it effortless.

In a Christendom culture, baptism can be immediate because it's easier to be conformed to the mind of Christ. In a post-Christendom culture, catechesis often precedes baptism, and it may take years.

For postmoderns, participation and conversation come before conversion. Mike Foss of Prince of Peace Lutheran Church in Burnsville, Minnesota, invites members of his congregation to come to the table with these words: "Come and hold in your hand and taste on your lips the love which we cannot comprehend."

GET AHEAD OF IT! ~ *SoulTsunami* is designed and dedicated not only to helping you predict, but to helping you intervene spiritually and socially to invent and prevent the future. The future is ours by design or default. In spite of that ubiquitous question "Where is technology taking us?" technology is not taking us anywhere. Technology is not some discrete, autonomous force that functions as an independent variable in history. As anthropologist Robert McC. Adams argues so convincingly, technology is best approached as a "field of interaction" that is only given shape and form by social, economic, and political context.[52]

No one "discovers" the future. The future is not a discovery. The future is not a destiny. The future is a decision, an intervention. Do nothing, and we drift fatalistically into a future not driven by technology alone, but by other people's need, greed, and creed. The future is not some dim and distant region out there in time. The future is a reality that is coming to pass with each passing day, with each passing decision.

Postmodern Christians are spiritual interventionists. The Postmodern Reformation Church will consciously intervene to help design this new world. There are many futures out there. The future is not a "single state," but a scenario of possibilities. There is a struggle between opposing visions of the future. It is not too late to choose which one we shall get. The future is a function of our choices and creations.

The world is where it is today because certain people imagined a world outside the standard models. Luther imagined the world differently and helped to change it. John Wesley imagined the world differently and helped to change it. Phoebe Palmer imagined the world differently and helped to change it.

> The best way to predict the future is to invent it.
>
> Allen Kaye, father of the personal computer

You can be the last of a dying breed of ministers, those left standing on a burning platform. Or you can be the front-guard of a new breed of ministers. You can be a dinosaur in the tar pit, or you can be the frontline of a new kind of leader for the church. You can be the church in a world you wish you had, or your faith can face the world the way it really is.

Which will it be? Will the church get ahead of it?

FROM HOUSE CALLS TO MOUSE CALLS AND HOME DELIVERIES ~

When my mother built a home that was open to the world with a wide front porch and an open-door policy to strangers. In doing so, she was perpetuating a millennia-old tradition of hospitality. In the 1500s, one German family reported, on a single Saturday, visits by peddlers, a jester, ice merchants, knife sharpeners, various servants' friends, a glass repairman, neighbors, a baker's apprentice, neighborhood children, the leech carrier, and the priest.[53]

Today parents build homes not to let the world in, but to keep the world out. Postmodern households are not set up to receive "house calls." The only ways into the home are now through mouse calls and home deliveries. Jeffrey Stratton, a pastor in Round Lake, New York, calls the latter "Domino's Evangelism." Domino's Pizza made a fortune on two words: "We Deliver." Postmodern churches have learned not to make house calls on their members, but to make daily mouse calls and periodic home deliveries.

Turn your church's "reception desk" into a Welcome Wagon, where guests are made to feel special and where special packets are prepared based on what's going on in the local newspaper, both for visitors to the church and for delivery to people in the community who are moving in, up, out—in their houses, jobs, family life, and special times and needs in their lives. Soup up a minivan as your Welcome Wagon vehicle and model it on the old-fashioned ice-cream trucks. Equip it with minifreezers and microwave ovens for meals-on-the-run and other home deliveries. Find excuses to communicate with people by word of mouse; spread positive gossip across the postmodern fence—the digital grapevine/e-mail. Make a ritual of home deliveries of baptismal, wedding, and other rites-of-passage video momentos, all produced by your Media Ministry Team and your ministers of videography and photography.

DOUBLE-RING MINISTRIES ~

Christianity is still the religion of choice for USAmericans. This nation has the largest number of professing Christians per capita of any nation in the world. Yet we must get used to living in a world in which biblical standards no longer matter and where the deck is stacked against Christians.[54] Similarly, in the 20th century the Christian religion became a truly global faith. Evangelical Christianity was the fastest-growing religion in the world during the century, especially in Latin America, where evangelicals multiplied at four times the rate of population growth.[55]

Islam is the world's fastest growing religion of the 21st century. While Western Christianity accounted for 26.9% of the world's population in 1900 and peaked at about 30% in 1980, the Muslim population increased from 12.4% in 1900 to as much as 18% in 1980 with well over 1 billion adherents by the mid-1990s. The percentage of Christians in the world will probably decline to about 25% by 2025, the slack largely taken up by Muslims. Muslims are already poised to outnumber Jews in the United States and become the nation's second-largest faith by 2010.

> Nothing is impossible for the man who will not listen to reason.
>
> John Belushi
> in *Animal House*

Every pastor is involved in new church development. Every church should make as one of its biggest mission projects a new church plant—right where you are.

The first words spoken on the moon were in what language? English. Did England get there first? No, one of it's colonies did.

In the same way, the mother church may not be the one carrying the flag into the 22nd century. It may be only through its "plants" that the mother church gets there.

MAKE DOGMA DRAMA ~ Theology is not boring. In the words of Dorothy Sayers, "It is the dogma that is the drama—not beautiful phrases, nor comforting sentiments, nor vague aspirations to loving kindness." Postmodern Christianity must engage the intellect, must have edge, must be conversant with the sciences, and must not be afraid of intellectual fire. Nothing pushes postmoderns' nausea button quicker than sermons that are pure didactic cardboard or psychological mush. They know better than "if you learn these seven points, then surely goodness and mercy will follow, along with success and salvation." Camille Paglia was introduced before a lecture at Harvard as "an enemy of the namby-pamby, the hoity-toity, and the artsy-fartsy." Her motto is "Hate dogma. Love art. Love learning."

"Dogma" must be approached less from a "doctrinal" standpoint than from a "teaching" perspective. Postmoderns are drowning in an avalanche of information. They feel the lack of a world of wisdom, rituals, and content. They are curious about strong moral codes and the strictly ordered life. Postmoderns are hungry for "teaching," but not for "doctrine."

> It is far better to soak in five pages of substance than to read 500 pages of fluff.
>
> Author Richard Foster[56]

The word *doctrine* is used 49 times in the New Testament, while *teaching* is used 93 times. If postmoderns choose to become disciples of Jesus, they will want to know the teachings of Jesus and his best students. What is the difference between John Calvin's and John Wesley's interpretation of Jesus' teachings? And what was behind this dispute between Erasmus and Luther? What made Erasmus a skeptic who always suspended convictions, while Luther said, Nonsense, the Holy Spirit is no skeptic?

The return of "dogma" to the church is part of the postmodern preference to go to the table than to the mat. Anyone who has spent time around Gen-Xers knows that round-the-clock ear-bendings are part and parcel of everyday life. But "dogmas" for postmoderns are less back-then "answers" that can be recited than bone-deep "convictions" that can be questioned and explored. In many ways, the best days of "dogma" may be ahead of us if only the church can learn to nutshell dogma and present the drama of learning in postmodern forms.

One futurist, who himself has no interest in religious traditions and hopes they die out, nevertheless has the sneaking suspicion that his descendants may think differently and reconnect on higher levels with ancient teachings like the doctrine of the Holy Trinity.

One scientist sees this idea, which seems so alien to us with our hierarchical structures of command, as a "revolutionary form of logic which is ideal for new forms of computing." His idea ... is to have three master-chips controlling a computer in equal authority, instead of a single one—the "central processing unit" that prevails in present computer architectures. Each would function as a separate entity. When the machine had to make a decision, the outcome would be decided by a vote between the three instead of a directive from one. This would give the computer an unheard-of degree of independence and flexibility.[57]

Most of us, however, cannot remain high spiritually on Theological Studies for long. Unless dogma becomes drama, it is full of sound and fury, signifying little.

COMING ANTI-CLERICALISM ~

"Do you know why clergy are just like diapers?" a woman asked me teasingly after one of my presentations. "They need to be changed often—and for the same reason."

This will not be the first time in history that the church had to contend with anti-clericalism. In the latter half of the 19th century in Paris, one *communard* suggested bagging up the bodies of the city's 60,000 priests and using them as barricades. A 24-year-old Prefect of Police, Raoul Rigault, renamed the Boulevard Saint-Michel the Boulevard Michel and wanted to issue a warrant for God's arrest. "Whom do you serve?" he asked one of the many priests he arrested. "God," replied the accused. "Where does he live?" "He lives everywhere." Rigault turned to his scribe: "Write down: Serves God, a vagrant."[58]

There is anger over the hogging of ministry by professionals; anger over not empowering all Christians for ministry; anger over not releasing the spiritual potential in every believer.

Anglican Bishop Rowan Williams warns preachers that the biblical verse "We are treated as impostors, and yet are true" (2 Cor. 6:8) is being fulfilled in our lifetime: "We are not merely harmless spinners of fantasy; we are *deceivers*, seducers, frauds, misleading men and women in the most significant and vulnerable areas of their lives."[59]

TURN STAINED-GLASS WINDOWS OUTWARD ~ In a Doonesbury comic strip by Garry Trudeau, the first panel begins: "You know, popster, you guys ought to get married on the space needle! And have fireworks or something!"

Second panel: "Or have it at a cyber café, so all the guests can play on the Web! Or at sit&spin, where everyone can dance and do their laundry after the ceremony!"

Third panel: "Um . . . Actually, we were thinking of a church."

"A church? What do people do at a church?"

Fourth panel: "Get married."

"PERFECT!"

We can assume only two things about postmodern culture in its views toward Christians. First, church is seen as a scary place. Almost half (46%) of Britons say they never set foot in a place of worship except for an occasional wedding or funeral.[60] This makes "vestibule evangelism" a key component of postmodern ministry.

Part of pre-Christian evangelism is finding ways to get the unchurched into church in the first place and to make them feel comfortable once they are there. "Come As You Are or As You Please" is the motto of one church that has understood the importance of vestibule evangelism. Christmas pageants, seminars, and tournaments are other vestibule events that make church culture less frightening.[61] The 14,000-member Prestonwood Baptist Church in Dallas, Texas, attracts over 30,000 people to its six-day, nine-show, sell-out Christmas pageant, charging visitors from $10 to $13 a seat to listen to 400 choir members, live elephants, five sheep, a donkey, and three Wise Men atop camels.[62] People who would never set foot in the door of a church have trouble resisting the appeal of this Broadway-sized production, and the church has found that once they get them in the door, they stay.

In a Christendom culture, to ask all guests and visitors to stand was to pay them a compliment. In a post-Christendom culture, such an invitation is likely to drive people to worship at the altar of St. Mattress and to exhibit greater devotion to Our Lady of the Pillow. Therefore, at Peachtree Presbyterian Church in Atlanta, Dr. Frank Harrington asks each Sunday, "Will all the *members* please stand?" Steve Stroope of Lake Pointe Baptist Church in Rockwall, Texas, modified the traditional "altar call"; it changed from an appeal to come forward in front of 4,000 people and say "I'm a mess" to meeting in a glass-enclosed "hospitality center" after the service for coffee, counseling, and prayer. Other churches, knowing the colon-churning sound of those words "small group" to male culture, calls their disciple-making ministries *anything but* "small groups."

Second, postmoderns are totally unfamiliar with our language, rituals, and beliefs. The Bible isn't closed—it's unknown. Biblical illiteracy is such that 12% of the American people think Joan of Arc was married to Noah. Eight out of 10

US adults claim to be "Christian," but they are hazy and lazy about their faith. Four out of 10 Christians are unable to name the four gospels.[63] Only half of those who claim to be "born again" read the Scripture during the week.

Jay Leno periodically does "man-on-the-street" interviews. One night he asked questions about the Bible. "Can you name one of the Ten Commandments?" he asked two college-age women. One replied, "Freedom of speech?" Leno then asked the other student: "Complete this sentence: Let he who is without sin . . ." "Have a good time" was her response. Leno then turned to a young man and asked, "Who, according to the Bible, was eaten by a whale?" The confident answer was "Pinocchio."

> They laughed at Joan of Arc, but she went right ahead and built it anyway.
>
> Gracie Allen (of Burns and Allen comedy team)

Canadian theologian John G. Stackhouse Jr., tells of sitting next to a passenger and talking about his faith. Finally the passenger interrupted him and said, "Who is this 'apostle Paul' you're referring to?" This widespread ignorance, even among the educated, leads Stackhouse to conclude:

> Too much of our Christian witness today concentrates upon trying to convince people that Christianity is true. We need instead to consider two prior problems. First, most Americans and Canadians are ignorant of even the basics of authentic Christian faith. And second, most people think that they do understand Christianity and thus feel entitled to dismiss it out of hand.[64]

FORGET EVANGELISM TRAINING ~ Our problem in evangelism is not a lack of training. The problem in evangelism is that we don't love enough. Do you need training to talk about your grandchildren? You love them so much you can't stop spreading the good news and new pictures with everyone who will listen. Do you need to attend workshops to talk about your hobby? Your collection of Beanie Babies or Barbie Dolls is always on the tip of your tongue, ready to come tripping off at the drop of a hint of interest.

Evangelism doesn't require training. Evangelism requires love. Lack of evangelism means lack of love.

SERVE BREAKFAST IN BED ~ It was my first "fireside chat" with seminary students at Drew. It proved to be more a fireside "roast" than a "chat," and "roast dean" was the favorite dish of the evening.

At issue was the use of Drew Theological School as one of the locations for the shooting of Woody Allen's movie *Deconstructing Harry.* Did I know that Drew University was going to be used that way? No, I said. Should I have known, or been asked permission, for Drew to be used that way? No, I said. Had I ever seen a Woody Allen movie before? No, I said. Did not I have an obligation to review the script of the movie before allowing a Woody Allen movie to be shot on campus? No, I said. Should Drew accept Mr. Allen's money for his use of the campus? Yes, I said. I didn't care about money's pedigree, only about its destiny.

And so it went. At the end of the "chat," after everyone had left Asbury Hall, one of our brighter, younger students (Todd Jordan) lingered behind and said, "Dean Sweet, I think I can learn something from you."

"That's nice, Todd, that you feel that way. What could you have possibly learned from me this evening?"

"I learned that when people throw at you rotten eggs and tomatoes, you can serve them breakfast in bed."

When postmodern culture throws at Christians rotten eggs and tomatoes, barbs and subpoenas, can we serve it breakfast in bed? Can the church serve this pre-Christian culture not just breakfast in bed, but eggs Benedict in bed?

In 1996 NPR commentator and writer Andrei Codrescu did a satire on the Christians and their views of eschatology on *All Things Considered.* Not only did he ridicule the varieties of millennial views (the premillennialists, the postmillennialists, the amillennialists, etc.), but those who believed in the Rapture received a special spanking. As far as he was concerned, he said, "the evaporation of 4 million who believe in this crap would leave the world a better place."[65] NPR has since apologized to the Christian community. The commentator has refused. Why?

He refuses because he is more convinced than ever that he's right. After the NPR broadcast, was Codrescu flooded with "breakfast in bed" letters that read "Dr. Codrescu: I can certainly understand why someone not familiar with Christian theology would be confused and even bemused by the bewildering variety of views on Christ's second coming. But if you would give me a moment, let me tell you what it means for me to say on a daily basis 'Maranatha,' and what this doctrine of hope does for my life"?

Is that the kind of letter Mr. Codrescu received from Christians?

Andrei Codrescu got hate mail from Christians. He got death threats from Christians. He got such an inundation of vituperation and venom that he's more convinced than ever that the "evaporation" from earth of those who believe such things would "leave this world a better place."

As far as I'm concerned, the only thing worse than Mr. Codrescu's commentary was the reaction of Christians to Mr. Codrescu's commentary.

WHEN "HAIL HIM" TURNS TO "NAIL HIM" ~ More and more, postmoderns are not throwing rotten tomatoes and eggs and other garbage at us. They are throwing sticks and stones and other things that can break our skin and bones. The question becomes, when postmodern culture throws nails at you, can you not spit nails back?

There is a host of new Sauls "breathing threats and murder" on the road to Damascus (Acts 9:1). Indeed, the increased persecution of Christians throughout the world is the great untold story of our time. In Pakistan, Ethiopia, Egypt, Saudi Arabia, Iran, East Timor, China, and North Korea there is a rise of persecution that is terrifying. The more the balance of power in the Middle East shifts from secular to Islamic governments, the more Christians are in jeopardy. Sudan is notorious for its treatment of Christians. Convert to Islam, get out of the country, or be sold into slavery (Christians can be bought for slave labor at $15 a head) and sometimes killed.[66] Children are routinely starved to death if their Christian mothers don't convert to Islam.[67]

In Egypt, 18 Christian Copts were massacred in early 1997, reportedly by Islamic extremists. In Algeria, seven Trappist monks had their throats slit by Muslim guerrillas in 1996. In Saudi Arabia, citizens receive $3,000 "rewards" for informing on Bible studies. There are more Christians in jail for their faith in China than in any other country. Arrests, beatings, confiscation of books and personal property, and demolition of church property take place almost daily.[68]

David Barrett, professor of missiometrics at Regent University, claims that about 156,000 Christians were martyred worldwide in 1994 alone. From a global perspective, Barrett's statistics conclude that "One in every 200 Christians can expect to be martyred in his or her lifetime."[69]

You don't believe Barrett? Log on and download some of the prayer requests from the mission fields. You can get in touch personally with missionaries whose lives are in danger, and you can find names of most recent martyrs. Add these people to your prayer list. Honor persecuted Christians worldwide on 29 September, which has been designated by World Evangelical Fellowship as "Persecution Sunday." Don't be surprised if Christians turn out to be the first colonizers of the moon. Why? Because we will be motivated to take the risks of such a hazardous undertaking to escape religious persecution.

How ironic: Amnesty International seems more concerned about increasing persecutions of Christians around the world than we Christians do.

How ironic: Michael Horowitz, a Jewish lawyer, is beating down Christian doors because he believes Christians could be the Jews of the 21st century.[70] Horowitz of the Hudson Institute and John Hanford, an aide to Sen. Richard Lugar, argue that "On a worldwide basis, Christians are the most persecuted major religion in terms of direct punishment for practicing religious activities—public worship, evangelism, charity."

How ironic: Jews are coming to the aid of Christians. At a conference in March 1997 hosted by Washington's Center for Jewish and Christian Values, a bill was proposed creating a White House adviser on religious persecution. Subsequently, in July 1998 Robert Seiple, former head of the relief organization World Vision International, was named to that position by President Clinton.[71]

How ironic: U.S. News & World Report does an article on why "the ongoing repression of Christians worldwide receives scant notice." Why the indifference of Christians to Christian persecution? Nina Shea of Freedom House says the reason is "secular myopia": "There's a view that someone who stands before Army tanks in Tiananmen is a hero, while someone willing to lay down his life for his religious faith must be a zealot."[72]

John Buchanan is senior minister of Fourth Presbyterian Church in Chicago. He was chosen Moderator of the Presbyterian Church (USA) for 1996–97, meaning that he was forced to take a leave of absence from his pulpit for that year. On Stewardship Sunday he returned to preach and let his parishioners know how upset he was that they were doing so well without him.

He entitled his sermon "The High Cost of Believing" and shared with his people how he had learned the "high cost of believing" when he signed just the past week a letter to Ayatollah Ali Khamani and President Rafsanjani of Iran on behalf of the PC (USA), "expressing sadness at the death of an Iranian Christian pastor who disappeared and was hanged two weeks ago." He then told of one of the earliest trips he took as Moderator, a trip to Cuba.

> We were dinner guests in the apartment of the Moderator of the Cuban Church General Assembly and his wife. When I was assured I could ask anything I wished, I asked about how the state applied pressure to believers. The Moderator's wife told me about her son, a good student at the University of Havana and a fine athlete and basketball player. Because the team represented the university and the nation, he was thrown off the basketball team and allowed to return only if he quit the church and renounced his faith. The young man did. What parent could not understand and feel deeply this Cuban family's agony? There was a lot of pain in her voice when she told me he had moved to Germany and they had not seen him for a long time. "We have talked about our faith for years. Now we have had to learn how to live it," she said.[73]

We must re-read Paul's declaration: "I am not ashamed of the gospel" (Rom. 1:16). Our marginality may turn out to be Christianity's greatest source of strength. At least Martin Luther King Jr. found it so. The more he was oppressed and persecuted, the more oppressed blacks were liberated. Likewise, the more Soviet dissidents were hunted down and imprisoned, the more dissension rippled through the hearts of the Russian people. The longer Nelson Mandela spent on Robben Island, the less the stranglehold of apartheid choked to death South Africans.

We must come to terms with Stephen and Thecla, the church's first martyrs. We must reread 1 Peter, where the church was struggling with ignorance (2:15), curiosity (3:15), suspicion of wrongdoing (2:12; 4:14–16), and aggressive hostility (3:13, 14, 16). We must reread 1 Peter, where "Christ's people" must confront persecution in the form of slander and verbal abuse (4:4, 14), accusations of actual wrongdoing (2:12; 3:16), even so far as legal proceedings (3:15).

Will you put Christ first, whatever the cost? We don't need to be "gluttons for punishment." "When they persecute you in one town, flee to the next" (Matt. 10:23). But can disciples expect better treatment than their Master (Matt. 10:16–25)? Should the treatment we receive differ from his? "If they persecuted me, they will persecute you" (John 15:20). To some you will be a "savior of life unto life"; to others "of death unto death."

Our kids are preparing for this world better than we are. At least they know what to expect. The contemporary gospel group BTR (Big Tent Revival), in its Top 10 album *Open All Night,* concludes the CD with a song that group member Steve Wiggins wrote: "If Loving God Was a Crime."

> If loving God was a crime, I'd be an outlaw
> I would join the fight
> They could not shut me down;
> I would stand tall for what I know is right.[74]

Hans P. Ehrenberg, in his *Autobiography of a German Pastor,*[75] tells how it happened that his church was instrumental in establishing the "Confessing Church," the group that refused to accept Hitler.

Ehrenberg tells how every Thursday evening people from his church met to immerse themselves in the tradition and in the classic creeds and Reformation confessions of faith. He calls these meetings a "rehearsal" for whatever might be coming:

> We came to realize that instruction itself already contains the seeds of fellowship, of true community. In our case it was important as the final rehearsal of the orchestra: a sort of "performance before the performance."

The common people learned to discern the spirits within such groups: "It was only *within* the Church, if I may put it this way, that individual witnesses of the Confessional Church learned to resist the enemy, to attack, to condemn, to exorcize, to overcome in actual places, such as the concentration camp." (Ehrenberg had just described the reaction of a railway man in his parish to the teachings of a pro-Nazi pastor in the neighborhood.)

Ehrenberg, who himself was eventually dispatched to a concentration camp, describes something happening at a summer camp for teenage girls that says it all. A "united service" for Catholics and Protestants was held in a room dominated by a large picture of Hitler set up on a table. A young Lutheran girl, recently confirmed, could take it no more, tore down the picture, and smashed it against the wall, shouting the words, "Thou shalt have no other gods but me." Ehrenberg observes,

> The remarkable thing was not that she smashed Hitler's picture, nor even that she had the courage to confess the First Commandment, but that she was *prepared beforehand* to do both.

What was it that made her "prepared beforehand"? The church! It is the only community on earth that can confront the evil one. For it is the only community on earth to whom the keys of the kingdom were given.

The gates of hell can prevail against anything and everything . . . but the church.

say what? 1. Want an example of the pre-evangelism of John-the-Baptist ministries? The youth of Frazer Memorial Church in Montgomery, Alabama, decided to raise money for something other than a trip for themselves. They raised money to throw a party for some of the most forgotten, overlooked, marginal people in our society today—carnival workers. Listen to the tape of their pastor, Johnny Ed Mathison, tell the story of how they rented a tent and threw a sit-down-service, real-silver-tableware, filet-mignon meal for 400 carnival workers at which each person was given a long-stemmed carnation and presented with a real leather Bible and a T-shirt that said "Friends Forever."

All they wanted to do was to show how much God loved and cared for some of God's forgotten children.

Log-on to my Web site to hear Dr. Mathison personally tell this John-the-Baptist ministry story: www.leonardsweet.com/.

2. Discuss this thesis: Christianity is true, not to the degree that it points to itself, but only to the degree that it points to its Lord and God who stands in judgment over it just as God stands in judgment over every other religion.

The love of God gets particularized in the cross of Christ, and then expands outward again to the world. Duke theologian Tom Langford uses the image of the hourglass to portray the particularization of God's love in the cross and then back again to the world. Get out an hourglass. If you do not have access to one, you may use a picture or drawing. Do you like its symbolism?

3. Listen to the country and western song "We're Not in Kansas Anymore" and relate it to life ring #10.

4. Listen and discuss Grover Levy's new disc *Wrestling Angels* (Myrrh), which has a song ("If You Want to Lead Me to Jesus") that takes the perspective of the unbeliever.

5. Read and discuss Paul Marshall's *Their Blood Cries Out: The Untold Story of Persecution Against Christians in the Modern World* (Dallas: Word Books, 1997) and Nina Shea's *In the Lion's Den: A Shocking Account of Persecution and Martyrdom of Christians Today and How We Should Respond* (Nashville: Broadman & Holman, 1997). Why do you think American institutions—media, academe, denominations, government—have largely been silent in the face of Christian persecution?

6. Obtain the 83-page document "United States Policies in Support of Religious Freedoms Overseas: Focus on Christians," which outlines religious

persecution, especially against Christians, in 78 countries. The report criticizes China most heavily, but it takes to task Austria, Belgium, Bulgaria, France, Germany, and Greece as well. It was released by the State Department's Bureau of Democracy, Human Rights, and Labor Affairs on 22 July 1997. As of this writing, the report has been forwarded to Secretary of State Madeleine Albright and President Clinton. It is available online at

www.state.gov/www/global/human_rights/970722_relig_rpt_christian.html.

7. From your own experience, give some examples of church-bashing that you have encountered.

8. Bob Guccione Jr., 39-year-old publisher of *Spin* magazine, explains his commitment to Catholicism and his weekly attendance to Mass this way when asked "what's the appeal of Catholicism for you?"

> Well, it's just that which I grew up with. It's not so much like I chose Catholicism off a shelf of possible religions in a supermarket of spirituality. I grew up with Catholicism. And I believe in God. And I just happen to believe in it in a Catholic way because that was my experience, and I get a lot out of it.... I don't get something from Mass every Sunday.... But, again, the importance is the fact that there's an overall certitude in my life, an overall discipline that no matter where I am in the world, I go to Mass on Sunday.... It's an anchor. And it gives you the foundation to be able to tap into this subscription, if you like, of spirituality. I'm a subscriber. It's like getting online.[76]

There it is. It's no longer "membership" in a church; it's "subscription" to a service—an online service—and the subscription runs out periodically and one needs to reup. What are the implications of this "subscription" model of church membership?

9. What is your church doing to get ready for the increased likelihood of vandalism and vituperation?

10. What might the insights of contemporary Judaism into persecution have to say to us about how to deal with both subtle and obvious persecutions?

11. Read and react to Foxe's *Book of Martyrs*. (An in-print edition of the book, edited by W. B. Forbush, is published by Zondervan.) There were times in the history of the church when the only good reformer (read "Protestant") was a dead one.

12. Do a Bible study of 1 Peter 4:12–13.

13. Where would you stand, how would you fare, if you had to face what Christians faced in Nazi Germany during WWII, or more recently in Sudan and China?

14. Obtain the book by Dr. Seuss, *Oh, the Places You'll Go* (New York: Random House, 1990). What is the "waiting place" he writes about? Does postmodern culture need "waiting places" for people to go to figure things

out and sort through competing claims? Is the church as a "waiting place" an appropriate way for it to connect with postmodern culture?

15. Social scientist Mark Granovetter says that a characteristic of postmodern institutional life is "the strength of weak ties."[77] Whereas in the past we enjoyed deep and lasting relationships, fleeting and functional relationships are increasingly the norm. Do you agree? What does this mean for the church?

16. Kristin Anderson and Ron Zemke[78] have started a *Knock Your Socks Off Service* series (New York: AMACOM, 1996). Read one of these volumes and discuss how the church might "plunder the Egyptians" in learning how to serve postmodern culture breakfast in bed.

17. The Islam law known as *sharia* prohibits interest earnings as well as investments in "sin" industries like gambling and alcohol. Once limited to the Persian Gulf, Islamic banks (which grew 15% annually for the past decade) are now opening divisions in Europe and the United States. If one opened in your community, would you be a customer?

18. In 1995, 150 international missionaries from various countries were murdered on the field.[79] Is spreading the gospel in the most unreached and hostile reaches of the globe worth dying for?

19. In Woody Allen's *Deconstructing Harry* (part of which was filmed at Drew University), there is this exchange between the liberal-minded title character and his sister, a devout Jew:

> "I'm a Jew," she declares. "I was born a Jew and you hate me for that."
>
> "And if our parents had converted to Catholicism a month before you were born, we'd be Catholic and that would be the end of it. They're all clubs. They're exclusionary, all of them. They reinforce the concept of the Other so you know clearly who to hate."

Do you know people who share this distrust of organized religion? What is your church doing to diminish the mistrust?

20. Read Gore Vidal's "Monotheism and Its Discontents," in his United States: Essays: 1952–1992 (New York: Random House, 1993), 1048–56, in which he calls monotheism "the great unmentionable evil at the center of the culture," a kind of "sky-god" totalitarianism that supposedly fosters "racism, sexism, the regulation of private morality, the sacking of the environment, wars and empire-building." How would you answer Vidal's charge?

21. Discuss whether or not you think Paul R. Sponheim is predicting a new inquisition with these words: "As the world collapses, it is not strange that the people of God will argue among themselves about where God is to be heard and obeyed. In the loss of worldview the communication of the very content of the faith that we believe (the *fides quae creditur*) is at risk." See his *Faith and the Other: A Relational Theology* (Minneapolis: Fortress, 1993), 15.

now what? See the Net Notes in http://www.soultsunami.com

NOTES

1. R. U. Sirius, "The Last Judgment," *21C* 25 (1997): 8.

2. Margaret Daphne Hampson, *After Christianity* (Valley Forge, PA: Trinity Press, 1996). See also the writings of Barbara Tuchman, who has an absolute contempt for Christianity and dismisses it as meaningless, superstitious, and worthless except to give history grief and pain.

3. As quoted in "Seeking Christian Interiority: An Interview with Louis Dupré," *Christian Century* (16 July 1997): 654.

4. For books that applaud the end of Christendom as a hope for the church, see Mike Regele, *Death of the Church: The Church at the End of the 21st Century* (Grand Rapids: Zondervan, 1997), and Rodney Clapp, *A Peculiar People: The Church as Culture in a Post-Christian Society* (Downers Grove, IL: InterVarsity Press, 1997).

5. P. J. Kavanagh, "Bywords," *TLS, Times Literary Supplement* (6 Mar 1998).

6. Diana L. Eck, "Exploring the New Religious Landscape of the US: A Preliminary Report on the Pluralism Project," *Church and Society* 83 (Sept-Oct 1992): 4–8.

7. For a restatement of Sorokin's classic *Social and Cultural Dynamics*, see Anne Glyn-Jones, *Holding Up a Mirror: How Civilizations Decline* (London: Century, 1996).

8. "Evangelism and Accountability," *Barna Report* 1 (1997): 4–6.

9. This marked a 5% increase from the last Roper survey in 1976.

10. *Wall Street Journal* (2 Dec 1994): B1.

11. These figures are from the comparative study conducted by the Independent Sector (Washington, DC) in 1996 called "Giving and Volunteering in the United States," as reported in "Calling All Volunteers," *The Boomer Report* (Dec 1997): 2. See also George Barna's research, which reveals that the church in the US has not grown at all since 1980, with the proportion of USAmericans who claim to be "born again" a constant at 32%. Also see David Dunlap, "The Myth of 'Growth,'" *Uplook* 64 (Nov 1997): 4–5.

12. Bill Leonard, "What Kind of Church Will Survive and Grow in the Next Millennium," *Baptists Today* 14 (26 Sept 1996): 9–12.

13. C. Kirk Hadaway and David A. Roozen, *Rerouting the Protestant Mainstream: Sources of Growth & Opportunities for Change* (Nashville: Abingdon Press, 1995), 44–45.

14. Kavanagh, "Bywords," 16.

15. The highest "apostate" rates are for Episcopalians, United Methodists, Presbyterians, and UCCs. See William S. Korn and Giles Asbury, "So Long, Mom: High School's Out, and Church May Be, Too," *Plumbline* 25 (Winter 1998): 4–12.

16. Alison L. Boden, "Spirituality," *Plumbline* 25 (Winter 1998): 13.

17. Quoted in Dimitri Ehrlich, *Inside the Music: Conversations with Contemporary Musicians about Spirituality, Creativity, and Consciousness* (Boston: Shambhala, 1997), 157.

18. Ehrlich, *Inside the Music,* 220.

19. Ehrlich, *Inside the Music,* 225.

20. As cited in Paul Heelas, *The New Age Movement* (Oxford: Blackwell, 1997), 129.

21. Sandra Loh, *Depth Takes a Holiday: Essays from Lesser Los Angeles* (New York: Riverhead Books, 1996).

22. The only novelist present is Umberto Eco, although he's not there for his novels. See "NB," *TLS, Times Literary Supplement* (5 Sept 1997): 16.

23. Jacques Derrida, *The Gift of Death* (Chicago: Univ. of Chicago Press, 1996), 2. See also Benjamin Hutchens, *TLS, Times Literary Supplement* (2 Feb 1996): 32.

24. Ian S. Markham, *A World Religious Reader* (Cambridge, MA: Blackwell Publications,1996).

25. Stephen Logan, "In Defense of C. S. Lewis," *TLS, Times Literary Supplement* (21 Feb 1997): 25.

26. Henry Louis Gates Jr., "Hating Hillary," *New Yorker* (26 Feb 1996), 116–23.

27. Dan Wakefield, "Clear Vision," interview of Reynolds Price in *Common Boundary* (July-Aug 1996): 27. Naomi Wolf says similar things in "Coming Out for God," *Mademoiselle* 103 (Sept 1997): 158ff: "Admitting to an interest in God is . . . something that provokes the social embarrassment that used to be caused by a boorish, off-color joke."

28. Robert Wuthnow, "Tour of the Believers' Underground," *In Trust* 2 (New Year 1991): 12, 13.

29. Ehrlich, *Inside the Music,* 79.

30. Ehrlich, *Inside the Music,* 78.

31. With thanks to David A. Lord of Valley View United Methodist Church in Clinton, TN, for this Twain reference.

32. With thanks to S. Wesley Ariarajah, "Ministerial Formation for the 21st Century," 130th Matriculation Address, Drew Theological School.

33. Bill Easum and Thomas Bandy, *Growing Spiritual Redwoods* (Nashville: Abingdon Press, 1997), 152.

34. George Hunter and Bill Easum also argue for this category of "pre-Christian." See George G. Hunter's work *Church for the Unchurched* (Nashville: Abingdon Press, 1996), and *How to Reach Secular People* (Nashville: Abingdon Press, 1992). Easum's most elaborate treatment of this theme is in *Growing Spiritual Redwoods.*

35. The Barna Research Group survey as summarized in *Baptist Standard* (15 Apr 1998): 6. For more information contact Barna Research Group, 5528 Everglades St., Suite B, Ventura, CA 93003.

36. As quoted in the Leadership Network *Net Fax* 93 (16 Mar 1998): 1.

37. John Weever, *Ancient Funeral Monuments* (repr., Amsterdam: Theatrum Orbis Terrarum, 1979).

38. In the same way, scientists are now having to escape their toilet training in an old scientific method with its radical anti-religion bias. Now many of the world's top physicists are religious in one way or another. One out-there physicist has even designed and patented a "God Phone"—a machine designed to decode faster-than-light (FTL) communications, since experiments conducted by Alain Aspect in the early 1980s proved that instantaneous transfers of information across the space-time matrix are theoretically possible. See for example: Bill Easum's *Sacred Cows Make Gourmet Burgers* (Nashville: Abingdon Press, 1995) and *Dancing With Dinosaurs* (Nashville: Abingdon Press, 1993).

39. Mike Regele, *Death of the Church* (Grand Rapids: Zondervan, 1995), 20.

40. Robert Morales, "Toni Morrison: The VIBE Q," *VIBE* (May 1998): 98.

41. Michael Gantt, *A Nonchurchgoer's Guide to the Bible* (Intercourse, PA: Good Books, 1998).

42. *Newsweek Interactive Boards*, "Religion: The Meaning of the Holy Spirit: Your Take," 8 Apr 1998: from New4911, Message-id:(1998040816470501.MAA12038 @ladder01.news.aol.com).

43. As found in "Media Diet" section of *Utne Reader* (May-June 1995): 106.

44. Paul Monette, *Last Watch of the Night: Essays Too Personal and Otherwise* (New York: Harcourt Brace, 1994), 256.

45. David McCumber, *Playing Off the Rail: A Pool Hustler's Journey* (New York: Random House, 1996).

46. The Congress took place on 13 April 1996 in Barnesville, Ohio.

47. Case Ventura, "An Ill Wind Blows Thru the Pru," *Communications Week* 12 (Feb 1996): 70.

48. *USA Today* (14 Oct 1996): 3C.

49. The words of the filmmaker are quoted by David Nokes, "It Isn't in the Book," *TLS, Times Literary Supplement* (26 Apr 1996): 12.

50. As found in Edward Norman, "Cape Englishman," *TLS, Times Literary Supplement* (9 Dec 1994): 30.

51. See Elvin W. Janetzki, "Christian Living and Christian Witness," *Lutheran Theological Journal* 19 (Aug 1985): 80–86.

52. Robert McC. Adams, *Paths of Fire: An Anthropologist's Inquiry into Western Technology* (Princeton: Princeton Univ. Press, 1997). See especially the concluding summary, 276–77.

53. David Bodanis, *The Secret Family: Twenty-four Hours Inside the Mysterious World of Our Minds and Bodies* (New York: Simon & Schuster, 1997), 63.

54. For further insights into this phenomenon, see Hunter, *Church for the Unchurched,* 23, and Eddie Gibbs, *In Name Only: Tackling the Problem of Nominal Christianity* (Wheaton, IL: BridgePoint Books, 1994).

55. David Shibley, "The Holy Spirit Around the World," *Charisma* 21 (Jan 1996): 31–33.

56. Richard Foster, "A Pastoral Letter," *Prism* 4 (Mar-Apr 1997): 8–10.

57. Adrian Berry, *The Next 500 Years: Life in the Coming Millennium* (New York: W. H. Freeman, 1996) 258. Berry is referencing the work of W. I. McCaughlin, "Reusable Ideas," *Spaceflight* (May 1995): 167–68.

58. Rupert Christiansen, *Paris Babylon: The Story of the Paris Commune* (New York: Penguin Books, 1996), 301–2.

59. Rowan Williams, *A Ray of Darkness* (Cambridge, MA: Cowley, 1995), 160.

60. "British Religious Practice Lags Far Behind the US," *Emerging Trends* 18 (Sept 1996): 4.

61. Charles Arn, "Keep Them Coming Back," *Worship Leader* 6 (July-Aug 1997): 26–30.

62. Here is a church that doesn't ordain women but has five-month-old girls playing the role of Baby Jesus.

63. Larry Witham, "Bible Lessons Still Relevant," *Insight* 13 (30 June 1997): 39.

64. John G. Stackhouse, Jr., "Why Our Friends Won't Stop, Look, and Listen," *Christianity Today* (3 Feb 1997): 49.

65. As quoted in *National and International Religion Report* 10 (8 Jan 1996): 5.

66. Stan Guthrie, "Evangelicals Respond to Unabated Persecution," *Evangelical Missions Quarterly* 32 (Oct 1996): 460–67.

67. Tom Bethell, "Saving Faith at State," *American Spectator* 30 (Apr 1997): 20–21. See also Nina Shea, *In the Lion's Den: A Shocking Account of Persecution and Martyrdom of Christians Today and How We Should Respond* (Nashville: Broadman & Holman, 1997).

68. Mindy Belz, "The Party Rules," *World* 11 (15 Mar 1997): 12–17.

69. Kim Lawton, "Killed in the Line of Duty," *Charisma* 21 (Oct 1995): 54–59.

70. See, for example, Michael Horowitz, "Continuing Christian Persecution: Breaking the Chains Around the Gulags of Faith," *Vital Speeches* (15 May 1997): 466–72.

71. "Seiple Named to Post for Religious Liberty," *Christian Century* (1 July 1998): 641–42.

72. Dorian Friedman, "Sharing the Lessons," *U.S.News & World Report* (31 Mar 1997): 15.

73. John M. Buchanan, "The High Cost of Believing," 20 October 1996, Fourth Presbyterian Church, Chicago, Illinois.

74. "If Loving God Was a Crime," in the CD by Big Tent Revival, *Open All Night* (Memphis: Ardent Christian Music, 1996).

75. H. P. Ehrenberg, *Autobiography of a German Pastor* (London: N.p., 1943), 48, 50, 64: as cited in Rowan Williams, *A Ray of Darkness* (Cambridge, MA: Cowley, 1995), 42–43.

76. James Morgan in conversation with Bob Guccione Jr., *Mondo 2000* no. 14 (Spring-Summer 1995): 103.

77. Mark Granovetter, "The Strength of Weak Ties," *American Journal of Sociology* 78 (1973): 1360–80.

78. Recent volumes of this series by Kristin Anderson and Ron Zemke include *Coaching Knock Your Socks Off Service* (New York: AMACOM, 1997); *Delivering Knock Your Socks Off Service,* rev. ed. (New York: AMACOM, 1998); and *Tales of Knock Your Socks Off Service: Inspiring Stories of Outstanding Customer Service* (New York: AMACOM, 1998). Also available is the *Knock Your Socks Off Service Video Training Series* (Los Angeles: Mentor Media, 1993), based on the 1991 edition of *Delivering Knock Your Socks Off Service.*

79. According to Global Evangelization Movement, as reported in *The Baptist Standard* (Texas) 110 (18 Mar 1998).

IS THIS A GREAT TIME, OR WHAT ?

Get Chaordic

"CHAORDIC" CHURCHES AND
"CHAORDIC" LEADERS

or what? It is time for the church to get wet! In fact, if the church is to survive, it had better get wet in ways it has heretofore never even dreamed of. For only water quenches people's eternal thirst.

In the Hebrew Scriptures, and in many other cultures, water is a symbol of chaos. Yet all of the traditions that relate Jesus to water present water in a positive way.

Chaos is the word of the 21st century. It is associated with water.

The central mystery of the gospel is the essence of water and the essence of chaos: A thing can change and still be the same. It is the symbol of the fountain:

We're always changing.
We're always the same.
We're the chaos church of Jesus Christ.
We're always in motion, going somewhere.
We're always in rest, going nowhere.
We're the chaos church of Jesus Christ.

Both continuity and change are essential to an institution. How can the church express continuity through change? How can the church catch the waves of change without abandoning the tides of continuity?

> If there is magic on this planet, it is contained in water.
>
> Anthropologist
> Loren Eiseley[1]

The gospel is like "living water" (*hudor*), Jesus told the Samaritan woman. Water fills any receptacle without retaining the form of any. The container doesn't matter. Content stays the same, containers change. Using 21st-century containers are first-century imperatives.

Jesus told us *what* we should be doing: "Go into all the world and proclaim the good news to the whole creation" (Mark16:15). He didn't say *how* we should be doing it.[2]

The *how* of ministry has changed. The *what* of ministry has remained the same. The modern world was grounded. Its favorite definition of God was "Ground of Being." Its basic metaphors were drawn from a landscape consciousness that didn't trust water. Scholars are trained to keep categories clean and "watertight." We were taught to be careful not to "water down" our

> In order to stay the same, a thing must change often.
>
> John Henry
> Cardinal Newman

insights. The surface on which we lived was solid, fixed, and predictable. We could get "the lay of the land," mark off directions where we were headed, and follow maps, blueprints, and formulas to get where we are going. A lot of time was spent on boundary maintenance and border issues.

Postmodern culture has marched off all maps. A seascape, its surface is fluid, not fixed, changing with every gust of wave and wind, always unpredictable. Maps and blueprints are useless on the water, never the same. The sea knows no boundaries. The only way one gets anywhere on the water is not through marked-off routes one follows but through navigational skills and nautical trajectories.

NO CHANGE, NO FUTURE ~ What is the difference between a living thing and a dead thing? How to tell one from the other? "Locomotion" and "consciousness" always appear high on the list of identifiers. But in the medical world, a clinical definition of death is a body that does not change. Change is life. Stagnation is death.

If you don't change, you die.

It's that simple. It's that scary.[3]

In molecular biology the world revolves around the cell. In the time it takes you to read this chapter, of the 100 trillion cells that make up your body, hundreds of millions will have died. Your body, with five pounds of dead cells already sticking to it, will have flaked them off or flushed them out.

You say, why am I not shrinking with that kind of cellular change? Because for every one of those cells that dies while you're reading this, another cell divides to replace it with a new one. Skin replaces itself every month; the stomach lining, every five days; the liver, every six weeks; the skeleton, every three months; cheek cells, three times a day. Ninety-eight percent of the atoms in your body are replaced every year—your whole body every five years (men) or seven years (women).

> The cells change completely
> every seven years.
> That's so your skin doesn't keep
> the bruises
> where people touch you
> and hurt, you
> can start again
> fresh you see
>
> Dennis Scott, "Time piece"[4]

Biologists are only now beginning to study this cell death phenomenon, partly because, as one biologist says, "It is too intimately tied to our own mortality."[5] Woody Allen said it best: "It's not that I'm afraid to die. I just don't want to be around when it happens."

But for many years developmental biologist H. Robert Horvitz and his colleagues at the Massachusetts Institute of Technology have been challenging their colleagues to ask such questions as "Why do your cells suicide?" "Why is there a death wish in every cell?" "Why is the human body both old and new at the same time?"[6]

Their answers to these questions, albeit preliminary, are provocative. Even at a cellular level, the body has a kind of collective awareness.[7] Every cell contains within itself poison-pill proteins that are ready to be released unless told otherwise by the body itself. Your body triggers these poison pellets for certain reasons:

1. Sculpture. Cells sculpt body parts. Our feet are weblike creatures; our toes take shape only as the cells between them die. Your body and mine would have died in the womb without cell death.
2. Obsolescence. When a cell is no longer contributing to the larger body. Cells know when they are no longer needed.[8] Our bodies have been programmed so that when a cell is obsolete or obstinate or offensive, it dies.
3. Self-sacrifice. Cells sacrifice themselves to protect the larger organism. If a cell is invaded by a deadly virus, it will trigger its own self-destruct mechanism, called apoptosis, preventing the virus from spreading further.
4. Isolation. When neighboring cells exercise the ban on a cell; when the cell's neighbors do not affirm it and encourage it and tell it how much it is needed, it dies. Only when it is connected and contributing to its partners do its apoptosis inhibitors kick in.

> Change is good.
> You go first.
>
> Bumper Sticker

Your body is here today because it is constantly changing and because those parts of it that can't keep up and contribute to the whole are constantly dying. Death and changelessness go together. I love the story of the letter returned to the post office, marked on the envelope: "He's dead." The post office messed up and sent the letter again to the same address. It was duly returned with the blunt comment,

> Change is good.
> Unless it happens.
>
> Bumper Sticker[9]

"He's still dead." The English poet Samuel Rogers used to say, "It does not much matter whom one marries as one is sure to find the next morning it is someone else."[10]

CHANGE OR BE CHANGED ~ In the old ecology of nature, change was seen as abnormal. In the new ecology of nature, change is life's natural, normative state. It used to be that the natural condition of nature was seen as one of equilibrium and "steady-state" (see the "steady-state economics" of Herman Daly).[11] Now change is normalized. Change is seen as the natural ecology of nature. Daniel Botkin of the University of California at Santa Barbara writes about how ecosystems actually work:

> You live by shedding.
>
> Robert Frost

Change now appears to be intrinsic and natural at many scales of time and space in the biosphere. Nature changes over essentially all time scales, and in at least some cases these changes are necessary for the persistence of life, because life is adapted to them and depends on them.[12]

Why do organizations disappear quickly? Of the Fortune 500 companies on the 1955 list, 70% are now out of business. Of the Fortune 500 companies on the 1979 list, 40% no longer exist as corporate entities. One-third of the Fortune 500 companies are nowhere to be found seven years later. The average Fortune 500 company today can expect to enjoy a lifespan of about 40 to 50 years.[13]

What works today won't work tomorrow. Or as a friend put it, "Every time I figure out 'where it's at,' they move it." Don't believe me? Ask Diana Shepherd. In 1996 she launched a quarterly magazine *Divorce* to cater to the two million of us who divorce every year. She was previously associate editor of *Wedding Bells*.

One book on "change management" theory opens with this quiz: "Try to think of a major industry [in the 1990s] that is *not* experiencing profound upheaval."[14] The wonder is that churches are not in more disarray. The problem is that most churches aren't experiencing *enough* upheaval. They are standing pat, opting to uphold the status quo rather than undergo the upheaval. The more we shrink in timidity, the more we sink into rigidity and slink behind an *ancien régime* that is being swept away.

Is it any wonder that 85% of the mainline church is in serious decline? Kenneth L. Woodward writes on the subject "Dead End for the Mainline?" that "From every angle Protestantism is gripped by crisis: of identity and loyalty, membership and money, leadership and organization, culture and belief."[15] Is it any wonder that the oldest denominations in terms of the average age of membership are, in descending order, the Christian Scientists, the PCUSA Presbyterians (average age 65 and rising), and the United Methodists? The Presbyterians are in special peril, a victim of their unparalleled success in claiming a print culture for the gospel.[16]

> I'm no longer in the mode of trying to change people. I'm in a mode of finding a way to enable them to change. Because it's going to happen naturally.
>
> Arian Ward,
> Hughes Space and
> Communications Company

Postmodern culture is a change-or-be-changed world. The word is out: Reinvent yourself for the 21st century or die. Some would rather die than change.

The lengths we will go to not to change, the excuses we will muster to defend the status quo, are illustrated by a little-known fact about the Civil War. Shortly after the war began, gun manufacturers introduced new rifles that were easier and quicker to load than the standard muzzle-loading ones. But officers on both sides resisted changing their rifles and gave lots of excuses: Easy-loading guns encouraged wasting of bullets; guns that allowed one to shoot lying down would cause soldiers to refuse to stand up, and so on.

It has not been easy for the church to make change. But Jesus did not call us to live easily or painlessly. All discovery, every birth, is disorderly, ragged, and messy. Death is neat and orderly. But birth is slimy, bloody, sweaty, oozing primordial juices and elements. Change is messy—never neat. Change is not premeditated. Change does not follow precise, predetermined paths or rational routes.

HORNS OR HOODS ~ We are living in a world of quantum changes, of macro change. The whole world is changing. And we aren't?

We are already living in the 21st century. Our 22nd-century kids[18] (think about this: the movie *Lost in Space* was set in 2058) will see changes in their lifetime that are beyond our comprehension. Already the changes that have exploded us into this new world are as important as the commercial revolution of the 13th century, the intellectual revolution of the Renaissance and Reformation, the industrial revolution of the 18th century. Indeed, the changes we are now undergoing may be more important than these earlier upheavals because they affected only "the West." This one is global.

> It's not that the business environment is changing. Change *is* the business environment. And it's not that every company is undergoing change. Change has overtaken every company. Creating change, managing it, mastering it, and surviving it is the agenda for anyone in business who aims to make a difference.
>
> Charles Fishman[17]

Change can have either horns or hoods. *Change* is a loaded word. There are at least three kinds of change: conversions, subversions (change that takes place underground), and reversions. On top of these three kinds of change we must distinguish whether they are Virtuous Change or Virus Change. Virtuous change is where change is positive, creative, considered, and cautious. Virus change is where change is negative and cancerous, driven by political, economic, or consumerist considerations.

Virus change is change for change's sake, or change as another change-by-numbers program. Cancer cells are cells that change, not for the good but for the worse. Change can be diabolical or divine, bad or good. There are changes taking place in our weather—warming atmosphere, breaking up of ozone shield; these are not good changes. There are changes taking place in our environment—disappearing species, exhausted, weakening soils; these are not good changes.

> At 200 miles per hour, you're covering a football field every second. You have to know where you're going before you get there.
>
> Race car driver Al Unser Jr.

We must also remember that not everything changes, as the cartoon character Shoe reminds us: "The more things change, the more my salary stays the same."

CHANGE HAS CHANGED ~ So far, so good. But we have not gone very far yet. This book is built on a critical distinction between change and transition. William Bridges is known for his distinguishing the differences between change and transition. In his

> We will all be changed.
>
> The apostle Paul
> (1 Corinthians 15:51)

view, "It isn't the changes that do you in, it's the transitions." For Bridges the difference between the two is that "Change is situational: the new site, the new boss, the new team roles, the new policy. Transition is the psychological process people go through to come to terms with the new situation."[19]

With due regards to Bridges for his helpful contribution to seeing change as external and transition as internal, I want to make an even more critical distinction between "change" and "transition." For the purposes of *SoulTsunami*, here is the difference: Change is incremental. Transition is supersonic change at the edge of chaos that phases from incremental to exponential.

Change is when you have to do better what you already know how to do.

Transition is when you have to do what you don't know how to do.

Change has always been with us as the one "constant of history." The society painters of the 1770s and 1780s, for example, were presented with a constant challenge: Hair fashions changed so rapidly and wildly that clients brought their portraits back and asked to have their heads "updated."

Transition is when change changes, when change is no longer incremental but exponential. One of the key features of the day in which we live is the accelerating pace of change itself.[20] Some experts are no longer talking about "change," but "churn" and "blur."[21] In 1989, people bought vinyl albums; no one bought CDs. Within seven years vinyl albums had become collector's items purchased by jazz aficionados and club DJs who still spin wax. In 1991, my favorite TV station, the Weather Channel, didn't exist. Five years later, an estimated 200,000 homes tuned to the Weather Channel daily.[22] Inventions used to generate profits for decades. Now many inventions, especially in electronics, have a typical life span of two months. The pace of change is so fast on the Internet that it is said that cyberspace time must be reckoned in dog years: Just as one year of a dog's life is like seven years of our lives, so one year on the Internet is like seven years in real life.

Postmoderns live on a different planet from their modern parents and grandparents. "We're at a point of absolute, supreme discontinuity," global consultant and futurist Watts Wacker proclaims. "Human beings were not built to process what we're going through now. Two generations ago people didn't move more than 50 miles away from where they were born. Today if you live in New York City, you see 8,000 commercial messages a day."[23] A little more than a hundred years ago, people were put in prison if they couldn't pay their debts. A little less than a hundred years ago, all of a woman's property became her husband's legal property when she married, and even she was considered property.

The speed of life is leaving skid marks. Scientific information doubles every 12 years. General information doubles every two-and-a-half years.[24] We know the first law of computer programming: "Any given program, when running, is obsolete." "Moore's Law" (named after Gordon Moore, co-founder of Intel Corporation), which says that the power of computer chips doubles every 18 months, is much too conservative. Since the late 1950s, there has been a 100,000-fold rise in computer power *times* a thousandfold drop in cost.[25] In fact, Intel now boasts that it is *doubling* the computing power of the world every year.[26]

The half-life of education is getting shorter and shorter. The shelf-life of resources is getting narrower and narrower. Only the after-life is getting longer and longer—and that's because our information base is a graveyard of rotting doctrines and after-life ideas that we continually resurrect no matter how rancid they are.

> **Make haste slowly.**
>
> Motto of the printer Aldus

What we read about in science fiction is soon fact. In fact, science fiction has become more science than fiction. More information is generated in one hour than you can take in over the course of one life. A weekday edition of the *New York Times* now carries more information than the average person in the 17th century would digest in a lifetime. In some ways, in fact, the knowledge race has replaced the arms race.

Up until now, the computer revolution was more change than transition. Computers spelled not a revolution in what we do so much as a speeding up of what we have always done. We are now using computers to do what humans have never done before.

In February 1996 the most powerful chess computer (Deep Blue) took on world champion Garry Kasparov and won one and tied two of six games. It lost, by the way, because it was too logical—the human edge was intuition.[27]

When the computer played the rematch with the human in April 1997, it didn't make that mistake again. And it won. (Interestingly, the Hal 5000 was born on the date of 20 April 1997 in the movie *2001: A Space Odyssey*.) But even more "transitional" was what happened at the Web site IBM put together to enable the world to follow each move as it happened and to play along virtually. Five million "hits" took place on the first day, bringing the IBM server to its knees. Hundreds of thousands of people from 75 countries played along with the computer and Kasparov.[28]

Here's the difference between change and transition. Pretend you are making an omelet. What kind of instrument do you pick out of the drawer to begin the omelet? A whisk or fork is Standard Operating Procedure (SOP). Then you add equal amounts of air and fat, and stir the air and fat together:

air, fat, air, fat, air, fat. For a period of time all you are doing is stirring more air and fat, air and fat together. That's change.

There comes a time, however, when you stir one more increment of change—air, fat—and change becomes transition. Once you pass through a threshold, a whole new world is created. Liquid becomes solid. The old SOPs which worked so well in a change/liquid world mess things up in a transition/solid world. Once you cross a threshold, new Standard Operating Procedures are required. A lot of churches are doing whisk ministry in a spatula world.

> You can't make a Hamlet without breaking eggs.
>
> Michael Foley[29]

Pretend you are a photographer. Adding a few frames per second only speeds up your work. Ten frames per second: photography. Fifteen frames per second: photography. Twenty frames per second: photography. By adding more frames per second, I am only changing the speed of my craft. But there comes a time—21, 22, 23 frames per second—when I cross a threshold—24 frames per second—into a whole new world. Change becomes transition. Photography becomes cinematography. Stills become cinema.

What is good cinematography is different from what is good photography. One evaluates each genre on its own terms, in terms of its meanings, its references, and how these are materially embodied and how they are to be understood. To judge the art of cinematography by the standards of the art of photography is to engage in categorical imperialism. We imperialize one art form when we impose it on another art form.

There are many print-culture imperialists writing in the church today. They judge what is good ministry in postmodern, electronic culture by what is good ministry in modern, print culture.[30]

> Such is the nature of custom, that it causeth us to bear all things well and easily, wherewith we have been accustomed, and to be offended with all things thereunto contrary.... But such as will persist in their wilfulness, I must needs judge, not only foolish, forward, and obstinate, but also peevish, perverse and indurate.
>
> Archbishop Thomas Cranmer in his Preface to the *Great Bible*[31]

CHOOSE RESILIENCE OVER STABILITY, CHAOS OVER ORDER ~ You can't grow without making changes. You can't live without making changes. Or in the words of Peter Drucker, "Every organization of today has to build into its very structure . . . organized abandonment of everything it does."[32] A world of discontinuous change elevates resilience over stability as one of its highest attributes.

When asked to explain the stability of their life and customs, the Greeks had a saying:

"tsi ta vrikame, étsi tha t'afisoume"

"That's how we found things, that's how we'll leave them."

No longer. Even the Greeks willy-nilly are leaving things different than they found them. Arguably the most change-resistant institution in the world, the British monarchy, is finding that it has to change if it is to survive into the 2K and 21-C. The monarchy has had to change. Welfare, health care, and the workforce have had to change. The world is changing all around us, and we in the church think we don't get our turn?

Chaos is a better strategy for survival than order. It is not just that order can be reached out of chaos, or that one can only perceive chaos in relation to some perceived order. The emerging science of complexity, the generating science of postmodernity, argues that chaos is essential to the emergence of order. Chaos and order coexist and emerge from one another.

The modern era of Newton and Locke was an era of Order: a world of natural laws, of hard facts, of well-defined structures operating with clock-work precision. The Protestant Reformation adapted the Christian faith to this highly ordered, linear universe, and those brands of Protestants, like the Puritans first and the Methodists second, who were best able to highly order and structure their disciplines of belief and behavior fared the best.

Moderns were taught that this world-machine evolved with highly set regulations and rules of the game. If we follow the regs and play by the rules, then predictable things happen in life. Go against these laws or break the rules, and predictably unbalanced things will happen. It was a cost-benefit exogenous theology where we were on the outside looking in, rather than a part of what we are looking at.

The postmodern era is dominated by metaphors of chaos and complexity, not law and order. Complexity theory is the study of systems that behave orderly even though you might expect them to be anarchic (weather, rain forests, the stock market, the job market). Advanced micro- and macro-physics has given up its love affair with logical and mathematical consistency and rational prediction and control—it now embraces chaos, uncertainty, and complexity.

What complexity theory is teaching us is that we are living "on the edge of chaos" in a world that is ill-defined, out of control, and in constant flow and flux. We live in a world that is more weird than we ever imagined—a world that is fractal, self-replicating, inflationary, unpredictable, and filled with strange attractors. We do not live in linear time and space, but in curved time and space and nonlinear iterative processes. The modern world taught that this is a causal universe. We know now that this is actually an ever-curving universe. Rather than stasis and order, the dynamics of life-systems are non-linear, where the rules of the game keep changing because the game keeps changing. One plays on the run and while everything is moving. Rather than set goalposts, processes and patterns are the name of the game.[33]

In a state of equilibrium, nothing happens! Enduring organisms embrace a strategy toward a life of disequilibrium over stability. They expect and sustain disruption. Organisms that stagnate and die settle into equilibrium and harmony. Stability is less to be desired than resilience.

In postmodern culture, fluidity wins out over fixity. Instead of "structuring" and "ordering" and "solidifying" reality, cyberspace "bends" and "blends" and "melts." Life is a fluid realm. But fluid does not mean "anything goes," as any captain of a boat can tell you; fluid is a different kind of going.

Stability is the capacity of a system to return to equilibrium after it has been disturbed. Resilience is the "measure of the persistence of a system and its ability to absorb change and disturbance." An organism's adaptive response depends on its agility in getting outside of itself and seeing from different angles and patterns.[34] Not to be able to get one's way is a recipe for survival.

CHAORDIC LEADERSHIP ~ Change leaders and change teams operate on the boundary of chaos and order—or what Dee Hock, the man who created the trillion-dollar Visa credit-card empire, calls the "chaordic" zone.

A "chaord" has been defined as "a self-organizing, adaptive, nonlinear complex system (whether physical, biological or social) that simultaneously exhibits characteristics of order and chaos, that exists between rigidity and flexibility." The church is by its very definition a chaordic organism—an organic, free-form community driven by mission and responsive to its indigenous environments. The early church was almost a textbook definition of "chaordic": fluid, flat, fast off its feet, and strong on its feet with control at the edges only.

Any network or partnership, any alliance or institution, can become "chaordic" if it in some ways fights the forces of order and planners and embraces change and chaos.[35] Chaordic leaders see change and chaos as their friends, not enemies.

> Art is order, made out of the chaos of life.
>
> Novelist/Nobel Laureate
> Saul Bellow

The most creative places in nature, where life is born and renewed, are "chaordic" zones.[36] The most creative times in history are those hinge moments when chaos and order overlap. Historian Gordon Wood has argued that "the time of the greatest religious chaos" in America was also the time of the greatest "originality in American history."[37]

"Chaos theory" is a relatively small subset of the science of complexity. "Chaos"—or as Katherine Hayles puts it better, "chaotics"[38]—is the study of systems that are so sensitive to minuscule influences that they appear random and capricious but aren't. In fact, there is harmony amid the chaos, and stability can both inhere in and issue from disorderliness. "Universality" is an aspect of chaos theory that is overlooked but is perhaps its most important feature. "Universality" means that transitions from order to chaos and vice versa are both predictable and universal. The lower the complexity, the higher the predictability. Transitions from order to chaos are the result of the increased complexity of a system.[39]

Chaotics teaches us that if you add a little more chaos into a chaotic system you get order. In fact, physicists now believe that a little disorder can nudge organizations out of turbulence into order.[40] This is the key theological insight of chaotics: sensitive dependence on initial conditions. The uniqueness of complex systems resides in the way in which small changes in a dynamical system can generate exponential outcomes, even divergent outcomes. Small changes in one world can create massive changes in another world.

What does all this stuff about "chaordic" and "chaotic" mean?

It means that unfathomable possibilities are at your fingertips at every moment. It means that what you do can literally change the world.

Don't believe me? Try this thought experiment. Air molecules are colliding all the time in a room. Imagine God removing *one* electron from the edges of the universe. Its effect is to lessen the gravitational force on the air molecules bouncing in the room. After only 50 collisions, two molecules that would have collided if God had not removed that one single electron now miss hitting one another. After only a fraction of a second, the trajectories of two electrons are different because of God's removing one electron at the edge of the known universe.

Still don't believe me? Try this experiment. Set aside 15 minutes a day to read a book. Now calculate how many books that becomes in a year? Two dozen. How many books in a lifetime? One thousand—or five times what you read in college.

The church is missing the boat on what it means to be a leader. Our problem is not a need for leadership to add sanity and order to an insane, irrational system. The church is bursting at the seams with rationality, decency, order, dignity, and predictability.

> Order generated without design can far outstrip plans men consciously contrive.
>
> Economist/Nobel Laureate Friedrich August von Hayek[41]

What it needs is the holy intoxications of foolishness, humor, craziness, outrageousness, creative disorder, and passion. T. Scott Gross, whose book *Positively Outrageous Service* is a key look at the future, tells the story of an Italian restaurant that began its business by putting all its money into one form of advertisement: randomly selecting an evening every month when everyone ate free, without advance notice. Business is still booming.[42]

Vinod Khosla, cofounder of Sun Microsystems, isolates the key to keeping Sun innovative: the ability to integrate and celebrate the "flakes" within the system. "You have to be willing to put up with some unusual people because some of the most creative people are very unusual."[43] Can your church celebrate those who are unusual, zany, "flaky"? Chaordic leaders call each of us to let the unusual in us out—to launch out into the deep, to lift anchor, to climb out on the edges, to live our passion, to forget moving mountains and try moving molecules, even at the outer edges of the known universe.[44] Or in the words of the Bonaro Overstreet poem, "To One Who Doubts the Worth of Doing Anything If You Can't Do Everything":

You say the little efforts that I make
will do no good: they never will prevail
to tip the hovering scale
where justice hangs in the balance
    I don't think
I ever thought they would.
But I am prejudiced beyond debate
in favor of my right to choose which side
shall feel the stubborn ounces of my weight.[45]

INFORMATION SUPERHIGHWAY AND INFORMATION COWPATHS ~

Do you own a computer? No?

Hello?! You don't own a car then?

Do you own more than one computer? No?

Hello?! Then you don't own a car either. For today's cars contain at least 30, and some as many as 100 computers. Anyone who owns a car less than 10 or 12 years old owns at least 30 computers. Some people are well into the computer age and don't know it.

How do you like cyberspace? No, you've never been in cyberspace?

> Managing in this world is a lot like playing three-dimensional chess where you've got to see both near and far at the same time as you prepare to move up, down, across, and sideways.
>
> Ian Morrison, president,
> Institute for the Future (IFTF)[46]

Hello?! You don't own a phone? Where do you think you are when you're on the telephone? You're in cyberspace!

The invention of the microprocessor will have a greater impact on planet Earth than the invention of fire. And this nascent technology has only just begun to transform our social, political, cultural, and economic worlds.

Your remote? That remote control you fight over while watching TV is the electronic equivalent of the stone ax. It will shrink in size as it increases in importance for a "ubicomp" future.[47] Computers are doing a disappearing act. In the words of Kevin Kelly, "as the size of the silicon chips shrinks to the microscopic, their costs shrink to the microscopic as well. They become cheap and tiny enough to slip into every—and the key word here is *every*—object we make."[48]

That is why "dead" objects are coming alive, becoming responsive to human needs and emotions. More and more computers are becoming "unseen," invisibly linked together. Called "embedded systems," millions of tiny computers are everywhere, implanted into everything we use, hardwired into everyday products and dedicated to performing specific functions. "Already 90% of the world's microprocessors are used not in PCs, but are hidden inside common household or electronics products."[49]

Your school textbook? When the half-lives of information are getting shorter and shorter, and the time it takes to download text from data bases is getting faster and faster, that bound biology text that took years to prepare will appear as a stone tablet to future generations.[50]

Your modem and URL (Uniform Resource Locator)? All that typing you do to get online—http://www . . .—will be looked on by our grandchildren as we looked on our grandparents' cranking of the model-T ("You mean, Grandpa, you actually had to do that to get the car started?") or as our children look on our TV-watching ("Tell me again, Mom, what it was like when you were a kid and had to walk across the room to change the channel?").

Your watch? The digital watch you now wear on your wrist contains more computing power than existed in the entire world before 1961.[51]

Your birthday card? That card with a 10-second message prerecorded by your granddaughter contains more processing power than all the vacuum-tube computers in 1950.

Your car? It has more computational power to get it down the street than all the computers combined in the Apollo 11 spacecraft that carried Neal Armstrong and Buzz Aldrin to the moon.[52] Ditto that one computer on your lap.

Your pager? That pager that vibrates to inform you that your table is ready at Outback Steak House, or that your baby is crying in the nursery at Prince of Peace Lutheran Church in Burnsville, Minnesota? We are now living in a world where it is cheaper, faster, and safer to send a signal over 20,000 miles up to a satellite and back again than it is to walk the 50 feet to tell you that your child is crying or your table is ready.

There are computers that say "thank you" and "have a nice day" with more sincerity than some people I run into. While most of us only use 5,000 words on a regular basis, already some speech recognition systems recognize 230,000 words with 95% accuracy.[53] The problem with voice recognition is that 95% accuracy means that every 20th word must be repeated or spelled. "Recognition speech" and "wreck a nice beach" sound the same to a computer.

By the year 2000, fiber optic transmissions systems will permit us to send one terabit of information per second. That's the equivalent of 200 million fax messages, 660,000 video conferences, or 20,000 TV channels. Already in the pipeline is a 160-gigabit fibre capable of transmitting the text of 35,000 full-length novels every second.

By 2000, everyone reading these words will have an e-mail address.

By 2000, all checks coming from the federal government will be distributed electronically. One billion federal payments each year (including social security) will be made electronically.

By 2005, everyone who has a calling card will have a Web site.

By 2005, no kid will ever be able to say, "We don't have any books at home to do this homework." Every home will soon have at its beck and call entire libraries, if not one day soon the entire Library of Congress.

By 2010, everyone online will have an "avatar" (a word that, when I first used it in a graduate school paper, brought the accusation that I had "graduate school mouth"), which will become to your virtual world what your social security number is to the real world—an absolute reference point. Soon avatars will merge with what are now variously called "information butlers," "cyber valets," and "know-bots" that will prowl the Web for you when you log off and then feed information back to you upon your return in three-dimensional audio, video, and "bodyo" (sensory stimulations that encompass smell, taste, and touch).[54] Avatars are already replacing "emoticons"—those shorthand symbols for specific emotions that you get on e-mail.

Before too long, your computer will speak, your TV will listen, and your telephone will show you pictures. Or as a cartoon puts it, "Answer the television, honey, I'm watching the phone."

In China, there are 84 people who own a TV to one person who has hot running water. In USAmerica, more homes have telephones and televisions than have toilets or running water. Some 93% of families officially classified as poor have color TV sets, 72% have automatic washing machines, and 60% have VCRs and microwave ovens.[55] Nearly every eligible USAmerican has a driver's license (175 million in 1994), with the number of vehicles (198 million in 1994) exceeding the number of drivers. All Americans in the future will have a computer. What all Americans don't have is an understanding of the new world that the computer has generated.

The number of people using computers rose from 100,000 in 1970 to 76 million in 1990. Of the 6 billion people on the planet, only 10% have a telephone. That's probably the percentage of the planet who will have a computer in 5–10 years. Already over half of US households with children have personal computers, and if these children are asked, "Which would you rather keep, your TV or your PC?" 71% say their PC.[56] One cannot compete in the future without computer skills. Perhaps that's why a Roper Starch Worldwide survey revealed that computer owners would sooner give up their stereo, dishwasher, or television before they would give up their computer.[57]

And by the way, everything you have read above, by the time you read this book, is probably already out of date.

DUMB COMPUTERS ~ It had been a longer than usual flight from Seattle to Newark. I had used up two battery packs when the flight attendant instructed us to put away all electronic equipment as we approached the airport. I grumbled to myself in frustration as I put my ThinkPad through its shutdown paces.

It shouldn't be this tedious. Why can't I just tell it to shut off? For being so smart, my computer is really dumb.

Upon landing, I hurried to the men's room. As I entered, I started laughing. All of a sudden it hit me: I am living in a world of dumb computers and smart toilets. As soon as I enter that men's room, a toilet starts to have a relationship with me. It knows I exist. It responds to my presence. It knows what to do and when to do it. And that brief encounter with that toilet was of such caliber that when I turn my back on it to walk away, it weeps.

When someone wakes up and realizes that he or she could actually make smart ThinkPads, it will be the end of WIMP computers (windows, icons, menus, pointers).

We Boomers, now the graybeards of the generations, think we are being digital when we use e-mail—which is nothing but print on screen. Our Buster and Net-Gen kids communicate with us through e-mail. But to communicate with each other they use chat rooms and computerized MUDS (multi-user domains, where there is synchronous chat).

When my parents' generation purchases electronic technology for the church (really for their grandchildren), they think of it like buying a piano, whereas it's really more like buying a car or carpet. Computers become landfill in a decade or less. Supreme Court Justice Antony Scalia throws his computer away every five years.

The church is still on dirt roads, or worse yet, cowpaths. We are trying to pave cowpaths with asphalt when we should be building the superhighway with electronics. And when we do use computers, we are simply computerizing old ways of doing business much as earlier auto makers designed their machines as "horseless carriages."

Consider the Internet.

The Internet is revolutionizing everything, from medicine[58] to marketing, from government[59] ("Netizens") to ethics ("Netiquette"). The Internet was the creation of the government (living proof, one wag has said, of what the government can do when it doesn't know what it is doing). It was born in 1969 as something called "ARAPnet" by its sponsors, the Pentagon, with a purpose initially to build a user-friendly communication link between the research companies and their employees engaged in military projects. Some 500 computers were connected to the Net in 1983. Four years later, the number had grown to 28,000. Today there are over 6 million hosts on the Net, with 50 different search-engine providers. By the year 2000 there will be at least 500 million hosts.

The Internet, the most important USAmerican export in history, "is like a freight train roaring along while people are laying tracks in front of it. It's not just gaining on those laying tracks; it's gaining on the steel mills."[60] In 1995 the Internet had only 31 million pages. By 2001 the number of Internet accounts will equal the total world population.

MEDIA IS NOT A ZERO SUM GAME ~ As post-modern culture shifts away from print-based sources of information and entertainment, it is important to remember that old media don't die; they just play musical chairs. Radio didn't kill newspapers; TV didn't kill radio or movies; cable-TV didn't kill broadcast networks; the digital age didn't kill vinyl (with 2,200,000

> You must be the change you wish to see in the world.
>
> Mohandas Karamchand Gandhi[61]

vinyl albums sold the first six months of 1997). When there is a media revolution, one does not so much lose a past media form as gain new ones. Media is not a zero sum game. As Walter Ong is wont to remind us in his lectures on the complex relationships between literacy and orality, people who write talk more than people who don't.

Whatever happened to that "paperless" society some pundits were predicting? People are using more paper than ever before.

You think the MTV generations are ignoring traditional print media? Why else would 30 new magazines be launched between 1993 and 1996 targeted at Generation X?

Whatever happened to that Internet-dominated world without magazines? The year 1996 witnessed the launching of more new magazines than ever before, with underground "zines" flourishing.[62]

What about the demise of newspapers? From mid-1996 to mid-1997, the shares of Gannett, Knight Ridder, the *New York Times*, the *Times Mirror*, and the Washington Post Company all hit historic highs.

Many people are worried about the loss of print in an electronic culture. Gore Vidal has said that as the number of readers in the world shrinks, the number of writers increases. The warnings that we are becoming "alliterate" (alliteracy is being able to read but not doing it) seem louder each passing day.

Nothing could be further from the truth. The whole debate about "the end of the book" is ridiculous.[63] People are buying more books than ever before, especially—note—on the Internet.[64] Oprah Winfrey tells her 20 million viewers to turn off their TV sets and read books. Book groups are as hot as can be. A thousand new titles are published every day, with the total of all printed knowledge doubling every five years. Total adult book purchases in the US rose from 776 million in 1991 to 1 billion in 1995, a 32% increase.[65]

A new medium doesn't banish its precursor, but alters its purpose. When the printed book emancipated itself from the medieval manuscript around 1480, new kinds of manuscript books made their appearance as well. People's reading patterns and purposes are different. Either it's the "dip and skip" reading equivalent of channel-surfing, or it's the slow-read, savor-the-book baths in Don DeLillo, Thomas Pynchon, Peter Nadas, and so on. The Gallup Poll gauges reading habits by how many Americans complete a book, a figure which is down to 24% in 1990 from 30% in 1975.

The kinds of books people read are different; indeed, many of them now start as movies. New kinds of publications are appearing all the time—"the book of the film," texts of radio plays, magazines that specialize in film, radio, and television. Why is Jane Austen being read in the original like never before? The originals are purchased after screen successes like *Pride and Prejudice* and *Sense and Sensibility*. There is a booming business in reprinting 19th-century fiction, although fiction in general is losing ground to nonfiction. The religious books category has racked up the top rate of growth, followed by technical and science books.[66]

In USAmerica some 60,000 audio books are available. The "Books on Tapes" company alone has some 29,000 titles. There is even talk now of simultaneous tape editions of new books, which some say could account for 10% of the print-run. Truck drivers are among the biggest consumers of tape books. Expanded sales of audio books has not detracted from book sales, demonstrating that multiple media forms are complementary rather than competitive.

> We have reached a crucial stage in the history of life. The face of the Earth has changed dramatically . . . and it is changing ever faster. What would have taken one thousand generations in the past may now happen in a single generation.
>
> Biologist Christian de Duve[67]

Finely bound books and books that are works of art are all the rage. Marshall McLuhan predicted this in his contention that as various media become outdated they suddenly become an art form. As people use them less, the media increase in importance as objects and artifacts (e.g., LP records and 45s).

so what?   ANCIENTFUTURE METHODOLOGY FOR MINISTRY ~

Out walking one day, Alfred Lord Tennyson spotted General William Booth, the founder of the Salvation Army. "General," yelled Tennyson, "what is the news this morning?" "The news, sir?" replied Booth. "The news is that Christ died for our sins and rose for our justification." "Ah," replied the poet, "that is old news, and new news, and good news."

While modernity sought to bury the past, postmoderns start chaordic journeys on ancient paths. In the words of biblical scholar Gary Phillips of Holy Cross, "The postmodern names . . . an epochal shift in the conditions by which we are coming to know ourselves and the world we inhabit differently. And, on the other hand, the postmodern announces a reimagining of forgotten and ignored faces lived out now according to different aesthetics and indigenous politics."[68] Postmodern pilgrims are chronological snobs of a reverse order. The wisdom of the future is found afresh in the past. For the postmodern leader, the ancient will always be the future. An ancientfuture methodology seeks to create stock situations anew, not do away with the old or introduce the novel. The key to contemporaneity will always be continuity.

> Just because everything is different doesn't mean anything has changed.
>
> Mabel Boggs Sweet

The more authentically traditional one becomes, the more relevant one's ministry. Good news is old news. The Postmodern Reformation aspires not to create a church that is "good as new," but "good as old." "Good as old" is better than "good as new." The problem with the church today is not that it is "too traditional"; the problem with the church today is that it is not traditional enough. It has held the future to a frozen version of the past. It has reduced the rich, full tradition of the Christian faith into a bounded set of rituals, formulas, or principles—liberals call them "stands," conservatives call them "fundamentals."

Postmodern leaders are visionaries spellbound by the past. An ancient-future faith unapologetically lives out of "the faith that was once for all delivered to the saints" (Jude 3 NKJV). Postmodernity is becoming more ancient and more future at the same time. Postmodern leaders keep the past and the future in perpetual conversation—like the COMPAQ ad in which a futuristic car is set in the middle of an antique-paneled library reading room with the caption "Introducing a Traditional Notebook with Complete Disregard for Tradition." This is how we distinguish genuine newness from nowness.

Poet/graphic designer William Blake admonished his readers to "Drive your cart and your plow over the bones of the dead."[70] Modern society was a culture that consumed its own past. In contrast, postmodern pilgrims honor those "bones of the dead" and make those bones live (Ezek. 37). "Moses took with him the bones of Joseph," reads Exodus 13:19. Moses didn't leave without taking his past with him. Those bones were the symbol of the Hebrews' history, prompting them in their struggle to remember, equipping them in their war against forgetting.

In a digital culture that erases memory so quickly, memory becomes one of our most prized possessions. Is it any wonder that recycling of the past through "memory marketing" can be so successful—witness the Volkswagen back-to-the-future Beetle?

Postmoderns who are Christian must not go anywhere without carrying the bones and stones of memory with them: the memory of our past, the memory of our ancestors, and the memory of our holy

> Understand, therefore, beloved, that the Paschal mystery is both new and old; eternal and temporary; perishable and imperishable; mortal and immortal. It is old as regards the law, but new as regards the Spirit; temporary in respect of the model, but eternal because of grace; mortal because of the Lord's burial in earth, yet immortal because of his rising from the dead.
>
> Melito of Sarcis' Paschal Homily, from about a century after St. Paul[69]

places. To abandon the past is to forget what we know. Those bones and stones are the memory of the future. At the heart of worship is deep anamnesis, or re-membering.[71] It is anamnesis that births the new postmodern song:

- "Sing to the LORD a new song" (Ps 149:1).
- "I will make a new covenant with the house of Israel and the house of Judah" (Jer. 31:31).
- "A new heart I will give you, and a new spirit I will put within you" (Ezek. 36:26).
- "For I am about to create new heavens and a new earth" (Isa. 65:17).
- "I am about to do a new thing" (Isa. 43:19).

Postmodern pilgrims strive to embody an ancientfuture faith. Like the French composer Saint-Saens, who adhered to classical principles of music while at the same time functioning as a formal innovator of surprising resourcefulness, an ancientfuture faith brings together tradition and newness, institution and inauguration, innovation and consolidation. "Jazz" may be the ultimate postmodern genre because it brings together both tradition and contemporaneity; it is highly disciplined while at the same time spontaneous and unpredictable; it constantly surprises yet is highly structured.

The Very Reverend Alan Jones, dean of Grace Cathedral in San Francisco where a "rave Mass" wedded the ancient liturgy to an electronic setting filled with jazz, rock music, and dancing, says that "to be innovative is to be traditional. But most institutional churches are deeply ignorant of their own traditions."[72] A sort of romanticized search for tradition and connectedness is also reflected in popular culture. Much of *Sister Act's* popularity in the '90s revolved around its popularizing and revitalizing an ancient faith.

One creates the future by wrapping traditional functions into new delivery systems. The admixture of old-fashionedness with newfangledness, the old and the yet to be born, is the only sure-fire recipe for stability and strength amid changing times. The church exists as a preservatory of the past as well as a laboratory of the future.

Postmodern culture performs historical lobotomies very quickly. Postmoderns are continually being admonished to "Forget What Is. Create What Will Be" (Sony). The Postmodern Reformation road to the future starts with a speed bump that slows down rather than steps up the distinctions and discontinuities between new and old, between future and past, between innovation and tradition. This is in severe contrast with movements of the modern era, whether in architecture or literature or religion, which took an especially cavalier attitude toward the past. Where a depreciation of the past marked the modern era, the postmodern sense of organic connectedness extends to the past and ushers in renewed metaphors of the church as "body."

This is somewhere the rootless, ruthless path of the modern era never went. For this reason, "uprootedness" was a key image in the writings of modern novelists and essayists such as Bertolt Brecht and Leo Tolstoy. To be "radical" in the postmodern era means not to tear up the roots, in the root-canal fashion of the '60s, but to "go to the roots" and there find the direction, energy, and nutrients necessary for growth and movement. Postmoderns don't "go back" to the roots so much as they "go forward" to the roots.

The more multicultural the world becomes, the more imperative it is that we stay attached to our roots. One does not respect another culture by repudiating one's own. To be proud of Western culture, its intellectual energies, and advances is not to deny respect for Eastern culture.

> Slow me down, God, and inspire me to send my roots deep
> into the soil of life's enduring values
> that I may grow toward the stars
> and unfold my destiny.
>
> Poet Wilfred Peterson[73]

FROM MAINTENANCE TO MISSION ~ The Christian tradition is open to change. In fact, that's one of the things that distinguishes it from other religious traditions. The closest thing Islam has to the Western notion of "heresy" is the Arabic word for "innovation." Fear of the new, aversion to change, and intolerance for disagreement mark many other religious traditions much more than the Christian tradition.

How ironic it appears that the *New York Times* on its front pages has identified Christians as "the chief roadblocks to new ideas and change in our society."[74] How do we help the church be true to its own heritage and lead this Postmodern Reformation? How do we prepare Christians to respond effectively to change, to feel good about change, to embrace a transition agenda? How can we help move the church from a maintenance culture to a missional/innovation culture?

To prepare for and lead ongoing adaptive change, the church grafts new ministries onto old roots. The church lives out of tradition, not on tradition. The church builds on tradition; it doesn't live on tradition. Churches that live on tradition die on tradition. There is an old Chinese saying about clinging to tradition just because it is tradition that reminds us of the reason for spiritual practice in the first place: "It's like carrying a raft on your back after you have crossed the river." Tradition is important, but it's not God; it is a route to God.

Transition leaders need to be "turnaround" (that is, *metanoia*) artists. But it is God who effects the turnaround. Religious leadership is less about turning around or turning ahead and more about turning toward God. These 25 transitions from modern to postmodern ministry are an attempt to turn toward what God is already doing in this new world. Each transition is addressed at length in the various chapters of this book. Here they are in abbreviated form:

From Modern to Postmodern Is to Transition . . . ~

1. From critique and pick-apart to celebrate and pick-up; from verbal critics to aesthetic ethicists.[75]
2. From pyramid to pancake/from ladder to web/from cog-and-wheel machine to organic garden.
3. From representation to participation.
4. From institutional "Here-I-Stand" Churchianity (maintenance) to "There-We-Go" Christianity (mission); from inwardly mobile to outwardly mobile ministry; turn the headlights on (not the dome lights).
5. From eye to ear; from structure to rhythm; from seeing to hearing.
6. From printed page to screen; from consecutive/linear to concurrent/field; from word to image; from "in rows" to "in the round."
7. From control to out-of-control; from program to manifestation.
8. From authority structures to relational structures.
9. From "Does it make sense" to "Was it a good experience?"; from information processing, that accesses through critical thinking, to modulating.
10. From excellence to authenticity.
11. From performance to realness.
12. From theology of giving to theology of receiving.
13. From hi-fi to stereo and surround-sound spirituality ("the postmodernist always rings twice").
14. From planning to preparedness and prophesying your way forward (a.k.a. dine out on dreams—backcasting).

> We are writing more and more books that are read by fewer and fewer people with less and less impact on the culture.
>
> Media expert
> Thomas E. Boomershine Sr.[76]

15. From politics to bionomics to culture clash.
16. From church growth to church health.
17. From standing committees to moving teams; from independence to interdependence (synergy and serendipity).
18. From denomination to tribe; from nation state to mega-state (European Community, NAFTA) and micro-tribe; from national to uni-global and multi-tribal/pan-denominational.
19. From mass to demassed structures (e.g., from congregational to cellular thinking).
20. From illustration to animation.
21. From think big and simple to think small and complex.
22. From boundary-living to frontier/border living.

23. From Christendom culture (churchbroken) to pre-Christian mission fields (the unchurched and overchurched).
24. From pastoral care to ministry development.
25. Wild card: From "Re" words to "De" words.

W³ MINISTRY ~ In the media world, "W-cubed" means whatever, wherever, whenever it takes. In the religious world, W-cubed means the gospel is communicated in whatever, wherever, whenever form. Jesus told us *what* to do: Go into all the world and tell my story. Jesus never told us *how* to do it.

If Jesus were here today, what would he say to invite others to follow him? Would he say, "Follow me and I'll take you fishing"? No doubt Jesus would say many things to postmodern culture, but one thing he would say to a world where 10% of its population is using the computer in one form or another is, "Log-on." Go whole hog and log-on. Don't click on to me. Log-on to my life, and you'll go Web-casting.

> *Piscator no solum Piscatur.*
>
> **"There is more to fishing than catching fish."**
>
> 15th-century sportswoman
> Dame Julina Benere

FROM FISHING NETS TO INTERNET ~ Bishop Francis Asbury, the "George Washington of Methodism," was such a familiar figure that he once told a correspondent that he could be found simply by addressing a letter to "Bishop Asbury, America."

The Internet brings us back to Bishop Asbury's world—except you can leave off the "America." Type in leonardsweet anywhere in the world, and you can find me. Type in the name of a church anywhere in the world, and you can visit it—listen to its choir, visit with the pastor, hear a daily devotional delivered by one of the ministers, find out a schedule of ministries, and add your name to the church's prayer list.

The Web is not about technology. The Web is all about relationships and communication. That's why churches need Web sites and Web ministers—not to have the latest technology, but to have the highest levels of connectivity and communications possible. It's not the interactive technology that's significant; it's the interaction of Christians who are finding new ways to meet, to pray, to make decisions, to study the Bible, to do church. Christians do not need physical computer skills so much as intellectual knowledge skills and spiritual skills to use this revolutionary medium.

This collaborative technology is inventing new ways of ministering that we haven't even dreamed of yet. Ministry through the Internet at least includes the following interactive features, each one of which is discussed at length in this book:

1. Living room: basic facts about Christianity, Bible search-engines, "This is my story, this is my song" features of people in the church,

in-home videoconferencing that helps church families (especially youth) stay connected.

2. Kitchen: body-building; who's sick, who needs prayer, pictures of newest members, obituaries, e-mail of everyone in church.
3. Bedroom: r&r, meditation, sabbaticals.
4. Study: distributed learning, seminary education, virtual bookstore-library, continuous learning.
5. Front porch: map to church, bulletin board of what's going on, basic information on history of church.
6. Bathroom: clean-up, confessional.

For the first time in the history of the church, Rick Warren has made it a mission project of Saddleback Church to make every member of his church a part of a password-protected intranet. An intranet is a highly secure member-only service dedicated entirely to Saddleback Church. One can only anticipate what new heights of communications and service to a congregation will emerge, now that 9,000 members are connected to each other and to the church staff. One thing is sure: Olan Mills had better reinvent its business or it will go the way of Smith Corona. With every Saddleback family having its own Web page, and with members changing daily, one could print out a new church directory every single day and it would be different from the one before.

> The bend of the road is not the end of the road unless you fail to make the curve.
>
> Anonymous[77]

ON THE LINE ONLINE ~ Digital interface is both the new market space and the new public space. Can the church be the conscience behind/within the computer? Can we find ways to join mind and heart electronically in what St. Thomas Aquinas once called "a word breathing out a love," an "enlightenment of mind and enkindling of affections."[78]

The Internet, that network of networks, was created organically, from the bottom up. There is no hierarchy of knowledge; it has a "federal ethic," which means that each page, each item is equal. So then, where is the process of "peer review" in the Net?

There is a general crisis of epistemology—how do we know, and how do we know different kinds of knowledge? Elementary schoolkids in USAmerica are facing epistemological and bibliographical questions that most of us didn't face until graduate school.

LEARN YOUR LIVING: GET SMART, CHURCH! ~ Flight attendants give the following instructions to airline passengers: "For those of you traveling with small children, in the event of an oxygen failure, first place the oxygen mask on your own face and then place the mask on your child's face."

In ministry we spend almost all our time placing oxygen masks on parishioners' faces while we ourselves suffocate. The Postmodern Reformation Church knows it must keep fresh, keep current, keep that supply of oxygen strong if it is to help its people. The church is a learning culture. One essence of leadership is to make sure the church knows itself as a learning organism, and then for the leadership to embody those characteristics that make it unique.[80]

> **Your career is only as healthy as your learning curve.**
>
> Program director/Career Action Center staff member Betsy Collard[79]

The major source of wealth creation in the future is not land or labor or capital, but what some would call "worthless matter"—our creative minds, our intellectual and spiritual capital. As business is finding out, training people is expensive. But untrained people are even more expensive. In the same way that knowledge is a key resource of the new economy, so knowledge is a key spiritual resource for postmodern ministry. I shall never forget the time a pastor took me aside after my presentation and asked for help in interpreting something. He said he had brought best-selling author Bill Easum to his church and was beseiged afterwards by grateful parishioners thanking him for such a "good job" and expressing deep appreciation for his ministry. He looked at me quizzically and asked, "What did I do? I didn't do anything but sit there and listen to Bill, and yet I got all the credit as if I had done it myself."

In the industrial economy, value is measured in tangible assets like cash, accounts receivable, buildings, inventory, and machines. In an information economy, value is measured in intangible assets such as information, loyalty, and innovation. Information is more than power. Information is value, especially information that becomes knowledge, that is integrated and insightful. And those who broker information that leads to understanding and usefulness (i.e., knowledge) will be rewarded.

No learning, no movement. Ministry, like information, needs to be "refreshed" or it decays and stagnates. Unfortunately, much of the church has a brain like Einstein—it's been dead since 1955.

Charles G. Finney and Billy Graham are bookends. What Charles G. Finney, the father of modern urban mass evangelism, started, Billy Graham ended. Yet how many of our churches are trying to do "mass evangelism" as Finney and Graham have done it? Wayne Bristow, president of Total Life International Ministries, says that 50% of what he is doing around the world today in mass evangelism he has never done before. In 10 years he expects that figure will rise to 90%.

> **Every living thing that moves has a brain.**
>
> Cybernetician/biologist Francisco Varela

To incorporate the new learning into the life of faith is not to get dumbed down but smartened up and niced up. Ignorance and impotence go together.

"The future of work consists of *learning* a living," argued Marshall McLuhan. A "knowledge society" requires a knowledgeable ministry. An "information society" requires a church that is always in-formation. The Postmodern Reformation Church is a learning church. Its yearning for learning is unquenchable. Its learning curve will not just be single-loop learning—change what you do—or even double-loop learning—changing what you think and do. It must also be open to triple-loop learning—changing the assumptions and perspectives that determine who you are. In a world of continuous improvement, the famous line is "there is no finish line."

The information superhighway is making it possible for the church to drive into some of the roughest terrain it has ever encountered. If all four wheels are to be engaged, we will need mentors or coaches to tutor us in all-terrain driving. We will also need personal learning plans that can teach us the ATV options and skills we are going to need for our next ministry/job/assignment.

Are you taking charge of your own ministry? Are you planning your second-ministry even while you're knee-deep, if not neck-high, in your first ministry? Virtually all jobs in the future will require continuing education and retraining.

One feature of taking responsibility of your career with a personal learning plan will be "distributed learning." Even though I am vice president of a university, I do not believe in "alumni." To acquiesce in the category of "alumni" is to acquiesce in dangerous notions about "graduation" from education. I tell Drew students that we "commence" them but don't "graduate" them. They will always be students, and we hope that throughout their lifelong learning they will connect with Drew through distributed learning opportunities that enable them to keep fresh and smart without ever leaving home. More than 30 business schools in the US (including Harvard and Stanford) are already offering part of the MBA course work online to get their students used to distance learning. Through CUSeeMe technology I can have a "class" of 25 students from around the world and see and talk to all of them simultaneously, and they to me. What if churches were to connect with seminaries, and with each other, to provide lifelong learning to their members?

MINISTRY AS QUICK-CHANGE ARTISTRY ~ In this new world and new economy—where companies launch 25,000-plus products every year—speed is essential. Speed must become a mind-set of ministry and part of the delivery system of ministry itself. Are you revved up to the ministries you do at any time, at any place, for any one? Everything now comes with a use-by date. What things in your church have passed their use-by dates?

> Human history becomes more and more a race between education and catastrophe.
>
> H. G. Wells

The keys to postmodern ministry are adaptability, flexibility, and speed, which might be defined as the ability to change midstream. Pope John Paul II names this gift of the church *aggiornamento,* or "updating." *"Aggiornamento* does not only refer to the renewal of the church; nor only to the unification of Christians, 'that the world may believe' (John17:21)," he writes. "It is also, and above all, God's saving activity on behalf of the world."[81]

Intel head Jim Zurn compares most big organizations with top-down management to aircraft carriers. "You turn the wheel and it sort of turns ... real ... slow. We're more like a school of fish. A school might have tens of thousands of fish in it, but they can change together, instantaneously, and go in a new direction."[82]

> History now comes equipped with a fast forward button.
>
> Novelist Gore Vidal

United Parcel Service, the US Postal Service, and Emery Air Freight all thought of the idea of overnight nationwide delivery before Fred Smith conceived of Federal Express. But he was the first to see that just because no customers had ever asked for it doesn't mean there wasn't a need for it. The issue isn't a shortage of ideas for creative ministries. The issue is a shortage of people who will change direction and act with dispatch on creative ministries.

Quick change doesn't mean quick fix. Fast learning doesn't mean fast-and-loose knowledge. David Orr distinguishes between "slow knowledge" and "fast knowledge." "Fast knowledge" is technologized knowledge—knowledge that enables us to keep up and ahead in this fast-paced, always changing knowledge culture. "Fast knowledge" is an education that prepares us for *living* in the world we're in today. "Slow knowledge" is contextualized wisdom—knowledge that is "shaped and calibrated to fit a particular ecological and cultural context." "Slow knowledge" is an education that prepares us for *life* in the world we're in today.[83]

No matter how quick-change or fast-on-our-feet we become, we must never forget that we are all slow learners. Nietzsche's little known aphorism—"Philosophy is the art of slow reading"—deserves better. It is slow knowledge that gives our lives meaning and purpose and dignity; it is slow knowledge that can bring us into the aesthetic, social, and spiritual dimensions of life.

> There's no success like failure and failure's no success at all.
>
> Bob Dylan

SAFE-TO-FAIL CHURCH ~ Not only will change not be top down; it will also be top-notwithstanding. Can church culture become a change culture? Can the dynamics of change become a vital and visible component of our life in the body of Christ?

Postmodern culture has moved from "trial and error" to "trial and success." Can the culture of the church change from safety-first, risk-free to risky, frisky innovation and unplanned experimentation?[84] Can the church arrange its life differently than it has in the modern world? Only if it can give up the

"M" word—management—and give up control of our lives, give up command and control of our ministries, give up command and control of our churches, to God. To a church filled with people playing control games, Jesus says "If you want to save your life, lose it" (see Matt. 10:39). If you want to have control in life, go out-of-control. Our only control in living comes from going out of control and giving up control to God.

The Internet shows just how far we've come from the command-and-control structures of the Industrial Age. The Internet was established on the principle of mutuality and reciprocity: If you pass on my message, I'll pass on yours. As mentioned earlier, its origins lie in 1969, when the Pentagon established the ARAPnet computer-communication scheme that was designed to survive nuclear attack because it was beyond any central control.[86] Nobody owns it; nobody controls it; nobody runs it; nobody can turn it off. The Net is all about chaos—the safety of being out-of-control.

> Managers still talk about the people who "report" to them, but that word "report" should be stricken from management vocabulary. Information is replacing authority.
>
> Peter F. Drucker[85]

There is no such thing as safe sex or safe religion. Postmodern culture dictates a different dynamics to being and doing church: multiplicity, connectedness, plurality, resilience, chaos, entrepreneurship, risk-taking. An overmanaged church, like an overmanaged corporation, is mired in the modern paradigm. In fact, stockpiling safety systems, as the airline industry has discovered, increases the likelihood of breakdowns and accidents, not diminishes them.[87] The risk-averse pursuit of safety is the quickest path to disaster.

Anyway: Since when did Jesus call his disciples to lead a risk-free, safety-first life? Isn't the human race "God's risk" (Johann Gottfried Herder's phrase), the divine hazarding of a drama that is still being played out? During times of plague Christians exhibited higher-than-average survival rates. Why? Because the Christian ethic of compassion and care for the sick meant that Christians were exposed in higher numbers to the disease, which had the paradoxical effect of developing greater immunity among those who survived than those who fled the plague and vacated the cities.[88]

Kenwyn Smith of the Wharton School distinguishes between those institutions that seek to create a predictable environment—a "fail-safe" world—and those that expect the unexpected and hence create an open-ended, "safe-to-fail" world.[89] Remember the Michael Jordan commercial for Nike: "I've missed more than 9,000 shots . . . failed over and over . . . that is why I succeed"?

Jesus didn't say, "Come follow me, and I will make you . . . feel good."

Jesus didn't say, "Come follow me, and I will make you . . . rich."

Jesus didn't say, "Come follow me, and I will make you . . . successful."

Jesus did say, "Come follow me, and I will make you . . . fishers of men and women."

Jesus did say, "Come follow me, . . . take up your cross."

The divine is present in the world in complex ways. The notion that you're going to have

> Chaos should be regarded as extremely good news.
>
> Tibetan Buddhist meditation master
> Chögyam Trungpa Rinpoche

an ordered and orderly life as a disciple of Jesus Christ is bunk. You want a conventional, convenient, consistent, predictable life? Then don't follow Jesus. There is a complexity of referents if you're a Christian. For the disciple of Jesus, God can be as present in tragedies, defeats, conflicts, and crucifixions as in victories, successes, and resurrections. (Matthew 11:12 NIV says, "From the days of John the Baptist until now, the kingdom of heaven has been forcefully advancing, and forceful men lay hold of it.") You follow Jesus, and you *will* be tried and you *will* be tested.

The trial for Jonah was gurgling around in the belly of a fish.

The trial for Noah was building an ark amid sneers and jeers.

The trial for Jacob was wrestling with an angel.

Jesus said that if we are to turn things around, we must first turn things upside down—including our life itself. Our God is a wild and creative God. Our God is an awesome and unpredictable God. "Our God is in the heavens; he does whatever he pleases" (Ps. 115:3).

God breathed in Isaiah—and he stripped off all his clothes and walked around the town naked and barefoot for three years (Isa. 20:2–3).

God breathed on Ruth–and she was widowed and departed from her familiar native Moab to the unknown land of Judah (Ruth 1:1–18).

God breathed on Paul—and he changed his plans after having a vision of a man from Macedonia, and off he went to Macedonia (Acts 16:9–10).

God breathed on you—and you . . .

Can you trust the Spirit? Can you believe that the invisible is more real than the visible? Can you believe that what is most real about you is not your flesh, but your soul?

say what?

1. In D. H. Lawrence's novel *Women in Love*, Rupert Birkin says the following:

> God can do without man. God could do without the ichthyosauri and the mastodon. These monsters failed creatively to develop, so God, the creative mystery, dispensed with them. In the same way the mystery could dispense with man, should he too fail creatively to change and develop.[90]

To what extent is the decline of establishment religion a symptom of the church's "failure" to be creative and develop?

2. When you stand at the Pearly Gates, would you rather be told you believed too much or you believed too little?

When you stand at the Pearly Gates, would you rather be told you cared too much or you cared too little?

When you stand at the Pearly Gates, would you rather be told that you tried too hard or you didn't try hard enough?

When you stand at the Pearly Gates, would you rather be told that you were too forgiving or you were too judgmental?

When you stand at the Pearly Gates, would you rather be told, "Well done, thou hyper-hopeful and risk-taking servant," or "Well done, thou sober and play-it-safe servant"?

3. One of my favorite motivational posters is simply this:

IYAD

WYAD

YAG

WYAG

In small print there is the translation: "If You Always Do What You Always Did You Always Get What You Always Got."

4. Entrepreneur/philosopher Steven Holtzman is president and CEO of Perspecta. He has a Ph.D. in computer science and a background in philosophy. How do you react to his statement?

> Kids who grow up in information spaces using nonlinear tools like Perspecta, and those brought up on MTV's sub second splices, perhaps won't know how to use a pen to write a story from A to B. But they *will* have the skills to do 10 things at once and create something where people will say, "Holy _____, that's amazing!" Is this less "deep"? Only in the dimension of traditional linear logic.[91]

5. Here's an experiment for your group to try and then report back on the consequences. For one week turn off the TV. Declare a "Week of Jubilee" by unplugging all screens and leaving them unplugged.[92] "Use the freed-up time to do things you have needed or have been planning to do. Get more sleep. Read something. Have a really good conversation."[93] Then report back on what you learned from this "Week of Jubilee." Is this something you would/should do again?

6. Ask the question Peter Drucker made famous. Ask of every activity in your church: "If we did not do this already, would we do it now, knowing what we now know?"[94]

7. Try the "Worst Idea" exercise. What it involves is for everyone in the room to come up with his or her worst idea. This exercise gets people thinking new thoughts, makes people laugh, and brings together opposites—the

worst idea inspires the best. The best example here is the campaign for California raisins:

> When copywriters Seth Werner and Dextor Fedor were trying to brainstorm a campaign to promote California raisins, they were getting nowhere. Until, that is, they went over to a friend's house to work, and Werner happened to mockingly propose having the raisins "do something stupid, like singing, 'Heard it through the Grapevine.'" Everyone laughed and forgot about what was obviously a ridiculous idea until the next morning, when, upon reflection, absurd as it was, the idea seemed to have some merit. It wasn't long until Werner and partner Fedor had contacted Claymation creator Will Vinton, and one of advertising's most memorable and effective campaigns was born.[95]

8. Church consultant Lyle Schaller argues that the church is beginning to face the challenge of change, but has not yet come to deal with the reality of discontinuity. What are the discontinuities?

9. Richard Moran, for many years the national director of organizational change for Price Waterhouse, has put together a book in which he outlines the timeless truths of leadership. He calls the book *Cancel the Meetings, Keep the Doughnuts, and Other New Morsels of Business Wisdom*. Which of these maxims does your church need to pick up and use?

- "When there are tons of sarcastic, cynical cartoons in everyone's cubes and offices, there is probably a problem."
- "Fear is not a good motivator. It only works in the short term."
- "Self-directed work teams require lots of direction."
- "Leadership is more about communication and credibility than it is about policy and performance."
- "Give people space when talking."
- "Not utilizing the skills of employees is the worst crime of management."
- "Don't go on Oprah's or Geraldo's show when they're talking about Bosses from Hell unless you've just won the lottery."
- "Manage the morale, the messages, and the doughnuts. Everything else will fall into place."[96]

10. "We're looking both backward and forward at the same time," says spokesperson Bette Kahn for Crate & Barrel, which sells retro-inspired furniture. Bring in one of their catalogs and explore their tapping into this "ancient-future" hermeneutic.

11. For an excellent series of hands-on activities for learning change, see the "Do It" section of chapter 10, "Welcome Change," in Thom and Joani Schultz, *Why Nobody Learns Much of Anything at Church: And How to Fix*

It (Loveland, CO: Group Publishing, 1996), 279–86. A marvelous role-play scenario for small groups is on page 285.

12. Do we resist change or making changes? You doubt it? How many of you have changed your mind on something significant in the past year? On anything in the past year? When he was dean of the chapel at Howard University, Howard Thurman used to tell the students that every New Year's Day he wrote down what he believed about God and compared it with what he had written the year before. He said that if the two papers said the same thing, he'd know that he had lost a year.

13. John Petersen, president of the Arlington Institute, challenges us to think about "wild cards," which he defines as low probability but high impact changes that could drastically impact the way we live, think, and do church. Petersen gives as some examples of "wild cards" human cloning, an asteroid slamming into the Earth, or time travel. He argues that "in the coming years, wild cards will only get wilder and come faster, and people who recognize and learn to make sense of them will have a real advantage." He calls this "surprise management."

What are some "wild cards" that could fundamentally change your environment and identity? What wild cards could change your denomination (e.g., for United Methodists, the end of guaranteed appointments)? How can we anticipate wild cards? Are there early indicators? What have been some wild cards in the past?

14. Baseball umpire Durwood Merrill tells of his rookie year of umpiring, his first time calling a game in which fastball pitcher Nolan Ryan was on the mound. The second pitch of the game was so fast, Merrill never saw it. He froze, unable to make the call. Finally he yelled, "Strike!" At which point the batter backed out of the box and said, "Ump, don't feel bad. I didn't see it either."

Is this a good metaphor for what is happening in the world today? Change is occurring so fast that none of us can see it clearly, yet all of us have to make vital calls every day. What calls are we making—in the worlds of government, finance, church, family life—that we can't see clearly, but must say something?

15. The president of the National Education Association, which represents the nation's 14,600 school districts, has declared that "we must change the way we do business." After admitting that the factory-model mentality must be overturned—"the structure of most of America's public school system is similar to a traditional assembly line"—he then repents of the way the NEA "too often" became "focused on the welfare of our members to the exclusion of that of our students. . . . We refuse to do this any longer. . . . We understand that America's public schools do not exist for teachers and other employees. They do not exist to provide us with jobs and salaries. Schools

exist for the children. And children must be our bottom line. And so, we are changing."[97]

Can you see this change occurring on a local level?

16. A young man walked into a recruiting station and asked to reenlist. When asked why he was returning to the Marine Corps, the man replied: "There's no one in charge on the outside."

Is it worse to have one person in charge on the outside, or no one in charge? Is anyone in charge of the Internet? Does one person always have to be "in charge"?

now what? See the Net Notes in http://www.soultsunami.com

NOTES

1. Loren Eiseley, *The Immense Journey* (New York: Random House, 1957), 15.

2. I want to thank Doris Buchanan Johnson, a seminary student at Virginia Theological Seminary, for showing me the relevance of this text to the discussion of content/container. See her "God However Met," *In Trust* 9 (New Year 1998): 16.

3. Studies have shown that the younger you are, the more open you are to change, although overall USAmericans are split almost 50/50: Half say they "prefer to keep things in my life constant," while the other half say they "like to make changes in my life."

4. Dennis Scott, *Dreadwalk: Poems 1970–78* (London: New Beacon Books, 1982), 28.

5. Martin C. Raff, "Death Wish," *The Sciences* (July-Aug 1996): 36–40, 38.

6. See, for example, *Abstracts of Papers Presented at the 1997 Meeting on Programmed Cell Death, September 17–September 21, 1997* (Cold Spring Harbor, NY: Cold Spring Harbor Laboratory, 1997), and *A Nematode as a Model Organism: The Genetics of Programmed Cell Death* (New York: Cognito Learning Media, 1996): videocassette.

7. For more on the body's collective consciousness, see Sherwin Nuland, *The Wisdom of the Body* (New York: Knopf, 1997), esp. 84–85.

8. "When a tadpole turns into a frog, its thyroid gland secretes a hormone into the bloodstream. In most of the tadpole, the hormone encourages cells to divide, but in the tail it orchestrates a mass cell suicide. The tail, now useless, withers and disappears."

9. "Attitudes and Values," *American Demographics* 16 (Sept 1994): 12.

10. As quoted in *Current Thoughts and Trends* 10 (Sept 1994): 11.

11. Herman E. Daly, *Steady-State Economics: The Economics of Biophysical Equilibrium and Moral Growth* (San Francisco: W. H. Freeman, 1977).

12. As quoted in Walter Truett Anderson, *Evolution Isn't What It Used To Be* (New York: W. H. Freeman, 1996), 171.

13. Arie de Geus, *The Living Company* (Boston: Harvard Business School Press, 1997).

14. Donald C. Hambrick, David A. Nadler, and Michael L. Tushman, *Navigating Change: How CEOs, Top Teams, and Boards Steer Transformation* (Boston: Harvard Business School Press, 1998), ix.

15. Kenneth L. Woodward, "Dead End for the Mainline?" *Newsweek* (9 Aug 1993): 46.

16. The percentage of older adults in an average congregation is usually 10% higher than the general population. Biblical scholar/media specialist Thomas E. Boomershine Sr. calls the Presbyterians "the most high literate Church in the whole of Christendom" and argues forcefully that the renewal of the church depends on "its power to communicate the gospel in

ways that are meaningful in the emerging electronic culture." See "The Polish Cavalry and Christianity in Electronic Culture," *Journal of Theology* 95 (1995): 92, 90–100.

17. Charles Fishman, "Change," *Fast Company* (Apr-May 1997): 66.

18. The life expectancy of most Net-Gens will see them through the 21st and into the 22nd century.

19. William Bridges, *Managing Transition* (Reading, MA: Addison-Wesley, 1991), 3.

20. Peter N. Stearns, *Millennium III, Century XXI: A Retrospective on the Future* (New York: Westview, 1996), 152.

21. Kevin Kelly uses the example of the dropping in half since 1970 of the half-life of Texas businesses: "That's change. But Austin, the city in Texas that has the shortest expected life spans for new businesses, also has the fastest-growing number of jobs and the highest wages. That's churn." See his "New Rules, New Economy," *Wired* (Sept 1997): 196. For "blur," see Stan Davis and Christopher Meyer, *BLUR: The Speed of Change in the Connected Economy* (Reading, MA: Addison-Wesley, 1998).

22. Prudential Securities' *Future Shocks* (29 Feb 1996): 46.

23. Watts Wacker as quoted in David Diamond, "What Comes After What Comes Next," *Fast Company* (Dec-Jan 1997): 74. The argument that change is discontinuous has never been made better than by Charles Handy in *The Age of Unreason* (London: Business Books, 1989).

24. George Thomas Kurian, ed., *Encyclopedia of the Future* (New York: Macmillan Library Reference USA, Simon & Schuster, Macmillan, 1996).

25. George Gilder, "Happy Birthday Wired," *Wired* (Jan 1998): 40. From 1965 to 1995, information processing capacity, relative to cost, has increased one millionfold!

26. This is the boast of Avram Miller, "The Fast Pact," *Fast Company* (Feb-Mar 1998): 140.

27. Langdon Winner, "It Plays Like God," *Technology Review* (May-June 1996): 68.

28. Quoted in "You Like to Watch," *Wired* (June 1996): 69.

29. As quoted in D. J. Enright, *Interplay: A Kind of Commonplace Book* (Oxford: Oxford Univ. Press, 1995), 8.

30. See, for example, Marva Dawn, *Reaching Out Without Dumbing Down: A Theology of Worship for the Turn-of-the-Century Culture* (Grand Rapids: Eerdmans, 1995).

31. Thomas Cranmer, *Cranmer's Selected Writings*, ed. C. S. Meyer, ed. (London: SPCK, 1961), 2.

32. Peter F. Drucker, *Post-Capitalist Society* (New York: Harper Business, 1993), 59.

33. Michael Rothschild, "Want to Grow? Watch Your Language," *Forbes ASAP* 152 (25 Oct 1993): 20.

34. For an excellent discussion of the difference between stability and resilience, see Richard Tanner Pascale, *Managing on the Edge* (New York: Simon & Schuster, 1990), 262.

35. "What Al Qöyawayma Taught Me About Leadership," *Sweet's SoulCafe* (Oct-Nov 1996): 13.

36. M. Mitchell Waldrop, *Complexity* (New York: Simon & Schuster, 1992), 12.

37. Gordon Wood, "Evangelical America and Early Mormonism," *New York History* 61 (Oct 1980): 362.

38. Katherine Hayles, ed., *Chaos and Order: Complex Dynamics in Literature and Science* (Chicago: Univ. of Chicago Press, 1991), 1–36.

39. For more on "universality," which deals a death blow to scientific determinism, see John D. Eigenauer, "The Humanities and Chaos Theory: A Response to Steenburg's 'Chaos at the Marriage of Heaven and Hell,'" *Harvard Theological Review* 86 (Oct 1991): 455–69. In fact, universality shows that modern reductionism isn't exactly wrong so much as it is "the long way to the answers."

40. Reported in *Nature* (10 Nov 1995) and in *Science News* 148 (9 Dec 1995): 389.

41. Friedrich A. von Hayek, *The Fatal Conceit: The Errors of Socialism,* ed. W. W. Bartley III (Chicago: Univ. of Chicago Press, 1988), 8.

42. Cited in James C. Collins and William C. Lazier, *Beyond Entrepreneurship: Turning Your Business into an Enduring Great Company* (Englewood Cliffs, NJ: Prentice Hall, 1994), 164.

43. Collins and Lazier, *Beyond Entrepreneurship,* 165.

44. For more along these lines, see Chip Bell, *Managers as Mentors: Building Partnerships for Learning* (San Francisco: Berrett-Koehler, 1996), 3.

45. Bonaro Overstreet, "Stubborn Ounces," in his *Signature: New and Selected Poems* (New York: Norton, 1978), 19: with thanks to Jack Harnish of Tampa, Florida, for pointing me to this poem.

46. Ian Morrison, *The Second Curve: Managing the Velocity of Change* (New York: Ballantine, 1996), 2.

47. The future will be ubicomp (ubiquitous computers) even though no one can yet document the payoff of information technology. Nobel economist Robert Solow is famous for saying, "You see computers everywhere except in the productivity statistics." Ditto Peter Drucker.

48. Kevin Kelly, "New Rules, New Economy," *Wired* (Sept 1997): 141.

49. David Kline, "The Imbedded Internet," See *Wired* (Oct 1996): 98, 100.

50. This analogy I stole from Mary Meeham, Larry Samuel, and Vickie Abrahamson, *The Future Ain't What It Used to Be: 40 Cultural Trends Transforming Your Job, Your Life, Your World* (New York: Riverhead Books, 1998), 199.

51. This is according to Morley Winogrod, vice president of AT&T.

52. A late-model Ford car already contains some 50-plus tiny computers.

53. Naturally Speaking by Dragon Systems (617-965-5200). IBM's Simply Speaking Gold lets users "voice surf" the Internet. See www.software.ibm.com/is/voicetype.

54. For more on this, see Michael L. Dertouzos, *What Will Be: How the New World of Information Will Change Our Lives* (San Francisco: HarperEdge, 1997), 56ff.

55. "How Poor Are the Poor?" *American Enterprise* (Jan-Feb 1996): 58–59.

56. See the semi-annual Consumer Technology Index study by Computer Intelligence of La Jolla, California.

57. For the full report called "The Lexmark Report on Computing and the American Family," call 212-599-0700.

58. The 10 million men who suffer from impotence in America now have their own Web page: www.impotent.com. The impotence drug Caverject sponsors the page, which greets you with this: "Welcome. You are person 34,824 visiting this site." The number grows daily.

59. Voting by modem as well as ballot box is within a decade of reality. Your Congressperson will be able to hold town meetings electronically, at which you will be polled as to how she or he should vote. Of course, whether true democracy is a computer democracy is another matter.

60. Matt Mathis, as quoted in *Wired* (Aug 1996): 109.

61. With thanks to Ted Yaple, who has this quote over his desk.

62. There were 933 new magazines launched in 1996, a record number and an 11% increase over 1995. See *The 12th Annual Samir Husni's 1997 Guide to New Consumer Magazines* (New York: Oxbridge, 1997). The top categories were (in descending order) sports, epicurean, special interest, computers, sex, crafts (games, hobbies), home, media personalities.

63. See T. D. Max, "The End of the Book?" *Atlantic Monthly* (Sept 1994): 61–71.

64. Amazon (www.amazon.com) has more books than anyone can count. All of the advertised books can be ordered over the Internet and most will be shipped by the next day. The site also publishes book reviews and makes recommendations.

65. As referenced by Rebecca Pirto Heath in "In So Many Words: How Technology Reshapes the Reading Habit," *American Demographics* (Mar 1997): 39. See also the annual consumer research study of book purchasing by the Book Industry Study Group, Web site www.bisg.org.

66. Religious books are in fourth place (after fiction, cooking, and general nonfiction) in terms of what books people buy. When combined with psychology/recovery books, they constitute a 13% share of all book purchases in 1995. See "Book Worms," *The Boomer Report* (July 1997): 7.

67. Christian de Duve, *Vital Dust: Life as a Cosmic Imperative* (New York: Basic Books, 1995), 271.

68. Gary A. Phillips, "Drawing the Other: The Postmodern and Reading the Bible Imaginatively," in *In Good Company: Essays in Honor of Robert Detweiler*, ed. David Jasper and Mark Ledbetter (Hillsboro, OR: American Academy of Religion, 1994), 404.

69. As quoted in John Barton, *People of the Book?* (London: SPCK, 1988), 10.

70. Quoted in Denis Donoghue, "The Book of Genius: Harold Bloom's Agon and the Uses of Great Literature," *TLS, Times Literary Supplement* (6 Jan 1995): 3.

71. Alas, the extent of the knowledge of many Christians about their heritage reaches all the way back to the last denominational conference they attended.

72. As quoted in Andrea Young Ward, "Treasures Old and New," *Common Boundary* 13 (May-June 1995): 51–52.

73. As quoted in Elizabeth Roberts and Elias Amidon, *Honoring the Earth* (San Francisco: HarperCollins, 1994), 70.

74. As quoted in David L. Larsen, *The Evangelism Mandate* (Wheaton, IL: Crossway Books, 1992), 154.

75. For an aesthetic theory of morality, see Colin McGinn, *Ethics, Evil, and Fiction* (Oxford: Clarendon Press, 1997).

76. Thomas E. Boomershine Sr., "Reforming the Church," *Circuit Rider* (June 1996): 12.

77. My thanks to Professor Charles Courtney for finding this reference.

78. Thomas Aquinas, [*Summa* I, Q.43, Art.5.] as recorded in *Summa Theologiae: A Concise Translation,* ed. Timothy McDermott (Westminster, MD: Christian Classics, 1989), 80.

79. Betsy Collard, as quoted in "Unit of One Handbook," *Fast Company* (Feb-Mar 1997): 101.

80. See Leonard Sweet, *Eleven Gateways to a Spiritual Awakening* (Nashville: Abingdon Press, 1998).

81. Pope John Paul II, *Crossing the Threshold of Hope* (New York: Knopf, 1994), 76.

82. Quoted in Roger Dow and Susan Cook, *Turned On* (New York: Harper Business, 1997), 257–58.

83. David Orr, "Slow Knowledge," *Resurgence* 179 (Nov-Dec 1996): 20-32, quotes on 30-31.

84. John P. Kotter calls it *Leading Change* (Boston: Harvard Business School Press, 1996).

85. T. George Harris, "Interview with Peter Drucker [1993]" *Executive Book Summaries* 20 (May 1998): 8.

86. For more, see Howard Rheingold, *The Virtual Community* (New York: Summit Books, 1994), 7–8.

87. See Yale sociologist Charles Perrow's *Normal Accidents: Living with High-Risk Technologies* (New York: Basic Books, 1984).

88. For more, see Rodney Stark, *The Rise of Christianity: A Sociologist Reconsiders History* (Princeton: Princeton Univ. Press, 1996), 76–94.

89. Kenwyn K. Smith, "Epistemological Problems in Researching Human Relationships," in *The Self in Social Inquiry: Researching Methods*, eds. David N. Berg and Kenwyn K. Smith (Newbury Park, CA: Sage Publications, 1988), 128.

90. D. H. Lawrence, *Women in Love* (New York: Modern Library, 1949), 545.

91. John S. Couch, "The Artist of the Future Is a Technologist," an interview with Steven Holtzman, *Wired* (Dec 1997): 257.

92. The best argument by a non-Luddite for periodically going off-line is Gene I. Rochlin's *Trapped in the Net* (New York: Wiley, 1997).

93. John Ortberg, *The Life You've Always Wanted* (Grand Rapids: Zondervan, 1997), 77.

94. Drucker, *Post-Capitalist Society*, 59.

95. Bryan W. Mattimore, *99% Inspiration: Tips, Tales and Techniques for Liberating Your Business Creativity* (New York: AMACOM, 1994), 177.

96. Richard Moran, *Cancel the Meetings, Keep the Doughnuts, and Other New Morsels of Business Wisdom* (New York: Harper Business, 1995), no. 4, 10, 38, 86, 134, 137, 236, 308.

97. Robert Chase, "Changing the Way Schools Do Business," *Vital Speeches of the Day* 64 (1 May 1998): 444–45.

Get Glocal

THE GLOBAL RENAISSANCE

or what? Why does a glass of water not explode when I move it? Why does a glass half full of water not become a quarter glass of water when I pour another half glass into it?

I am asking some of the most gnarly questions of quantum physics. The stability of matter, and why matter neither collapses nor explodes, is referred to as "a foundational problem" of contemporary physics. Mathematical physicist Mary Beth Ruskai at the University of Massachusetts, Lowell argues that "classical physics can't account for the fact that matter is stable and occupies space."[1]

Water is nothing but trillions of molecules—each one containing two hydrogen atoms and one oxygen atom. These molecules are running into one another at breakneck speeds. So why when I move this glass doesn't it cause an atomic-bomb-sized explosion?

"In some poetic sense, it's a miracle, says Elliott H. Lieb, a mathematical physicist at Princeton University; when you consider all of the physical forces at work in matter, even in something as simple as a glass of water, it's sort of miraculous that everything doesn't just collapse and then, releasing huge amounts of energy, blow up."[2]

And what are molecules but a void, basically empty space? So why do these two water glasses combine to make a full glass rather than a quarter glass of "compact" water that might be twice as dense as the originals?

But matter is stable. If it weren't, we'd risk setting off nuclear-sized explosions every time we put a glass of water down on the table.

GET IT? ~ On 5 August 1996, the American Heart Association journal *Circulation* announced that a drug, poloxamer 188, helped reduce the severity of heart attacks.[3] On 6 August 1996, NASA scientists announced the discovery of evidence supporting simple life forms on early Mars. On 7 August 1996, *Nature* magazine published the first example of an autocatalytic protein. On 8 August 1996, the *New England Journal of Medicine* announced a "new era" in treating sickle cell disease with the discovery that bone marrow transplants can cure the disease in some children.[4]

You get the picture. Almost every day is like this. Bombs drop daily from the sky—some new discovery; some tremendous advance in space, medicine, or manufacturing; some new opportunity to get rich—each one capable of generating fallout that utterly transforms the way we live.

Could this be the dawn of a new global renaissance?

No, it's close to midmorning. It's way past dawn.

We are on the verge of another culture-shaping, value-changing renaissance. Planet Earth is entering one of the most exuberantly creative periods in all of history, a period of artistic and intellectual exploration and discovery similar to the outrageous styles, financial energies, and individual geniuses that characterized the Renaissance in Europe in the 14th through 17th centuries.

The 21st century has the potential to be a time of galactic imagination, artistic flowering, deep and wide connectivity, and rich new intellectual veins for exploring and expanding the meaning of life. One scholar has already named the period of 1993–1998 "the five best years that humanity has ever experienced," and goes on to claim that "we are squarely in the midst of the most amazing upsurge of knowledge and wealth ever seen on Earth."[5] Whether or not we will turn these "best years" into a New Renaissance depends on the choices we make in the next few years.

Humans will enjoy a greater ability to shape the future than ever before by controlling the development of nature and ourselves. Along with expanding wealth, goods, services, there will be breathtaking breakthroughs in medical science—especially in longevity. There is already taking place an extension of the human lifespan beyond our wildest dreams. Some people born in the next 30 years could expect to live to be 200 or more. Chances are your children under 10 will witness the turning of two centuries, not one.

> We are watching the beginnings of a global economic boom on a scale never experienced before. We have entered a period of sustained growth that could eventually double the world's economy every dozen years and bring increasing prosperity for—quite literally—billions of people on the planet. We are riding the early waves of a 25-year-run of a greatly expanding economy that will do much to solve seemingly intractable problems like poverty and to ease tensions throughout the world. And we'll do it without blowing the lid off the environment.
>
> Peter Schwartz and Peter Leyden[6]

But the most revolutionary developments are occurring in our changes of perspective and modes of thinking. The Watergate trial's ontological question, "What did he know, and when did he know it?" has been eclipsed by the O. J. Simpson trial's epistemological question, "What do you think you know, and why do you think you know it?"[7] The *terra firma* pronouncement of Walter Cronkite—ending each evening's narrative on the day in his basso profundo voice by laying claim to "the truth" with the calm certainty, even smug confidence, of "And that's the way it is . . ."—has been succeeded by Dan Rather, whose *terra* is never *firma* but always *excessa*, ever *incognita*: "Well, that's part of our world tonight. . . ."

One of the greatest changes in perspective is the postmodern redefinition of size at both the gargantuan and the minuscule levels. Physics is increasingly becoming the study of matter so small (is it a wave? is it a particle?) as to become the study of consciousness. In other words, physics is becoming metaphysics. The nanotechnology revolution makes possible machine parts the size of atoms and molecules that can build anything and everything. This matter of "perspective" has been immortalized in film in the 1997 summer hit *Men in Black*—where an entire galaxy is held in the bell of a cat's collar.

The 20th-century Christian mystic Padre Pio of Pietrelcina liked to tell a folktale to illustrate how a change in perspective is necessary for us to begin to understand the mysteries of life:

> There is a woman who is embroidering. Her son, seated on a low stool, sees her work, but in reverse. He sees the knots of the embroidery, the tangled threads. . . . He says, "Mother, what are you doing? I can't make out what you are doing!" Then the mother lowers the embroidery hoop and shows the good part of the work. Each color is in place and the various threads form a harmonious design. So, we see the reverse side of the embroidery because we are seated on too low a stool.[8]

What stools do you need to get off of that you might see the big, beautiful picture of your life? What glasses do you need to put on that can enable you to see more *sub specie aeternitatis* and less sub-standard or sub-zero? What angles do you need to look from to switch from seeing life in lines to life in the round?

But there I go again: too far, too fast.

THE DOUBLE RING ～ Millennium Three is a wildly exciting time in which to live, but at the same time a wildly disconcerting and confusing time. "Never before in human history," argues CEO Leslie Danziger of LightPath Technologies, "have people had access to all the information they could possibly ever need."[9] Her "never before" could be multiplied many times over. Postmodern culture is both heady with itself and with the new candor, wit, and iconoclasm that comes from this period of great genius. But the sense of being overwhelmed by the profound cultural upheaval is itself overwhelming.

Previous eras (like the Victorian era of intellectual life) have witnessed a general unsettling of perspective. But with the historical rupture that has occurred in our lifetime, the unsettling has become an upsetting of perspective. Time itself seems out of joint. The world has become unhinged. Doors that used to open and close no longer work. And if they do work, they creak and shriek while closing. In the words of *Sojourners* founder Jim Wallis: "The world isn't working. Things are unraveling, and most of us know it."[10] In the words of art critic Eleanor Heartney, "There is a growing sense, inside and outside the art world, that something is out of joint."[11]

Everything is breaking up and up for grabs. Most of our institutions are adrift, washed up at sea, or abandoned ashore, beached by the tide of history, turning to "dust and crashes." Why the surprise at the success of a movie about the world's most famous shipwreck? The metaphor of "rearranging deck chairs on the Titanic" was in circulation long before the movie.

We know less than we thought we did. More than that, we know too many things that aren't true. The major political and economic assumptions of the last few hundred years, the Industrial Age, can no longer be taken for granted. That Age of the Machine could count on order, rationality, coherence, and certainty. The Age of the Network can count on none of the above. As we have seen, the basic postmodern paradigms are now chaos, complexity, risk, and uncertainty. Discoveries about "nonlinear dynamical systems" are destabilizing life, dissolving illusions, and shattering dogmas.

History used to be seen as driven by laws (principles) and jaws (power). We are living in a world where the old rules no longer apply, where the old laws and jaws no longer work, and where just about all the cards are wild. There is no longer any united vision of what anything means—whether it's what it means to be human, what it means to be male or female, what it means to be Christian or pagan. Leszek Kolakowski writes how "sometimes it seems as if all the words and signs that make up our conceptual framework and provide us with our basic system of distinctions are dissolving before our eyes."[12]

Things don't work as we expect them to. Everything now seems upside-down and topsy-turvy.

Take Braess's Paradox. This phenomenon is named after Dietrich Braess, a German operations researcher who has shown that adding routes to a congested network actually slows the network down, not speeds it up.

Or take the fact that hydrogen (H) burns and oxygen (O) sustains burning—but put the two together (H_2O) and it extinguishes burning.

Or take the phenomenon whereby, just when democracy is triumphing around the world, our American democracy is in trouble and "on trial," as Jean Bethke Elshtain puts it.[13]

Or take Thomas Hine's memorable phrase of what it means to be a human being, which he defines as "little more than a cloud of information."

Is it any wonder that people are shaken and in shock? Is it any wonder that people are finding life confusing, baffling, beyond comprehension? This stressed and strained world of accelerating change, unforgiving competition, where social, economic, and political institutions are being shuffled and rearranged, is a genuine shock to the system. Who among us is not shaken?

As the Unabomber wrote in his manifesto, "We aren't the first to mention that the world today seems to be going crazy."

> Everything in the universe is subject to change and everything is on schedule.
>
> Bumper sticker

The problem is that the "crazies" are proving to be right. After one of Linus Pauling's papers was heavily criticized at a scientific meeting, another Nobel Laureate, Niels Bohr, said, "I think we are all agreed that our young colleague's latest theory is crazy: The question is, is it crazy enough to be true?"

CHANGE VELOCITIES ~ It's crazy: Life has become one big blur.

The velocity of change takes the breath away. Changes erase themselves before they even have a chance to take shape. And it's slower now than anytime in the future. Do you think there will ever come a time in your life when there will be *less* change than there is today?

It has been estimated that more information has been generated in the last three decades than in the previous 5,000 years. Over 1,000 books are published every day. One weekday edition of the *New York Times* includes more information than the average person encountered in his entire lifetime in 17th century England.[14] The average consumer will see or hear one million marketing messages in a year. That's almost 3,000 per day.

The early space flights generated information that is forever lost. Why? Because the means of retrieving that information are now gone. The government produced research two decades ago that we can no longer access. Why? Machines to read that information no longer exist. I have lost an entire manuscript entitled *Mother Goose Models of Church* (perhaps it's better lost). I wrote it six years ago, put it away on disc, and then returned to it recently only to discover that there are no machines to read it.

The accelerated speed of change is mixing with an accelerated speed of time. Technology speeds up time, even to the point where some have suggested that we have now moved out of the age of speed and into the age of "real time," a single "world time."

There comes a time when the ability of the human species to accommodate such speed and change is maxed out. In times of acute social stress, some will want to turn back the clock. Others, shell-shocked by the exploding bombs all around, use drugs to mask the challenges of life.

POWER VORTICES ~ It's crazy: The movers and shakers have moved on or gotten quiet.

Old centers of power are being undermined, and old systems of authority are being challenged. New vortices of power are emerging. Newspaper readership is falling. Social clubs like the PTA, Red Cross, League of Women Voters, and Boy Scouts are barely making it. The only reason Kiwanis clubs have not gone the way of the Jaycees (lost 44% of members since 1979) and Masons (down 39% since 1959) is that the adding of women has stabilized their membership. The Elks are down 21%, the Lions down 12%, since 1983. The Moose, Eagles, and Falcons need to be placed on the endangered species list. Labor unions are almost as much in decline as the animal clubs. At the same time, other groups are gaining members, both old (the Knights of Columbus, celebrating values and immigrants, have mushroomed) and new (Promise Keepers attracts over 700,000 per year; logged-on groups have exploded, where virtual interactions through electronic on line communities take place).

Some argue that the greatest threat in the future is the breakdown of those institutions modern society created—business, government, public education, the family. Even those who don't go that far are nervous over the general alienation from traditional ways of doing things as postmodern society ruthlessly carts away many of the modern assumptions. As Michel Foucault warns, "Those who have been in positions of power feel vulnerable and fragile."[15] In those seeds of vulnerability and fragility are unpredictable fruits.

> I once said, perhaps rightly: The earlier culture will become a heap of rubble, and finally a heap of ashes, but spirits will hover over the ashes.
>
> Philosopher/logician/professor Ludwig Wittgenstein[16]

IDENTITY VERSIMO ~ It's crazy: Just who do you think you are?

What does it mean that gender is socially constructed, even provisional, almost daily redefined (e.g., plastic surgery, prosthetics, the body recombinant)? The erosion of traditional gender roles has brought on a crisis in masculinity. The 20th century has proved an acid bath for the male psyche. Male identities are crumbling on almost every front, not the least of which is the process of revision from a lifetime "career" to multiple career-roles and multiple income streams.

SOUL VERTIGO ~ It's crazy: The world has come to an end.

The world I grew up in is over. Everyone's [[]] world is over. The church of my childhood is doomed. Since the "olden" days when I was born, the world has changed almost beyond recognition, leaving us dizzy, dislocated, and open to requiems for a lost civilization.

Change or transition? It is not simply economically that the US is a different place from the world of the 1950s, although I'm not sure every generation in American history has gone through this amount of change in this span of time. When I was born, movies were 75 cents, a new Chevy was $1,220, a new pair of jeans $3.50. When I was born, a gallon of gas was 23 cents, a year's tuition at Harvard $525, a round of golf at Pebble Beach $2. When I was born, a Coke was 5 cents, a Hershey's chocolate bar 5 cents, a cup of coffee 5 cents, a box of Crayola crayons 15 cents, a first-class stamp 3 cents, a record album 1-3 dollars. When I was born, a teacher earned $2,640, 9% of the households owned a TV, and your most basic computer cost $500,000.[17]

Change or transition? I was born in the "olden" days when you could count on, in the famous words of Blanche DuBois (*A Streetcar Named Desire*), "the kindness of strangers." I was born into a blue-laws, 9-to-5, 5-day-a-week, workday world. I now live in a nonstop society, a 24-7-365 all-the-time world: People expect to be able to do anything 24 hours a day/7 days a week/365 days a year. Consumers are taught to expect anything, anytime, anyplace in a world where 24-hour employment is fast becoming the norm. Roy Speer and Lowell Paxson saw that people liked to shop, people liked to watch TV, and they liked to do both 24 hours a day. So they founded the Home Shopping Network. In a 24-7-365 world, how many churches are still 1-1-52 (1 hour, 1 day a week, 52 weeks a year)?

Change or transition? In the "olden" days just before I was born, 22% of American troops in Germany agreed that "the Germans under Hitler had 'good reason' for the persecution of the Jews."[18]

Change or transition? In the "olden" days when I was born, white supremacy was the law of the land. A couple years before I was born, Jackie Robinson was barred from playing baseball in the Jacksonville, Florida, city park because he was black. The Pentagon in Arlington, Virginia, has twice as many bathrooms as necessary because when it was built in the 1940s, the state still had segregation laws requiring separate toilet facilities for blacks and whites. In the 1950s, 44% of whites said they would move out if a black person moved next door, a figure that in 1997 was down to 1%.[19] The percentage of whites who would vote for a black presidential candidate rose from 48% to 89% between 1963 and 1996. Blacks and whites have really only been listening to one another for half my life.

Change or transition? In the "olden" days when I was born, the kids who were lucky enough to have TV watched heavy-duty *Howdy Doody.* Today kids play Super Mario and Yoshi for hours on end. My favorite playthings were an invention of Frank Lloyd Wright's son, called Lincoln Logs, and an Erector Set. My son's favorite "playthings" are a CD-ROM game called *Construction* and *The Magic School Bus* books and CD-ROMs.[20]

Change or transition? In the "olden" days when I was born, "close enough for government work" was the ultimate in engineering excellence and high-standard performance. Today one of the great lies of our time is "I'm from the government, and I'm here to help you."

Change? Transition? In the "olden" days when I was born, penicillin had just been synthesized for the first time. Today scientists around the world are cloning sheep, cows, and pigs.

Change? Transition? In the "olden" days when I was born, you could go to jail for playing lotteries and numbers games. Today games of chance are government monopolies. The biggest bookie around is the state.

Change? Transition? In the "olden" days when I was born, my generation had at least one set of grandparents who were still tied to the farm in some way, giving us some memories of farm living. In the 2000 US census they aren't even counting farmers because there are so few of them (under 2 million, with anticipations of only 600,000 farmers by the year 2020.) Average age of farmers today? 60.

Change? Transition? In the "olden" days when I was born, abortions were illegal except for life-saving situations or rape and incest. Today abortions are performed on demand, having increased to almost 2 million a year, with tax-payers picking up the tab for many of the poor.

Change? Transition? In the "olden" days when I was born, "shotgun wed-dings" were common. Nowadays the number of children born out of wedlock has increased eightfold from 1950 to 1991 (from 146,000 to 1,151,000). Three of every 10 children born in the US during 1991 were born to unwed mothers.

Change? Transition? In the "olden" days when I was born, pornography was seen as smut and repressed. Today you can take your car to "adult" car washes or hire nude cleaning services.

Change? Transition? In the "olden" days when I was born, we snuck bub-ble gum to school. Now schools are equipped with metal detectors, surveil-lance, frisking, and locker searches to keep out guns, knives, and other deadly weapons.

Change? Transition? In the "olden" days when I was born, spanking was proper punishment for misbehavior. Today spanking is child abuse.

Change? Transition? In the "olden" days when I was born, loan sharks were the only ones charging usurious rates of 15–20%. Now credit card com-panies and banks routinely charge rates around 20%.

Change? Transition? In the "olden" days when I was born, there were not even fences around airports. They first put up fences so the planes wouldn't run over the children playing in the fields.

Change? Transition? In the "olden" days when I was born, wireless phones were not even conceived of. In the 11 years I was president of a seminary in Ohio, the number of cellular subscribers worldwide skyrocketed from less than 1 million to more than 90 million. By 2010 at the latest, there will be equal numbers of wireless and wired subscribers.

Change? Transition? In the "olden" days when I was born, "real estate" was one of the best investments one could make. Now "unreal estate" has become the dominant form of property in the world, and the economic value of knowledge trumps the economic value of land (Japan, anyone?). The planet's largest landlord? Bazillionaire Bill Gates.

Change? Transition? In the olden days when I was born, the United Nations had 56 members. There are now 185 nation-states in the world, over 100 of which did not exist when I was born.

Change? Transition? In the "olden" days when I was born, well over 25% of the English language was not invented yet—it has been created in the last 20 years. Wayne Bristow of Total Life International Ministries suggests that I will die speaking English, but I will die having spoken four different English languages if anyone but my generation is to understand my preaching. We need new English translations of the Bible, it has been argued, for the same reason we need new clothes—our bodies change, and the old clothes sim-ply don't fit as well as they used to.

Change? Transition? In the "olden" days when I was born, my West Virginia Gramma cooked on a wood stove. She refused until the day of her death to cook on anything but a wood stove. When Gramma said "Log on," she meant "Make the wood stove hotter." When she told my brothers and me to "download," she meant for us to get the firewood off the pickup.

Change? Transition? In the "olden" days when I was born, a "crack salesman" meant that someone was really good at what he did.

Change? Transition? In the "olden" days when I grew up, only 4% of church members had been raised in a different denomination from what they were in then. Today that figure has risen to 40%.[21]

Change? Transition? When I graduated from high school, all I wanted was a Smith Corona electric typewriter. I had to wait for one, the orders were so backed up. In 1995, Smith Corona filed for bankruptcy as it could not stem the tide of personal computers even after moving its manufacturing operations in 1992 from Cortland, New York, to Tijuana, Mexico, as a way of saving about $15 million a year in wages.[22]

> The more things change, the more things stay the same.
>
> French proverb

Change? Transition? In the "olden" days when I was born, weather forecasting was a joke. Well, some things never change.

Seriously, however, because of computer modeling, satellite imaging, simulation games, and such, weather forecasting has become accurate enough that farmers can plan, if not a few years in advance, at least a few hours. Weather prediction can still be a joke, but it's not a standing joke.

CONSTANT REINVENTION AROUND THE CORE ~ When I went to college, my classmates and I looked forward to "lifetime employment" with one company. Anyone now who thinks he's got a job for life has been in a coma for 10 years or is a tenured university professor. Before he retired, Lou Holtz admitted that his "lifetime contract" with Notre Dame meant "I can be declared legally dead at any time."

From 1920 to 1980, the American Dream was to choose a career and get a lifetime job with one corporation. In the 1980s the dream cracked. There is no such thing as a "career." "Career" went the way of "job security" and "lifetime employment." Everything now is temporary.

Fifty percent of the jobs in the classified ads won't even be around 10 years from now. The top endangered careers?[24] In order, accountants, bank tellers, government bureaucrats, telephone linemen and operators, factory workers, computer data entry personnel, mechanics, library researchers, and middle managers. At the top of the most desired list?

> The bad news is that there are no more jobs. The good news is that there are no more jobs.
>
> Joe Dolce, editor-in-chief of Buster magazine *Details*[23]

Computer animators and database administrators. Second in line? On line content producers and computer engineers. Third? Systems analysts.[25] Other desirable "jobs" weren't even in the dictionary when I was born: "learning brokers," "coordinators," consultants, catalysts, linkers, matchmakers, netweavers, integrators, animateurs, celebritizers, evangelists,[26] counterparts (liaisons), investigators, disseminators, developers, and spook-busters.

Let's face the truth: One cannot function in this new world with low levels of computer literacy (which I call *graphicacy*), just as one could not function in the modern world with low levels of print literacy. Health care services and computer technology jobs are hot. Ministry and manufacturing jobs are not. In fact, the US Department of Labor in *The Occupational Outlook Handbook, 1996-97 Edition* gives a special warning to mainline Protestant ministers: There are tough times ahead unless you're willing to work part-time or go to rural congregations. No wonder pastors have been designated "the single most occupationally frustrated professionals in America."[27]

Postmoderns live their lives in chapters, not in one lifetime chunk.[28] There is only one permanent career I can think of: career counselors who can help people upgrade their skills, become self-employed, and develop multi-careers and multiple income streams. Owning one's own business as a secondary source of income will be as common in the 21st century as a second car is today. (By the way, the emphasis in the Bible is on being self-employed: Paul the tentmaker, Jesus the construction worker, etc.). Constant reinvention is required for a changing workplace. Jack Welch, GE CEO, used to be known as "Neutron Jack." Now he's called "Transformational Jack." Even CEOs are reinventing and redesigning themselves.

> When you are green you grow, but when you become ripe, you begin to rot.
>
> Old southern saying

In the future everyone will have personal agents—people who will help us negotiate this hunting and gathering, telecommuting economy. In the US the number of telecommuters has increased threefold from 1990 to1995; by 1997 nearly 8 million Americans telecommuted to work. From spring 1996 to the end of the year, the number of Americans who claimed a designated room in their house as an office jumped from 24% to 31%, with the home office market expected to expand at 7% a year through 2000.[29]

"WHAT A DIFFERENCE A DAY MAKES" ~ People do not understand what is happening to them. One day people are being shot trying to cross the "no-man's-land" between East and West Germany; the next day, tourists are picnicking there, and East Germany has ceased to exist. I fully expect that I wake up every morning to a different world from the one I went to sleep in—change is happening that fast.

People are crazed and dizzied by the velocity, vortices, versimo, and vertigo of change. They are suffering from IFS (Information Fatigue Syndrome). They are dazzled and dazed by the new art forms, new literature, new perspectives on values, new thoughts, new aesthetics, new behaviors (e.g., the Rodman Delay in Chicago). Cubs reliever Bob Patterson, describing the pitch that the Cincinnati Reds' Barry Larkin had hit off him for a game-winning home run, said, "It was a cross between a screwball and a change-up. It was a screw-up."

That's how people are feeling: fed up, messed up, screwed up. Many are confused, angry, disgusted, and pessimistic about the future. Alienation abounds, even in church. Church people are irritable, cranky, angry, with notoriously quarrelsome dispositions and unruly polyphony. Sometimes it seems as if the cynics and critics are inheriting the church, if not the earth.

FIN-DE-SIÈCLE ANGST ~ In 1792, during the French Revolution, Germaine de Stael wrote to Edward Gibbon and said, "Men will go mad; most heads are not organized to *cope* with all these shocks."[30]

Those shocks are nothing compared with the ones we are experiencing in this "interregnum," as Antonio Gramsci calls the time in which we are living. All around us, he notes, "a great variety of morbid symptoms appears." Expressions of *fin-de-siècle* angst, of cultural crisis, are everywhere. The latest *Diagnostic and Statistical Manual of Mental Disorders* (4th ed.; 1994) includes the standard "disorders" like depression, schizophrenia, but also "oppositional defiant disorder" (won't obey instructions), "conduct disorder" (bad interpersonal relations, including bullying and intimidation), "fictitious disorder" (pretending to be sick), "amnestic disorder" (unable to absorb or tolerate new information), and "narcissistic personality disorder" (self-absorption). Some are even talking of "vacation disorders," which helps explain the growing trend toward businesses offering sabbaticals.

Coping with this blitzkrieg of change is destabilizing for people and for organizations. There is a classic television episode of *I Love Lucy*. Lucy and Ethel go to work in a candy factory where their job is to take pieces of candy off a conveyor belt and put them into boxes. Everything starts out hunky-dory, but then the belt begins to speed up. They grab the lever to slow the conveyor belt down, but instead it just accelerates. At first, Lucy and Ethel solve the problem by working faster and popping candy into their mouths to keep the pieces from falling off the end of the belt. But they can't keep up. Candy and boxes fly everywhere.

> Wildlife is decreasing in the jungles, but it is increasing in the towns.
>
> Mohandas Karamchand Gandhi

We know how they feel. Information is overwhelming us, and we can't keep up. But it's more than candy and boxes that are flying everywhere. Did you see the cinematic carnage of David Cronenberg's *Crash*? Or perhaps the *X-Files*, which is watched by 16 million people each week and was the most watched TV show for 18–49-year-olds in 1996. Both are true postmodern media—suspicious, ironic, cynical, gruesome. The grime and gloom are everywhere.

Can you blame people for withdrawing from civic culture and building their own islands of safety and privacy? *jiwak* my parents created a household that welcomed the world. As economically impoverished as we were, our front porch was open, not just to our neighbors on "Hungry Hill," but to the world.

We now live in a world where people build homes, not to welcome the world in but to keep it out. This is what some are calling the "forting of America" or "Fortress America"[31] as our living spaces look more and more like the walled cities and castles of medieval Europe. The percentage of us who live behind gated communities is skyrocketing; 28 million USAmericans already live in gated or walled communities (including guarded apartment dwellings), a figure expected to double in the next decade. In fact, homes behind walls appreciate in value much faster than those outside walls.[32] Gated communities are not just for the rich. In Dayton, Ohio, gated streets and alleys were installed to fight drugs and prostitution in the city's Five Oaks neighborhood.

EVERYDAY TERRORISM ~ Russian historians talk of times of "letting out the red rooster." These were spontaneous eruptions of peasant fury that would lead to the slaughtering of the lords and ladies and the burning of their manors. British historians narrate how the disruption released by the first Industrial Revolution required Britain's government in London to nationalize local militia for seven straight years to keep the peace.

Postmodern culture is seeing the "letting out the red rooster" in compensatory behavior—teenage suicide, teenage violence, domestic violence, rising crime rates, drug abuse, divorce, civil unrest, civil disorder. Look at the numbers of environmental and political and economic refugees.[33] Organized armed conflict is now not warfare but criminality. Almost half of US teens say they are likely to be mugged, and 33% say that it's likely they will be shot or stabbed in their lifetime.

Apparently the "No Fear" generation has a lot to fear.

Violent upheaval is already here in arson fires, militia movements, terrorism. But the breakouts of riots and mayhem and the outbreaks of hysteria, resignation, and delirium are only the beginning of what can be anticipated on an unprecedented scale as violence will become an everyday terror.

Some of the everyday terrorism will be random violence, á la the conventional bombings of the Olympics in Atlanta and the federal building in Oklahoma City. One can expect marked increases in carjackings, drive-by shootings, holdups, drug warfare, and terrorism—especially biological and nuclear terrorism. A biological terrorist strike is almost a certainty for the future, and nuclear terrorism becomes more likely in the light of fewer controls on suppliers of nuclear technology to terrorist states.[34]

Much of the everyday terrorism will be homegrown—angry white males are already flocking to militia groups and venting their anger. There is increasing violence among classes in this country—not violence against other countries so much as civil warfare within this country. According to one analyst, Gerald Celente, "Never before in American history have so many people from so many different classes been so disillusioned with so many of society's institutions at once." Much of postmodern violence will be a reactionary *cri de coeur* against a televised world in which some people thrive like gods while other people die like flies. We are

> bombarded with news of dysfunction: Waco, Ruby Ridge, Whitewater, Vincent Foster, Mark Fuhrman, Bob Packwood, the Mexican bailout, fraudulent FBI lab reports, social welfare cuts, corporate welfare gains, unchecked business monopolies, massive business downsizings, environmental degradation, immigration pressures, unwed teen mothers, pedophile priests, militia groups, terrorist cells, severe punishment for petty perpetrators, full protection for powerful offenders, a failing public education system, the bribery of public officials through campaign contributions.[35]

Some of the violence will be international. Professor Aaron Friedberg of Princeton University recently listed the border disputes in just the Pacific Rim: "Japan against Russia, Russia against China, China against India, Japan against South Korea, Laos against China, China against Burma, India against Pakistan, Cambodia against Vietnam, China against Vietnam, China against Taiwan, Indonesia against Timor, Malaysia against the Philippines, and in the case of the Spratly Islands in the South China Sea, which may hold a bonanza of oil, we have seen war before over oil, China against Vietnam, against the Philippines, against Malaysia, against Taiwan."

Much of the everyday terrorism will be religious, such as the nerve-gas attack in a Japan subway, the bombing of the World Trade Center in New York City, the raid on the Branch Davidians in Waco, Texas, the "militia" activities in USAmerica, ethnic cleansing in former Yugoslavia, and terrorist attacks by extremists in and from Algeria. Some of the everyday terrorism will take the form of information warfare, whose destructive potential for social regression is greater, some say, than if it were biological and chemical weapons.[37]

REALITY CHECK ~ This is a "killing society." But this is not the one and only "killing society" in history. Violence, like poverty, has always been with us. Lawmakers complain about the streets of Washington, D.C., but Queen Victoria was attacked three times on Constitution Hill in London. People were more than 10 times more likely to meet a violent, unexpected death in the England of 700 years ago than in the England of today. It was more dangerous to walk the streets of Britain in the 1860s than it is today.[38] Jerry Springer ghoulishness has also been a long-standing problem; on Fleet Street in London, the public hangman sold his rope for sixpence an inch on execution days.

> While the long-term future of the human race may be great, for the next 20 or 30 years, in several dozen countries, there is going to be a big mess.
>
> Robert Kaplan, contributing editor, *The Atlantic*[36]

USAmerica is now seeing some of the lowest levels of violent crime in years. But this is a matter where perception is everything, and even though the statistics don't warrant the fears and paranoia, the perception is real. Nurses in emergency rooms are already wearing their name tags upside down to keep patients from identifying them. By the mid-70s, private police officers outnumbered public police officers better than three to one.[39] Security guards are being commando-trained, hardly the gentlemanly retired police officers of the past. Companies are already selling bullet-proof ("SafeShield") panels that can be installed with drywall to make homes and offices bullet-resistant. One survey revealed that 43% of consumers have stopped shopping at night because of the fear of crime.[40]

Issues of crime are, above all, issues of security. Places we have traditionally considered safe—home, auto, workplace—are now threatened by drive-by shootings, kidnappings, carjackings, "going postal." The criminals as well as the yuppies are moving into communities that were free of crime just years ago. People feel as if they are losing control of their destinies, and they are reaching out for securities—occupational security, health security, personal security.

GLOBAL FEATURES OF RENAISSANCE ~ Before you leave the house in the morning, you experience how global this world has become. You make that first cup of coffee—but only with the help of four states and six foreign countries.

Who owns Firestone? Japan's Bridgestone.

Who owns Dr. Pepper? Britain's Cadbury/Schweppes.

Who pushes the buttons of the Pillsbury Doughboy? Diageo, a company created by Guinness (what country owns Guinness?) and Grand Metropolitan.

"Globalization" is more than the preeminent economic trend of the 21st century, with a thriving global investment culture. It is also a new way of living and being in the world.

The coming together of the new biology and the new physics is providing the basic metaphors for this new global civilization that esteems and encourages whole-brain experiences, full-life expectations, personalized expressions, and a globalized consciousness.[41]

It is hard to underestimate the *unprecedented* nature of this global civilization. We have an interdependent, interlocked economic system in which everybody in the world participates. Global integration is becoming almost universal, with the Net the main medium. Everyone on the planet is participating in the same images and metaphors, even lauding the same heroes. "Transgovernmental" global systems (such as the World Trade Organization, World Intellectual Property Organization, the Kyoto Conference on Global Warming) are starting to do the work previously done by governments, a phenomenon called "the nationalization of international law."[42] Judges from around the world are now citing the US Supreme Court in their decisions. All this can only be described as unprecedented.

We are confronting problems that we cannot begin to imagine and for which we are not prepared.[43] No wonder Busters are more afraid of the future than they are of death. In the words of American-Liberian pastor Alex Benson, "There is helplessness about the present and hopelessness about the future."

THE NEW URBAN RENAISSANCE ∼ The biggest losers in the future are the suburbs, not the cities. Postmodern morphing is leading to an urban revival and a potential rebirth of American cities. Cities are either becoming, along with Smalltown USA, the most desirable places to live, or they are becoming last-place-to-live sites.

A 40-year trend of urban flight is reversing. Cities have become hot spots again for art, entertainment, food, morphed cultural experiences, and an emerging global culture that prizes information sharing, spiritual growth, community development, and no lawns. Graying Boomers, especially those facing empty nests, long commutes, and sagging siding, are heading for the 'hoods of older cities and fleeing the deteriorating suburbs.[44] Here is where a new global population that revels in fine art, culinary experiences, cosmopolitan tastes, and diverse entertainment is being born. Global citizens want to live together. The early 20th-century Chicago School of Urban Theory defined the city as "the concentration of difference," a place where encounters of race, class, and religion take place.[45] In this new urban wave, postmoderns, tired of the sameness of the suburbs, flee either to small towns or to cities.

But it is in the cities where trend-setting—especially morphing components to culture like fusion cuisine, fusion music, fashion fusion—first gets its road-test and roadworthiness. As Tommy Hilfiger knew from the start, the hip-hop fashion among white suburbanite kids started in the cities. Three-quarters of rap albums sold in 1994 were to white consumers.

What is Promise Keepers but a postmodern urban camp meeting that is doing for our day what camp meetings used to do for our ancestors?

The new urban renaissance is already under way in Cleveland, Milwaukee, Kansas City, Memphis, Chicago, Philadelphia, Detroit, Boston, New York City, Seattle, Miami, Minneapolis, and San Francisco.

Any consideration of the future that fails to take account of the urban scene is "futopic" and thus doomed to failure. Today 51% of the world's population lives in cities, and the number gets bigger every year; 388 cities already report a population of more than 1 million.

GOING TO MAYBERRY ~ What we said would happen in *FaithQuakes* has occurred with greater force than anticipated.[46] The return to sidewalks from parking lots has become a stampede.

Small towns in the US are growing at a rate of twice that of urban growth—4.9% per year. One out of 4 USAmericans resides in a town of 2,500 people or less. In virtually every category—population, income, jobs, recreation, retirement base—small-town America is on the rise. The long slide of the '70s and '80s is over. People are migrating to small towns and rural areas, especially "recreational counties" with a recreation and retirement base.[47] Unlike suburbs, where people's lives overlap but don't connect, in small towns they interact and intertwine.

The fastest-growing counties in the US are nonmetropolitan recreational counties.[48] "Micropolitan areas" are outpacing metropolitan centers for growth. "Micropolitan" cities are places with at least 15,000 residents within a surrounding county of at least 40,000 residents (including the central city). More than half of small cities are within 50 miles of a metropolitan city center.[49]

Postmoderns want the benefits of big cities but would rather live in small towns.

RURAL REBOUND ~ Postmoderns are striking out for the wide open spaces. According to the US Bureau of Economic Analysis, incomes in rural areas (5.5% growth) began outstripping urban areas (4.8% growth) between 1990 and 1992. Some 54% of the nation's 2,304 nonmetropolitan counties lost population in the 1980s; between 1990 and 1992, 64% of them gained. In these three years, rural areas had a net gain of 377,000 people. Between 1990 and 1996, these nonmetropolitan counties gained nearly 3 million residents.[50]

Farm-based Midwest communities continue to lose population, but rural areas that are near coastal areas, airports, or recreation are becoming rural boom towns. Henderson, Nevada, once a backwater butt of jokes for gamblers in Las Vegas, has now pushed its glitzy neighbor aside as the country's fastest-growing city. What demographers call the "mild wilds" are the hottest properties of the 21st century.

People are cashing out to the country. Postmoderns define success as being able to say "Good morning" to the butcher, the baker, and the Fed Ex driver. They want to live in areas where the seasons of the year are not totally independent of the seasons of nature—the seasons of our cities are more fiscal seasons and shopping seasons (consumer-driven, holiday-making) than natural seasons. In *Country Home* magazine, readers were asked to chose their ideal home out of the following: a Beverly Hills mansion, a four-bedroom Tudor in the suburbs, a sleek designer loft in Manhattan, or a country farmhouse on a few acres with a pond. More than 50% chose the farmhouse. You can see the "country pipe dream" in the cars people are buying (four-wheel drives, pickups, Hummers), the shoes people are wearing (hiking boots), and the food people are eating (southern cooking, as Cracker Barrel can attest).

Without breathing in "futopia," we must hear the double ring of Michael L. Dertouzos: "People of the twenty-first century will find themselves leading a somewhat schizophrenic life characterized by virtual urbanity and physical parochialism."[51] "Rurban" is the name for the new breed of postmoderns who live in rural areas but have an urban mindset. Dertouzos calls people of the future "urban villagers—half urban sophisticate, roaming the virtual globe, and half village, spending more time at home and tending to family, friends, and the routines of the neighborhood."[52] I am a bicoastal "rurban," a postmodern "urban villager." I work outside of New York City, but I am a legal resident of the San Juan Islands in the state of Washington. I'm half urbanite, half islander.

so what? PASSION PLAY

~ "Work Doesn't Work Anymore," complains Elizabeth Pearle McKenna in her attack on modern culture. Postmodernism sounds the death knell of the Protestant "work ethic" and the emergence of a post-Protestant "play" ethic. The big blur between work and play can be seen in the "social perks" that companies are now offering: company choir (Hewlett Packard), bowling league, ballroom dancing club, trails for jogging, biking, skating, horseback riding (Baan), and "morale budgets" (DreamWorks Interactive).

One of the most significant cultural transformations with profound implications for the church is this shift away from the modern world's emphasis on work, which was tied to the materialistic values of accumulation and economic growth. Postmodernization means a cultural leaning towards postmaterialist values of self-expression, aesthetic interests, and quality-of-life issues like environment, health, and spirituality.[53]

Postmoderns are learning to play, playing to learn, and learning how to make work play.[54] In the upcoming renaissance, people will have to spend less time in paid work and will have more time for neighboring each other and the earth. In fact, postmodern fulfillment is found more in play and contemplation than through work and labor. Concepts of work and play are morphing into each other. Some say the days of work are

> Do not lions lounge? Do not gulls drift effortlessly on the winds? Do not dolphins play endlessly in the oceans? Are we less deserving than our fellow creatures to partake of the joys of life and the wonders of the planet and human society?
>
> The Leisure Party Manifesto[55]

over, that we don't need better "work habits," but better "play habits." Post-moderns will work their heads off, but they need certain assurances: (1) that you care, (2) that there's something in it for them, and (3) that they can *make work play.*

The Christian life is Passion Play.

Jesus may have been the first postmodern. He displayed a genius for never growing up. He didn't have much use for work. In fact, he attracted his disciples by calling them from work: "Let others work, even bury their dead. You follow me" (see Matt. 8:18–22).

Ask someone born before 1964, "What do you do?" and you will find out where they work, what their title is, what they "do" for a living. Ask someone born after 1964, "What do you do?" and you are as likely to find out that they dirt-bike, mountain-climb, net-surf, sea-kayak—in other words, they define themselves more by "life first" than "work first" commitments. Already the resumes of Gen-Xers are reflecting this new importance to play. Many that I have seen have two parts with equal billing and attainments: "At Work" and "At Play." What's *your* play job to go with your day job?

Corporate guru Tom Peters tells of having in one of his London seminars an international banking executive who runs a successful operation in Asia. When the seminar was over, the executive showed Peters his business card. It read: "Playground Director." The man explained, "I seek out the best, slightly offbeat talent I can find, then I give them the best tools in the world and tell them to go play/explore in the markets. What else can I do?"[56]

If you want to make a violin sing, do you "work" at it? No, you "play" a violin. It takes a lot of "practice," but the "practice" leads to "playing" the instrument. I want my marriage to sing. That's why my wife and I don't "work" at our marriage; we "play" at our marriage. I don't go to Drew to "work"; I go to Drew to "play." I don't want the Scriptures to "work" in my life; I want the Scriptures to "play" in my life.

What if the church were to turn its day-care centers into "play-care" learning centers? What if the church itself were to be a center for dare-care learning and spirituality?

ETERNAL SECURITIES ~ Steve Allen tells of a conversation between two upper-middle-class suburbanites bottoming out on bottom-line living. It goes something like this:

> DANNY: I feel guilty about being dissatisfied with my life. After all, what right have I to expect things to be better than they are? Everybody in my neighborhood tries to live the way the people do in *Good Housekeeping* magazine. We're all like bees in a giant hive, mowing our lawns and going to our supermarkets and bowling alleys and movies. Who am I to say this isn't really what life is all about?

HANK: You're asking some pretty subversive questions. You start knocking power-mowers and TV sets and you're shaking the foundations. The fact is, we're all hung up with things and stuff. We feel secure when we're just saving money or buying a new car. And then, too, a lot of people retreat further from what is really important by leaning on religion.

DANNY: Don't you think religion has a reality of its own?

HANK: Sure, but there isn't one churchgoer in a thousand who ever perceives what the founder of his or her religion had in mind. Your average churchgoer is not looking for enlightenment; your average churchgoer is looking for security.

Is Hank right?

Have you noticed the growing number of gated churches that match our gated communities? Expect churches in the future to come fitted with bullet-proof windows, surveillance cameras, alarm systems, and special tests to screen out candidates with psychological propensities toward violence and sexual abuse.

But wait: We already have these pseudo-securities that tempt us to trust the benefits over the Benefactor. Yet the real security packages are not those of Wells Fargo; the real securities are not those of Shearson Lehman. The real securities are the moral and spiritual securities that go with being a disciple of Jesus.[57]

It's time to take back our streets. It's time to take back our homes.

Let others talk about making a difference in the world. It's time for the church to make a different world.

Don't make a difference in the world. Make the world different. Redeem and redream your world.

MAKE THE WORLD MAKE SENSE ~ How many times have you heard (or said) "Hello!"? How about "Go figure!"?

People are having trouble making sense of their world. I grew up in a world where we taught kids the values of the wider culture. Now we raise kids in a world where we teach them how not to succumb to the values of the wider culture. It's not so much that people don't have principles any more as that their principles have changed beyond any recognizably moral form. This is especially true in USAmerica, where a nation has lost faith in itself and major discontent marks everyone and everywhere.

The CTV (Canadian Television) marketing slogan is more a therapy than an ad campaign: "Making Your World Make Sense." In this time when the ancient maxims are undergoing rethinking and there is no coherent moral universe, the role of the church to help people understand what is going on around them is greater than ever. If we don't do it, the media will (and indeed already is doing it).

Here is indeed the challenge of our time for the church of Jesus Christ:

- Can we give postmoderns the intellectual framework by which they can make sense of the world and the social scaffolding by which they can change the world?
- Can we give postmoderns the right pair of glasses by which to view and bring into focus the changes that are going on all around them?
- Can we offer a biblical worldview that shows how all that exists is the gift of a Creator whose definitive revelation is in Jesus the Christ?
- Can we move the church from a shallow cultural Christianity to a deep and wide faith that hoists life's cocktail of hope and despair but downs only hope and drowns despair?
- Can we show how to develop a spiritual mind that makes sense of life and makes life make sense from a biblical framework?
- Can we seek solutions in the crisis to which we are headed, not in political institutions but in spiritual forces?

LISTENER-FRIENDLY ~ "Their mouths lay claim to heaven, and their tongues take possession of the earth" (Ps. 73:9 NIV). This may be history's best definition of an ivory tower.

Two paths have been taken by intellectuals, argues medieval historian Jacques le Goff.[58] First is the pursuit of knowledge by a secluded, scholarly oligarchy. Much of modern learning has taken place behind the walls of academe, sealed off from the people at large, with intellectual activity shut inside specialist bunkers and scholars seldom coming out from behind their high barbed-wire barriers of specialization that surround disciplinary citadels. Most scholars' writing is tightly wrapped in academic bands. Only rarely do they unbutton into street dress, and even then they come out looking like this memo written by the New York City Board of Education: "The management of information requires organizing and structuring data into conceptually clear and logical component ideas that can be transmitted in forms that are user-friendly."[59]

The second path taken by intellectuals is learning that can connect the masses to a wider world. Le Goff argues that intellectual activity is most intellectual when it takes place in a "proletarian" milieu wherein "one of the primary tasks of the intellectual . . . was to have contact with the masses, to connect their knowledge with teaching."

Walter Benjamin says that Berthold Brecht kept a toy donkey on his desk with a sign around its neck: "I too must understand." There has been no spiritual awakening in history without preaching, teaching, and healing that connects with questions asked by ordinary persons in ordinary life. Every great preacher in history has been adept at being led by the audience. Great Awakenings have been led by the "learned" who never lost the common touch or by the "unlearned" who established an almost mystical rapport between themselves and the people.

The Bible says of Jesus that "the common people heard him gladly" (Mark 12:37 KJV). Preachers have three different accountabilities: one to their subject (God), one to their public (listeners), and one to their colleagues (other preachers). Postmodern preachers can not meet any of these accountabilities unless they take seriously bar-room philosophies and gas-station jeremiads; unless they give up NOSP (Not Our Sort of People) preaching; unless they communicate so that "the common people hear them gladly."

> Never perform for other comedians, perform for the audience.
>
> Danny Thomas's advice to young comedians

G. K. Chesterton once described Oscar Wilde's need to aphorize for the common person—"he stoops to conquer"—as the easy victory, the swift clinch, the playing to the grandstands.

It's time to stoop, church.

No one cares whether or not you can tell what Paul Tillich said.

No one cares whether or not you can explain Nicholas Wolterstorff.

But everyone cares whether or not you love your subject and can love-lock them.

Archbishop William Temple once said that the Church of England was in danger of dying of good taste. So may be the entire organized church.

RENAISSANCE MEN, RENAISSANCE WOMEN ~ Pioneer software developer Pattie Maes, associate professor at the MIT Media Lab, says her chief ambition in life is "to do a lot of different things and do them well: being a mother, a wife, a career woman, an academic, an entrepreneur, an inventor, an artist, an intellectual, a traveler. . . ."[60]

> Metaphysics are in the street.
>
> Philosopher/social critic Friedrich Wilhelm Nietzsche

Notice the slashing throughout this book, something I started in *Quantum Spirituality*. No one is ever one thing: Postmoderns are many, many things. Will the church help them be many things and direct their manyness toward the glory of God?

Partially paid sabbaticals are being offered by corporations to enable workers to recharge physically, mentally, spiritually. Can your church put these people to ministry? Can your church provide sabbatical space for postmoderns to develop their renaissance interests?

For outer-beauty shopping, go to your mall. For inner-beauty development, go to your church.

SAVE OUR CITIES—FROM DRUGS TO HUGS ~ St. Catherine of Siena believed that "the city is the image of the soul." If she's right, our soul is in mortal danger. Our virtual urbaneness may make us more insensitive to the plight of the cities. The problems of the inner city are potentially fatal. Here is where a lot of kids are being sentenced to death at birth—crack babies, kids having kids, abused children.

Is there hope for our cities, riddled with AIDS, drugs, poverty, racism, crime? Ray Bakke argues that the hope for our cities is the "entrepreneurial church" that ministers "simultaneously for the salvation of persons and the social transformation of places."[61]

The church holds the keys to saving the world's troubled cities. What if the church were to deploy its own version of the Peace Corps—a "Shalom Corps" of young Christian urban missionaries who would take a bite out of the white suburban doughnut that encircles the urban "black hole" by "re-neighboring" our cities?

THEOLOGY CAFÉ ~ Something strange is popping up in France, Belgium, England, Greece, Switzerland, and Japan. It is being called "the philosophy café." With everything in flux and Western civilization in transition, people are sensing a need to get together to chew about the gristly issues of life such as

"Why was there Adolf Hitler?"
"Why was there Mother Teresa?"
"Do I have a body, or am I a body?"[62]
"Do I have a soul, or am I a soul?"

There is no easy escape from familiar habits, and people seek comfort in comfort foods (soups), "childhood memory" meals as well as counsel and guidance from one another in safe comfort zones like cafés. Have you noticed how sewing clubs and quilting bees are coming back with a vengeance?

In USAmerica more and more philosophers are hanging out their shingles. Philosophical counseling is replacing psychotherapy's "medical" approach that treats everything as a disease. In fact, the philosopher practitioner movement[63] is so strong, don't be surprised to see philosophy kiosks in airports the way one now sees massage parlors.

> It's not enough to have the courage of your convictions. You have to have the courage to have your convictions challenged.
>
> Nietzsche's dictum

BE AUTHENTIC ~ Of the nine definitions of "authentic" that one can find in the *Oxford Dictionary of the English Language*, the one that is deemed most "archaic"—real, true, sincere, as opposed to imitative, contrived, phony—is the one that is most meant when postmoderns talk about "authenticity."[64]

Postmoderns want to be original, not an imitation. One of the reasons for the success of the Broadway musical *Friends*, which is to Gen-Xers what *Godspell* was to Boomers, is the fact that the cast members basically reworked the writing for each show. They generated their own substance and delivery, making it authentic. Postmoderns develop their own personal style out of real-life experience, not contrived or copied.

It is not easy, and the church must help them. Don't believe me? Let's try a little experiment. Finish this sentence:

"Winston tastes good . . ."[65]

Or try this one:

"Plop, plop, fizz, fizz, . . ."[66]

How'd you do? Got them both? The last time those commercials aired was more than 30 years ago. How did these messages get burned into your brain? How did cigarettes and antacids get seared into your soul?

As one scholar puts it, "What is at stake here is the possibility of authentic experience in a world where all our dreams, desires, and fears seem manipulated by external forces. According to Lionel Trilling, the modern ideal of authenticity stands in stark contrast to the older notion of sincerity. Whereas sincerity suggests a way of being in harmony with one's surroundings, authenticity posits a radical disjunction between individual and society. The authentic individual achieves his state not in society but in spite of it, and he is ever at war with the homogenizing tendencies of the group."[67]

The church can create a space in which authenticity can thrive. The church can provide the authenticating experiences of empathy ("I've been there") and understanding ("I know how you feel"). It can also help identify the signifiers of authenticity that have been drawn from the experiences of those who have followed Christ in history and today. For the disciple of Jesus, authenticity is not the self-expression of a private vision, but the divine impression of a community's expressions and identity. The church can also show postmoderns how to resist the evangelism industries of advertising, television, and the movies that seek to infiltrate our consciousness with their values, turning us into grist for the market mills.

> To be natural is such a hard pose to keep up.
>
> Oscar Wilde

HOW TO SURVIVE INQUISITIONS ~ The more unsettling the new discoveries, the more upsetting will be the battles between the defenders of established opinion and the discoverers of new orthodoxies. There are many people in the church who want to make every little thing a test of orthodoxy.

Robert Frost has a character say in one of his poems:

Right's right, and the temptation to do right
When I can hurt someone by doing it
Has always been too much for me, it has.[68]

There is no love for enemies in this new world. New inquisitions are not just possible—inquisitions in the church, inquisitions in the academy[69]—they are an already established fact.

There was only one way that people emerged unscathed from the Salem witchcraft trials of the late 17th century. The only people who survived this inquisition were those who did not let the inquisitors define the issues or the terms.

QUALITY OF LIFE INDEX ~ The Gross Domestic Product (GDP) is useless as an indicator that measures a nation's progress. Our nation's GDP has been climbing while our illiteracy rates, crime problems, neighborhood health, and educational systems were deteriorating—not to mention our environmental health.[70]

What if the church were to push for a quality-of-life GDP?[71] If the magazine *American Demographics* can propose an "Index of Well-Being" that addresses the inadequacy of a single economic indicator (GDP) by combining income/employment data with information about the social and physical environment, consumer attitudes, leisure, productivity, and technology, why can't the church devise something that asks similar questions but factors in moral and spiritual values?

Time, not money, is the currency of the 21st century. The "new poverty," according to Jacob Needleman, is time starvation. People have chosen to embrace things over time, the material over the spiritual.[72] We can do things faster, but is our life better for the speed? Does an increased pace of social life add or detract from human existence?

The key words for philanthropy in the future are "impact" and "choices." Traditional revenue streams are drying up and taking new directions. People want to make a difference with their giving, and they want an experience of the difference they are making.

BUILD A BRIDGE AND GET OVER IT! ~ Information inequity is a painful but inescapable byproduct of the Information Age. The growing gap between the knows and the know-nots will exacerbate the rich-poor problem. In fact, the gap between the knows and the know-nots is more crucial than the wealth gap. In this one fact of postmodern life there is tremendous instability and danger.

The bridge between "the connected" and "the unconnected/disconnected" is getting bigger all the time. "Never before in our history has a medium so sharply divided the population along generational lines. The use of computers and online technology is overwhelmingly dominated by Boomers and young adults, with older Americans greatly under-represented in what is being called the Digital Nation."[73]

The connected get their information and look at life differently from the unconnected: Their attitudes are different. Alas, in this generational divide, our churches are strongest with the least-connected segment of the US population—the segment that doesn't "get it."

Given the immense improvement in the ability of the rich to reach their goals, even if the poor stand still, in relative terms they are falling exponentially behind. By 2000, only half of the world's population will have ever made a telephone call. Only 12 phones exist for every 100 people globally. In China and India, there is one phone for every 100 people (in USAmerica, 60 per 100).

But don't ever overestimate the problem. We can either be astonished that the majority of people in the world have never made a phone call, or be amazed that there are 700 million telephones in the world. As of 1997, with the cost of computers continuing to fall, "an adequate used computer and online access for a year can be had for the cost of a year's subscription to the *New York Times*."[74]

Part of my family hails from West Virginia, where the state flower is the satellite dish. Favellas in Rio de Janeiro, one of the poorest places on the planet, have no running water but they do have satellite dishes. I shall never forget traveling up the Rio Negro to a remote Amazonian village, where the entire community gathered to watch the one TV hooked up to a generator, their eyes glued to the number one television program in the world: *Bay-Watch*.

LIGHTEN UP! ~ Children laugh an average of 400 times a day. Adults need at least 50 laughs a day to stay healthy. How are you doing?

One of C. S. Lewis's greatest insights was that the devil has no sense of humor. One of the great signs of evil is the absence of humor.[75] The early Protestant Reformers' use of laughter as a weapon against the wisdom of the world remains an untold story in the emergence of early modern Christianity. All Reformers better know how to laugh—at themselves, at life, at the church—if evil is to be thwarted.

> When the going gets tough, the tough lighten up.
>
> Entertainer Lily Tomlin

Workaholism is a social disease and a mental disorder. In Japan they have even given it a name: *karoshi,* death from overwork. Japanese researchers who have studied the phenomenon have identified five fatal habits of movers and shakers who die of *karoshi*: long hours, night work, no holidays, high pressure, and demanding physical labor. They omitted a sixth fatal flaw: no sense of humor.

Lord, save us from these movers and shakers.

Lord, save us from humorless theological pedants and biblical scholars who spend their lives correcting grammatical errors in love letters.

To be sure, humor is not always appropriate. Hilbert J. Berger tells of one time beginning an offering: "O Lord, no matter what we say or what we do, Here is what we think of You. Amen."[76] Or my own saying, "The Lord loves a cheerful giver, but the Lord accepteth from a grouch." Witty, clever, humorous—but inappropriate. Such humor creates a wrong mood for the presentation of our tithes and offerings. But better to be skilled in making the cat laugh than in making it cry.

> **Madness:**
> **To be utterly**
> **Without humor.**
>
> Welsh poet Robert
> Minhinnick[77]

INTEGRATE THE BIG THREE ~ Make Morals into Art into Science.

1. Strengthen the Moral Immune System. Postmodern culture has the flu—the morals flu. Walter Yetnikoff, former head of CBS records, met poet/novelist/composer Leonard Cohen in an elevator one day. Yetnikoff is supposed to have said to him, "I know you're great, Cohen, but I just don't know if you're any good."

A healthy human immune system is able to identify and attack alien invasions and encroaching disease. A healthy immunological environment is not disease free, but disease resistant and disease smart.

A similar situation exists for the moral immune system, which needs vaccinations into violence to activate its immune system into developing resistance. We must carefully inject stories at strategic points in the development of moral systems that can introduce children to the reality of violence and the enormity of evil. The worst thing a system can do is to not understand its own cells and attack itself.

We are living in a world that is trying not just to find out what it's like to live, not under conditions of zero gravity, but under conditions of zero morality.[78] What were once seen as stone tablets coming down from the mountain are now seen as sand castles built along the seashore. Why does satire fare so poorly in postmodern culture, while one-liners, sarcasm, and detached irony flourish? Because satire requires a moral standpoint. Moral wobbling hobbles deep humor.

There is a moral vacuum at postmodernity's core that cries out for filling. Will the Postmodern Reformation church step into this void of moral sewage and social vampirism and establish a kind of spiritual copyright over the moral hygiene of postmodern culture? Will the church lead the quest for moral orientation, even moral consensus?

What difference did your day make?

2. Art Your Church, Art Your Life. Where would you go to see the church's greatest treasures? I would pick the Louvre first. My Louvre favorites? Cimabue's *Madonna of the Angels* is a late 13th-century icon that moves. In Andrea Mantegna's 15th-century painting *Calvary,* the rocks are woven into the story of the

Crucifixion, with the mineral universe yet to cry out, as Jesus prophesied it would. Of the literal handful of Joseph/Jesus scenes in the history of the church, Georges de La Tour's *Saint Joseph the Carpenter* is my favorite.[79]

We could spend all day—all year—a lifetime—at the Louvre. But to really discover the church's art treasures one needs to go to what started out as the private art collection of the Tsars, known today as the State Hermitage in St. Petersburg, Russia. Its 3 million art works on display qualify it for the title of "The World's Greatest Museum." My favorite Hermitage heirlooms? The Italian painter Titian (1488–1576) painted perhaps the greatest portrait of Mary Magdalen in existence; *Mary Magdalen in Penitence* (c. 1560) reaches out and grabs you by the soul.[80] Raphael painted 36 Madonnas; *The Contestible Madonna* (between 1502 and 1505) was his first Madonna *en tondo*.[81] The scintillating colors in El Greco's *Apostles Peter and Paul* (1587–97) are matchless; of the two elongated figures, Paul's face bears a mysterious likeness to El Greco himself, whose real name was Domenikos Theotokopoulos (1541–1614).

We could go on and talk about Rembrandt, who is called "the painter of the soul," or Michelangelo, whose frescoes on the ceiling of the Sistine Chapel in Rome stir the heart. Do you have a favorite face of Jesus? Mine is *The Holy Countenance* (1912) by Georges Rouault (1871–1958), which you can see at Winterthur, Switzerland; there is both suffering and compassion in the face, which radiates an inner peace.

A little-known Christian artist is Robert Thompson (1937–1966), an African-American expressionist painter who died tragically at age 29. Born in Louisville, Kentucky, he grew up drawing on anything he could find—including window shades. Thompson played off the old masters, as he did in my favorite *Expulsion and Nativity* (1964).[82] One of the church's greatest female art treasures is Elizabeth Gardner Bouguereau (1837–1922), a New Englander who broke the male barricades of the Parisian art academies by getting one of them to agree to let her attend classes if she dressed like a man. Her *Shepherd David Triumphant* (1895) demonstrates her love of painting Old Testament themes.[83]

But wait a minute!

Are these really the greatest heirlooms in the history of the Christian church? You think these are really the greatest art treasures of the church?

You don't have to go to the richest museum in the world, the Louvre, to see them. You don't need to visit the Vatican to view the greatest art treasures in the history of the church. If you want to see the church's greatest art treasures: *Go Home. Stay Home. Look Around You.* Open your eyes to the acts of service, the acts of grace, the acts of compassion going on all around you by heirs of Christ. Didn't Jesus himself say:

> "I was hungry and you gave me something to eat, I was thirsty and you gave me something to drink, I was a stranger and you invited me in, I needed clothes and you clothed me" (Matt. 25:35–36 NIV).

God did not send the Spirit only to inspire Michelangelo.

God did not send the Spirit only to inspire Rembrandt.

God did not send the Spirit only so that Rouault could paint Jesus' portrait.

God did not send the Holy Spirit only to inspire artists and musicians.

God sent the Spirit to be born in you.

God sent Jesus to be born in you. In the words of onetime Methodist Vincent Van Gogh, Christ lived

> as a greater artist than all other artists, despising marble and clay as well as color, working in living flesh, that is to say, this matchless artist . . . made neither statues nor pictures nor books. He loudly proclaimed that he had made . . . *living men,* immortals.[84]

God is calling *your church* to be the greatest art treasure.

God is calling *you* to be the church's greatest art treasure. To paraphrase Ephesians 2:10, "*You* are God's masterpiece." Or as some translations render it, "*You* are God's poem" and others, "*You* are God's handiwork" which really means "You are God's artwork."

The Christian life is a work of art. Ministry is a work of art. The self is a work of art. The Creator chose creation as the artistic medium for the divine to become human—a medium of wood, stone, color, and texture.[85] The philistinism of the inartistic modern church contrasts sharply with the Medieval church, where the arts were taken seriously and honored for their own sake.

If the medieval church was a patron of the arts, the Postmodern Reformation church must reconceive itself as art. When life is lived from the inside out, it becomes an art form.

Pentecost connects us to the continuing artistry of the Creator. We live in the sort of cosmos that encourages risk and co-creation and freedom. Because we as human beings are blessed with consciousness, our participation in this creativity is necessarily self-conscious: One of the forms it takes is called art.[86]

Can the church encourage the artistic expression of its people: poetry, painting, sculpture, photography, videography, mime, dance ("praise in motion" and "physical prayer"), temporary icons, new forms of music like rap (which has achieved the impossible, combining poetry, politics, popularity, and music). I love processionals because they bring many of the arts together in one ritual act.

My eight-year-old son, Thane, is already a published author. How was his first book published in first grade? His teacher had an Author's Corner in class where kids outlined their book, composed it, illustrated it, submitted it to peer review, edited it, printed it, and published it. Why can't churches "publish" the writings of members of its congregation?[87] Why can't churches celebrate and produce the Amy Grants and Michael W. Smiths in our midst, the Jars of Clay that didn't "make it" on the charts but are charting new worship courses for the congregation?

The postmodern renaissance will be led by artists who love God. Is your church celebrating the artisans in its midst? Have you turned your corridors and classrooms into art galleries where your artisanship can be displayed? But be forewarned: True artists don't meet needs so much as create new cravings.

3. Make Friends with Science. Philosopher Ken Wilber believes that there is "no more important and pressing topic than the relation of science and religion."[88] The separation of the two, he writes, is a "massive and violent schism and rupture in the internal organs of today's global culture, and this is exactly why many social analysts believe that if some sort of reconciliation between science and religion is not forthcoming, the future of humanity is, at best, precarious."[89]

In the same way the arts and sciences have come together in a way unparalleled since the Renaissance—when "discoveries" by Leonardo da Vinci, Filippo Brunelleschi, Masaccio, Leon Battista Alberti, and so on were scientific as well as artistic breakthroughs—so science and spirituality are opening in conjunctions not seen since the 1600s. I now read scientific studies for their spiritual insights as I used to read theological tomes.

It is time to take religion and science out of the cold-war refrigerator they have been chilling in for the last 500 years. It is time to unfreeze facts and values, science and spirituality, and mix them together without spoiling either of their truths.

During the modern era, what science thought was a cure, religion deemed a curse, and vice versa. For Descartes, "seeing is believing." For Jesus, "believing is seeing" (see John 11:40; 20:24–29). The nescience of science required total allegiance, and so did religion. So when science and religion were not spitting tantrums of jealousy over each other's place in the modern world, attacks from either side were piling on in a relentless flurry of heavy punches, terminating long after decency and mercy would allow. One modern scientist, in an oft-quoted remark, revealed the depth of the blood feud when he boasted, "This is the sort of thing I wouldn't believe, even if it really happened."

After slugging it out for much of the modern era, science and spirituality are back together again. Since the 1960s, the warring camps of sacred teaching and scientific learning have started knocking on each others' doors to come out and play. For theologians, the "data" of truth includes the natural sciences. For scientists, the "data" of truth includes faith perspectives. Can you find a scientist today who does not believe in spirit?[90]

say what? 1. It is time for us to read Joseph Heller's tragicomic masterpiece *Something Happened* (London: Cape, 1974) to study how others handled life when their world collapsed around them.

2. Do you detect our language becoming more violent in its metaphors and expressions? For example, some upper-management lingo for dealing with nonperformers is "drive-by shootings" to "take out" those who can't keep up. Then they'd "drag the body around" to make an example to everyone else. Is this common? Can you come up with other examples?

3. What is the essence of leadership in a time of cultural renaissance? Make a list of "essences," and then prioritize them. How important is picking the right people, and then helping them succeed, to postmodern leadership? How accessible should a leader be? What is the difference between a leader who is a catalyst and a leader who is a controller? Which do you tend to be?

4. What would you say to the thesis that every age is equidistant from eternity? Is any age really privileged? Or might every age be a "progress" from the one preceding it, but every age brings with it and introduces unique challenges that make it at the same time better and worse than the one preceding it. Discuss Ken Wilber's maxim: "We are all tomorrow's food."

5. If you still don't think the global nature of the future is significant, take this as an example: You can hire a Ph.D. in physics from an American university for between $70,000–100,000. You can hire a Nobel Prize winner in physics from the old Soviet Union for between $100–150 per month. Which do you think is going to get hired? Centralized communist countries couldn't run an economy if they tried; but they ran some great school systems. Studies have already showed that high school students from formerly communist countries are far better educated than average American high school students.[91]

6. Greg Blonder speaks of "exponential change," in which "exponentials start slowly and remain disarmingly out of sight. Yet they build strength relentlessly until they grow too large to ignore. By then, whole industries have changed and whole cultures have fallen." Does this way of phrasing the world in which we live excite and exhilarate you, or enervate and depress you? Consider Blonder's example:

> Imagine that the price of automobiles [unlike computers, whose cost and intelligence improve by a factor of two every 30 months] drops exponentially. At US$200,000, a Rolls Royce is large, expensive, and unaffordable. You'd never even consider a Rolls as the family sedan. But say the Rolls drops in price by a factor of two each year.
>
> After one year, it costs $100,000—still out of price, out of mind. In the second year, at $50,000, the car stays parked in England. In the third year, at $25,000, you start comparison shopping: the Rolls versus the Taurus. In the fourth year, the kids take one with them to college. After 11 years, the Rolls costs less than $100. Now, instead of renting a car on vacation, you buy a Rolls at the airport and leave it with the redcap in lieu of a tip on your return. In 20 years, Rolls Royces cost less than a quarter; they are soon repurposed as ocean breakwaters and highway barriers."[92]

7. Have someone read and review Norman Crampton's book *The 100 Best Small Towns in America* (New York: Macmillan, 1995, 2d ed.). Why do you think eight of the top dozen communities are in snow country?

8. Move art in your church from the margins to the mainstream by creating a church art gallery. Showcase artists in your church as well as artists in your community. Feature a "discovery" of the month, including children whose artistic skills deserve cheerleading.

9. How can your church give permission for adults to be kids again? How about a Sunday where the adults came forward for the children's sermon and the kids stayed in the pew? What about singing Christmas carols in June and July? What if we were to give everyone a children's bulletin and a few crayons in church? What makes us afraid to have fun in church?[93]

10. The 18th-century poet/former slave-trader/hymn writer William Cowper talked of "the inborn inextinguishable thirst/Of rural scenes"

And they that never pass their brick-wall bounds
To range the fields and treat their lungs with air
Yet feel the burning instinct . . .[94]

How do you explain the "cashing out to the country" phenomenon. Is it simply country nostalgia? Is it "inborn," as Cowper suggests, or is there something more going on here?

11. Use as a study book Robert E. Webber's 13-session workbook *Enter His Courts with Praise: A Study of the Role of Music and the Arts in Worship* (Peabody, MA: Hendrickson, 1997).

12. True or false: There are more government bureaucrats employed in the US than there are laborers employed in the manufacturing sector.[95]

13. More and more people feel that the public schools are failing them. Discuss whether or not you feel that your public school is failing the children of your community. How might your church become a safe learning place for kids?

14. Bring in a week's worth of the *New York Times* newspapers. Can you duplicate the same exercise with which this chapter began?

15. Biblical scholar/media expert Thomas E. Boomershine Sr. makes an intriguing analogy of the church and the Polish army in September 1939 when Hitler's blitzkrieg was hurled against it.

> Hitler sent 14 armored divisions across the Polish border. The Polish army was committed to the traditions of the cavalry and sent 12 cavalry brigades against the German tanks. In the tradition of the great cavalry divisions of the Prussian army, the Polish cavalry was molded for warfare as it had been fought in the 18th and 19th century. When the divisions of German armor came streaming across the border, therefore, the Polish generals sent

wave after wave of cavalry, men mounted on horses, against the tanks. The battle lasted about three weeks. The fields of Poland were choked with the bodies of horses and brave men who had gone into battle with a strategy formed for warfare in a previous period.

Today the Church goes into spiritual battle in an electronic culture, seeking to communicate the gospel in a new cultural environment. In a culture dominated by television, films, CDs, and computers, the Church continues to pursue its strategies that were developed for a culture in which books, journals, and rhetorical addresses were the most powerful means of mass communication.

Like the Polish cavalry, [mainline Protestant churches] are dying in this culture . . . empty and abandoned Protestant churches [strewn across] America's landscape like the horses and men of the Polish cavalry on the fields of Poland.[96]

What does Boomershine's analogy portend for the church's worship? For the sermon?

16. "If you have a new world, you need a new church." Discuss this thesis of Brian McLaren, as found in his book *Reinventing Your Church* (Grand Rapids: Zondervan, 1997).

17. "If you come to the ball park today, you won't have any trouble recognizing me," Jackie Robinson said to his wife on that historic day in 1947 when he started with the Dodgers, the first black American to play Major League baseball. "My number is 42."

Discuss how black-white relations have changed in your community in the course of your lifetime.

18. Send for a free sample of *Science and Spirit* magazine by ordering online at www.science-spirit.org or by calling 800-782- 3235. The Templeton Foundation is encouraging these across-the-table discussions between scientists and theologians and has funded an edited and moderated free e-mail service, called "Meta," for this to take place. For more contact with others involved in this dialogue go to http://www.templeton.org/meta or grassie@voicenet.com.

19. For more on the intersection of faith and work, see the excellent publication *The Life@Work Journal*. For subscription information call 1-800-739-7863.

20. To see how important it is to understand and critique alternative worldviews, see the debate between evangelist Jimmy Swaggart and Islamic writer Ahmed Deedat that took place many years ago at Louisiana State University. In contrast to Deedat, who quoted extensively from the Old Testament, the New Testament, and the Koran, Swaggart admitted he knew virtually nothing about Islamic thought. You can obtain a videotape of *Is the*

Bible God's Word: Swaggart vs. Deedat Debate (Baton Rouge: Louisiana State University, 1986) from the Islamic Teaching Center, where it is used as a Muslim evangelistic tool.

now what? See the Net Notes in http://www.soultsunami.com

NOTES

1. Mary Beth Ruskai, as quoted in Richard Lipkin, "The Stability of Matter: Why Matter Neither Collapses Nor Explodes," *Science News* (14 Oct 1995): 252.

2. Elliot H. Loeb, as quoted in Lipkin, "The Stability of Matter," 252.

3. The findings sent researchers back to the laboratory, as the drug was shown to cause some kidney damage in some of the patients.

4. See M. C. Walters et al., "Bone Marrow Transplantation for Sickle Cell Disease," *New England Journal of Medicine* (8 Aug 1996): 369: as reported in *New York Times* (8 Aug 1996): A1.

5. Julian Simon, "The Five Greatest Years for Humanity," *Wired* (Jan 1998): 66.

6. Peter Schwartz and Peter Leyden, "The Long Boom," *Wired* (July 1997): 116.

7. For more of this, see Kurt Andersen, "The Age of Unreason: Welcome to the Factual Free-for-All," *The New Yorker* 72 (3 Feb 1977): 40–43.

8. C. C. Bernard Ruffin, *Padre Pio: The True Story* (Huntington, IN: Our Sunday Visitor, 1991), 143.

9. As quoted in Patricia King, "Photons: Coming Even Faster to a Computer Near You," *Newsweek* (20 Apr 1998): 13.

10. Jim Wallis, "Restoring the Soul of Politics," in *Nourishing the Soul*, eds. Anne Simpkinson et al. (San Francisco: HarperCollins, 1995), 252. See also his *Who Speaks for God?* (New York: Delacorte Press, 1996), 2, where he observes how "most people, religious or not, sense that something is wrong in America.... Things seem to be unraveling and coming apart. The values and bonds that hold life, families, and communities together feel like they are collapsing."

11. Eleanor Heartney, *Critical Condition: American Culture at the Crossroads* (New York: Cambridge Univ. Press, 1997), 1.

12. Leszek Kolakowski, *Modernity on Endless Trial* (Chicago: Univ. of Chicago Press, 1990), 70.

13. Jean Bethke Elshtain, *Democracy on Trial* (New York: Basic Books, 1995).

14. Twenty years ago there were only 300 online databases; now 7,900 such databases store literally billions of bits of information. For more such statistics see *Executive Book Summaries* (Feb 1996): 2.

15. Michel Foucault, *Power Knowledge: Selected Interviews and Other Writings 1972–77*, ed. C. Gordon (New York: Pantheon Books, 1980), 80.

16. This comes from Wittgenstein's posthumously published book *Culture and Value*, ed. G. H. von Wright (Oxford: Oxford Univ. Press, 1980), 3e.

17. These statistics come largely from "Then: Now," *Kiplinger's Personal Finance Magazine* (Jan 1997): 124–26.

18. As quoted in David S. Wyman, "From Curiosity to Remorse: The Struggle to Establish the Truth About the Holocaust," *TLS, Times Literary Supplement* (7 Mar 1997): 5.

19. As quoted by Rex Teixeira in *Mother Jones* (Sept-Oct 1997): 42.

20. The furniture of my mind is different from that of my kids:

Old	New
Brawn/Metal Bending	Brains/Mind Bending
Mass Production	Small Lots
Competitive standards based on cost	Competitive standards based on quality, variety, timeliness
Standardization	Customization
Hierarchies	Teams
Job security—seniority	Job security—skills
Job specific skills	Broad skills
Limited competition	Global competition
One employer career	Multiple employers
Benefits tied to employer	Benefits that are portable
Pay for time served	Pay for performance
Big bureaucracies	Small, flexible entities
Government solutions	Public/private partnerships
"Go it alone"	Strategic alliances

21. As quoted in *Current Thoughts & Trends* (Sept 1997): 21.

22. Smith Corona is attempting to resurrect itself through marketing to small firms cordless phones, fax machines, and other telecommunications products.

23. "Editor's Letter," *Details* (Apr 1997): 34.

24. For one list see Eva Pomice, "Annual Pick of 10 Career Fields to Get Into," *P.O.V. (Point of View)* (May 1996): 55–62.

25. "Five Occupations with the Fastest Employment Growth, 1996–2006," Bureau of Labor Statistics. Fourth and fifth are personal and home-care aides and physical therapy assistants.

26. "Evangelists" is what Apple Computer and Play Technology call their salespersons-models.

27. George Barna, *The Index of Leading Spiritual Indicators* (Dallas: Word, 1996), 118.

28. This was the conclusion of the Chicago-based International Survey Research Corporation after polling 2.2 million US workers.

29. See the Wirthlin Worldwide Home Office Trends study, reported in the *Wirthlin Report*, as summarized in Matthew J. Cravatta, "Everybody's Doing Homework," *American Demographics* (July 1997): 35. (The report is available online at www.wirthlin.com.) Also see Kathi S. Allen and Gloria Flynn Moorman, "Leaving Home: The Emigration of Home-Office Workers," *American Demographics* (Oct 1997): 57–61, quote of numbers on 61.

30. Germaine de Stael, *Delphine*, trans. Avriel H. Goldberger (DeKalb: Northern Illinois Univ. Press, 1996): quoted in *TLS, Times Literary Supplement* (31 May 1996): 10.

31. Edward J. Blakely and Mary Gail Snyder, *Fortress America: Gated Communities in the US* (Washington: Brookings Institution Press, 1997). Eight out of 10 middle-class housing developments now come with iron gates, wire fences, private security guards, and close-circuit cameras. The authors put the numbers of gated communities in the US at 20,000.

32. Edward J. Blakely and Mary Gail Snyder, "Places to Hide," *American Demographics* (May 1997): 22.

33. "The Human Consequences of a Consumer Society," *Green Cross* 2 (Summer 1996): 13.

34. Benjamin Netanyahu, *Fighting Terrorism: How Democracies Can Defeat Domestic and International Terrorists* (New York: Farrar, Straus & Giroux, 1995).

35. Gerald Celente, "U.S. Trending Toward National War," *The Trends Journal* 4 (Fall 1995): 4.

36. As quoted in Michael Cromartie, "New World Disorder," *Books & Culture* 3 (Mar-Apr 1997): 26.

37. Walter Laqueur, "Postmodern Terrorism," *Foreign Affairs* (Sept-Oct 1996): 24–36.

38. See Linda Grant, "Violent Anxiety," in *The Age of Anxiety*, eds. Sarah Dunant and Roy Porter (London: Virago, 1996), 21–39.

39. According to the Rand Corporation, by 1987 $14 billion was spent annually on all public police officers, but the US spent $21 billion on private-sector security services and hardware.

40. The higher your income, the less likely you are to shop after dark; 80% of people with incomes of $75,000 or more don't shop at night. For more, see *John Naisbitt's Trend Letter* 14 (2 Mar 1995): 5; and 14 (8 Dec 1995): 3.

41. I like what power guru Terence McKenna says about the easy familiarity of New Age with physics: "I'm a little suspicious of the New Age's appropriation of the language of quantum physics, because I think most of these people couldn't solve a partial differential equation if their lives depended on it; they're just surfing on the obfuscation of quantum physics that its mathematical basis provides." Interview with Mark Dery, *21C* 3 (1996): 42.

42. See the work of Harvard Law School professor Anne-Marie Slaughter, "The Real New World Order," *Foreign Affairs* (Sept-Oct 1997): 183–97.

43. Peter Senge, "Through the Eye of a Needle," in *Rethinking the Future: Rethinking Business Principles, Competition, Control and Complexity, Leadership, Markets and the World,* ed. Rowan Gibson (Sonoma, CA: Nicholas Brealey, 1997).

44. Corrie M. Anders, "Suburban Flight," *San Francisco Examiner* (11 Jan 1998): E1, E3.

45. Richard Sennett touts this definition and the work of Robert Park in *The Conscience of the Eye: The Design and Social Life of Cities* (New York: W. W. Norton, 1992).

46. Leonard Sweet, *FaithQuakes* (Nashville: Abingdon Press, 1994), 125–38.

47. Some 93% of the nation's 285 nonmetropolitan recreational counties gained population between 1990 and 1996.

48. "Redefining the Best Years," *The Boomer Report* (Sept 1997): 4.

49. Kevin Heubusch, "Small Is Beautiful," *American Demographics* (Jan 1998): 43–49. For more information read *The New Rating Guide to Life in America's Small Cities*, available for $34.95 by calling 800-828-1133.

50. "A New Era for Rural America," *American Demographics* 19 (Sept 1997): 30.

51. Michael L. Dertouzos, *What Will Be: How the New World of Information Will Change Our Lives* (San Francisco: Harper Edge, 1996), 280–81.

52. Dertouzos, *What Will Be,* 305.

53. For more on this trajectory, see Ronald Inglehart, *Modernization and Postmodernization: Cultural, Economic, and Political Change in 43 Societies* (Princeton: Princeton Univ. Press, 1997), esp. 324ff.

54. For the academic grounding of this statement, see D. W. Winnicott, *Playing and Reality* (London: Tavistock, 1980); John Caldwell Holt, *How Children Learn* (Reading, MA: Addison-Wesley, 1995); and Seymour Papert, *Mindstorms: Children, Computers, and Powerful Ideas* (New York: Basic Books, 1993).

55. As printed in "Workers of the World Relax: The Leisure Party Manifesto," *Wired* (Special edition 1995): 109.

56. Tom Peters, "Let Chaos Reign," *Forbes ASAP* (26 Aug 1996): 113.

57. Instead of talking about moral absolutes, I prefer to talk about moral securities.

58. Jacques le Goff's argument spans the 9th to 16th centuries. See *Les Intellectuels au Moyen Age* (1957) or, in its English translation, *Intellectuals in the Middle Ages* (Oxford: Blackwell, 1993).

59. Ross Petros, *The 776 Stupidest Things Ever Said* (New York: Doubleday, 1993), 168.

60. As quoted in Marguerite Holloway, "Pattie," *Wired* (Dec 1997): 239.

61. Ray Bakke, "The Entrepreneurial City Church," *International Urban Associates* (Fall 1994): 1.

62. This was the question posed by *The Economist* (8 Feb 1997).

63. Joe Sharkey, "Philosophers Ponder a Therapy Gold Mine," *New York Times* (8 Mar 1998): sect. 4:1, 4.

64. A pioneering discussion of "authenticity" and its role in popular culture is Richard A. Peterson, *Creating Country Music: Fabrication Authenticity* (Chicago: Univ. of Chicago Press, 1997), esp. ch. 13, "Authenticity: A Renewable Resource," 205–20.

65. ". . . like a cigarette should."

66. ". . . Oh, What a Relief It Is."

67. Eleanor Heartney, *Critical Condition: American Culture at the Crossroads* (New York: Cambridge Univ. Press, 1997), 13.

68. Robert Frost, "The Pauper Witch of Grafton," from "Two Witches" in *The Poetry of Robert Frost*, ed. Edward C. Lathem (New York: Holt, Rinehart & Winston, 1969), 207.

69. Allucquere Rosanne Stone, *The War of Desire and Technology at the Close of the Mechanical Age* (Cambridge, MA: MIT Press, 1996), 178: "Now that we live, tentatively but inescapably, at the threshold of a new and unsettling age, perhaps it's time to reimagine the scholarly enterprise in terms of this new age—terms under which academics in the humanities and social sciences cannot be conservators of stable know ledges [sic] that are crystallized in books and belief systems, but rather in which the critical importance to human growth and fulfillment that the humanities and social sciences provide within the university structure can drive the institution of higher education to reemerge in a form that can carry it beyond the so-called information revolution, without compromising its mission as conservator of the best of whatever this brawling, struggling thing we call humanity is or may yet come to be."

70. Herman E. Daly, John B. Cobb, and Henry George studied the GDP for the USA from 1970 to 1980, when the total of goods and services grew an annual average of 2.04% per person. When environmental factors are included, the statistics showed an average annual *decrease* of 0.14% per capita during the same time.

71. Hazel Henderson, a longtime critic of the GDP, proposes a Country Futures Indicators. For more, see her *Building a Win-Win World: Life Beyond Global Economic Warfare* (San Francisco: Bartlett-Koehler Publishers, 1996), esp. 238–40.

72. Jacob Needleman, *Time and Soul* (New York: Doubleday, 1998).

73. "Digital Nation," *Boomer Report* (Mar 1998): 1–3.

74. David Boaz, "Creating a Framework for Utopia," *The Futurist* (Nov-Dec 1997): 39.

75. C. S. Lewis, *The Screwtape Letters* (London: Collins Fount, 1977), 26.

76. Hilbert J. Berger, *Now, Concerning the Offering* (Nashville: Discipleship Resources, 1987), 15.

77. Robert Minhinnick, "The Hot-House," Sect. 1, in *The Looters* (Bridgend, Wales: Seren Books, 1989), 21.

78. Leonard I. Sweet and Elizabeth Rennie, "The Gravity of Grace," *Homiletics* (July-Sept 1997): 15–23.

79. Rubens mastered the light of the sun and the moon. The Dutch Masters mastered the clouds. De La Tour (1593–1652) mastered artificial light, the mysterious shadows, and shadings of candlelight.

80. If Titian's style looks familiar, it is because it was mimicked for the Godfather movie series.

81. Note how Mary inclines her head slightly to read to her Son while he fingers the edge of the book, as if following the text with his mother.

82. Martha Jackson Gallery, New York. For more on Thompson, see Elsa Honig Fine, *The Afro-American Artist: A Search for Identity* (New York: Holt, Rinehart & Winston, 1973), 243–44; his *Expulsion and Nativity* is illustrated in Plate 27, p. 237.

83. See the *National Museum of Women in the Arts* (New York: Harry N. Abrams, 1987), 46–47.

84. Vincent Van Gogh, "Letter to Émile Bernard, June 1888," in *The Complete Letters of Vincent Van Gogh* (Greenwich, CT: New York Graphic Society, 1959), 3:496.

85. A specialist with many good things to say about the arts in worship is Robert E. Webber, *Blended Worship: Achieving Substance and Relevance in Worship* (Peabody, MA: Hendrickson Publishers, 1996).

86. Sara Maitland, *A Big-Enough God* (New York: Henry Holt, 1995), 121.

87. John Fischer, "In Praise of the Unrenowned," *CCM Magazine* (Oct 1997).

88. Ken Wilber, *The Marriage of Sense and Soul* (New York: Random House, 1998), 3.

89. Wilber, *The Marriage of Sense and Soul*, 4.

90. See Sharon Begley, "Science Finds God," *Newsweek* (20 July 1998): 46–51, and Kenneth L. Woodward, "How the Heavens Go," *Newsweek* (20 July 1998): 52.

91. For more on this discussion, read Lester C. Thurow's *The Future of Capitalism* (New York: Morrow, 1996).

92. Greg Blonder, "Faded Genes," *Wired* (Mar 1995): 107.

93. I am grateful to John Whitehurst for this question.

94. William Cowper, "The Winter Evening," book 4 of *The Task: A Poem* (London, 1785), as reprinted in *The Poetical Works of William Cowper,* ed. H. S. Milford (New York: Oxford Univ. Press, 1934), 199.

95. True, according to George Marotta, research fellow at the Hoover Institution.

96. Thomas E. Boomershine Sr., "The Polish Cavalry and Christianity in Electronic Culture," *Journal of Theology* 95 (1995): 97–98.

Life ring #7

IS THIS A GREAT TIME, OR WHAT?

Get Dechurched

DE-EVERYTHING

or what? Organized religion now stands at the bottom of the information food chain. Denominations today are living in the Digital Dark Ages. Why?

It will not be easy or fun answering this question. In fact, this chapter is both the hardest and most helpful one in the book. Unlike Truman Burbank in *The Truman Show*, there are good reasons for agoraphobia among believers. Before Christians venture into the postmodern waters, we need to understand the above- and below-ground weather patterns that created the tsunami in the first place. So let's get busy. We have a heavy burden of theory and other meteorological timber to come to terms with and clear out of the way before we can get down to picking up the lumber for a new ark.

TOXIC INFORMATION ~ There is a saying making the rounds: "God created the world in six days, but God didn't have an installed base." What prevents the church from being future-fit is less its installed base of industrial plants and factory-model facilities than its installed base of obsolete thinking and low-grade, even bad information.

In the modern age it was said, "What you don't know can't hurt you." In the postmodern age, what you don't know, or what you know wrong, *can* hurt you. It can also kill you. One of our greatest killers is the notion that what we don't know isn't worth anything. One of our greatest challenges is how to come to terms with what we don't know and the too many things we know that aren't true. Because the church has failed to be both a learning organism and an unlearning organism, our intellectual capital is steadily depreciating.

The Information Age is over. As we seek to live and minister in the Digital Age of Innovation and Imagination, the quantity of information has never been greater, but its quality has become problematic. We are swimming in a sea of information, the quality of which is often poor, rotten, or evil.

We would be better off with less quantity if the quality information were high-grade knowledge or holy wisdom. What does it profit a postmodern if he or she gains an Information Age and loses quality information? Information is tyranny unless there's talk about the quality of global connectedness, the quality of inner consciousness, the quality of commitment to Christ, and so on.

Forbes magazine was built on the economics of industrial capitalism: "Bigger is better." *Fast Company* announced on day one the cardinal tenet of postmodern economics: "Better is better." The qualitativists have already won in the economic world. Why are the quantitativists still winning in the church? Corporate culture is moving from quantity to quality, from profit-driven/market-driven (quantity) to values-driven (quality) economics. Postmodern companies seek "qualitative development rather than quantitative growth"; they admit that, to use Barbara Brandt's words, "growth is meaningless as an overall measure of well-being."[1] I use toothpaste created by entrepreneur Tom

Chappell ("Tom's of Maine"), whose business goal is "a bottom line with a heartbeat."[2]

Bad information is toxic. Get the wrong information, and it poisons the entire system. This principle of toxicity is behind how pesticides work. An herbicide kills because it is a hormone that gives the plant bad information. It tells the plant to grow faster than its capacity to absorb nutrients allows. It literally grows itself to death because its information base is wrong.

Ministry out of an information base of "re" words and "growth" concepts is toxic to the body of Christ. For the re-words to rise again, the church must de-everything.

THE POSTMODERN DEFORMATION ～ "Re-naissance," "re-formation," "re-volution": The modern era was structured around "re" words like these and more (revitalization, revival, renewal). The doors of the postmodern era are being opened up to new experiences and expressions by "de" words. If postmodernity is basically about "re-enchantment,"[3] to get to the "re" words one first must pass through the "de" words.

Postmodern culture is building a new digital civilization, constructed with sand (silicon), glass (fiber), air (wireless), and DNA (genes). The human species is on a journey that will create some of the most profound changes ever witnessed in human history. Religious leadership must bring to this creation the full creative potential with which God has gifted the human species. Before there can be a Postmodern Reformation, however, there must first be a Postmodern Deformation. Structural *deformation* leads to spiritual *formation*, which leads to ecclesial *reformation*.

Ever notice how no one is "fired" any more? One is now "deselected" (the position is abolished) or "dehired" (classic firing) or "decruited" (laid off) or "delayered" (reengineered downsizing)[4] or "dejobbed" (moved to temporary "work assignments" rather than full-time, life-time jobs with benefits)[5] or "delocated" (one's job has moved to another nation/state). From theories of "decoherent histories"[6] and "decoherence physics"[7] to studies of "decolonization;"[8] from calls to "derisk" our initiatives[9] to politicians calling for government to be "deinvented:"[10] no one seems able to pick back up the "re" words without going through the "de" words. All of the hottest intellectual theories specialize in the "de" prefixes. Even many of the theorists themselves have names beginning with "De"—Jacques Derrida, Manuel DeLanda, and Gilles Deleuze (the first philosopher of the Cinematic Age).

Hear some "de" words of the worlds we have lost. How many have you ever heard?

Decubation—the act of laying down
Defossion—the punishment of burying alive
Dejerate—to solemnly swear

Hear some "de" words of the world we have gained. How many do you re-cognize?

1. *Decapitalization*—a spiraling worldwide phenomenon whereby varieties of capital (natural, human, local) are being converted into financial capital and concentrated by institutional investors (corporations, pension funds) into investments that continue this cycle.
2. *Demanufacturing*—the recycling of industrial parts, especially computer hardware.
3. *Democide*—governments putting to death groups of their own people. (More people have been killed by their own government in the 20th century than have died in wars.)[11]
4. *Destressing*—cool-down massages, vacations, spas, beauty aids, coffee bars for our frazzled nerves—anything that helps people come together before they go to pieces.
5. *Delurking*—emerging from the online "lurking mode" either to make your presence known ("Hello, room. I just had to delurk and say ...") or to flame something or someone.
6. *Designosaurs*—an almost extinct species of designers who refuse to use computers.
7. *Dehumanization*–what happens when people apply technological solutions to social and spiritual problems; stated in classic form in Francis Bacon's *New Atlantis* (1627), where the consequences of the Fall are allegedly overcome by technology.
8. *Deforestation*—the disappearance of more than 50% of the forests of the world (half that amount in the 20th century alone) and the devitalization of much of what little forest remains. Every year some 40 million acres (the size of Florida) of tropical rain forest are lost, a rate that will in 50 years wipe out all tropical rain forests, where more than half all known species live.
9. *Deregulation*—the relaxing or removal of government controls over industries that are supposed to be essential public services or "natural monopolies."[12] Regulation is difficult in an increasingly "isonomous" ("no-rule") culture, Hannah Arendt's word for the postmodern state in which all rules or no one rules.[13] Arguably the biggest deregulation of the day, however, is a moral deregulation.

> If you had to trace a missing package, would you rather deal with the US Post Office or Federal Express? If you had to correct an error on your retirement account, would you rather deal with Social Security or your mutual fund?
>
> Michael Rothschild, president,
> Bionomics Institute

THE SECOND GREAT DEPRESSION ~ As a church leader, I am living through an era of institutional decline and degradation some are calling the "Second Great Depression." As a historian of American religion and culture, I am privileged to live in one of the greatest spiritual awakenings in American history, a time some are calling America's "Fifth Great Awakening."

What irony that in the midst of a spiritual heat wave in the culture, in the church it's a deep freeze. Establishment religion now looks back nostalgically at a wonderful past and looks forward anxiously at a frightening future. The problem is even deeper than the statistics of 25 years of mainstream membership loss reveal.

TOP 10 DE-WORDS FOR A DEFORMATION CHURCH ~ Lord Byron kept a skull on his desk. Postmodern leaders need to keep these ten de-words in our skulls. The point of each of these de-words is to move a de-spirited church to the re-word that follows it. Can you hear the double ring?

1. Deconstruction. One of postmodernism's favorite expressions in literary and philosophical circles (indeed, for some scholars "postmodern" equals "deconstruction"), "deconstruction" is technically associated with Jacques Derrida in France and Paul de Man in North America. Its melancholy slogan "There is nothing outside the text" has become a call to arms for postmoderns to satisfy themselves with playful process, to stand within the text and not attempt futile efforts to get "beyond" or "behind" the text to some "outside" reality.

In the same way consciousness fails to coincide with identity, deconstructionists argue, so words and language fail to coincide with what they represent. Thus, nothing can be said to be truly "real," since everything we think or perceive is a cultural and linguistic construct. In other words, deconstructionism demolishes virtually every intellectual girder that held up the modern era in general and "the American Way of Life" in particular.

At its best, deconstruction has demanded the development of a new set of reading practices that can enrich the intellectual and spiritual life. It has given rise to a uniquely postmodern hermeneutic—there is no understanding without standing under—that insists that everything must be entered in order to be understood, whether a text or a television show. It is profoundly pessimistic about rationally grounded truth and "totalizing" theories. Indeed, the traditional charge against deconstruction—that it is indifferent to values— lies precisely in its radical critique of reason. Whereas Nietzsche critiqued rational argument as an effect of self-interest, Foucault critiqued rational truth as an effect of power.

As literary theory, "deconstruction" is dead, though its impact on philosophy and theology has been significant.[14] Postmodernism has gone past literary deconstruction,[15] but deconstruction can also be viewed as a philosophical endeavor in social critique.[16] Philosophical deconstructionism can be as life-denying and home-destroying as the scientific modernism it aims to replace, leading some to suspect that "postmodernizers are really only modernizers in another guise."[17]

Only a few have seen deconstruction as an attempt at moral philosophy. One of those is biblical scholar Gary A. Phillips, who argues that "deconstruction invigorates the ethical question" based on the double proposition—"both affirming and analytic"—that "whenever we read we necessarily mark up the text and are in turn marked by it."[18] According to this College of the Holy Cross scholar, deconstruction is "an active engagement—an ethical engagement, a signing on—by the reader *with* a living text and the Other that comes to the reader as a gift and a challenge."[19]

If deconstruction as literary theory is dead, and deconstruction as moral philosophy is alive, deconstruction as a strategy for change is only now coming into its own. "Deconstruction" is used in this book as another way of conveying Joseph Schumpeter's idea coined half a century ago of innovation as "creative destruction." Is it any wonder "composting" has become a favorite metaphor for "creativity"?

Anyone doing ministry during transitions is in the business of deconstruction. To "deconstruct" is to "make the familiar strange." Jesus' use of parables did precisely this: They made the familiar strange. Biblical parable and metaphor work to shock us into new awareness.[20] They break open our "structures of expectation" and make us receptive to new and fresh insights.[21]

> If it's not going to matter in five years, it doesn't matter now.
>
> Entertainer Cher's mother's advice

This is what historians claim to do: defamiliarize a period or person so that the "pastness" of that period or person can emerge and the strangeness of the everyday be restored.

This is what Shelley claimed for poetry: It "strips the veil of familiarity from the world."

This is what Russian formalist critic Victor Shklovksy claimed for art (*ostranemie* in Russian means to "make strange").[22]

This is what John Naisbitt claimed for businesses in the '90s: deconstructing their one-size-fits-all outlooks and reconstructing as self-renewing "networks of small, autonomous units catering to diverse and specific needs."[23]

If we are to move beyond scientism (the claim that science is the only valid method of acquiring knowledge and discerning truth) and the Western worldview that began with Bacon, was empowered by Descartes, and achieved self-doubt through Kant, a great deal of deconstruction is a necessity. Contrary to perception, to be deconstructive by design is not to be destructive by nature.

The proof's in the bunny: the drum-banging Energizer Bunny. This advertising creature, which made the Top 10 list from 1989 to 1993, is a perfect image for deconstruction as "creative destruction."[24] The bunny's secret is this: A commercial interrupts your program, you check it out and begin to check out because you've seen this commercial a thousand times before, when at the bottom of your screen appears a bunny banging a big base drum. Suddenly you're interested again—"This is not what I thought it was, something else is going on here"—so your mind returns to the commercial with new attentiveness and awareness because of this bunny's "creative destruction." That is, he destroyed the commercial in order to invite you back into the commercial. The rabbit deconstructs the normal so that a release of creativity can come as we see the same things differently: That's why the brand is called Energizer.

Every church needs at least one drum-thumping cottontail in every ministry. Why are "children's sermons" so popular with congregations? These times with children are Energizer Bunnies that serve to deconstruct worship so that something spontaneous and unplanned can take place.

But beware: Deconstructionists are easily misunderstood and maligned, especially when they become the subject/hero and not merely a servant/pointer. In the "Kill the Bunny" ads, the Energizer Bunny was attacked by King Kong and Ernst Blofeld (the evil genius of James Bond spy novels). The response of the establishment to deconstructionists is to knock them off.

> Science can purify religion from error and superstition, and religion can purify science from idolatry and false absolutes. The unprecedented opportunity we have today is for a common interactive relationship in which each discipline retains its integrity and yet is radically open to the discoveries and insights of the other.
>
> Pope John Paul II[25]

2. Dematerialization. The fundamental fact of life in the modern era was the tyranny of matter. "Modernism" was in many ways a word for totalitarianism, and one of the most totalitarian states has been the state of materialism. Moderns were trained in materialistic categories and taught to think that matter is more important than spirit, that the most powerful forces in the world are those that are visible.

In postmodern culture the universe is disappearing. Everything solid is melting into thin air, including the traditional solid pillars of space and time. Everyday life is now lived as much on the screen as anywhere. The 20th century has been the story of multiple dematerializations: the dematerialization of science—matter is now seen as but a more fancy form of energy; the dematerialization of business—one of the hottest business seminars of the '90s has been, not how to fire unproductive employees, but how to fire employees with bad spirits (foot-dragging employees, know-everything employees, whining, negative employees variously dubbed The Jabbermouth, The Shark, The Snoop, The Politician); the dematerialization of everything.

> Nothing is too wonderful to be true.
>
> 19th-century physicist
> Michael Faraday

The default assumption of the modern church was a material theology that said "Got a problem, get a program." For the church to minister in postmodern culture, it must dematerialize its thinking. The truth is, it should never have materialized it. Zechariah 4:6 espoused a dematerialized theology when the prophet warned that it is "not by might, nor by power [not even by programs, one might add], but by my spirit, says the LORD of hosts." The apostle Paul elaborated a dematerialized spirituality like this: "We look not at what can be seen but at what cannot be seen; for what can be seen is temporary, but what cannot be seen is eternal" (2 Cor. 4:18). In a spirituality where faith is "the substance of things hoped for, the evidence of things not seen" (Heb. 11:1 KJV), the spiritual is more to the point than the physical. Prayer moves things in another world, an unseen world—a world more real, more powerful, and more lasting than this one.

If we dematerialize our thinking, then . . .

Faith is the art of hearing the invisible.
Hope is the art of believing the invisible.
Love is the art of trusting the invisible.

At the same time the world is dematerializing all around us, people want and need to materialize. They need hands-on experiences and physical interactions. Automated systems are sufficient for routine transactions, but when there's a problem, people want people. Could this be the double meaning behind the phrase "in your face"?

"In-your-face/With-God's-grace" is the motto of Sam Williams and his church plant in San Francisco. We dematerialize to rematerialize in the lives of people and the life of the world. Tattooing and piercing phenomena are an expression of and reaction to these twin forces of de- and re-materi-

> When the devil decided that nothing was to be done, he formed the first committee.
>
> Old adage

alization. Kids especially are trying to "cope with a sense of emptiness by punching holes in their bodies, a kind of self-inoculation, and covering their skin with tattoos, simultaneously denying and affirming corporeality."[26]

3. Decentralization (sometimes called Decentration). This is the art of relishing relinquishment—of success, of self, of control, of peak products, of ministry. Every organism must learn how to devolve—to "let go at the top," to lose control, to cell out,[27] to reverse oneself and become less optimal, less efficient, less fit, less ordered and organized.

Also known as "the Devolution Revolution," decentralization is the push of power downward from the center to the margins, from vertical to horizontal, from "command-and-control" organizations to "cultivate and coordinate"[29] empowered organisms. All the employees at the Ritz-Carlton in San Francisco, bellhops and housekeepers included, can spend up to $2,000 to fix a customer's approval.

Decentralization makes strange bedfellows out of *Wired* editor Kevin Kelly, futurists Manuel DeLanda and Heidi and Alvin Toffler, intellectuals Gilles Deleuze and Felix Guattari, Republican Congressman Newt Gingrich, militias,[30] and novelist Don Delillo, whose work problematizes the notion of a stable center and opens up the periphery.

> There is no alternative ... to leaving behind perfectly good products, expensively developed technology, and wonderful brands and heading down to trouble in order to ascend again in hope. In the future, this forced march will become routine.
>
> *Wired* editor Kevin Kelly[28]

To see the postmodern forces of decentralization at work, one need only look around. Look what's happened to American evangelicalism: decentralization. Kenneth Offner, who works with InterVarsity Christian Fellowship at Harvard, says there are really now 12 different types of evangelicalism.[32]

> The future belongs to crowds.
>
> Don Delillo, *Mao II*[31]

Or look what's happened to that invention of modernity, the nation-state: decentralization. The teetering and toppling of one centralized body (the nation-state) in favor of multiple centralized bodies such as multinational corporations, city-states, or individuals is evident in the growing number of countries in the world from fewer than 50 at the close of World War II to nearly 200 today.[33] The devolution revolution is adding more small entities to the world scene, entities that may be small but are paradoxically enormously powerful in politics and economics and are pushing themselves forward to center stage—Estonia, Croatia, and Ireland, to name a few. Even the US itself will be forced to deal with decentralizing pressures to expand the number of states beyond 50, if not to allow outright secession itself—in Texas, in the Pacific Northwest, or in California.

Or look what's happened to the Third Sector: decentralization. In 1975 there were only 3000 NGOs (nongovernmental organizations) worldwide. In 1998 there were more than 25,000. This growth of the Third Sector, not government, is increasingly responsible for social change and transformation.

Or look what's happening to philanthropy: decentralization. The future of philanthropy is not in the Lillys or Rockefellers or Carnegies. It is in small, family foundations, community development corporations, and local community philanthropic efforts—like churches.

Or look what's happening at your local supermarket: decentralization. A decentralized marketing system for food is increasingly being called for, and more and more locally raised organic products people can trust are being sold to local markets.

Or look what's happening to businesses: decentralization. Small businesses are the driving force of the new economy. Two of every three new jobs come out of small businesses. We are fast approaching a self-employed world where every person will be a "small business."

> I half cherish the hope that the end of history will be Swissness.
>
> Jan Morris[34]

In a decentralized world, the "small numbers" are no longer small. If "all is one," then one is all: it's the "law of small numbers."

Small inputs can have massive consequences. On the Web, small companies have the same standing as the big ones. It matters not how many hundreds of millions you've spent on distribution infrastructures; the Web neutralizes all previous distribution investments. One lone individual can have a Web site that looks as impressive as General Motors or even Microsoft. One rural church can have a Web site that is more stellar than Willow Creek. A key postmodern strategy for success is to figure out how to do what you're already doing, except better and on a smaller scale.

> Let us hope the 21st century seeks universality at the smallest scale, that it recognizes that the fullness of existence is contained in the tiniest of spaces.
>
> Professor/"Small Is Beautiful" proponent Leopold Kohr[36]

World Vision International produced a poster that asks in stark white letters against an all-black background: "How do you feed two billion hungry people?" A small picture of a tiny boy and his rice bowl appears at the bottom of the poster with the caption, "One at a time."

In a world of bits-bites-bots, you can be small and global at the same time. Small things can have big effects. Your own consciousness is powerful enough to effect massive change. You can change the world, literally. *Schindler's List* was right: "Whoever saves one life, saves the world entire."[35]

4. Deconversion. Postmodern culture is undoing one massive deconversion—from modern ways of living and thinking to postmodern ways of living and being in the world.

USAmerica is becoming de-Christianized. We are now living in a post-Constantinian church. Can we de-Westernize the gospel? Can we de-Westernize Christianity? Can we deconvert the church?

Why? People need to be deconverted from what Christendom culture has taught them a Christian is.

Religion is not harmless. I have seen all sorts of lives absolutely shipwrecked by Christian belief—their pride, their arrogance, their guilt, their hatred. Some of us need to be converted *away from* Christianity. Philosopher William P. Alston tells of his leaving the church, and then coming back, in terms of being "attached to Christianity for the wrong reasons, for radically wrong reasons." When that is the case, "the best thing to do may be to get out and give yourself a chance to make a fresh start under new circumstances at some later time."[37]

> Give up your good Christian life and follow Christ.
>
> Author/entertainer
> Garrison Keillor

Deconversion will take place through the development of "a folk apologetic" (George Hunter's phrase)—a folk theology that is built on narratives, not concepts or categories. People are not prone to move away from one home unless they see a good alternative available. A "folk apologetic" is not a "for-all-time" systematic theology but a "for-now" piety that is built on "as-they-should-be" beliefs.

5. Dealignment (also called Decoupling or Deinstitutionalization). Social structures and political systems (e.g., the two-party system) are buckling under the pressures of decomposition, dealignment, and disintegration. Both ideas and institutions are taken up, toyed with, dropped, and resuscitated with alarming alacrity.

The institutional church is also coming apart in states of discordancy, groaning under modernity's toll of disintegrating structures and ideas.

Eight of 10 adults believe you can be a good Christian and not go to church.

Eight of 10 adults believe you should arrive at your own faith apart from the church.

The linkages are growing between popular culture and religious expression.[38] "What do you think of the resurrection of the body" is now a pick-up line. Even the once highly unified and tightly centralized religion of Catholicism is now dealigning into a diverse assortment of Catholicisms around the world, all resisting attempts by the Vatican to reimpose centralized authority.

> Will anyone lying on their deathbed wish they had had the chance to go to more church meetings?
>
> Christopher Levan[39]

6. Demoralization. This is what happens to demythologized, devitalized institutions.[40] Feelings of displacement and diminution are everywhere. Radical alienation is obvious not just in the near anarchy of the world's cities, but also in the near anarchy of the thought of the world's greatest postmodern philosopher and literary critic Jacques Derrida, whose intellectual enterprise of building a nonconceptual world, as Martha C. Nussbaum reveals, is without any moral philosophy or moral judgments or any help whatsoever with the question: "How to live."[41]

Pauline Rosenau draws an important distinction between "affirmative post-modernists" and "skeptical post-modernists." In the former, represented by Stephen Toulmin and Willis Harman, there are attempts at new constructions of science and human engagement based on new paradigms. In the latter, represented most particularly by Derrida, Jean-Francois Lyotard, and Jean Baudrillard, there is a rejection of constructivist proposals as naive and intellectually adolescent and a reveling in defamations.[42]

In the high modern era the media lionized and mythologized our American institutions (government, judiciary, FBI). In the postmodern era we have learned that the FBI was really headed by a transvestite, that the government could kill not just others but even its own citizens, and that our civil "servants" wouldn't serve.

How many denominations do you know that aren't having "morale problems"? How many pastors do you know who aren't singing and sighing for that "Balm in Gilead":

Sometimes I get discouraged

and think my work in vain. . . .

7. Democratization. If there is anything that the implosion of the Soviet Union, the smashing of the Nicaraguan Sandinistas at the polls, and the rapid adoption of free-market economics by Latin American (and other) governments has proven, it is that democracy is the wave of the future. The number of democracies in the world has risen dramatically, doubling in the past quarter-century. Since the conclusion of the Cold War, more than 30 countries have adopted democratic political systems.[43]

So complete is the democratic victory that Mexican leftist scholar Jorge G. Castaneda argues that if the left is to be reinvigorated, it must immediately do two things: first, profess unconditional allegiance to democracy with no ifs, ands, or buts; second, embrace the primacy of the market in most situations.[44] The future promises to even be more democratic. Electronic media, especially the Net, are the most democratizing, empowering media ever invented; the Net puts power into the hands of the people more than any other medium of history.

> You rarely leap off one trapeze unless you know the other one's coming at you.
>
> Dominican Sister Miriam McGillis

8. Deprivatization. Religion is returning to public life. It is once again exercising its political voice. Just when secularization theory seemed to have won, all of a sudden religion gets deprivatized and rediscovers civic responsibility.[45] But the church has no role in public culture unless it is present in the media. To be without media presence is to be voiceless and powerless in postmodern culture.

Just because the number of churches isn't withering away does not prove that it is sacred needs rather than secular needs that are being met by them. There remain secular, civil reasons for going to church. In some locations, going to church still brings secular rewards and is an expression of civic responsibility.

9. Dedifferentiation. This is the "Everything Goes" phenomenon whereby everything goes together: the interchangeability of shopping, sports, leisure, eating, education, and so on. World fairs, World Series, World Olympics are blending together, resembling each other, and becoming increasingly difficult to distinguish.

Maya Lin, who designed the Vietnam Veterans Memorial—what is she? An artist? a sculptor? an architect? a funerary artisan? a designer?

As a Yale graduate school student in architecture who saw herself as all of the above, Lin was seen as out in left field for her refusal to honor established boundaries between these disciplines. Criticized by her professors for playing with art and not being serious enough about architecture, only architect Frank Gehry gave her encouragement. "Don't worry about the distinctions," he kept saying to her. "Do what you need to do."[46]

One of the fastest-growing industries in the future—tourism and travel— is a good example of dedifferentiation. Half the world's vacationers head to the sea each year, and half the world's people live within 50 miles or so of saltwater.

Ever notice how tourism now gets connected to other social phenomena like sports, shopping, education, health, and vacation?[47] When you go to the Mall of America, eat at Café Odyssey, and try out gear at REI, what are you— a shopper? an athlete? a tourist?

Postmodern organizations are becoming "boundaryless," more networked and distributed, less confined and defined. Even religion:

Religious mingles with secular, churches become businesses, Christ dispenses grace and miracles on TV, preachers call themselves CEOs and run for President, faith healers build ultramodern hospitals, AT&T hires New Age consultants and churches hire religious market analysts, creationism calls itself a science, scientists discover the ineffable, narrators become characters, and fictions come true. If something is ending, it is the world in which the things forming these zany amalgamations were kept apart, separated, in their place, properly ordered and moving progressively toward some end.[48]

10. Demassification. The Tofflers coined the phrase "demassification" in 1980. It is one of the most important of the "de" words and refers to the collapse of big middles, trends, "typicals," averages, generals, and ordinaries.

There is no "normal" anymore. We are ruled by the abnormal. Many have felt this in terms of tremendous economic displacement and loss as new kinds of jobs are being created and old kinds of jobs are being abandoned.

In this Digital Age, the monolithic mass markets of the mid- and high-modern era have broken up and diversified.[49] We have gone in my lifetime from a mass market to a micromarket to new mass customized market. We have moved from mass to micro and are now moving into mass customized in everything. Sales of mass beers like Budweiser and Miller are flat; sales of Samuel Adams and Rappahanock Red Ale are skyrocketing. Sales of Maxwell House and Folger's are stable; sales of Starbucks, SBC (Seattle's Best Coffee), and Gevalia are skyrocketing. As hard as some features of postmodern culture may try, postmoderns will not be pounded into a common pulp.

Even Billy Graham has recognized the shift. His three-day crusade on 16–18 March 1995, called Global Mission, which broadcast to countries comprising 70% of the world's population, was billed as "not mass evangelism," according to BGEA spokesman Larry Ross, but "personal evangelism on a mass scale."

Everything is devolving into the smallest niches; even niches within niches. Have you bought potato chips recently? You can choose from sweet potato chips, yucca chips, and parsnip chips (Terra Chips has all three flavors). Reebok and Nike, who niched the shoe into the sneakers, are now niching sneakers—we are being told we can't play basketball in the same sneaker we play tennis in or jog in or climb a mountain in.

"Standardized" items, from the nuclear family to general stores, have demassified. There are now two-career couples, childless couples, fissured families (divorced, remarried).

DOUBLE-RING MINISTRIES ～ It is not true that pomo culture isn't massifying. In fact, by the time you read this book there may be only one bank left in the world (I suspect it's the case already). Your newspaper most likely announced some mega-merger this past week.

Look at the global media consolidation, a monopoly that some have argued has "drifted out of democratic reach" (George Gerbner). At the same time that there are demassifying forces at work, there is also a polar tendency toward massification and monopoly. The world's tallest building went up in Kuala Lumpur. Plans for building Europe's flagship skyscraper, the "Millennial Tower," have been announced in London.

The big brands are getting bigger: Coca-Cola? Nike? Disney? McDonald's alone already feeds 7% of the US population every day. In a world of impermanence and instability, brands are consoling constants. Similarly, there are the superstores on the one hand and the boutiques and ma-and-pa shops on the other.

The Postmodern Reformation church must learn both to decentralize and centralize; both demassify and massify. Some areas of ministry call for hypercentralization and massification. Other areas of ministry call for decentralization and demassification. Postmoderns are slashers (and/also), not binaries (either-or). We are both consumer and producer, both buyer and seller, both top-down and bottom-up. Can the church bring together top-down thinking and bottom-up thinking, top-down technology and bottom-up technology?

So what? **LEARNING TO TRIANGULATE** ~ Postmodern circuit riders who will venture into 21-C mission fields and frontiers are engaged in an act of creation: a Postmodern Reformation Church. The key to ministry in this next reformation is intellectual capital in general, and innovation and creativity in particular.

In the new world one thing is certain: What works today won't work tomorrow. The galelike forces of technology and globalization are turning the world upside-down and inside-out. The most successful churches at the close of the 20th century weren't even a glint in some guru's eye 50 years ago.

The need to prepare for ongoing adaptive change makes *innovation* and *creativity* the key survival skills in navigating the chaotic world of the 21st century. How embarrassing that the institution that worships the Creator is so often bankrupt of creativity! Where ought the world's most creative space to be if not the church? The definition of "creativity" used throughout this book is that of critical creativity: It aims not at novelty, but at innovation that specifically continues the divine work of creation. Not everything "new" is creative. To be truly creative, one has to be in touch and in tune with the ongoing mysterious, miraculous powers of divine creation.

Have you ever gone to a mall and stumbled over people staring meditatively at a picture on a tripod? However much it may appear that these contemporary hunters and gatherers are eyeing weird wallpaper or buying psychedelic art, they are actually participating in a postmodern tribal ritual. These experiences in three-dimensionality are more than an electronic culture's equivalent of Industrial Age dioramas or children's "pop-up" books. "Magic Eyes" are the first low-tech vestibules to virtual reality available to postmodern culture.[50]

The methodology for "Magic Eye" seeing is precisely the methodology of doing creative ministry in a de-everything world. If we know how to view these colorful but chaotic computer-generated fields, dazzling three-dimensional images suddenly materialize out of the Jackson Pollock-like swirls, dots, and blobs splashed across the page. If we master these three steps, a whole new world of meaning and understanding opens before our eyes. In postmodern culture, what you see is *not* what you get. There is always more hidden and more to be revealed.

The choice of ministry is this: deep vision or shallow perception. If religious leaders can master a triangular methodology of ministry, they will experience a ministry "deep and wide" in creativity and imagination. The choice is ours: flat-surfaced ministry and random, confusing dots, or creative ministry amid dancing, meaningful patterns and images. Leaders of the Postmodern Reformation do not look at different things; they look at the same things differently.

TAKE THREE LOSSES ~ Jesus said if we want to save our life, we must first be willing to lose our life. Here are the three "losses" that can transform a flat plane of ministry into the creative deep of multi-dimensionality that transports and transposes ministry into new realms of space and service.

1. Lose Focus. If you try to see it, you'll never see it. You first must loosen up and let things get cloudy. Deconstruct your world. Give up preconceived notions of how to do ministry:

Picasso's dictum that "every act of creation is first of all an act of destruction" and that "a painting is the sum of destructions" is profound. Deconstruct your old way of seeing and hearing and doing. Give up preconceived notions of how to do ministry. "Fuzzy" is good.

In the biblical story of the man born blind, Jesus speaks of why he came into this world: "So that those who do not see may see, and those who do see may become blind" (John 9:39). Our problem is not that we can't see, but that we don't want to become blind to old ways of seeing. We must first do some unlearning before learning to see anew. We "know" too many things that aren't true or that are partial truths.

In a world where intellectual capital steadily depreciates without constant updating, the church must be an unlearning organism before it can become a learning organism.

2. Lose the "M" Word. Give up the "M" word—Middle. Take up the "H" word—Higher. Go from Middle Ground to Higher Ground. The culture in which God has called us to minister forces us into Trinitarian thinking and Trinitarian theology. Monoliths and simple polarities are replaced by trinities.

> Being in the middle of the road is probably the worst thing you can say about anyone.
>
> Singer Phil Collins[51]

Cross the crowded ways of life. Look at multiple points at the same time; either by crossing your eyes, or diverging your eyes in walleyed fashion. Bring your field of vision to a critical focus too soon, and you'll never see it. Allow your vision to diverge from the norm. Let your brain work at cross purposes. Trust your brain to merge the different perceptions of each eye into a single picture. Minister on the boundaries of difference, not sameness.

Only the opening of that second eye, which both sees something that the first eye doesn't and which works in harmony with the first eye, can bring out depth. When both eyes look at two contrasting points long enough—one eye fastening on some point on the hidden image, with the other eye landing on some point in the random pattern—and the brain has sufficient time to make connections between the two (a process that neuroscientists still don't fully understand), a three-dimensional image suddenly pops out and up.

Dead Center. The modern era apotheosized the center. In postmodern culture there is a decentering into moving foci,

Ellipsis: double foci, double ring.

Historian Ann Douglas calls this "the exaltation of the average." The modern era's riddle of the middle brought everything to a single point. "I propose one single building for all nations and climates," said Le Corbusier, the leading figure in modern architecture. He almost did it through his gray, high-rise concrete monoliths that litter our urban landscape. Modern cultures made a holy grail of "middle ground," and those who were most successful (the "moderates") claimed to have found that elusive but long-sought-after *via media* between right and left, liberal and conservative, rich and poor.

Today there is a mitosis of the middle. The middles are separating. "Mediating institutions" are in trouble, declining and decaying (e.g., political parties, denominations, TV network news). How are these "middles" doing?

- Middle-brow?
- Middle-class?[52]
- Middle management?
- Middle-man?
- Middle-size?
- Mainstream music?
- Mainstream media?
- Mainstream religion?
- Mainframe computers?

The center is not holding. Or, in the words of that southern gospel song, "There ain't no middle ground." If you keep looking for the middle, or hugging the middle of the road, you will run our churches right off the postmodern cliff. Be a "middle-of-the-roader," and you will get run over by both sets of oncoming traffic.

Triangulation in a postmodern context does not yield a triangle. When one brings two ends together postmodern style, one creates a figure eight: the double-helix, the symbol of all life.

In a world where gray is such a dull, drab, lukewarm color that there is a new name that tries to save it—"Black Forest Smoke"—don't blend black and white into fence-sitting gray. Bring black and white together into "white chocolate." Triangulate the ebony and ivory in all of their mutual attraction and opposition, and you get the double-helix energy of Paul Celan's celebrated poem "Black Milk" (*Todesfuge*), which has almost become the anthem of post-war Germany.

In a world where the rich are getting richer and more numerous and the poor are getting poorer and more numerous, what are the very two groups the church is least prepared to minister with? The rich and the poor.

In a world which is becoming more "natural," more "unplugged," more back-to-nature and out-of-doors while at the same time more high-tech and computerized, why is the church becoming more and more the product of the great indoors and less willing to embrace a culture of the screen? Instead of hugging middles, why not bring the rich and the poor together, as Habitat for Humanity has done? Instead of hugging middles, why not bring the dying and the well together, as Hospice has done? Instead of searching for a *via media*, the Carnegie Corporation program "Science rich/Science poor" links "science rich" sectors of society with "science poor" communities.

Postmodern culture is obdurately oxymoronic: and/also, not either-or or even both/and. Postmoderns bat on both sides of the plate; they have double vision. Their patron saint might as well be Leonardo da Vinci, who sketched with his right hand while he wrote with his left—simultaneously. Opposite things happen at the same time without being contradictory—for example, postmodern economies globalize and localize at the same time. The church of the Postmodern Reformation embraces the planet on one hand and embraces our tribe and bio-region on the other. The church of the Postmodern Reformation brings together and bridges reason and passion, the fundamental and the fancy, the liturgical and the Pentecostal, the unchurched and the overchurched, the Boosters and the Busters, the one and the many, the tough-minded and the tender-hearted, the exquisite and the everyday.

The postmodern era is binocular, not monocular. Postmoderns are anti-cyclopean. They have given up a one-eyed view of the world for "whole-sight"—both eyes, both heart and head, both body and soul, both left brain and right brain. Some authors are now calling this "peripheral vision." I prefer "complexity vision." Peripheral presupposes a "center that holds." Yet the central focus is not what is already there, but is what you create when you bring two things together. Complexity is bringing together two rational processes simultaneously—differentiation and integration. Differentiation is the ability to embrace diversity and uniqueness and be responsive to the external environment; integration is the ability to achieve harmony and oneness and to bring into unity the coordinates of consciousness.[53]

The essence of complexity is the ability to look at many things at once, to think more than one thought at a time, to abandon old fixations and make new connections, following your intuitions and trusting the Spirit.

3. Lose Control. Relax! Look through the picture, not at it. Peer into the distance. Become wide-eyed at what is before you. Even when your eyes want to go back and focus on the image at hand, resist the temptation to peer closer and keep your focus on the deep, distant future that you know is out there. The brain is curious; it will immediately want to make sense of what is in front of your face. Resist the temptation of the immediate for the satisfaction of the ultimate. Defer your mental gratification for the moment and trust the future.

At this point you will have the visual experience of "losing it." Every one who has ever seen a stereogram (and 2% of us are stereoblind) can testify to the panic of almost "losing it." Many people refuse to pass through the pain of losing control and hence can never see what life has to offer. If you will allow yourself to be "lost in wonder, love, and praise," as the hymnwriter said, and pass through the pain of losing control, an image will suddenly float in front of your face and the world will expand right before your eyes.

If you pass through these three stages, your perception changes. What appeared at first glance to be a flat, bland surface of random dots suddenly becomes a three-dimensional universe and ministry. The key to navigating postmodernity's choppy, crazy waters is not to seek some balance or "safe middle ground," but to ride the waves and bridge the opposites, especially where they converge in reconciliation and illumination.

COMING TO TERMS WITH JESUS ~ We fear postmodernity's collapse of the middle more than we need to because we haven't come to terms with Jesus. Jesus dealt with the first and the last; he never liked middles. Jesus never left anyone neutral; he taught of a God who hated lukewarms. Jesus recognized the double-sidedness to the universe, the spiral structures of the mind, body, and spirit: The full is carried in the empty, and strength is found in weakness.

Heraclitus, in one of the earliest definitions of Logos, said that Logos is that which holds contradictions and opposites together. He used Apollo's instruments to explain. A stick is but a stick, Heraclitus said. But triangulate that stick's extremities, and one has the lyre and the bow. Extremes, when "strung" under the power of the divine Logos, produce harmony and balance.[54]

Our logo is the Logos: Jesus the Christ, the triangulation of God and the Holy Spirit, the unity of opposites—"omnipotence in bonds," as someone has called him. He laughs, he weeps; he is tender, he is aggressive; he has a free spirit, yet he is obedient to God. He is as "wise as serpents and innocent as doves" (Matt. 10:16). One minute he walks on water, the next minute he washes his disciples' feet. One minute he is executed on the cross, the next minute he rises from the dead. Jesus, the Lion and the Lamb, is the one who has come, and the one who is coming. Christ reigns—from a cross.

These are the best of times for ministry. These are the worst of times for ministry. We must live the double-helix.

FAULT LINES BECOME FRONT LINES OF MINISTRY ~ Within the span of my lifetime I went from sharing common media experiences with my friends (we all read the same daily papers, watched the same programs on network TV, and read the same newsmagazines) to living in separate worlds, as information now splits along demographic, generational, religious, and cultural fault lines.

Postmodern culture revels in the riches of niches. The editors of *Chicken Soup for the Soul* understand this, with 17 niche books already in print (e.g., *Chicken Soup for the Global Soul, ... the Pet Lover's Soul, ... the Country Soul*) and 74 more planned (e.g., *Chicken Soup for the Grieving Soul, ... the Erring Soul*, etc). There is even a niche for those fed up with chicken—*Chicken Poop for the Soul: Stories to Harden the Heart and Dampen the Spirit: A Parody* by David Fisher (Pocket Books, 1997). ᵂᴵᵂᵃᵏ I grew up in a Robert Young/*Marcus Welby* world of general practitioners. I am now living in a *Chicago Hope/E.R.* world where the "generalists" have all become "specialists." But in the same way the G.P. in medicine became extinct, only to come back as a speciality in Family Medicine, so the church must give up congregational, mass thinking and learn to niche the "generals" it took for granted.

One of the biggest lines along postmodern faults range is generational. For the first time in history we are living in a world where seven generations are living side by side, a world the Iroquois could only think of in futuristic terms. They made no decision until they factored in its impact on as far into the future as they could imagine: the Seventh Generation. The fault lines between generations are getting larger and more numerous. One of the great challenges for the church, therefore, is to niche multigenerational worship, multigenerational missions, multigenerational education.

The multigenerational niche is not achieved by putting all the generations into a blender and pouring out a solvent that pleases no one. Watch carefully the Gaither Homecoming videos. What is the secret of their phenomenal success? The legends of gospel music's old guard—the aging Happy Goodman Family, only Vestal able to sing any longer; the legendary Hovie Lister; and Jake Hess—all gathered around a piano with the succeeding generations of musicians, including the young turks like Russ Taff and the Martins.

The multigenerational "Environmental Mentor Program" in Ohio pairs a town's seniors with young people. Together they walk around the town and talk about how it used to be, where the rivers ran and what they were like, where wild spaces existed, where children played, what buildings are still in use and what ones are gone. The children learn the history of their town, and the older people discover the changes the town's children are going through. Both generations are sensitized to the experiences of the other.

How small a niche? In a culture that has shifted from mass to micro cultures, you can't establish too small a niche.

Passenger: "I'd like a glass of water."

Flight Attendant: "Plain, St. Croix, sparkling, tonic?"

In fact, with each "micro" possessing its own "Sisberts" (a new word named for the movie critics Siskel and Ebert, who are anointed to evaluate and validate movies for their niche communities), there's a "Sisbertizing" niche ministry within every niche. "As We Change" is a mail-order catalog targeting women in menopause. This is a culture that revels in quality coffee: There were 200 coffeehouses in the US in 1989, almost 10,000 just 10 years later; each week more than 5 million people visit a Starbucks outlet. Where, invariably, is the worst coffee to be found in any town on Sunday morning? The church kitchen (except in Phoenix, where the Dove of the Desert Church boasts "the best coffee in town on Sunday morning").

> This fundamental preference for truth over tradition is . . . a hallmark of Christianity, and any abandonment of this characteristic of what is authentically Christian would lead eventually to the disintegration of the Christian faith.
>
> Martin Henry[56]

A graphic portrayal of the Chinese-box style niche within niches is in the area of "youth ministry." **WIWAK** I grew up in a youth group ghetto where the idea was to sequester the kids in the basement and give them some musty, mildewed room they can call their own. Traditional "youth ministry" won't work any longer. Nor does the entertainment/message model of the '60s and '70s. Nor does the "trickle-down" strategy of Youth for Christ, in which you attract the most popular kids, the "group" that is "in," and you've got everyone else. Why?

No one "group" is "in" anymore; groups have demassified into affinity communities. There is no one "youth ministry" possible anymore because there is now not one "youth group" anymore. Besides the jocks, there are now the bands, blacks, blonds, brains, computer people, cools, crews, dorks, druggies, floaters, FOBs (fresh off the boat), friendlies, groovies, hippies, jocks, losers, nerds, nobodies, normals, overly violent ("regular violence was okay; you just couldn't be overly violent"), partiers, peace freaks, pom-poms, rappers, richies, scumbags, sluts, smokers, snobs, stoners, tides, trendies, wannabes, wavers, weirdos, and yuppies.

FAULT LINES BECOME BATTLE LINES ~ Demassification and decentralization are polarizing churches over such things as abortion, homosexuality, economics, lifestyles, and the allocation of resources between the young and the old. Church warfare in the postmodern era is less over theological issues than social and stylistic issues. Each side boasts a politically correct and theologically correct position.

Abortion threatens to be second only to slavery as the greatest disturber of civil peace in USAmerican history. The only thing that might save the abortion issue from splitting this nation in the future is either a technological or philosophical change: the former in the shape of "the abortion pill," the latter in the abandonment of rights discourse as the only public discourse of political morality.

The claims of communities and local identities must be featured as well as the rights of individuals. We need churches and leaders willing to take experimental antibiotics against the "them" versus "us" virus that is plaguing society. We need communities of faith and faith leaders who will not discover an Enlightenment-style *via media* between the competing pro-choice/pro-life ideologies, for example, but will pioneer a *modus vivendi* through irreconcilable and intractable forms of belief that cannot be harmonized or balanced, only bridged.

FROM THINK-BIG-THINK-SIMPLE TO THINK-SMALL-THINK-COMPLEX
~ Complexify, complexify, complexify! There was a boy who brought his report card home from school, and it was underwhelming. Noticeably absent were the first three letters of the alphabet. The little boy looked at his distraught father and said: "What do you think, Dad. Is it environment, or heredity?"

During a wedding ceremony, the minister asked the bride, "Do you take this man for richer or for poorer?" The bride thought for a minute, then replied, "For richer."

The truth is in the complexity. Why is Sally (Kristen Johnston) on *Third Rock From the Sun* such a hit with TV viewers? She is perhaps the most complex, even oxymoronic character ever to appear on television: a male alien trapped in a female human's body, the strongest and weakest person you'll ever want to meet.

The smaller you get, the more complex you become. The smaller things get, the more complex they become. So says the sciences of complexity—nonlinear dynamics, molecular biology, artificial life, cognitive science, fuzzy logic, computational mathematics, material science, ecology. These generating sciences of the future are moving the modern paradigm of "Think Big, Think Simple" to "Think Small, Think Complex." Forget KISS: "Keep It Simple, Stupid."

The science of chaos or complexity suggests that the universe is endowed with an "innate tendency to develop ever more complex structures." Nature strives towards complexity. There is a natural bias towards complexity—

almost as if God hard-wired into nature the emergence of sentient, self-reflective beings.

In a world of increasing complexities of structure, in which emerging "wholes" are greater than their component parts, we must learn to trust the complexity. In fact, part of the problem with too much "contemporary worship" is that there is insufficient complexity rich enough to express the involution of Christian doctrine.[57]

Postmodern ministry is the parting of the commonplace to reveal the complex. In a world opting for the simple Boy Scout handbook—whether it's "seven habits" or "22 vital traits" or "one-minute manager" or leadership lessons from Star Trek, Attila the Hun, and Winnie-the-Pooh—the church refuses to sell out to the simple and chooses the complex over simple, chaos over order, ambidextrous over one-sided, and/also over either-or.

The wonder of Jesus is not either-or. The wonder of Jesus is and/also. He was the most complex person who ever lived, which enabled him to live the most simple life that's ever been lived.

> "It is hard to be brave," said Piglet, sniffing slightly, "when you're only a Very Small Animal."
>
> Rabbit, who had begun to write very busily, looked up and said: "It is because you are a very small animal that you will be Useful in the adventure before us."
>
> Novelist/playwright/children's author A. A. Milne[58]

FIND THE SIMPLICITY ON THE OTHER SIDE OF COMPLEXITY ~ Jeff Davidson, head of the Breathing Space Institute,[59] tells of the mid-'80s film *Moscow on the Hudson,* starring Robin Williams. In one scene Williams's character is shopping in a Manhattan supermarket when he comes to a giant coffee display. There's freeze-dried, rich blend, Colombian coffee. You can buy your coffee in cans, pouches, glass, canisters, cartons. You can choose a whole host of colors. Williams's character has lived all his life in a world where there were two choices—coffee or no coffee. Faced with all these choices, he suffers an anxiety attack—and he pitches forward, faints, and knocks over the whole display.

There was an amusing *Reader's Digest* article not too long ago about a man visiting a restaurant with his wife, to be greeted with the pleasantry, "Would you like to sit by the window, the balcony, or in the back?" When the waiter appears, the diner is asked, "Would you like your water with ice, without ice, sparkling water, or water with lemon?" The list of appetizers takes a page, the entrees four pages. And then when you order something like a potato, will it be baked, mashed, boiled red, or french fries? Baked? Then with chives, sour cream, butter, plain, with cheese, with broccoli? The story goes on to document how the man's enjoyment of the meal vanishes in the confounding number of choices he is forced to endure in the course of getting through one simple meal.

Finally, after the waiter asks him for one more decision, the diner loses his cool and challenges the waiter to a fight—only to be asked if he'd like to fight at the table or in the lobby or would he rather step outside.

People are desperate for simplicity, for closure, for comfort, for endings. They want choices, but are tired of making choices, overloaded from too much suspense, too many "new and improved" products, too many beginnings and not enough endings. Coping with overload was the topic that generated the strongest emotional reaction among teens, according to one study.[60] Complexity physicist Stuart Kauffman talks about "complexity catastrophe"—what happens when an organism is forced to process more information than its system will allow. And what often does happen is fibrillation—"a purposeless, resource-expensive quivering that usually culminates in system collapse."

Many of our denominations, organizations, and institutions—not to mention many individuals—have already reached this state of connection crash. It's enough to make postmoderns long for less. Hence the appeal of fundamentalisms, of sports, of gambling, of games, of lists, of count-downs. People are looking for the tried and true, the familiar and the trusted, known quantities.

Postmoderns understand that the truth is both far simpler and a great deal more complicated than anything the modern world offered. Postmoderns are not afraid of getting complex to get simple. The modern church sought the simplicity of laws that explained everything—as Archimedes' principle of the lever did, as Newton's theory of gravitation did. The church seeks the simplicity on the other side of complexity. Postmoderns are hungry for this postcomplex simplicity.

FAST-TRACK THE SLOW TRACK ~ Bored with excitement, jaded by the discovery that nothing fails like success, fogged-in by clouds of information, our circuits overloaded by an overabundance of choices, people are opting for "Downward Nobility" (Watts Wacker's phrase), repudiating status for satisfaction, keeping up for keeping body and soul together. When it comes to "high-value, low-maintenance" lifestyles, why isn't it the church that is helping the culture to *Want What You Already Have*, to *Simplify Your Life*, and to find *Simple Abundance* (all titles of recent bestsellers)?

Everywhere you look, people are paying big bucks for simplicity—especially technology that makes our lives more simple, not more complicated. (Want a simple way to record a TV program for later playback, anyone?) This back-to-basics movement can also be seen in the clothing trend toward the casual, comfort-

> Generally, my feeling is towards less: less shopping, less eating, less drinking, less wasting, less playing by the rules and recipes. All of that I want in favour of more thinking on the feet, more improvising, more surprises, more laughs.
>
> Musician/composer Brian Eno[64]

able, and rugged (Timberland boots, Patagonia jackets). But remember this, church: Back-to-basics is a personal statement of faith that requires even more customization and individuality, not less.

If we are the sum of the choices we make, some postmoderns' choice is in not making a choice. Jean Rostand, the early 20th-century French writer, argued that "far too often the choices reality proposes are such as to take away one's taste for choosing."

Sometimes you have to go slower to go faster. Can the church help people slow down, even shut down? Can the church help people "simplify" their lives? One futurist organization says that "never before, in the Institute's 17 years of trend tracking, has a societal trend grown so quickly, spread so broadly and been embraced so eagerly."[61] Bookstores now have whole sections devoted to "Simple Living." Why can't the church? A daily devotional called *Simple Abundance* pops in and out of the *New York Times* bestseller lists.[62]

The editor of *Simple Living: The Journal of Voluntary Simplicity* says that the real desire in the "simple living" phenomenon is not simplicity so much as freedom. Simplicity is not sensory deprivation, but "it is having everything you need with the bonus of being able to find it."[63] Personal "downsizing" is not about depriving oneself and removing things so much as it is adding certain elements to life—like joy, peace, love, relationships, authenticity. Aren't these really the bailiwick of the church?

A thirsty cowboy walked into a saloon. The bartender said, "Care for a drink, stranger?" The cowboy responded, "What are my choices?" The bartender answered, "Yes or no."

CUT THE JARGON ~ You can hear the cry for post-complex simplicity in the summary dismissal "that's what _____ is all about." You can see it in the one-syllable names that are the badge of the late '90s: Cort, Wren, Lark, Pierce, Skye, Geige, Quest, Thane. You can sense it in the growing roster of single-name performers: Dino, Sting, Pavarotti, Madonna, Prince.

You can find it in the grassroots campaigns to "simplify government" and "simplify preaching" (both of which often confuse complexity with verbosity). Politicians and preachers on both the right and left must realize that "less and better" go with the words

Lord's Prayer: 66 words
Gettysburg Address: 286 words
10 Commandments: 179 words
Declaration of Independence: 1,300 words
Pythagorean theorem: 24 words
Archimedes' Principle: 67 words
US Govt. Regulations on sale of Cabbage: 26,911 words[65]

"government" and "church." Plain-talk has become the new watchword and song of scientists, medical professional, even government bureaucrats. Got that, theologians? Get that, preachers!

After an interminable luncheon speech, the guest speaker turned to toast-master Will Rogers and said, "I'm sorry that I went beyond my limit, but I left my watch at home." Will Rogers responded: "Don't you even have a pocket calendar?"

Sometimes the "simple" things have the greatest complexity. Postmodern culture constantly plumbs new shallows. But the shallows can be surprisingly deep.

The simple life of faith can be lived only by passing through immense complexities. Simplicity is not the starting point, but the ending point.

Faith is not simple. Faith can only *become* simple.

DECANT AND RECANT ~ Christianity is the first religion that was not temple based. Jesus decentralized the temple. He made every local expression of the church an expression of the temple (1 Cor. 3:16). To what degree is your church apathetic about its apostolic heritage? To determine to what degree your church is temple based, look at your budget and figure out what percentage of your money is spent on maintaining your temple.

Nor was Christianity priest based. The decentralization of ministry in the glocal church means a decentralization of leadership and responsibility. Modern versus postmodern ministry is the difference between creating a church

> I have aimed at ease of Numbers and Smoothness of sound, and endeavour'd to make the sense plain and obvious. In [*sic*] the Verse appears so gentle and flowing as to incur the Censure of Feebleness, I may honestly affirm that sometimes it cost me Labour to make it so.
>
> Dissenter/printer/hymn writer
> Isaac Watts in his "Preface"[66]

that reaches out to the world and creating mature believers who team together to reach out to the world.

How can you decentralize church (dechurch, if you will)? It can be as complicated as multiple sites and campuses, to multiple worship services and home-based worship and discipleship experiences. St. Michael's Episcopal Church in Dallas conducted its 1997 Christmas and Easter services in the homes of 100 parishioners. The church was divided into 100 zones, and a family hosted the worship in their home.[67] As the "American Dream" has now expanded from a second car to a second home, why not help your members living this dream do church in their home-away-from-home hideaways?

Dechurching can be as simple as planning a church picnic that isn't based on a central table to which everyone brings something. Make the church picnic a tailgate party. Or help your people create sacred space in their homes. (Our ancestors were actually better at this than we were, with in-home altars, kneeling benches, and prophet's chambers.)[68]

FROM BOUNDARY LIVING TO FRONTIER/BORDER LIVING ~ The church must begin to wander outside its usual haunts. Can it go "over the wall"? The dedifferentiating phenomenon is breaking down the walls between highbrow and lowbrow, between public and private, performer and audience, high or fine art and pop art, "foreign" and "domestic" policy,[70] data processing and data communications, "men's work" and "women's work," carrying information and providing it (e.g., the electronic bulletin board), between original and copy, between nature and mimesis. Can we become an over-the-wall church?

All boundaries of space and time (whether walls separating privacy of home and outside world or walls separating nation-states from neighbors) are coming down or blurring, thanks to telecommunications and the microchip. Dedifferentiation is blurring the delineations between the sacred and profane, the worldly and the godly, church and state, politics and entertainment, the serious and the trivial, the quality and the tabloid,

> When people say, "I know how to set a boundary," what they often mean is, "I read in a pop-psychology book that I can control a situation by saying, 'I need to make a boundary.'"
>
> Mariana Caplan[69]

the real and the imaginary—all boundary-defined categories that are legacies of the past.[71] Feminist essayist Catharine MacKinnon's argument that there is difficulty drawing the line between sex and rape is reflective of the degree to which even obvious boundaries have become problematic.

Postmodernism crosses boundaries and flouts genres until their generic uniqueness is shattered. It plunders and parodies with abandon until "nothing is inappropriate, all is appropriated, excorporated; the exclusive is included, distinctions and categories dissolved into coequal fragments."[72] In the movie *Who Framed Roger Rabbit?* do you remember moving in and out of human worlds and cartoon worlds, *ficta* and *facta*—fitfully at first, then effortlessly by the time the movie ended? In this world where the lines separating places, times, subjects, readers, experiences, and realities are not tightly drawn and "constantly leak through,"[73] there is a need for new categories that approach politics, society, economics, and religion as interconnected wholes rather than rigid categories.

Here is a new entry into our postmodern lexicon: "globalnomics."[74] The Swedes are subsidizing Poland's clean-up costs for Polish industry's pollution of the Vistula. Why? Because Swedish interests in reducing pollution in the Baltic are better served paying for the sins of others than allowing those sins to go unaddressed.

Here's another candidate: "cosmopolitics," as developed by the philosopher Isabelle Stengers. As the Hong Kong "bird flu," the British "mad cow disease," and the Kikwit "Ebola virus" make clear, microbes are no respecters of national boundaries or even most natural boundaries.

One more new term: "intermestic," which brings together "foreign" and "domestic." When foreign policy can get you fired, hired, or mired in high interest rates, what's the difference between "foreign" and "domestic" policy? There isn't one. Everything now is "intermestic." Anyone for Intermestic Missions?

The church should not be afraid of a border world. We are a water people, and unlike the land, the sea knows no boundaries. In a boundary world, life is predictable, controllable, familiar, and well-delineated. In a border world, life is ill-defined, diffuse, anxiety-ridden, riddled with uncertainty—and often violent. Jesus ministered on the borders; he dissolved and crossed boundaries. In his healing he crossed boundaries between Jew and non-Jew, male and female.[75] He healed in gentile areas and rejected old categories of "clean" and "unclean," "Jew" and "Greek."

THE MIXING DESK ~ If you have ever been in a radio or TV studio, you've seen a mixing desk. Many churches that have electronified their worship have installed these electronic instruments called "mixers," in which different things—songs, words, images—come together to be blended. To do ministry in a border world is to be a master mixer. Mixing is at the heart of postmodern ministry.[76]

Postmodern leaders need not be afraid of fuzzy ministry or mixed ministry. Fuzzy is good, as "fuzzy logic" has now instructed us. Mixed metaphors are good, despite the admonitions of your sixth-grade grammar teacher to "never mix your metaphors." In a culture of mix masters, leadership requires paradox making, the ability to put things together in odd, original ways. As well as being one of the keys to "genius," the ability to mix metaphors is essential to communications theory itself.[77]

What Christian Scientist artist Joseph Cornell (1903–1972) did with his collage boxes—mixed up media in strikingly original ways[78]—postmoderns are doing with everything. Just look at the book titles: *Frugal Indulgences*; *Simple Abundance*. More and more entrepreneurs are finding fortunes in mixed metaphors and postmodern culture's love of oxymorons—like TCBY's "White Chocolate Mousse" Yogurt, or like Snapple, which took iced tea and mixed it with peach or raspberry or strawberry or kiwi. One of my favorite novelists, Michael Malone, easily mixes genres in his writing.[79]

The entwining of disparate academic disciplines provides another example of postmodernity's stint at the mixing desk. Scholarship is now being recast through interdisciplinary studies, merging biology with physics and chemistry; putting together literary theory and anthropology and feminist studies; joining economics with biospheric studies and cognitive psychology. This phenomenon is more than adventurous scholars jumping over the barbed-wire disciplinary barriers to cooperate with other scholars on a project and then jumping back over again. Rather, the borders are coming down, and the crossing of the boundaries is leading to the transformation of the disciplinary horizons themselves.

It is not merely postmodern culture that is a farrago of mixed metaphors. Postmoderns themselves are mixed metaphors. In business language post-moderns are MPCs (multiple-profile consumers)—the person who wears a Rolex and shops at Rite-Aid and Wal-Mart; drives an Alfa Romeo and clips grocery coupons; gives extravagant amounts of money away, and lives in gen-teel poverty. MPCs have a taste for the finer things of life; they prize value, but they also prize bargains and practice little economies. They save "mad money" so that they can spend on quality. Postmoderns lead laminated lives.

Mixing metaphors is a key to ministry in postmodern culture: mixing order and chaos, form and energy, spirit and structure. One of the greatest masters of the mixed metaphor was the apostle Paul. In 2 Corinthians 4:16–17 he tes-tifies to the cross's "weight of glory." Paul held both images together. He felt the heaviness and the buoyancy at the same time. Indeed, it was the heavi-ness that made him buoyant, like gravity in the water that lifts us up.[80]

Canadian communications theorist Donald F. Theall calls this way of liv-ing "the poetic," which he defines as "an art of assemblage." A "poetic min-istry" would not be afraid of any and all possible combinations of words, images, objects, gestures, sounds, smells, and tastes. To demonstrate just how far the lines of demarcation have fallen, Theall makes it clear that the poetic includes drama, film, dance, sound and video recordings, mime, hypermedia and hypertext, as well as all the other arts and crafts, including comic books, television, and advertising.[81]

THE PANTY HOSE PRINCIPLE ~ There is a story set in King Arthur's court. A pure knight is forced to marry an ugly woman over a point of honor. As they lie together on their wedding night, the ugly woman offers her reluctant husband a choice. Since he's been so honorable, she has the capacity to be beautiful half the time—either by day, when everyone else will see her, or by night, when only he will. Which will it be?

The puzzled man finally says, "You choose, dear."

You guessed it: There is a happy ending. The woman becomes beautiful all the time.

You want your church to be beautiful? Give the people the power. Let them choose. The church for too long has lived by the one-size-fits all "Panty Hose Principle." It is time to move to "the Platinum Rule." It's a gift to us from Jesus.

THE PLATINUM RULE ~ JOY was one of the first plums I learned to pull out of the pie of piety. In Sunday school, JOY was more than a word in a verse ("Rejoice in the Lord always") or a phrase in a song ("I've got the JOY, JOY, JOY, JOY down in my heart . . . WHERE?"). JOY was a biblical way of living in the world. A JOY lifestyle meant that one put in place a threefold ranking of priorities: Jesus first, Others second, and You last.

In growing up to adulthood, the pie kept getting thrown in my face. I had the JOY drummed out of me. What drove the JOY from my life was another lesson I also learned in Sunday school: the Golden Rule, which taught that we should "Do unto others as you would have them do unto you." In other words, we are to live our lives in such a way that we treat others the way we ourselves would like to be treated.

The JOY method didn't stand a chance of winning over the Golden Rule lesson, because the latter was constantly reinforced by the wider culture. In playing sports I learned Lou Holtz's "Three Simple Rules" of sportsmanship: (1) Do right; (2) do your best; (3) treat others as you would like to be treated. In classrooms and practice rooms, on stage floors and dance halls, in sanctuaries and fellowship halls, after a pat on the head I was sent on my way with the words of the Golden Rule ringing in my ears.

One problem in the church today is that it is attempting to live by the Golden Rule when, in fact, Jesus came to repudiate it. He knew of the rule and referred to it (Matt. 7:12). But he also announced that he came to give us a "new commandment." Jesus came to cut a "new covenant" with us. And this new covenant was not based on doing unto others as we would have done unto us.

The problem with the Golden Rule is that it places first what the JOY method rightly says should come last: me. The Golden Rule places my likes and my preferences at the center of the universe. The need for something that goes beyond the Golden Rule can be seen in the dead-end street even others-oriented communitarians like Amitai Etzioni have landed in: Respect and uphold society's moral order as you would have society respect and uphold your autonomy to live a full life.[82] If one didn't know in advance, one would think such a declaration came from the libertarians, not the communitarians.

Nor is Jesus' principle based on doing unto others as others would have us do to them—now a cardinal tenet of the new "customer-driven" corporate mentality. Rather, the "new commandment" Jesus left us in his farewell discourse is this: "Do unto one another as I have done unto you." Or in the exact translation, "I give you a new commandment, that you love one another. Just as I have loved you, you also should love one another" (John 13:34–35).

For Jesus, there was something beyond "gold" status. Jesus demanded a "platinum" discipleship. There is something beyond the Golden Rule, and it is "the Platinum Rule." The "new commandment" for a demassified church is this: "Do unto others as Christ would have you do unto them."

And how has Christ done unto us? He loved us so much he "laid down" his life for us. "I am the good shepherd. The good shepherd lays down his life for the sheep" (John 10:11). In Jesus' "greater love" doctrine, nothing can be greater than that we be willing to lay down our lives for another. Jesus willingly laid down his life for his friends (John 15:13); Jesus made us *his* friends by laying down his life for us (Rom. 5:8). The fundamental issue of the Platinum Rule is, what are you willing to "lay down" that others may pick up the life of faith?

One reason I call this the Platinum Rule is that the generations who most need to learn this rule are the precise generations most likely to have the one card in their wallets and purses that trumps a "gold card"—the platinum card.

Want to test out the Platinum Rule and see how it works? The next time you are in front of a crowd, ask those present who have grandchildren to please raise their hands. You will see a lot of proud hands go up very quickly. Now ask those with their hands up if they want to reach their grandchildren for Jesus? "How many of you want the church to be as central to the lives of your grandchildren as it is for you?" Once again you will see every hand raised high. The Platinum Rule then asks the question, what are you willing to lay down? If you are doing unto others as Christ has done unto you, then you are laying down some things to reach these grandchildren for Jesus.

Like Peter ("Lord, . . . I will lay down my life for you"), these generations quickly boast that they would give their lives for their grandchildren. They would sooner do that than lay down some other things—their musical preferences, their worship styles, their institutional control, their hard-earned reputations. The Golden Rule taught them that what was good enough for them is good enough for their grandchildren. Hence, ghetto the kids in the basement or give them some musty, mildewed room they can call their own.

The Platinum Rule challenges us to do unto succeeding generations as Christ has done unto us. Every generation has different cultural experiences, knowledge bases, and aesthetic sensibilities. Each generation operates in a different linguistic, sartorial, and myth system from the preceding generations.[83] In religious terms this means that every generation must be reached for Christ differently. If we are to pass the baton of a living faith in Jesus Christ on to the next generation, we must find ways of handing it off to them in ways whereby they can receive it. Just as Jesus "laid down" his life for us, so we are to "lay down" some things in order to pass the gospel "from generation to generation."

How would you like to sit for two hours and be a part of a Gen-X service? Take the youth church in Mount Prospect, Illinois, founded by Ed and Cathi Basler. How comfortable do you think you'd feel during one of their "Souled Out" services? How comfortable do you think Gen-Xers feel sitting through your service?

One church consultant recommends that church leaders watch MTV for one hour. We may have to tie each other into the chair, but we must not get up until the hour's over. MTV has captured the sight-and-sound generation. Has the church lost them? How might we recapture them?

THE VEGGIE PRINCIPLE ~ How do we know we are living up to the standards of Jesus' Platinum Rule? The generation degeneration is what I am calling the Veggie Principle. I have a seven-year-old and a three-year-old who can't get enough of Veggie Tales videos. Frankly, if I have to listen to Bob the Tomato one more time, I'm going to squash him. I have already been caught trying to strangle Jr. Asparagus. Veggie Tales drive me right up the wall. Veggie Tales do to me what a red rag does to a bull, what fingernails do to a blackboard. But who are Veggie Tales for? Even though I can't stand them, I thank God for Veggie Tales and can't wait to purchase each new video for my kids.

The Veggie Principle tests the operation of the Platinum Rule in your home and church. How do you know if you're "doing well" reaching another generation for Jesus? Do *you* like it? Then who's it for? Are you willing to lay down your money to purchase electronic equipment you think is totally irrelevant? Are you willing to lay down your time to do things at church you would never think of doing at home?

How do you know if you're doing well with your children's ministry? Do *you* like it? If there are parts of it that drive you right up the wall, well done!

How do you know if you're doing well with your youth ministry? Do *you* like it? If some of the songs they sing, some of the things they do, some of the language they use drives you crazy, well done!

How do you know if you're doing well with your singles' ministry? Do *you* like it? Then your singles' ministry is in trouble.

How do you know if you're doing well in reaching the lost? Do *you* like it? Does it minister to your needs? If you don't find your church doing things and offering rituals you find shallow and unnecessary, then whom are you really reaching?

The same person who gave us the Platinum Rule also pioneered the Veggie Principle. Jesus was masterfully adaptable and flexible—yet all the while the central core of his message remained unchanged. Jesus communicated a gospel that was always the same and always changing. He sent us out into the world instructing us *what* to do. He never told us *how* to do it. The what remains the same. The how is always changing.

Does your church have the Joy, Joy, Joy, Joy down in its heart? Really?

say what? 1. Here is a thought experiment for you or your group: Your house is on fire. Whom do you call—the professional firefighters, or the volunteer firefighters?

Let's get more specific. In Vestal, New York, a community outside Binghamton, there are eight professional firefighters who are paid full-time to work 24 hours a day. You could call them and be guaranteed that someone would show up. Or you could call the volunteer firefighters and get no such guarantee. But know this: When you call the volunteers, 200 firefighters will get beeped to respond to that fire. All 200 will decide at that moment whether to respond or remain. If your fire occurs during the day, many of them will have to leave work to respond. But chances are, you'll get 20–30 who will show up. At night, 50–60 may show up. And never has no one shown up.

It's your house. Whom do you call? A handful of ordered professionals, or two or three dozen unpredictable volunteers?

2. What was your earliest postmodern experience? What was your first "de" memory?

3. "The electronic technology is re-moulding and restructuring the usual schemes of social interdependence and every aspect of our personal life. It pushes us to reconsider almost every thought, every action and every institution which were evident before." These words from Marshall McLuhan (1964) were printed on the front page of the first issue of the '90s magazine *Wired*. Discuss their significance.

4. What would it mean for you to "speak audiovisual"?

5. Joseph Turow, a professor at the Annenberg School for Communication (University of Pennsylvania), argues in the book *Breaking Up America* that niche marketing has an underbelly that is frightening:

> Segment-making media are those that encourage small slices of society to talk to themselves, while society-making media have the potential to get all those segments to talk to each other. In the ideal society, segment-making media strengthen the identities of interest groups, while society-making media allow those groups to get out of themselves and talk with, argue against, and entertain one another.[84]

The problem, Turow contends, is that we are focusing on the trees and losing sight of the forest. Do you agree?

6. Challenged to justify yet another round of restructuring, Wally's boss in the comic strip "Dilbert" asks, "When a car gets a flat tire, what do you do?" Answers Wally: "Well, if I'm you, I rotate the tires and drive home."

To what extent is this picture true in the world of the church? Are we really getting our hands dirty and facing the issues before us, or are we switching fads and fancies?

7. At its most "bureaucratic" heights, the Roman administration boasted only about 30,000 civilian officials—one for every 2,000 subjects.[85] Today there is one government "bureaucrat" for every 35 US citizens. Admiral Hyman Rickover once said, "If you have a choice of sinning against God or the bureaucracy, sin against God, because God will forgive you and the bureaucracy will not." Do you have any stories to share from personal experience that prove Rickover right or wrong? When did you last have a pleasant trip to the Division of Motor Vehicles?

8. Have someone in your group look up Arthur Koestler's concept of the "holon." One good discussion is found in Steven Rose's *Lifelines: Biology, Freedom, Determinism*. As rose puts it,

Wholes, emerging, may in themselves constrain or demand the appearance of parts. Arthur Koestler . . . described each "level" as having a Janus-like relationship to the others. To that immediately below it, it was unitary (or as he named it, a holon) while to that above it, it was assemblage of components. The ontological level of the universe then consists not of a pyramid of levels, but of a nested hierarchy of holons.

Rose elaborates,

Unless you know the function of the parts in the system, you can't understand what they are for or how they fit together. . . . That is, to understand any piece of machinery you need to know not merely its composition but its role in the larger system of which it is a part.[86]

How is your church like a holon? How useful is the holon metaphor for understanding our postmodern world?

9. Listen to the song called "Hand in My Pocket" on Alanis Morisette's CD named *Jagged Little Pill*. Can you find the litany of generational double rings in the lyrics? How about the title itself: "I've got one hand in my pocket, and the other's giving a high-five"? Do you see other evidence that Gen-Xers show confidence with one hand while guarding their wallets with the other?

10. Evaluate this thesis by Bill Easum and Thomas Bandy:

Worship form or style is no longer specific to certain generations. At one time, it seemed safe to assume everyone born before 1946 would automatically value organs, printed liturgies, stately movement, and solemnity. And it seemed safe to assume everyone born between 1946 and 1965 would appreciate guitars, praise choruses, spontaneity, and constant activity. Then a whole new "generation of seekers" emerged after 1965 for whom the only safe assumptions were that worship style would be "extreme" and "extremely diverse." It is becoming increasingly clear, however, that differentiating worship form and style *by generation* no longer fits our cultural experience. A new generation emerges every three years—not every thirty years.

Easum and Bandy suggest, however, that three distinct traits will characterize worship for the next 20 years: *traditional, praise,* and *sensory* (which they believe will eventually become the dominant form of worship experiences).[87]

11. Have members of your congregation bring their favorite Gaither Homecoming videos. View them and discuss reasons for their popularity. In the later stages of Alzheimer's disease, my Aunt Margaret could only be roused from her living death when my Uncle Theodore would sit down with

her on the couch and put on these videos. It was the only connection he truly had with her during the last five years of her life. Can you tell similar stories?

12. The best single study of postmodernism from a Christian perspective is Stanley J. Grenz, *A Primer on Postmodernism* (Grand Rapids: Eerdmans, 1996). Spend some time as a group reading and discussing this book.

13. Bishop Robert H. Spain warns postmodern circuit riders that our revered forebears who rode the violent, frontier circuits of the 1790s and early 1800s had it easy compared to what God has chosen their descendants to do in the 1990s and early 2000s: "I doubt there has ever been a more demanding time for those in our calling than now."[88]

Industrial Age circuit riders had to contend with such changes as this one announced in the 16 November 1912 edition of the *New Jersey Times*:

> It has been suggested that the Thanksgiving services be held on Thanksgiving Eve, Wednesday evening the 27th, instead of Thursday (Thanksgiving Day). We are inclined to think that a change would greatly increase the attendance at this important service. We are living in a progressive age and the church ought to keep in step with the times.

Discuss what changes postmodern circuit riders and churches must deal with. How much more substantial, more destabilizing, more adventurous might they be than whether services should be on Wednesday or Thursday evenings (or Saturday or Sunday evenings)?

14. Create a one-page resume for your church as if it were a person applying for a job. Include experience, education, accomplishments, and references.

15. For a mixed-metaphor literary experience, read C. S. Lewis's famous university sermon "The Weight of Glory" in his *The Weight of Glory and Other Addresses* (New York: Macmillan, 1949), 1–16.

16. Look into the Seeds of Simplicity children's program out of Cornell University's Center for Religion, Ethics and Social Policy. Its aim is to help children not blow their allowances on junk.

17. Decentralized education has exploded to the point where more than 1 million USAmerican children are receiving home schooling. This does not include the millions in private and parochial schools. What can your church do to assist the variety of decentralized educational programs for its 22nd-century kids?

18. Purchase for your church the excellent video *Postmodern Pilgrims* featuring the gifted ministry of Mark Driscoll at Mars Hill Church in Seattle. (Call 206-570-9467 for a copy.) Discuss in particular the niche-within-a-niche "Skate Church" ministry to postmoderns introduced in the video. Wowak hayrides brought kids together. How different is this?

19. The *Star Trek* dematerializing transporter recreates each atom of the body in precisely the same chemical state of excitation as the atoms are at

present. Is this what happens when you die, or are we more than the sum of our parts? What does the Bible teach?

20. Discuss the devolution revolution at work in the United Kingdom. The UK is no longer a unitary state where what it means to be English and British are virtually indistinguishable. Now the "United Kingdom" has become a multinational state where the English, the Welsh, the Irish, and the Scottish share distinctive identities and heritages and competing memories.

now what? See the Net Notes in http://www.soultsunami.com

NOTES

1. Jessica Lipnack and Jeffrey Stamps, *The Age of the Network* (Essex Junction, VT: Omneo, 1995), 216.

2. For his book that outlines ways to bring together human dignity and human utility, values and profit, see Tom Chappell, *The Soul of a Business: Managing for Profit and the Common Good* (New York: Bantam Books, 1995).

3. So argues Zygmunt Bauman in *Postmodernity and Its Discontents* (New York: New York Univ. Press, 1997).

4. Often through "chain-saw consultants." Some 1.4 million managers have lost their jobs in America in the last five years. Reengineering is at base the organization around processes (selling and making) rather than function (accounts and advertising).

5. Don Peppers and Martha Rogers call the dejobbing of the workplace the ascending power of the hunter-gatherer: the independent contractor, the freelancer, the self-employed consultant. Technology is turning postmodern culture into a hunting and gathering economy. "Instead of eating what the landowner allows us to keep, or what the capitalist pays us for our time, we eat whatever we can forage for ourselves" (Don Peppers and Martha Rogers, "Hunter-Gatherers of the World, Unite!" *Wired* [April 1995]: 107–8). See also William Bridges, *Creating You and Co.: Learn to Think Like the CEO of Your Own Career* (Reading, MA: Addison-Wesley, 1998).

6. Victor J. Stenger, *The Unconscious Quantum: Metaphysics in Modern Physics and Cosmology* (Buffalo, NY: Prometheus, 1996).

7. Roger Penrose et al., *The Large, the Small and the Human Mind* (Cambridge: Cambridge Univ. Press, 1997).

8. Roderick Braithwaite, *Palmerston and Africa: The Rio Nunez Affair* (London: British Academic Press, 1996).

9. Gary Hamel in C. K. Prahalad and Gary Hamel, *Competing for the Future* (Boston: Harvard Business School, 1997), 286.

10. Governor Jeb Bush of Florida is betting his political future on his charge to lead a revolution to "de-invent government": "To bring about a genuine political realignment, Republicans must kill the Government Goose that Lays the Golden Eggs—the very Goose they have fought so hard and long to possess. They must not reinvent government; they must *de-invent* it in order to succeed at governing." See Jeb Bush, "Deinventing Government," *The Best of Imprimis,* vol. 11 (Nashville: Knowledge, 1996), cassette tape 1.

11. Pete de Pont, "When Nations Snuff Out Their Own Citizens," *Insight* 13 (27 Oct 1997): 30.

12. In the US, five industries have been deregulated successfully—airlines, natural gas, railroads, telecommunications, trucking—with savings to consumers of between $40 and

$60 billion a year. (This is the estimate of Robert Crandall of the Brookings Institution and Jerry Ellig of George Mason University.) The major example of an unsuccessful deregulation is that of the savings and loan industry.

13. Andrew Shanks, *Civil Society, Civil Religion* (Oxford: Blackwell, 1995), 33.

14. "[Jesus] may or may not have escaped decomposition," writes scholar Stephen D. Moore, "but how could he escape deconstruction?" (Stephen D. Moore, *Mark and Luke in Poststructuralist Perspectives: Jesus Begins to Write* [New Haven: Yale Univ. Press, 1992], xiii).

15. For an excellent montage of what postmodernism can mean, see the quote from Dick Hebdige in John Frow, *Time and Commodity Culture: Essays in Cultural Theory and Post-modernity* (Oxford: Clarendon Press, 1997), 18: "the décor of a room, the design of a building, the diegesis of a film, the construction of a record, . . . a fascination for 'images,' codes and styles, . . . the collapse of cultural hierarchies, the dead engendered by the threat of nuclear self-destruction, the decline of the university, . . . or even a generalised substitution of spatial for temporal co-ordinates." This originally appeared in Dick Hebdige, "Postmodernism and 'The Other Side,'" *Journal of Communication* 10, no. 2 (1986): 78.

16. Thus Rodolphe Gasche, "Deconstruction as Criticism," in *Johns Hopkins Textual Studies* 6 (1979): 177–215; Christopher Norris, *Against Relativism: Philosophy of Science, Deconstruction, and Critical Theory* (Malden, MA: Blackwell, 1997), and Christopher Norris, *Reclaiming Truth: Contribution to a Critique of Cultural Relativism* (Durham, NC: Duke Univ. Press, 1996).

17. Roger Scruton, "In Inverted Commas," *TLS, Times Literary Supplement* (18 Dec 1992): 3. This is also the argument of theologian Marjorie Suchocki (personal conversation with author).

18. Phillips places deconstruction in sharp contrast to historical-critical and new literary-critical methods. For more, see Gary A. Phillips, "The Ethics of Reading Deconstructively, or Speaking Face-to-Face: The Samaritan Woman Meets Derrida at the Well," in *The New Literary Criticism and The New Testament*, eds. Edgar V. McKnight and Elizabeth Struthers Malbon (Valley Forge, PA: Trinity Press, 1994), 283–325.

19. Phillips, "The Ethics of Reading Deconstructively," 287.

20. For the importance of deconstruction in developing a constructive theology, see Sallie McFague, *Models of God* (London: SCM Press, 1987), esp. 24–28.

21. Sallie McFague has taught us this in *Speaking in Parables: A Study in Metaphor Theology* (Philadelphia: Fortress Press, 1975).

22. Victor Scklovsky, "Art as Technique," in David Lodge, ed. *Modern Criticism and Theory* (New York: Longman, 1988), 16–30.

23. *The Trend Letter* 13 (3 Mar 1994): 2.

24. See Richard L. Nolan and David C. Croson, *Creative Destruction: A Six-Stage Process for Transforming the Organization* (Boston: Harvard Business School Press, 1995).

25. As quoted in Chet Raymo, *The Virgin and the Mousetrap: Essays in Search of the Soul of Science* (New York: Viking, 1991), 150.

26. James R. Rosenfield, "'Millennial Fever': Packaging, Processing, and Passion," Internet (Oct 1996).

27. For more on "celling out," see Leonard Sweet, *11 Genetic Gateways to Spiritual Awakening* (Nashville: Abingdon Press, 1998), 55–68.

28. Kevin Kelly, "New Rules, New Economy," *Wired* (Sept 1997): 194.

29. This is the phrase of MIT's Thomas W. Malone. See the interview between Peter Schwartz and Malone, "Re-organization Man: Thomas Malone Explores Tomorrow's Professional Guilds, Multi-lifetime Employment and the Arrival of Virtual Countries," in *Wired* (July 1998): 135.

30. Militias are based on the principle of "leaderless resistance"—small cells that know nothing about each other, other than they are out there in growing numbers.

31. Don Delillo, *Mao II* (New York: Viking, 1991), 16.

32. Kevin Offner, "A Typology of Evangelicalism," *First Things* 37 (Nov 1993): 48.

  1. Reformed Evangelicalism—thinking Christianly, transforming culture, changing institutions, opposed to dualism

2. Anabaptist Evangelicalism—community, counter cultural, pacifist, servanthood vs. authority

3. Neo-Orthodox Evangelicalism—knowing God vs. knowing about God, narrative theology vs. propositional theology

4. Charismatic Evangelicalism—expecting Signs and Wonders, personal experience, God speaks afresh today

5. Theonomist Evangelicalism—God's unchanging law, salvation as God's lordship, postmillennial, America as Christian country

6. Fundamentalist Evangelicalism—antiliberal, biblicist, seriousness of (external) sin, everything is black and white

7. Dispensational Evangelicalism—nondenominational, pro-Israel, grace vs. works

8. Pro-American Pietist Evangelicalism—America as Christian country, civil religion, personal piety, power of politics

9. Anti-American and Anti-Pietist Evangelicalism—sinfulness of capitalism, anti-rules, anti-Right, anti-Fundamentalist, freedom is what counts

10. Therapeutic Evangelicalism—inner healing, sin as sickness, evil as dysfunction, self-knowledge

11. Social Action Evangelicalism—priority of the poor, physical-spiritual unity, works vs. faith

12. Liturgical/Sacramental Evangelicalism—tradition, sacraments, ordered worship, respect for the mystical.

33. For the sharpest consigning of the nation-state to the dustbin of history, see James Dale Davidson and William Rees-Mogg, *The Sovereign Individual: The Coming Economic Revolution* (New York: Simon & Schuster, 1997).

34. Jan Morris, *Fifty Years of Europe* (New York: Villard, 1997), 125.

35. Thomas Keneally, *Schindler's List* (London: Hemisphere Publications, 1982).

36. One of the last interviews with Leopold Kohr (1909–1994) was given to Marilyn Berlin Snell, who quotes this toast that Leopold made at the end of their conversation: as quoted in "Leopold Kohr: Visionary Economist," *Utne Reader* (Sept-Oct 1994): 44.

37. William P. Alston, "A Philosopher's Way Back to the Faith," in *God and the Philosophers*, ed. Thomas V. Morris (New York: Oxford Univ. Press, 1994), 25–26.

38. "Religion is no longer always 'contained' by formal institutions; a variety of symbol systems may function to create identity and meaning just as traditional religious systems do" (Paul Nathanson, *Over the Rainbow: The Wizard of Oz as a Secular Myth of America* [Albany: State Univ. of New York Press, 1991], 14).

39. Christopher Levan, *Living in the Maybe: A Steward Confronts the Spirit of Fundamentalism* (Grand Rapids: Eerdmans, 1998), 130.

40. See Gertrude Himmelfarb, *The De-Moralization of Society: From Victorian Virtues to Modern Values* (New York: Knopf, 1994).

41. See Martha C. Nussbaum's insightful treatment of Derrida in *Love's Knowledge: Essays on Philosophy and Literature* (New York: Oxford Univ. Press, 1992).

42. Pauline Rosenau, *Post-Modernism and the Social Sciences: Insights, Inroads, and Intrusions* (Princeton: Princeton Univ. Press, 1992). Unfortunately, Rosenau is fairly hostile to religious faith and criticizes the affirmative post-modernists for their openness to spirituality.

43. See the *Journal of Democracy* published by Johns Hopkins University Press. Here is where the widely discussed article by Robert Putnam, "Bowling Alone: America's Declining Social Capital," was first published (6 [Jan 1995]: 65–78). For more see http://muse.jhu.edu/journals/journal_of_democracy/.

44. See Jorge G. Castaneda, *Utopia Unarmed: The Latin American Left After the Cold War* (New York: Knopf, 1994).

45. This is the argument of Jose Casanova, *Public Religions in the Modern World* (Chicago: Univ. of Chicago Press, 1995).

46. Maya Lin tells this story in Charles Gandee, "The Other Side of Maya Lin," *Vogue* 1 (Apr. 1995): 403.

47. John Urry, *The Tourist Gaze: Leisure and Travel in Contemporary Societies* (London: Sage Publications, 1990), 135.

48. Susan Harding, "The World of the Born-Again Telescandals," *Michigan Quarterly Review* (1988): 539.

49. With perhaps one exception: the dual-income Boomer market.

50. The ritual is global. In Japan, where Tom Baccei published the first *Magic Eye* book in 1991, 750,000 sold in 8 months; 200,000 sold in Korea during the first month of publication. Well over 1 million books have been sold in the US. The "Magic Eye" peers out from everywhere—cards, posters, neckties, bathroom tiles, college dorm rooms, newspapers. We can even create and print our own autostereograms with such programs as I/O Software's Stereolusions for Windows.

51. As quoted in "Q+A Phil Collins," *Time* (18 May 1998): 102.

52. The middle class is shrinking, as the top fifth of the population earns well over 10 times more income than the bottom fifth. (In 1968, the ratio was 6 to 1.) Since 1969, incomes in the top quintile have shot up over 600% (Lynn Ehrle, "The Myth of the Middle Class," *The Humanist* 56 [Nov-Dec 1996]: 17–20).

53. For a more in-depth discussion of the dual requirements of complexity, see Mihaly Csikszentmihalyi, *The Evolving Self: A Psychology for the Third Millennium* (New York: HarperCollins, 1993).

54. Martin Heidegger, in his classic essay on Heraclitus (*Heraklit,* vol. 55 of his *Gesamtausgabe* [Frankfurt: Klostermann, 1979]), said that this notion of Logos as basically speech and discursive reason is too one-sided. It suppresses the more intuitive, more experiential sense of "letting-lie-before" (or, in its verb form, *legein*). In other words, for Heidegger Logos means as much "listening" as "speaking," a "harkening" as much as a "happening," an allowing of things to "come into presence" as much as a controlling and ordering of things into logistics and schematics.

56. Martin Henry, *On Not Understanding God* (Dublin: Columba Press, 1997), 102–3.

57. For the position that humans are doxological beings, see Catherine Pickstock, *After Writing: On the Liturgical Consummation of Philosophy* (Oxford: Blackwell, 1998).

58. A. A. Milne, *Winnie-the-Pooh* (New York: E. P. Dutton, 1926), 94.

59. You can find out more about the Breathing Space Institute through www.BreathingSpace.com.

60. Sue Shellenbarger, "Teens Following Parents' Habits," *Arizona Republic* (4 June 1998): D1, D3.

61. Gerald Celente of The Trends Research Institute predicts that by the year 2000, 15% of Boomers will have embraced the simpler life. See *The Trends Journal* (Winter 1997): 7.

62. Sarah Ban Breathnach, *Simple Abundance: A Daybook of Comfort and Joy* (New York: Warner, 1995).

63. Victoria Moran, *Shelter for the Spirit: How to Make Your Home a Haven in a Hectic World* (New York: HarperCollins, 1997).

64. Brian Eno, *A Year with Swollen Appendices* (Boston: Faber & Faber, 1996), 16.

65. Roger Dow and Susan Cook, *Turned On* (New York: HarperBusiness, 1996), 96–97.

66. As reprinted in Selma L. Bishop, *Isaac Watts, Hymns and Spiritual Songs, 1707–1748: A Study in Early Eighteenth-Century Language Change* (London: Faith Press, 1962), liv.

67. Personal communication with St. Michael and All Angels Church (11 June 1998).

68. A home with a "prophet's chamber" for preachers to stay was called a "Shunammite household." For the resurgence of family sanctuaries, much of it inspired by New Age and Eastern spirituality, see Peg Streep, *Altars Made Easy* (San Francisco: HarperCollins, 1997) and Jean McMann, *Altars and Icons: Sacred Spaces in Everyday Life* (San Francisco: Chronicle Books, 1998).

69. Mariana Caplan, *Untouched: The Need for Genuine Affection in an Impersonal World* (Prescott, AZ: Hohm Press, 1998), 202.

70. The 1992 Report of the Carnegie Endowment for International Peace in its foreign-policy-for-the-'90s blueprint.

71. The elision of categories is evident in the way "celebrities" (supermodels, politicians, sports heroes, etc.) are writing "novels," which people read because they might be "true." For the blurring of the boundaries in novels between male and female, even animal and human, see Mary Flanagan, *Adele* (New York: Norton, 1997). Part of the appeal of *Beauty and the Beast* lies precisely in this.

72. John Fiske, *Television Culture* (New York: Routledge, 1987), 254–55.

73. Gary A. Phillips, "Drawing the Other: The Postmodern and Reading the Bible Imaginatively," in *In Good Company: Essays in Honor of Robert Detweiler*, ed. David Jasper and Mark Ledbetter (Hillsboro, OR: American Academy of Religion, 1994), 418.

74. An excellent book that details the power of concentrated economic interests to organize politically and generate social change (for good or ill) is Tim O'Riordan and Jill Jager, eds., *Politics of Climate Change: A European Perspective* (London: Routledge, 1997).

75. Harold Remus, *Jesus as Healer* (New York: Cambridge Univ. Press, 1997), 34–36.

76. Pierre Babin first pointed this out to me at a conference at United Theological Seminary. His paper was never published, but for his remarks about mixing as the essence of media ministry, see "The Spirituality of Media People," *The Way* Supplement 57 (Autumn 1986): 50. "Many different items come their way and so they are mixed beings with diversified tasks, varied people to meet and a flexible programme.... Moreover, they are never on one track only, they are inquisitive beings who go wherever there is human interest and who cross from one track to another. What is the principle behind the mixing? The gospel! And that is the challenge. I sometimes say to students of communications: 'Be all things to all people. Do not belong to anyone–except to God. God is the principle of your mixing, the one who gives it its direction and who brings it all together.'"

77. Joshua Meyrowitz uses three different metaphors for media—as vessel or conduit (content), as language (grammar), and as setting (context)—and shows that "when each is pushed to its limit, it shades into the next." No category is discreet; all are continuous. No metaphor functions in isolation. See his "The Questionable Reality of Media," in *Ways of Knowing (The Reality Club)* (New York: Prentice Hall, 1991), 158–59, quote on 141. For Howard Gardner's work in the capacity of creative people to "combine different modes" in their thinking by flouting conventions and crossing frames of reference, see *Creating Minds* (New York: Basic Books, 1993).

78. For more, see Deborah Solomon, *Utopia Parkway: The Life and Work of Joseph Cornell* (New York: Farrar, Straus & Giroux, 1997).

79. Read, for example, Michael Malone, *Dingley Falls* (New York: Harcourt Brace Jovanovich, 1980).

80. For an example of preaching mixed metaphors, see Leonard Sweet, "Gravity of Grace," *Homiletics* 9 (July-Sept 1997): 15–19.

81. See Donald F. Theall, *Beyond the Word: Reconstructing Sense in the Joyce Era of Technology, Culture and Communication* (Toronto: Univ. of Toronto Press, 1995), 8.

82. Amitai Etzioni, *The New Golden Rule:Community and Morality in a Democratic Society* (New York: Basic Books, 1996).

83. Donna Gaines, "Border Crossing in the U.S.A.," in *Microphone Fiends: Youth Music & Culture*, eds. Andrew Ross and Tricia Rose (New York: Routledge, 1994), 229.

84. Joseph Turow, "Breaking Up America: The Dark Side of Target Marketing," *American Demographics* (Nov 1997): 51. See also his *Breaking Up America: Advertisers and the New Media World* (Chicago: Univ. of Chicago Press, 1997).

85. J. E. Lendon, *Empire of Honor: The Art of Government in the Roman World* (Oxford: Clarendon Press, 1997).

86. Steven Rose, *Lifelines: Biology, Freedom, Determinism* (New York: Oxford Univ. Press, 1998), 94–95.

87. Bill Easum and Thomas Bandy, *Growing Spiritual Redwoods* (Nashville: Abingdon Press, 1997), 51–55.

88. Robert H. Spain, *Getting Ready to Preach* (Nashville: Abingdon Press, 1995), 20.

L ife ring #6

Get EPIC

HOT (HANDS-ON TRUTH) CHURCHES FOR A
HOT (HIGH-ONLINE TECHNOLOGY) CULTURE

or what? A "hot" word, according to Sigmund Freud, is a word that means one thing and *at the same time* its exact opposite. For postmoderns that word "HOT" means "high-online technology." For the church that word "HOT" must *at the same time* mean "hands-on truth," high-touch experiences, or what George Steiner calls "real presences."[1]

Scholar/mythologist Joseph Campbell told TV journalist Bill Moyers that the vast majority of his friends were living "wasteland lives." They were confused, baffled, "wandering in the wasteland without any sense of where the water is—the source of what makes things green."[2]

Only a HOT church can lead a HOT culture out of the wasteland and into the place of water—the source of all things green.

FROM AUTHORITY STRUCTURES TO RELATIONAL STRUCTURES ~
The "dark prince of American letters," William S. Burroughs, tells in his journal of his lifelong quest for truth, for "the secret of the universe" or at least "a fraction of that secret."

How did Burroughs search for that "secret of the universe"? Not through the authoritative modern paths of reason, reflection, and "Enlightenment," but through the relational postmodern paths of experience and encounter: "I have tried psychoanalysis, Yoga, Alexander's posture method, done a seminar with Robert Monroe, taken journeys out of the body, an est in London, Scientology, sweat lodges, and a Yuwipi ceremony."[3]

The Postmodern Reformation fundamentally reframes questions of power and control and redefines authority. In the modern era, power was understood as a relationship of authority. In the postmodern era, power is understood as an authority of relationship. Power now inheres less in knowledge than in the linking of knowledges and the intimacy of those linkages.[4]

Postmoderns are the first people in history who do not need authority figures to access and process information. In fact, the information universe of the digital young is not just beyond the control of their elders, but also beyond their elders' reach. Information travels up and down the superhighway in ways their elders don't understand.

> The relations between objects are more important than the objects themselves.
>
> French painter
> Paul Cézanne

Every generation before now learned about the world directly from authority figures through seat-based learning. Parents, teachers, and priests, among others, were the credentialing gateways to knowledge: social and academic and religious. Now kids learn about the world on their own from people they don't know, never see, and can't touch.[5] Authority figures have lost their authority.

Authority increasingly is something earned, not learned. All traditional authority figures are toppling. The Drudge Report now has as much standing as the *Wall Street Journal*. Postmoderns don't want to "study under" any authority figure; they want to study the authority figure. They don't need "authorities" to help them gain information. But ironically, they need "authorities" more than ever before to mentor them in how to use, perform, and model the information. Hence the interest in preaching, teaching, and healing as performance rituals.

CONNECTEDNESS ～ There are times to be literal, and times to be figurative. It is time to get literal about human connectedness. The church has talked the language of interconnectedness, but it has been a sappy, figural connectivity. In its unveiling of the illusion of separateness, postmodern science is turning us into literalists about Jesus' words: "Inasmuch as you have done it unto the least of these, you have done it unto me" (see Matt. 25:40).

> A religion is, at its heart, a way of denying the authority of the rest of the world; it is a way of saying to fellow human beings and to the state those fellow humans have erected, "No, I will *not* accede to your will."
>
> Yale law professor Stephen Carter[6]

Two similar experiments have moved us beyond a cause-and-effect universe into a holographic universe where there is an interconnectedness to all things. First is the experiment by Alain Aspect and a team of physicists at the University of Paris in 1982 in which it was discovered that when a molecule is moved in one spot, any molecule one observes anywhere in the universe registers that movement.

The second experiment is called the Bell Effect. It discovered much the same thing—that what happens to a particle in one part of the universe affects a companion particle in any other part of the universe without any cause-and-effect linkages or nothing-travels-faster-than-the-speed-of-light time delays.[7]

THE EXPERIENCE ECONOMY ～ In the course of my lifetime the world has moved from an "industrial economy" to a "service economy" to an "experience economy."[8] In fact, some strategic thinkers believe we are already moving beyond an "experience economy" to a society in which the dominant characteristics are "emotion" (a heightened concern for personal and spiritual well-being) and motility (fast movement and rapid change). They call it "the Emotile Era."[9]

Why are fast foods the #1-selling foods in USAmerica? Because they're fast, or because "fast food" is finger food that offers people a food experience. Why is fried chicken becoming supercrispy, yogurts more crunchy, and meats dry-rubbed in spices and crusts or marinated in exotic juices? Because people are looking for sensual and tactile stimulation at mealtime.

John Naisbitt, who coined the term "experience economy," describes the phenomenon this way:

Economic activity starts with *raw commodities* that are transformed into *goods*, which are then wrapped in *services* and eventually turned into *experiences*. Each level increases the total value to the customer and, therefore, the total price. . . . A cup of coffee requires about a penny's worth of coffee beans (the raw *commodity*) and about a nickel's worth of coffee grounds (a packaged *good*). If you purchase a cup of coffee at a diner, though, you will pay around 50 cents for the *service*, and, at a fine restaurant, as much as $2 to $3 for the *experience*.[10]

To be sure, postmodern culture boasts different kinds of Experiencers. Already in the marketing world we are being divided up into Full-blooded Experiencers, Latent Experiencers, Extreme Experiencers, True Experiencers, with a lot of categories in between and to follow. But the bottom line is this: We are all "experiencers." For postmoderns, television is not a medium of information but a medium to be experienced and inhabited.

> I never say no to a new experience.
>
> Dove soap commercial

The experience economy is euthanizing retailing as we know it.[11] With every passing year, the number of retail stores closing their doors is almost doubling. The Chicago-based retail-consulting firm of McMillan & Doolittle says that "Americans are spending one-third less time shopping now than a decade ago."[12] What is the problem? There are approximately one million shops in the US, and they are all selling basically the same stuff and providing the same one-note experience. Stores that sell products are an endangered species. Stores that sell values and experiences are poised for the future.

The demallification of America is taking place even faster than we anticipated in *FaithQuakes*.[13] The mall concept is here to stay. But mall-crawling the 42,000 malls scattered across the US for retail purposes is coming to a crawl. Fewer USAmericans are going to malls, and those who do are spending less and less time there.[14]

What is even of more concern to mall magnates, people are entertained by mall shopping less and less. In 1995 more than half of shoppers aged 15 and older said they go to the mall with a specific store or product in mind, a percentage that is climbing every year. Mall shopping as entertainment was half as popular in 1996 as it was in 1990. Boomers are demalling faster than all age groups, opting for open-air and village-like ventures if not village-life. Parking lots are giving way to sidewalks, mall stores to corner stores, back patios to front porches.

Little wonder pension funds have started either tearing down retail malls and putting up in their place quick-in-and-out power centers (category killers like Home Depot and Toys'R'Us). Or they are building "new malls" (e.g., the Mall of America in Bloomington, MN; Canada's West Edmonton Mall; the

Forum Shops at Caesar's in Las Vegas), which are less retail centers than gigantic experience and entertainment centers, a kind of postmodern world's fair. Visit Café Odyssey on the third floor of the Mall of America. It seats 365, with different themed environments: the Explorer's Club, Machu Picchu, the Lost City of Atlantis, and the Serengeti. If patrons get an experience, visitors will pay more for the meal and buy the T-shirt as a remembrance of what happened.

> The only real question to be asked of another is: what are you experiencing?
>
> Religious writer/activist/mystic
> Simone Weil

Only those malls will survive that provide a new café society and its mature consumers, not products to buy but social and cultural experiences to share or to buy. Gift giving itself is transitioning away from "goods" and toward good experiences. Instead of the bike, the kids get a hike in Yellowstone Park. Enjoyable family outings and novel experiences are the most prized possessions of postmoderns, and not just on their birthdays—witness the Michael Douglas movie *The Game.*

Jointly backed by Sega, Universal Studios, and DreamWorks SKG, GameWorks opened in March 1997 in Seattle (with 40 of them planned by the year 2000). Part café, part club, part book store, part 21st-century arcades, GameWorks is perhaps best described by Steven Spielberg as a "collection of experiences." It boasts an interactive game designed by Spielberg himself, called "Vertical Reality," in which the player's bubble-chair rises with each new skill level to a height of 24 feet . . . and then drops in free fall if he loses.

What does Planet Hollywood or Hard Rock Café deliver?

Great food? They serve experiences.

Have you heard the Toyota Avalon commercial? "It's an experience, above all else."

> What is important now is to recover our senses. We must learn to see more, to hear more, to feel more. Our task is not to find the maximum amount of content in a work of art, much less to squeeze more content out of the work than is already there.
>
> Philosopher/novelist/filmmaker
> Susan Sontag[15]

EXPERIENCE BRANDING ~ In the modern era, a "brand" was a "name," a name often created through mass media advertising campaigns. "Brands" were bought because the names were respected and familiar.

Postmodern "brands" are active experiences created through the interchange of producer and the customers they have made partners. Wjwak my parents didn't buy a product without looking for the Good Housekeeping Seal of Approval. They trusted that seal, even though I'm sure they didn't know who or what was really behind it. The seal "branded" a product as trustworthy.

That seal is still around. It appears in postmodern culture in the form of Martha Stewart. Encounters with her cheery face and gentle demeanor have become the brands around which we decide what products we need to do "good housekeeping." The difficulty of branding without personalities was pointed out to me by Stewart M. Hoover, head of the Center for Mass Media Research at the University of Colorado, who spoke at a United Methodist Communications gathering.

> On NBC's *Saturday Night Live,* the Irish pop singer Sinead O'Connor, who was a guest host of the program, ended her last song by holding up a photograph of John Paul II, tearing it in half, and saying "fight the real enemy." This sent shock waves through a predominantly young audience which had for several years been consuming images of Madonna's cavorting with the crucifix with little reaction. In contrast, the reaction to O'Connor's act was huge—and telling. The cross, as an object of history and tradition, had lost much of its power to shock and convict. The Pope, by contrast, was someone known, in the here and now, and understood via his media presence to be a real human being.[16]

Through sports figures, celebrities, and created personalities, companies like Coca Cola ("Always Coca Cola") are taking products and transforming them into experiences and relationships. What do Coke and Pepsi make? Not soda pop. They manufacture culture. They create logos from which people can share experiences, logos that nourish communal identities and a distinctive sense of belonging. Alas, the "brand name" denominations—United Methodists, Southern Baptists, Nazarenes, Presbyterians, Lutherans, Episcopalians, United Church of Christ, etc.—have done little "branding," while off-brand groups such as the Mormons and the Scientologists have branded big-time. If denominations are to survive, they must become less a bureaucracy and more a brand.

> Our machines are disturbingly lively, and we ourselves frighteningly inert.
>
> Feminist philosopher Donna Haraway[18]

Space at vacation resorts, summer camps, and "brand events" now need eight-month advance arrangements because a lot of postmoderns want the same one-of-a-kind experience at the same time.

Is there anyone left who really thinks that electronic culture will obliterate magazines or make ink addicts an endangered species? Boomers and Gen-Xers are collecting the magazines *Wired* and *Fast Company* the way our parents and grandparents used to collect *National Geographic.* In 1995 there were 850 gay and lesbian newspapers and periodicals circulating to 2 million readers.[17] Why? We read magazines to be part of an ongoing conversation and brand community. Support groups and special-interest groups (book clubs, travel societies, dinner circles) will proliferate.

GOING TO EXTREMES ∼ In the modern world we were taught to "avoid extremes" and find the *via media*. William Hazlitt's essay on the "common-place critic" talked about those who searched for truth "in the middle, between the extremes of right and wrong." It is in the very nature of postmodernity's adrenalin-rush culture to go to extremes. In fact, it is less accurate to say that postmodern culture takes you from one extreme to another in the blink of an eye than that pomo culture does both extremes simultaneously.

Bingeing and bunjee-jumping are classic symptoms of an attempt to come to terms with extremes. Postmodern culture is more bulimic than anorexic. Anorexia nervosa was first described in 1868; bulimia nervosa—alternative binge-eating and binge-evacuation (mostly by self-induced vomiting)—is a recent addition to medical nosology. As many as one in a hundred women is anorexic, but three to four in a hundred are bulimic.[19]

The more virtual the world becomes, the more physical become people's needs and wants. Far from being a substitute for the real world, cyberspace actually stimulates people's desires for real-world, extreme-themed, get-physical experiences. "Surfing" the Net only makes people want to surf Maui more or "theme out" at some surfing theme park. The MTV generation and the Net generation greet traditional Olympic sports with a yawn. It must be labeled "extreme" or it's boring.

Look around you. Have you noticed a sudden appearance of the word *extreme* almost everywhere?

- FedEx sends packages that are "extremely urgent."
- NASA sends up a new satellite called the "Extreme Ultraviolet Explorer" (EUVE).
- At Boston Market you order an "Extreme Carver" sandwich.
- At Taco Bell you order an "Extreme Combo Meal."
- Pontiac announces that it's "taking it to the extreme."
- Blue Byte produces a 3-D action adventure game called "Extreme Assault."
- Nynex promotes a discount calling plan with the slogan "Extreme Dialing."
- "Slim Jim X-treme Stick."
- The best cigar lighter is made by Colibri and is called "Xtreme."
- Mattel's successor to the "Street Sharks" series is "Extreme Dinosaurs."
- *Fortune* magazine has a cover article on "eXtreme investing" by "cool companies," and *Inc.* magazine the same week does a cover article on "Extreme Managing."[20]

There is even now a book of readings called *Extremism in America: A Reader,* which examines the growth of extreme groups like survivalists, as well as other extremists.[21] Infoseek found 141,737 pages containing the word *extreme,* including Extreme News, eXtreme Books, "Extreme fragrances," extreme catalogs, Extreme Pinball, X-Treem Caffeine beverages, Extreme Sports Network.

Extreme sports (snowboarding, ice biking, skydiving, rock climbing, and "multisport" sports like sky surfing and skijoring) are already replacing baseball and football as the quintessential American sports. Don't believe me? Watch ESPN's Extreme Games series, or rent movies like *Cliffhanger, Point Break, Terminal Velocity,* and *Drop Zone.* There are niches within each extreme sport—e.g., skydiving is divided up into six disciplines, including sky surfing, free flying, free style, etc. There are many reasons for the phenomenal growth in extreme sports—improved equipment, increasing income levels, boomeritis. But the experience economy is surely one of the most important factors behind the popularity of the X Games: inline skating, wakeboarding, sport climbing, bicycle stunt riding, skateboarding, street luge, sky surfing, and snowboarding.

> Happiness is not around the next corner. It *is* the corner.
>
> BMW commercial

DOUBLE-RING MINISTRIES ~ With millions of people at our fingertips, our fingers need to grasp tightly and intensely a handful.

The average USAmerican spends eight whole years of life watching electronically how other people live; 50% of all USA families have three TVs or more. Postmodern culture creates a population that is, in the words of Andy Warhol's motto, "bored but hyper." Postmoderns are hungry for "real" epiphanies; they are ravenous for "real" experiences—for sensory stimulation and socialization and emotional fulfillment. Hence they are "cutting loose" in a new activism, hitting the streets, theaters, cafés, bars, and bistros.

Telecommuters working inside their homes can be rabid out-of-door types: bladers, bikers, hikers who are both Net savvy and nature loving. The more wired the culture becomes, the more outside recreation and extreme sports become the norm. And they lure not only the young.

Michael L. Dertouzos, while understanding that information technologies will enable "each church to reach hundreds of millions of people with information about their beliefs and functions," doesn't get it when he argues that "we cannot foresee any ways in which the Information Marketplace will affect the spirituality of people one way or another, except perhaps indirectly by exposing many more people to the various options for spiritual fulfillment."[22] The Information Marketplace will transform spirituality in the same way print culture altered Christian spiritualities.

Here's another double ring: Family household size is getting smaller and smaller while the homes people build are getting bigger and bigger. Perhaps the best way to understand the "homes" we are building today is to compare them with the medieval castle. The function of a castle was to protect one's family and friends from the chaos and violence of an outside world. Hence the moat, the drawbridge, and the elaborate turrets and security systems. USAmericans are cantilevering their mansions (or McMansions, since so many of them look exactly alike), much like patricians did in the late 18th century, the splendor within only matched by the squalor without. We are forting up electronically, our ark-compounds and high-tech workplace/playgrounds pre-occupied with hypersafety and PHAST systems.[23] No wonder martial arts were the second-fastest-growing business category in the US in 1994.[24]

Rival futurists Faith Popcorn and Richard Celente are both correct. People are both "cocooning" (Popcorn) and "de-cocooning" (Celente) or "bunkering" (*Iconoculture*) at the same time. We are "cocooning" in our smart castles and telecom-muting from them, but at the same time we are tired of being cooped up and bolting from them with increasing velocity. Ray Oldenburg, in his book *The Great, Good Place*, argues that people have three primary places of human contact. The first two, where we work and where we live, are increasingly one.[25] Upwards of 50 million USAmericans are now working out of their home full- and part-time, up from 11 million in 1985.[26]

> Without experiences there is no wisdom.
>
> Ancient Chinese proverb

Where we gather socially, what Oldenburg calls "third places," have become endangered by urban planning, materialistic values, suburban car-culture, social disorder, and fear of violent crime. Just when our culture needs "third places" the most, they are most in peril. We have pagers, answering machines, e-mail, phones, cellular phones, and modems. We're more connected than ever before, and we're more lonely than ever before. Gadgets have enslaved us, not freed us. We can't complete the circuit.

We are awash in missed connections.

The Web is being transformed into a global third place—a city square, café, cocktail lounge, and social club. Remember: Electronic media both globalize and individualize. Why are people surfing the Web? They are look-ing for experiences to go along with their information. University of Chicago scholar Mihaly Csikszentmihalyi argues that true postmodern Web sites are not about delivering content, but about staging experiences. The reason why America Online has more subscribers than *Time, Newsweek,* and *U.S. News & World Report* combined is that people are desperate for connectedness.[27]

People are using the Net as they used to use the picket fence in the back-yard—to talk across and neighbor. This bias in favor of chat over commerce is one reason that corporate America has had such scant success in selling products over the Web. That will change. What won't is this: The Internet will be a key source for relationships in 21-C. Postmoderns are developing rich, varied, and complex online lives.

Author Anthony Burgess sneered at CD-ROMs when they first came out—
"metallic beer mats," he jeered. It's a cheap shot to degrade the emerging
new forms of placeless community, many of

> Happiness isn't good enough
> for me! I demand euphoria!
>
> Comic strip character Calvin
> ("Calvin and Hobbes")

which violate our inherited geographical concepts of community. Postmodern communities
are comprised less of place than of people with
collective interests and shared heroes, hopes,
and icons. Already there are more than 140,000
networks that can be contacted through the Internet. These telecommunities
will not replace traditional communities, but they will transform the world in
which we live.

It is hard for us to "get it," but "get it" we must in a world where a message was posted about Leonardo DeCaprio on AOL *every ten seconds* when
the *Titanic* film fever broke.[28] Fewer and fewer of our "keyboard kids" are living in geographical communities anymore. I know kids whose diversification
of communities is such that their best friends are people they have never met
face to face. They have a shared identity that is not geographic bound.

A father asked his kid one day, "Who's your best friend?" The exchange
that followed is classic postmodern.

The kid replied, "Jonas."
"Where does Jonas live?"
"Jerusalem."
"You can't mean Jerusalem, as in Israel?"
"Yep."
"What about Peter next door?"
"I don't have anything in common with Peter."[29]

We are now living in a world where it is possible for people to have more
in common with someone halfway around the world than the person next
door.

SO What? MORE TECHIE, MORE HUMIE ~ The more hard-core
"techie" the church becomes, the more soft-core "humie" the
church must get. A culture hotted by high-online technologies requires HOT
(hands-on-truth/high-on-touch) churches. Humies must become Techies, and
vice-versa. Postmoderns are famished for closeness, starved for contact. In a
world where touch-crimes are increasing, we are a touch-starved people.

If your worship isn't good enough, you're not close enough. You're not
in touch.

The worst thing the Postmodern Reformation church can do is to get more
techie and less humie. This voice-mail message at the Cathedral of the Holy

Spirit–Chapel Hill Harvester Church, Atlanta, is a graphic example of a teckie-tacky thing *not* to do:

> "If you are calling about a death in the family, press 9."

ŵïŵäk , in the West Virginia county where our family homestead was situated, there were 4R's to be learned: Reading, 'Riting, 'Rithmetic, and the road to Roanoke.

Postmoderns are also growing up in a 4R's world, except the 4ᵗʰ R for them is Relationships.

> **If your pictures aren't good enough, you're not close enough.**
>
> Magnum photographer
> Robert Capa[30]

RELATIONSHIP MINISTERS ～ When God "knew" God, the Creator "conceived" and the universe was born. When Adam "knew" Eve, they "conceived," and a child was born. From a biblical perspective, knowledge conceives. Knowledge is a relational category. Relationship is the central reality in both physical and spiritual existence.

In his journey through life, singer Frank Sinatra amassed more fortune, fame, and followers than all but a handful of 20ᵗʰ-century folk. But at the end of the journey it was relationships—with God, with family—that mattered. Sinatra's last words? "O my Lord, . . . my Mother."

When Jesus was asked to name the greatest commandments, he cited the *shema*—"love God and love others." When Jesus was asked how to pray, he defined God in terms of a relationship: *abba*. Jonathan Edwards, perhaps the greatest theologian this country has produced, said that "being is relation."

Jesus pioneered a relationship ethic based on compassion. Being a disciple means building relationships—with the Creator and with all creation and creatures.

Relationships rule postmodern life. Hope College Chaplain Ben Patterson tells of meeting a physician who had grown up in the Midwest, attended the University of Chicago Medical School, and now practiced in Portland, Oregon. When Patterson asked him what had made him choose Portland as a place to practice, the physician's answer was striking. He didn't mention the beauty of the Northwest. He didn't mention Portland's ranking as one of the best places to live in America. He didn't mention the healthy economies of the Pacific Rim. What he mentioned was once meeting a young seminary student while in Chicago. When that student decided to go to Portland after graduation and start a new church, this physician wanted to help him in his ministry. So he chose Portland as a place to practice medicine.[31]

There is a new saying in the conflict management field: "You can be right, or you can be close." Postmoderns would rather be close than right. They are more interested in being there than going there or getting there. Every self-help group screams our desperation for relationships. The dating service industry has doubled in size in the past seven years, with 3,000 agencies nationwide. Love-by-the-line personal ads add $5 billion a year to the newspapers' coffers. Someone spent $35.50 per 36-character line to put in this one:

NO RECENT PAROLE VIOLATIONS! White male, 37; likes to wear black socks, sandals, extremely baggy Bermuda shorts, mutter aloud on city buses. Recently obtained proof of government plot to steal my ears. Seeking compatible woman.[32]

The business world now has positions called "relationship managers," "relationship management," and "relationship investing."[33] Even "PR" (Public Relations) is being given a face-lift and name change: Personal Relationships.

Postmodern evangelism also can be summarized in one word: relationships. According to the Billy Graham Evangelistic Association, 80% of adults coming to faith in Jesus Christ do so as a result of the influence of a friend. Whereas churches reaching moderns organized around function—missions, finances, worship—churches in mission to postmoderns must organize around relationships—relationships with God, with each other, with the community, and with creation. Whereas people used to go to church to meet old friends, they now go to church to meet new friends.[34] Church is relationship building. "The most radical thing you can do is to introduce people to each other," argues Glenn Hilke.[35]

Steve Stroope, pastor of Lake Point Church in Rockwall, Texas, expects each of his members to maintain a list of three non-Christian friends for whom they are praying and seeking to lead to faith. Gated churches, insulated from nonbelievers, are the least able to lead postmoderns to a living faith.

The seat of the soul is not inside or outside a person, but the place where people overlap. The soul is less the space within or without as between. A soul becomes a soul through other people. A soul becomes itself through tapping and trapping the heart of another.

What does it profit . . . if you gain the whole world, like Charlie Chaplin, and all eight of your children unanimously hate you?

DE-STUFFED SHIRTS ~ There is a rumor that the devil now makes his postmodern home in either Boring, Oregon, or Normal, Illinois, having moved there from Doubting, Alabama.

The modern age robbed people of their eccentricities. Postmoderns are preeningly odd and original. Moderns didn't want anything that parts the hair. Postmoderns do not suffer boredom easily or quietly. Reynolds Price's phrase that "some of them boring as root canals" describes the pain postmoderns feel in the presence of too many Christians.[36] Better for the church to be anything—quirky, nerdy, *anything!*—than "boring." Stuffed shirts have a negative witness in postmodern culture. Why?

Walker Percy's definition of boredom is classic: "the self *stuffed with the self.*" The church must find ways of "un-stuffing" people's lives with things and stuffing people with God.[37] Will the church point them to the real "stuff" of life—the stuffings of the Spirit. How can your church help "un-stuffing" postmodern lives?

POSTMODERN MAMMONISM ~ "Success" in the modern world meant one or both of two words: profession and possessions. To be "successful" one either had mastered professional skills associated with some guild, or had accumulated great possessions. The exchanges of the modern world were exterior capital—money, power, and status.

"Success" in the postmodern world means lifestyle: a life of balance, harmony, health, security, and control, and most importantly, a life that amasses a wealth of experiences, stories, and relationships. "Success to me is knowing that fun is a major portion of my paycheck," one Gen-Xer contends.[38] The exchanges of the postmodern world are interior capital. We have moved from a balance of power world to a power of balance world.

But each one of these capital components of a postmodern lifestyle can be turned into its own obsession. If moderns were fetishizers of commodities—the obsessions of possessions and professions—postmoderns are fetishizers of experiences.

Postmoderns can be as fanatically acquisitive as moderns. An ad that debuted in late 1997 for the Mercury Mountaineer begins with a drawer pulled out filled with "collectibles": coins, stamps, keys, and other symbols of success. The copy above the panel teases "Imagine collecting something more valuable." The next panel reads simply "Experiences" and shows an all-wheel-drive Mercury Mountaineer reflecting the shimmering sun of the desert Southwest. The final copy makes the message of experience consumption explicit: "Maybe the greatest possessions aren't the ones you hold in your hand. At Mercury, we believe they're the images and experiences you collect in your travels."

> Don't let anyone steal your spirit.
>
> Actor/comedian Sinbad

For postmoderns, greed centers less in collecting estates and "toys" than in collecting experiences, friends, and stories. The pleasures to be derived from possessing jewels are nothing beside the pleasures of possessing experiences. Postmoderns are expert miners; they possess a keen eye and sharp shovel for digging experiences from anywhere and everywhere and then stacking them up for all to see, sparkling and dazzling in the sunlight. The church must help postmoderns live experience rather than consume experience.

If "to get a life is to get an illness,"[39] the scourge of modern life was depressive disorders. The scourge of early postmodern disorders is addiction.

Anything that offers an experience can quickly be turned into a pathology of the self. Helping people "get free" of addictions is a primary ministry of the Postmodern Reformation church.

EXTREME DISCIPLESHIP ~ The gospel evokes extreme reactions. Wherever Paul went, it has been said, there was either a riot or a revival. Whenever Wesley moved his ministry toward the people and took the gospel to the streets, it caused a commotion. Where's the commotion, church? Silver and gold we have aplenty. But where are the wind and fire of Pentecost?

What if the church were to "get extreme?" By this I don't mean "going off the deep end" at either end, but triangulating the ends into double-helix discipleship. What if the church were to embrace extreme worship (the free-form and the liturgical), extreme learning (ink and light), extreme confirmation, and so on? What if the church were to be open to the extemporaneous and serendipitous? Any community without the tang of "realness" is too insipid for postmodern tastes—not to speak of Jesus himself. What if the church were to really get jazzed by Jesus?

WIWAK a bishop touted the three "unforgivable S's" to his clergy: "No surprises, no subversion, no sinning," in that order. Moderns disliked surprises because they shattered the illusion that we are in charge. Surprises challenge our cause-and-effect thinking, which is a frontal assault on the ego of power and control.

I tell people I am "dangerously Christian." I proclaim a "shock gospel." I confess to being an "out-of-control disciple." Until we can hear "out-of-control" as positive, not as negative, we will not have understood what it is to minister to postmoderns.

With every passing whim satisfied by consumer capitalism, postmodern comfort and boredom create a craving for unnatural and destructive forms of stimulation. People look for empowerment from wherever they can find it, and it's time the church admitted that purchasing is a form of empowerment. Shopping is an adventure. The credit-card click is a rush. People get emotional highs from consumerism. It's a cheap high, a faux empowerment, a skin-deep rush—but it's better than nothing.

It is up to the church to offer postmoderns adventures that are difficult, demanding, spiritual, and true. Want cheap experiences? Then don't get jazzed by Jesus. The church of Jesus Christ specializes in earned experience, deep experience, authentic experience.

Here's a motto for some church: The Adventure of a Lifetime Begins Here.

> He is The Way.
> Follow Him through the Land of Unlikeliness;
> You will see rare beasts and have unique adventures.
>
> W. H. Auden[40]

FROM "DOES IT MAKE SENSE?" TO "WAS IT A GOOD EXPERIENCE?" ~
Postmodern spirituality is different from modern spirituality. A continental drift
of the soul has taken place whereby spirituality is less creedal, less propositional, more relational, and more sensory.[41] Logic is no longer converting anyone—only the transforming experience of the living Christ.

Scholars are calling this lived religion, experienced religion, "vernacular
religion," a spirituality "more internal than external, more individual than
institutional, more experiential than cerebral, more private than public."[43]
Harvey Cox calls the new mode of spirituality "experimentalism," and says it
is "emotional, communal, narrational, hopeful, and radically embodied."[44]
Whatever you call it, one thing is certain: Postmodern spirituality mistrusts
our rational powers as incapable of telling the whole story, the whole truth.

Samuel Beckett talked in an early poem about "a world politely turn-
ing/From the loutishness of learning." That "turn" has become a rout. The
insufficiency of reason alone to nourish the soul, or even the inaccessibility
of faith to reason, is simply assumed. The sin of scientism—the notion that if
we can't understand something, then it's nothing—has given rise to a new
modesty of the mind, a renewed tilting of the head to the heart.[45]

Of course, we distrust reason even as we reason, as Ved Mehta has
observed,[46] and it is reason itself that helps to teach us
to distrust it. Scientists themselves have uncovered
the sin of scientism with their admission that there is
not a physicist alive who fully understands gravity,
particle physics, or electromagnetics—yet there is
something called gravity, particle physics, and electromagnetics. A new convert to Eastern Orthodoxy,
Yale church historian Jaroslav Pelikan, reminds us that "the recognition that
reason does not exhaust the range of meaning in human life is itself an accom-
plishment of reason."[47]

> It's hard to imagine a
> scholar kneeling down.
>
> Emil Cioran on his fellow
> Romanian colleague
> Mircea Eliade[48]

It is not your job to help people decide what is right and wrong. It is your
job to help bring people to Christ, who through the Holy Spirit can reveal to
them what is right and wrong.

It is not your job to teach people what is "good church music." It is your
job to help people have an experience of God.

Churches in postmodern communities will be built, not around great
preachers, but around great experiences. Preaching must cease to be the "big-
jug/little-mugs" presentation of points of view or the representation of arguments that can be verbalized; rather, it must become a rushing mighty wind
that blows through the congregation and makes it glow with an incandes-
cence that cannot be ignored.

FROM ILLUSTRATION TO ANIMATION ~ A sign posted on the glass door
of a bankrupt bookstore told the whole story: "Words Failed Us."

In the modern world, the word was the primary unit of cultural currency. In the postmodern world, the image is the primary unit of cultural currency. In the modern world, preachers exegeted words to make points. In the postmodern world, preachers must learn how to exegete images to create experiences. Preachers are connoisseurs of biblical images, for it is the image that fixes the subject in postmoderns' mind and memory. A course in metaphor is as important a part of a preacher's education as a course in exegesis or church history.[49] One "illustrates" points. One "animates" experiences. Facility with metaphors and images, which link reason and imagination, which yoke the conceptual to the perceptual, can help transition the church from modern to postmodern.[50]

Illustrations are about as appetizing and cold as yesterday's mashed potatoes. The difference between illustration and images-in-motion animation is graphically portrayed by Thom and Joani Schultz in their narrative of the funeral of Joani's 94-year-old grandmother.

> The preacher described how this beautiful Christian woman died while serving others. She collapsed while making popcorn balls for neighborhood children. That was a perfect parting picture of this lifelong servant of God. The preacher could have galvanized that point in his listener's minds forever by the simple use of a visual. If only he'd brought out Grandma's last batch of popcorn balls at that moment.[51]

Christianity is now undergoing visual metamorphosis. In the modern era, the more abstract the words, the more sophisticated and scientific the thought. Metaphors were suspect. Their ability to layer meaning and convey two or three things at the same time were seen as negatives, not positives. Provocative, open-ended, and fuzzy, they were deemed inferior methods of discourse. So-called postmodern deconstructionists like Jacques Derrida are really hypermoderns, not postmoderns. They live in utter fear that literary images and visual metaphors are so narcotic that they disarm the critical senses and cramp rationality—so they would remove all images and return us to words and more words, putting the intellect clearly in the driver's seat. How many books and articles have you sloshed your way through, no metaphor in sight? This is why university presses seldom ran pictures of their authors throughout the 20th century. Without an image of an author, the words on the page seem more impersonal, more dispassionate—more universal principles, more incontrovertible truths.

> "What is the use of a book," thought Alice, "without pictures or conversations!"
>
> *Alice in Wonderland*[52]

Postmoderns rely on emotions for evidence, metaphors for truth, and myth for direction. Postmoderns live in metaphors and dwell in parables. They have a highly developed visual sense. Disraeli boasted that "with words we govern men." More precisely, with metaphors postmoderns are governed. I have an academic friend who offers her ideas free of charge for the taking, but woe betide the person who steals her metaphors, examples, and anecdotes. She's not joking. The most revealing part of oneself is the imagination. The most powerful arguments one makes is through metaphors. Metaphors are best seen as "eggs," Russell Lockhart argues, "eggs ... that carry life, that give birth." He quotes Gaston Bachelard in support: "For a word dreamer there are words which are shells of speech. Yes, by listening to certain words as a child listens to the sea in a seashell, a word dreamer hears the murmur of a world of dreams."[53]

Preachers are more than word dreamers. They are image dreamers, story dreamers who hear in an image and story the sounds of God's DreamChurch.

I made two mistakes immediately upon becoming dean of Drew Theological School. Either one could have ruined me.

My first stupidity was when I walked into my office and saw a desk so large it reminded me of an aircraft carrier. I remarked, "I don't do desk," and asked the faculty, "Anyone want it?" How dumb can you be—like tearing out the pulpit before preaching one's first sermon at a new church. My second stupidity was remarking in a committee meeting that "the only power I want as dean is the power to choose the metaphors." The university grapevine is one of the wonders of the modern world. Information passes among us at speeds that defy Einstein's long-held maxim that nothing can travel faster than the speed of light. When this word spread, what spread alongside it was that I wasn't taking my job seriously, or that I was a pushover because "Sweet's not into power."

The truth is that I'm so "into power" that I repent almost daily of my power-mongering ways. In the modern world there was "agenda power"—the leader's right to set the agenda for the organization, the power to establish goals and strategies. In the postmodern world there is "metaphor power"—the leader's right to choose the metaphors for the organization, to establish the dreams and language.

Which power would you pick?

We know now that metaphors are not "just" metaphors: They are the software of thought. Metaphors do more than add to the cognitive impact of language. Metaphors are the stuff of which our mind is made to begin with. In our mental encyclopedia, concepts like "chair" are not based on abstract sets of necessary and sufficient conditions, but on prototypes, best examples, images. Ezra Pound called an image "that which presents an intellectual and emotional complex in an instant of time."[54] Images do the same as dreams, which, in Emily Bronte's words, "go through one's life like wine through water." When someone is in a position to choose the metaphors, that someone is in a position to mess with your mind, to change your perspectives, to generate new dreams.

Again: Which power would you pick?

METAPHORIC CHRISTIANS ～ The image of images must be altered. Post-moderns are hypermediated, metaphoric believers. The church has been slow to come to terms with postmodern culture's preference for the perceptual over the conceptual. This is partly due to the Protestant bias against the visual. In her book *Image as Insight*, Margaret Miles reminds us of the impact of Luther's words: "The ears are the only organs of a Christian."[55] Following Luther, Calvin, and Zwingli, the Protestant Reformation developed aesthetic principles that emptied visual culture from liturgical space. The role of visual images like painting and sculpture in communal ritual and liturgy was severely circumscribed. It still is. In our attitude toward the media, our minds are still inhabiting the Orwellian nightmare of the all-observing screen while people all around us, and we ourselves, are living out the dream come true: That screen Orwell prophesied is a word processor that helps us write our papers and books, check our spelling, keep our accounts, and file our thoughts.

> The soul never thinks without a mental picture.
>
> Aristotle

What images we allow are primarily written images, but even here there is an aversion to the visual. In preaching, we still think that people are moved by impeccable logic, powerful reason, and scientific thinking. The modern era got right to the point. In fact, it began in 1517 with a 95-point sermon, and we are still preaching "points" (although now they're down to three in club-sandwich sermons) through Enlightenment-based linear exegesis as opposed to image exegesis. Seminaries still compete with one another to be *The* Logical Seminary.

The problem is that clarity about God is no longer transmitted to post-moderns by impersonal, sequential logic. To modernity's pointy finger, post-modernity gives a shrug. Making points no longer makes points. Or as my wife puts it less charitably, "Sweet, your sermons are pointless." The step-by-step, point-by-point language of analytic discourse no longer has the power it once did. The linearity of sermons had better be deceptive.

It was not historical happenstance that the founder of modern, urban revivalism was a lawyer trained in the art of logics. Charles G. Finney used to move thousands to tears and the altar by some of the most intricately reasoned and brilliantly argued sermons ever preached in America. We read these sermons from the Second Great Awakening today, and they leave us cold. Why? Because in a visual culture, the people are visually literate. We think more in terms of concrete images than abstract ideas. The reason that has power in a visual culture is the reason that is fashioned by and formulated into images and metaphors.

This is not to make the case for the Romantic era over the Enlightenment. It is, however, to deny the distinction between reason and emotion, between *muthos* and *logos*, or myth and logic. We must go beyond those who decry myth as illogical—go beyond even those like Levi-Strauss who see myth having a logical structure all its own—and realize the significance of Marcel Detienne's work on pre-Classical Greece, recently translated into English, that demonstrates conclusively that the very distinction between *muthos* and *logos* is a not-so-felicitous fiction invented in Greece by Thucydides and Plato and carelessly picked up by modern theorists.[56]

What makes the cultural change of mediatization so absolute is that it reinforces organic predispositions. It takes the brain longer to process and read a digital watch than an analog watch. The left brain is digital; the right brain processes an analog. The digital is math, logic; the analog is symbol, pattern, image. The mind responds quicker to image than to logic.

Poets and religious thinkers have sensed this idea intuitively from the beginning of time. Why do people follow various pied pipers who are blatantly charlatans, crooks, cranks, and crackpots? The poet Yeats answered the question in his own life, writing that he preferred "the violent expression of error to the reasonable expression of truth." G. K. Chesterton said that he distrusted anything that could not be told in stories or colored pictures. One of William Blake's ubiquitous visions insisted on the supremacy of the symbolic over the scientific:

> What it will be Questioned When the Sun rises
> Do you not see a round Disc of fire somewhat like
> a guinea, O no no I see an Innumerable company of
> the Heavenly host crying Holy Holy Holy is the
> Lord God Almighty.[57]

JESUS' PARABOLIC PREACHING STYLE ~ The greatest exponent of images, metaphors, and animations was Jesus himself. Metaphors and animations were more than oases so his listeners, and we readers, would keep on the journey. They *were* the journey.

The communication style of Jesus was a narrative style in which the truth lies in the telling, literally. That telling was dominated by mental pictures that conveyed more than words. Jesus taught in parables, analogies, figures of speech, and startling metaphors to stir the sediment of people's hearts and open their eyes to the deeper meanings of life. We now know that Jesus' aphorisms, metaphors, and parables were the ballast, not the bubbles of his teaching. For Jesus, anecdotes were antidotes, healing balms that detoxified life. Read no further than the gospel of John and its rapid succession of "I am" images. Or go from the beginning of the Bible to its ending in a bewildering dazzle of images and symbols.

The two best definitions of Jesus' parabolic preaching style are these: first, a parable is a narrative metaphor; second, a parable is fuzzy logic. Paul Ricoeur has shown us that parables combine metaphoric process with narrative form.

In other words, a parable is a narrative metaphor grounded in experience and carrying heavy symbolic cargo.[58]

Religious leadership in postmodern culture is a symbolic activity. We snickered and jeered at former President Reagan, who couldn't remember facts to save his life, who never could put two logical sentences together, who was the last person in the world even his friends would call a mental giant. Yet no one snickers and jeers at his skill as a storyteller. This President will go down in history for moving and governing this nation, defining controversial policies, and twisting the arms of the Congress through his skill and mastery at creating compelling images that moved and bound people. He is the best 20th-century example of a political leader who knew the root meaning of the word *communication:* to bring together in one. If you doubt the power of parables in postmodern culture, stop at your local bookstore, order a double tall split skinny wet cap, and chase it with one helping of *Chicken Soup for the Soul.* Some 27 million of these books of parables have already sold, with no slackening of appetite in sight.

> In the wonderful word of television, anything is compatible with anything else. The one continuity is discontinuity. The flow resembles that of a mountain stream, complete with white water. What kind of social education, what type of character formation, occurs when there are so many stories and each one is constantly interrupted, is soon over, and flows immediately into an unrelated story that, in turn, is swallowed up by the next? In an earlier era, even the uneducated American could know well, and reflect upon a small stock of stories—in particular, the Bible and Shakespeare.
>
> Todd Gitlin[59]

The church is now faced with the challenge of helping postmoderns to think and feel again through metaphor. Religious leaders who will best build up the body of Christ are those who can image forth the Christian life and imagize prayer. By this I mean generate memorable images, provide people with an array of metaphors that testify to meaningful relationships between word and experience, and root out the images by which people live and die.

METAPHOR IS METAMORPHOSIS ~ George Steiner says that "metaphors can kill." He points to Hitler for proof.[60] "Norma" is my glass-case exhibit.

Norma was an archetypal church treasurer—tight-fisted, bitter, distant, cranky, intimidating. Even I was afraid to approach her. Then, after years of being Norma's pastor, I discovered something that no one else in the church knew: She had lost a child in infancy. On the anniversary of the child's death, I called on her and revealed my knowledge of her whole story. She seemed relieved that I knew. I then asked her how she had dealt with her only daughter's death, and why she didn't let anyone know about it. Norma replied, "Someone told me something I'll never forget. It's the only thing that makes sense. They said, 'Sometimes God gets tired of having faded roses around all the time. Sometimes God wants to smell little rosebuds instead.'"

Horrified at this image of God, I first said nothing. But I began working with Norma to get her to see God in new images, through new lenses. I soon came to understand for the first time in my ministry that metaphor is metamorphosis. Once I realized that my people were receiving their sense of life and death from images and metaphors, and that my ministry was to help them grasp life-enhancing images by which to live and face death, I began to see ways of healing people through images and emotion.

Metaphor is metamorphosis because animations create illusions. They redraw the map; they put boundaries in different places; they free people from destructive patterns of belief and behavior. Metaphors function in life the way what scientists call "Strange Attractors" function in physics: These singularities bring order out of chaos, organize the conscious mind, provoke rational faculties, and engender survival skills.

> Images are ... bridges thrown out towards an invisible shore.[62]
>
> Carl Jung

"A world ends when its metaphor has died," says a poem by Archibald MacLeish.[61] The world of an abusive God ended for Norma when her rosebud metaphor died.

WHAT THE REMOTE HATH WROUGHT ~ The issue in education (or worship) is not one of "dumbing down" or "slacking off" or "I'm entitled" or "microsecond attention spans." The issue is the wiring and firing of neurons. There is a postmodern sensibilty[63] in which new logics and logistics, new accessing and processing of information, apply in a world wired for instant communication.

My 22nd-century kids are natives of the Net. I am a naturalized citizen of the Net.[64] Their brains are wired differently from mine, although mine is being rewired all the time. The more the neurosciences tell us about the brain, the more we understand how "neural networks" are shaped by cultural and technological contexts. In earlier periods of history the cerebral circuitry was different, necessitating ways of knowing marked by remembering, then critical thinking.

The new *terra incognita* of human-computer symbiosis is what happens to people's brains (and human organizations) when computers disappear into the background through voice recognition and become invisible ("ubicomp"). What then?

The cerebral circuitry of postmoderns is different from yours and mine. A new "sensorium"[65] and circuitry of consciousness has been created by electronic culture. This does not mean we no longer need memorization skills.[66]

Nor does it mean we can jettison critical thinking skills. God did not put us through the last 500 years for no reason. A future that doesn't stare down the past is no future. But what it does mean is that the neural habitat for post-moderns is what some have called "curvilinear logic," others the "sigmoid curve,"[67] others "modulating."

As long ago as 1980, German scholar Frederic Vester[68] did work on the thinking of cybernetics, which is radically different from Aristotelian logic that connects cause and effect in straight lines. Cybernetic thinking operates in circular motions, or "closed control loops" where causes become effects and effects causes and where one can enter the loop from any entry point. Reasoning now takes place, not in logical, linear fashion, but through a series of links and a multitude of connections, juxtapositions, and adjacencies.

> Cells that fire together
> wire together.
>
> Neurobiological axiom

Postmoderns can't draw a straight line. This is good news, as the mind does not work in linear but in spiralic fashion. Throw a ball and catch it: That's ministry in the modern world. Now let loose an inflated balloon and catch it: That's ministry in the postmodern world. Life is no longer a billiard ball/cause-and-effect/straight-lined world (if it really was). Life is an inflated balloon/ricochet-around-the-room/loopy world.[69] It is the character of chaotic, high-dimensional, complex systems like the weather, the economy, and the stock market to be loopy. Of the 20 students who received theoretical physics doctorates from Stanford between 1989 and 1994, only two or three are still in physics. The majority of the others are trying to beat financial markets.[70]

If the culture is *thinking* in "control loops," what does it mean to *communicate* in "control loops?" Well, what do you think Jesus was doing when he said, "Want to be first? Be last. Want to be greatest? Be least. Want to find yourself? Lose yourself" (see Matt. 16:24–26). Here is Loop Theology at its highest, a hermeneutic circle in which mutual processes of interaction with the environment and subsequent modification customize discipleship into the image of Christ.

If postmodern rationality is post-linear, postmodern "literacy" is the literacy of cyberscapes, or what I call "graphicacy." Just as Sunday school was designed to bridge the worlds of the rich and the poor through "literacy training," what if postmodern Sunday schools were to bridge the economic chasms of your community and teach computer skills and graphicacy training?

GET LOOPED — MOVE STORYTELLING FROM CONSECUTIVE/LINEAR TO CONCURRENT/FIELD ~ ꟿ the big debate was between the inductive styles of narrative storytelling (á la Fred Craddock) and deductive models of sermon delivery. Postmodern storytelling is a plague on both houses; it is *ab*ductive—concurrent, stacked, loopy, nonsequential, and image-based.

The church has yet to discover the abduction methodology of Charles Sanders Peirce, the towering philosopher of the 20th century. Some have called him "the American Aristotle." But in contrast to Aristotle as the master of "points" and "propositions," Peirce is the master of images and metaphors. What Peirce has done in philosophy, George Lakoff and Mark Johnson have done in cognitive linguistics. "The conceptual systems of cultures and religions are metaphorical in nature."[71] Or, "the most fundamental values in a culture will be coherent with the metaphorical structure of the most fundamental concepts in the culture."[72]

Joseph R. Jeter Jr., who distinguishes between "image-based sermons" and "traditional sermon illustration," gets right to the "point": "It makes little difference whether we move *from* the point (deductive) or *toward* the point (inductive)—the illustration still functions in service of the proposition."[73]

[I]Wak my brothers and I sat glued to the screen and watched *Bonanza* and *The Millionaire* (my favorite show—I'm still listening for that knock). We were able to sit still and follow a one-hour linear, consecutive, sequential narrative. *Laugh-In* and *M.A.S.H.* changed all that. Now when I turn on *Chicago Hope, E.R.,* and *The Practice,* I am watching stacked narratives, stories lasting no longer than three to four minutes that loop in and out of each other in spiralic fashion.

Have you tried watching some of those old shows in reruns? It's not easy. It's like going back to a typewriter after working on a PC for years. When Harold Brodkey tried to return to a typewriter, he confessed, "It's h_____. Nobody's mind works that way."[74] Marshall McLuhan argued that print media *created* our sequential, linear ways of thinking. It was the technology of print itself that made us label, classify, list, become detached. Electronics is making us look at the world in more natural, organic, less unitary ways.

Hypertext is the narrative mode and model of postmodern culture. Whether this is "the biggest upheaval in narrative form since written language itself," in hypertext the text is composed of light rather than ink; the reader shapes the story with the author; there is movable text instead of movable type, as the text won't stay still and can't be seen in its entirety. Without beginnings, middles, or ends, the same text is never read twice the same way.[75] There is no one right way through the hypertext; there are many best ways.

No wonder some are giving this genre of cyborg textuality—including hypertext narratives, collaborative Internet texts such as MUDs, computer games, etc.—a new name: "ergodic literature."[76] Nonlinear interactive electronic literature is already taught by more than 40 colleges.[77] But it is available to the church through the American Bible Society's CD-ROM electronic translations of the Bible, where there are trapdoors in and out of the story of the Gerasene demoniac, you can switch from "healing" to "pig" with the click of a mouse, and categories are "hotlinked" to one another in an instant of time.[78] As I experienced the Bible this way for the first time, I was struck by how medieval it felt: Medieval illuminated manuscripts were prototypes of hypertext, replete with extensive, artistic marginalia, collaborative authorships, multivocal interactivity, and multiple links between thought and image.

TALK IN CIRCLES — MOVE FROM "IN ROWS" TO "IN THE ROUND" ~

Circles are the basic forms of creation—whether in the macro world of stars, planets, and galaxies or in the micro world of cells, atoms, and DNA. In the apostolic period, the circle symbolized the infinite mystery of the universe.

By the time we moved from the apostolic to ancient to medieval to modern period, the circle had been squared. The modern world was heavily linear and hierarchical in all its forms—from rows of seats bolted to the floor facing a singular power podium, to power pyramids and boxy skyscrapers that dominate urban landscapes. The square, which some have called "the most artificial of shapes," is symbolic of the modern quest for quantification and abstract reasoning. In the modern world people got a "square meal," a "square deal," got things "straight," and gave it to each other "straight."

Postmodern culture has given up squaring the circle and has started circling the square. After thousands of years, the exact value of *pi* (the ratio of the circumference of a circle to its diameter) is still a mystery. Even the computer can't fathom the mystery of the circle. In July 1997 a Japanese scientist spent 29 hours on a Hitachi SR2201 and gave up after 51.5 billion decimal places.[79] Postmoderns bring the circle and the square together in ellipses, spirals, and spins. They have come to terms with the fact that *pi* is, like much of life, an irrational and transcendental number.

Note how everything now is being designed to be rotund, globular, and curved? Straight ends and lines are out. Look at the Bose Wave radio. Rounded objects have appeal—mobile phones, fax machines, TVs, VCRs, even Ford Tauruses are reflecting this new shape. In fact, this book, like my earlier *Quantum Spirituality,* is written in somewhat of a circle: It ends up where it began.

GET OVER IT — THE PENTECOSTALS AND EASTERN ORTHODOX/EPISCOPALIANS HAVE WON ~

The church is preoccupied with problems of meaning when the culture is very little concerned with meaning. What preoccupies pomo culture is the quest for experience, especially experiences with a purpose, and the reveling in full sensory immersion rituals, signs, and symbols that connect to the divine.

Not meaning but purpose in life is the key to pomo self-identity.[80] People are looking for primal experience. People long for the mystery and mysticism of an encounter with God and expect the church to help them get in touch with their experiences. Hence the growth of primal spiritualities like Pentecostalism, the fastest-growing and most important religious movement of the 20th century.[81] Pentecostalism has grown from 3.7 million at the turn of the century to around 450 million today, with a growth rate of about 20 million per year. Much of the growth has occurred in Latin America, Africa, Asia (especially Korea), and North America. Several Latin American countries are approaching Pentecostal majorities. About 25% of the world's Christians are Pentecostal or charismatic.

Harvey Cox, who has studied this Pentecostalization of Christianity, says we have an "ecstasy deficit." He argues that the attraction of drugs "in a culture that doesn't provide this in a religious setting is that people find a kind of pseudo-ecstasy. But chanting, fasting, mantras, music, meditation, and prayer can also create altered states of consciousness."[82]

Sociologist Donald E. Miller, in his study of "a new paradigm of church" that is revolutionizing American Protestantism, has found that although places like Calvary Chapel, Vineyard Christian Fellowship, and Hope Chapel have electronified worship, "One reason for the growth of new paradigm groups is that their organizational form enables people to experience the sacred more directly than is possible through the more pyramidal and reified forms of the mainline church."[83] It matters less whether the churches are highly liturgical or highly informal, according to Miller's study. "The question is whether the people, including the clergy, are having life-transforming experiences in worship. Are these churches, and their clergy, mediating deeply moving experiences of the divine?"[84]

What would happen if we truly expected that in worship someone was going to be transformed? What joy if we *really believed* in the transforming power of God's presence in worship? What difference would it make if worshipers could expect in worship to come to "*know Christ*" and "experience the power of his resurrection" (Phil. 3:10 NEB)? What if we, the worshiping subjects, positioned ourselves to be constituted in and through worship?

The two groups who have the greatest mastery of EPIC (Experiential, Participatory, Interactive, Communal) worship are the Pentecostals and the Eastern Orthodox.

What happens in an Episcopal church? The first thing you do upon entering is kneel in the aisles and gesture. As soon as you find your pew, you get back down on your knees and gesture some more. The entire service finds the worshiper getting up and down, gesturing, interacting, and responding antiphonally to the liturgist. No Episcopal service ends without an altar call, and the majority of the congregation streams down the aisle and kneels and prays at the altar.

What goes on at Pentecostal worship? The same thing. Not necessarily the same movements and gestures, but movements and gestures nonetheless. We could say that the Episcopalians are the realist worship artists, the Pentecostals the abstract artists. Neither Episcopalians nor Pentecostals do sit-and-soak worship. They don't countenance pew potatoes. They engage in highly experiential, interactive, participatory, communal worship.

Why is Eastern Orthodoxy growing—among evangelicals, among Busters, among nonethnics? The English composer John Tavener has become a convert to the Orthodox church—not just because it is an "Eastern" version of Christianity, though that has something to do with it, but because in the Orthodox church one doesn't come to church to understand God, but to encounter God and be united with God. The Eucharist itself invites everyone present to become a "participant."

The Eastern church has understood better than the Western that the fastest way to reach the emotions is through smell.[85] Postmoderns want a God they can feel, taste, touch, hear, and smell—a full sensory immersion in the divine.

EMOTION WORK — CAN YOU FEEL IT? ~ If the church is to reach postmoderns, it must come to terms with mood and emotion. The modern world wanted little to do with emotions. Huxley called emotions "the sticky overflowings of the heart," as if synonymous with syrupy sentimentality. The modern era aimed to produce deep thinkers. It feared strong feelings and maligned those who blubbed into their handkerchiefs. It found all sorts of numbing agents to ward off feelings.

In postmodern culture, feelings are as important as thoughts. Deep feeling is as important as deep thinking.[86] Emotion work leaves people not just thinking differently but feeling differently. The postmodern challenge of theology is not to help people "think critically," but to both "feel critically" and "think creatively."

In fact, feelings now constitute a key mode of experiencing life, and they are key to our storytelling. Miss Manners received a letter from the parents of a seven-year-old boy. They refused to let him visit an injured friend because they believed his motives were more to see his friend's injuries than to visit a friend in need. Miss Manners voiced her objections to the parents' decision in a section of her book entitled "When Form Precedes Feeling."

> Miss Manners disagrees with your decision not to allow your child to visit his friend because his motives were not noble. Send him off with strict instructions to pretend to be sympathetic with the illness, but apparently not unduly curious. (Some interest in the nature of the illness is usually agreeable to patients.) Perhaps his sympathies will truly be aroused.
>
> In the event of a worst-case scenario—the child's motives were not changed—"he still will have done better by his friend than he would have by ignoring the friend. Form comes first . . . and while one hopes that feeling will follow, going through the form well without it is more acceptable . . . than eschewing the form because the feeling is not there.[87]

Emotions often follow motions, even when the motions are merely those of form.

KINESTHETIC WORSHIP ~ The Protestant Reformation transformed popular worship. The Postmodern Reformation is also transforming popular worship.

Preachers must learn how to body forth their sermons. When reaching postmoderns, it's not enough to know how to "write sermons." One must now learn how to create experiences—or more accurately, work collaboratively with a team to construct spaces in which the Holy Spirit can create authentic experiences of God. That's why music is more important to worship than ever before. The Protestant Reformation spread through hymn-singing. The Postmodern Reformation is spreading through praise music and other forms of spiritual songs and hymns (which British historian Ian Bradley calls aptly "the folk songs of the church").[88]

The modern church has been too sparing in its liturgical excitements. Folk theologian/philosopher/storyteller Garrison Keillor contends that "if you can't go to church and, for at least a moment, be given transcendence; if you can't go to church and pass briefly from this life into the next; then I can't see why anyone should go. Just a brief moment of transcendence causes you to come out of church a changed person."[89] If people leave church and haven't encountered God, what have we accomplished?

Few would disagree with the need to encounter God. But many would disagree on what it takes for postmoderns to experience "transcendence." Worship is the art of transcendence-releasing. The smaller question is, Can you release transcendence in a burst or bubble? The larger question is, Can you deliver an experience? The frontiers of worship lie in helping postmoderns move, breathe deeply, express emotion, and touch the divine. Postmodern leaders create in the church and especially in worship an "experience economy."

I learned in seminary how to craft sermons. I am learning now how to craft experiences. These experiences are more than a pew rub, more a body-and-soul rub. To "get real" means to "get physical" and "get spiritual" at the same time. Postmodern preachers are visual poets, experts in kinetic and kinesthetic worship where bodily knowings are acknowledged and affirmed.

Many attention-deficit-disorder kids are really multiple kinesthetics: postmodern, electronic kids who learn not through lockstep, lecture-drill-test marches of the Industrial Age but through multisensory webs of stimulation and inspiration.

Virtual Reality is itself being forced into tactile, interactive directions. It is not enough to put on passive gloves and helmet and body suit. There must be a more interactive relationship between the person and the computer. In other words, all the senses must be present for an authentic virtual experience, even the sense of touch.

Hence the emerging field of "haptics," coined from the ancient Greek *haptein*, which means to hold fast or to bind. Haptics makes physical interaction with virtual environments possible. Through both tactile feedback and force feedback—the former providing a sense of touch and the latter muscular resistance—haptic interfaces transfer motor commands from the user into sensations of touch back to the user. The field of haptic virtual reality is growing, and its companies are prime investment opportunities of the future.

Modernist production churches that cling to sit-and-soak worship are not understanding the hands-on character of the future. "In fact, for worship in the 21st century," write Bill Easum and Thomas Bandy, "if you can say it all with words, you've missed the point!"[90] Experiential worship is enactive worship; it requires the use of the body.

In postmodern worship there is more liturgy, pageantry, creed recitation, vestments, use of spectacle, and gestures, not less.[91]

Postmodern spirituality is somatic. It values the body as an expression and experience of aliveness and attunement.

Worship is bodywork as well as mindwork and soulwork.

"Hands-off" worship where the congregants treat each other as untouchables may have been possible in the modern world. Not now. Postmoderns relish physicality and relax with it. They are more in tune with the informal nature of early Christian worship without abandoning the highly formal nature of later Christian worship.

FIRE-AND-ICE WORSHIP ~ Bring the emotional fire of the Pentecostals and the intellectual ice of the Orthodox/Episcopalians together.

But be careful.

A man is in a hardware store and sees on a shelf an item he does not recognize. He stares at it for a while until a clerk approaches and asks if he can offer any assistance.

"What is that thing?" asks the man.

"It's a vacuum bottle."

"And what does it do?"

"It keeps hot food hot and cold food cold."

"What a great idea!" says the man. "I'll take one."

The next day at lunch, the man proudly displays his purchase to his co-workers. "This is my new vacuum bottle," he tells them. "It keeps hot foods hot and cold food cold."

"What a great idea," says one friend. "So what are you having for lunch today?"

"Chili and Jell-O."

ELECTRICIANS ~ Beat poet Bob Kaufman called saxophonist Charlie Parker "an electrician" because the musician "went around wiring people." He meant not only that Parker's music had "electricity" (shocking and exciting), but also that Parker was an energy source, connecting people to power supplies they knew not of.[92]

Postmodern evangelists are electricians—they go around wiring people to the Spirit, getting them connected to holy energies. The power of connectedness is this: The more connections there are in a system, and the greater the strength in those connections, the greater the intelligence and the greater the consciousness. This is called neural-net technology. It might also be called neural-net ecclesiology.

What if the church were to sponsor the real Power Lunches and Power Breakfasts—times that connect people to the Real Power?

Electricians who specialize qualify as explosives experts. This is the essence of postmodern preaching: to help the Scriptures go off in people's lives. Preaching is as related to biblical awareness as "Toe Poppers" and "Bouncing Betties" were to the land mines of the Vietnam war.

> Those in the power given to praying for the pastor are like poles which hold up the wires along which the electric current runs. They are not the power, neither are they the specific agents in making the Word of the Lord effective. But they hold up the wires upon which the divine power runs to the hearts of men."
>
> Pastor/Confederate Army Chaplain
> E. M. Bounds[93]

The NY Yankees had a slogan a few years ago: "At any moment, a great moment." Electricians help people make holy moments, holy memories, and holy meaning. Making moments, memories, and meaning is the fiber of the Spirit's webbing.

DON'T AMUSE, BUT DO "EDUTAIN" ~ An experience culture is easily amused. That word *amusement* comes from *a* ("not") and *muse* ("to ponder"). Literally, *amusement* means "not to ponder"—which is the problem with amusement. There is no evaluation, no critical faculty, no judgment. Amusement is the dominant ideology of postmodern culture.

Entertain, don't amuse. Do not be afraid to add to education the component of "entertain"—hence the monstrous word "edutainment." Moderns have serious problems with that word *entertain*. No modern leader likes to be seen as an entertainer, or doing entertainment.

Entertainment literally means "holding the attention of." You don't want to be an "entertainer"? You don't want to "hold the attention of" your people? You don't want to be a "crowd pleaser"? You want to antagonize, alienate, displease your congregation?

We "entertain" people in our homes all the time. We judge hosts on how well they have "entertained" or hosted us. We are the hosts of God's house; we had better know how to "entertain" postmoderns in God's house.

HOT MISSIONS ~ HOT politics is what Wade Clark Roof calls a "politics of the spirit," which he sees exemplified best in the "Hands Across LA" chain of bodies that spanned all theological and doctrinal distinctives. Political action for postmoderns is involvement in small, community-based initiatives—such as the Christian Community Development Association based in Chicago, Illinois, and Jackson, Mississippi, which builds networks among the plethora of Christian groups working in community development.[94]

HOT missions are what lie behind the success of ministries like Habitat for Humanity, Pax Christi, Hospice, and Bread for the World. Missions are changing from sending-money to mission-sending agencies, to personal involvement in mission projects and local initiatives.[95] Can your church partner with a local travel agency to combine adventure tours with mission projects? Spirituality-based camps that integrate mission projects into the experience are like catnip to postmoderns.

> It's all very well in practice, but will it work in theory?
>
> French management saying

TELLING LI[V]ES — FROM EXCELLENCE TO AUTHENTICITY, FROM PERFORMANCE TO REALNESS ~ [96] Even though "virtual" realities are becoming more real than reality itself, postmoderns want the real. They're tired of "virtual life." They aren't into "performances." They want the real thing.[97] Look at our booming outdoor activities or the new socializations in coffee bars, brew pubs, block parties, and ethnic festivals. The rage in musical recordings is "living room records," defined as "a collection of songs so intimate and telling that it's hard to imagine them being performed as much as being *shared*."[98] No wonder one author talks about "the return of the real"— in art and theory.[99]

Part of postmodern authenticity is unpackaging, unplugging, deprocessing: Always tell the truth. You don't always have to tell the whole truth. Do you really think anyone believes you when you ask to be excused from the table to "powder your nose"? Worship leaders at Hillsongs Australia made a compilation of their past songs. It is raw, underproduced, and recorded in a small church where you can hear, if you listen closely enough, congregation members singing off-key.[100]

But to "get real" in postmodern terms means to "get spiritual," not "get physical." To "get real" in 21-C does not mean to "Show Me the Money" or "Help Me Make Money" but "Show Me the Way" or "Help me Make Life."

Cyberspace (a "consensual hallucination," according to William Gibson, who coined the term) should never replace life in the real world. Part of the Postmodern Reformation church's message is that real life is more interesting and more important than anything you'll find on a screen or in a headset. There are a lot of people for whom online community is an upgrading of their social life. The church can do better.

We must not be afraid to announce that it is time to turn the computer off, just like the TV. The computer is not to master us; we are to master it. Sometimes you log-on; sometimes you go on foot. But mainly, you go EPIC. The church must go EPIC.

AN EPIC CHURCH: EXPERIENTIAL, PARTICIPATORY, INTERACTIVE, COMMUNAL ~ *Experiential.* The Way is not a method or a map. The Way is an experience. Postmodern leaders are experience architects.

In the modern world, explanation came to substitute for experience. The church in mission to postmodern culture must leverage spirituality out of the rational crack the modern world has wedged it into—wedged it so hard, in fact, that

> Board broken. Message inside.
>
> A church's outdoor sign

the last place anyone today expects to have a religious experience is in church. Who among postmoderns can say that they found in worship the most luminous and liberating experiences of their lives?

Postmoderns don't come to worship for something to believe in. They believe in everything and anything. When a British insurance firm offered coverage for alien impregnation called "Virgin Birth by Act of God," 300 women signed up the first week to pay $3 a week with the possibility of collecting $1.5 million if she were impregnated by an "Act of God."

Postmoderns don't even come to church "to explore three words, 'Is it true?'"[101] Postmoderns come to church to explore "Is it real?" When postmoderns say "Get real," they don't mean "Prove it!" and they don't mean "Give me the Truth." They mean "Give me an experience, and then I'll see whether or not I believe it." For something to be real, it doesn't need to be proven—only experienced. Logic neither convicts nor convinces—only the experience of a faith that "works" and "plays."

> For many years now I have taken to going to church less and less because I find so little there of what I hunger for. It is a sense of the presence of God that I hunger for.
>
> Theologian/author
> Frederick Buechner[102]

Try-before-you-buy postmoderns will not first find the meaning of faith in Christ and then participate in the life of the church. Rather, they will participate first and then discern the meaning of faith. Truths about Christ must first be "lived" before they can be embraced. If postmodern souls are to be dense with being, they first pass through the delectations of experience. Or, in the words of the Jewish theologian Abraham Heschel, "First we sing. Then we believe."

The good news is that truths do not need to be proven before they can be believed. Invitation to discipleship is not made through propositions or arguments, but with feelings, moods, music, and energy.

Postmodern preaching draws fewer conclusions than it does entertain possibilities. It is the preaching of departures, beckonings, thresholds . . . to a people On The Way.

Participatory. The late Mickey Mantle was once asked what kind of compensation he would have demanded had he played in today's era of super-sized salaries. The Mick said, "I'd have knocked on the owner's door and said, 'Howdy, partner.'"

The Protestant Reformation notion of the "priesthood of all believers" (see 2 Cor. 3:6; 1 Peter 2:5, 9) was a doctrine that stubbornly refused to grow in the modern world.

It is now time to disestablish the clergy in the church once and for all.

Postmodern culture is an "age of participation," an "age of access." The modern world was an "age of representation," its goal to "represent" to the people "the best that has been thought and said" (Matthew Arnold). The postmodern world is a karaoke world. Peter Greenaway films (*The Draughtsman, Prospero, The Baby of Macon*) specialize in demonstrating the inadequacy of any representation (whether maps, films, or men and women) to embody and do justice to the reality.

Alas, the economic world is far ahead of the church in transitioning from representation to participation. The participative customer-focused organization has been the watchword of the business world since the 1980s. The three biggest developments in management theory in the past 15 years, according to Harvard's Rosabeth Moss Kanter, have all been a means of coming to terms with an ethic of participation: (1) customer-focus, (2) employee involvement, and (3) partnerships with other companies.[103]

Kids have already shifted from representation to participation, and corporate America knows it. H. J. Heinz asked America's children to create new labels for its ketchup bottles; Crayola has asked children to help design some of its new products; Levi Strauss & Co. has a 500-kid Trend Advisory Panel called "cool consultants."

If the business world is finding out that it's not "put customer first," but "put people first," why can't the church learn to put people before program? For too long people have been on behalf of program. "Communication" does not mean delivering a message. It means "to make common to many," to evoke a common experience, "to participate." True communication and participation are more synonymous than we ever imagined.

> In some strange sense, this is a participatory universe.
>
> Physicist John Wheeler

The degree to which postmodern culture has gone karaoke can be seen in the television shows we are now watching. We have gone from soaps to talk shows, from *Candid Camera* to *America's Funniest Home Videos*, from *Dragnet* to *COPS*, from *Emergency* to *911*, from *Ozzie and Harriet* to MTV's *Real People,* from *Gunsmoke* to *America's Most Wanted.*

Are any of your kids making a video diary? Everyman/Everywoman is making their own movies, with them as star (much as book diaries were in early print eras). When my first child was born, I couldn't get anywhere near the hospital delivery room. A bunch of us had to fret in a "Father's Waiting Room." With my only daughter's birth, who showed up 11 weeks early, I stood by my wife during her Caesarean surgery. At some hospitals, relatives are being allowed into emergency treatment rooms during resuscitation attempts.

> Information retrieval is not about finding out how much tannin there is in an apple. It's about letting everyone publish.
>
> Wide Area Information Services founder Brewster Kahle[104]

Who are the traffic patrolers that keep more and more cities alert to emerging commuter difficulties? Commuters themselves. Listen in to San Francisco's KGO's "Newstalk" on 810 sometime. Steven Rosenbaum's Broadcast News Networks (BNN) is founded on the belief that viewers want to be active participants in what they watch. "Put someone in front of a TV and they're a couch potato," Rosenbaum says. "Put a camera in their hands and they're a storyteller."[105] Here's an entire news company that owns only one Betacam. By deprofessionalizing storytelling and making it first person, they encourage viewers to pick up their digital video (DV) cameras and take over TV. MTV was the first to hire Rosenbaum to put on the consumer-as-producer model "MTV News UNfiltered." CBS's cable channel features them in the series "I-Witness."

Every professional guild is being turned on its ivory-towered head by this wave of participation. In fact, the best definition of leadership I know of comes from Max De Pree, chair and CEO of Herman Miller: A leader is someone who develops other leaders. Or to put it in his words, "The signs of outstanding leadership appear primarily among the followers. Are they reaching their potential? Are they learning?"[106]

The key distinguishing characteristic of the "new paradigm church" that is revolutionizing religion in America, according to Donald E. Miller, is "the level of lay involvement in leadership and program development."[107] Lay empowerment is not some kind of "pastor dust" (Martie Cladis) you sprinkle on folks and suddenly they become a minister. The church must create a learning environment in which ministries can be embraced and explored.

> They put us on a pedestal, and we like the view.
>
> Pastoral counselor Stuart Rothberg

Who are the basic caregivers of the church? In the words of church consultants Bill Easum and Thomas Bandy, "The transition from congregations dependent upon clergy for pastoral care and leadership, to congregations that rely on gifted, called, and equipped laity for pastoral care and leadership, is the greater paradigm shift that lies behind the growth of cell groups."[108]

But the larger issue here is not one of "clergy" and "laity." The Postmodern Reformation church will once and for all abolish the laity.[109] Of course, in saying that, I have also said something else: The Postmodern Reformation church will once and for all abolish the clergy. There is no biblical ordering of the church into "clergy" and "laity." Only "ministers," which one becomes at one's baptism, and those set apart and ordained for the "equipping of the saints" for their ministries.

Paul did not have a firm ranking or final number of ministries. In fact, there is an almost unlimited variety of ministerial functionings. In Romans 12:6–8 there is one list; in 1 Corinthians 12:28 there is another; in 1 Corinthians 12:7–11 still another; in Ephesians 4:7, 11–12 one more. We find in the Scriptures references to *episkopoi* (bishops), *presbyteroi* (elders), and *diakononi* (deacons), but they are never mentioned in the same place.

> To sum up, my friends: when you meet for worship, each of you contributes ...
>
> The apostle Paul
> (1 Corinthians 14:26 NEB)

The people want in. They want out of the bleachers and onto the court. This does not mean the ordained give up long-term involvements in people's lives. But those involvements take place with sacramentally significant days and ways—baptize youth, officiate at weddings, confirm children, and so on. Moreover, the ordained did not relinquish their baptismal consecration into ministry when the body set them apart to educate and empower the people for ministry.

3. Interactive. One of the biggest lies ever foisted on us is the notion that electronic culture creates "couch potatoes," "vidiots," and passive people. The truth is exactly the opposite. Electronic culture stimulates activity and interactivity, not passivity.

Postmodern is another name for *interactive everything*. We have even made soda cans and candy bars interactive—with toll-free numbers and Web site addresses where you can talk to the manufacturer. Microsoft is investing $400 million in interactive media development for a reason. Interactive Technology is enabling and enhancing an Interactive Society. Part of the appeal of the casino culture is the interactivity of its games.

Televisions are on for longer hours, and people are paying less attention to it than ever before. The sets are on, but the eyes are off. The audience for children's network television is plummeting; in 1997 alone, network TV ratings for children's programming declined by as much as 61%, according to Nielsen Media Research. More Net-Gens say they could get by without a TV than say they could get by without a computer.[110] If any generation has come to have a head the shape of a television, it is the Boosters.

Kids make things that aren't interactive, interactive. Notice how they watch television. When Barney is on, they're not "glued" to the screen; they're in front of it dancing and fencing and doing whatever it is Barney and friends are doing. When I couldn't watch the final NBA championship game with my son Thane, I made him promise he'd watch it for me. My phone call awoke him the next morning, and he told me what an exciting game it was. I asked what happened in the final seconds with Michael Jordan.

He said, "Sorry, dad, I missed it."

"But I thought you said you watched the game!"

"I did," he insisted. "But that's when I was out on the deck shooting baskets."

Thane couldn't even watch basketball without making the game interactive.

One day I asked Thane's older brother to give me his opinion of some of the 11,000 United Methodist and 10,000 Southern Baptist Web sites. Justin clicked onto one and announced, "Dad, this is not a Web site." He clicked onto another and made the same pronouncement. After a dozen or so visits to "Not-a-Web-site" Web sites, I insisted he tell me in words I could understand why these Web sites weren't Web sites.

After some struggle, he said, "Because nothing moves."

"So what?"

"Dad, I can't see it if it doesn't move."

Interactive learning[111] is to postmoderns what blackboard-based, lecture-drill-test methods of learning were to moderns. I grew up in a learning style in which you didn't "do it" until you "got it right." Then after much trial and error on your own, you finally "did it." Interactive learning prizes "do it" experimentation, trial and success, enterprise, and making do with whatever you've got to work with. In the culture of the screen, one first learns by doing rather than by rote or rules.

Games are usually how we get introduced to a new technology—how we first let it into our homes. Our children are growing up with interactive games (videogames, computer games) the way we grew up with blackboards and our parents grew up with "Old Maid" and marbles. Videogames and computer games bring music, art, and narrative together into one of the highest aesthetic forms of postmodern culture.

Thane knows more about the human body at his age than I do at mine, thanks to a *Magic School Bus* CD-ROM game that teaches physiology through game learning (Thane is partial to the liver game; his best friend Merrick likes the kidney game). When we played the "Operation" game. Remember that red plastic saw and the red light? Thane plays a game and says, "Let's take it up to the next level. Make it harder." I don't ever remember saying, "Give me another worksheet; make it harder."

Our museums are doing better than our schools and churches in pioneering some of the best forms of interactivity out there. Visit the Museum of Science in Boston. Its Leonardo da Vinci exhibit[112] boasted 13 different interactive stations where visitors could explore Leonardo's life and work through hands-on, multimedia, and multi-sensory interactivity. Unfortunately, our churches are even further behind our schools in claiming interactive learning for our children. As many as 50% of teachers have little or no experience at all with interactive classroom technology; only 18 states require technology training for teacher certification as of this writing.[113]

> Tell me, and I will forget,
> Show me, and I may not remember.
> Involve me, and I will understand.
>
> Native American proverb

How many interactive learning instruments is your church offering its 22nd-century kids? We've always known that interactivity increases retention, which is why people like humor so much. Humor is by nature interactive, which is the secret of comedy's ability to "turn ha-ha into aha."[114] I love what children's ministries specialist Philip Schroeder says about his work with children in worship. "I usually provide the plank for us to walk off and let the sea do the rest." I cannot think of a better definition of interactive worship than that.

A HOT church is an interactive medium between two worlds.

4. Communal. There is a legend that at the entrance to heaven, two questions will be asked of everyone seeking admittance. The first is, "Did you come alone?" If your answer is yes, the second question is, "How could you?"

One of the rarest things in the cosmos is a soliton—a chronically solitary particle which remains unaffected even when it collides with another. According to the scientific evidence, God made only a handful of solitons in the entire universe. Humans are not one of them.

The declining quality of human relationships makes people yearn for community all the more. Opportunities for personal contact in American life are diminishing. It is increasingly difficult to have personal relationships with each person in your life—bank tellers, mail carriers, shoe repairers, dry cleaners. We've already lost paperboys, telephone operators, door-to-door salespeople. A TV crew recently filmed an actress, posing as an elderly woman, falling down in a variety of street locations. It took only two minutes for someone in a village to come to her aid, compared with 45 minutes in an urban shopping mall.

The relational anorexia of postmodern culture[115] was brought home to me during a time when I was away from my family for three weeks and almost constantly on the road. I found myself actually looking forward to and finding comfort in the sound of Sprint's double-ring "thank you" beeps when you input your PIN. I was so lonely once, I dialed home, knowing no one was there, just to hear the electronic "thank you." Roper Starch Worldwide polled USAmericans on how many friends, excluding family members, they had seen in the past two weeks. In 1983 the median number was 5.4. In 1995 the median number was 4.0. That's more than a 20% drop.[116] More than 70% of pastors claim to be without a single friend.

In the midst of a culture of communal anorexia, there is a deepening desire for a life filled with friends, community, service, and creative and spiritual growth. The church must provide its people with a moral code, a vision of what gives life value, and an experience of embeddedness in a community to which one makes valuable contributions. Personal relationships are key in postmodern ministry. Can the church foster close, supportive, confiding, confining relationships? When Jesus completed most of the training of his disciples, like parents training their children, he announced their commencement by graduating them to the status of "friends" (John 15:15).

> I can never be what I ought to be
> Until you are what you ought to be
> And you can never be what you
>   ought to be
> Until I am what I ought to be.
> This is the interrelated structure of
>   reality.
>
> Martin Luther King Jr.
> at Drew University

The church must help people build a communal life full of deep and rich personal relationships. This is one reason that performance- and program-based ministries are being turned into relational cell-based ministries all over the globe.[117] This is especially how postmodern youth are being reached—not through big concerts, but small groups and clubbing. The number one issue of Gen-Xers is in fact, "I want to have a relationship with God. But I don't know how."

When Ezra Earl Jones, General Secretary of the Board of Discipleship, asks laypeople in the United Methodist church this question—"What's working?"—the top five responses are these: (1) Emmaus; (2) Disciple Bible Study; (3) Covenant Discipleship and other small group experiences; (4) VIM—Volunteer in Missions; (5) Camping. What's the common denominator? All of them are relation-based.

A HOT Christian will be an "entrenched transactor"—that's banking jargon for people who refuse to stop using the more expensive human tellers. We will use ATMs and automatic checkouts at the supermarket, but every chance we can get we will make a financial transaction at the checkout counter into a personal relationship of trust and compassion.

> Don't judge a life good or
> bad before it ends.
>
> Sophocles

Postmodern leadership requires HOT skills—the ability to pamper people, to make them feel important, to make them laugh, to build community, to give them the personal touches that are the "my pleasure" signatures of Ritz-Carlton.

A HOT church will superconnect its people, stimulating and shaping an online community that is as vibrant and vital as its physical community. A HOT church will take up the challenge of creating Christ-body communities in cyberspace and make the Web a gathering place for Christians. Intimacy used to be experienced in love feasts, class meetings, and camp meetings. The cyberspace equivalents of these are only now being discovered. A survey found that, by a two-to-one ratio, "superted" people—those who regularly exchange e-mail and use a laptop, cell phone, beeper, and home computer—would rather stick with one employer for 20 years than have five jobs for four years each.[118] Postmodern loyalty comes to those who enable superconnectedness—"access of everyone to everyone, everything to everything, and everything to everyone," as Watts Wacker and Jim Taylor put it.[119]

Finally, part of the communal experience is the establishment of healthy artisan relationships with objects. Creative pastors such as J. Ellsworth Kalas have always found ways to highlight their people's artisanship and creativity through special weekends of displays. Gallery your people's collections in a room dedicated to that end—whether their collections be pigs or frogs, rocks or clocks. Every church needs a special room set apart for the display of its people's artisan relationships.

TWO EPIC PARABLES ~ Two parables tell the story of an Experiential, Participatory, Interactive, and Communal culture. They are from real life, from your life, from the most opposed proposed memorial in America and the most famous traffic accident in history. Hear what they might be telling us about ministry in a postmodern culture.

EPIC Parable 1. In 1980 President Carter signed a bill that provided the land for a Vietnam memorial monument, funded by private sources. A nationwide panel of architects, designers, and academics was created to jury the design competition. There were 1,421 entries to the competition, but the unanimous winner of the commission was an architect/sculptor/student at Yale University named Maya Ying Lin. Still in her 20s, Lin proposed for the Vietnam Veterans Memorial a mirrorlike wall of black granite that never rises above ground level. In chronological order of death there would be engraved on this geode the roll call of deceased soldiers, with every name beckoning you to touch it and in reaching see reflected your own image in the polished granite. "I believe in the touch of the human hand," Lin explained.[120]

When Maya Lin's design was first unveiled, the backlash took everyone by surprise. One veteran called it "a black gash of shame." Tim Carhart, a member of the Vietnam Veterans Memorial Fund (VVMF), called it "the most insulting and demeaning memorial to our experience that was possible," a "degrading ditch" whose black color said it all: "Black is the universal color of shame, sorrow, and degradation in all races, all societies worldwide." Of Chinese descent, Lin took hits like "How could they let a gook design this memorial?" Even activist Phyllis Schlafly took swipes at it, calling it "a tribute to Jane Fonda"[121]—the actress who expressed her protest by visiting North Vietnam during the war.

Writers who had been Vietnam veterans also attacked it. Al Santoli called it "a place to go and be depressed." James H. Webb Jr. used the *Wall Street Journal* as a platform to announce his resignation from the National Sponsoring Committee of the Vietnam Veterans Memorial Fund because of the "travesty," the "denigration," the "rubbing of the world's face into the grisly shame of the deaths" and a "nihilistic statement that does not render honor to those who served."[122]

Businessman Ross Perot and former White House aide Pat Buchanan in particular rose to support the veterans who opposed Lin's design. Besides being black and abstract, the memorial didn't hoist a flag.[123] Buchanan alleged that the selection panel was infiltrated by Communists. Perot called the memorial "a slap in the face" and funded a poll of 587 ex-POWs to show that the majority of them didn't want Lin's design.[124]

Secretary of the Interior James Watt entered the fray and formed an ad hoc committee to reach a compromise. The committee's solution was to authorize the commissioning of a second memorial. A panel consisting entirely of Vietnam veterans selected the entry of architect Frederick Hart. His monument, "The Three Servicemen," was a traditional, oversized, representative statue of three soldiers much more in keeping with the Marine Corps Monument, with its bronze soldiers raising the flag over Iwo Jima, except this time what was stressed was not triumph but vulnerability and camaraderie.

Hart explained the difference between his "populist" statue and Lin's "elitist" statue: "People say you can bring what you want to Lin's memorial. But I call that brown bag esthetics. I mean you better bring something, because there ain't nothing being served."[125] Hart was paid $200,000 for his design; Lin had received $20,000 for hers.

For more than three years the fight raged over these two memorials. First critics tried to dismantle the competition process. When that didn't work, they tried to block construction of the winner. When that failed, they attempted to install what they were sure would become *the* memorial—Hart's representative statue.

Lin's memorial was unveiled and dedicated on November 13, 1982. Veterans groups didn't want her to be at the dedication service; not wishing to cause trouble, she hid out in the press box.[126]

Maya Lin fought the concept of a "second" memorial, or what some were calling the "real memorial." When it became clear that the issue had become such a political hot potato that the only way to get Lin's sculpture built was to put in the other one, the question was where.

Opponents wanted it placed in the vortex of the V-shaped wall, with a flag stuck on top. In a moving speech before the government commission, Lin stood her ground and refused to change her design. Finally Lin agreed to this compromise: Go ahead and install the Hart's representative statue near the entrance to the memorial site; but don't invade the wall's space and give people enough space to experience, participate, and interact with my monument. And so Hart's work was placed on the memorial site on Veterans Day 1983.

The outpouring of emotion that greeted Maya Lin's memorial continues to this day. It has become USAmerica's version of a wailing wall. It has done more to heal the oozing wounds of the Vietnam War than any other single thing. The Vietnam Veterans Memorial Collection now contains more than 250,000 items, artifacts, and mementos left behind by pilgrims to the wall. Ironically, Lin's greatest critics have now become her greatest fans. Vietnam vets now see her as one of them, and every major veterans group has passed resolutions either apologizing for their earlier treatment of her, or thanking her for hanging in there when their own members mercilessly attacked her.

Have you been to the Vietnam Memorial? Did you even know there was a second "Vietnam Memorial"? How many people did you see there? A handful at best? That offers an image for your church if you don't transition to EPIC ministry.

EPIC Parable 2. What killed Princess Diana (besides sin)? What was the major contributing factor to her death? What really killed her?

I watched her memorial service along with a good slice of planet Earth. We never knew her. We never spoke to her. We never heard her speak. We never read a word she wrote. What were *we* doing at her funeral?

I had a better excuse than you did. As a historian, I told myself, I was witnessing history. Who would have predicted you and I would live through an English revolution? Yet we did. Of course, there was no Cromwell or a king's head rolling to the floor. But the British people brought the monarchy down, at least as far down as its knees. The monarchy capitulated to every one of the people's demands. As the Queen admitted through clenched teeth, the monarchy agreed to change its arrogant ways and be more accessible to the commoners, and in return it got a good-behavior lease on life in the emerging culture. A bloodless revolution, but a revolution nonetheless.

Then it hit. What was at the heart of the Dianamania phenomenon? You and I are now living in a world where, for the first time in history, there are "global" celebrities—individuals who for one reason or another have ignited the interest of people from a majority of the world's cultures, languages, and countries. As the walls of flowers got higher, and the online waits to sign her memorial book got longer, it became obvious that Princess Diana was one of these. The entire world was fascinated by this princess, and we couldn't get enough of her. We could not stop participating in her life. You and I literally loved her to death.

Not me, you say! Really? I confess: I can remember times when I actually chose the longer checkout lines at supermarkets to have more time to scan the rag racks. I don't confess to ever buying one of those filthy gossip magazines, but I do remember once picking one up. Its Princess Diana headlines obstructed by the rack's bar, with ice-tongs for fingers I lifted up the magazine high enough to see and then dropped it back down.

Once the only person to speak at funerals was a clergyman. Participation was limited to the organist and sometimes a soloist. On rare occasions someone besides the priest would read the Scripture, but basically it was a ritual presided over by the person who gave the memorial meditation and eulogy as one.

What speech do you remember being delivered at Princess Diana's funeral? You found the Archbishop of Canterbury's homily riveting, didn't you? Hello?! Like most funerals today, the memorable moments come from those members of the family who are increasingly eager to participate in the service. And that is why something happened at this memorial service for Princess Diana that had never occurred in the long history of worship at Westminster Abbey. It wasn't after Lord Spencer's speech. But after rock singer Elton John offered his gift of song in celebration of "England's Rose," centuries of tradition were broken. The people clapped. Remember? It started from outside. And the people inside couldn't resist the wave of the future. It wasn't just the British monarchy that couldn't resist becoming more EPIC. The Church of England was hit by the EPIC tidal wave, and it too changed.

THE LAST WORD — GOD'S EXPERIENCE OF US ～ In an experience economy, what poet Les Murray calls "eventless experience" becomes all too easy. The purpose and meaning of the experiences we have make a world of difference. Journalist Pete Hamil likes to point out that the market may be giving people what it wants, but so, too, does a Colombian cartel.[127]

What ultimately matters in life is not our experience of God, but God's experience of us. In all the postmodern rush to perceive the sublime and experience the divine, the church must point people beyond our experience of God to the God of our experience and then to God's experience of us. One day we will hear one of two things—the best thing we could ever hear, or the worst thing.

The best? "Welcome! Well done! Your life has brought me great pleasure" (see Mark 1:11).

The worst? "Depart from me! Your life has brought me no pleasure." (see Heb. 10:38).

Here are the hottest words the church can teach postmoderns to say or pray: "Please God." Unless these two words "Please God" are put together, without a comma between them, heaven remains heaven, and earth earth.

> A perfect Judge will read each work of Wit
> With the same Spirit that its Author writ.
>
> Alexander Pope (1711)[128]

say what? 1. How pivotal are surround sound systems in the new church? If music must be felt even more than heard, shouldn't money that was once spent on pipe organs be redirected to audio and video systems?

2. Discuss Bill Easum and Thomas Bandy's argument that the integration of images into worship will be one of the most time-consuming parts of worship. "Tech rehearsals must replace choir practices. . . . Tech rehearsals will be needed due to the many technical issues involved in integrating the visuals with the songs, announcements, dramas, interviews, conversation pieces, and any other part of the service. Worship teams will include graphic artists and audio technicians."[129]

3. Dennis Shock, pastor at the Churubusco United Methodist Church in Indiana, relates,

> I was visiting a 99-year-old woman in the nursing home, the mother of one of our parishioners, and she indicated she wanted to join our church because her little country church had closed and she had no church home. I said it would be no problem, and returned shortly, gave her the vows in the nursing home, and gave her Communion. Then I arranged for her granddaughter to videotape her testimony. The following Sunday I announced we had a new member, and I wanted the congregation to meet her. Our screen came down, and we projected our newest member (Eva Egolf) offering her testimony. People were mesmerized as Eva narrated her involvement with the church over the years from teaching infants to teaching the "old people" (laughter), and now not being able to do much besides pray. She ended: "And now I'm happy to have a new church. Thank you for having me." The congregation applauded the video. Eva has since turned 100 and, thanks to technology, still feels a part of our church even though she cannot get out to worship with us.

Could you do this in your church?

4. Explore a copy of the magazine *Storytelling* (423-753-2171), a trade journal for the emerging profession of storytellers who are already being widely used in schools, libraries, and story-telling festivals. Find out who in your church are the storytellers, and ask them to share some of their stories.

5. Rent the video of Jim Henson's TV program *The Storyteller*. What wisdom is being conveyed through these nine folktales? Should the primary mission of storytelling be amusement, entertainment, or wisdom keeping?

6. The percentages of US households with electronic products, as of 1995:[130]

Television: 98%	Computer printers: 34%
Home radios: 98%	Camcorders: 23%
Telephones (corded): 96%	Cellular telephones: 21%

VCRs: 88%	Computers with CD-ROM: 19%
Answering machines: 60%	Modems: 16%
Telephones (cordless): 59%	Caller ID devices: 10%
Home CD players: 48%	Home fax machines: 8%
Personal computers: 40%	Laserdisc players: 2%

Changes have been dramatic in just two years since the survey. For example, camcorders in 1997 were in 1 out of every 4 US households, up from 1 in every 5 three years ago, 1 in every 10 five years ago.[131] What other changes do you see happening to make this 1995 survey dated?

7. In back-to-back fashion, listen to a piece of classical music (such as Beethoven's *Fifth Symphony)* and an example of "ambient" music (such as Tom Vedvik's *Slowdiver* [Malibu, CA: CyberOctave Music, 1996]). Describe and discuss the difference in music that is designed to produce sound and music that is designed to produce an experience.

8. Climb up a mountain in the night and reach the top at dawn.

9. What shapes the life of your church—meetings or memories? Meetings issue forth more meetings. Only experiences issue forth memories. Can you think of one meeting that promotes a more vital faith among your people?

10. Get a copy of the Leadership Training Network (LTN) *Starter Kit for Mobilizing Ministry.* Call 1-800-765-5323, ext. 104. Web site is www.leadnet.org.

11. Use the Native American tradition of the "talking stick" to discuss one of the above questions. First, get in a "talking circle," where there is no top or bottom, first or last, better or worse. Then pass around a "talking stick" with the understanding that whoever holds the stick can speak for as long as he or she wishes, while everyone else listens with respect and attention. Native American leader Manitonquat, who conducts monthly "talking circles" in prison sweat lodges all over the country, says that the cardinal rule of the talking stick is that "no one will interrupt, and no one will argue with a previous speaker, or with any other individual. You respect him by listening and keeping your mind open to hear his words, as well as to feel his heart and what lies behind the words. Each person holding the talking stick is asked only to be honest."[132]

12. Have someone read and review Rudolf Otto's book *The Idea of the Holy,* which was first published in 1917.[133] Why might theologians have dismissed his ideas so readily earlier in the century? Are there some perspectives here that might be useful in this experience economy?

13. Read and review any or all of these three books on the power of touch: Christine Caldwell, ed., *Getting in Touch: The Guide to New Body-Centered Therapies* (Wheaton, IL: Quest Books, 1997); Mariana Caplan, *Untouched: The Need for Genuine Affection in an Impersonal World* (Prescott, AZ: Hohm Press, 1998); and Ashley Montagu, *Touching: The Human Significance of the Skin* (New York: Perennial Library, 1986). Did Jesus have a touch ministry?

14. What is your church doing to un-stuff people's lives? Listen to and discuss Sinead O'Connor's song, "I Do Not Want What I Haven't Got." (on the album of the same name [New York: Ensign Records, 1990]).

15. Gather a group to attend the National Storytelling Festival in Jonesborough, TN. At its 25th anniversary in October 1997, more than 12,000 paid to join in the festivities.[134] Or, if you can't send a delegation, hire one of the 500 people who work full-time as "tellers," or ask a member of one of the 300 storytelling organizations that is nearest you to give a "telling" to your group.

16. G. K. Chesterton once said that "mankind doesn't need art, what he needs is stories." Is he right? Is there a difference? Are stories not an art form, and storytelling an artistry? What influence do you think Jesus' artistry in wood and stone had on his artistry as one of history's greatest storytellers?

17. In the entire repertoire of Rolling Stones discography, there is only one song about Jesus. It is called "Just Wanna See His Face" and was written by Mick Jagger and Keith Richards. Listen to it on the CD *Exile on Main St.* (Beverly Hills, CA: Virgin, 1994). Do you agree with their contention that there are sometimes when "you don't want to walk and talk about Jesus,/You just want to see His face./You don't want to walk and talk about Jesus,/You just want to see His face"? Are postmoderns more interested in the talk, the walk, or "seeing his face"?

18. Have someone read and review Ivan Illich's *In the Vineyard of the Text* (Chicago: Univ. of Chicago Press: 1993). It tells the story of a 12th-century monk, Hugh of St. Victor, who experienced the art of reading in very different ways from us. For him, reading was a way of life. Each word, says Illich, was like a grape picked from the monastery vineyard. Reading from line to line was a spiritual experience as well as a physical experience. To the extent that the university is a place of learning that revolves around the book, to what extent is the university dead? To what extent does your church revolve around the book?

19. The best introduction to emerging brain research is Sharon Begley's outstanding article called "Your Child's Brain" (*Newsweek* [19 Feb. 1996]: 55–62). Get copies of it for your cell to read and discuss.

Research in neurobiology demonstrates how at the level of nerve cells and molecules the brain's circuits form from the experiences of childhood. A person's "perceptual map" (which neurons your brain uses) is "programmed" into your brain by childhood experiences as a "programmer" works at a keyboard inputting into a computer. The brain has 100 trillion connections. Only the main circuits are determined by genes, the rest by the environment.

Furthermore, once the brain has been hardwired, there are "critical periods" or "time limits" or "windows of opportunity" that "nature flings open, starting before birth, and then slams shut, one by one, with every additional candle on the child's birthday cake." There are different auditory maps, and that is why some children are "functionally deaf to sounds absent from their native tongue," an auditory map that is virtually completed by the first birthday. "By 12 months," says Patricia Kuhl of the University of Washington, "infants have lost the ability to discriminate sounds that are not significant in their language, and their babbling has acquired the sound of their language." That's why learning a second language after the first rather than with the first is so difficult. Yet we wait until junior or senior high to teach a second language, after the "windows" are closed.

The cortical map shapes our sound life. Music trains the brain for higher forms of thinking, especially mathematics. Hence the "Mozart Effect"—the idea that the earlier you train the child musically, the higher the child's ability to reason. The emotional map is one of the hardest to rewire, as the emotional circuits harden quick and firm. Almost all the brain's windows close before we're through elementary school. "Children whose neural circuits are not stimulated before kindergarten are never going to be what they could have been."[135]

Discuss the implications of all this for the way you do children's ministry. What about "spiritual windows"? To what extent does your curriculum for infants and children integrate our new understanding of how the brain works?

20. List your church's relationship ministries. Where are the strengths and weaknesses?

21. For the best postmodern children's learning curriculum available, see Group Publishing's "Hands-On Bible Curriculum." Their box of gizmos called the "Learning Lab" takes out-of-the-box thinking literally. (Group Publishing, 1515 Cascade Avenue, P.O. Box 481, Loveland, CO 80538; telephone: 800-447-1070; e-mail: innovatr@grouppublishing.com.)

22. Have someone bring an EPI-Pen to your group. What is the function of an EPI-Pen? It provides emergency medication for life-threatening allergic reactions. What does "EPI" stand for? What if "EPI" were seen as an acronym for "Experiential, Participatory, Interactive"? What ministries in your church need a shot of EPI? Is there any ministry you can think of that doesn't need an injection?

23. Rent Freida Lee Mock's 1994 Academy Award-winning feature-length documentary *Maya Lin: A Strong Clear Vision* (Santa Monica, CA: Sanders and Mock Productions, 1995), about Maya Lin's work on the Vietnam Veterans Memorial.

24. Have a competition to see who can come up with the longest list of nonlinear design appliances, stereos, etc. Somebody in your church may even have Microsoft's "Natural Keyboard," which was introduced in October 1994. It looks like a wave, with palm rests, split keyboards for comfort, and built in supports. It was designed in cooperation with the University of California—San Francisco Ergonomics Laboratory and retails for about $100.

25. Gregory Wolfe, publisher and editor of the journal *Image: A Journal of the arts and Religion,* argues that "Conservative Christians have become traumatized by the social changes of the 20th century. Unfortunately, these conservatives have failed to cultivate the arts and the intellectual life as a means of embodying their vision and persuading others that this vision is compassionate and just. Instead, they've retreated into a fortress mentality that is highly politicized and brittle."

Do you agree?

Take a little quiz: Do more USAmerican adults who enroll in universities choose courses in

_____ (a) creative writing, or (b) literature
_____ (a) more studio arts, or (b) art history
_____ (a) filmmaking, or (b) film criticism or cinema studies
_____ (a) performance or composition, or (b) music appreciation

In a culture of participation, option *a* would be the most preferable—which it is now, in every case.

26. For the story of Lutherans, Baptists, Pentecostals, and others leaving their denominations to become Eastern Orthodox, read and review Peter Gillquist, *Becoming Orthodox* (Ben Lomond, CA: Conciliar Press, 1992).

now what? See the Net Notes in http://www.soultsunami.com

NOTES

1. George Steiner, *Real Presences* (Chicago: Univ. of Chicago Press, 1989). Steiner would have us run from postmodern culture because he sees it as a sort of *Bucherdammerung.*

2. In Joseph Campbell and Bill Moyers, *The Power of Myth* (New York: Doubleday, 1988), Campbell defines the wasteland as "a land where everybody is living an inauthentic life, . . . doing as you're told, with no courage for your own life" (196), and "The world without spirit is a wasteland. . . . The thing to do is to bring life to it, and the only way to do that is to . . . become alive yourself" (149).

3. William S. Burroughs, "Last Words," *The New Yorker* (18 Aug 1997): 37.

4. Jean-Marie Guehenno, *The End of the Nation-State?* (Minneapolis: Univ. of Minnesota Press, 1995).

5. No wonder the commitment of high school students is "at an all-time low." So argues Laurence D. Steinberg in *Beyond the Classroom: Why School Reform Has Failed and What Parents Need to Do* (New York: Simon & Schuster, 1996). The vast majority of students call their studies "boring," and 40% of those interviewed say that they are "just going through the motions." More than one-third said they don't do assigned homework. Most appalling, more than half said that their parents wouldn't get upset if they brought home grades of C or worse. For a proposed remedy, see Lynn Olson, *The School-to-Work Revolution* (Reading, MA: Addison-Wesley, 1998).

6. Stephen L. Carter, *The Culture of Disbelief: How American Law and Politics Trivialize Religious Devotion* (New York: Doubleday, 1994), 41.

7. For more on the nature of a holographic universe, see my book *Quantum Spirituality* (Dayton, OH: Whaleprints, 1991). For a further description of the Bell Effect, see Ernest C. Lucas, "The 'New Science' and the Gospel," in *The Gospel in the Modern World: A Tribute to John Stott,* ed. Martyn Eden and David F. Wells (Downers Grove, IL: InterVarsity Press, 1991), 129.

8. This is the phrase of B. Joseph Pines II, author of *Mass Customization* (Boston: Harvard Business School Press, 1993). See also John Naisbitt, "Beyond the Service Economy," *John Naisbitt's Trend Letter* (15 Dec 1996): 1–4.

9. See Edith Weiner and Arnold Brown, *Insider's Guide to the Future* (New York: The Boardroom, 1997).

10. Naisbitt, "Beyond the Service Economy," 2.

11. Some 4000 retailers went kaput in the US in 1995, another 7000 in 1996.

12. As quoted in *Hemispheres* (Sept 1997): 36.

13. See Leonard Sweet, *FaithQuakes* (Nashville: Abingdon Press, 1994), 23.

14. In 1990 Americans were spending 12 hours less per month in a shopping mall than they were in 1980. In 1987, 16% of USAmericans said they shopped often at malls. In 1994 that number was down to 10%. Today the percentage is in single digits. The number who say they don't go to malls at all (24%) doubled in that same time frame (*Current Thoughts and Trends* [Sept 1994]: 4). In fact, one in three Boomers, the hard-core mallers, is going to the mall less frequently than a year ago (*The Boomer Report,* "Will Boomers Emerge from Their Cocoons?" [Apr 1996]: 1). See also the 1997 Maritz Marketing Research Ameripoll, as reproduced in "Shopping Mall Blues," *The Boomer Report* (Sept 1997): 6.

15. Susan Sontag, "Against Interpretation," in her *Against Interpretation, and Other Essays* (New York: Farrar, Straus & Giroux, 1966), 14.

16. Stewart M. Hoover, "Religion, Media, and The Center of Gravity," Unpublished address given to the foundation for United Methodist Communications (7 May 1998).

17. Rodger Streitmatter, *Unspeakable: The Rise of the Gay and Lesbian Press in America* (Boston: Faber & Faber, 1995).

18. Donna Haraway, *Simians, Cyborgs, and Women: The Reinvention of Nature* (New York: Routledge, 1991), 152.

19. J. Kevin Thompson, ed., *Body Image, Eating Disorders, and Obesity: An Integrative Guide for Assessment and Treatment* (Washington, DC: American Psychological Association, 1996), 177–223.

20. 6 July 1998.

21. Lyman Tower Sargent, ed., *Extremism in America* (New York: New York Univ. Press, 1995).

22. Michael L. Dertouzos, *What Will Be: How the New World of Information Will Change Our Lives* (San Francisco: HarperEdge, 1997), 201–2.

23. PHAST is an acronym for Practical Home Automation Systems Technology. The company's premier product is the PHAST Landmark System, a command and control of one's castle that functions as drawbridges and turrets did in the past.

24. According to American Business Information, a business-research organization.

25. Ray Oldenburg, *The Great Good Place: Cafés, Coffee Shops, Community Centers, Beauty Parlors, General Stores, Bars, Hangouts, and How They Get You Through the Day* (New York: Marlowe, 1997), 16.

26. The widely quoted figure is that one-third of all employees work at least part of the time out of their homes.

27. Howard Rheingold, *The Virtual Community: Homesteading on the Electric Frontier* (New York: Harper Perennial), 1994.

28. This amazing statistic I found buried in Brad Stone and Bronwyn Fryer, "The Keyboard Kids," *Newsweek* (8 June 1998): 72.

29. For a similar exchange quoted by Watts Wacker, see William C. Taylor, "What Comes After Success," *Fast Company* (Dec 1996-Jan 1997): 84.

30. Russell Miller, *Magnum: Fifty Years at the Front Line of History* (New York: Grove Press, 1998).

31. Ben Patterson, *Serving God: The Grand Essentials of Work and Worship* (Downers Grove, IL: InterVarsity Press, 1994), 57.

32. Jeffrey Kluger, "Love by the Line," *Discover* (Mar 1996): 42.

33. Two of T. Boone Pickens's former aides, David Batchelder and Ralph Whitworth, have started a new fund called "Relational Investors" to practice "relationship investing." What they do is buy 3-to-10% stakes in a midsize company and then work with management to make decisions in the interest of employees and shareholders rather than in management's interest (Seth Lubove, "The King Is Dead, Long Live the King," *Forbes* [15 July 1996]: 64).

34. Lyle Schaller makes a big deal of this change in "Twenty-One Changes for the 21st Century," *Clergy Journal* (Feb 1995): 44–46.

35. Mary Pipher, *The Shelter of Each Other: Rebuilding Our Families* (New York: Grosset/Putnam, 1997), 140.

36. The phrase comes from Reynolds Price, *A Whole New Life: An Illness and a Healing* (New York: Atheneum, 1994), 182.

37. For "un-stuffing" our lives, see John C. Ryan and Alan Thein Durning, *Stuff: The Secret Lives of Everyday Things* (Seattle: Northwest Environment Watch, 1997).

38. As quoted in *Details* (June 1997): 24.

39. The phrase is that of Mark S. Micale in "Strange Signs of the times," *TLS, Times Literary Supplement* (16 May 1997): 2.

40. W. H. Auden, "The Flight into Egypt," in his *For the Time Being* (New York: Random House, 1944), 132.

41. Albert Borgmann, *Crossing the Postmodern Divide* (Chicago: Univ. of Chicago Press, 1992).

43. Sociologist Wade Clark Roof, "God Is in the Details: Reflections on Religion's Public Presence in the United States in the Mid-1990s," *Sociology of Religion* 57 (1996): 149–62, 153.

44. Harvey Cox, *Fire from Heaven: The Rise of Pentecostal Spirituality and the Reshaping of Religion in the Twenty-first Century* (Reading, MA: Addison-Wesley, 1995), 319.

45. Of course, the modern approach to knowledge also known as critical reasoning is based on a concept of logic successively *disproved* by Frege, Russell, and Whitehead early in this century, and earlier by Wittgenstein (*Logico-Tractatus*), Kurt Godel ("Incompleteness Theorem"), Werner Heisenberg ("Uncertainty Principle"), by mathematical intuitionists Weyl and Brouwer, and long, long ago by Zeno.

46. Ved Mehta, *The New Theologian* (London: Weidenfeld and Nicolson, 1966), 172.

47. Jaroslav Pelikan, *The Melody of Theology* (Cambridge, MA: Harvard Univ. Press, 1988), 70.

48. As quoted in Martin Henry, *On Not Understanding God* (Dublin: Columba Press, 1997), 48.

49. Physicist Chet Raymo argues the equal importance of metaphor and mathematics in a scientist's training in *The Virgin and the Mousetrap* (New York: Viking, 1991), 178. For a preacher who is a master at exegeting images, although I'm not sure he knows exactly what he's doing and why he's doing it, see Robert Farrar Capon, especially his George Craig Stewart Lectures for 1996 at Seabury-Western Theological Seminary, *The Foolishness of Preaching* (Grand Rapids: Eerdmans, 1998).

50. I want to thank one of my doctoral students, Phil Schroeder of Atlanta, Georgia, for helping me formulate this distinction.

51. Thom and Joani Schultz, *Why Nobody Learns Much of Anything at Church: And How to Fix It* (Loveland, CO: Group Publishing, 1996), 251.

52. Lewis Carroll, *Alice's Adventures in Wonderland and Through the Looking Glass and What Alice Found There* (London: Oxford Univ. Press, 1971), 9.

53. Russell Lockhart, *Words as Eggs: Psyche in Language and Clinic* (Dallas: Spring Publications, 1983), 85–111; Gaston Bachelard, *The Poetics of Reverie*, trans. Daniel Russell (Boston: Beacon Press, 1969), 49.

54. Ezra Pound as quoted in the Introduction to *Poets on Painters: Essays in the Art of Painting by Twentieth-Century Poets*, ed. J. D. McClatchy (Berkeley: Univ. of California Press, 1988), xi.

55. Margaret R. Miles, *Image as Insight: Visual Understanding in Western Christianity and Secular Culture* (Boston: Beacon Press, 1985), 95; see also 95–118.

56. Marcel Detienne, *The Masters of Truth in Archaic Greece* (New York: Cambridge Univ, Press, 1996).

57. William Blake, "A Vision of the Last Judgment," in *The Complete Poetry and Prose of William Blake*, ed. David R. Erdman (Berkeley: Univ. of California Press, 1982), 566.

58. See Paul Ricoeur, "Biblical Hermeneutic," *Semeia* 4 (1975): 129–48.

59. Todd Gitlin, "Flat and Happy," *The Wilson Quarterly* (Autumn 1993): 52.

60. George Steiner,"The Scandal of Revelation," *Salmagundi* (Spring-Summer 1993): 68–70.

61. Archibald MacLeish, "Hypocrite Auteur," in his *New and Collected Poems, 1917–1976* (Boston: Houghton Mifflin, 1976), 415.

62. Carl G. Jung, "On the Relation of Analytical Psychology to Poetic Art," in *Contributions to Analytical Psychology*, trans. H. G. and Cary S. Baynes (New York: Harcourt Brace, 1928), 239.

63. John Leo, "No Books, Please, We're Students," *U. S. News & World Report* 121 (16 Oct 96): 24.

64. John Perry Barlow calls those of us over 30 "immigrants" of cyberspace. The image of "naturalized citizen" is that of Sherry Turkle, the chief anthropologist of cyberspace, who summarizes it like this: "The precedence of surface over depth, of simulation over the real, of play over seriousness" (as quoted in Pamela McCorduck, "Sex, Lies, and Avatars," *Wired* [Apr 1996]: 108). See also Turckle's *Life on the Screen: Identity in the Age of the Internet* (New York: Simon & Schuster, 1995).

65. See Walter Ong, *The Presence of the Word: Some Prolegomena for Cultural and Religious History* (Minneapolis: Univ. of Minnesota Press, 1967), 87–92.

66. The English philosopher John Locke proposed that I am what I remember myself being. There are some wonderful Bible memorization software programs available. Memory is more, not less important, in the future, as my kids remind me every time I marvel and wince at their ability at memorizing lyrics. An excellent case for memorization has been made by Milton J. Coalter, "The Craft of Christ: Imperfect Tailors," *Theology Today* 50 (Oct 1993): 387–96.

67. Charles Handy advocates this method of thinking for the business world in *The Age of Paradox* (Boston: Harvard Business School Press, 1994).

68. Frederic Vester, *Neuland des Denkens* (Stuttgart: Deutsche Verlags-Anstalt, 1980).

69. This is a favorite teaching device of complexity physicists like Doyne Farmer, as quoted by Kevin Kelly in *Out of Control: The Rise of Neo-Biological Civilization* (Reading, MA: Addison-Wesley, 1994), 421.

70. Kevin Kelly, "Cracking Wall Street," *Wired* (July 1994): 132.

71. George Lakoff and Mark Johnson, *Metaphors We Live By* (Chicago: Univ. of Chicago Press, 1980), 40.

72. Lakoff and Johnson, *Metaphors We Live By,* 22.

73. Joseph R. Jeter Jr., "Revelation-Based Preaching: Homiletical Approaches," in *Preaching Through the Apocalypse*, eds. Cornish R. Rogers and Joseph R. Jeter Jr. (St. Louis: Chalice Press, 1992), 19.

74. David Gates and Ray Sawhill, "Of Texts and Hypertexts," *Newsweek* (27 Feb 1995): 71–72.

75. Ford Maddox Ford's masterpiece *The Good Soldier* (New York: Vintage Books, 1951) is a narrative that moves backward and forward in time and earned a reputation for being unconventionally nonlinear 50 years ago.

76. Espen J. Aarseth, *Cybertext: Perspectives on Ergodic Literature* (Baltimore: Johns Hopkins, 1997).

77. Eastgate Systems of Watertown, MA, is pioneering publication of state-of-the-art hypertext fiction.

78. *Out of the Tombs: A Scripture Translation of Mark 5:1–20* (New York: American Bible Society, 1991), videocassette.

79. David Blatner, *The Joy of PI* (New York: Penguin Press, 1997).

80. An excellent beginning discussion of this phenomenon is Richard J. Leider, *The Power of Purpose: Creating Meaning in Your Life and Work* (San Francisco: Berrett-Koehler Publishers, 1997).

81. Gary Burge, "Are Evangelicals Missing God at Church?" *Christianity Today* (6 Oct 1997): 21–27.

82. Harvey Cox shows how and why Pentecostalism has become the fastest-growing religious movement in the world today. See his *Fire from Heaven,* 279.

83. Donald E. Miller, *Reinventing American Protestantism: Christianity in the New Millennium* (Berkeley: Univ. of California Press, 1997), 156.

84. Interview with Donald E. Miller in *Next* (Nov 1997): 4.

85. This is the contention of Dr. Alan R. Hirsch, founder of the Smell and Taste Treatment and Research Foundation in Chicago. See also *Sweet's SoulCafe* 3 (1997).

86. Robert H. Hopcke, *There Are No Accidents: Synchronicity and the Stories of Our Lives* (New York: Riverhead Books, 1997), 32.

87. Judith Martin, *Miss Manners' Guide to Rearing Perfect Children* (New York: Athenaeum, 1984), 322.

88. Ian Bradley, *Abide With Me: The World of Victorian Hymns* (London: GIA Publications, 1997), xvi. For the importance of music in this postmodern transition, see my "What Emmanuel Levinas and Bill and Gloria Gaither Have Taught Me About Prayer," *Sweet's SoulCafe* 3 (1998). Also see Leonard I. Sweet, *11 Genetic Gateways to a Spiritual Awakening* (Nashville: Abingdon Press, 1998), 154–69.

89. Garrison Keillor, "Door Interview: Garrison Keillor," *The Wittenburg Door* (Jan-Feb 1985): 16.

90. Bill Easum and Thomas Bandy, *Growing Spiritual Redwoods* (Nashville: Abingdon Press, 1997), 51.

91. See Tex Sample, *White Soul: Country Music, the Church, and Working Americans* (Nashville: Abingdon Press, 1996).

92. See Andrew Ross and Tricia Rose, eds., *Microphone Fiends: Youth Music and Youth Culture* (New York: Routledge, 1994), 25.

93. As quoted in *Current Thoughts and Trends* (Jan 1995): 26.

94. "Can Churches Save America?" *U. S. News & World Report* (9 Sept 1996): 46–53. The article describes some of the hands-on missions of America's congregations.

95. So says Bill O'Brien, executive director of Samford University's Global Center, as cited in *Baptists Today* (7 Nov 1996): 2.

96. With thanks to Alison Lee, *Realism and Power: Postmodern Fiction* (New York: Routledge, 1990), 29.

97. "Americans Out of Cocoon," *Trends Journal* 5 (Summer 1996): 1, 6.

98. Dwight Ozard, "Music Notes," *Prism* 4 (Mar-Apr 1997): 32.

99. Hal Foster, *The Return of the Real: The Avant-Garde at the End of the Century* (Cambridge, MA: MIT Press, 1997).

100. See Darlene Zschech, "I Believe the Promise" (LCMC/Integrity Music, 1998).

101. So insists my fellow church historian Martin E. Marty.

102. As quoted by John M. Buchanan, "Water to Wine," Fourth Presbyterian Church, Chicago (18 Jan 1998): 8.

103. Interview with Rosabeth Moss Kanter in *Soundview* (Oct 1997): 7.

104. Brewster Kahle in Steve G. Steinberg, "Seek and Ye Shall Find (Maybe)," *Wired* (May 1996): 182.

105. Rob Walker, "He's Making News—for the Future," *Fast Company* (Apr-May 1997): 42.

106. Max De Pree, *Leadership Is an Art* (New York: Doubleday, 1989), 10.

107. Miller, *Reinventing American Protestantism,* 15.

108. Easum and Bandy, *Growing Spiritual Redwoods,* 122.

109. For greater definition of what this means, see Sweet, *11 Genetic Gateways to Spiritual Awakening,* 116.

110. The poll was conducted by CNN and *USA Today,* as reported in *Newsweek* (8 June 1998): 72.

111. For an excellent brief summary of "interactive learning," see chapter 7 of Schultz and Schultz, *Why Nobody Learns Much of Anything at Church,* 179–94.

112. The exhibit entitled "Leonardo da Vinci: Scientist, Inventor, Artist" was on interactive display from 1 March through 1 September 1997.

113. William E. Rodrigues, "Raising the Bar, Lowering the Barriers," *Vital Speeches of the Day* 63 (1 Apr 1997): 376.

114. This is the mantra of Dr. Joel Goodman, director of the Humor Project, an organization based in Saratoga Springs, NY.

115. A frightening look into the future is Steven Levy, *Hackers* (New York: S. French, 1986), in which the dysfunctionality in personal relationships highlights almost every page.

116. *The Boomer Report* (Apr 1996): 8.

117. For more, see *CellChurch* magazine, published by Touch Ministries, founded by Ralph Neighbor and headed now by his son, Randall Neighbor. www.touchusa.org/cellchurch/.

118. The survey results are printed in John Katz, "The Digital Citizen: The Wired/Merrill Lynch Forum," *Wired* (Dec 1997): 68–82, 274–75.

119. Jim Taylor and Watts Wacker, "Speak the Future," *Wired* (June 1997): 100.

120. Charles Gandee, "The Other Side of Maya Lin," *Vogue* (1 Apr 1995): 403; see 346–53, 402–3.

121. Elizabeth Hess, "A Tale of Two Memorials," *Art in America* (Apr 1983): 121–26.

122. James H. Webb Jr., "Reassessing the Vietnam Veterans Memorial," *Wall Street Journal* (18 Dec 1981): 22.

123. For an "insider" view of the controversy, see Robert W. Doubek, "The Story of the Vietnam Veterans Memorial," *The Retired Officer* 39 (Nov 1983): 17–24.

124. Nicolaus Mills, "Architectural Politics: The Vietnam Memorial," *Dissent* 31 (Winter 1984): 24–26.

125. Elizabeth Hess, "An Interview with Frederick Hart" in Hess, "A Tale of Two Memorials," 124.

126. Gandee, "The Other Side of Maya Lin," 353.

127. Pete Hamil, "Crack and the Box," *Esquire* (May 1990): 64.

128. Alexander Pope, *Pope's Essays on Criticism,* ed., with introd. and notes by John Churton Collins (New York: Macmillan, 1896), 8.

129. Easum and Bandy, *Growing Spiritual Redwoods,* 71.

130. According to the Electronic Industries Association.

131. According to the Consumer Electronics Manufacturers Association (CEMA).

132. As quoted in *EarthLight* (Winter 1997–98): 9.

133. Rudolf Otto, *The Idea of the Holy: An Inquiry into the Non-Rational Factor in the Idea of the Divine and Its Relation to the Rational,* trans. John W. Harvey (New York: Oxford Univ. Press, 1958).

134. For the dates of the next National Storytelling Festival, contact the NSA at www.storynet.org or call 1-800-525-4514.

135. Sharon Begley, "Your Child's Brain," *Newsweek* (19 Feb 1996): 62.

WE INTERRUPT THIS BOOK TO DELIVER
AN IMPORTANT DOSE OF REALITY

A minister about to baptize a baby turned to the father and asked, "What is this child's name?" The father answered, "Justin Winthrop Charles Adam Lucius McWilliams." The minister then turned to the assistant and said, "A little more water, please."

When the lightning strikes and the thunder rolls, it's time to turn to God and say, "A little more water, please. A little more faith, thank you."

That time is now.

Biotechnology, genetic engineering, artificial life, bionic medicine, nano-technology—these are the flagship technologies of the 21st century. Post-modernity is a culture of unnatural acts and highly contrived processes. Scientists are now back to non-backroom conversations about "utopian eugenics." What was once unthinkable is now the usual.

Biotechnotopia is a world created through the synthesis of biology and technology. We are leaping into a new world biologically and technologi-cally. Yet we are crawling backward into the caves of an old world philosophically and spiri-tually. Technology is outrunning our theology and ethics, leaving us panting, helpless anachronisms. Whether it is the devilment or the divinity within human knowledge that is way ahead of human ethics and wisdom depends on us.

> Once we understand DNA, it will make the electronics revolution look like a flash in the pan.
>
> Geneticist Jim Ostell

Biotechnology is the fastest-growing industry in recorded history.[1] Nothing more need be said about why the powers that be refused to sign a biodiversity treaty at the 1992 Earth Summit in Rio De Janeiro. Very shortly the biotech industry will surpass the computer indus-try; by 2022 it will be a trillion-dollar business.

The awesome power of this emerging new molecular biology is hard to overestimate. "The new biology is now poised to move into the field, or the barnyard, or the home."[2] It can be seen in the reproductive revolution going on all around us. Issues of abortion, genetic engineering, euthanasia, designer genes (even "designer fetuses"), genetic surgery, and fetal tissue transplantations all are but faint and primitive signals of this biotechnological revolution in the making.[3]

It also can be seen in the development of DNA computers,[4] molecular computers, optical computers, and quantum computers. Nanotech computers and nanotech robots are being designed to work in tandem. To be cured of cancer, "swallow the surgeon," as Richard Feynman puts it.

Ed Regis, author of *Virus Ground Zero*[5] and an expert in biotechnology, was hired by the US Department of Defense as a consultant. He emerged from the Pentagon with deep creases in his brow "in the realization that some of the world's farthest-out, cutting-edge, and high-technodazzle biotech thinking was now being done not by scientists or academics, but by the military."[6]

Welcome to the future! It is at this point in our journey that we may be tempted to abandon altogether the search for a church that can be in mission to postmodern culture. But disciples of Jesus the Christ cannot just jump ship or abandon post. In the motto of the Coast Guard,

> You have to go out;
> You don't have to come back.

English cultural anthropologist Nigel Barley sums up the enterprise known as "fieldwork" on the last page of his "Notes from a Mud Hut." It's in the form of an exchange:

> "Ah, you're back."
>
> "Yes."
>
> "Was it boring?"
>
> "Yes."
>
> "Did you get very sick?"
>
> "Yes."
>
> "Did you bring back notes you can't make head or tail of and forget to ask all the important questions?"
>
> "Yes."
>
> "When are you going back?"[7]

Jesus did not call us to hug harbors. We're all in the Coast Guard. It's time to head out for the deep.

And deep the waters are.

NOTES

1. Michael W. Fox, *Superpigs and Wondercorn: The Brave New World of Biotechnology and Where It All May Lead* (New York: Lyons and Burford, 1992), 6.

2. Oliver Morton, "Overcoming Yuk: It May Be Unnatural, But Encouraging Genetic Choice in Humans Is Not All Bad," *Wired* (Jan 1998): 44.

3. An excellent preliminary look at this subject is J. Robert Nelson's *On the New Frontiers of Genetics and Religion* (Grand Rapids: Eerdmans, 1994).

4. Computer scientist Leonard Adelman (University of Southern California) solved complex mathematical problems using a DNA computer in 1994. Whereas silicon-based computers manipulate information through strings of zeros and ones, DNA computers manipulate information using strings of adenine, cytosine, guanine, and thymine—the four nucleotides that form DNA. The computer itself is a test-tube soup of DNA molecules. DNA-based computing means a trillion operations per second (a thousand times faster than the best supercomputers, a billion times more energy-efficient than conventional computers). For Adelman's own account of his biological computer, see his article "Molecular Computation of Solutions to Combinatorial Problems," *Science* (11 Nov 1994): 1021–24.

5. Ed Regis, *Virus Ground Zero* (New York: Pocket Books, 1996).

6. Ed Regis, "Bio War," *Wired* (Nov 1996): 153.

7. Nigel Barley, *The Innocent Anthropologist: Notes from a Mud Hut* (New York: Henry Holt, 1983), 190.

L ife ring #5

Get Bionomic

THE LOSS OF GENETIC INNOCENCE

or what?

What happens when the computer meets the gene? What happens when we turn "hardware" into "wetware" (biological life)?

Will we have crossed the Rubicon, opened Pandora's box, entered into a Faustian pact? We can't rebottle the genie, so we had better come to terms with the human itch to "try all things possible" (Francis Bacon).

"The line must be drawn *here*," says Jean-Luc Picard, master of the USS *Enterprise-E*, the best ship in Star Fleet. With these words he drew the line against the Borg, a race of cybernetic creatures that take over and morph every culture and species in the universe into one undifferentiated blob.[1]

Physics was the science of the 20th century. Biology is the science of the 21st century. Biology is the basic metaphor of the new civilization. The "biologizing" of life has only just begun.

FROM POLITICS TO BIONOMICS ~ In the modern era, the power paradigm was politics. In the postmodern era, the power paradigm is economics. The corporation is a key postmodern social form. To see how economics has taken over from politics, compare the financial sections of newspapers. I first remember them as being thin and sickly; now they are robust and thick.

To understand the power of economics in postmodern culture, think of the power of the church in the Middle Ages. Consider the power of the nation-state in the modern age. That's the power of the corporation in our world today.

You still don't believe me about the power of economic over political forces? Just $500 worth of cocaine or heroin in some place like Bolivia, Colombia, Peru, or Mexico will bring around $100,000 on the streets of any American city. Do you think any army in the world, much less law enforcement agencies, can intercept this flow? Hello?! It's a matter of economics.

Let's come at it another way. The gay and lesbian market stands at something over $500 billion. (Some say it's double that.) Like it or not, that's arguably a bigger market than the 15.6-million member Southern Baptist Convention. If a denomination decides to play the economic game and boycott Mickey Mouse, one must be prepared that the sanctions don't have the opposite effect and make you look ridiculous. Get your Donald Ducks in order before jumping off the deep end, church.

But here's the really hard part to get: Economics is becoming almost coincident with electronics. It costs $1 to process a check and 25 cents to handle

> You know, if this stuff were going to happen in a thousand years, I could regard it with some fond equanimity. But the thought that it could happen in 10 or 20 years makes me kind of nervous.
>
> A friend of mathematician/computer scientist Vernor Vinge[2]

a credit card transaction. Our choices for payment today may be cash, check, credit card, ATM direct debit card. But soon most every payment will be made electronically—money cards, "smart" cards, and virtual digital cash on the Internet (although we will never go totally "cashless," thanks to the IRS). The postmodern economy is based not on nuts and bolts or on bits-bites-bots, but on DNA and bioelectronics: hence "bionomics." After all, what is a gene but information?

BIONOMICS ~ Bionomics[3] is literally the merger of biological and economic theory, or the coming together of the world of the born and the world of the made. Everything is becoming more biological, even economic systems. Economics does not relate only to material progress or materialistic politics.

We have defined technology as anything that humans make. Premodern technology was integrated into nature. Modern technology distanced itself from nature. Postmodern technology once again is enveloped within nature— and that means biology. Technology now is not something separate from ourselves, but an extension of ourselves. The friendlier technology is to humans, the more biological it becomes.

We are creating things that behave as if they are alive: organically grown networks (like the Internet), with computers writing their own software. The old saying that a computer is only as smart as the person who programmed it is no longer true. It hasn't been true since 1987, when computer scientist John Holland first discovered that he could let computer programs evolve, which turn out to be better than human programmers but also beyond the comprehension and control of humans. Already we are flying on airlines that run on software that no human mind or human pilot can understand, much less control.

Kevin Kelly, executive editor of *Wired* magazine, has written an entire book showing that the more human-made things are becoming lifelike, the more life is becoming engineered.[4] In the words of "the Thomas Jefferson of the Internet," John Perry Barlow—also lyricist for the rock group Grateful Dead and cofounder of the Electronic Frontier Foundation, "We've spent the last two hundred years trying to turn people into machines, and we're going to spend the next two hundred years trying to turn machines into people."[6]

> The things that haven't been done before
> Are the tasks worth-while to-day;
> Are you one of the flock that follows, or
> Are you one that shall lead the way?
> Are you one of the timid souls that quail
> At the jeers of a doubting crew,
> Or dare you, whether you win or fail,
> Strike out for a goal that's new?
>
> Edgar Guest[5]

What does it mean that humans will now be able to control their own biology? In biology, including the biology of the unborn, there are not just biomaterials but biomining and bioelectronics—connecting biological neurons and microchips through something called "biochips."

HELLO, DOLLY ~ Dolly standing there, staring at us, is about as perfect a symbol of the emerging culture as we're going to get. First, Dolly's natural— just another sheep. Second, Dolly's unnatural—the first clone. The born and the made, nature and technology—a wolf in sheep's clothing?[7]

Of all the "boundary less" distinctions we have mentioned in this book, the most threatening of all by far are the dissolving distinctions between the born and the made, between human and machine, between nature and culture. Indeed, the transubstantiation of the made into the born, and vice versa, is one of the dominant features of postmodern life. Even species boundaries are dissolving and being breached. Doctors have transplanted a baboon heart into a human baby. Firefly genes have been transplanted into wheat, fish genes into corn, human genes into E. coli bacteria. No wonder the question of human identity will be one of the key issues in the future.

> We are, after all, giants—a modern American uses as many calories of energy each day as a sperm whale. But giant people possess giant brains, big enough to figure out ways around any of our problems.
>
> Essayist/naturalist Bill McKibben[8]

Remember how mad our ancestors got when they were told they were related to apes? How disturbed are you to be told that one day you may be related to the computer, a sibling of a biochip, or kin to other A-Life creatures?[9] At San Francisco's Advanced Communication Technology Laboratory, old-style "selves" with single skins like you and me are already being referred to as "BUGS"—body units grounded in a self.[10]

The new biology will challenge deeply ingrained assumptions about life, death, health, disease, personality, and personhood. Issues of death and dying are becoming enormously complex and socially problematic.

TECHNOLOGY 'R' US ~ We are at a crossroads in the definition of what is "human." Our upgrading through gene therapy, artificial organs, low-level eugenics, plastic surgery, and biotechnology is allowing people the ability to fashion themselves. The self is now a story that is continually being edited and revised. Philosopher Donna Haraway wrote in her 1985 "Manifesto for Cyborgs": "I would rather be a cyborg than a goddess."[11] Perhaps it is time to take seriously the Borg on *Star Trek*—that half-computer, half-human creature that symbolizes the ultimate cyborg (shorthand for cybernetic organism).

My preacher mom, Mabel Boggs Sweet, was a cyborg when she died. In fact, she had been living in cyborg reality for 10 years—ever since she received her pacemaker, which made her part human, part machine.

One could make a case for peg legs, hook arms, and eyeglasses creating the first cyborgs. But we leaped into cyborg space in 1953, the date of the first polio vaccination, and in 1958, when a human received the first heart pacemaker. Perhaps the first cyborgs were the bodybuilders, who are arguably more artificial than human; their mass is the result of vitamin supplementation. But if you have contact lenses, breast implants, a myoelectric arm, or a titanium alloy knee joint, you're also a cyborg.

French polymath Paul Virilio argues that there are "three industrial revolutions." The first industrial revolution (the Industrial Era) gave machines muscle and power. But machines needed human intelligence (ergo human operators) to give them a brain. The sound of the first industrial revolution was clanging steelworks.

The second industrial revolution (the Information Era) gave machines more than muscles and power. It also gave them intelligence and senses, producing less need for human operators. In the Information Era, the primary economic resources were no longer land or labor or capital, but knowledge. The culture's move from brawn to brain led Peter F. Drucker to call it a "postcapitalist" society.[12] A little belatedly, *Newsweek* devoted an entire issue to "the Big Bang of our time," or what it dubbed "the Bit Bang." The sound of the second industrial revolution is clicking keyboards.

The third industrial revolution (the Bionomic Era) brings together brain and biology. In the lifetime of our 22nd-century kids, silicon chips will be outmoded by DNA logic gates.[13] Biophysicists at the Naval Research Laboratory in Washington, working collaboratively with scientists at the National Institutes of Health and at the University of California–Irvine have reported that they have taken a "key first step toward creating electronic microchips that use living brain cells," according to the *Wall Street Journal*.[14] DNA (which stores information) and microchips (which process information) are now being combined, with the flow of information going from one to the other.[15]

Perhaps it's time to take a new look at the film *Blade Runner* (1982) and its population of "replicants"—robots that are almost indistinguishable from human beings. Have you noticed the steel-and-girder backgrounds to movies such as *Batman?* This industrial memory speaks of a yearning for "a world where the girders show" (Samuel Delany) in an electronic culture where everything is intangible. The sound of the third industrial revolution is the human voice ("Call home").[16]

The miniaturization of nanotechnology is virtually limitless. "In case I should be accused of exaggeration, it is worth noting that a prize has *already* been claimed for building an electric motor 1/25 of a centimeter in width, and a book page has been reduced to 1/25,000 of its original size," says Adrian Berry.[17] K. Eric Drexler argues that it may be possible to shrink the component parts of computers to the size of molecules. Scientists are now working on what they call "quantum computers," in which information is stored on atoms themselves. If each atom could store one bit of information, a single grain of salt could contain as much information as the RAM in all the computers in the world.[18]

THE GRAY WAVE ~ When she reached 98, the son said, "Mom, I think you're going to make 100."

She replied, "What am I going to make of it?"

> Now I don't have to buy antiques to sit on something 90 years old.
>
> US Senator Strom Thurmond, celebrating his 90th birthday

Part of postmodern ministry is helping post-moderns come to terms with life in all its forms and stages—including death. The tail end of life got short shrift in the modern world. That tail is becoming longer. It will be the tail that wags the dog in the future. Whereas modern psychiatrists spent years studying *Young Man Luther*,[19] post-modern scholars will be more prone to study Classic Luther (a "classic" being something that grows fresher with use while everything around it wears out with use).

We now live in the Age of the Aged.

A textbook Boomer, I asked my barber not too long ago: "What would you call the color my hair is turning? Silver?"

"I'd say it was more gun-metal gray," she replied.

Even after I give people their lines they refuse to give them back to me.

All of Charlie's Angels turned 50 in 1998, as did 50,000 other Boomers every single day. With the Boomers, a new breed of senior citizen is emerging. Forget every image you ever had of the elderly as dribbling, doddering, Depends-wearing dotards. Although Boomers don't look any more like Michelangelo's *David*—if they ever did—they continue to want to be like younger flatbellies. As fitness-conscious Boomers and Busters age, these affluent, energetic "seniors" share little in common with their predecessors in terms of either how they look or how they act.[20]

The "compression of morbidity" before death predicted long ago[21] has come true. All sorts of studies have revealed a fall in the prevalence of

> Gray hair is God's graffiti.
>
> Comedian Bill Cosby

disability in old age despite an increase in life span. In fact, from an actuarial standpoint, those age 45 and above are the healthiest age group in USAmerica.[22] Contrary to the stereotype, centenarians ("the oldest old") are often healthier than people 20 or 30 years younger.[23] Centenarians are a special segment of the population—they enjoy health, sex, and the out-of-doors. The Willard Scott club is also the fastest growing segment (percentage wise) of the population.[24]

A revolution has snuck up on us unawares. Erasmus's best-known poem "On the Troubles of Old Age"[25] was written when he was nearly 40. In 1506 that *was* old age. For postmoderns old age begins at 80, not 65. Middle age is now 50–80. Boomers are the original "youth generation." In fact, Boomers are still the "youth" market, or what has been called the "mid-youth" (*not* "mid-life") culture.[26]

What moderns looked like at 65, postmoderns will do anything *not to* look like until the day they die. Baby Boomer deaths will not arrive when anticipated. New treatments and technologies will push death closer to age 100 than any of us can even imagine.[27]

Boomers will do anything to resist aging. Of the 17,000 new products introduced in the grocery stores in 1995, between 4000 and 5000 were in the "natural products" (i.e., health foods) category.[28] A significant percentage were also de-aging products, from lotions to lingerie.

RETIRE RETIREMENT ~ Retirement is a thing of the past. It stands as a prime example of a form of social engineering that is installed by one generation and obsolete by another. Far from what we think, "retirement" is not a citizen's "right," nor a part of natural law. What retirement is can be seen in terms of quite specific generational traits from the high modern era:

> In the dim and distant
> When life's tempo wasn't fast,
> Grandma used to rock and knit,
> Crochet, tat, and babysit.
> When the kids were in a jam,
> They could always count on Gram.
> In an age of gracious living,
> Grandma was the gal for giving.
> Grandma now is at the gym,
> Exercising to keep slim.
> She's off touring with a bunch
> Taking clients out to lunch.
> Driving north to ski or curl,
> All her days are in a whirl.
> Nothing seems to stop or block her,
> Now that Grandma's off her rocker.
>
> "Times Are Changing," Anonymous[29]

1. Housing boom—Boosters built the suburbs, which they then sold at enormous profits to their Boomer children. Homes bought for $15,000 in 1950 sold for $150,000 in 1980. Whereas for Boosters it was a seller's market, for Boomers it is proving to be a buyer's market. Boosters could expect a huge real estate payback; Boomers can't.
2. Postwar boom—Boosters saved financially. Those who are currently retired saw their income balloon 524%, in real terms, between the ages of 20 and 30. In contrast, Boomers saw a 34% increase.[30] It should not surprise us that Boomers have trouble saving.[31] Their real salaries have been stagnant since 1973. Moreover, they are having kids later and later in life; some are just now starting their families.
3. Government aid boom—The GI Bill helped Boosters get a degree. Social security was launched in 1937. Boosters paid a maximum

contribution of $30 per year into social security until 1949. Today one-third of the workforce pays more into social security than into the IRS. Actuaries have advanced the date of insolvency for the system with increasing rapidity. In 1985 social security was supposed to go broke in 2049. By 1993 it was to crash in 2036. The 1994 report jumped the system's "exhaustion" to 2029. One wonders what the actuaries will predict by the year 2000.[32]

4. Demographics—According to Lydia Bronte in *The Longevity Factor*, and Catherine D. Fyock in *Unretirement*, the ultimatum of retirement is built on four demographic premises—all of which are false for Boomers.[33] First, age 65 is old. But Baby Boomers will live two-to-four decades longer than their parents; people retiring at 65 today have 25–30% of their adult life still ahead of them, making it unlikely that they will receive government funding. Second, leisure is more fulfilling than work. For Boomers, work is still a positive source of satisfaction. Third, older people should move over for the next generation. This all-or-nothing mentality allows for no phasedown, part-time, or tent-making labor. Fourth, people over 65 are worse workers than those under 65. We know now how far this can be from the truth.

Even Boomers who are "retiring" are not retiring where their parents retired. Retirement developments filled with the age groupings of their parents' are the least likely sites for Boomers. Boomer "retirements" will not be stopping work so much as stopping work on things they don't want to do, and working only at things that give them joy and pleasure. Boomers are looking for a better quality of life, which they define in terms of relationships, culture, creativity, and experiences.

Bored with suburbia, Boomers are already third-aging to one of two places: (a) downtown condominiums and lofts in Urban Renaissance cities such as Boston and Chicago; the hottest properties in the future are inner-city homes in populations under 300,000; and (b) small towns, especially in the rural and semirural southern US and West, choosing what demographers are calling "sunspots" over "sunbelts." Some of those "sunspots" are in the North (e.g., Cape Cod) and Northwest (Puget Sound). Boomers will settle in for the final chapters at places where they had good vacation experiences and where they can live the last years of their lives to the hilt with a lilt. Good-bye, non-stop leisure and shuffleboard. Hello, education-service-experience settings, where what matters most is access to the arts, ongoing work, social and intellectual stimulation, and learning.

Here's a checklist. See how you do. Hint: Postmoderns like to stack (that is, do multiple things at once).

Is your church in a small town? You're ministering on the cusp of the future.

Is your church in a county seat/small town? You're ministering on the cutting edge of the future.

Is your church in a county seat/small town where there's a college/university community? You're ministering on the bleeding edge of the future.

Is your church in a county seat/small town with a college feel that boasts some recreational component or tourism attraction? You're ministering so far out on the frontier of the future, you're almost falling in.

FOREVER FORTY ~ More than half the people in history who have reached the age of 65 are alive today. A postmodern world can expect an increase not just in world population, but in the proportion of older people—whether at home or in "a home."

When Bismarck, the inventor of the pension system, set the retirement age at 65 in 1891, life expectancy for the average German male was 45. The equivalent of Bismark's retirement age today is 95. Are you prepared for retirement at 95? Are you prepared to live to 120?

Life spans are increasing, not just in Western nations but in most of the world.[34] The lifetime of the average USAmerican has lengthened in the 20th century by more than 60%. The Social Security Administration has been officially warned: You're dangerously underestimating longevity among the elderly. The population of those over age 65 will grow by at least 60% between now and 2020 and will double within 50 years.[35] Most members of the Net-Gens will live to be 100-plus, and a few perhaps 200-plus. We have argued that they are really 22nd-century kids. For the first time in history, six and even seven generations are now living side by side.

A new journal has appeared in the medical profession: *The Journal of Anti-Aging Medicine*. Anti-aging medicine will become the top medical specialty of the 21st century. Cellular and molecular degeneration are not automatic or universal, as US Senator John Glenn symbolized when he returned to space at 77. To be sure, many of our internal organs shrink with advancing age. Our brain, liver, lungs, and kidneys are all getting smaller; the only body parts that do not shrink with age are our ears, nose, and fat. The smaller our organs get, the fatter and more sluggish we become. But not all of the cells of the body deteriorate. In fact, many of our body parts show no evidence of aging at all—blood-making stem cells, sperm-producing cells, cells lining the intestinal tract. Other cells undergo perpetual birth from within—heart and brain cells last a lifetime.

So why not Methuselean dreams? Why not 300-, 400-, 500-year-olds? There are two main reasons why not. One is the raging aging diseases: cancer, heart conditions, Alzheimer's. Scientists dealing with angiogenesis genes, which tell the body how to grow new blood vessels, are working on the cusp of an era of regenerative medicine whereby we would literally molt our bodies as we grow older. Genes with guided instructions would be placed into our bodies, repairing and rejuvenating damaged organs.

The other reason is the body's on/off switches for the aging genes. Our bodies turn on some of these switches automatically; our cells boast chromosomal clocks (telomeres) that age and die according to preset ticking. Again, scientists are already at work to shut off the switches. Some are tinkering with telomere "caps" that would keep the clock from ever winding down. To prove it can be done, scientists have expanded the maximum life span in two species: the fruit fly (doubled) and the nematode worm (six times its normal life span).[36] Then there is the Geron Corporation, the world's first biotechnology company devoted to developing genetically engineered products to retard or reverse the aging process.

Aging is already more in our control than we can imagine. The new science of psychoneuroimmunology makes it possible for us to measure our increased or decreased resistance to disease and our ability to heal based on what is in our mind and souls. This is spawning whole other empires of medicine: stress reduction, alternative medicine, preventive medicine, anti-aging foods, diet and nutrition, food and water monitoring, faith healing.

Diet. This bulge in the population called "Boomers," their favorite food "seconds," are now finding themselves bulging out all over. Too many (myself included) have as their favorite ethnic food heart-stopping southern cooking. Yet at least a third of us is on a diet at any given time. We're both "health conscious" and "junk food loving."

> The only way to keep your health is to eat what you don't want, drink what you don't like, and do what you'd rather not.
>
> Mark Twain[38]

What and how much we eat has everything to do with what we look like[37] and how long we live. In the future, chefs won't recommend dishes; they will prescribe entrees based on our wellness profile. Chefs, nutritionists, and pharmacists are becoming one and the same: specialists in foodaceuticals (or what some are calling "nutraceuticals")—foods that have scientifically proven health benefits that prevent or treat disease. Foodaceuticals officially began when the Food and Drug Administration proclaimed oatmeal and oat-based cereals good for the human heart.

The research of Roy Walford and others shows that reduced food intake through calorie-restricted diets dramatically increases longevity as well as enhances DNA repair. Mutual of Omaha reimburses patients who participate in a preventive program that combines diet, medication, exercise, and support groups to reverse heart disease.

Exercise. I shall never forget hearing a sermon delivered by the courageous Los Angeles Baptist pastor Amos Brown in which he lambasted his own African-American community for their horrendous eating habits and lack of exercise. It was the most silent congregation of Black Baptists I had ever witnessed.

> By design, the body should go on forever.
>
> Stanford University biochemist Elliott Crooke[39]

Study after study has demonstrated that exercise is the closest thing we have to a magic bullet against aging. Even 90-year-olds were freed from their wheelchair imprisonment by special exercise programs. According to one group of Tufts University researchers, "The bottom line: it's never too late. Your body is always ready to give you another chance."[40]

Intimacy. The issue isn't so much what we're eating as what's eating us. In this dog-eat-dog/eat-or-be-eaten world, intimacy is being shown to have positive effects on health and heart. Positive experiences of community, good social relationships, and reduced stress keep the heart healthy and the arteries free-flowing.[41]

WHAT CAN BE DONE WILL BE DONE ~ There has been no historical evidence that humans will not do what can be done. No hospital ethics committee can stop revolutions from doing whatever can be done at least once. There is historical evidence that revolutions can be stopped from doing something twice.

Medical scientists are already developing cloning techniques. Genetic screening and the use of fetal tissue for disease prevention are here. Human DNA strands have already been patented by the government and numerous pharmaceutical companies.

You say cloning hasn't been done with humans? Hello, Dolly?! We didn't know a sheep was cloned until three months after the fact. Cloning is so absolutely irresistible—it's a low-cost, low-tech procedure—that cloning humans will be done and probably already has been.

Gene therapy is being carried out not just in rabbits, but in humans as well. "Gene jockeys" and "Biotrekkers" (named after "Star Trekkers") are but two of the names given to scientists who are creating new forms of life that enrich and extend the known forms. The names "B. t. Cotton" and "Ice-Minus" will be as common as Nike and IBM in the future. Foods are now being genetically engineered by outfits that are not so much corporations or megacompanies as they are "life sciences conglomerates."[42]

SCIENCE FICTION/FACT ~ Reading scientists today is little different from reading science-fiction novelists. Doubt it? Tulane University physicist Frank Tipler predicts that "in an extremely remote future all the people who have ever lived will be resurrected because the beings who live in that far-off epoch will have immeasurably powerful computers." In a closed universe collapsing in on itself (which is what he believes ours to be), "*no information would be lost.*" No thought or deed that has been expressed or carried out by any person in any Age could escape the detection of the computers. It's all there, somewhere, in the form of radiation that is undetectable to present-day machines. Tipler concludes his rhapsody in science, "If any reader has lost a loved one, or is afraid of death, modern physics says: 'Be comforted. You and they shall live again.'"[43]

Still think I'm exaggerating? Scientists are already talking about how to transfer a complete human mind from one person to another. Call it MIND-COPY:

No such mental copying is *now* possible, because the memory storage capacities of computers are immeasurably smaller than that of the human brain. The most powerful personal computers can only store some 200 to 500 million bytes—or characters—of data. . . . Yet the human mind is generally considered to possess the equivalent of a trillion bytes. . . . Every year, data storage capacity roughly doubles and its price halves. This means that, unless some fundamental obstacle is encountered, it *will* be possible before the middle of the next century at least to store—if not to reproduce entirely—a human personality electronically.[44]

Philosopher/neuroscientist Paul Churchland (University of California–San Diego) sees no reason why immortalizing the mind and the consciousness isn't philosophically or technologically possible: "The speed of a human brain is about 100 meters per second—tops. The speed of transmission in a copper wire is a million times faster. If you've got a machine that can *think* a million times faster, then it can *learn* a million times faster—if you can feed it the information fast enough."[45]

Here is a criminal activity your kids may have to worry about: Erase the minds of the young and insert one's own in its place. The computer command *DISKCOPY*, which copies all information from one disk to another, could be matched by a computer command to *MINDCOPY*. Copy all the information in one mind into a computer, and then into the brain of another human being or robot.

So here we are where we began this chapter: a postbiological world where our artificial progeny take pride of place.

So what? FROM CHURCH GROWTH TO CHURCH HEALTH ~

Health—physical, mental, spiritual—is, alongside globalization, the number one trend of the 21st century. Already an astounding 15% of the gross domestic product comes in the form of direct and indirect health-related expenditures.

The church must transition its ministry beyond a "church growth" mentality into a "church health" mentality.[46] The promise of the gospels is not "growth." The promise is health—a healthy relationship with God, and a healthy lifestyle of wholeness or holiness, where spirit, mind, and body work and play together.

The church-growth people have hold of a profound half-truth: Numbers are important. But they are also tricky. They fool you. One must be careful of numbers. Statistics can be used to prove almost anything. The Centers for Disease Control and Prevention has started releasing statistics with this notice: "Figures should be interpreted with caution."[47]

Or to translate this into a more biblical context: God expects fruit! The season for figs has come. But at the same time (and where the other side of the half-truth comes in), who can measure the fruit of one's ministry? Who really succeeds and who fails? Have you noticed anything that doesn't only get so big and then it tops you out? Everything has limits.

> There are reasons why trees don't grow to heaven.
>
> Danish proverb

Our job is to cultivate the soil and plant seeds, to tend seedlings. Whether there is a garden this year or we are planting for future seasons is not ours to say, nor often ours to see. What we need is endurance, encouragement, and hope. I see my own ministry as taking to church leaders a seed catalog (which is apocalyptic literature), out of which they can choose what they think will grow in the soil God has given them.

If the body of Christ is an organic entity, then "church growth" will be no different than "biological growth." This is the thesis of Christian Schwarz, who leads the Institute for Church Development in Germany. He argues that our aim should not be to "make" the church grow, but to release the growth hormones through which God builds the church.[48]

Do you know the famous parable of the Chinese bamboo tree? The story goes like this: A farmer plants the bamboo seed, then waters and fertilizes it. For the first four years there is no visible growth. During the fifth year, things change, rather dramatically: The Chinese bamboo grows a staggering 90 feet in nine weeks.

What is going on? Well, not as much as the parable would suggest. First, bamboo is a grass, not a tree—no matter how high it grows. Second, if any seed doesn't sprout in the first year and shoot above ground, it will die. The story is great morality and bad biology.

But the larger part of the parable remains. The root system of some bamboo grass grows those first four years down and out more than up and up. The apostle Paul had a Chinese bamboo grass ministry. His first labors were so uneventful in converts and results that it is easy to overlook the small shoots. But the seeds Paul planted, others watered and nurtured until the sprouts of Christianity spread like kudzu throughout the ancient Greek and Roman worlds.[49]

JESUS' HEALTH MINISTRY ~ Jesus did not have a church-growth ministry. He had a health ministry. Jesus' teachings are a prescribed health regimen. The Sermon on the Mount is a prescription for a healthy lifestyle.[50]

Jesus was given three years by his Father in which to save the world. So what did he spend his three years doing—growing a big church or a mega-following? He spent it training his small team of 12 for ministry. From the cell context to his ministry, Jesus preached to large crowds (Mark 12:37), often with his small group by his side. But after three years of intense ministry he could claim an intimate group of 12 key associates and at the very most 500 followers.

> And he sent them out ... to heal.
>
> Luke 9:2

You can't have a smaller or more humble beginning than the Jesus movement—little in time (three years); little in geography (the countryside of an occupied Israel); little in leadership (12 disciples); little in followership (120–500?); little in results (an execution).

Today this little-or-nothing band of Jesus' disciples has become 1.8 billion professing Christians around the globe.

The people Jesus chose may have been unlearned and undesirable by worldly standards (Acts 4:13), but they were teachable and he established an intimate relationship with them. In this "Jesus Seminary" he gave them peripatetic courses in lifestyle, healing, and leadership and mentored them in "the mysteries of the kingdom of God" (Luke 8:10 KJV).

Jesus used the Socratic method in his teaching: "Who is my mother?" "Who are my brothers?" "What did you go there to see?" "What do you do more than others?" "Who do you say that I am?" "What are you looking for?" He then gave them periodic tests to see how they were doing. He gave them stories and images from which to draw. He gave them downtime from which they could draw breath and inspiration. He protected them and mentored them. Within the team of 12, he spent intensive time in leadership development with Peter, James, and John. The closer his crucifixion drew near, the more time he spent with the Apostle TeamNet.

The genius of Jesus' method is that he spent his entire ministry majoring in the quality of disciple making, not the quantity of disciples. Jesus did not have a self-conscious strategy for growing his movement. Growth simply happened as a result of the mysterious work of the Spirit from the contagion of the quality of life in Jesus Christ. Jesus spent more time on shaping his disciples for leadership than on their pastoral care.

It was a powerful strategy. This small band of believers turned the world upside down and inside out (Acts 17:6).

What is more, Jesus handled his "succession" crisis in this highly original way: "It is for your good that I am going away" (John 16:7 NIV). Why? Because, to paraphrase Jesus' words, "I will send you a successor, and you will be able to do under that successor what you never did with me" (see Acts 1:8). Jesus didn't see the Promised Land of Acts 2. Jesus measured his success in terms of succession ministries, not present achievements.

But sure enough, when Jesus sends his successor, what happens? It all collapses? It implodes? There's a sacrificial lamb? No, Jesus' ministry explodes. We read about that explosion in Acts 2. Was it a vertical explosion? The gospel explodes outward to girdle the globe.

WAY STATIONS TO WELLNESS ~ Rush your bleeding three-year-old to the emergency room, and the first thing you hear today is not, "What's wrong?" but "Where's your insurance card?"

In a world where the password to success is "quality"—quality of care, quality of life, quality of relationships, quality of family, quality of death—the church that fastens on quality ministry honors its pedigree and dignifies its destiny.

It is time that the church understood itself as a leader in the quality "health" business. The phrase that embraces this more holistic vision of health is "wellness." The church is a wellness center. There were 12,000 health clubs in the US in 1993, with 18.2 million members, up 10% from 1992. The biggest health club of all, however, is the church.

Jesus is the Great Physician. We are to be the physicians of our people. But postmodern physicians work harder to keep people from getting sick than making sick people well. Most fundamentally, faith does not so much make sick people well as keep well people from getting sick. It is time to move the church from a sickness paradigm to a wellness paradigm, from a sin para-digm to a holiness paradigm. It is time for our churches to "go holistic" and move from being Illness Centers to Total Wellness Centers.

You've heard it quoted many times: "The church is not a museum for saints, but a hospital for sinners." No wonder we're in such a fix: We're more fixated on sin than sainthood. We specialize more in disease than in health.

We're not the only ones. We have discovered that the conventional wis-dom on the making of babies is backwards, according to a new study by the National Institute of Environmental Health Sciences. Epidemiologist Allen Wilcox was asked why it took so long for scientists to uncover this basic fact of human biology. The way medical research works is that we are pretty good at studying diseased people, but what happens in ordinary healthy people is much more elusive.[51] By contrast, Chinese medicine revolves around health rather than disease.

Someone once called the family the original Department of Health, Education, and Welfare because its health function is preventive rather than curative. Departments of health look and feel different from departments of disease. If we do not build communities based on creativity, holiness, and health, then our foundation is built on unstable compounds of disease, weakness, and sickness.

Wholeness consists of illness and health, independence and dependency. Disease is more than the breakdown of a particular system; many times it's the expression of a struggle between competing organisms. Disease has functions as well as causes—the germs wins, the body dies. In the words of Susan Sontag,

> Illness is the night-side of life, a more onerous citizenship. Everyone who is born holds dual citizenship, in the kingdom of the well and in the kingdom of the sick. Although we prefer to use only the good passport, sooner or later each of us is obliged, at least for a spell, to identify ourselves as citizens of that other place.[52]

To move from church growth to church health is to move from taking care of people who get sick to stopping people from getting sick. Let's stop getting sick. What if our churches became Wellness Centers, Holiness Stations on the King's SuperHighway?

THE HOLISTIC CHURCH ~ Bringing the name of Jesus to others (Acts 19:1–18) meant (1) preaching, (2) teaching, and (2) healing in his name. Most of the healers of Jesus' day were not teachers. Jesus was all three—healer, teacher, preacher. Unlike other healers of his day, Jesus charged no fee for his services. Also unlike other healers of his day, Jesus' healing concern was for both individual illnesses and social illnesses. Healing includes deliverance from marital problems, racism, sexism, unemployment, and so on.

Healing people and healing the planet, according to Jesus, are both expressions of the same impulse.[53] Further unlike other healers of his day, Jesus placed a "supportive community" at the heart of the healing act. From the use of oil by the elders (James 5:14–16) to Jesus' valuation of "*their* faith" in Mark 2:5, the role of the community in healing is featured in the biblical portrait of the church's healing ministry.[54]

Students who come to seminary dream of becoming a "great preacher." After three or more years of intense faculty prodding, they may come to realize the importance of the rabbinical role of becoming a "great teacher." But very few leave seminary wanting to become a "great healer." If I had to rank the three in importance to postmodern culture, it would be in the exact opposite order: (1) healing; (2) teaching; (3) preaching. Ministries of healing, health service, and health care are at front and center in the church reaching out to postmodern culture.

Perhaps you think, "I can't be a healer. I need healing myself." Paul, who was a healer (2 Cor. 12:12), could not heal himself either (2 Cor. 4:7–12; 12:7–10). Know a preacher that also doesn't need preaching? Know a teacher that also doesn't need teaching?

People are picking up "home remedies," "alternative medicine," self-care, and self-healing with breathtaking speed. *Physicians' Desk Reference,* the Bible of the medical profession, is booming in sales to laypeople. One in three of us is putting our money down on alternative health-care remedies alone. Can we replace self-healing programs with church-healing ministries? Where are our triage ministry teams? Why aren't we assigning "care partners" for the sick? Three-quarters of the elderly don't exercise regularly, and one-third don't meet minimum RDA nutrition standards, and 75% don't take their medicine properly—so why aren't we assigning care partners for the not-yet but soon-to-be sick?[55]

And what about the young? Recent brain research highlights the "windows" of the brain that open and close in the early years, making these developmental, preschool years more high risk than we ever imagined. Brain development depends on the kind of stimulation and environment a child receives in the first three years of life, when a lifetime of synapses is produced.

Enlist the church in providing children with a healthy and spiritually stimulating environment, one that can open windows to eternity.

HEAVEN'S MIDWIVES ~ Gertrude Stein liked to joke about Picasso's reply to her complaint that his portrait of her didn't look like her. He said, "It will."

No matter how healthy the body, it's a condemned building. Christians need to learn and live the art of dying well (*ars moriendi*).

Don't count on the funeral industry to be of help. The only industry more "out-of-it" for postmodernism is perhaps the banking industry. The funeral industry is proving to be its own best listener. With space burials soon becoming cheaper than traditional land funerals,[56] the handwriting is on the wall.

There are now more than 10,000 health and medical Web sites. One health management organization (HMO), Kaiser Permanente, is spending $1 billion in 1998 to put its clinical records online. The Internet's role in grieving and "Cybermourning" has only just begun. One can already find Web memorials that point the way. So a powerful ministry awaits those who would make the creation of a Web Heaven part of the church's Web site.

Here's how a sample Web Heaven would work. An angel could take a child that wanted to visit Grandma to Web Heaven. There he could click on a video clip of Grandma holding him in her arms, or click on an organ that would play Grandma's favorite hymns, or click on an ever-growing memorial register that collects the memories and accolades of those who knew Grandma, or click on other markers that remind visitors to Web Heaven that the majority of the church is underground. The gravestones of the future are online as well as above ground.

What this means is that the Postmodern Reformation church loops back to the past, when graveyards were an extension of the church.

More and more people are deciding to die at home, surrounded by loved ones. Home hospices cannot be founded fast enough. Establish in the church a variety of heaven's midwives—ministry teams to surround the dying, some to surround them with music, others with art or prayer or simply love.

Make special efforts to celebrate birthdays and check in on people after their birthday. Why are birthdays so special? A person is more likely to die during his or her birthday week than any other time (men more likely just before, women more likely just after).

IN TOUCH WITH TOUCH ~ Lack of touch is as serious to our health as a lack of sun. In a touch-starved culture that is more and more touch-free—with touch-free bathrooms and touch-fear connections—the church must be a place that does not lose touch with touch.

> I'd rather be dead than singing "Satisfaction" when I'm 45.
>
> Mick Jagger (now 55) early on in his Rolling Stones career

Touch Therapy: What if the church were to set up a booth at the local fair and offer "FREE! 8-MINUTE THERAPEUTIC MASSAGE"? Or church-sponsored "holdings," especially for the older members of the community, who agree to relax and be held while the holder prays for them, whether in silence or in speech. What would it take to make your church less user-hostile as a spiritual spa where leisure and learning, relaxation of body, and rejuvenation of soul were combined?

PRAYER ~ The results of scientific research into the medical benefits of prayer are so overwhelming[57] that physicians who don't integrate it into their treatments are liable to malpractice suits.

What does prayer do? Does prayer keep us healthy and whole, or does prayer heal us? Some say it does the former. Some say it does the latter. I say it does both.[58]

When someone says, "I'll be praying for you," and really means it, you can rest secure that you are in great shape. For no matter who, where, or what such people are, their energies will enter your body, activating your immune system and animating the healing resources of your body.

In 1998, at least a dozen out of 125 medical schools in the US offered specific courses on "Prayer and Healing."[59] (I am afraid to tally a comparison with North America's 200-plus divinity schools.) Shouldn't the church be a training ground or resource for medical professions in the spiritual practice of prayer?

In mature years, and especially among the housebound, prayer is a niche ministry. Only 25% of people aged 55 to 64 say they always feel rushed, compared with 40% of people aged 25 to 54. Call them "prayer warriors" or "prayer partners" or whatever you want—the mature Christian and the housebound Christian boast a congenial climate for prayer, for reflection, for lifting up others' arms for ministry, for making your church a praying church.

Individual churches have established niche ministries for everything else, so why not prayer? Churches have endowed chairs in seminaries for everything else, so why not Professors of Prayer? How else can your church be a health place where faith is based, love is laced, and hope is faced? How else can your church be a healing place where people can break the walls down, build the body up, bridge the gaps across, bring the poles together?

QSL STANDARDS ~ Instead of working on "mission" or "vision" statements (didn't Jesus give us those—the Great Commission and John 3:16?), establish what could be called "QSL" ratios—Quality of Spiritual Life Standards. What would the spirit of a church "thoroughly equipped for every good work" (2 Tim. 3:17 NIV) be like?

SpiritMatters. The Word becomes flesh. Itemize how the energy of each "spirit" would issue in specific "matterings" in the body of Christ. Here is a suggestion of 12 QSLs, which you can adapt for your unique setting. On a scale of 1–10, how is your church doing? Try to keep out of your mind specific matterings in worship, mission, ministry development, community growth, personal disciplines, giving, networking with other churches, or good administration. Here we are after "spirit" stuff.

1. Confidence—"I can do all things . . ."
2. Humility—". . . through him who strengthens me"
3. Prayer
4. Reverence for the Scriptures
5. Repentance
6. Compassion
7. Passion
8. Endurance
9. Joy
10. Openness to diversity
11. Adaptability
12. State of being out of control

GENETHICS ~ If there are, as some have argued, two "wilderness areas" left—space and genetics—do we leave the genetic wilderness wild, or do we cultivate and colonize it, as we are already doing with space?

The real question is what biotechnologies will we choose to embrace in the 21st century? Can biotechnology work for life, not against life? What kind of production of genetically engineered life-forms should we allow? Will we allow genetic commerce to spell the end of nature?

> The trouble with always trying to preserve the health of the body is that it is so difficult to die without destroying the health of the mind.
>
> G. K. Chesterton

But we're more than a little out of our depth, you say? I say how else do we learn to swim? We have been shaping our descendants for decades. Louise Brown, the first child of in vitro fertilization, is now in her third decade, with thousands born after her since 1978. It is long overdue to integrate genetic counseling into premarital counseling.

If the church doesn't establish moral handrails for the enterprise of choosing our descendants, who will? The biological entrepreneurs—roboticists, cyberneticists, artificial-intelligence researchers, artificial-life researchers? But they are looking religion's way for guidelines and guardrails. Even though I do not agree with Jerry Mander's position on biotechnology, I like his principle for where we should be now in the development of this technology: "Guilty Until Proven Innocent."[60]

Biotechnology boasts great potential. It can be a dream come true for the starving people of the world who must raise more food on the same land or from less land. But at the same time biotechnology raises enormous ethical questions, and not simply for those with religious dietary laws and allergies.

Biotechnological advances have so far outpaced ethical guidelines and societal regulations governing their use that we're playing serious catch-up. Biologist Wes Jackson, who calls for a hybrid discipline called "agroecology" rather than biotechnology, cites the latter as "the current extension of the human cleverness approach to arranging the world." He questions the hubris of biotechnologists in supposing "they can avoid producing the negative impacts comparable to those created by chemical and nuclear technologies."[61] Yet, from time immemorial our ancestors have played with the biotic processes of microorganisms. In fact, in a technical sense supplemental estrogen treatments are actually a kind of gene therapy.

There is cause for alarm. A lot of biotechnology is now hooking our dependency even deeper to "the _____-cides": pesticides, fungicides, herbicides, weedicides, insecticides. Five billion pounds of poisons are already being manufactured by chemical companies each year, lethal substances that must go somewhere and go most often into our air, soil, or water.

Can biotechnology lead the way to sustainable agriculture and value-added crops? Or will biotechnology become a substitute for sustainable agriculture or sustainable methods of controlling weeds and crop disease? Then a dream will have become a nightmare.

Consider this modern Arab folktale:

A sheik's four sons returned from studying at a Western university. The sheik took his sons on a trip through the desert to test what they had learned.

First they came upon a pile of bones. "Son," the sheik asked his first-born, "what did you learn?"

"Those are the bones of a six-foot, 300-pound lion," the young man replied.

The father was impressed. He asked his second son, "Son, what did *you* learn?" That son took the bones and reassembled them into the carcass of a lion.

When he asked the third son the same question, he took some hide and put it over the frame of the lion.

When it came time for the fourth son to show what he had learned, he touched the lion and gave it life.

Whereupon the lion rose up and ate all five of them.

There is a new phenomenon in American culture: beeper-bearing ethicists on call. "WANTED: Bioethicist. So many ethical questions, so few to lead the debate" is how Iconoculture ends its chapter on "Healthwatch."[62] Should the church be a part of this growth industry? Whom would you rather have training the genethicists?

HANDICAPPED ALL ~ A school in Virginia offered the course "Home Economics for Boys." No one enrolled. Then the dean renamed the course "Bachelor Living," and 120 signed up.

Can the church be this creative in getting people to come to terms with their native disabilities? Once we lose our genetic innocence, and the Human Genome Project is complete, we will stand genetically naked. Then we shall discover that we are, one and all, biologically challenged and thus ontologically disabled. There are as many as 4000 diseases caused by a single defective gene. Some of these can be avoided through genetic engineering. Others can't.

To inhabit this new world where everyone gets the handicapped parking space, the church needs to get busy and teach some things that it already knows:

1. *A new respect for variety.* Genes show just how different people actually are and the endless combinations in which the image of God can become incarnate. Variety is as important to social ecosystems as to biological ones. A healthy anything needs diversity, which is why cloning is so unhealthy.

2. *A new respect for equality.* Nature doesn't ever provide equality; society does. But it is this equality of opportunity that protects and cherishes difference and even weakness. Do you really want to live in a world where Down's syndrome kids are forbidden? (We're almost there now, as 95% of pregnancies diagnosed with Down's are aborted.) And what genetic defect comes next to be outlawed?

3. *A new respect for autonomy.* People need the freedom to find ways to overcome their genetic handicaps in ways that may not seem "appropriate" and "seemly" to some.

THINK IT AND SINK IT ~ No remains of a soldier will be placed in the Tomb of the Unknown Soldier ever again. In fact, the remains of the last soldier, placed after the Vietnam War, were removed from the Tomb in Arlington Cemetery because DNA testing has developed to the point where he could be identified simply from a strand of hair. There can be no more "unknown" soldiers.

In postmodern culture, nothing is "unknown." Everything is known. There is a saying of postmodern life: "Do nothing you would be ashamed to see reported on page two of the *New York Times*." In the global village, everybody "knows about" everyone.

Because everything and everyone is so easily known, issues of privacy and anonymity will become more urgent than ever. Already the US government has more files, more data, more scoop collected on its citizens than any other totalitarian government in the past or the present.[63]

> We share each other's woes,
> Our mutual burdens bear;
> And often for each other flows
> A sympathizing tear.
>
> John Fawcett[64]

In the midst of a glass culture of gossip and innuendo, the church must protect and preserve people's privacy on every front. The Mafia has a code of silence, called Omerta. If anyone ought to know the meaning of Omerta, it is the disciples of Jesus. People should trust Christians enough to tell us things we will share with no one—not even our spouse. I will die with information people have told me burning holes in my heart. Each one of us will turn to Mary again and again and live out the meaning of these words: "But Mary treasured all these words and pondered them in her heart" (Luke 2:19). None of us will go very far from that old hymn, "There's not a friend, like the lowly Jesus, No, not one! no, not one!"

A postmodern motto of privacy-enhancing ministry is this: Think it and sink it.

One of the due-process reforms of the '60s was the Miranda Rule: The reading of Miranda rights is required for every person arrested. The Miranda warnings inform suspects of their right to remain silent (or have a lawyer present), for what you say can and will be used against you.

Too much of the body of Christ is living out a mirandized ministry—whatever we say to a brother or sister can and sometimes will be used against us. A colleague from another Methodist annual conference started telling me one day some things that I thought were better left unsaid.

I asked, "Are you sure I ought to know this?"

He replied, "Well, the person told me not to tell anyone."

"Then why are you telling me?"

"Come on, Len," he countered. "Whenever anyone comes to you and says, 'Now this is between us—don't tell anyone,' they really are asking you to tell people. Don't you know that by now?"

Sorry, but no, none of us should know that by now. If there ought to be any exception to the Robert Burns Rule ("I've never confided anything to any-one without having regretted it ever afterward"), it ought to be us Christians. There is enough hearsay, rumor, and gabble of gossip going on behind our backs in the world without our colleagues in the church adding more to the pile. The congregational grapevine is strangling the body of Christ. It deserves not our ears, but our shears.

If we must gossip, gossip the good news—first about Jesus, then about each other:

- Have you heard how the Lord is working at so-and-so's church?
- Have you heard how many hearts so-and-so has turned toward the ministry?
- Did you hear what an incredible worship experience her church had last week?
- Can you believe how the Lord is working at that church?
- You'll never believe what I heard. So-and-so's people got so upset when they heard the pastor might have to move out of the parsonage that they almost rioted. They must really love their pastor.

THE TABLE IS PREPARED ~ The four words every postmodern mother says before meals are "Get in the car."

The church can help families prepare a healthy table. WholeDining Suppers: an eco-experience perhaps featuring Amish-raised chicken from "Whole Foods, this country's biggest co-op chain," a meal where everything served would be organic with no pesticides. If your church uses wine in the Eucharist, make sure your people know that the wine the church uses is free of the sulfites and antifungal sprays that cover the vineyards.

In 1996 the US spent $76 billion on "nutraceuticals," according to *Nutrition Business Journal*, testifying to our growing awareness of the connection between diet and disease. One-third of all adults choose foods for specific medical purposes on a daily basis.[65]

To scientists who say that genetically engineered foods are better, I say "Hello?!" Look at overbreeding, hormone-injected cattle, factory-farming, Mad Cow disease. And have you tasted that tomato? It's tasteless—looks good, but it's tasteless.

CARBON CHAUVINISM ~ Christians should proceed with "no fear" to "bio-ize" ministry and "bio-ize" the church—on one condition. We have to remain "carbon chauvinists." We do not want to wrest control of the creation from the Creator. The word *creativity* is often used much too loosely. By many definitions of the word, Hitler was one of the most "creative" leaders this world has ever seen. The church must tie the ropes of creativity around its original moorings.

The word *creative* was initially used in the exclusive context of the divine creation of the world. *Creation* and *creature* have the same root stem. This context remained normative until at least the 16th century, when the major transformation of thought that we now call Renaissance humanism[66] expanded the word to include and indicate present or future making—that is to say, the making of, by, and for humans.

> Had another of Leopold Mozart's sperm cells won the race to the egg cell produced by Anna Maria Pertl sometime around May 1, 1755, some of the most beautiful music in the world would never have been written.
>
> Belgian cytologist/biochemist Christian de Duve[67]

In sum, the context of creativity went from one Creator, and our embellishments and embroideries of that Creator's work, to two creators, each of which operated on separate "creations": the divine Creator, and the human creator, the latter totally dependent on human actions and capacities, with no reference to divine intentions or past actions.

Biblical "creativity" is *critical* creativity. It aims not at novelty, but at innovation that specifically continues the divine work of creation. Not everything "new" is creative. To be truly creative, one has to be in touch and in tune with the ongoing mysterious, miraculous powers of divine creation.

THE NEW PREDESTINARIANS ∼ Are you depressed? Don't blame it on your parents, your unemployment, your abusive relationship, or your rat-race scrambles. You're depressed because your brain has a chemical imbalance or your genes are defective.

There is a new genetic determinism abroad in our land: "my-genes-made-me-do-it" biologism. Biologism is a kind of fate faith in which we are what we are and believe what we believe by the forces of nature. Who would have guessed that Social Darwinism, which we thought was finally defeated after Hitler's death in 1945, is making a comeback in the aftermath of the Cold War?

The major proponent of this new predestinarianism is Edward O. Wilson. Wilson would deny and fight the discrimination angle. Wilson is also correct about our environmental offenses. But he posits so strong an automatic linkage between genes and character that he ends up in neuroendocrinological determinism. He greatly overinterprets our genetic endowments. In his book *Sociobiology: The New Synthesis,* Wilson argues a hardline genetic predestination. Everything is in the genes. Our parents' genes wanted to reproduce themselves—therefore you and I exist. Our prime motivation is to reproduce our genes, and there are genes "for" intelligence, aggression, depression, homosexuality, alcoholism, altruism, drug dependency, and so on.[68]

Wilson is wrong. Culture can trump biology. Genes are not predictable. They do not unveil a predictable destiny. They exist in intimate interaction with their world, but they do not control it. They permit, they limit, but they don't dictate. Ian Steward and Jack Cohen call the multiplicity of influences that shape our character and constitution "complicity"—the interaction of "two or more complex systems [e.g., environment, genes, chance, fetal development] in a kind of mutual feedback."[69] Someone else has compared genes to the Freudian notion of the "subconscious"—"a strong influence on a person's life, but normally hidden."

The great American dancer Isadora Duncan allegedly once suggested to George Bernard Shaw that they have a child together. "Just imagine," she said, "a child with my beauty and your intelligence." To which the celebrated Irish playwright, notorious for his ugliness and his wit, is said to have replied, politely declining, "What if it should have my beauty and your intelligence?"

> Aged to Perfection
>
> Boomer T-shirt

But Wilson is right. We ignore biology to our detriment.

The church must fight both the determinism and the discrimination that comes willy-nilly from being defined by our genes. The number one prejudice of the future will be genetic discrimination.

If anyone should uphold a sense of human freedom and the special value of human life and experience, it is the church. If anyone should not succumb to the "victim" cop-out, it is the church. If anyone should not be afraid to explore questions of how God acts in the brain and the brain-soul link, it is the church.

"AGED TO PERFECTION" MINISTRIES ~ Postmoderns embrace the wisdom but not the wrinkles of age. A favorite e. e. cummings poem replaces the old laws of "thou shalt nots" with one new commandment: "you shall above all things be glad and young."

> you shall above all things be glad and young.
> For if you're young, whatever life you wear
> it will become you; and if you are glad
> whatever's living will yourself become.[70]

Postmoderns are above all aging "glad and young." In the words of writer/actor Robert Benchley, "As for me, except for an occasional heart attack, I feel as young as I ever did." In 21-C, older is cooler than younger.

Angelo Roncalli kept a journal for more than 65 years. At age 64, Roncalli meditates on the challenges of aging and his futile attempts to maintain earlier levels of vitality and vigor. His becoming Pope John XXIII is still 13 years away. In 1961, three years into his world-changing pontificate, he writes this:

> When on 28 October 1958, the Cardinals of the Holy Roman Church chose me to assume the supreme responsibility of ruling the universal flock of Jesus Christ, at seventy-seven years of age, everyone was convinced that I would be a provisional and transitional Pope. Yet here I am, already on the eve of the fourth year of my pontificate, with an immense programme of work in front of me to be carried out before the eyes of the whole world, which is watching and waiting. As for myself, I feel like St. Martin, who "neither feared to die, nor refused to live."[71]

Can your church help postmoderns "neither fear to die, nor refuse to live"? Walt Schoedel divides the aging into the go-gos, the slow-gos, and the no-gos.[72] The go-gos and the slow-gos want help in becoming "aged to perfection." Can the church help people see aging as a gift from God with a spiritual purpose (see the aging Psalms 71, 90, 92)? Or must postmodern culture's hunger for new ways at looking at aging be met only from such people as Betty Friedan, who in her book *The Fountain of Age* presents a vision of aging where getting old is not a process of deterioration but an adventure in redefining oneself for the future.[73]

Lifelong learning is one of the biggest growth industries in the church. Elder care will be to 21-C what child care has been to 20-C. But elder care will look and feel more like a college town than a nursing home. "Grackers" (gray hackers) is a word coined by the Iconoculture team to describe people 65 or older who would rather join a computer club than a shuffleboard club.

Knowledge is a powerful resource at every age, and the need for the church to develop info-structures for every age is more acute than the development of infrastructures. The church must resource a senior citizen wanting to be "an educated person" with electronic learning and up-to-date and continuing understanding of what is going on and preparation for what is coming.

"Everyone who lives and believes in me will never die," Jesus said to Martha (John 11:26).

You will never die. You will live forever. You are not getting old. Your body may be getting old. But you—the you you will take into eternity—need not get old. It need get wise. It need get smart.

Nothing dies. It just changes form, or is resurrected.

The final vision of the Bible (Rev. 22) brings everything together in the final victory of Jesus. The language of "victory" is not that of politics or philosophy or economics or military force. The language of victory is that of biology. There are no borders to defend or guards to protect. There are no walls for keeping out or gates for control. There is no temple to divide the sacred and the profane.

What there is, is water ("the river of life") with trees ("the tree of life") on each side of the river. There is growth and fruit and holiness and "healing of the nations" (vv. 1–2).

RE-THATCHING ~ The '80s brought us "the Me Generation." The '90s brought us "the We Generation." The emerging culture is bringing us "the Re Generation." The church's traditional views of aging need taking out—to the curb at least, and preferably to the dump.

Larry Krause, warning of the dangers of "retirement," is making a fortune getting people to think "regeneration" rather than "retirement." The Postmodern Reformation church should be the one giving the mature market a regeneration kick in the posterior. The last third can be the best years of one's life—the years when we make our biggest contributions to make the world different.

"Re-thatching" is a boom ministry for the Postmodern Reformation church. Instead of complaining about the sea of gray heads out there, we ought to be celebrating them, finding more of them, and deploying them for ministry.

At the same time, the church can resource this group through what one should never call "elderly assistance": vacation planning, personal gophering, money management, and surrogate grandparenting.[74] With so many children growing up without two parents, much less grandparents, the Grammy Rewards for seniors willing to invest in particular children are bigger than ever. It is no accident that Mattel has come out with Grandma and Grandpa versions of Ken and Barbie.

The church's greatest contribution to re-thatching may be helping people come to terms with their different rates of aging physically, socially, psychologically, and spiritually.

Sister Mary Martin Weaver has been a Catholic nun all her adult life. At the age of 55, when many of us begin thinking about retirement, she began thinking about athletics. She began training and now has won 44 gold, silver, and bronze medals in the Rocky Mountain Senior Games and the U.S. National Senior Olympics. Her specialties include snowshoe racing, speed and figure skating, basketball free throws, shot put, ice hockey, and the 5,000-meter race walk. She said,

> People have gotten flabby, and I don't mean just physically. Anything that's too much, people just don't want to do. But there are no rewards in anything unless you try. Age should never be a barrier to full participation in life. What's most important is to enjoy life to its fullest, to do things for and with others, and never, ever be afraid to stretch your limits.[75]

FAITH AND FINANCES ~ The mysterious Watergate informant known as "Deep Throat" was right. "Follow the money," he told reporters Bob Woodward and Carl Bernstein. "Follow the money."

It's a lesson the church, fixed on the power of politics in a world where the power paradigms are economic, has yet to learn. No church should be without a Minister of Planned Giving or a Minister of Estate Planning. Their role is *not* to raise money for the church; it is to help the church's members "give it all away." The words Jesus spoke to the rich young ruler are not for him alone, but for each one of us (see Luke 18:18–25). None of us gets out of life without giving everything we have away. We all die broke. The Minister of Estate Planning helps Christians decide who gets what they have and helps people pass on their inheritance while they are still alive.

The whole issue of fund-raising is such a serious issue for every denomination that, given their financial future, governing bodies should be meeting in Lourdes praying for a miracle instead of Los Angeles praying for majority rules. Who is supporting the church today? Boosters—those born before 1946. One study by the Southern Baptist Convention found that 80 cents of every dollar given to the church comes from Boosters, especially older Boosters.[76]

With memories shaped by the Great Depression and World War II, Boosters know what it is to sacrifice and save. In many ways, each generation is best defined by what it says no to. Busters say, "No fear"; Boomers say, "No problem"; and Boosters liked to say, "No sweat"—but did, plenty. In their "sweating" for others, Boosters learned the art of deferred gratification. One happy result of this hard work and sacrifice is that they have amassed for themselves quite a fortune. Boosters are the most well-off generation in history. In the next 10-to-15 years, between 10 and 15 trillion dollars will pass to the next generation—the largest generational transfer of wealth in the history of civilization. There is only one thing more fraught with pain than the transfer of power from one generation to another: the transfer of wealth.

Yet Boosters might not have as much to leave as everyone suspects. First, their wealth is heavily annuitized, which means income streams end with their death. Furthermore, their well-being is subsidized through government programs and pensions—social security, Medicare—none of which can be passed on. Second, Boosters are starting to spend more, and not just on medical care. The bumper sticker "I'm Spending My Kid's Inheritance" trumpets a new kind of Booster who is done saving and has started spending. Some of them may be spending their own children's inheritance, but they are protecting their grandchildren's inheritance. The majority of Boosters are passing on their accumulated wealth. Who is going to get this money, and what will the people who get it do with it? Right now, institutions—museums, hospitals, and especially churches—are getting a large share. An unselfish, parsimonious generation, Boosters think institutionally and have no trouble handing over money to institutions, trusting them to spend their hard-earned money wisely.

The Boomer children of the Boosters, in hock to their eyebrows, are salivating in expectation of getting their share. Studies have shown what they plan on doing with their portion, estimated at an average of $90,000 per Boomer. (The average net worth of Boosters is $290,000, with an average of three kids.) Boomers say that, first, they will pay off their credit card debts (in other words, they've already spent their inheritance); second, prepare for their kids' college education; third, buy a new toy (a second home, boat, or new car).

Whatever Boomers end up doing with however much they end up with, we know enough about their finances to make some preliminary predictions. Unlike their Booster parents, Boomers aren't good savers; the average Boomer's rate of savings (4%) is less than half of what their parents saved. Boomers are said to be saving at one-third the rate necessary for their retirement.[77]

Unlike their Booster parents, Boomers distrust institutions. They are already not taking their parents' place as patrons of the arts. Boomer attendance for ballet, symphony, opera, jazz, musicals, and theater has declined sharply over the past 10 years, according to one study by the National Endowment for the Arts.[78]

Boomers have good reason for their distrust of institutions, as summarized in a couple of defining Boomer events that dealt severe blows to our moral nervous system: Vietnam and Watergate. What Boomer can forget the sick-to-the-stomach feeling after learning that Charles Van Doren had cheated on the TV quiz show *Twenty-One?*[79] As the legendary batboy said to his hero, "Say it ain't so, Joe."

Moreover, Boomers have little faith in government solutions to problems.[80] They don't profess organizational loyalty easily, and they reject authority structures. Boomers have not returned to organized religion in anything near the numbers predicted of them, but even when they do, they are still less "religious" than their parents. They may be more "spiritual" than their parents, but they are less "religious" in an organized or formal sense.

Boomers particularly don't like the idea of giving to an organization and letting that organization decide how to spend their money ("apportionments"). Boomers (doubly for Boomer women) want to see where their money goes and choose how it gets there. They expect an accounting for every dollar. In their skepticism toward authority, they want to be personally involved in the distribution of their money. Boomers give more to causes than institutions.

At the same time, the Boomers, the flower children of the 1960s, want their resources to help people and make a difference. The 1994 Wingspread Conference on philanthropy compiled the following characteristics of Boomer giving:

- They prefer cause-related giving over institution-based giving.
- They prefer smaller, community-based groups over large, bureaucratic institutions.

- Giving that makes a difference and promotes fairness and equality is very important.
- Leaving a legacy perpetuating their family name is unimportant.
- Having some voice and control and participation in their charity is crucial.
- They have high concern for the character and integrity of grantees.
- Boomer women are active, independent, and powerful contributors.
- African-Americans are engaging in philanthropy in record numbers.[81]

One reason why support for missions work is declining among Boomers is that old methods of raising missions money don't work on them. What does? The two top Boomer fund-raising organizations are Habitat for Humanity (which between 1975 and 1995 had built 30,000 single-family homes and is ranked 17th among the nation's top home builders) and Hospice. Boomers have also proved eager to support the environmental movement, which for the knock-it-all-down-and-start-again Boosters is a blind spot. Indeed, Boosters are generationally tone deaf on this issue of creation; unlike the Boomers, they have little "ecological ego," a sense of ethical responsibility to nature.

FROM A THEOLOGY OF GIVING TO A THEOLOGY OF RECEIVING ~

The tithing system is based on a "theology of giving." That is, God calls me to give 10% of what is mine to the work of the kingdom. There are two main problems with this theology of giving that has undergirded church fund-raising in the modern era.

The first is revealed by a simple question that tells more about someone's mental and spiritual health, the state of a soul and body, than anyone will care to have known: "Can you accept praise?" Or, "When the affirmation we all want comes to us, how do we accept it?"

Most people in the pews have one of the greatest spiritual problems anyone can have: They are better givers than receivers. Clergy especially suffer from this disease. I confess: I am a better giver than receiver. I don't celebrate birthdays for a lot of reasons (I gave up birthdays when I turned 40), chief among them the fact that I am uncomfortable receiving. I love to give presents; I am awkward and ill-at-ease in receiving them. For me, the joy is in the giving, not the getting.

My soul is in mortal danger every day. I pray daily over this debilitating spiritual disease that imperils my very soul. Why? What is my fundamental category in relationship to God, and vice versa? God is the giver; I am the receiver. The very best things about Len Sweet are what I have received. I can love because "Christ first loved me." The fact that for me the joy is in the giving, not the receiving, means that I don't like my category of receiving. I'd much prefer God's category of giving.

In other words, I have a "god-complex." And there are few more dangerous spiritual conditions than this.

The modern world built a "stewardship ethic" on a deeply flawed foundation: the theology of giving. The fact that the phrase "the joy is in the getting" grates on our spiritual nerves testifies to the very nature of our problem with basic theological doctrines of divine grace, love, and providence. It is time to build a postmodern "stewardship ethic" on the foundation of a theology of receiving rather than a theology of giving.

Here is the most fundamental insight of a faith that is postmodern: All is a gift. Everything! Here is the most elemental biblical attitude toward life: God is the owner. I am the ower. When King David dedicated to God everything and everyone who was a part of building the first temple in Jerusalem, he offered this prayer:

> Yours, LORD, is the greatness and the power, the glory, the splendour, and the majesty; for everything in heaven and on earth is yours;. . . Everything comes from you, and it is only of your gifts that we give to you (1 Chronicles 29:11, 14 REB)[82]

God owns everything. You and I own nothing. All I think I own, I owe anyway. The best things about Len Sweet are not what I am able to give, but what I have already received. This has perhaps never been expressed in community life better than the membership commitment of the Church of the Savior in Washington, DC.

> I commit myself, regardless of the expenditures of time, energy, and money to becoming an informed, mature Christian. I believe that God is the total owner of my life and resources. I give God the throne in relation to the material aspect of my life. God is the owner. I am the ower. Because God is a lavish giver I too shall be lavish and cheerful in my regular gifts.

The second major problem with a theology of giving is that it deludes us into believing that what we are giving God is ours to begin with. *Stewardship* is more than a stale word that conveys to the hearer a host of couldas, wouldas, shouldas. More is at stake in the word *stewardship* than nomenclature; the entire stewardship metaphor is anachronistic and arrogant.

The anachronism comes from the cultural irrelevance of the word itself. There are no stewards around anymore. In an agrarian culture, a steward—literally, a "keeper of a pigsty"—was a term ladled in meaning and laden with power. We named our church treasurers "stewards." We named our caretakers in flight "stewardesses." A "steward" was someone to be trusted.

The only "stewards" postmoderns come into contact with are at 5-Star restaurants—and they're the ones giving out the libations. The word itself has lost its rich referents to creation and life. "Stewardship Sunday" is now not about costly care for creation, but the cost of keeping church and fund-raising. If anything, modern stewardship appeals have separated people from creation more than connecting them to whole-life discipleship. Stewardship means "money." For postmoderns, the currency of the future is time more than it is money.

Biologist Lynn Margulis hammers home the arrogance problem:

> The idea that we are "stewards of the earth" is another symptom of human arrogance. Imagine yourself with the task of overseeing your body's physiological processes. Do you understand the way it works well enough to keep all its systems in operation? Can you make your kidneys function? Can you control the removal of waste? Are you conscious of the blood flow through your arteries, or the fact that you are losing a hundred thousand skin cells a minute? We are unconscious of most of our body's processes, thank goodness, because we'd screw it up if we weren't. The human body is so complex, with so many parts, . . . a system which is far more complex than we can fully imagine. The idea that we are consciously care-taking such a large and mysterious system is ludicrous.[83]

Even if we were to argue that it's a viable metaphor intrinsically, stewardship is not a metaphor that works. "Stewardship" is like trying to reach people for Christ in postmodern culture with a button or bumper sticker that says "Jesus Saves" or through the "Four Spiritual Laws." I once was in a car with some Gen-Xers who cracked up in laughter when a radio program came on. The Christian broadcast was introduced with organ background music, with the announcer saying, "Welcome to New Testament Light." Of course, the kids didn't hear "Light"; they heard "Lite."

Two Greek words in the New Testament are translated "stewardship." One is *epitropos*, which means "manager, foreman, steward, governor, procurator, guardian." The other, more common word is *oikonomos*, which also means "manager, steward, administrator"; it is formed by combining two words: *oikos* (house) and *nomos* (law).

I wish to argue that the best postmodern translation of both *epitropos* and *oikonomos* is "trustee." For the former, see Galatians 4:1–2: "What I am saying is that as long as the heir is a child, he is no different from a slave, although he owns the whole estate. He is subject to guardians and trustees until the time set by his father" (NIV). For the latter, see 1 Corinthians 9:17: "If I preach voluntarily, I have a reward; if not voluntarily, I am simply discharging the trust committed to me."[84]

> What wee gave, wee have;
> What wee spent, wee had;
> What wee left, wee lost.
>
> Epitaph for Edward Courtenay,
> Earl of Devon (d. 1419), and
> his wife at Tiverton, England

Postmoderns understand the complex nuances and connotations of "trusteeship." Many are on the boards of trustees of local organizations, including the church. Many themselves are trustees of estates. Whereas "stewardship" has been stripped of all legal overtones and fiduciary consequences, postmoderns understand that the trustees are the legal guardians of that organization or estate. They do not "own" it, but they are legally accountable for its health and well-being. If the church is sued, it is not the pastor who will go to jail, nor the members of the congregation whose money is on the line—it is the trustees. Once again, in the words of Paul, "It is required that those who have been given a trust must prove faithful" (1 Cor. 4:2 NIV).

The fundamental question of anyone who is a trustee of an estate is not "How much do I give away of what is mine?" but "How much of this estate do I receive for myself so that the estate might grow and prosper and do good?" The language of trusteeship is the language of receiving first, and only after the receiving question is settled does it become the language of giving.

> "Give as you have received ..."
>
> Jesus (Matthew 10:8 PHILLIPS)

The issue of receptivity was central for Jesus' ministry. Jesus demonstrated a marvelous capacity for receiving: "I was hungry and you gave me food, I was thirsty and you gave me something to drink, I was a stranger and you welcomed me" (Matt. 25:35). To see this theology of receiving at work in his life, theologian Elizabeth Barnes turns to the story of the hemorrhaging woman (Mark 5:24–34), which illustrates Jesus' "reciprocal giving and receiving of gifts." Barnes contends that

> Jesus felt the exchange between them precisely because she also gave something back to him. . . . He has been the grateful *recipient of her trust.* Many, no doubt, had jostled against him in the press of the crowd. But she had touched him with intention and hopeful trust. So doing, she has given to him, as well, a precious gift, even as he returns a priceless gift to her. Something truly human and healing *for them both* has occurred in this exchange. . . . she gives to Jesus—needful of human community as much as she—the incomparable gift of trust, confidence in him and all that he is and his healing power in relation to her.[85]

Or consider the story of the woman at the well near Sychar (John 4:1–42). Jesus is exhausted and parched. When a Samaritan woman approaches the well, Jesus asks her for a drink, for she had a bucket. Maria Teresa Porcile of Uruguay retells the story this way:

> In the shanty-town there was no water. . . .
> It was evening, and the day had been very hard. . . .
> And Jesus said: "Give me a drink."
> A woman passed that way, coming from afar. She was a stranger, someone they didn't know and she carried a bucket. She went up to the well

where the children were sitting, and the old people and the men and women, looking at the water in the well—the water, so near and yet so far.

And Jesus said: "Give me a drink."

And the woman answered: "Why do you ask me for a drink? You are poor and I am rich. You are thirsty but the bucket is mine."

And Jesus said: "Woman, what of the well? Whose well is it?"

And the woman's eyes were opened and with her bucket they began to draw water for the whole district.[86]

I am not the first, of course, to argue for a trusteeship ethic and its concomitant transition from giving to receiving. Andrew Carnegie, who slept all his life on his poor-boy's metal cot, expressed his wealth ethic in 1889 in precisely these terms of "trusteeship":

> This, then, is held to be the duty of the man of wealth: To set an example of modest, unostentatious living, shunning display or extravagance; to provide moderately for the legitimate wants of those dependent upon him; and, after doing so, to consider all surplus revenues which come to him simply as trust funds, which he is called upon to administer . . . to produce the most beneficial results for the community.[87]

Albert Einstein orchestrated his life from a self-composed receiving ethic: "A hundred times every day I remind myself that my inner and outer life depend on the labours of other men, living and dead, and that I must exert myself in order to give in the same measure as I have received and am still receiving."[88]

More recently, Harry Wendt, president of Crossways International in Minneapolis, argues, like me, that the whole language of "giving" needs to be abandoned in favor of what he calls "Christian distribution."

> When we place our so-called "gift" on the offering plate, we are not giving God anything. . . . [W]e are not *giving God but God's own!* We are merely getting our grubby little hands off what has always belonged to God. In short, we are not called to practice Christian *giving*, but Christian *management* and Christian *distribution*, and this applies not merely to what we "give" on Sundays, but to our total use of life as we manage this planet to the glory of God and for the good of all.[89]

In a theology of receiving, the first question is not "How much do I give to God of what is mine?" but "How much of God's do I keep for myself?" At various times in my life I may need to receive from the estate that has been entrusted to me almost 100%. At other times I may need to receive for myself less than 10%. But whatever our stage of life, one thing is clear: All that we have is a trust from God. We came into this world with nothing, and we leave this world with nothing. What Jesus told the rich young ruler, "You must give it all away" (see Luke 18:22), Jesus says to every one of us. None of us leaves life without having given it all away—to someone, to somewhere.

Humorist Erma Bombeck was continually asked if she saved up her best ideas for the next column, or how she parceled out and dribbled them out. Before she died, she answered these queries in a column entitled "What's Saved Is Often Lost."

> Be forewarned: Man and money cannot remain together forever. Either the money is taken from the man, or the man is taken from the money.
>
> Rebbe Nachman of Breslov[90]

I don't save anything. My pockets are empty at the end of a week. So is my gas tank. So is my file of ideas. I trot out the best I've got, and come the next week, I bargain, whimper, make promises, cower and throw myself on the mercy of the Almighty for just three more columns in exchange for cleaning my oven. . . .

Throughout the years, I've seen a fair number of my family who have died leaving candles that have never been lit, appliances that never got out of the box. . . .

I have learned that silver tarnishes when it isn't used, perfume turns to alcohol, candles melt in the attic over the summer, and ideas that are saved for a dry week often become dated.

I always had a dream that when I am asked to give an accounting of my life to a higher court, it will be like this: "So, empty your pockets. What have you got left of your life? Any dreams that were unfilled? Any unused talent that we gave you when you were born that you still have left? Any unsaid compliments or bits of love that you haven't spread around?"

And, I will answer, "I've nothing to return. I spent everything you gave me. I'm as naked as the day I was born."[91]

As Jesus sent forth his disciples, he said to them, "Freely ye have received, freely give" (Matt. 10:8 KJV). It is only in having been blessed by God's gifts that it is more blessed to give than to receive.

We cannot give until we have first received. We cannot bless others until we first receive for ourselves God's blessing. And out of that receiving, we give—most importantly ourselves (2 Cor. 8:5), and then our trust.

When he first became a Christian, John Wesley had a salary of 30 pounds per year. He lived on 28 pounds and gave two to the church. When his salary was increased to 50 pounds per year, he lived on 28 and gave 22 to the church. When his salary was increased to 100 pounds per year, he lived on 28 and gave 72 to the church.

> The flowing out of God always demands a flowing back.
>
> Jan Van Ruysbroeck
> (1293–1381)

We are not called to give. We are called to invest what is God's in the work of his kingdom.

God did not call us to "have dominion" over the earth; he called us to be trustees of his estate.

Whether the church's economic deployments begin with a theology of receiving or a theology of giving is important because where one begins alters the spirit in which the church's economic life takes place. And spirit matters. In a study for the Center on Philanthropy, Boston College sociologist Paul G. Schervish has found that charitable giving has very little to do with income or wealth. Rather, it has everything to do with one's associations, attitudes, faith, and ability to identify with the needs of others.[92]

Jesuit theologian John Haughey contends that

> it is absolutely false to ever use the words "my wealth." It is radical fallacy to consider wealth as mine. It is not my wealth! This is a lie hot from hell! "My" does not fit on the world "wealth." "Nation's wealth" is a lie! "Corporation's wealth" is a lie! Whatever wealth I have disposition over is not my wealth. It is the wealth of the Owner. If there is anything worth hearing, it is this statement: "My" must never again be attached to the noun "wealth." It's NOT my wealth. Rather, it's my responsibility about the Master's wealth.[93]

say what? 1. Consider EFT (electronic funds transfer): EFTs moved $271 trillion in the US in 1996, 3.6 times the value of all checks. By 2000, almost all federal payments will be by direct-deposit transfers. More than that, if a business submits more than $50,000 in federal payroll taxes, it *must* file taxes electronically as of 1997. If you have questions, you may want to call the Electronic Funds Transfer Association (703-435-9800; www.efta.org).

2. Do a Bible study on the story of Elisha and the chariot that transported him to heaven (2 Kings 2:1–13). Each of us will one day ride such a chariot. For some, that chariot is cancer; for others, a heart attack; for others, Alzheimer's; for some, an accident. If you could choose your chariot, which would it be? Any premonitions about what your chariot might actually be?

3. One biotech researcher made some off-the-record predictions for *Wired* magazine. Here is what he is predicting.

2003	Human-genome sequencing completed.
2000+	Artificially engineered DNA used routinely to treat defects in human cells.
2000+	Desktop genetic testing available in hospitals and clinics.
2000+	Genetic therapy for cancer and other genetic diseases becomes widespread.

2000+ Inherited traits in mammals successfully altered in the laboratory.

2010+ Alteration of inherited traits in mammals is routine.

2010+ Complex (polygenic) human traits, including intelligence, are fully understood.

2010+ Alteration of inherited traits becomes a major political issue.

2015+ Genetic engineering widely used to eliminate disease-causing defects, paid for by public-health programs and private health insurance.

2020+ Inherited human traits are routinely altered for nonmedical reasons.

2030+ First generation of children altered for intelligence, longevity, and appearance approach maturity; genetic engineering begins to have profound impact on the human experience.[94]

What about this scenario excites you, and what frightens you?

4. In what ways is the "medium" the amplification and the modification of the body?

5. One of Philip Larkin's most masterful small poems, "Days," asks the question, "Where can we live but days?" The attempt to answer that question

Brings the priest and the doctor
In their long coats
Running over the fields.[95]

What is the difference between the answers of the priest and the doctor?

6. Is there anyone who doesn't get some short straws in life's lottery? If we were to get rid of everyone with dirty genes, wouldn't it mean that we would have to get rid of each and every one of us?

7. Rent Andrew Niccol's cautionary film *Gattaca* (Columbia Pictures, 1997)—the acronym comprises the four chemical letters of DNA—and discuss its theological implications about the Bionomic Age. How "distant" in the future is this separation of "valids" and "in-valids"?

8. Thanks to the 1982 experiments at the University of Paris by Alain Aspect and his team of physicists, and thanks to what is known as the "Bell Effect," we have moved from a cause-and-effect universe into a holographic universe where there is an interconnectedness to all things. Physicist Ernest C. Lucas describes the Bell Effect as follows:

Sometimes a sub-atomic event produces a pair of particles which fly off in different directions. Quantum theory predicts that, from then on, the characteristics of these two particles will be linked, however far apart they go. For example, sub-atomic particles have a characteristic called "spin." If, when the two particles are produced, one of them has a spin of 2 and the other has a spin of −1, throughout their lifetime their combined spin will always be zero. Now it is possible to change the spin of a particle. If the spin of one of the pair is changed from 1 to –1, quantum theory predicts that the spin of the other will instantaneously change from –1 to 1, even if it is millions of miles away. This is inexplicable by the normal law of causality. According to this, for one even to cause another, information must travel between them. But the theory of relativity says that this cannot happen faster than the speed of light. . . . So how is the Bell effect produced? No one knows. . . . What happens to a particle in one part of the universe affects a particle in another, far-distant part without any physical cause-and-effect link.[96]

What does it feel like to live in a universe that is getting stranger and stranger?

9. Have you heard the "parable of the lily leaf"? Let's suppose that the lily leaf doubles in size every 24 hours. That means that on the day before it completely canopies the pond, the water is only half covered. Two days before the pond is completely choked, the water is only a quarter covered; the day before that, only an almost imperceptible eighth. All summer long one doesn't notice the growth of the lily leaf until its "sudden" manifestation. By then, however, it is too late.

What are some examples of the "parable of the lily leaf" you can think of?

10. The social and technological realities of the 21st century are redefining "family" beyond the nuclear definitions we came to live with from the '50s on. From surrogacy to single motherhood through artificial insemination, there is a whole host of new definitions of "family." Where do you come down?

11. Do you agree with Robert Heilbroner's presentation of the problem, as made in a 1975 article in the *New York Times Magazine*?

> Will mankind survive? Who knows? The question I want to put is more searching: Who cares? It is clear that most of us today do not care—or at least do not care enough. How many of us would be willing to give up some minor convenience—say, the use of aerosols—in the hope that this might extend the life of man on earth by a hundred years? Suppose we also knew with a high degree of certainty that humankind could not survive a thousand years unless we gave up our wasteful diet of meat, abandoned all pleasure driving, cut back on every use of energy that was not essential to the maintenance of a bare minimum. Would we care enough for posterity to pay the price of its survival?
>
> I doubt it.[97]

Poll your congregation to see how many have given up the use of aerosols.

12. Have someone read and review Steve Jones's *In the Blood: God, Genes and Destiny* (New York: HarperCollins, 1996), a book that was written to accompany a BBC television series with the same title. What in this book is dated? You can also check out Jones's Web site at www.euro.net/markspace/SteveJones.html.

13. Gandhi claimed that there is a kind of "wild card" within each of us, a wellspring of strength and creativity we don't know even exists until we learn how to tap into it through spiritual practice. How well are you accessing your personal "wild card"? Where is your church's "wild card"?

14. Is it modern, or postmodern, to give precedence to rights over responsibilities, freedom over fidelity?

15. Some excellent resources for the study of the genesis of Dolly and her scientific achievement are Gina Kolata (a *New York Times* reporter), *Clone: The Road to Dolly and the Path Ahead;* Lee Silver (a Princeton ethicist), *Remaking Eden: Cloning and Beyond in a Brave New World;* and Carson Strong (an ethicist at the University of Tennessee), *Ethics in Reproductive and Perinatal Medicine.* Strong asks the basic question, "Who gets to have a baby using whose genes?"[98]

16. Someone has said that FEAR is an acronym for False Evidence that Appears Real. But aren't there some things that we *should* be afraid of? Isn't the world *really* a fearful place? From a biblical perspective, what is it that overcomes fear?

17. Will the potential of longer and healthier lives heighten people's interest in spirituality, or lessen it?

18. What does it mean that corporations are now securing patents to cells, mircroorganisms, and genes? What does it mean for someone to have a license to live? To own life?

19. Jeremy Rifkin believes that "the biotech revolution will affect every aspect of lives: the way we eat; the way we date and marry; the way we have our babies; the way our children are raised and educated; the way we work; the way we engage in politics; the way we express our faith; the way we perceive the world around us and our place in it. . . . The Biotech revolution will force each of us to put a mirror to our most deeply held values, making us ponder the ultimate question of the purpose and meaning of existence."[99]

Is he exaggerating?

20. Physicist Stephen Hawking is already on record as claiming that computer viruses should count as a form of life—they duplicate themselves, live off another's metabolism, etc. "It says something about human nature that the only form of life we have created so far is purely destructive," says Hawking. "We've created life in our own image."[100]

What do you think about Hawking's thesis?

21. How would you answer these questions posed by futurist Faith Popcorn?

> You're pregnant and a horrible disease is expected to show up in, say, your baby's fourth year. Four precious years, but too short for a full life. What do you do?
>
> What if you find out the disease is slated to show up by age 70? And degenerate into a terrifyingly painful ending? Then what?
>
> How would you handle it if there was only an 80% chance of the problem manifesting itself at all? 48%? 30%? 20%?[101]

22. "In my esteem, age is not estimable," wrote Lord Byron. Is "ageism" a problem in your faith community? The anti-ageist tract by Michael Young and Tom Schuller, *Life After Work: The Arrival of the Ageless Society* (London: HarperCollins, 1991), argues the case that just as we have the right to change our birth certificate and choose our name, so we ought to have the right to change our birth certificate and pass ourselves off as "ageless."

Is there anything ironic about their argument? What do you think of it?

23. Ken Dychtwald, head of the Age Wave Institute, makes a comparison based on the fact that age 50 is the entry level for membership in the American Association of Retired Persons (AARP), which boasts more than 33 million members: "If AARP were to become an independent nation, it would be the thirtieth-largest nation in the world, with a population only slightly smaller than that of Argentina."

Do you think Boomers and postmoderns will become card-carrying members of AARP? When you are 50, will you start asking for "senior citizens discount, please"?

Dychtwald also concludes that "if the nation were now to pick one age group for special economic treatment because it was poor and has bleak prospects for the future, statistics show that this group would not be the old, but the young."[102]

What might the implications of this one statement alone be for your church?

24. Read and review as a group Ted Peters's *For the Love of Children: Genetic Technology and the Future of the Family* (Louisville: Westminster/John Knox, 1998) or Arthur L. Caplan's *Am I My Brother's Keeper? The Ethical Frontiers of Biomedicine* (Bloomington: Indiana Univ. Press, 1998). Draw up a list of advances where biomedical technology is outpacing our ethical guidelines.

25. Discuss:

> We are going to have to redefine our notions of what motherhood, fatherhood and pregnancy are. Some women will become biological mothers

but won't get pregnant, hiring a birth mother instead. Other women will choose to become pregnant later in life, after their careers and even after menopause, either by carrying their own embryo conceived years earlier or by buying eggs from another woman. Some women will become pregnant without meeting the father. Men will become biological fathers without meeting the mother. Some babies will be born without anyone becoming pregnant at all! And there are other permutations as well.

Undoubtedly, many of us will initially find these ideas too abhorrent, too foreign to the basic human way of life. What right do science and medicine have to intrude upon this most natural of life processes and make it so unnatural?[103]

now what? See the Net Notes in http://www.soultsunami.com

NOTES

1. See *Star Trek: First Contact* (Hollywood, CA: Paramount Pictures, 1996).

2. As quoted in Mark Dery's "Immortal Thoughts," *21C* 23 (1997): 41.

3. Michael Rothschild, *Bionomics: The Inevitability of Capitalism* (New York: Henry Holt, 1990).

4. Kevin Kelly, *Out of Control: The New Biology of Machines, Social Systems and the Economic World* (Reading, MA: Addison-Wesley, 1994).

5. Edgar Guest, "The Things That Haven't Been Done Before," in his *A Heap o' Livin'* (Chicago: Reilly & Lee, 1916), 173.

6. Stoll/Barlow Debate 97: "NetHype vs. Digital Revolution," *Web Fanatic* [Buzz Webster] Special Edition.

7. Morton, "Overcoming Yuk," 44, 46. See also Jeremy Rifkin, *The Biotech Century: Harnessing the Gene and Remaking the World* (New York: Jeremy P. Tarcher/Putnam, 1998).

8. Bill McKibben, "Ocean Solitaire," *Utne Reader* (May-June 1998): 103.

9. For Bruce Mazlish, the elimination of "the Fourth Discontinuity" between humans and the things humans create will shock us as strongly as Galileo, Darwin, and Freud did. The first three "egosmashings" have placed the human creation on a continuum in relation to the universe (Greek physicist philosophers), to the rest of the animal kingdom (Darwin), and to humans themselves (Freud). See Mazlich's essay "The Fourth Discontinuity," in *Perspectives in the Computer Revolution,* ed. Zenon W. Pylyshyn and Liam J. Banon (Norwood, NJ: Ablex Publishing, 1989), 71–83, esp. 73.

10. Allucquere Rosanne Stone, *The War of Desire and Technology at the Close of the Mechanical Age* (Cambridge, MA: MIT Press, 1995).

11. Donna J. Haraway, "Cyborg Manifesto: Science, Technology, and Socialist-Feminism in the Late Twentieth Century," ch. 8 of her *Simians, Cyborgs, and Women: The Reinvention of Nature* (New York: Routledge, 1991), 181.

12. Peter F. Drucker, *Post-Capitalist Society* (New York: HarperBusiness, 1993).

13. A paper describing the work of the University of Rochester researchers into this is available on the Web at www.cs.rochester.edu/users/faculty/ogihara/research/pubs.html.

14. *Wall Street Journal* (1 Feb 1994). The progress report on which the *Journal* based its report is found in Clarence A. Robinson Jr., "Bioelectronics Computer Era Merges Organic, Solid State," 15–17, and "Selective Biological Cells Grow as Neural Networks," 19–20, *Signal* (Feb 1994).

15. The technology of wiring up molecules is already being experimented with by Thomas Meade of the California Institute of Technology.

16. "The first important revolution on the technical plane was that of transportation. The second, which was almost concomitant, was the transmissions revolution, including Marconi, Edison, radio, television. The third, which we are on the verge of, is the revolution of transplantations. All these technologies of telecommunications that had been employed in aviation and missiles favor nanotechnology—the possibility of miniaturizing technology to the point of introducing it into the human body. . . . We are on the verge of the biomachine." See James Derian, "Special Pollution," an interview with Paul Virilio, *Wired* (May 1996): 121.

17. Adrian Berry, *The Next 500 Years: Life in the Coming Millennium* (New York: W. H. Freeman, 1996), 91.

18. As computed by Seth Loyd in Charles Platt, "A Million MHz CPU?" *Wired* (Mar 1995): 125.

19. Erik Erickson, *Young Man Luther: A Study in Psychoanalysis and History* (New York: Norton, 1958).

20. In 1997, CBS's top hit, *Touched by an Angel,* generated revenue of $90,000 per 30-second spot. Fox's series *The X-Files* charges $278,500 for a 30-second spot for a much smaller audience. Why the difference? Advertisers, used to paying more to reach "younger generations," haven't wakened up to the fact that the always-young generation with mega-purchasing power now is the aging Boomers. For more, see Carter Henderson, *Funny, I Don't Feel Old: How to Flourish After 50* (San Francisco: Institute for Contemporary Studies Press, 1997).

21. James F. Fries and Lawrence M. Crapo, *Vitality and Aging* (San Francisco: W. H. Freeman, 1981).

22. Larry Laudan, *The Book of Risks* (New York: John Wiley, 1994), 81: "Although those over 45 are much more likely to have chronic diseases, their incidence of humdrum infections such as colds, sore throat, and flu is much lower than that for younger folks."

23. Thomas T. Perls, "The Oldest Old," *Scientific American* (Jan 1995): 70–75; Richard M. Suzman, David P. Willis, and Kenneth G. Manton, *The Oldest Old* (New York: Oxford Univ. Press, 1992). The centenarian population grew by 160% in the US during the 1980s. The oldest old men (those over 90) become less and less likely to develop Alzheimer's disease with every passing year. "Gender crossover" (whereby the advantage goes to men having better cognitive and physical condition than women) doesn't occur until after 85. Men comprise 20% of 100-year-olds, but 40% of 105-year-olds. After 85, men live healthy and active lives longer than women.

24. Charles Handy, *The Age of Paradox* (Boston: Harvard Business School Press, 1994), 4: "If we have not died by the age of 50 we are unlikely to die before 75, unless we do something silly."

25. Erasmus, "On the Troubles of Old Age," in *Collected Works of Erasmus,* trans. Clarence H. Miller (Toronto: Univ. of Toronto Press, 1993), 72:13–25.

26. Cheryl Russell, *The Mid-Youth Market: Baby Boomers in Their Peak Earning and Spending Years* (New York: New Strategist Publications, 1996).

27. This case has been made most powerfully by Marvin Cetron and Owen Davis, *Cheating Death: The Promise and the Future Impact of Trying to Live Forever* (New York: St. Martin's Press, 1998).

28. As quoted by Walt Schoedel in "The Graying of the Church," *Vital Ministry* (May-June 1998): 49.

29. For more statistics from the trade journal *Natural Foods Merchandiser* (NFM) and *The Hartman Report,* see the cover story "Health Food Goes Mainstream," *Boomer Report* (July 1997): 1–2.

30. As quoted in Stephen M. Pollan and Mark Levine, "The Rise and Fall of Retirement," *Worth* (Dec 1994-Jan 1995): 69.

31. "In 1960, fully 92 percent of men aged 55 to 59 were in the labor force. By 1993, the figure had fallen to 78 percent. Among men aged 60 to 64 it fell from 81 to 54 percent. In the 1950s, a majority of men aged 65 to 69 were still working. Today, only one-fourth are in the labor force" (Cheryl Russell, "The End of Early Retirement," *Boomer Report* [Aug 1994]: 4).

32. According to C. Eugene Steuerle and Jon M. Bakija, in *Retooling Social Security for the 21st Century* (Washington, DC: Urban Institute Press, 1994), the average single American male who retired in 1980 will receive checks from social security worth $39,000 more than their contributions and the interest they might have earned. An average Boomer retiring in 2010 will suffer a lifetime loss of $38,000. A Buster retiring in 2030 will lose $62,000. These numbers are only going to get bigger. At the inception of social security in 1935, each American retiree was supported by 42 workers; by 1995 the figure had plummeted to 3.2.

33. See Lydia Bronte, *The Longevity Factor: The New Reality of Long Careers and How It Can Lead to Richer Lives* (New York: HarperPerennial, 1994); see also Catherine D. Fyock and Anne Marrs Dorton, *UnRetirement: A Career Guide for the Retired—the Soon-to-Be Retired— the Never-Want-to-Be Retired* (New York: American Management Association, 1994).

34. The world average life spans increased from 46 years in 1950 to 65 years in 1993, according to Gary Lee, writing in the *Washington Post Weekly* (1 Aug 1994): 40. Of course, in some areas it is getting worse. AIDS is taking a gruesome toll in Thailand, Uganda, and other parts of Africa. Environmental collapse is taking a toll in Russia.

35. The Popular Reference Bureau, a Washington think tank, says that by the year 2025, Americans over 65 will outnumber teenagers by more than two to one.

36. Michael Fossel, "Reversing Human Aging: It's Time to Consider the Consequences," *The Futurist* 31 (July-Aug 1997): 25–28.

37. USAmerican men are now two inches taller than they were, on average, in 1960, and they weigh 27 pounds more. USAmerican women are also two inches taller, but only one pound heavier.

38. Mark Twain, *Following the Equator* (New York: Harper, 1899), 2:137.

39. Jeff Lyon and Peter Gorner, *Altered Fates: Gene Therapy and the Retooling of Human Life* (New York: Norton, 1995), 517.

40. As quoted in Lyon and Gorner, *Altered Fates,* 523.

41. See Carolyn R. Shaffer and Kristin Anundsen, *Creating Community Anywhere: Finding Support in a Fragmented World* (New York: Putnam, 1993), and Robert E. Ornstein and Charles Swencionis, eds., *The Healing Brain: How Your Mind Can Heal Your Body* (Emmaus, PA: Rodale Press, 1986).

42. See Pamela Weintraub, "The Coming of the High-Tech Harvest," *Audubon* 94 (July-Aug 1992): 92–103.

43. Frank Tipler, *The Physics of Immortality: Modern Cosmology, God and the Resurrection of the Dead* (New York: Macmillan, 1995), 1.

44. Adrian Berry, *The Next 500 Years: Life in the Coming Millennium* (New York: W. H. Freeman, 1996), 86–87.

45. As quoted in Max More, "Thinking About Thinking," *Wired* (Dec 1996): 252.

46. My recent book *Health and Medicine in the Evangelical Tradition* (Valley Forge, PA: Trinity Press International, 1994) helped me work out some of these thoughts from a historical perspective. See also my audio book with Richard Warren, *The Tides of Change: Riding the Next Wave in Ministry* (Nashville: Abingdon Press, 1995).

47. See the table on diseases reported by the CDC in the 1995 Statistical Abstract of the United States (1995).

48. Christian Schwarz offers six "biotic principles" for natural development of the body of Christ in *Natural Church Development: A Guide to Eight Essential Qualities of Healthy Churches* (Carol Stream, IL: ChurchSmart Resources, 1996).

49. Ron Archer with Janet Bond, "Lessons from the Chinese Bamboo Tree" in *On Teams* (New York: Irwin Professional Books, 1996). But see Lisa Chadderdon, "The Big Bamboozle," *Fast Company* (Nov 1998): 62.

50. For more along these lines, see my book *The Jesus Prescription for a Healthy Life* (Nashville: Abingdon Press, 1997). The importance of "health" as a religious category is

explored in Leonard Sweet, *Health and Medicine in the Evangelical Tradition* (Valley Forge, PA: Trinity Press International, 1994).

51. "Breakthroughs," *Discover* (Mar 1996): 12.

52. Susan Sontag, *Illness as Metaphor* (New York: Doubleday, 1990), 3.

53. Harold Remus, *Jesus as Healer* (New York: Cambridge Univ. Press, 1997), 115.

54. Remus, *Jesus as Healer*, 114–15.

55. "Taking a Look at the Future of Medicare," *Boomer Report* (Dec 1995): 3.

56. According to the National Funeral Directors Association, the national average cost for earth funerals in 1995 was $4,624. Houston's Celestis (713-522-7282) would have buried you in 1998 on board satellite-bearing rockets for $4,800.

57. In *Prayer Is Good Medicine* (San Francisco: HarperSanFrancisco, 1996), Larry Dossey has collected more than 130 scientific studies that document the power of prayer.

58. In this I agree with Larry Dossey, *Healing Words: The Power of Medicine and Prayer* (San Francisco: HarperCollins, 1994).

59. Interestingly, this is the same number of medical schools that require courses in gerontology.

60. Jerry Mander, *In the Absence of the Sacred: The Failure of Technology and the Survival of the Indian Nations* (San Francisco: Sierra Club Books, 1991), 161–77.

61. Wes Jackson, "Listen to the Land," *Amicus Journal* (Spring 1993): 33.

62. Mary Meehan, Larry Samuel, and Vickie Abrahamson, *The Future Ain't What It Used to Be* (New York: Riverhead Books, 1998), 46.

63. David Ronfeldt, "Cyberocracy Is Coming," *Information Society* 8, no. 4 (1992): 243–96.

64. John Fawcett, "Blest Be the Tie That Binds," *The United Methodist Hymnal: Book of United Methodist Worship* (Nashville: United Methodist Publishing, 1989), 557.

65. Alison Stein Wellner, "Eat, Drink, and Be Healed," *American Demographics* (Mar 1998): 56.

66. Raymond Williams, *Keywords: A Vocabulary of Culture and Society*, rev. ed. (New York: Oxford Univ. Press, 1985), 72.

67. Christian de Duve, *Vital Dust: Life as a Cosmic Imperative* (New York: Basic Books, 1995), 264.

68. Edward O. Wilson, *Sociobiology: The New Synthesis* (Cambridge, MA: Harvard Univ. Press, 1975), 3–6, 547–75. Wilson argues genetic predestination especially in the first chapter ("The Morality of the Gene") and the last ("Man: From Sociology to Biology").

69. Ian Stewart and Jack Cohen, *Figments of Reality: The Evolution of the Curious Mind* (New York: Cambridge Univ. Press, 1997), 63. For more about what these influences might be, see Walter Bodmer and Robin McKie, *The Book of Man: The Human Genome Project and the Quest to Discover Our Genetic Heritage* (New York: Scribner, 1994), 4–5.

70. *E. E. Cummings: Complete Poems 1904–1962*, ed. George J. Firmage (New York: Liveright, 1991), 484.

71. Pope John XXIII, *Journal of a Soul* (London: Geoffrey Chapman, 1965), 264.

72. More seriously and substantively, the "gerontographics" life-stage model proposes four groups for older adults: (1) Healthy Indulgers (18% of the 55-plus population), who behave like younger people except are more well-healed and more settled; (2) Healthy Hermits (36%), who are withdrawn socially and psychologically because of divorce, death, disease, or retirement; (3) Ailing Outgoers (29%), who have health problems and life-stresses but still don't let it get them down; they live life regardless; and (4) Frail Recluses (17%), who accept old-age status and have adjusted their lifestyles to almost invalid dimensions. For more see George P. Moschis, *Gerontographics: Life-Stage Segmentation for Marketing Strategy Development* (Westport, CT: Quorum, 1996).

73. Betty Friedan, *The Fountain of Age* (New York: Simon & Schuster, 1993), esp. ch. 18, "Age as Adventure," 571–612.

74. Jay Kesler, "Surrogate Grandparents," *Vista* (19 Feb 1995): 4–5.

75. *Parade Magazine* (15 July 1990): 10.

76. Bobby L. Eklund and Terry Austin, *Partners with God: Bible Truths About Giving* (Nashville: Convention Press, 1994), 6.

77. A study by Arthur D. Little, Inc., revealed that Boomers with pensions are still 40-to-50% shy of what they need; those without pensions are 70-to-80% shy. This study, however, did not include housing wealth, which if factored in would bring that figure to three-fourths of what is necessary.

78. "Culture Shock," *Boomer Report* (Dec 1995): 4.

79. This event is memorialized in the 1994 movie *Quiz Show*.

80. Twenty-one percent of Boomers believe the American Dream is dead, and 61% believe that their children will not enjoy their standard of living (*Boomer Report* [Oct-Nov 1994]: 6).

81. *Lessons from Wingspread: The Ten Trillion Dollar Intergenerational Transfer of Wealth—A Philanthropic Game Plan.* A Report of Recommended Strategies for Promoting Philanthropy Developed at a Wingspread Conference. September 1994 (Boston: The Philanthropic Initiative, 1994), 12–13.

82. See also these texts:

"All the earth is mine" (Ex. 19:5 RSV).

"The silver is mine, and the gold is mine, says the LORD of hosts" (Hag. 2:8 RSV).

"Know that the LORD is God! It is He that made us, and we are His" (Ps. 100:3 RSV).

83. See the interview with Lynn Margulis in Jonathan White, *Talking On the Water: Conversations About Nature and Creativity* (San Francisco: Sierra Club Books, 1994), 76.

84. For other examples see Matt. 20:8; Luke 12:42–43; 16:1–2, etc.

85. Elizabeth Barnes, *The Story of Discipleship* (Nashville: Abingdon Press, 1995), 53–55.

86. As quoted in John S. McClure, *The Round-Table Pulpit* (Nashville: Abingdon Press, 1995), 106.

87. Andrew Carnegie, *Gospel of Wealth and Other Timely Essays* (Cambridge, MA: Belknap Press of Harvard Univ. Press, 1962), 25.

88. Albert Einstein, *The World As I See It* (New York: Covici, Friede, 1934), 1.

89. Harry N. Wendt, "Second Presentation, June 14, 1997," to the Chicago Synod Assembly, ELCA, 7–13. See also H. N Wendt, *The Divine Drama* (Indianapolis: Shekinah Foundation, 1983), 293–303.

90. Moshe Mykoff, ed., *The Empty Chair: Finding Hope and Joy: Timeless Wisdom from a Hasidic Master, Rebbe Nachman of Breslov* (Woodstock, VT: Jewish Lights Publishing, 1994), 22.

91. As quoted by John M. Buchanan, "Give It All," Fourth Presbyterian Church, Chicago, Illinois (23 Oct 1994): 1.

92. See the working document "Wherewithal and Beneficence: Charitable Giving by Income and Wealth" (Indiana University Center on Philanthropy, n.d., 317-274-4200).

93. Father John Haughey, S.J., as quoted in *Ministry of Money* 98 (Oct 1995): 5.

94. "Man and Superman," *Wired* (Oct 1997): 193.

95. Philip Larkin, "Days," in *Philip Larkin, Collected Poems,* ed. Anthony Thwaite (New York: Farrar, Straus, Giroux, n.d.), 67.

96. See Ernest C. Lucas, "The 'New Science' and the Gospel," in *The Gospel in the Modern World: A Tribute to John Stott,* ed. Martyn Eden and David F. Wells (Downers Grove, IL: InterVarsity Press, 1991), 129.

97. Robert Heilbroner, "What Has Posterity Ever Done For Me?": as quoted in Joseph Petulla, *Reading the Signs of the Times: Resources for Social and Cultural Analysis* (New York: Paulist Press, 1993), 186–87.

98. Gina Kolata, *Clone: The Road to Dolly and the Path Ahead* (New York: Morrow, 1998); Lee Silver, *Remaking Eden: Cloning and Beyond in a Brave New World* (New York: Avon Books, 1997); and Carson Strong, *Ethics in Reproductive and Perinatal Medicine* (New Haven: Yale Univ. Press, 1998).

99. Jeremy Rifkin, *The Biotech Century: Harnessing the Gene and Remaking the World* (New York: Jeremy P. Tarcher/Putnam, 1998), 326–27.

100. Stephen Hawking, as quoted in Mark E. Johnson, "Are Computer Viruses a Form of Life?" *USA Today* (3 Aug 1994): 1A.

101. Faith Popcorn and Lys Marigold, *Clicking: 17 Trends That Drive America* (New York: HarperCollins, 1996), 244. Popcorn's immediate response: "Welcome to the next century's sleepless nights."

102. See Ken Dychtwald, *Age Wave: How the Most Important Trend of Our Time Will Change Your Future* (New York: Bantam, 1990).

103. Dr. Jeffrey A. Fisher, as quoted in Walter Truett Anderson, *Evolution Isn't What It Used to Be* (New York: W. H. Freeman, 1996), 93.

L ife ring #4

Get Deidolized

THE GODLET PHENOMENON

or what? Question: Do you have any idols lying around the house?
[Caution to reader: It's a trick question. Remember—idols come in varied forms, and John Calvin called the heart a veritable "factory of idols."]

Answer: We are our new idols. Every age has its golden calves, and ours is ourselves.

- When Katherine told her father Ira wanted to marry her, her father asked, "Is Ira religious?"
  "Oh yes," replied Katherine. "In fact, he thinks he's God Almighty."
- Said the psychiatrist to the patient, "I'm not aware of your problem, so perhaps you should start at the beginning."
  Said the patient to the psychiatrist, "All right. In the beginning I created the heavens and the earth . . ."

A GENIE OUT OF THE BOTTLE ～ Ira's problem, and that patient's problem, is the godlet phenomenon of postmodern culture: the misguided notion that we are gods or can be as gods. The title of a 1996 album from the "trip-hop" acid-rock group Tricky tells it like it is: *Nearly God.* So does the 1997 movie *Playing God.*[1] Who knows what the next few years will bring? The godlet genie is out of the bottle. It must be recorked. The self must be dethroned.

Postmoderns now have unprecedented powers—power to change life, to change themselves, to change the world. Postmodern culture is a sucker for the serpent's lie: "You will be like God" (Gen. 3:5). Long after history's first temptation, physicist J. Robert Oppenheimer predicted that the ancient hubris would raise its head with renewed force. In the mysterious atmospherics of that afternoon testing of the A-bomb in New Mexico, he claimed, we have become as gods. Since then, what has our technological exploration of outer space become if not a search for "contact" with higher beings that could "godify" us? Since then, what has our technological exploration of inner space become if not a search for a higher consciousness that could goddify us? Little wonder that postmodern spirituality is more about self-knowledge than about God-knowledge.

> For my people have committed two evils:
> 　they have forsaken me,
> the fountain of living water,
> 　and dug out cisterns for themselves,
> cracked cisterns
> 　that can hold no water.
>
> 　　　　　　Jeremiah 2:13

We call "gods" ofttimes "celebrities," sometimes "stars"—and every single one of us is trained to imagine oneself as one of them. Europeans are fond of saying that, judging from what they read in the newspapers, the US is composed entirely of celebrities and serial killers. In a culture where more than 65 million USAmericans have had a personal involvement with stardom—i.e., they or a member of their family has appeared on the TV screen, were seen on the local news—it is no wonder that being a star has been described as "our number one mass motive."[2] Andy Warhol was more right than he knew. Every one of us can look forward to being a one-night celebrity, or at least a legend in our own lunchtime.

> Q: How does a soprano change a lightbulb?
>
> A: She just holds on and the world revolves around her.

For most of history, athletes have received the goddifying treatment of the masses. Now every commercial pays homage to every person's divinity. We increasingly believe the goddifying messages that come down from Madison Avenue:

It is you who are running the show.
You are the one calling the shots.
You are the most important person in the world.
What you want, you get—anytime, anywhere, anyplace.
Have it your way.

Do you want thick crust, thin crust, spiced crust, stuffed crust, or double-stuffed crust? And that's just at Pizza Hut. We live in a "you want it you get it" world that drives us increasingly inward. Here is a print commercial for a Hummer in *The Economist*.

You Are Invincible.
You Are All-Powerful.
You Are Unstoppable.
You Are on Your Way to the Grocery Store.

Pretty soon the grocery store will be on its way to us. A digitized future, in which computers are so small and cheap, they will be in everything, promising to make us even more godlike. When our appliances talk to us and to each other, they will know exactly how strong we like our coffee, how burnt we like our toast, how *al dente* we like our vegetables. Everything will be ours how we like it, when we like it, and where we like it. Every detail will be within our control.

The digital world empowers the individual to be more than captain of the ship; we can become masters of the multiverse, of self-made galaxies. It used to be we lived a life where others (politicians, conglomerates, middlemen) made decisions for us. The digital domain gives each of us complete control over life's decisions. A computer hacker told author Steven Levy, "You could be God."[3] Cyberspace philosopher Michael Heim argues that the very nature of the hypertext itself, with its infinite reaches within finite grasps, breeds a drive toward "omniscience"—which he defines as "the confidence that we can really express and gain an adequate grasp of almost anything."[4] In other words, we can attempt to be God. Cyberculture critic Mark Dery warns that behind our quest for cyborg status and digital butlers lurks "a misguided hope that we will be born again as 'bionic angels' . . . a deadly misreading of the myth of Icarus [that] pins our future to wings of wax and feathers."[5]

> Man has as it were become a prosthetic God.
>
> Sigmund Freud [6]

The secret appeal of the serpent's lie is that, if we are gods, if we are sole authors of our lives, then we can do anything we want, create any religion we want. One hospital chaplain was instructed by a spiritual guide that "if you can't find a religion that supports you, start your own."[7] In a culture of do-it-yourself spiritualities, it is no wonder that tradition-based religions are having a hard time of it.

Not all postmoderns are as egotistical as Nietzsche, who wrote to a concerned publisher in Leipzig that he had the distinction "of publishing the foremost human being of all millennia" (even though only a handful of Nietzsche's books had been sold).[8] Not all postmoderns are as self-preoccupied as James Joyce, who, safely ensconced in Zürich, condemned the outbreak of the Second World War as a plot to glean attention from the publication of *Finnegan's Wake*.

Postmoderns suffer from such delusions of grandeur that we flit from god-obsession to god-obsession—with people, places, projects—abandoning each when it fails to meet our needs or live up to our heavenly expectations. Pomo culture jerks its knee at the very mention of "self." Autobiographies by postmoderns increasingly read more like a valentine to oneself than anything else.

> I, Janet Downs, take myself with all of my strengths and faults . . .
>
> Janet Downs exchanging vows with herself in front of a mirror and 200 friends in Bellevue, Nevada[9]

Even in church we are prone not to worship someone other than ourselves. Our worship impulse constantly snags on shadowy, darker reefs. We go to worship mostly to feel good about ourselves. We want every sermon to be a self-hug. We want every worship experience to pump us up and make us happy. We have created a Sunday supplement of what scholar Paul Heelas calls "the Self Religions."[10]

ME, INC.® ~ The new economy is focused on the individual, not on the masses. In postmodern culture, everyone is a free agent. Everyone is a corporation, with one's own self securitized. The stock market of the future will be stock in a person. There is already a David Bowie bond, and perhaps by the time this book is published there will be a Michael Jordan stock.

Faith Popcorn calls these forces of molecularization "ego-nomics"—"giving the customer custom design and individual treatment."[11] Other seers give it a double ring—"mass customization"—as people are delivered only what information or products conform with their predetermined wishes and distinctive sizes. A company called MySki sells designer skis created for a market of one; you can custom design your skis right down to the graphics. The founder, Chris Jorgensen, hopes to open soon MyBike, MyFurniture, MyName-the-product-and-we'll-customize-it-for-you.[12]

An aberration? Mass customization is taking over the marketplace.[13] Dell Computers will produce a "customer-configured" PC

> A Christian is a perfectly free lord of all, subject to none.
> A Christian is a perfectly dutiful servant of all, subject to all.
>
> Martin Luther[14]

eight hours after you order it. Made-to-order jeans and shoes are already here: Levi's "Personal Pair" jeans uses computer hip and leg measurements; Custom Foot shoe stores use infrared scanners on both left *and* right feet. College professors can create their own textbooks using McGraw-Hill's Web site.[15] Imagine Radio lets each listener design his or her own Internet Radio station through downloading a software "tuner."[16] Upscale stores (Saks Fifth Avenue, Nordstrom, Bloomingdale's) offer private, one-on-one service through "personal shoppers." Discovery Communications' new Your Choice TV cable service lets you view any program at any time for 99 cents. Microsoft promises us that in the next few years our computers will become "intuitive," automatically conforming to our tastes, needs, and even personalities. "Pharmacogenics" is the fancy name the biotech industry has given customized drugs—drugs that are designed expressly for you to ensure that it will work and you will not have adverse reactions.

Postmoderns buy for style, not for logos. Postmoderns increasingly don't want corporate logos or designer names on their clothes unless they can at the same time express their identity, their "unique ethnicity" in style and form. If you are Latino/Latina, you expect to read about what is going on in the world in a form that is tailored to your cultural traditions: your specific needs and preferences, your skin tones and taste buds. Hence there is Spanish radio and Spanish television, Hispanic newspapers (from 232 in 1970 to 406 in 1995, with a combined circulation of 8.1 million), and Hispanic magazines—*Latino Style* (Washington, DC), *Si* (New York), *Moderna* (Texas), *People En Español* (Spanish-language edition of *People*).

Mass customization is designed to make you feel as if you're the only person on earth. Postmoderns are not only being treated like gods and encouraged to have unlimited and illimitable ambitions; they are actually getting more and more autonomous, displaying more and more powers that are so unprecedented, even godlike, they compare only to the way gods functioned in the Greek and Roman worlds. We are pressed on every side, to live, to die, "as becomes a god."

> Just because some of us can read and write and do a little math, that doesn't mean we deserve to conquer the Universe.
>
> Kurt Vonnegut[17]

Postmoderns can live in a world largely of their own making. The postmodern national anthem was introduced by Frank Sinatra in his 1969 ballad "My Way." The Industrial Age gave power to big machines—big unions, big government, big cities, big corporations, big hierarchies. The Information Age is giving power to the individual. A networked society shifts the power from the producer to the consumer. People are experiencing that redistribution of control and power, away from hierarchies and toward networks and individuals.

UNIT OF ONE ~ In our lifetimes we have moved from mass markets to regional markets, then to niche markets, and now to demassed customers. Mass products, mass media, mass production, mass distribution are now all giving way to virtually one product per person, micromedia, personal customization, and even point-of-sale customization (beyond boutiques and specialty stores).

Postmodern culture is more populist, more Jeffersonian, than even Jefferson could have imagined. *Fast Company*, the corporate magazine of 21-C, talks about this being a "unit-of-one" world. No longer does the economy revolve around "big" organizations. Rather, the new economy revolves around the individual, the unit-of-one. Even agriculture has gone to "precision farming," in which personalized attention is given to each shovelful (sometimes spoonful) of dirt.[18]

We are living in the Age of the Personal, which one analyst sees as a key explanation for the rise of evangelicalism as the new mainline religion in the US. Ron Sellers writes,

The Evangelical mindset focuses on personal change, personal spirituality, personal salvation. Mainline Protestant groups often tend to focus more on societal change, and an emphasis in Catholicism is the Church itself. . . . while mainline Methodists and Presbyterians were trying to ban the bomb and fight for the homeless, . . . Evangelicals were telling people that they could have a personal relationship and experience with God—and people were listening.[19]

Postmodern culture is so personalized that it has moved from mass-produced to mass customized to the point where the latter are giving way to one-on-one relationships. This shift from customized to personalized is manifest in the appearance of designer sex, designer spirituality, designer education, and so on. The personalized touch has gone so far that some people are making a good living as "wine counselors" or "image consultants" or "personal agents." Soon everyone will have their own "personal agent."

To see the unit-of-one revolution at work, consider the kinds of lives home-based "micropreneurs"[20] are living. Information technologies allow people to design their own worlds and play god in them. Superstring physics reveals that the center of one atom is the center of all atoms. Imagine that atoms are people, and it is no wonder postmoderns get giddy about themselves and their place in the universe.

> **I couldn't have done it without me.**
>
> Bumper sticker

Oscar Wilde's aphorism that "self-love is the beginning of a life-long romance" applies with equal force to the beginnings of literally lifelong religions. Spiritualities that encourage self-divinization will flourish (Jungian psychology is especially adept at facilitating the view of one-self as a god), which is what makes New Age spiritualities (especially pagan-ism) and Eastern Orthodoxy[21] like catnip to postmoderns.

POWER OF ONE ~ I wouldn't go so far as George Gilder in saying that the Internet multiplies the input and power of a single person at a computer by "a factor of millions."[22] But I do believe in the exponential power of ONE. The Michael Jordan brand has a $10 billion impact on the economy.[23] In many ways, what Bill Gates and Steven Spielberg and Oprah Winfrey are doing and where they are going is more important than what most corpora-tions and countries are doing. When Oprah declared to her 15–20 million daily viewers that she lost 67 pounds in four months, the manufacturer of the Optifast protein drink Sancoz Nutrition got 200,000 calls. When Oprah and Don Imus feature a book on their programs, they can increase sales by 250,000 copies overnight.[24]

Even columnist Ann Landers can create a bestseller. University presses are notorious for selling books that don't sell, but once in a great while one of them makes a killing. In 1990, Johns Hopkins University Press received the "Golden Fluke Award" for the book *Staying Dry: A Practical Guide to Bladder Control.*[25] Turned down by 49 commercial houses, it sold over 100,000 copies in a single year—when Ann Landers endorsed it in her syn-dicated column.

In his classic discussion of fifth-generation supercomputers, computer expert Marvin Minski argued that the new freedom electronics gives us will enable every individual to organize and live life exactly according to one's own wishes.[26]

This is the first time in history that people can (or at least believe they can) design their own lives according to their preferences. Never before have people been able to live designer lives, to customize their preferred lifestyles. Rather than standardize life according to set, established norms, we now can customize life according to our wishes. Indeed, every group is increasingly liv-ing in a parallel universe; every person almost lives in a parallel universe.

TECHNICISM ~ "Technicism" is the ideology of technology. It is the notion that science can solve any and all problems, even the one that it itself creates. Or, in its best defined form,

> Technicism is the human pretension to be able to autonomously bend all of reality to our will through the use of scientific-technological control and in doing so to solve any problem that arises and hence to guarantee material progress. The assurance is that even the problems technicism creates can in turn be mastered with new or proven scientific-technological solutions.[27]

The ideology of technicism was invented in some way by René Descartes, who argued that "nature is a machine, as easy to understand as clocks and automata, when one but investigates it carefully enough." As an ideology it has been warned of by philosophers like Heidegger, Ellul, Sachsse, Staudinger, Horkheimer, Ihde, and many others. This false faith in technology may have found its classic expression at the World Food Conference in 1974, when Henry Kissinger went on record saying, "In ten years no child will go to bed hungry."

Technicism is especially dangerous today when the object of our technicism—genetic engineering—has become *us.* Humans are technologizing nature. I believe that the kingdom of God has computers. But I also believe that computers *serve* heaven and don't rule the kingdom. God is not calling everyone to be a "computer person," but he is calling all of us to be persons with computers.

One day they built the ultimate computer. It took up five city blocks and was 10 stories high. When it was completed, the dignitaries from near and far gathered around the giant structure. They had agreed ahead of time that the first function of the computer would be to answer the most important question ever asked: "Is there a God?"

They fed the question into the machine, and its lights flashed and the inner workings hummed, and after a few breathless minutes, out came the answer: "There is now!"

Legendary filmmaker Jim Cameron, whose real expertise lies in computer-generated morphing, sacrificed a fortune to produce the Oscar-winning movie *Titanic.* For him, the faith that the experts put in the *Titanic* in 1912—"an almost unshakable faith that science and technology would deliver us to a better Age and a better life, with no penalty paid"—is an all-too-perfect cognate of the faith people are putting in technology and the information superhighway.[28] The metaphor *"Titanic"* is an enduring symbol of human ingenuity (the White Star Line claimed it was "unsinkable") frustrated by forces of nature and unpredictability.[29]

so what? **THE CHRISTIAN SELF** ~ The Delphic oracle's "Know Thyself" has become Deepak Chopra's "Create Thyself." The "crisis of modernity" was largely a crisis of self—a self conceived of in exclusively individualistic terms, created by self-authority and "self-trust." The postmodern self is even more self-reverencing and self-referential. The irony is that the more the culture fixates on the self, the weaker and more weightless the self becomes.

The very density of the postmodern "network consciousness" can be retarding to a healthy individual identity. A hive consciousness asks the self to play dead. Concern about the erosion in the sense of self, and the potential for the zombification of the church, is echoed in the cyberculture through Sven Birkerts's warning that "our spells of unbroken subjective immersion will become rarer and rarer, and may even vanish altogether." Steven Johnson fears that already "our own sense of self has been whittled away by the dark forces of perpetual connectedness."[30]

A cartoon in *The New Yorker* shows a new person being introduced to hell, with fire and devils bearing pitchforks everywhere. A friendly devil says to him, "You'll find that down here there is no right and wrong. It's just what works for you."

Hell is getting what *you* want. Hell is doing only what works for *you*. Hell is building a self based on a foundation of one. Heaven is being the self God made you to be and the self you can't become without God and the church. Heaven is living a self-identity that is God-given, not self-constructed, a self built with communal and familial scaffolding and an identity moved beyond self-fulfillment and self-gratification. The search for self-fulfillment can only be met in the context of belonging and contributing to a community where the common good takes precedence over the self.[31]

There are four dimensions to a Christian self. First, the depth of a heartfelt faith in which our identity is reconfigured in Christ's image. Second, the height of a Christ-body community in which discipleship is lived out in the context of a community. Third, the breadth of a transforming witness that lifts up and lives out of the Cross. Fourth, the whole-is-greater-than-the-sum-of-its-parts dimension of spirituality where mystery and miracle reign.[32]

A man was asked why he did not weep at a sermon when everyone else was shedding tears. He replied, "I don't belong to the parish."

COACHING ~ Auto racer Stirling Moss was once asked where he learned the most about driving. He replied, "The best classroom of all time was the spot two car-lengths behind Juan Manuel Fangio. I learned more there than I ever did anywhere else."

As horizontal functioning changes the us-them control paradigm to a commitment paradigm, leaders must switch from supervisory roles to mentoring roles, taking people from where they are to where they want to be. The political, social, and organizational lessons of the day teach us that people at work are demanding less control from others and more power for themselves. Postmoderns resent the "boss" mentality of traditional management. But they truly welcome mentoring.[33]

Mentoring has been defined as "a relational experience through which one person empowers another by sharing God-given resources."[34] But mentoring skills, which are now being taught virtually everywhere[35] but the church, can be best defined through the etymology of the word *coach*. The word *coach* first occurred in English in the 1500s in reference to a particular kind of carriage. The root meaning of the verb *to coach,* therefore, is to convey a special person from where he or she is to where he or she wants to be. Not until the 1880s was *coach* used in an athletic sense (to describe a person who was tutoring rowers on the Cam River near Cambridge University), and then it retained its connotation of moving a person (the athlete) from one place to another.

A horizontal coach instructs, trains, and guides performers in some particular activity or endeavor. The coach's job is to identify the individuals' blind spots and provide whatever will enable performance beyond previous limits. The assumption is that this mutual commitment to performer and coach—this partnership—is what breaks down us-them barriers to horizontal activity.

Michael Hammer, named by *Business Week* as one of the preeminent management thinkers of the '90s and by *Time* magazine as one of America's 25 most influential individuals, uses the model of an American football team to describe the 21st-century corporation. There is a lot wrong with football. (George Will says it's the same thing that's wrong with American culture: too violent and too many committee meetings.) But a big thing right about football is its coaching structure. There is a head coach for the entire team, but the team is organized around functions: an offensive, defensive, and special team function.

> A coach is somebody who makes you do what you don't want to do so you can be what you want to be.
>
> Football coach Tom Landry

Each one of these functions has its own coaching structure. Then within each function there are specific positions, each with its own coach: line, quarterback, back, ends. Then every person on the team is given a personal trainer who coaches in the basics of conditioning. This does not even take into consideration the way teammates coach each other during the game.

Every member of a football team is multiply coached. Hammer concludes, "It is this simultaneous focus on both the process and the team collectively, as well as on the individual and his or her capabilities, that I think is the model for where we're heading in terms of organizational structure."[36]

Perhaps the mentoring role can best be illustrated by the Greek myth of Pygmalion, a sculptor who carved a statue of a beautiful woman who was subsequently brought to life. The central idea of George Bernard Shaw's play *Pygmalion*—in spite of the macho-qualities of the musical *My Fair Lady*, which is based on Shaw's work—is that one person, by effort and skill, can mentor another person into a more alive and useful being. Mentors or coaches have Pygmalion-like ministries in nourishing and nurturing souls that have depth and resonance.[37]

> The customer is in charge in the new world disorder.
>
> Dieter Huckestein,
> executive vice president
> of Hilton Hotels Corporation

Sam Williams, who works as a seminary professor (Golden Gate), a pastor (Bay Marin Community Church), and a consultant, has implemented the "spiritual fitness" model of discipleship training in his church. The life of faith is not a linear baseball diamond, where, if you don't make it to second on time or correctly, you get thrown out. Indeed, not everyone even needs to start on first base. Given how God has worked in their lives, some people should be able to go to the outfield first. The people of Bay Marin Community Church are each assigned a spiritual trainer who helps them assess what areas of their life need work if they are to be in mission for God at home or in the world: For one it may be cardiovascular, for another it may be nutrition, for another it may be daily hygiene. They go there first with a spiritual coach.

What if our churches were to form something like Coach University, founded in 1992 to work with families, companies, and business teams to help them gain the art and skill of coaching. Specialties within the coaching profession include communication, business planning, career planning, and spirituality.[38] Specialties in the church's Coach University would include the brain-bending work of Nancey Murphy (Fuller Theological Seminary) and the body-

> I never vote for anyone. I always vote against.
>
> W. C. Fields

mending work of Roger Barrier (Tucson, AZ) and the mission-sending work of Sam Williams.

FROM CRITIQUE AND PICK-APART TO CELEBRATE AND PICK-UP ~
From Verbal Critics to Aesthetic Ethicists: Here's another little quiz for you. This one's easy.

Q: Who are the worst people in the world to listen to sermons?
A: Preachers.

Why is it that we who preach have such difficulty receiving God's word from other colleagues? Because we have been trained to "critique," not celebrate.

Psychologists warn us that our first impulse when we meet people is to decide whether we like them or not by setting ourselves over and against them: "I hate that voice." "What an arrogant attitude." "She's more attractive than I am." "Why can't I be that bright?" In other words, our initial response is the critique that separates, not the celebration that unites and harmonizes.

Whether it was the art of homiletics or the art of life, our learning was based on the academic fallacy of the modern world: the presumption that a negative voice is superior to a positive voice. The modern world was temperamentally allergic to praise.

One of the great academics of the modern world, Henrik Ibsen, was gravely ill. A nurse commented that he "seemed a little better today." Ibsen growled, "On the contrary," and died.

The scientific method was built on the power of those words "on the contrary." Moderns were taught to "think critically," to doubt the senses, and to distrust the emotions. Descartes was so addicted to doubt that to see whether animals had souls, he sliced open a live dog to see if he could find it.

Everything about the Postmodern Reformation is built on a postmodern, postcritical epistemology. Churches of the Postmodern Reformation subscribe to a postmodern scientific method (sometimes called "participant-observer") that combines the head (think creatively) and heart (feel critically), a method in which there is no understanding without standing under. Unlike the critical method, which taken to an extreme results in scientism ("the irrational belief in the rational"), in postcritical studies first you believe it, then you see it.

Illustrator/painter Gustave Doré, one of the patron saints of the Dream-Works team of Spielberg/Katzenberg/Geffen, was handed a painting of Jesus just finished by one of his students. Asked for his critique, Doré studied it, his mind searching for the right words. At last he handed it back to the student. "If you loved Him more," he said, "you would have painted Him better."[39] The modern era produced a lot of master critics; it was woefully short of master builders. If moderns had built as much as they tore down, we would not be facing many of the problems we are today.

Lovers understand better than haters. The Postmodern Reformation church leans on and learns from a small but growing confraternity of scholars who have gone beyond the historical-critical method of biblical interpretation and are "returning" to the text as "postcritical" scholars whose relationship to the Scriptures for many of them is one of deep respect, faith, and love as well as scholarship and exegesis. For these scholars, to be Christian means to experience life and oneself on Christians terms,[40] terms that I would argue are more incarnational than creedal.

Two New Testament scholars, Gary A. Phillips and Stephen D. Moore, and two Jewish scholars, Harold J. Bloom and Peter Ochs, are pioneering this postcritical approach to the text. In spite of the fact that "except for a handful of exegetes, the postmodern divide is a landmark event which modern biblical scholarship by and large has ignored," Phillips argues that "from a postmodern perspective, the sense of the biblical text and of reading religiously stand on very different epistemic, aesthetic and political grounds."[41] The first scholarly task in a postmodern reading of the Scriptures is a "letting be"—letting the text speak and be heard on its own terms. "Postcritical" for Phillips doesn't mean anti-critical, but being critical in a different way from the modern method.

In *The Book of J*, Bloom challenges us to go beyond the horizons of modern knowledge by trusting the text where it stands and by letting it lead us where it will. He admonishes us to let the text surprise us. Suspicion is not the attitude in which to read anything—especially the Bible. Whenever the text puzzles us, Bloom says, let's not presume that the text is faulty. Let's not read it from a suspicious standpoint. Rather, he suggests that we place ourselves under its authority and let it speak to us.[42]

Peter Ochs of the University of Virginia lambastes old-style, positivist biblical critics as

historical-critical scholars [who attempt] to locate some higher science of history and reason that can mediate disputes between those who dogmatically affirm the fact and character of biblical revelation and those who dogmatically deny our capacity to have any positive knowledge of such a thing. Such scholars . . . arrogate to themselves the authority to separate the language of the Bible from the facts—of history and moral truth—to which that language ultimately refers. In this way, the scholars tend ultimately to make their higher sciences higher than the Bible—higher sources, that is, for evaluating what the Bible says, what it says to do, and what it means.[43]

Ochs contrasts "higher criticism" with postcritical theorists whose task

is to relocate the Bible's meaning within the biblical text itself . . . to recover the premodern practice of reading the biblical text as "realistic narrative." The Bible is to be read as a collection of stories that are "history-like," not because they point outside themselves to some events more important than the Bible itself, but because they function for the community of biblical interpreters as history does, narrating the community's literary and religious inheritance and, thereby, shaping the way community members live their lives today.[44]

Ochs takes his postcritical stance to the point where he argues that even modernity needs our compassion, understanding, and love. "To criticize modernism [as the enemy or as erroneous] is to reinvoke the law of the excluded middle on which modernisms of all sorts stake their claims."[45]

In postcritical scholarship, one does not have to dissect an author before quoting him affirmatively or picking up her work. In postcritical ministries, one does not have to critique a colleague before cheerleading her or partnering with him.

I can enjoy and quote Nobel Prize-winning author Elias Canetti without embracing (or even mentioning) his sincere belief that he was never going to die.[46] I can learn from and be instructed by the theology of Martin Luther without embracing his beliefs about the evil of the Jews or his rejection of Copernicus. Ninety percent of Isaac Newton's writings consist of treatises on theology, alchemy, and mysticism. They are basically blather. Does that mean that his scientific colleagues should have dismissed his scientific work as worthless? Any visit to the Christian Hall of Fame (Hebrews 11) reveals a gallery of greats who didn't have it all together or get it right, either.

In fact, one of the great needs of the church is for Barnabas Ministries, Cheerleaders, and Mentors (á la Barnabas "the Encourager"—see Acts 4:36). A 21st-century leader has been defined as someone who stands on the sidelines with a Bible in one hand and pom-poms in the other. In spite of what the modern world taught us, criticism is not one of the gifts of the Spirit.[47]

> We sit down before a picture in order to have something done to us, not that we may do things with it. The first demand any work of art makes upon us is surrender. Look. Listen. Receive.
>
> C. S. Lewis

The distinction between critics and mentors is this: Critics give advice to detract; mentors give advice to care and nurture and wish you well. British theater critic Kenneth Tynan calls critics "people who know the way but can't drive the car." Mentors give advice, and are generous in giving advice, because they actually care that you are going the wrong way and can show you how to turn the car around.[48]

My favorite e. e. cummings poem expresses this postmodern transition from critique to celebrate: "I'd rather learn from one bird how to sing/Than teach ten thousand stars how not to dance."[49]

FIT TOGETHER ~ Ministry needs to be contextually determined. It is no longer enough to offer programs that people can "fit in." People want to fit together. "Fit in" was the mantra of the command-and-control structures of the Industrial Age. "Fit together" is the mantra of the decentralized, out-of-control systems of the postmodern era. The pigeonholing of people is at an end. Part of soccer's surge of popularity among the Net-Gens is precisely this: Everybody is trained in all positions, and everybody is playing almost all the time.

Postmodern systems staff the process, not the position. That's why "job descriptions" need to be blurred or replaced by "spirit descriptions." Job descriptions fit you into someone else's categorical cubbyhole, then post "No Trespassing" signs all around the hole warning you to stay in and others to stay out.[50]

In indigenous ministries to postmoderns, "spirit descriptions" will be so basic to the body of Christ that people will be hired for ministry solely on the basis of their spiritual energies. "I have no idea how we are going to use you, but I know this church can't be without you. Why don't you join us as the 'Minister of I-Don't-Know-What'?" Come join the Church of God-Knows-What.

> I, you, he, she, we.
> In the garden of mystic lovers,
> these are not true distinctions.
>
> Persian poet/Sufi mystic
> Jalal ud-din Rumi (1201–1273)

There are two mechanisms of "fitting together": teams and webs. Teams are project-oriented, goal-driven, and mostly short-lived. Webs evolve slowly and are based in relationships and connections that have little hierarchy and constantly shifting centers of power.[51] The church must learn how to fit people together into teams and webs. But teaming entails all sorts of new muscles, new spirits, new skills, new thinking. Who has trained us how to "think together"? It's a whole new kind of thinking, this team thinking.[52]

FROM STANDING COMMITTEES TO MOVING TEAMNETS ~ In the Postmodern Reformation church, the fundamental organizing principle of ministry is "I can't be me without you." *Me* needs its flip-side *we* if we are to *be* what God is calling us to *be*. Collectively we are better than any of us individually.

A moving TeamNet can be formed for every ministry. How is a TeamNet different from a committee? Committees take minutes, vote, make decisions and recommendations. TeamNets fix problems. TeamNet members are self-directed, empowered, and "trust one another." It is the TeamNet that becomes the hero, not a presiding chairperson or lone hero.[53]

Since when does leadership need to "come to a single point," as Jessica Lipnack and Jeffrey Stamps put it in their book *The TeamNet Factor?*[54] Our only single, sharp point is Christ. The biblical model as implemented in the early church was a plurality of leadership.

It is instinctive with postmoderns that one-person shows ultimately become no-shows. Gen-X pastors start out with the assumption that there's a team and that they're a part of it. Boomer pastors talk the team talk, but struggle to walk beyond solo.

Once again, the business world is doing a better job at modeling patterns of multiple leadership than the church. Lipnack and Stamps write, "While many know about such celebrated instances of multiple top leadership as the Intel triad, including president Andrew Grove, few are aware how dramatic a trend there is toward teaming at the top in the United States. In the 20 years from 1964 to 1984, American executive team arrangements in large companies tripled from 8 percent to 25 percent."[55] Another team of management experts coined the phrase "democraship" (a combination of democracy and leadership) to emphasize a decision-making process and style that is team-based, but whose recommendation is then credentialed and authorized by the leader.[56]

The late, great football coach Paul "Bear" Bryant revealed his "secret formula" just before retirement.

> I'm just a plowhand from Arkansas, but I've learned how to put and hold a team together. I've learned how to lift some individuals up and how to calm others down, until, finally, they've got one heartbeat together, as a team. To do that, there's just three things I'd ever have to say: If anything went wrong, I did it. If it went semi-good, then we did it. If anything went *real* good, then you did it. That's all it takes to get people to win for you.[57]

We now know how wrong people like Thomas J. Watson Jr., the former CEO of IBM, was when he said "the best way to motivate people is to pit them against one another."[58] Why do we pay basketball players like Michael Jordan such megabucks to run around in their underwear and throw balls through narrow hoops? Because they have mastered the art form of Fitting Together. The concept of Fitting Together is what helped Ervin ("Magic") Johnson and the Los Angeles Lakers win five league titles; it is what helped Michael Jordan and the Chicago Bulls win three titles; it is what helped Larry Bird and the Boston Celtics win three titles. Moving the ball and hitting the open man is the art form of Fitting Together.

WJWak   Bob Cousy and the Boston Celtics were in the '50s and '60s what Michael Jordan and the Chicago Bulls are today. The only difference is that Cousy was paid peanuts in comparison to present-day salaries. Yet Cousy argues that, if anything, Larry Bird, Magic Johnson, and Michael Jordan were underpaid. What saved basketball and, during the last 15 years, made it into the number one sport in fan popularity among professional sports? Superstars. A team that is afraid of superstars is a team that is afraid of success.

But what was each of these superstars known for? His team play. Cousy credits Bird and Magic for the "turnaround." In his words, "they reawakened the passing game. The big thing to sell in the NBA is still the creative part that comes from ball handling, passing, and play development. Bird and Magic were masters of this. The fans worshiped them."[59]

A "DreamTeam" is a TeamNet of superstars where everyone is a first among equals. The difference is that real superstars are willing to play backup, ready to come to the fore depending on the nature of the challenge or crisis. In other words, a postmodern superstar like Larry Bird, Magic Johnson, or Michael Jordan is a leader and a follower at the same time.

To bring TeamNets alive in the church, with their retinue of superstars, we will have to overcome huge reservoirs of envy—the envy in all of us, the envy between pastors, the envy between conferences and dioceses and associations, the envy between pastors and bishops, the envy between the ordained and the unordained, the envy that leads us to lop the heads off "long-stemmed red-roses" and to fell the tallest trees.

New leadership structures based on networks, not ladders, are needed in the church. In contrast to what many people think, networks are not "leaderless." They are "leaderful." Without leaderful structures, networks soon become notworks (a network in its nonworking state). But postmodern leaders are adept at followership as well as leadership.[60]

Peter Drucker's favorite model of leadership is the orchestral conductor.[61] I favor more of a mixed-metaphor model for leadership: A knowledge-based, networking church is a mixture of an orchestra, a basketball team, and a jazz combo.[62]

RESPECT THE CHILDREN ~ A sign in the window of a Maryland store reads: "Wanted: Permanent Part-Time Adult." I wanted to apply for that job.

Postmodern economies respect children for the wrong reasons. Too many churches respect children for the wrong reasons as well—to hook Boomer parents or to exploit their economic power. You don't think children have economic power? Ask McDonald's about "kidfluence." Children 14 and under spent $20 billion in the US in 1998 and will influence another $200 billion—figures expected to increase in the next few years to $35 billion and $300 billion respectively.[63] Teens spend $89 billion a year, $57 billion of it their own.

The new marketing motto is "If you don't have a kid's product, get one."[64] The Beanie Babies phenomenon—100 stuffed creatures that became bigger than Hula Hoops, Cabbage Patch Dolls, anything else in history, partly because they were brilliantly priced at a kid's allowance of $5—screamed loudly about the economic and cultural power of the Net Generation.[65] Children's aggregate spending doubled during each of the decades of the '60s, '70s, and '80s. It has tripled in the '90s, prompting one marketing expert to claim that "America's kids, while not actually sitting in the driver's seat, more often than not are directing where the car goes."[66]

Three out of four of the nation's 67 million children have baby-boom parents. Boomers eventually get it right and raise great kids—it just takes them a couple of tries. Boomers are raising their last crop of kids very differently from the way they raised their first. Boomer parents are spending more money than ever on their children. The church must help these same parents to spend more time than ever with their children and show them how to teach the sex appeal of virtue.

Keep children in worship. Just as kids sit at the same table with the adults, even though they may eat different food, so kids should enjoy worship with the adults, even though they may sing different songs.

After the Second World War, Pablo Picasso was viewing a British Council show of children's drawings. He observed to his companion, Herbert Read, "When I was the age of these children I could draw like Raphael. It took me many years to learn to draw like these children."[67] Growth in faith is both going up into more elemental realms of consciousness and going down into more elementary levels of consciousness. When Jesus said, "There will be no grown-ups in heaven" (see Mark 10:14–15), he was telling us that the language of faith is the language of children.

THREE DOUBLE-RING MINISTRIES ~ 1. Postmodern evangelism is first of all telling people how special they are, how much God loves them, how unique each and every one of them is. The fourth-century theologian Athanasius said in one of his letters that God became one of us "that he might deify us in himself." Similarly, elsewhere he wrote that Christ "was made man that we might be made God."[68]

Yes, a human being is a noble thing. We were born to be companions of God, even "capable of God" (*capax Dei*). As St. Leo put it in a Christmas sermon, "For if we are the temple of God and the Spirit of God dwells in us, what each believer has in their heart exceeds the marvels of heaven."[69] Or, as Victor Hugo put it in one of his poems, when a person dies, the whole universe is decapitated.

But no, the human is a cussed thing, the "greatness and garbage of the universe" (Pascal). Cut from "crooked timber" (Kant), we are not fit to be God. Created slightly lower than the angels (Ps. 8:5), we have lowered ourselves to the point where, in the 20th century alone, we killed 10 million combatants in the First World War, 50 million in the Second World War (many of them civilians), and another 50 million in the hundred or so conflicts between 1950 and 2000. The 1998 movie *Saving Private Ryan* is powerful testimony, not to the onward march of civilization through time, but to the fact that we stand in need of a Savior. The writer of Ecclesiastes put the two together: "[God] has put eternity in man's mind, yet so that he cannot find out what God has done from the beginning to the end" (Eccl. 3:11 RSV).

Henri Nouwen has argued that we now need to "forgive each other for not being God."[70] We need to forgive each other for not being perfect, for making mistakes, for being fallen but redeemed.

When the people asked John the Baptist, "Who are you?" he knew what they were really asking. That is why he did not say, "I am John the Baptist." He said rather, "I am not the Messiah" (see John 1:19ff.). God is God and I am not. Postmoderns need the message of *Elyeh Asher Elyeh* (Exod. 3:14): "I AM WHO I AM." Through water and the Spirit we can become "children of God," even "sons and daughters" of God—but not God.

2. Another feature of double-ring ministries is this: Yes, you are a minister. Yes, you are a doctor. Yes, you are a therapist. "Professionals" are not

those to whom people come for special expertise. "Professionals" are those who teach others how to develop that expertise in their life. Everybody's a minister. Everybody's a doctor. Everybody's a therapist.

But no, there are times when you need special ministry, special doctoring, special therapy.

3. Postmoderns declare themselves to be self-made men and women. The New Reformation church helps postmoderns declare themselves to be God-made men and women. Postmodern evangelism centers on the self at the same time it decenters the self in favor of God-centered service and selfhood. In the modern world there was simply too much *meum* and *tuum*—me and you.

> Give the mind two seconds alone and it thinks it's Pythagoras.
>
> Theologian/mystic/poet/ English professor/"EarthSaint" Annie Dillard[71]

DESIGNER CHURCH ~ In its special end-of-year theme issue on religion, the *New York Times Magazine* chose the title "God Decentralized" to describe a "new breed of worshiper" who is "looking beyond the religious institution" for a self-designed, do-it-yourself spirituality.[72]

People are hungry, but they don't want someone to feed them precooked meals. They want to feed themselves. Put them to work cooking. Give them the ingredients they need to make a meal. Let them decide how best to "do church." Create a designer church for them. Customize your ministry to every parishioner.

If I can order a "double tall split skinny wet cap" and have the person fix especially for me a cappuccino with one shot of espresso, one shot of decaffeinated espresso made of mostly nonfat milk but with a dollop of regular milk thrown in at the end, what can the church do to help people feel how special they are to God?

A fancy restaurant in Washington, DC, made headlines: "Man Thrown Out for Ordering Risotto." A customer saw risotto listed as an entree, but asked for a small portion as an appetizer. The waiter checked with the chef/owner to see what the man should be charged, and the boss sent the waiter back with the message, "I'm sorry, we do not serve risotto as an appetizer."

"Fine, I'll pay the whole entree price, but please bring it first as my appetizer."

"I'm afraid you don't understand, sir. We do not serve risotto as an appetizer."

"This is crazy! I just want risotto!"

The chef stalked out of the kitchen. "Risotto is not meant to be an appetizer," he said coldly. "It must be a main course."

"Give me a break! I'm the customer here. Bring me in the risotto!"

"You, sir, must leave my restaurant," the owner announced.

The incredulous patron refused to leave. The police were called in, and the unfortunate fellow was escorted from the premises for ordering risotto as an appetizer.[73]

We must begin to do church the people's way rather than expecting the people to do church "our way." In the modern world we were constantly being pounded into common pulps. Postmoderns need to feel special; they expect to be treated with respect. Postmoderns want to create the sort of lives they can't help but create. If you are to help them, you must be the kind of church you can't help but be and preach the kind of sermons you can't help but preach.

Only trust those who can help you live your own life, be your own church, preach your own sermons.

This means the Postmodern Reformation church has come to terms with the "M" word.[74] Gallup, the polling people, opened 21 offices in China. Their first two clients were the Chocolate Manufacturers Association and the Washington Apple Commission. Gallup's mission? To poll the Chinese to see if they even *like* chocolates or apples.

Do we care enough about postmoderns to even ask what they like and dislike? I have never seen this question on a hotel guest response card: "How well did you sleep?" How rare is this question in the church: "How well are you growing spiritually?"

How important is one person to you? Can your church put its arms around a visitor's shoulder and say, "I want to understand you; I want to hear who you are; I want to listen and hear *your* story, and how God is already working in *your* life. I want you to change *us* because you're here." The *Guerilla Marketing Newsletter* reports that American Airlines calculated that if they had one more customer on each flight in a given year, the difference in revenue would have been about $114 million. This is how much one customer is worth to American Airlines. How much is one new disciple of Jesus worth to your church?

CROSS-FRIENDLY, NOT CROSS-FREE ~ A godlet culture prizes self-fulfillment over self-sacrifice. Instead of choosing a church on the Cross-free basis of "Does this church meet my needs?" or "What's in this church for me?" we must train ourselves to ask the Cross-friendly question "What's in this church for God?" or "Does this church meet God's purposes for this world?"

Religion is not a matter of Burger King or Big Mac, red wine or white, flavored coffee or straight up. Religion is a matter of the way, the truth, and the life.

Religion is not some personal opinion or special preference. Religion is a penalty ("woe is me"). Religion is a purpose ("the way of the Cross").

"Please God." Hear that phrase in a new way, not as a petition but as a declaration. The Postmodern Reformation church goes beyond "gift-based" ministry to obedience ministry.

THEOSIS THEOLOGY ~ Christians need to get more comfortable with the shocking terminology of "theosis theology," a doctrine that, in its various versions, is at the heart of Eastern Orthodoxy and Wesleyan theology. Theosis theology presents as the heart of the human enterprise our "divinization," or "deification," or "Christification," or "participation" in God.[75] The key text in theosis theology is 2 Peter 1:3–4: The promise of the gospel is that "divine power has given us everything we need for life and godliness" so that we "may participate in the divine nature and escape the corruption in the world caused by evil desires" (NIV).

We prefer language of "likeness theology": becoming *like* Christ; taking on the *likeness* of Christ or the *mind* of Christ, following in the footsteps of Christ (e.g., 2 Cor. 3:18, where Christians, "who with unveiled faces all reflect the Lord's glory, are being transformed into his likeness with ever-increasing glory, which comes from the Lord, who is the Spirit" [NIV]).

Martin Luther talked about how the Christian becomes like "little Christs." But for early theosis theologians, "divinization" meant less taking on the divine attributes than taking on the divine ambition and activity in the world—compassion, outreach, and self-denial.[76] Christians can grow more and more into the likeness of Christ; become more godlike, and enjoy more communion with God, yet there is no ontological participation in the divine.

> He deigns in flesh to appear,
> Widest extremes to join;
> To bring our vileness near,
> And make us all divine;
> And we the life of God shall know,
> For God is manifest below.
>
> Charles Wesley

Theosis is more than imitation of Christ. It is manifestation of Christ's energies through the power of the Holy Spirit.

DON'T C3PO ME ~ C3PO of *Star Wars* movie fame had a mantra: "If you won't be needing me, I'll shut down now." Too many postmoderns expect their relationships to be like C3PO: Be there as long as I need you in my loneliness and loss, but then shut down. How many have succumbed to the fashionable needs-based religion touted by the reigning culture of the therapeutic?

A faith based on felt-needs leaves people feeling content with themselves and at peace with the world. Hello?! Forget felt-needs in favor of God-wants. The Greek godling Narcissus longed to be loved and ended only in loving himself. Faith is more than self-fulfillment. In fact, faith has nothing to do with loving oneself; faith is loving God and loving one's neighbor. Plato defined justice as friendship. Injustice is not being there for others when we are there for ourselves.

FROM INSTITUTIONAL "HERE-I-STAND" CHURCHIANITY (MAINTE-NANCE) TO "THERE-WE-GO" CHRISTIANITY (MISSION) ~ From
inwardly mobile to outwardly mobile ministry: Turn the headlights on (not the dome lights): The church must help teach godlings in all our micro-mega-lomania how to get *outside* the self, how to become self-overcoming. The church has become a save-yourself, save-itself society.

Our churches must be mission driven rather than ministry driven. The old distinction between ministry and mission—ministry is service *to* me, while mission is service *through* me—is as good today as when it was first introduced.

> Where I am folded in upon myself, there I am a lie.
>
> German poet Rainer Maria Rilke

The church of Jesus Christ exists today in four forms, in descending order of integrity and faithfulness. The first two derive directly from the two most influential churches in the New Testament, the church at Jerusalem and the church at Antioch.

1. Mission churches. Mission churches are movement oriented. The church at Antioch, unlike the Jerusalem church, began with nobodies and Gentiles. Here the dynamic of the gospel created a community that became the launching pad for the worldwide reach of the gospel.

2. Ministry churches. Even the church Jesus and the apostles founded, the mother church, did not fulfill its commission to evangelize. And even when it did attempt it, it reached out only to Jews, to people like themselves.

The key test of what kind of church you are is this: Listen to what people are talking about. Do they talk about the ministries that are going on in their churches and communities? Or are they talking about what is going on in the system? The Postmodern Reformation church is more concerned with what is happening in the world than what is happening in the church.

3. Maintenance churches. Housekeeping is important, but why are we keeping house? "Good housekeeping should never be an end in itself."[77] Deadbeat ministries can go either way, depending on whether the preservation of old customs becomes more central than ministry.

> God will have all, or none; serve Him, or fall
> Down before *Baal, Bel,* or *Belial*:
> Either be hot, or cold; God doth despise,
> Abhorre, and spew out all Neutralities.
>
> 17th-century English poet Robert Herrick[78]

4. Museum/monument churches. These churches are living off old memories and entrenched "traditions" that are best seen as bad habits. There are people who are relics even when they're still alive. Don Haynes says that what goes on in these churches is "bedpan" ministries. It is worth asking whether they aren't both deadpan and bedpan ministries. Those still spiritually alive in these gaunt and grave churches know firsthand the curse of being alive among the dead.

The problem with the last two especially, and also the second, is that they partake in what is the worst sin—as argued first by Augustine, then Luther—that is, "*incurvatus in se*," or turning in on oneself.

The Christian religion exerts a centripetal force in the world. Our organizations are built around the functions of keeping house, not working in the world.

During the reign of King Josiah, everyone had become so busy with repairing their worship buildings and worshiping in them that they had departed from the Word of God and their values and visions were far wide of the mark God's covenant had set for them. Then, while repairing the temple, someone found the scroll of the Law and brought it to the king, who then asked that it be read aloud. When hear-

> *Scientiae pars est quaedam nescire.*
>
> "Not to know certain things is a part of knowledge."
>
> Writer/traveler/priest Erasmus

ing the Word of the Lord, the king "tore his clothes" in repentance and ordered his staff to go and seek guidance of the Lord "for me, for the people, and for all Judah, concerning the words of this book that has been found" (2 Kings 22:11, 13). In the light of this new commitment to the Word of the Lord, they had an outpouring of God's Spirit that the Bible describes in the following terms:

> No such Passover had been kept since the days of the judges who judged Israel, or during all the days of the kings of Israel or of the kings of Judah. . . . Before him there was no king like him, who turned to the LORD with all his heart, with all his soul, and with all his might, according to all the law of Moses; nor did any like him arise after him" (2 Kings 23:22, 25).

Face outward! Move out! Become a movement church. Raise up movement people more than institutional people. Give up upward mobility for outward mobility. A church primarily concerned with itself and its needs is not healthy.

The church is where people like to go, not like to come.

KANGAROO THEOLOGY ~ Sometimes it's a good idea for the church to subscribe to "kangaroo theology." *Kangaroo* is an aboriginal name for "I don't know." When someone asked, "What are those things hopping around the countryside," Australian aborigines would shrug and say "Kangaroo." Hence the name.

The church has too many resident know-it-alls—theologians, preachers, consultants pontificating as if they possessed immaculate perceptions. The smarter you get, the more ignorant you know you are. "I don't know" is good theology. Sometimes it's the best theology. Pascal said that true eloquence is the abstention from all eloquence. Remember: Jesus once responded not a word (Matt. 27:12–14).

The wisdom of ignorance is illustrated by a story. The Delphic oracle was asked in the late fifth century B.C. to name the wisest man in Greece. The Athenian philosopher Socrates got the nod. When he was told of his selection, Socrates said, "Since the god proclaims me the wisest, I must believe it; but if that is so, then it must be because I alone of all the Greeks know that I know nothing."

Karl Weintraub of the University of Chicago has suggested that humans possess an as-yet-undiscovered organ he calls "the conclusion glands." He says they secrete a powerful hormone that makes us jump to conclusions that fly in the face of reality just because we're afraid to pass through the phase of "not knowing." But the basic insight on the biblical faith is the incomprehensibility of God. Moses was only permitted to look on the back of God—and the back of God, Gregory Nazianzus (329–389) wrote, is the world: "that Nature, which at last even reaches us . . . which He leaves behind Him, as tokens of Himself like the shadows and reflections of the sun in the water."[79]

> If you understand, it is not God.
>
> St. Augustine

Dan Johnson of Trinity Church in Gainesville, Florida, has a Ph.D. in Old Testament from Princeton. One day an elementary school student came to see him with a question. She said her parents and Sunday school teachers couldn't answer it, and they suggested she ask him. The question: "What do people eat in heaven?"

Dan had done his doctoral work in Isaiah, so he read Isaiah 25:6–10 to the girl. Then he gave a marvelous dissertation on the way the kind of food isn't nearly as important as the meaning of the feast, and on the importance of food as a spiritual reality. She thanked him politely and announced that he had done a pretty good job of tackling her question. But then he overheard the girl whisper to the church secretary, "He doesn't know either."

> So what it all boils down to is that no one's really got it all figured out just yet.
>
> Singer Alanis Morissette

Wislawa Szymborska devoted her 1996 Nobel Prize acceptance address to exploring the meaning of these three words, "I don't know."

Whatever inspiration is, it's born from a continuous "I don't know." That little phrase "I don't know" is small, but it flies on mighty wings. It expands our lives to include spaces within us as well as the outer expanses in which our tiny Earth hangs suspended. If Isaac Newton had never said to himself, "I don't know," the apples in his little orchard might have dropped to the ground like hailstones, and at best he would have stopped to pick them up and gobble them with gusto. Had my compatriot Marie Sklodowska-Curie never said to herself, "I don't know," she probably would have wound up teaching chemistry at some private high school for young ladies from good families and ended her days performing this otherwise perfectly respectable job. But she kept on saying, "I don't know," and these words led her, not just once but twice, to Stockholm, where restless, questing spirits are occasionally rewarded with the Nobel Prize.[80]

WEAR TO GO ~ Canadian philosopher Charles Taylor talks about a "politics of recognition" that is less something coming than something arrived. Attention is the most precious commodity of the future, as one is already seeing from the religious identities that demand recognition. Some are even abandoning the language of "information economy" for "attention economy."[82]

> You can't build a business. You build people.
>
> Enterpreneur/corporate magnate Spencer Hays[81]

How does one increase one's stock of recognition? Jean Beaudrillard established that modern society has become less a consumption of material objects than a consumption of symbols. We purchase, not to meet needs, but to gain the status indicative of power and wealth.[83]

In a recognition society, costumes are more important than ever. Everybody's dressing up, and not just for Halloween. The next time you are at a sports event, notice how supporters of teams "dress up," personalizing their enthusiasm for the team in what they wear and how they wear it. Who can forget the St. Louis Cardinals' sea-stadium of red that erupted after Mark McGwire hit his 61st home run against the Chicago Cubs on Labor Day 1998? Fans can even take support for teams to the grave with them. Funeral directors offer caskets that bear the colors and logo of their school—maroon-and-white coffins for Texas A&M fans, scarlet-and-gray coffins for Ohio State Buckeye fans.[84]

In a culture where there is no Logos without logo, colors, clothes, symbols, and attire are more important than ever. In short, clerical vestments will not go away—but they will be reborn as the people's wear.

GET AN ATTITUDE ~ One of the biggest changes in management theory in its adjustment to postmodern culture is its recognition that attitude more than skill and information is the key to leadership. Years ago, philosopher/psychologist William James wrote, "The greatest discovery of my generation is that human beings can alter their lives by altering their attitudes of mind."

> The last of the human freedoms is to choose one's attitudes.
>
> Neurologist/psychiatrist Viktor Frankl

Disciples of Jesus have an edge to them. It's not a chip on their shoulder, but an edge to their spirit. To put it bluntly, Christians have an attitude—some might even say an attitude problem.

Mark's gospel tells the story of Jesus not being able to do any healing ministry in his hometown (Mark 6:1–6). Why? His neighbors had a closed attitude, a shut-down faith. The attitude one brings to healing is key. Not even Jesus can succeed when the spirit is wrong. The healing of mind and body begins with a change of heart, a change of attitude, a right spirit.

> Create in me a clean heart, O God, and put a new and right spirit within me.
>
> Psalm 51:10

What is a "right spirit"? What kind of an attitude does a believer "get"? From a theological perspective, it is seeing yourself as God sees you: understanding God's delight in you and God's dreams for you. From a spiritual perspective, it is summarized in Psalm 51:10ff., which is but a variation of Micah 6:8, where we are summoned to do acts of justice confidently and walk humbly.

A right spirit from a biblical standpoint is the oxymoronic combination of confidence and humility, self-importance and self-mockery, the thumbs up and the bow down. In the language of Nehemiah, a right spirit is the ability to build new structures for our day with a sword in one hand and a trowel in the other (Neh. 4:16–18).

When Jesus admonished his disciples to get an attitude—"All who humble themselves will be exalted" (Matt. 23:12)—he was paraphrasing the paradoxical principle of an older contemporary. The great Rabbi Hillel (c. 60 B.C.– A.D. 20) said, "My abasement is my exaltation, and my exaltation is my abasement." First Peter 5:5–6 restates the attitude of the Christian with these words: "Clothe yourselves with humility toward one another . . . that he [God] may lift you up" (NIV). Jesus' art and artistry was in bringing together confidence and humility, self-expression and self-sacrifice. Through

> I try and create a spirit, and the spirit directs the movie.
>
> John Cassevetes

his artistry, common, ordinary things became magical and infused with grace. Even humble bread and wine become visitations of the Spirit.

The double ring of confidence and humility was fully developed by the time of the apostle Paul. "I can do *all things* . . . ," Paul claimed, but only ". . . *through him* who strengthens me" (Phil. 4:13). God doesn't ask or expect us to do "all things." But all the things he wants us to do, we can do through Christ's power in our lives.

HUMILITY ~ Humility is the full awareness of our fallibility and finitude. True religion begins with this sense that we have a lot to be humble about: "God, be merciful to me, a sinner!" (Luke 18:13). Paul called himself "the chief of sinners" (see 1 Tim. 1:15). No matter how gifted you think you are, no matter whether or not you can play every key in the keyboard, you are no better than anyone else. The fact that there may be a biological basis for Paul's crying out, "For the good that I would I do not: but the evil which I would not, that I do" (Rom. 7:19 KJV), only makes the doctrine of original sin all the more relevant.[85] Postmodern Christians are more prone to share their perplexities than their pretensions.

> Everyone must have two pockets, so that he can reach into the one or the other, according to his needs. In his right pocket are to be the words: "For my sake was the world created," and in his left: "I am dust and ashes."
>
> Jewish theologian Martin Buber[86]

We are guests in the world. We must treat everything our host bestows upon us with gratitude and respect, and receive it with humility. Billy Graham's mentoring of others was based on this mantra: "I'm going to pray for you. I think if you stay humble, God will use you."[87] What is the first step on the path to adultery? According to research, it is the notion of exceptionalism, the notion that you don't have to follow the rules like everybody else.

In the Jewish tradition there is the belief in "36 hidden righteous people" who uphold the earth. These are so in touch with God's Spirit that they are truly luminous. But these 36 people also have no idea that there is anything special about themselves. They don't see themselves as holier than anybody else, just ordinary. In fact, the moment they would even consider they might be one of the 36, they no longer would be. It is their humility that is the source of their enlightenment.

In Judaism, humility is the noblest of all virtues, the supreme human trait. Moses' only virtue singled out for mention was his modesty: "Now Moses was a very humble man, more humble than anyone on the face of the earth" (Num. 12:3 NIV). In a culture where humility is being elbowed to the side by rampaging self-esteem, we need to rediscover our Hebrew roots. God "detests all the proud of heart" (Prov. 16:5 NIV). "Do you seek great things for yourself? Do not seek them," God cautioned Baruch (Jer. 45:5).

You want to lead, Jesus said? Be willing to serve. The more you serve, the more humble you become, the greater you become, the more confident you can be. Appointed to lead means anointed to serve means ability to listen, to learn, to admit mistakes, to deny yourself, to let others get the credit. Postmodern leaders oppose the Darwinian "survival of the fittest" with the Christian doctrine of the survival of the weakest.

> Pride gives no food unless he can a feast:
> The quality of grace is goodness in the least.
>
> Poet/librarian Coventry Patmore[88]

There has never been a religious tradition in which its mystical masters have not made humility the open sesame to spiritual awakening. This is why kneeling is such a key humility exercise (along with remembering the fact that the number of people who come to your funeral will depend on how hard it is raining at the time). "Each human being goes through a door to the kingdom of God. This door is exactly as high as you are when you walk on your knees. If, in the pride of the ego, you stand up straight, you cannot fit."[89] Economist George F. Kennan once explained that the religious ritual he found most profound was kneeling: As a Christian he "welcomes" participating in the "equality of all naked human souls in the eyes of God" by

> I stand before you with humility and pride—but with much more of the former than of the latter.
>
> Bernard Baruch,
> upon receiving an award

> kneeling, together with anyone else who consents to kneel with similar humbleness, before the various symbols of faith. I find in this last, as do so many other people, support in the exercise of humility, which I regard as perhaps the greatest, certainly the closest to uniqueness, of the Christian virtues.[90]

CONFIDENCE ~ Confidence is not the same thing as arrogance or pride. "God opposes the proud, but gives grace to the humble" (1 Peter 5:5). "Pride goes before destruction" (Prov. 16:18); literally, nemesis (downfall) always comes in the wake of hubris (pride). Someone once said that "Satan courts the humble, the conceited are already corrupt enough."

The hubris of the modern project was the arrogance of "I can do all things ... through science." Historian Kenneth Clark deemed confidence the essence of civilization.[91] But the "confidence" of the Scriptures is not "I have the power to" or "I will do," but "I can have confidence in the Lord" (see Prov. 3:26). "We are always full of confidence," Paul insisted. "We walk by faith, not by sight" (2 Cor. 5:6–7).

Paul wanted a share in God's glory (Rom. 5:1–5). The glory of God in which we share is not arrogance or pride or celebrity status. It is the recognition in life that Christ changes the limits of the possible. In the words of an old Japanese proverb, "Ah, that's no problem, that's impossible." Bring the mind of Christ to a problem, and little is insolvable. Biblical scholar Joachim Jeremias distilled a lifetime of learning in this conclusion: "The fundamental note and inmost core of the message of Jesus, resounding in all his sayings about the Gentiles, is confidence in the reality of God and the vastness of God's mercy."[92]

After he lost a chance for the Utah Jazz to win Game 1 of the 1997 NBA Finals by missing two free throws late in the contest, Karl Malone tied the series at 2–2 in Game 4 by stepping to the line

> All you need to be assured of success in this life is ignorance and confidence.
>
> Mark Twain[93]

and, with 18 seconds left, sinking two shots. "This was the situation I was looking for," Malone said. "I said I wanted to be in that situation again."

Frank Berger used to talk about the true baseball player in these words: "You can never be a real ball player until you have the heart, the confidence, and the chutzpah in the bottom of the ninth with bases loaded, two outs and their best hitter at the plate to say: God, I hope he hits it to me."

Can the church have the confidence of "God, please use us to change this situation" or "God, we're ready to be deployed for you in this ministry"? Acts 4:31 portrays the church as the body of Christ moving under the guidance of the Holy Spirit to save the world. As one first-century person noted about these Christians, "they are a good people to know."[94] Are we a good people to know, church?

> **We are all struggling; none of us has gone far.**
> **Let your arrogance go, and look around inside.**
>
> 15th-century Indian philosopher Kabir

This doesn't mean that God will not use us unless we do something in a joyful spirit. What's most important to God is that we demonstrate our faithfulness and obedience. Jonah said yes to God even though he had no joy in it, but God used him anyway.

It also doesn't mean that we all end up with the identical same sweet spirit. Before his conversion, Paul was arrogant, aggressive, and deviously creative in his persecution of Christians. Guess what? After his conversion, Paul was arrogant, aggressive, and deviously creative in the cause of Christ. His temperament didn't change—but his motivation did.

We all have a lot to learn. We all have a long way to go.

say what?

1. Instead of starting worship with preludes, why not create "We Love You" reception parties so that when guests and visitors arrive, they feel as if they're at a party being thrown for them. They're treated like celebrities, and they feel like stars. Isn't that what the reception areas at Courtyard by Marriott are designed to do?

2. Have you noticed how more and more people are bringing their pets to work? Have you noticed how more and more animals are making their way into commercials (Budweiser frogs and ants, for example)? One way of making people feel special is to treat their pets special. Discuss the pros and cons of having a special service where people can bring their pets. Is the created order a part of the redemption story?

3. The Price Waterhouse team report called *The Paradox Principle* argues that team-based processes require more, not less, strong leadership at the center of the organization. Would your experience verify this "paradox" that the

more team-based our approaches, the more central strong leadership becomes?

4. One scholar of religion has argued that one of the appeals of Native American spiritualities is their emphasis on interconnectedness, their building a spirituality around

> relationships that are always reaching further and further out; relationships within the immediate family reaching out to the extended family, to the band, outward again to the clan, and to the tribal group; and relationships do not stop there but extend out to embrace and relate to the environment: to the land, to the animals, to the plants, and to the clouds, the elements, the heavens, the stars; and ultimately those relationships that people express and live, extend to embrace the entire universe.[95]

What do you think? Is this part of the appeal of aboriginal spiritualities? Are any or all of these elements present in Christianity itself?

5. What are some of the ways the oldest sin (pride) manifests itself in your life? (E.g., stubbornness? vanity? perfectionism?)

6. Have someone in the group review the book by Ernest Kurtz, *Not-God: A History of Alcoholics Anonymous* (Center City, MN: Hazelden, 1991). Why is the epithet "Not-God" so important to the recovery process?

7. Lewis Smedes tells a wonderful story about Pope John XXIII:

> A member of the curia was continually nagging him to fix this or that problem; this official lived as though he alone saw the severity of the problems facing the church and the world, and as if without his warnings everything would collapse. Finally the pope had had enough, so he took his hyper-conscientious advisor aside and confessed that he, too, was sometimes tempted to live as though the fate of the world rested on him. He was helped, he said, by an angel who would sometimes appear by the side of his bed and say, "Hey, there, Johnny boy, don't take yourself so seriously."[96]

What strategies do you have in your life, or what angels appear, to tell you that God is God and you are not—not to take yourself so seriously?

8. Here is one key test of how you are doing in not making yourself into a godlet: Are you open to the gifts that come from what you did not want to happen? Do your feet sometimes face directions in which you did not want them to go? Can you allow the story of your life to be written by serendipities, synchronicities, and other spiritual connections, or are you constantly appointing yourself the sole author of your story?

9. Give Peter Berger's "experience of alternation"[97] a test run. Open yourself to the possibility that the alternative to a belief you have may indeed be the truth; in other words, open yourself to the possibility that you may be wrong, or that the way you believe may need some correction. Can you do it?

10. Ask any group to form a circle and hold hands. Is that the only way you can form a circle? Why do we naturally make circles that look inward rather than outward? Is there a way to make a circle that looks *both* inward and outward at the same time? What kinds of circles is your church making?

11. Orthodox monks didn't just bow their heads in prayer. They inclined their heads to their hearts when they prayed, to pay homage to the head entering the heart, the mind paying its respects to the heart. Make it a spiritual practice to pray with your head bowed to your heart, and report on the difference it makes in your prayer life.

12. Listen to the music in church some Sunday morning. Does the music talk *about* God or talk *to* God? Which is better?

13. What do you think of William Faulkner's contention that "Unless you're ashamed of yourself now and then, you're not honest"?

14. Andrew Leonard, in his book *Bots: The Origin of New Species,* cites this quote:

> "Microcosmic Gods" [*sic*] is a science fiction short story by Theodore Sturgeon about an engineer so bored with engineering that he creates a race of tiny intelligent beings to do all his work for him, to solve any problem that he poses. He soon becomes rich and powerful by profiting from their invention and is considered a threat to the world's military and financial powers. The real threats, of course, are the hardworking creatures— the Neoterics. The engineer controls them by ensuring that each individual's life span is fleetingly short, but even so, their strength far outshadows his.
>
> "The question we have to ask ourselves," says Alex Cohen, onetime chief technical officer at the McKinley Corporation, "is, are we becoming microcosmic gods?"[98]

What do you think? Andrew Leonard asks, "Are we using our bot helpers to extend our power in the virtual realm to the point that our ability to inflict our will becomes godlike? And how do we restrain a world full of gods? And what happens when our helpers finally throw off their chains and sever their cyborg links?"[99]

15. Structuralist/anthropologist Claude Lévi-Strauss has argued that "the concept of humanity as covering all forms of the human species, irrespective of race and religion, came into being very late in history and is by no means widespread."[100] Can you verify Lévi-Strauss's assertion from your own experience, or is he exaggerating?

16. Have you noticed that the Net-Gens are communicating a much softer, friendlier image than their predecessor Gen-Xers? The anorexic, unsmiling, "heroine-chic" models of Calvin Klein have suddenly become friendly and fun. In fact, Estee Lauder introduced a fragrance for this generation called

"Happy." What do you think is going on here? What does this mean about these kids born after 1984?

17. Protestant Reformer Martin Luther's *Table Talk* for 1540 included these words:

Christ could have taught in a profound way but wished to deliver his message with the utmost simplicity in order that the common people might understand. Good God, there are sixteen-year-old girls, women, old men, and farmers in church, and they don't understand lofty matters! . . . Accordingly, he's the best preacher who can teach in a plain, childlike, popular and simple way.[101]

Are Luther's "common people" equivalents welcome in your church?

18. What would it mean for the church to distinguish between "who we are" and "how we function." How important is it to keep clear and clean the distinction between the two?

19. "To err is human, to forgive is not company policy."

To what extent does this sign on a company complaint board in Cambridge, MA, express the sentiment of too many churches?

20. Assign someone the 51st Psalm for a Bible study, especially verses 10ff. wherein the psalmist elaborates on just what is a "right spirit." Can you hear the double ring of confidence and humility?

21. Reebok, Pizza Hut, Honda, and Cap'n Crunch are investing six figures for kids to wear their logos in Little League Baseball, Pop Warner Football, American Youth Soccer, etc. Why can't the church put its money where its heart is and invest in kids' physical, mental, and spiritual fitness. What if your church fielded a soccer team that brandished your church logo?

22. Take a look at the provocative elaboration of the "one form of religious intolerance that does survive . . . the disdain bordering on contempt of the culture makers for . . . those for whom religion is not a preference but a conviction," as presented by Charles Krauthammer, "Will It Be Coffee, Tea or He?" *Time* (15 June 1998): 92.

now what? See the Net Notes in http://www.soultsunami.com

NOTES

1. *Playing God* (New York: Island Records, 1996).

2. David Diamond, "What Comes After What Comes Next: An Interview with Watts Wacker," *Fast Company Supplement* (1997): 33.

3. Andrew L. Shapiro, "Freedom from Choice," *Wired* (Dec 1997): 213.

4. For more, see Michael Heim, *The Metaphysics of Virtual Reality* (New York: Oxford Univ. Press, 1993). The quote comes from an interview in *21C* 25 (1997): 62.

5. As quoted in Andrew Leonard, *Bots: The Origin of New Species* (San Francisco: Hardwired, 1997), 84.

6. Sigmund Freud, *Civilization and Its Discontents,* trans. James Strachey (New York: Norton, 1961), 44.

7. Joseph Sharp, *Living Our Dying: A Way to the Sacred in Everyday Life* (New York: Hyperion, 1996), 56.

8. Lesley Chamberlain, *Nietzsche in Turin: The End of the Future* (London: Quartet Books, 1996), 201.

9. As cited in *Newsweek* (29 June 1998): 19.

10. Paul Heelas, *The New Age Movement: The Celebration of the Self and the Sacralization of Modernity* (Oxford: Blackwell, 1997).

11. Faith Popcorn, *The Popcorn Report: Faith Popcorn on the Future of Your Company, Your World, Your Life* (New York: Doubleday Currency, 1991), 46.

12. See www.myski.com/.

13. For an analysis of the trends feeding this customization frenzy, see "Customization's Powerful Pull," *Trend Letter* (2 Apr 1998): 1–4.

14. "Martin Luther's Treatise on Christian Liberty" [The Freedom of a Christian], in *Martin Luther's Basic Theological Writings,* ed. Timothy F. Lull (Minneapolis: Fortress Press, 1989), 596.

15. The Website is: www.mcgraw-hill.com/. This site links to 12,000 scholarly documents.

16. www.imagineradio.com.

17. Kurt Vonnegut, *Hocus Pocus* (New York: Putnam, 1990), 302.

18. Thomas Hayden, "A Brave New Farm, Tilled by Satellite and Robot," *Newsweek* (24 Nov 1997): 14.

19. Ron Sellers, "Nine Global Trends in Religion," *The Futurist* (Jan-Feb 1998): 24.

20. Michael LeBoeuf, *The Perfect Business* (New York: Simon & Schuster, 1996).

21. "It is not too much to say that the divinization of humanity is the central theme, chief aim, basic purpose, or primary religious ideal of Orthodoxy" (Daniel B. Clendenin, *Eastern Orthodox Christianity: A Western Perspective* [Grand Rapids: Baker, 1994], 120).

22. Quoted in Po Bronson, "George Gilder," *Wired* (Mar 1996): 188.

23. Ann Harrington, "The Jordan Effect," *Fortune* (22 June 1998): 128–38.

24. Oprah did this for Jacquelyn Mitchord's book *The Deep End of the Ocean* (New York: Viking, 1996). For Imus, see Ken Auletta, "The Don," *The New Yorker* 74 (25 May 1998): 59–61.

25. Kathryn L. Burgio, K. Lynette Pearce, and Angelo J. Lucco, *Staying Dry: A Practical Guide to Bladder Control* (Baltimore: Johns Hopkins Univ. Press, 1989).

26. Egbert Schuurman, *Perspectives on Technology and Culture* (Sioux Center, IA: Dordt College Press, 1995), 105.

27. Schuurman, *Perspectives on Technology and Culture,* 74.

28. As quoted in Paula Parisi, "Cameron Angle," *Wired* (Apr 1996): 132.

29. Seven survivors of the voyage were living as of 1996; one was 16 when the ship sank. For a homiletical interpretation of this theme, see Leonard Sweet and Elizabeth Rennie, "Titanic Possessions," *Homiletics* 10 (May-June 1998): 65–69.

30. Steven Johnson, *Interface Culture: How New Technology Transforms the Way We Create and Communicate* (San Francisco: Harper Edge, 1997), 218–19.

31. In the words of Christopher Lasch, the only route to self-fulfillment is "the selflessness experienced by those who lose themselves in their work, in the effort to master a craft or a body of knowledge, or in the acceptance of a formidable challenge that calls on all their resources. It is only in purposeful activity that we find a suspension of egoism that goes beyond conventional self-sacrifice" (Christopher Lasch, "Gilligan's Island," in his *Women and the Common Life: Love, Marriage and Feminism,* ed. Elisabeth Lasch-Quinn [New York: Norton, 1997], 126).

32. For a fuller elaboration of this four-dimensional psychology, see Leonard Sweet, *Quantum Spirituality: A Postmodern Apologetic* (Dayton, OH: Whaleprints, 1991). According to theologian Ellen T. Charry, there are "three distinguishing pivots" of the Christian self. First, above "self-expression" or "respect of others" is a "dwelling in the being of God." We can't "know ourselves" unless we first "know God." Second, the "call and cross of Christ," a singularity by which everyone and everything is reshaped. Third, "residence in the body of Christ." (See Ellen T. Charry, "The Crisis of Modernity and the Christian Self," in *A Passion for God's Reign: Theology, Christian Learning, and the Christian Self: Jurgen Moltmann, Nicholas Wolterstorff, Ellen T. Charry,* ed. Miroslav Volf (Grand Rapids: Eerdmans, 1998), 89–112.

33. Morris A. Graham and Melvin J. LeBaron, *The Horizontal Revolution* (San Francisco: Jossey-Bass, 1994), 181–82.

34. Waylon Moore, "Releasing Mentoring Power in Your Church," *Growing Churches* 8 (Spring 1998): 10–12.

35. Chip R. Bell, *Managers As Mentors: Building Partnerships for Learning* (San Francisco: Barrett-Koehler, 1996).

36. Michael Hammer, "Beyond the End of Management," in *Rethinking the Future: Rethinking Business Principles, Competition, Control & Complexity, Leadership, Markets and the World,* ed. Rowan Gibson (Sonoma, CA: Nicholas Brealey, 1997), 103.

37. Hammer, "Beyond the End of Management," 159.

38. You can access Coach University's training via the Internet at www.coachu.com or by phone at 800-48COACH.

39. As quoted in Ken Gire, *Windows of the Soul* (Grand Rapids: Zondervan, 1996), 172.

40. This is the contribution of postliberal scholars like George Lindbeck and Stanley Hauerwas. See Lindbeck's *The Nature of Doctrine: Religion and Theology in a Postliberal Age* (Philadelphia: Westminster Press, 1984) and *Theology and Dialogue: Essays in Conversation with George Lindbeck,* ed. Bruce D. Marshall (Notre Dame, IN: Univ. of Notre Dame Press, 1990). For Hauerwas see *In Good Company: The Church as Polis* (Notre Dame, IN: Univ. of Notre Dame Press, 1995); *Wilderness Wanderings: Probing Twentieth-Century Theology and Philosophy* (Boulder, CO: Westview Press, 1997); and Hauerwas and William H. Willimon, *Where Resident Aliens Live: Exercises for Christian Practice* (Nashville: Abingdon Press, 1996).

41. Gary A. Phillips, "Drawing the Other: The Postmodern and Reading the Bible Imaginatively," in *In Good Company: Essays in Honor of Robert Detweiler,* eds. David Jasper and Mark Ledbetter (Atlanta: Scholars Press, 1994), 408, 405.

42. Harold J. Bloom, *The Book of J,* trans. David Rosenbert, interpreted by Harold Bloom (New York: Grove Weidenfeld, 1990).

43. Peter Ochs, "Returning to Scripture: Trends in Postcritical Interpretation," *CrossCurrents* 44 (Winter 1994–95): 444. For more, see Peter Ochs, ed., *The Return to Scripture in Judaism and Christianity: Essays in Postcritical Scriptural Interpretation* (Mahwah, NJ: Paulist Press, 1993).

44. Ochs, "Returning to Scripture," 444. Ochs is using the argument of theologian Hans Frei, *The Eclipse of Biblical Narrative: A Study of Eighteenth and Nineteenth Century Hermeneutics* (New Haven: Yale Univ. Press, 1974), 66ff.

45. Peter Ochs, "Compassionate Postmodernism: An Introduction to Rabbinic Semiotics," *Soundings* 76 (Spring 1993): 139; see 139–52.

46. He was proven wrong on 14 August 1994. See "NB," *TLS, Times Literary Supplement* (7 Nov 1997): 18.

47. I want to thank Tom Becker of Knoxville, TN, for this insight.

48. My favorite definition of a critic is "someone who minds that it's rubbish" in Gilbert Adair, *Surfing the Zeitgeist* (London: Faber, 1997).

49. *E. E. Cummings: Complete Poems 1904–1962,* ed. George J. Firmage (New York: Liveright, 1991), 484.

50. It is instructive that people who work for DreamWorks SKG ("DreamWorkers") have no job descriptions or titles.

51. Sally Helgesen suggests we call these webs "webs of inclusion" in her book of that title, *The Web of Inclusion* (New York: Doubleday, 1995).

52. *Fortune* magazine surveyed CEOs across the world and found that 75% of them said they had become much more participatory, less hierarchical, and more consensus building in their approach to leadership. They also are learning "group thinking."

53. Dean Tjosvold and Mary Tjosvold, *Leading the Team Organization: How to Create an Enduring Competitive Advantage* (New York: Lexington Books, 1991).

54. Jessica Lipnack and Jeffrey Stamps, *The TeamNet Factor: Bringing the Power of Boundary Crossing into the Heart of Your Business* (Essex Junction, VT: Oliver Wright Publications, 1993), 47–48. They identify "Myth 4a, All leadership comes to a single point" as a common misconception about Networks.

55. Lipnack and Stamps, *The TeamNet Factor,* 96.

56. Gerald W. Faust, Richard I. Lyles, and Will Phillips, *Responsible Managers Get Results* (New York: AMACOM, 1998).

57. As quoted in Denis Waitley, *The New Dynamics of Winning* (New York: Morrow, 1993), 158.

58. Thomas J. Watson Jr., *Father, Son & Co.* (New York: Bantam Books, 1990), 291.

59. "Going Man-to-Man with Bob Cousy," *USAir Magazine* (Nov 1993): 82.

60. Elizabeth Lorentz at Yale says, "Leaders are expert followers, mapping the needs, resources and agendas of network members, so as to create good matches among people and organizations": as quoted in Lipnack and Stamps, *The TeamNet Factor,* 49.

61. I develop this more fully in Sweet, *Quantum Spirituality,* 153–61.

62. This is the suggestion of Charles Savage, *Fifth Generation Management: Co-creating Through Virtual Enterprising, Dynamic Teaming, and Knowledge Networking,* rev. ed. (Boston: Butterworth-Heinemann, 1996), ch. 2.

63. The numbers vary according to one's sources. See, for example, Gene Del, *Creating Ever-Cool: A Marketer's Guide to a Kid's Heart* (New York: Pelican, 1998), for figures that are a little lower than this.

64. James U. McNeal, "Tapping the Three Kids' Markets," *American Demographics* 20 (Apr 1998): 37–41.

65. According to the *Wall Street Journal,* nine of the 10 best-selling videos of all time are Disney animated films.

66. The 35 million USAmericans aged 4 to 17 spend about $9 billion a year of their own money and influence another $50 billion in purchases, according to Bernice Kanner, "Increasingly, America's Kids Are Steering the Economy," *Denver Post* (16 Nov 1997): 6H. To be sure, it was not just kids who collected Beanie Babies; witness a bumper sticker that read "Will Trade Husband for Beanie Babies."

67. Jonathan Fineberg, *The Innocent Eye: Children's Art and the Modern Artist* (Princeton, NJ: Princeton Univ. Press, 1997), 133.

68. As quoted in Robert V. Rakestraw, "Becoming Like God: An Evangelical Doctrine of Theosis," *Journal of the Evangelical Theological Society* 40 (June 1997): 257.

69. Pope Leo I, "Sermon 27, 25 December 451," in *St. Leo the Great: Sermons,* trans. Jane Patricia Freeland and Agnes Josephine Conway (Washington, DC: Catholic Univ. of America Press, 1996), 115.

70. "'Parting Words,' A Conversation on Prayer with Henri Nouwen," in *Fellowship in Prayer* 46 (Dec 1996): 18.

71. Annie Dillard, *Holy the Firm* (New York: Harper & Row, 1977), 68.

72. "God Decentralized," *New York Times Magazine* (7 Dec 1997): sec. 6.

73. As told in Roger Dow and Susan Cook, *Turned On* (New York: Harper Business, 1996), 104–5.

74. The "M" word here is "Marketing," not "Management," which was given in "Life Ring #9."

75. A. M. Allchin, *Participation in God: A Forgotten Strand in Anglican Tradition* (Wilton, CT: Morehouse, 1988). The best treatments of this doctrine and their relevance for today are by Daniel B. Clendenin, "Partakers of Divinity: The Orthodox Doctrine of Theosis," *Journal of the Evangelical Theological Society* (Sept 1994): 365–79; and Robert V. Rakestraw,

"Becoming Like God: An Evangelical Doctrine of Theosis," *Journal of the Evangelical Theological Society* 40 (July 1997): 257–69.

76. Rowan Williams, "Deification," *The Westminster Dictionary of Christian Spirituality,* ed. G. S. Wakefield (Philadelphia: Westminster Press, 1983), 106.

77. Stan Davis and Bill Davidson, *2020 Vision* (New York: Simon & Schuster, 1991), 112.

78. Robert Herrick, "Neutrality Loathsome," in *The Poetical Works of Robert Herrick,* ed. F. W. Moorman (London: Oxford Univ. Press, 1921), 343.

79. Gregory Nazianzus, "Second Theological Oration," in *Select Orations f Saint Gregory Nazianzen,* trans. C. G. Browne and J. E. Swallow, *A Select Library of Nicene and Post-Nicene Fathers of the Christian Church,* 2d ser., ed. Phillip Schaff and Henry Wace (New York: Christian Literature Co., 1894), 7:289. An editorial note adds: "His back parts are Creation and Providence, by which He reveals Himself."

80. Wislawa Szymborska, *Poems: New and Collected, 1957–1997* (New York: Harcourt Brace, 1998), xiii–xiv.

81. As quoted in William P. Barrett, "An American Original," *Forbes* (1 Dec 1997): 171.

82. Michael H. Goldhaber, *Reinventing Technology: Policies for Democratic Values* (New York: Routledge and Kegan Paul, 1986), esp. part 2, 121–244.

83. See Jean Beaudrillard, *Critique of the Political Economy of Sign* (St. Louis: Telos Press, 1981), ch. 9.

84. The casket company is Oak Grove International of Manistee, Michigan.

85. Quoted in Rabbi Joseph Telushkin, *Jewish Wisdom* (New York: Morrow, 1994), 90.

86. See Paul MacLean, *The Triune Brain* (New York: Plenum Press, 1990). I thank John H. Brand for pointing me to this reference.

87. Leighton Ford, *The Power of Story* (Colorado Springs: NavPress, 1994), 12.

88. *The Poems of Coventry Patmore,* ed. Frederick Page (New York: Oxford Univ. Press, 1949), 479.

89. Andrew Harvey and Mark Matousek, *Dialogues with a Modern Mystic* (Wheaton, IL: Theosophical Publishing House, 1994), 145.

90. George F. Kennan, *Around the Cragged Hill* (New York: Norton, 1993), 49.

91. Historian George Trevelyan thought it was curiosity.

92. Joachim Jeremias, *Jesus' Promise to the Nations,* trans. S. H. Hooke (London: SCM Press, 1958), 74.

93. As quoted in Jon Winokur, *Friendly Advice* (New York: Dutton, 1990), 244.

94. As quoted in R. E. O. White, *Luke's Case for Christianity* (London: Bible Reading Fellowship, 1987), 109.

95. Joseph Epes Brown, "Becoming Part of It," *Parabola* 7 (1982): 8.

96. Lewis A. Smedes, *How Can It Be All Right When Everything Is All Wrong?* (San Francisco: Harper & Row, 1982), 20.

97. Peter Berger, *The Precarious Vision: A Sociologist Looks at Social Fictions and Christian Faith* (Garden City, NY: Doubleday, 1961).

98. Alex Cohen, as quoted in Andrew Leonard, *Bots: The Origin of New Species* (San Francisco: Hardwired, 1997), 187. This is a reference to Theodore Sturgeon, "Microcosmic God," in his *Microcosmic God: The Complete Stories of Theodore Sturgeon,* ed. Paul Williams (Berkeley: North Atlantic Books, 1995), 2:127–56.

99. Leonard, *Bots: The Origin of New Species,* 187.

100. The quote by Lévi-Strauss appears as an epigraph in Justin Cartwright's *Masai Dreaming* (New York: Random House, 1995).

101. Martin Luther, *Table Talk,* no. 5047, in *Luther's Works,* ed. and trans. Theodore G. Tappert (Philadelphia: Fortress Press, 1967), 54:383–4.

L ife ring # 3

IS THIS A GREAT TIME, OR WHAT?

Get Green

SEVEN HEADS: ONE BODY

or what? **wiwak** card and board games were forbidden. Even Old Maid could open doors downward. So my brothers and I became experts in Paper-Scissors-Rock.

There is something that trumps all three, even rocks. That is water. In the modern world we thought in terms of foundational bedrocks to time. In postmodern culture we must think in terms of living flows of history.

It gets harder to think like water the less water there is in us to think. The human embryo is 97% water, a newborn 77%, an adult 60% and shrinking. But if we have been baptized by water and the Spirit, we not only can think like water but can thrive in the water and, when Jesus beckons, walk on water. We don't have to go through life walking on eggshells. We can become walk-on-water disciples.

But then we see the enormity of the challenge, and we begin to sink. A sign in front of a church featured the pastor's posting of the sermons for the next two Sundays. People did a double-take when one week the sign read:

August 18: "Jesus Walks on Water"

August 25: "Searching for Jesus"

This is the chapter where we begin to sink if we're not careful to keep our eyes fixed on Christ.

HYDRA-HEADED MONSTERS ~ Of the twelve challenges presented to the legendary Hercules, the slaying of the Hydra of Lerne was perhaps the most trying. Said to inhabit the depths of the marshy lake of Lerne in southern Greece, this monstrous sea snake had seven heads—some accounts say nine, 50, or even 100. As soon as Hercules severed one head, another one immediately grew back. Hercules was saved only because he mustered all the strength in his body and with one fierce blow shattered all the heads at the same time.[1]

In postmodern culture we are confronting multiheaded monsters. Many we have created ourselves. The monsters' names are legion, as legion as the names of Lucifer. Any one of these multiple menaces could destroy us.

Some of the greatest threats in the world today are the monsters of global warming, global cooling (which some tend to think more likely, but that's another story), asteroids, economic crashes, deforestation, desertification, potential for nuclear holocaust, worldwide plague, loss of biodiversity, exhaustion of natural resources, overconsumption of energy, poverty, the widening gap between the rich and the poor, environmental pollution, and humankind's own immunological deterioration.

No wonder postmoderns suffer from an almost human race hypochondria. Sometimes it seems we are afflicted with almost every known form of malady and it's only a matter of time until one of them takes us away.

One suspects the size of Hercules' brain. He may have had the body of a giant, but his mind was the size of a gnat. Instead of attacking the head, why didn't Hercules use his own head? Why didn't he attack the monster's body instead of each separate head?[2]

Fighting each head is fighting the symptoms, not the causes. Fighting all of them together can actually make the symptoms worse. The heart of the problem is the heart. Our true victory comes only if we go for the body. All the problems of postmodern culture stem from the same root cause: heart disease. Poet/politician Vaclav Havel, when asked how we can escape the horrors facing us in this new world, responds, "It is my deep conviction that the only option is a change in the sphere of the spirit."[3] Our problems are not "out there." Our problems are "in here." Berthold Brecht's dictum is correct: "Evil has a phone number."

> One ship drives east, another west,
> With the self-same winds that blow.
> 'Tis the set of the sails, and not the gales
> That tells them the way to go.
> Some ships sail east, and some sail west....
> And so it is, as we journey through life,
> 'Tis the set of the soul that determines the goal
> and not the calm, or the strife.
>
> Old poem

SPIRITUAL PROBLEMS REQUIRE SPIRITUAL SOLUTIONS ~ There was once a German mayor who had the honor of receiving to his small town a visit from the Holy Roman Emperor himself. The mayor was embarrassed, however, that he was unable to lay on the traditional 21-gun salute. He apologized to the emperor immediately.

"Sire," he said, "there are three reasons why we were unable to provide a 21-gun salute. The first is that we have no gunpowder—"

The emperor interrupted him. "My dear Lord Mayor, I think you might spare me the other two reasons, since the first is clearly sufficient."

Like that mayor, unless we attend to the spiritual crisis that is at the heart of all the other "crises" of our day, the tentacles of our troubles will run riot in many directions.

> A flower is your cousin.... Sometimes a person has got to take a life, like a chicken's or a hog's when you need it.... But nobody is so hungry they need to kill a flower.
>
> A Cherokee great-grandmother[4]

Don E. Eberly, a former White House aide, argues that "politics has been oversold." In his introduction to *Building a Community of Citizens*, he argues that America's most pressing need is for a reshaping of our hearts and habits that no politics of whatever brand can address.[5] An *Utne Reader* survey found that a majority think *the* most significant issue facing this country is not the deficit, racism, corporate downsizing, or the environment, but "spiritual and moral decay."

Monster #1: Climate Change. Have you noticed your wardrobe changing? The increased intensity and frequency of strange climate changes—from heat waves to frigid spells—is changing how we live on a daily basis.[6] When a summer heat wave hit the eastern and midwestern US in 1995, more than 500 people died. Climate change is now a public health challenge of the first order for the 21st century. Climatologists are our new apocalypticists, and their warnings are being ignored.

> The sky is not falling. The sky is filling up.
>
> Bill McKibben

Temperatures in the Northern Hemisphere have skyrocketed in the last decade to heights not seen since 1400.[7] So much arctic ice is melting that very soon we will have four seasons, warns Gene Perret: "summer, simmer, broil, and bake."

Want to see the effect of a runaway Greenhouse Effect? Take a look at Venus, which has winds of up to 100 meters per second and heated temperatures above 450 centigrade.

What happens when our biosphere breaks up? Enemies from the microbiological world get stronger and stronger. Mysterious viruses come out of nowhere and kill a half-million people a year. The first case of AIDS was diagnosed in 1981 at the Centers for Disease Control in Atlanta, but since then three other viruses as deadly as HIV have emerged: the Guanarito virus, a new arenavirus, and an unnamed Hanta virus.[8] Richard Preston's book *The Hot Zone* tells the story of two deadly viruses, Marburg and Ebola (a near relative of a flu), both fundamentally subcategories of environmental pollution.[9]

Global climatic change releases from the tropics diseases that would have stayed put if deforestation had not taken place. Scientists of the World Health Organization (WHO) are busy studying the impact of global warming on malaria, dengue, and yellow fever. The warming of just a few degrees Celsius, with a regional precipitation increase of just 7-15%, jump-starts these three diseases into temperate latitudes.

It is our choice: Either gear down deadly greenhouse gas emissions, or gear up to fight deadly tropical diseases.

New versions of old illnesses are popping up beyond the tropics. New strains of tuberculosis have emerged. The parasite responsible for malaria and two million deaths a year has been enormously successful in its attempts to overcome our most potent drugs. The hepatic C virus is spreading at an alarming rate. The plague is back in India, as is poliomyelitis in South Africa and Holland.

Monster #2: Species Extinction and Environmental Destruction. The largest creature ever to have lived on planet Earth was a female blue whale, killed in the Antarctic in February 1928. The people who sliced her blubber and

collected her oil hurried off to kill more of her companions. They did not preserve a single bone or record of the world's biggest leviathan.[10]

One hundred years ago 100,000 tigers lived in the forests of India alone.
They were part of a thriving tiger community that crisscrossed a continent.
Today there are fewer than 4000 left, tiny islands of "pocket tigers" surrounded by a vast sea of humans and forever isolated from each other. The
world will never again see tigers living as God created them to live.[11]

The only area where the centralized economies of Eastern Europe were
more efficient than capitalist economies of the West was in the destruction of
the environment. According to some, we are now
living in the midst of the latest and worst of planet
Earth's six extinctions. The planet is not suffering
from the explosive impact of a meteor from outer
space; it is suffering from the slow-motion impact
of a meteor called "homo sapiens."[13]

> The song of the Dodo, if it
> had one, is forever unknow-
> able because no human
> from whom we have testi-
> mony ever took the trouble
> to sit in the Mauritian forest
> and listen.
>
> Ecojournalist David Quammen[12]

Postmoderns don't face burning rivers, black
skies, or smoking exhausts as our Industrial Age
forebears did. Even the names Amoco Cadiz, Argo
Merchant, and Exxon Valdez don't begin to
address the worst spillage and pillage. Our threats
are more subtle and invisible: global warming,
ozone-layer depletion, endocrine disrupters, the paving over of our fruited
plains, lawn chemicals, overconsumption, and overpopulation. If there is one
thing we have learned in the '80s and '90s, it is that the quest for bigness and
growth is one of the greatest social and environmental disasters ever to hit
this planet.[14]

A billion homo sapiens are added every 11 years to the planet. The hyper-
trophy of a single species pushes other life-forms out of bed and into extinction. The decline of biological diversity is real and severe. The alarming loss
of soil fertility, forest cover, and coral reef viability and the release of fossilized
CO_2 that nature put away 300 million years ago in its march toward greater
diversity—all these "losses" and many others are the result of one life-form
annihilating other life-forms in its immoral confusion of "dominion" with
"domination."

Whether we are reading about animals or plants, the mantra is the same:
We are now living in one of the greatest periods of species extinction in the
history of the planet.[15] The normal "background" rate of extinction is one to
three species per year. Now there are 1,999 species lost a year, 1000 times
the normal extinction rate.

Of the 100,000 indigenous creatures in USAmerica that are found
nowhere else on planet Earth, 1500 one-of-a-kinds have been rendered
extinct in the last 100 years.

In tropical forests, 1,800 populations are lost every hour—some 16 million annually.[16] An inventory of species is almost too horrible to record:

- Birds: 11% officially threatened with extinction, but two out of every three species are in decline worldwide, including the largest and most unusual birds.
- Mammals: 25% of all mammal species are on an extinction course.
- Fish: 33% of all fish species are threatened with extinction.
- Amphibians: 20% of reptiles and 25% of other amphibians are threatened.[17]

All creation is crying out in agony and travail. "Sentinel species" like frogs are showing up with extra legs, two sets of hindquarters, three eyes. The handwriting is on the wall for those species that are diminishing more slowly. Like the tiger, all of nature now exists as islands cut off from each other. Biodiversity that is insular is unlikely to survive.[18]

In the words of biologist Christian de Duve,

The disappearance of living species is not just a blow to orchid growers, butterfly collectors, and beetle buffs. It is an irremediable loss of precious information, the biological equivalent of the burning of the library of Alexandria in 641. It is the destruction of a large part of the book of life before it can be read, the irreplaceable loss of vital clues to biological evolution and our own history. Resources of potentially great practical benefit may also be lost. With each daily shrinking of the biosphere, a valuable source of food or a molecule that could have cured malaria, AIDS, or some other scourge may be vanishing forever.[19]

Monster #3: Wealth Segregation. There is a joke among economists that if present trends continue, by the year 2010 the pay gap between executives and employees will exceed the spread between the wealth of King Louis XVI and the typical peasant just before the French Revolution.

> When everyone runs rather than walks, more people fall behind, even if all are advancing.
>
> Economist/global strategist Edward N. Luttwak[20]

It's no joke. In 1994, corporate executives averaged a 14% pay increase; workers barely got a 2% raise. That's a sevenfold salary growth differential. The ratio of multinational CEO salaries to employees' has jumped to 187 to 1 in 1995 from 41 to 1 in the mid-70s.

Part of the double ring of wealth segregation is that while the income gap between countries will diminish, the gap within countries will rise. The gap between rich and poor is wider in the US than in any of the top 20 industrialized nations. The US economy is the strongest it may have ever been in our history, and the number of personal bankruptcies is at an all-time high.

Twenty percent of the world's people organize their lives around cars, meat-based diets, and disposable products. Twenty percent of the world's population, born of want and worse, live in absolute deprivation.[21] In 1992, 2 billion people lived in countries with an average annual per capita income of $400; 2.6 billion reached $1,600; and only 830 million lived at income levels above $22,000. Among those 830 million, income inequalities are increasing and social gaps are widening. The gulf between the world's rich and poor has doubled in the last 30 years.[22]

> Sooner or later, we sit down to a banquet of consequences.
>
> Robert Louis Stevenson

Even those who debate the meaning of the income distribution gap agree that there is a widening gulf between the poorest and the richest.[23] In the early 1990s, "the richest 20 percent of the world's people earned 61 times more income than the poorest 20 percent," compared with a 30-fold difference in the 1960s.[24] The Urban Institute concludes that in the United States the top 20%, which had been four times richer than the bottom 20% 20 years earlier, was five times richer by the start of the '90s.[25] There are 625 US counties where the highest one-fifth in wealth live side-by-side the lowest one-fifth in poverty.[26]

During the '80s in USAmerica, the percentage of income received by the top 20% zoomed to the highest ratio recorded by the Census Bureau since it began counting in 1949.[27] Tensions are mounting between those on the upper rungs of the economic ladder and those on the bottom. No wonder some are predicting that the economy of the future is a "plantation economy." According to one survey, 70% of robberies and violent crimes are "vengeance crimes"—the unemployed taking it out on the rich.[28]

The good news is that more and more people are becoming rich. Those households earning more than $50,000 a year could easily grow 37% by the year 2005. Already one in 12 households in the US had an income of $100,000 or more in 1996.[29] The top 0.5% of US households own 40% of the nation's assets. John I. Clarke writes, "The assets of the world's 358 billionaires obscenely exceed the combined annual incomes of countries accounting for 45% of the world's population."[30]

The bad news is that more and more people are falling behind as well and the middle class continues its contraction that started in 1969. Economist Lester Thurow argues that "no country not experiencing a revolution or a military defeat with a subsequent occupation has probably ever had as rapid or as widespread an increase in inequality as has occurred in the United States in the past two decades."[31]

The more connected the planet becomes economically and technologically, the more socially and culturally fragmented it becomes.[32] Technology is creating economic and social distances that appear almost unbridgeable.

An underclass is emerging that cannot access electronic culture. One-third of the people of planet Earth still don't have electricity. Some estimate that the "worldwide" telecommunications network could actually bypass half the world as a winner-take-all-society is being created. For example, Africa, "the lost continent of telecommunications," possesses only 2% of the world's telephones. What telecommunications do exist in Africa are state controlled, badly managed, and rife with corruption.

Monster #4: Rampaging Microbes and Deadly Plagues. Whether they know it or not, Monster #4 is the #1 threat to the airline industry in the 21st century. It endangers the airline industry more than oil costs or government regulations or passenger fluctuations.

We are only beginning to understand something our ancestors knew only too well: how deadly infectious diseases actually are. Now the leading cause of death worldwide, infectious diseases both well known and unknown are reemerging. More than 30 new viruses have appeared around the world in the last two decades.[33] Infectious disease are a 21st-century national-security threat of even more momentous proportions than hostile states or terrorists.

> An imbalance between rich and poor is the oldest and most fatal ailment of republics.
>
> Plutarch

Indiscriminate use of "wonder-drug" antibiotics has left us weak to drug-resistant strains of bacteria, which could easily become a global epidemic without quickly developed DNA vaccines and new antibacterial chemicals.[34] Get used to the acronyms MCS and EI: We will be seeing a lot of them, because MCS stands for multiple chemical sensitivity and EI for Environmental Illness.[35] AIDS/HIV is spreading at a rate of 8,500 new cases per day, with more than 50 million infections expected by the year 2000.

We know that CJD (Creutzfeldt-Jakob disease), BSE (bovine spongiform encephalopathy), and Downer Cow Syndrome are prion diseases. Prions can somehow cross species barriers. But how, when, why, where? In USAmerica, 100,000 "Downer cattle" are melted down and fed to other cattle every year. Beef products can go into cough medicine, lipstick, certain sweets, and biscuits. To be on the safe side, Richard Rhodes suggests, we should also be avoiding milk, butter, surgical sutures, donated blood, and transplant organs.[36]

> Child to parent: "If your generation doesn't learn to save the planet, it won't matter if my generation can't learn to read or write."
>
> *Wall Street Journal* cartoon

Vegetarians: Think you're safe? Hello?! Organic vegetables are fertilized with the droppings of chickens fed on meat and bonemeal.

Gardeners: Think you're safe? Hello?! That rose garden can be deadly. Meat and bonemeal are routinely sprinkled on those flowers, and the dust can "get up your nose and, potentially, travel along the axons leading to your brain."[37]

One expert concludes that "everyone, everywhere who has been in contact with modern agriculture or medicine, is at risk."[38]

Monster #5: Violence Epidemic. We have endured an entire century of violence. We have been told to relax, please, and try to enjoy it—it's only to be expected.

Postmoderns are choking in abundance, creating an appetite for extravagance and a relish for violence. Crash scenes in movies bring the two together. As I watched director David Cronenberg's *Crash* (1997), I realized that here was the postmodern form of potlatch. Potlatch was a Native American ceremony where, to display a person's wealth, it was piled up and burned at a public ceremony. Disaster movies are postmodern potlatch.

The new postmodern forms of violence are dispersed, random, and frightening. The violence epidemic has many manifestations, from gun-toting grade-schoolers to gated communities with security guards to graffiti writing to gangsta rappers "talking back" to white society[39] to hate crimes to "clergy abuse"—people taking out their frustrations and anger on men and women of the cloth.

It is not simply a case of people being anesthetized to violence because of the media. People today are addicted to violence. Postmoderns easily become violence junkies. And violence begets violence.

> Ninety percent of war casualties at the beginning of this century were military combatants. As the century ends, 90 percent are civilians.
>
> David C. Korten[40]

Postmodernity's culture of violence started with John Wayne as the Ringo Kid (*Stagecoach,* 1939) and graduated to Marlon Brando as the Don (*The Godfather,* 1972). Violence affects kids regardless of gender. Studies of Gen-X women who grew up watching violent, heroic women on TV (*Charlie's Angels* and *Bionic Woman*) reveal that the more violence they absorbed in the late '70s, the more physically aggressive they became in adulthood.[41]

Few expressions of popular culture do not celebrate violence. Thanks to special effects technology, *Bonnie and Clyde* portrayed violence for the sake of violence for the first time. As British novelist Martin Amis put it, "In the cinema, if not anywhere else, violence started getting violent in 1966."[42] But even our music is getting more violent. Ice Cube, one of the premier gangsta rappers in '90s hip-hop, is only one of many. "We're gonna treat you like a king," threatens a white cop from the LAPD on the "Death Side" of Ice Cube's 1991 album, *Death Certificate.* "What g——king?" snaps the indignant rapper from South Central Los Angeles. "Rodney King! Martin Luther King! And all the other g—— kings from Africa!"

Violence has become such a staple of commonplace culture that in the future it promises to become almost a religious experience—the sacrament of violence, if you will. Like Aztec culture, our movies are preparing us to see the nobility and beauty of violence and to need periodic bathings in blood. It may be that media are giving people the rush and ritual that physical violence once provided to earlier cultures.

And we wonder why we are raising a generation of kids who seem strangers to remorse, to sensitivity to others' feelings, to basic human decency and civility.[43] Even more disturbing is the fact that for many kids and adults, organized violence brings order and betterment to their lives. Robert Kaplan points out that

> A large number of people on this planet, to whom the comfort and stability of a middle-class life is utterly unknown, find war and a barracks existence a step up rather than a step down. . . . Where there has always been mass poverty, people find liberation in violence.[44]

Hence the organized violence of ghetto gangs.

A plague of drive-by-hit-and-run hate radio testifies to the problematic nature of behavior and lifestyle diversity. With the rapid rise in homosexual households and a 10% decrease in married-couple homes, hate crimes are a growth industry.

If homosexuality will be the most difficult social issue of the first decades of the 21st century, varieties of terrorism will become the most explosive political issue.

"Briefcase warfare" is the name of a new kind of warfare in which courier-soldiers deliver cheap, portable weaponry that can be chemical, bacterial, or nuclear. One small suitcase carried by a "soldier" can contain enough biological weaponry to kill a half-million people. Forget "soldiers"—any biology student can make anthrax in a lab the size of a microbrewery.

Pipe and body bombs are obsolete, given high-tech guerilla weaponry. Bacteriological, chemical, and nuclear weapons are now available on the open market. In June 1997 two Russian technicians were apprehended while selling nuclear material to Iraq. Russia admits to losing track of "more than 100" suitcase-size nuclear bombs—each one capable of killing up to 100,000 people.

You do the math: 100 x 100,000 = 10 million people. Unless they were innocently taken to the dump (hello?!), weapons capable of killing 10 million people are now in someone's hands. If that isn't scary enough, 110 Stinger missiles are "out there" unaccounted for, ready to shoot down planes, even (especially) Air Force One, the President's plane. In the light of all these factors and more, war in the Middle East seems almost inevitable.

Monster #6: Overconsumption and Overpopulation. In 1992, two of the major scientific groups in the world—the US National Academy of Sciences and the Royal Society of London—issued a joint appeal to the world community. Here is the opening of the statement:

> If current predictions of population growth prove accurate and patterns of human activity on the planet remain unchanged, science and technology may not be able to prevent the irreversible degradation of the environment or continued poverty for much of the world.

All men and women whom I have faced at that final moment convince me that in what I have done I have not prevented a single murder.

Britain's last hangman,
Albert Pierrepoint[45]

The closing words of the document are even gloomier:

> Global policies are urgently needed to promote more rapid economic development throughout the world, more environmentally benign patterns of human activity, and a more rapid stabilization of world population. . . . Sustainable development can be achieved, but only if irreversible degradation of the environment can be halted in time.[46]

There is an old saying: Everybody worries about the population explosion, but nobody worries about it at the right time. Every second, three human beings die and six are born. Every year, 100,000,000 humans are added to the planet's population. In quadrupling over the past 80 years, world population is climbing to 8 billion. The equivalent population of the US is being added to the planet every three years.

In the words of comedian Sam Levenson, "Somewhere on this globe every 10 seconds there is a woman giving birth to a child. She must be found and stopped."

Why is population growing around the world? Less because people are having more children and more because fewer people are dying. There is a major decrease in mortality rates around the world. Between 1940 and 1960, Egypt's death rate dropped from over 25 per thousand to around 15 per thousand, yielding an increase in life expectancy of about 20 years. In short, the first half of the 21st century is facing the underpopulation of the developed countries—Japan and the nations of Europe and North America[47]—and the overpopulation of the rest of the globe.

Overpopulation and overconsumption together constitute the two most vicious of the Hydra's heads.[48] Too often the two are separated. Worldwatch Institute founder Lester R. Brown, a New Jersey tomato farmer, argues that we need to address the problems of overpopulation: "By far our greatest threat to food security is population growth." He gives an example from oceanic fisheries: From 1950 to 1989 the fish catch per person doubled, but since then the catch per person has fallen by 11% even though all fisheries are at maximum capacity.[49]

But "overpopulation" can be a code word for ignoring economic, social, and cultural issues that are even more basic.[50] We are all the products of lotteries, both genetic and environmental, that distribute benefits unequally. Everyone reading this book is a privileged citizen of an affluent society that is afflicted with the most virulent, most unvanquishable social disease ever to hit planet Earth: consumerism.

What some are calling "consumerism," others like Pope John Paul II are calling "superdevelopment," which the Pope defines as "an excessive availability of material goods for the benefit of certain social groups [making] people slaves of 'possessions' and immediate gratification, with no other horizon than the multiplication or continual replacement of the things already owned with others still better."[51] Humanity is hankering after junk and hunks of trinkets while truth lies unheralded.

> I had plastic surgery last week. I cut up my credit cards.
>
> Humorist
> Henny Youngman

If the world were a town of 1000 people, there would be 564 Asians, 210 Europeans, 86 Africans, 80 South Americans, and 60 North Americans. Seven hundred people would be illiterate; 500 hungry.[52] The 20% of the world's population who live in developed areas use more than 67% of the natural resources and generate more than 80% of the pollutants. The richest 25% of the world's population use 86% of all forest products, 75% of energy, 72% of steel production. The poorest who live in the world's most pinched and painful environments consume only 2% of our resources.[53]

On average, each USAmerican causes over 100 times more damage to the global environment than a person in a poor country. Each of us consumes five times more than a Mexican, 10 times more than a Chinese, and 30 times more than a person in India. Eighty percent of environmental damage is caused by the world's 1.1 billion overconsumers.

According to MIT economist Lester Thurow, the two extreme scenarios are as follows:

> ONE—If the world's population had the productivity of the Swiss, the consumption habits of the Chinese, the egalitarian instincts of the Swedes, and the social discipline of the Japanese, then the planet could support many times its current population without privation for anyone
>
> TWO—On the other hand, if the world's population had the productivity of Chad, the consumption habits of the US, the inegalitarian instincts of India, and the social discipline of Argentina, then the planet could not support anywhere near its present numbers.[54]

Harvard biologist E. O. Wilson did not, as the press first reported, announce at the 1993 Renewing the Earth Conference that the carrying capacity of planet Earth, at US levels of consumption of resources, was about 210 million. But he has since admitted that the figure is not an unreasonable one. In other words, planet Earth is already overpopulated by 5 billion persons.

Monster #7: Technological Evilution. Evil emerges in different times and places at different rates through different technologies. Whether it's the wheel or the Web, every technology can damage the organs of the body (especially the nervous system). When there are 20,000 pieces of technology the average American must learn to operate, there are bound to be some unfavorable, unexpected side effects.

Edward Wenk Jr. uses the "amplifier" metaphor for the impact of technology on people:

> Since prehistoric times, the lever and wheel have amplified human muscle. Today, the computer amplifies the human mind and memory. Because technology has such potent effects and is such a swift and powerful instrument of change, it also acts as a social amplifier. With death control through measures of public health not matched by processes of birth control, technology has spawned a population explosion. With modern telecommunication, interpersonal transactions are stretched in volume and distance. With rampant consumerism, sales techniques inflate material appetites, and television teaches all about the inequality of their satisfactions. With ballooning inequities come an increased number and diversity of conflicts. Finally, with technology imposing new demands on our social institutions, it exposes their weaknesses and the expanding power of technology's keepers.[56]

> Simplicity, moderation and discipline, as well as a spirit of sacrifice, must become part of everyday life, lest all suffer the negative consequences of the careless habits of a few.
>
> Pope John Paul II[55]

When everything everywhere is technology, there is all the more need for moral discourse about something that cannot tell us how to live our lives to good purpose.

Read the neo-Luddites. They are a healthy corrective to technological utopianism. "Luddites" is a term applied to those who blindly and wildly fear new technologies. It derives from the apocryphal figure of Ned Ludd, a British weaver who led riots that destroyed textile machines in the early days of the Industrial Revolution.[57]

> Home computer. Like new. Never been figured out.
>
> From the "For Sale" section of a daily newspaper

The neo-Luddites whom I respect the most are Jerry Mander, Chellis Glendinning, Jeremy Rifkin, Wendell Berry, Theodore Roszak, Dave Foreman, Langdon Winner, Stephanie Mills, Mark Slouka, and Kirkpatrick Sale. Sale is cut from the same cloth as the early temperance campaigner Carrie Nation, who toured the country "hatchetizing" kegs of liquor and entire saloons to the chopping chant of

"Smash! Smash! For Jesus' sake, Smash!" Sale enjoys taking a sledgehammer (this isn't technology?) to computers. He destroyed a computer on the stage of an *Utne Reader* forum in January 1995 after making a bet with *Wired* editor Kevin Kelly whether technology will have saved or wrecked the world by 2020.

You can join me in reading all about the Luddites—on their Web site! You can hear their warnings about what happens when "image replaces imagination," "when a quote is better than a thought," when "pictures are quicker than words."[58] I especially resonate with their warnings of an emerging barbarism that hijacks our creativity and homogenizes our dreams. The dangerous by-products of this new electronic culture can be seen in the rising incidence of addictions (including electronic addiction), depression, eating disorders. Or simply ask the people who know firsthand the meaning of a polarized economy and its imposition of involuntary simplicity in their lives.

Finally, read everything the three key cops of the silicon superhighway write: Sven Birkerts, Neil Postman, and Clifford Stoll. I sympathize with their concern that cyberspace will eliminate face-to-face contact, although I believe the truth is exactly the opposite. Another critic is Bill McKibben, whose works ought to be required reading as well.[59]

so what?   RETURN "EVIL" TO THE POSTMODERN VOCABULARY ~

The church must throw a searchlight on the human soul. It must show the folly of engaging in after-the-fact moral rectitude when what Pope John Paul II calls the "structures of sin" must be factored in from the beginning. Moral sewage must be taken into account and taken out on a daily basis.

The doctrine of original sin teaches postmoderns something important: The Alexander the Greats, Genghis Khans, Napoleons, Hitlers, Godfathers, Pol Pots, Unabombers, and Menendez brothers are more representative of the human species than Gandhi, Mother Teresa, and Martin Luther King Jr. The church must offer postmoderns a theological primer in the ABCs of absurdity, bigotry, and cruelty.

> Have faith in God, but tie your camels first.
>
> Old Sufi saying

The "hole in the moral ozone" is really what's behind the hole in the ozone. Anybody doubting our thinning moral air need only read a 1991 status report on American morality entitled *The Day America Told the Truth*. Its findings reveal that our moral cold has become the flu.

1. Nine out of 10 respondents admit to lying on a regular basis.
2. Only 1 in 10 believe all of the Ten Commandments.
3. Ninety percent say they believe in God, but for most "religion plays virtually no role in shaping their opinions on a long list of important moral questions."

4. One-third of married respondents admit to having committed adultery.
5. Twenty percent of female respondents testify to having been date-raped, with less than 3% of the rapes reported.
6. Twenty-five percent of respondents under 25 admit to having lost their virginity by age 13, compared with 10% for ages 45–64 and 5% for ages 65 and older.
7. One-third of the respondents own handguns, and 7% say they would be willing to kill a stranger for 10 million dollars.[60]

The human power of self-creation brings with it tremendous responsibilities. Postmoderns love the act of creating themselves and their world almost as much as they love to hide from taking responsibility for their acts, leaving to others the moral problems of what to do with their creations, whether wholesome or perverse.

At a time when moral issues are becoming more complex and difficult, our ability to engage in moral reasoning is becoming slighter and slighter. What an opportunity for the church to teach personal and social morality! If there is to be a shared culture and rich civic life and economic flourishing, the cultivation of morality is at the top of the church's ministry. Cranky moral crusades that mistake the larynx for the cranium are counterproductive. Can the church take its itchy fingers off the trigger of moral outrage long enough to help postmoderns devise moral markers and design moral emblems for an authentic 21st-century biblical faith?

MAKE WORK PLAY ~ "I have worked every minute of my life," creatologist/University of Chicago professor Mihaly Csikszentmihalhyi says, "And I never did a lick of work in my life."[61] What the "work ethic" was to the modern world, the "play ethic" will be to postmodern culture. Which will it be: homework or houseplay?

The Amish call house-raisings a "frolic." It's a frolic because it's the time when an entire community gathers for neighborliness and assistance. When it comes to building houses, the Amish don't "work at it"; they "play at it." How the Amish build barns and houses is how we must learn to build relationships and marriages and churches.

> When it comes to creativity, if you haven't learned how to play, you haven't learned how to work.
>
> Bryan W. Mattimore[62]

Tom Peters tells about a successful international banking executive who runs an operation in Asia. He attended one of Peters' London seminars, and after it was over, he chuckled as he showed Peters his business card. It read: "Playground Director."

GARBAGE IN–GARBAGE OUT ~ What plots do the film-going public flock to see? Stories about rapists, kidnappers, terrorists, vampiristic lovers, serial killers, child abusers, pornographers.[63]

Generation-X has witnessed more violence and murders than any generation in history. ᕩᓰᗯᵃᵏ, a sophomore in high school, to be exact, Linda Armstrong and I were asked to be part of a sting operation. (Life, Death, and Linda Armstrong were all about equal at that time in my teenage years.) We were recruited by the Kiwanis Club to go to a local cigar and magazine store and see if, being underage, we could purchase some *Playboy* magazines.

Now any 10-year-old can get on a computer and find material on sadomasochism, bestiality, vaginal and rectal fisting, pedophilia, and eroticized urination. Kids can (and—don't kid yourself, parents—do) download whole libraries of pornography, join sexually oriented chat lines, engage in tactile sexual encounters. The violence in CD-ROM and video arcade games has gone so far, and so low, as to require the use of a stomach pump.

Our kids' daily life percolates with media-driven stories of killings, kidnappings, rapes, riots, plagues, pollutions, battles, and bloodshed that are as pervasive as they are perverse.

Vice is a monster of so
frightful mien,
As to be hated needs but to
be seen;
Yet seen too oft, familiar
with her face,
We first endure, then pity,
then embrace.

Alexander Pope,
Essay on Man[64]

And we wonder why we are creating one of the most violent cultures ever to occupy planet Earth. Postmoderns may have strong stomachs, but also slushy minds. One of the phrases hammered into my head during childhood was "watch your language!" We should now be hardwiring into our kids' brains, "Watch your images!" It is not just "bad words" one should never say; there are "bad images" one should never see. What we allow ourselves to see and hear affects how we live. Elizabeth Newson's 1994 report, "Video Violence and the Protection of Children," states the obvious: If images don't influence human behavior, why are companies willing to spend billions of dollars a year on film and television advertising?[65]

The average teenager listens to four hours of music a day. Some of this music is indescribably degrading—for example, Prodigy's single "Smack My Birth Up" or Mo Thugs' "Don't Trust a Bitch" or Cannibal Corpse's songs "Orgasm by Torture" and "Stripped, Raped and Strangled." Nine Inch Nails' song "Big Man with a Gun" describes forcing a woman into oral sex and then shooting her in the head at point-blank range.

Such music may be constitutionally protected and perfectly legal, but it is absolutely immoral. Prohibition of violence doesn't work. Since the '50s, when the Comics Code was introduced that prohibits extreme violence in comic books, violence among young people has increased several *hundred* percent. The energies of the church in postmodern culture must be directed to teaching the difference between morality and legality.

Can we confront with courage the essential intellectual, social, and moral challenges of a rapidly changing society? Can we refuse to let postmodern vulgarity and violence, vacuity and vapidity, depress us? The church's vision of "nonviolence" and the dream of a nonviolent society have changed. The "nonviolence" movement used to be a protest movement that didn't approve of violence tactics. Today's nonviolence movement must be a protest movement that inverts, subverts, and ironicizes the dominant values of a culture of violence itself.

TRADITION BASED/TECHNOLOGICALLY SAVVY ~ Neo-Luddite poet and Kentucky farmer Wendell Berry is a personal mentor. He and his wife have hosted me at their table. His books are already classics. Wendell Berry says his opposition to machines is not superstitious: "I am not 'against technology' so much as I am 'for community.'"[66] So must be the church.

Berry's argument that possibility is not permissibility ought to guide everything we do with new technology. But Berry himself declaims against the computer and electronic culture while banging away on his 1956 Royal Typewriter. Isn't that technology? Back in the 19th century, many farmers stridently protested the steam locomotive, claiming that the locomotive's noise would prevent their chickens from laying eggs and their cows from giving milk. Other 19th-century critics of the Industrial Age warned that traveling faster than 20 miles per hour over extended periods of time caused one to go mad. (And when I look around at this culture, in my weaker moments I think they may have been right.)

I also don't hear any of these neo-Luddites wanting to return to "the good old days" when men worked at least 72-hour weeks, when life expectancy was 35 years (colonial America), when serial marriages were the norm (the average marriage lasted 12 years in the 1880s) because one-third of women died in childbirth, when domestic servants were the second-largest employee group in developed countries (1910), when 50% of the children never reached the age of two, when my son's epilepsy would have made him a social outcast and object of terror, when pneumonia, diphtheria, meningitis, and polio killed or crippled millions, when the victims of ergot poisoning were burned at the stake as witches. I could go on and on about the "good old days," but you get the point.

The church can be both tradition based and technology savvy, something that Arthur Kroker argues is a distinctive Canadian feature in the thinking of Harold Innis, Marshall McLuhan, and George Grant. Kroker says that "technology [exists] without a sustaining and coherent ethical purpose."[67]

Every technology leaves people with a weakened immune system in some part of the body. Leadership helps prepare people for the losses. What leadership does is help identify and isolate those fashionable mental and spiritual microbes that are damaging the organism and leaving us susceptible to social viruses and spiritual diseases and shutdowns. Leadership strengthens the internal defenses. Leadership helps people go against the grain, even shoves the "downside" in people's faces as a warning.

HIRE YOUR CHILDREN ～ If school boards can hire students to train teachers on how to use electronic technology, why can't churches hire its own kids to help it minister through the new technology? I am writing this book partly because a local church recruited my keyboard talents at 15 years of age when the official church organist eloped one weekend. What better way of evangelizing our children than recruiting them for ministry?

Auto mechanics are making better use of the Internet than are ministers. People fixing cars are better prepared for the future than people repairing souls.

Electronic technology is one area where we need to sit at the feet of our children. After all, according to humorist Dave Barry, who really runs the Internet anyway—the Mafia, the FBI, or a 13-year-old kid named Jason?

If you aren't comfortable hiring your own children, at least include them in the development of your Net ministries, whatever your current state of Web-ification. Ask them how to use a technology interface that speaks more than one language. Ask them how to use the Web to improve your church's relationship with your people. Ask them how to offer daily devotionals on your Web site, or how to install a prayer wheel and prayer wall. See what ideas they might have to use technology to advance world missions. With whom around the world does your church have regular contact, and how might those contacts be expanded through Internet connections, phone links, and the like?

Before long, there will be "virtual physicians" at accident sites. What about arranging for "virtual ministry teams" to be at crisis situations along with real ministry teams?

CHURCH STUDIOS ～ In the Enlightenment Era, pastors had "studies." In the high modern era they had "offices." In the postmodern era, pastors will have "studios"—spaces that are more like lobbies, living rooms, and cafés and less like "offices."[68] Such studios will facilitate team ministry done electronically with the help of teleconferencing and other communications technologies, while providing warm and accommodating space for people to come together face-to-face.

MEDITATION CAN BE BAD FOR YOU ～ There is something biblically troublesome about all this contemporary search for spirituality. The Greek ideal for life is encapsulated in the concept of *ataraxia* and *apatheia*. The former means tranquility, or undisturbedness. The latter, *apatheia*, means total peace, or beyond passion. *Ataraxia* and *apatheia* are the exact opposite of the biblical mandate. God wants us to be disturbed, passionate, and burdened; he does not want us to be "at peace" unless it is the "peace that passes understanding" (see Phil. 4:7). God is disturbed and passionate about the creation.[69] Michelangelo captured the God who is disturbed and passionate about creation better than perhaps any artist in history. In his frescoes for the Sistine Chapel ceiling (1508–12), the fourth picture in the center of the ceiling vault is the famous "Creation of Adam." God lets life flow into the already created body of Adam without their hands ever touching. Not until Jesus came did the fingers touch.

> God offers to every mind its choice between truth and repose. Take which you please; you can never have both.
>
> Ralph Waldo Emerson

Ask people what else they remember about this artistic masterpiece and they may note that the figure of God has the head of an old man with the body of a youth. One wonders if this isn't Michelangelo's way of conveying "eternity"—time beyond time, as in the youthful body, but time without end—hence the white hair.

But what is most amazing about Michelangelo's portrayal of God's creation of Adam, however, is the differing postures of God and Adam. A nonplussed, peaceful Adam reaches out, almost halfheartedly, his limp arm to a stretching, straining, passionate God.

One of the most haunting phrases in Matthew's passion story is this one: "sitting down they watched him there" (Matt. 27:36 KJV). A lot of postmodern spirituality is nothing more than "sitting down" and watching God work. James Hillman, former head of the Jung Institute, surveys postmodern culture with keen psychoanalytic eyes:

> I was at a talk in New York one day and this guy was speaking, a well-known Jungian analyst, about meditation, and I shouted out, "Meditation today is obscene." It just came out of me. I've thought about it ever since, and there's something absolutely wrong about meditation—I can't say what. If the ship is veering into the iceberg with a gaping hole in the hull, and you cross your legs and meditate—is that where you're supposed to be? . . . It's more important to face the ship going down. That's what will bring out the important virtues today. Not looking back on the good old days when the ship was sailing away. Now the *Titanic* is sinking. That calls forth the virtues of Joseph Conrad: courage, dignity, mourning, remembrance, ritual. All kinds of virtues which could come out of recognition of reality.[70]

It is possible to be deeply "spiritual" and never get your duff off the BarcaLounger. This makes a mockery of biblical spirituality. In the words of Rabbi Rami Shapiro,

> Hardly a week goes by without someone saying to me: "Rabbi, I'm not religious, but I am spiritual." They assume I will be happy about this. I always ask these people how much money they donate to help people in need.

Or about the last time they visited a hospital to see if anyone needed a sympathetic ear. Or about their diet, and what they are doing to minimize animal cruelty, environmental pollution, and exploitation of Third World laborers. The usual response is that these have nothing to do with spirituality. On the contrary, without care of the world spirituality is a self-serving waste of time.[71]

SOCIOLOGY OF SERVICE ~ Time for a quiz: What is the key to a postmodern kid's heart?

Music? Money? Guess again.

If you guessed "service," you pass.

For postmoderns, confession of faith is caring, compassion, and service, not creeds. Postmoderns don't want to be preached at; they want to be given a mission.

According to a 1996 Gallup Poll Youth Survey, the key to attracting the largest numbers of America's youth to church is to ask them to help less-fortunate people. Eighty percent of the teens said they are currently involved in "church-sponsored activities to help less fortunate people." Another study came up with much smaller numbers of teens actually involved in such church activities, but 60% said they would like to be.[72] An amazing 70% of college freshmen, according to one survey, are doing volunteer work. At my university, volunteerism is at an all-time high; Drew college students log 15–20 hours a week working at Habitat for Humanity, tutoring, or staffing homeless shelters and food banks.

The challenge for the church is that these same students are becoming socially involved while morally confused, unable to make basic moral judgments. Without any basis for making "right and wrong" statements, the Hitlers of history are not self-evidently "wrong."

If postmoderns are honest, is it because honesty is the best policy?

If they are pure, is it because purity requires less imagination?

If they are just, is it because justice garners more votes?

If they are noble, is it because nobility knows no greener pastures?

If they are gracious, is it because graciousness is the greatest crowd pleaser?

If they are lovable, is it because love is free?

One of the church's greatest contributions to postmodern culture may be its instilling in pragmatic, lack-of-sense-of-direction postmoderns a sheer love for truth, the moral banister to guide our steps up to the truth, and the ability to make urgent moral decisions even when the whole truth cannot be found.

HIGH-IMPACT DISCIPLESHIP ~ We need a new theory of church that is based less on budgets and baptisms than on community and service. In the theology of Jesus, you are saved to be spent. A missional church is one that orients itself to the needs of those outside it more than the needs of those inside it.

Our churches aren't sponsoring enough mission events and service projects such as kids helping the homeless on a certain day. Royal Palms Baptist Church in Phoenix, Arizona, required everyone who wanted to go on a 10-day mission trip to sign a covenant. Here are some of the terms of the covenant written by the youth pastor Phil Morgan:

—Must submit a written essay stating why they want to attend this trip, what they expect God to do, and how can they help in achieving these expectations;

—Must attend 5 of 6 training sessions through the months of March, April and May;

—Must go through a succession of three fasts: (1) a 24-hour fast from food; (2) a 3-day meal fast; (3) a 4-day media fast;

—No R-rated movies;

—Must show a consistent desire to grow as a Christian displayed by: (1) regular church attendance; (2) sharing their faith; (3) being in the Word; (4) praying.[73]

All this to go on a mission trip? Postmoderns are reached more by mission and service than by gimmicks and concerts or anything else. They want a faith that has depth to its discipleship. They want nothing to do with puny NIMBY (not-in-my-back-yard) solutions or BANANA (build-absolutely-nothing-anywhere-near-anybody) responses to the problems of the world.

Thomas Asacker, the founder of the medical devices company Humanfactor, writes in his diary about the "status quo living" of many of his acquaintances:

I'm amazed at how few interesting people I meet in my business life—for me a redundant expression. It seems that most of the people I run into simply want enough money and free time for things like annual vacations, watching television, surfing the Net, or kibitzing about this or that. Questioning the way things are and trying to improve them appears to be nothing but a waste of their "downtime."[74]

Now contrast Asacker's findings with the calls for ethical accountability beyond the marketplace that are coming from across the economic spectrum. The British management consultant Charles Handy is calling for a new theory of the corporation that is based less on property and profits than on community. He points out that the literal meaning of the word *company* is "the sharing of bread." "Profits are the lifeblood of any business," he states, "but life consists of more than keeping the blood flowing; otherwise, it would not be worth living."[75] Corporations are increasingly being judged on their bedrock values and initiatives for community betterment.[76]

"Political action" for postmoderns is more involvement in local service projects and small, community-based initiatives than in political parties and the so-called political process. To see a model of postmodern "political action" in the church, check out the Christian Community Development Association based in Chicago, Illinois, and Jackson, Mississippi. It builds networks among the plethora of Christian groups working in community development.[77] Did you know that Greyhound offers free transportation to runaways? Why not partner with your local Greyhound company so that these runaways can be helped in ways other than physical locomotion?

Philanthropy can constitute social warfare by another means. Why not create a Church and Community Foundation? Enlist your people in cause-related marketing, even "cause cuisine" fund-raising dinners that convey your church's commitment to service and community. Sponsor an annual awards banquet where local people are lionized and celebrated.

Here are two postmodern appeals based on a sociology of service. Test them out and see what the response is.

1. You think the challenge is too big for you? Guess what—it is. You think the challenge isn't too big for you and God to handle together? Guess what—it isn't.
2. When you get your 15 minutes of fame, will you use it to gripe about how bad the world has treated you and how hard you've had making it? Or will you spend your 15 minutes focusing on the needs of others and their difficulties?

CAESAR RENDERING TO THE CHURCH ～ In the 1996 welfare reform legislation passed by the US Congress, a provision called "charitable choice" made it possible for the government to send money directly to churches without the establishment of charitable subsidiaries known as CDCs (Community Development Corporations). What is more, church initiatives in the inner city don't need to be stripped of their faith components in order for the government to give the money.

Princeton political scientist John James Dilulio Jr., who created the phrase "superpredator," argues that the best thing the government could do for distressed communities and disadvantaged youth is to "let the churches have the inner cities" and to leverage faith-based initiatives and investments. Inner-city ministries have the best outcomes for USAmerica's meanest communities and vitality.

Dilulio's work proves that the intervention of 65,000 African-American churches do more for crime prevention and community health and vitality than any other secular or government agency. He defines "moral poverty" as "being without loving, capable, responsible adults who teach you right from wrong" and argues that "the evidence is compelling that the difference between at-risk youth who make it and those who don't is often but a single nurturing, capable adult who is there for the child on at least a predictable part-time basis."[78]

Government is less and less powerful as an agent of social change while the corporation and other economic instruments are becoming more effective and influential. The church is being invited to partner with these other agencies to improve our cities. Can the church come to grips with its own economic power? Can we engage in faith-based—faith-government, faith-corporation, faith-sports—partnerships?

CYBER-BOOST YOUR CHURCH ~ Public space is now graphic interface. Will the church enter this new public space and bring to bear a distinctively Christian perspective on this emerging postmodern culture? There are *enough* "private Christians" out there. The world needs the leadership of wise-as-serpents-innocent-as-doves "public Christians."

> It's become clearer and clearer to me that if families just let the culture happen to them, they end up fat, addicted, broke, with a house full of junk and no time.
>
> Mary Pipher[80]

It was the 18th century that redefined the relationship between individual and community. Until then, public debate was predominantly conducted in terms of the community.[79] The church can assist a culture with severely damaged familial and social support systems in conducting face-to-face and cyberspace public debate that brings the individual and the community into balance and harmony.

ᗯᎥᗯᗩᛕ my father worked a full-time job to make enough to support his family. Today parents don't have time for their children because it takes two incomes to support a family. What if the church were to sponsor an online town meeting and public discussion of tax credits for parents who wish to take care of their own children and forgo day care? The current tax laws, coupled with corporate subsidy programs, actually discriminate against families where one parent stays home to raise the children.[81] If the church has its way, the #1 status symbol in postmodern culture should not be a Porsche or a second home on the ski slopes, but a one-paycheck family (or at least a "family situation" that gives a newborn a minimum of two years of intensive parenting).

There are a few "dandelion children" out there—kids who survive and thrive even in a hostile atmosphere. But the discriminatory pavements against marriages and families embedded in government subsidies and tax laws needs public debate. David Ramsbotham tells of a conversation with a 19-year-old delinquent jailed for criminal activity. The first time in his life that anyone had taken any interest in him as a person, admitted the teenager, was when his parole officer sat down with him and talked about his sentencing.[82] James Prescott issued a challenge to the editor of the *New York Times*:

The legal-judicial and criminal justice system is challenged to find ONE murderer, rapist, or drug addict who has been breast-fed for "two years and beyond" (the recommended time) in any prison, jail or correctional facility in the US.[83]

The challenge stands to this day.

If even Club Med has discovered family values, why should the church not be a leader in the public arena for encouraging family-friendly practices? For example, covenant with your spouse to fast one meal a week and spend the time praying for your family, either together or apart. (In a postmodern world, you can be in India and your wife in Indianapolis, and you can do this.) Or launch a campaign for families to arrive at church 10 minutes before worship begins, not to chat with neighbors, but to sit in the sanctuary and pray quietly for the nation.

> The happiest moments of my life have been the few which I have passed at home in the bosom of my family. Public employment contributes neither to advantage nor happiness. It is but honorable exile from one's family and affairs.
>
> Architect/scientist/philosopher/statesman Thomas Jefferson[84]

Strange notions of "family-friendly practices," you say? The purpose of "family," whether nuclear, extended, or ecclesial, is not merely personal or private. Biblical parenthood is not the creation of comfy havens from a heartless world. Biblical parenthood, in Rodney Clapp's words, is the creation of "mission bases, mission bases that serve by acts of Christian imagination that range from family work at a soup kitchen to adopting a child who otherwise might have been aborted." In other words—and Clapp soars in elegance here—

Christian parenthood is a practice in hospitality, in the welcoming and support of strangers. Welcoming the strangers who are our children, we learn a little about being out of control, about the possibility of surprise (and so of hope), about how strange we ourselves are. Moment by mundane moment—dealing with rebellion, hosting birthday parties, and struggling with a toddler's nightmares—we pick up skills in patience, empathy, generosity, and forgiveness. All these are skills we can and must use to welcome other strangers, our many brothers and sisters in Christ.[85]

Or why not sponsor on the church's Web site a menu listing and linking various missions and ministries of your church and community? Families could talk about these over meals, and members could choose which projects they want a percentage of their contributions to go to. You might even want to list the 42 "pro-conscience" mutual funds in which one can invest.

This is not to suggest that there are no problems with cyberocracy, which decentralizes to the point that information, not money or power, is the driving force. In a cyberocracy, one person can shut down an entire system. Postmodern culture takes the power of one to an extreme never before seen in history.

Furthermore, nothing could be farther apart than church bureaucrats and church cybercrats. But the transition from one to the other, if the church can make it, is a trade-up. Church bureaucrats are good at channel keeping and tight leashes; church cybercrats are skilled at boundary hopping, roaming on long leashes. Church bureaucrats are skilled at establishing goals and priorities; church cybercrats are adept at multiple foci and entrepreneurial styles of leadership. Church bureaucrats are good at control and planning; church cybercrats are good at empowerment and preparedness.

FROM PLANNING TO PREPAREDNESS ~ If planning can be defined as "placing yourself in the path of serendipity," as William B. Rouse defines it,[86] then I am a planner. To others I am a preparer. Long-range planning, strategic planning is dead, church.[87]

The church that slays hydra-headed monsters needs to be in a preparedness mode for heads-up challenges that one could never predict. It won't be easy for the church to think in terms of ranges of possibili-

> Strategy is better than strength.
>
> Hausa proverb

ties, alternative futures, multiple scenarios, and multiple futures. Our peripheral vision has atrophied from all that modern focusing down and zooming in. But a 360-degree sweep of the radar screen is imperative to prevent collisions from becoming routine.

I have been influenced here by Clem Sunter of South Africa and by Peter Schwartz, president and a cofounder of the Global Business Network (GBN). His classic text *The Art of the Long View* challenges us to go beyond planning and to engage in "scenario" thinking.[88] Don't be surprised if soon virtual scenario thinking will be available for everything from outdoor dress to interior design—replete with outcome forecasts.

What is a scenario? My favorite definition of a scenario is "flight simulators to imaginative destinations to test real decisions."[89] Schwartz defines it as "a story that gives meaning to the future" and that "helps organize events that you already see into a meaningful pattern."[90]

Scenario thinking is not gee-whiz futurology. For the church it is nothing more or less than storytelling about plausible futures for functioning faith traditions and the priorities of denominational cultures. It is based on certain premises.

First Premise: Nonlinearity. The future never has been linear and never will be. We don't even know what one day will bring forth, much less one year. That is why rigidity and inflexibility spell danger in the mind as well as in the earth: Earthquakes are the result of brittle and unbending faults. Strategic planning was chained to generating the fixed conclusion. The planning model bets the whole enterprise on one pathway, one set of parameters, one "goal" or "objective" or "plan," one single desired future, one pinpointed trajectory that heads to the horizon.

Second Premise: Uncertainty. We live in a world where many things can happen at once and unexpected change happens routinely.[91] Most of life is beyond our control. Scenario thinking assumes that there will never be enough information on which to base a decision, if that decision requires certainty about the future.

Third Premise: Surprise. Surprise is one thing we can be certain about in the future. Look at the history of creations—"From Light Bulbs to Lasers," as Ira Flatow puts it in the subtitle to his most recent book about the inventions that have changed the way we live. Teflon, Velcro, saccharin, and the microwave oven have all come by accident and from scientists being surprised by something.[92]

Fourth Premise: Group Learning. Peter Schwartz argues that "never being wrong about the future is better than occasionally being exactly right." If we know many possible futures and can identify when we are moving toward one and away from another, we can develop the communal ability to morph into new forms as different scenarios present themselves.

"Scenario learning," pioneered by GBN, is a preparedness model of movement that involves the creation of a set of possible alternative futures, including both the thinkable and unthinkable, the optimistic, pessimistic, and status quo ("good, bad, middle").[93] The success scenarios are the most difficult to portray, the disaster scenarios the easiest. Scenario thinking helps people who are trained to think in straightforward, linear, reductionist, predictive fashion to think backward from the future to the present and explore what assumptions and agenda underlie each plausibility.

GBN is more a club, a connection, and a cause than a corporation. Founded in 1988, GBN has become the most successful, the most respected and the most mysterious consulting group in the world. With 90 network members and 55 paying customers,[94] GBN brings together the best linear thinkers with the best convergence thinkers and the best iconoclastic thinkers—all in a spirit of ruthless curiosity, fuzzy logic, informal open-mindedness, and omnidirectional intuitiveness.

More than anything else, scenario thinking can enable the church to formulate alternative strategies for differing realities and possibilities. Generalized scenarios of the major potential futures can be useful to make the complex manageable and prevent churches from becoming frozen in complexity and fear.

DUELING GOSPELS ~ The war of Evangels is being waged all around us. Two opposing gospels are fighting one another for the soul of our nation and, increasingly, the world: the gospel of consumption and the gospel of peace (Eph. 6:15).

What was the first question Columbus asked in the New World? When he landed in the Bahamas, he showed some gold to the first natives he met and asked, "Do you have any of this here?"[95] Or, in the language of postmodernity, "Show me the money."

Spanish conquistador Hernando Cortes told the Mexican ambassador at Vera Cruz in 1519 about a certain disease that afflicted the Europeans. Cortes called it a "disease of the heart, that infirmity, that we have, my companions and I, and that we cure with gold."[96]

To draw blood from the hydra-headed beast that is rampaging our planetary environment is to strike at consumerism, a blood disease that leads to addictions and a suicidal mania. The consumerist lifestyle—or what Dennis Potter calls consumerism's "shabby little gospel of greed and gain"—is suicidal to the soul and to the environment.

Consumerism is an even bigger beguiler of the Christian mind than Sophia or secularism or sexuality. Colossians 3:5 lists four sins of sensuality followed by "greed," or "covetousness" (KJV), or the drive to get and get, which is best defined as idolatry (see Eph. 5:5). Consumerist culture is even more of a master at marketing techniques for selling dead souls than Nikolai Vasilyevich Gogol.[97]

> **Annual lottery sales per capita:**
> **First: Massachusetts, $441**
> **Last: California, $66**[98]

Moses announced, "God is who God is [I AM WHO I AM], therefore we are." Descartes individualized the categories and pensioned God from the picture: "I think, therefore I am." We have taken Descartes one better: "I shop, therefore I am." The world is no longer going to hell in a handbasket; it is going to hell in a shopping cart.

Nestor Garcia Canclini names as the principal ethical contradiction of our times the contradiction between being a consumer and being a citizen.[99]

> Herein is revealed the tragedy of nearly fifty years of economic growth and national development. Rather than building societies that create a good life for sustainers and bring the deprived into the sustainer class, we have followed the path of encouraging over consumers to consume more, converting sustainers into over consumers, and pushing many of those in the sustainer class into the excluded class.[100]

The gospel of peace must use the weapon of *"subvertisements"* (Kalle Lasn's phrase). A subvertisement is anything that challenges and checks our overspending, that reduces the grip of television marketing on our lives. The more TV a person watches, the less that person saves—$208 less saved annually for each hour of television watched per week.[101]

Something like a "Buy Nothing Day" (the Friday after Thanksgiving) can deprogram people from their consumerist trances and pop our children out of the ideological toxic waste dump known as "children's programming." We need to teach our people media skepticism and find ways of loosening the media's consumerist noose around our children's necks.

One way is for the church to sponsor consumer education for children. To date, only 26 states require it, and often the curriculum for these courses is supplied by Visa and MasterCard. Hello?!

BUILD THE GLOBAL VILLAGE ～ The global village that everyone is talking about simply does not exist. In a village there is stability and sociability. Everyone knows one another and one another's uniqueness. Everyone is friends or at least friendly with one another. None of this is yet true globally.

Let us mobilize our churches to help create the global village of planet Earth. In so doing, let us not forget to address the issue of globalization's oppressiveness of the poor and marginalized, at least in some of its manifestations.

The Apple Hill Community in New Hampshire brings Jewish and Arab kids together to learn to play classical music and put on concerts. Apple Hill believes that even in the most violent corners, the global village can be built brick by brick, person by person, through the healing power of music. Its motto is "Together is much more than twice as good."

> Water and air, the two essential fluids on which all life depends, have become global garbage cans.
>
> Jacques Cousteau[102]

Oppose the Darwinian "survival of the fittest" with the biblical survival of the meekest. And make sure your global village doesn't exclude anyone. We are all in this together. On AIDS Awareness Sunday in 1995, Dr. Jeremiah Wright, pastor of the largest United Church of Christ congregation in the United States, asked all present to rise who had someone close to them die of AIDS. One-third of those present stood up.

BIGGER PIE, FEWER FORKS, BETTER MANNERS ～ Joel E. Cohen ends his book *How Many People Can the Earth Support?* with three choices we have in building the global village: "Bigger Pie, Fewer Forks, Better Manners."

1. Bigger Pie means the global diffusion of more and better technology and products.
2. Fewer Forks means the implementation of rigorous birth control and vegetarianism to reduce population and consume less of the planet's resources.
3. Better Manners means a political restructuring through either diplomatic civilities, global government, or the breaking-up of nation-states into smaller entities.[103]

In a Hobbesian universe, "when no other suit is called, clubs are trumps." In a postmodern world, however, other suits are constantly being called, and the range of cards in our hands grows larger with every passing moment. The answer lies in all three decks of cards: bigger pie, fewer forks, and better manners.

The church needs to put its greatest effort into #1: baking bigger pies. **WIWAK** my parents would take my brothers and me on Sunday afternoon drives. Some of our favorite places to go were in the rich parts of town, where we would gawk at houses that were beautiful beyond our wildest dreams. We did it enough that I learned an Appalachian saying when passing by a lavish mansion: "Some crook lives there."

Not true! It is not true that the rich are getting richer *because* the poor are getting poorer. The vast majority of those who have amassed huge fortunes did not get them unjustly. It is not true that all millionaires have airs—although stories abound that would make one think so, stories like that of Ivan Boesky, the global financier, who liked to order eight entrees from the menu at the exclusive Café des Artistes, sample each, and then decide which he would eat.

The social problem is poverty, not inequality. Actually, the world needs more accumulation, not less. Redistribution of wealth is a mistaken notion that misrepresents the problem.

GREEN CHURCHES AND GREEN CONGREGATIONS ~ Redefine missions to include the environment. People who minister worldwide to protect and conserve the environment are of no lower status than those who minister to plant churches.

It is time to repudiate the GDP (Gross Domestic Product), which measures consumption as something positive. A much more accurate index, and one that every church could track, is the GPI (Genuine Progress Indicator), which factors in the value of household work, costs of pollution, loss of forests, farmland, wetlands, ozone depletion, and so on. The GDP may be increasing, but the GPI has been dropping significantly since the early 1970s.

Do not doubt the importance of the environment to postmoderns. A Louis Harris poll in 1990 revealed that most Americans rate the environment more important than a satisfactory sex life. A poll of 145,000 kids discovered that they felt wildlife preservation was the biggest issue facing our world right now—hence the Earth Force campaign "Go Wild for Wildlife."[104]

For the first time in history, humanity is being asked to respond together to a global threat—if not global warming, then global something. We are used to tribal conflicts, with tribes gathering together to do war. But can the people of Earth gather together to do war against the global warming of the planet, the rising of the oceans, and the extinction of vast segments of God's creation?

In his 1990 World Day of Peace statement, "The Ecological Crisis: A Common Responsibility," Pope John Paul II said emphatically, "The ecological crisis is a moral issue."[105] Shrinking forests, expanding deserts, vanishing species, dwindling resources, rising greenhouse gases, a punctured ozone shield, polluted skies, poisoned water, stinking landfills, radiating wastes, mountains of garbage—these are but sociological names for moral issues.

There is a new role for the military in postmodern culture. Defense against other nations or peoples is no longer enough. Defense now must include the defense of planet Earth against things that would destroy it from within (such as chemicals) and without (such as asteroids), including ourselves.

> Every single creature is full of God and is a book about God.
>
> Meister Eckhart

Ever since 1969—the *annus mirabilis* of the environmental movement[106]—the greening movement has spread almost everywhere but the church. There are 15,000 environmental groups worldwide, with an annual income exceeding $1.5 billion and a combined membership equaling 10% of the Western world's population.

Can our churches become environmentally benign and beneficial communities? The institution of a certification process whereby churches could become "Green Churches" would go a long way. What would be some sample features of a Green Church?

1. A church that builds a future on walking, bicycling, public transportation. Can disciples of Jesus show the world how to start hoofing it? In only five big cities do at least one in 10 workers commute on foot.[107] Make your church as friendly to two-wheel travelers as to four-wheel travelers, with multiple bike-to-church ministries.[108]

2. A church that promotes recycling and uses recycling itself. In the United States the average person over the course of a lifetime consumes or accounts for the use of 540 tons of construction materials, 18 tons of paper, 23 tons of wood, 16 tons of metal, and 32 tons of organic chemicals.[109] To be sure, the 500 sheets of recycled toilet paper your church uses a week may not save the planet in and of itself. But your congregation's decision to use only recycled toilet paper creates healing energies for our planet.

3. A church that installs at least one "breathing wall"—indoor ecosystems of rocks, plants, waterfall, fish, and microorganisms that breathe in dirty air and exhale clean air. (The spider plant, berbera daisy, musa oriana, and potted mums all improve air quality.)

4. A church that rejects a monoculture of green grass in favor of creation-friendly lawnscapes. The total territory cultivated as lawn in the US adds up to an area the size of Indiana. The price of green lawns is too high, especially for churches. Lawn chemicals are killing bees, ladybugs, and butterflies and are poisoning our aquifers.

5. A church that either serves only the new four food groups (vegetables, whole grain, fruit, and legumes) or, when it offers meat, makes sure the chickens weren't caged all their lives in "egg houses" with five birds stuffed into spaces smaller than two sheets of typing paper.

6. A church with Ministers of Gardening. It shouldn't be hard to find such ministers, since 78% of the American population engages in some form of indoor or outdoor gardening to the tune of $21 billion a year.[110] Be laboratories of "permaculture gardening," which is to the natural world what "ancientfuture theology" is to the spiritual world. The word *permaculture,* formed from "permanent" and "agriculture," reflects a concept whereby one takes the best in traditional farming and yokes it to the latest technological developments.

> In the rustling grass I hear him pass,
> He speaks to me everywhere.
>
> Maltie D. Babcock[111]

7. A church that doesn't engage in greenwashing. If some chemical companies get their way, pretty soon we will have green agent orange, green chlorofluorocarbons, green herbicides. Just because your pickle jars are reusable doesn't mean you're green. Just because an oil company spends a few bucks saving ducks doesn't mean it's green. Just because your church recycles doesn't mean it's green.

8. A church that is a sustaining member of the Green Cross Society, the Land Institute,[112] or another ecological ministry.

9. A church that prays earnestly for all of creation, teaches others how to pray and fast, and encourages its members to join one of the 150-plus prayer organizations that have sprouted up in the past 10 years. ᴡᴵᴡᴀᴋ my mother treated Wednesday night prayer meeting as the most important service of the week. In postmodern culture, Jesus' words, "This kind can come out only through prayer" (Mark 9:29), apply to almost every problem. Be a church that believes that Prayer Really Can Change the World.

TAKE WATER WITH PRICE ~ Distilled drinking water is now more expensive than gasoline. It's worth the price. Our drinking water is filled with drugs, herbicides, and worse. One in five of us downs tap water that has lead, radiation, herbicides, or even feces in it. And that's not the "worse."

> To clasp the hands in prayer is the beginning of an uprising against the disorder of the world.
>
> Karl Barth

Herbicides run off from lawn and garden chemicals. They pollute our streams and watersheds and get into our drinking water and baby formula. They are bad enough—even worse than feces. Fifty to 90% of any drug can be excreted through urine and feces in its original unused or biologically active form. It goes back into the environment. Our antiquated and outdated waste management systems can't filter out these wonder drugs.

This is the "worse." Our drinking water is becoming a drug cocktail. Chronic exposure to this water contamination has unknown consequences on the species.[113]

The Bible says, "Take the water of life without cost" (Rev. 22:17 NASB). What if a church were to become a place where water flows—both the water of spiritual life and the water of biological life? What if the church were to partner with mountain communities with pristine springs, to bottle under sanitized, laboratory conditions the water of physical life for those who can't afford to drink gasoline?

PET FRIENDLY ∼ In the early days, Methodists insisted on bringing their dogs to worship, to the consternation of many circuit riders.[114]

Pets are no longer pets. They are life companions and healing attendants. Why shouldn't people be allowed to bring their pets to special services? If animals are welcome in homes, why shouldn't they be welcomed in God's house—not just pet blessing services, but pet-friendly worship?

This is not an argument for egalitarian attitudes toward animals. Richard D. Ryder coined the term *speciesism,* to exist alongside *racism* and *sexism,* to describe the human inclination to exclude other "animals" from moral consideration.[115] But one can critique the specious character of "speciesism" while advocating that the church not make pests of pets. Besides, there is something healthy about the cooperation and interaction of humans and earthlings in the church as well as in the outdoors.

FROM PERFORMANCE TO AUTHENTICITY ∼ As President Bill Clinton has discovered to his dismay, the secret of postmodern living is that there are no secrets. There is mystery aplenty, but no secrets.

Part of godliness is acknowledging one's sinfulness. The apostle Paul, who confessed to being "the chief of sinners" (see 1 Tim. 1:15), made the heart of Christian theology the fact that "*while* we still were sinners Christ died for us" (Rom. 5:8). There is no one, to use Kant's phrase, who is not cut from "crooked timber."

If the modern era valued performance, even contrived performances of soul making, the postmodern world values authenticity, even the authenticity of soul-making the sublime out of slime. The valuing of authenticity is evident in the "Been There/Done That/Worn That T-Shirt." Postmoderns want you to be real. They know all information to be blemished, partial, perspectival. They know all people to be blemished, partial, perspectival.

This is a flawed book. Know any book that isn't?

You are a flawed person. Know any person who isn't?

Is there anyone reading this book who hasn't been unfairly criticized? I say "unfairly criticized," because of course I've never been "fairly" criticized. Have you?

American citizens assume the worst about Bill Clinton, and still vote for him. People will assume the worst about you and your church, and still value you and even join your congregation—if they don't see you dancing in denial about what you've been or dancing on the hot coals of fads and fashions trying to be something you're not.

> There are no longer any saints without warts.
>
> Don Cupitt[116]

It's not so much that postmoderns cast a glassily amoral eye in the direction of hypocrisy and indiscretions as that moral issues in these flagitious, litigious times are understood to be more complex and difficult than the media make them out to be. What is more—again thanks to the media—human failings and defects now have all the opacity of a pane of glass. There is no place to hide. Being seen through glass is not the best way to find intimacy and joy and participation. Do you wonder why you constantly hear the sound of breaking glass?

Postmodern culture is creating a definition of "character" that is based more on becoming than being. Or, to put it in theological categories, "character" has more to do with the sojourn of sanctification than the state of justification. The poet John Ruskin captures character's essence: "The highest reward for a person's toil is not what he gets for it but what he becomes through it." Or, as Shakespeare's Duke Vincentio says in *Measure for Measure,*

Heaven doth with us as we with torches do,
Not light them for themselves; for if our virtues
Did not go forth of us, 'twere all alike
As if we had them not.[117]

say what? 1. Jacques Attali has written, "The problems that will plague millennial man require that we restore the idea of evil, the idea of the sacred, to the center of political life."[118] Do you agree? To what extent is the mystery of evil less good against evil than good against good? Discuss this statement by Boethius in the sixth century: "This discord in the heart of things, this endless war of truth with truth."

2. Invite someone in from your church to talk about Habitat for Humanity.[119] If your church isn't active in Habitat, why not get active? It took 10 years for Habitat to build 10,000 homes (1977–87); it took another 10 years to reach 50,000—that's 40,000 in one decade (1987–97). Habitat is now projecting that it will have built 100,000 homes by 2000—three years later. Why do you believe Habitat has registered such a phenomenal rate of growth?

Could it be because Habitat does more than swing swords—it connects head and heart?

3. Arrange to watch the PBS special *Affluenza*, which premiered on 15 September 1997. It is hosted by NPR's Scott Simon and reveals that each week 70% of USAmericans visit shopping malls—more than attend churches or synagogues.[120] Is consumerism the real "mainline" religion of this nation?

4. George W. S. Trow argues that "the important moment in the history of television was the moment when a man named Richard Dawson, the 'host' of a program called *Family Feud,* asked contestants to guess what a poll of a hundred people had guessed would be the height of the average American woman. Guess what they've guessed."[121] To what extent does a "survey says . . ." mentality govern politics and other aspects of postmodern life? When "survey says" dictates perspective, don't facts and truth and issues give way to polls and statistics?

5. Jonathan Kramer and Diane Dunaway Kramer have coined the phrase *moralectomy* to describe how we have removed the moral backbone from our lives and our communities, or how what moral muscle is there "remains undeveloped, along with our compassion, caring, and consideration."[122] What "moralectomies" have been performed in your community, as evidenced by the front page of the newspaper or by stories with which you are familiar? Are there different professions that are more subject to certain moralectomies than others? Have we already been led down the path of "moral mediocrity"?

6. This is the poetry of a street kid in one of our larger cities:

I'm falling
No gravity in my life
Like dust
Swept under the carpet.[123]

How do you feel about living in the richest nation in the history of the world that sweeps its own children under the carpet? What can the church do to reverse this?

7. Discuss Daniel Deudney's image of the 21st century as a fleet of stretch limos in New York City. Inside the limos are the air-conditioned cultures of North America, southern Europe, the Pacific Rim, and other scattered places connected by the information highway. Outside the limos, living in the streets and shantytowns, is the rest of the world living in Road Warrior Culture (Somalia), Totalitarian Regimes (Iraq), and Fascist Mini-states (Serb-held Bosnia)—fighting ethnic and cultural warfare with insufficient water, soil, and space. Inside the limo life is getting longer and better. Outside the limo life is, in Thomas Hobbes's phrase, "poor, nasty, brutish and short."

8. Explore the "Glauberg Intercession" movement, which started in Glauberg, Germany, in 1988. If someone in your church reads German, search "Glauberg" on the Internet and choose the appropriate entries.

Participants in the Glauberg Intercession movement, or those forming a local chapter, are encouraged to (a) pray for a specific animal you know personally that is being abused or is in need; (b) pray every Wednesday at 8 p.m. for animals in want everywhere, thus connecting to Glauberg prayer groups in Europe and around the world; (c) form a prayer group with other Christians who are concerned about animals in need; (d) request that prayers for animals be included sometimes in worship; (e) follow the "prayer plan for animals" that has been developed by the Glauberg Intercession movement.

The address of this movement is

AKUT e.V.
C. Appel,
Hauptstrasse 39
D–63695 Glauberg, Germany
Fax: 06041/6213

9. What do you think of the prospects of a "sin tax" (like that on tobacco and alcohol) on high-fat foods such as hamburgers, french fries, and pizza, which cause health problems ranging from heart disease and diabetes to cancer, hypertension, and stroke. Are our nutrition habits improving, or deteriorating? Would you personally support a bad-food tax, the proceeds of which could go to fund bicycle paths, recreation centers, nutrition education programs in the public schools, and so on?

10. Pass around a globe and pray for different countries.

11. How will your church provide leadership for the global crusade to clean up toxic wastes, conserve both temperate and tropical rain forests, and heal damaged environments? Has your church ever done a tree-planting?

12. Alan Wolfe, in his book *One Nation, After All,* has discovered a deep underground stream of nonjudgmentalism in postmodern culture. He explains this in part by saying that most people are too busy trying to make their own marriages work to lecture neighbors on what happens in theirs.[124] Has nonjudgmentalism now become a cardinal virtue? What is the difference between "nonjudgmentalism" and "tolerance," if any?

13. The private urban-policy Milton S. Eisenhower Foundation released a 1998 report called "The Millennium Breach," in which they conclude that "the rich are getting richer, the poor are getting poorer, and minorities are suffering disproportionately." The foundation isolated certain projects that are working to bridge the gap: Head Start, after-school youth centers, school-to-work programs.[125] How involved is your church in these reforms? What ministries might

your church unleash to assist inner-city economic development, crime and drug prevention, and on-job training, placement, and retention?

14. Is there any significance to this comparison: During the Great Depression, 1 in 215 USAmericans declared bankruptcy. In 1995 the ratio was 1 in 225. At the end of the first half year of 1998 (a period of economic boom), the number of filings for individual bankruptcies (702,716) almost equaled the total number for the entire year of 1995 (874,137).[126]

15. Discuss novelist Toni Morrison's lament that public spaces are increasingly being treated as though they are private: "Not homeless but *streetlessness* is what I call it. Privatizing all of public space: parks in which people are not welcome, streets that belong to the buildings."[127]

16. Do a Bible study of Judges 9:45 and the saga of what happened to Shechem, near Nablus in Jordan. It is history's first record of chemical warfare.

17. Do you want to see how the double ring works? Let's say you are in the market for the best air filter you can find for your home. You note that there are two "expos" in your city that weekend. One is for environmentally good and earth-friendly products. The other is for cigar afficionados. Which one should you go to?

The cigar one, of course. At the NYC Cigar Expo of 1998, next to cigars the only things more widely displayed were air filtering systems.

18. What do you think of the growing corporate employment of "ethics officers" to promote and enforce a company's policies? What does it say about the world in which we live?

19. Don Haynes, a colleague and friend from North Carolina, likes to ask the question, "If your church closed today, who would miss it besides its members?" How would you answer that question about your church?

20. What would you say if Chinese scientists came to your community, harvested a plant found only in your local ecosystem, and took it back to China, where it was developed into a $100-million-a-year drug—and your community received not a cent?

That is exactly what US drug companies do all the time. Lilly, for example, took the vinca periwinkle off the biodiversity-rich island of Madagascar and developed it into an immensely profitable chemotherapy treatment. The people of Madagascar, without sources of income, are chopping down their rain forests to plant crops to feed themselves.

What are the ethical issues involved for both parties? Is it right for Madagascar to cut down rain forests that might harbor cures for the world's cancer patients? Is it right for drug companies to hit-and-run?

21. Would you support the implementation of ankle/wrist monitors and other "house arrest" hardware for parents' usage with children? What about "nannycams," not just at day-care centers but at home, so parents can drop

in on latch-key kids or other problem situations? If not the parents, who should pay the social and environmental costs of children's truancy and delinquency?

22. Arrange for some of your church's college students to take summer field courses offered by the Au Sable Institute,[128] directed by Calvin DeWitt, wetlands ecologist at the University of Wisconsin. DeWitt likes to use Rembrandt as a way of helping us appreciate God's handiwork. "Is it conceivable," he asks, "that we could give acclaim to the artist but not to his masterpieces?" What is keeping you and your family from responding to God's creation with wonder and awe?

23. Is there a racial divide on the Internet in your community? National studies reveal that—

- Whites are more likely to own a computer and to use the Web than blacks.
- In households earning more than $40,000, blacks were more likely than whites to have a computer at home.
- Of those families not online, more blacks than whites wanted to be.
- In homes without computers, black students were only half as likely to have used the Internet (16% vs. 38%) than whites—that is, whites are finding access to the Internet that is denied blacks.[129]

Discuss this issue: Should our communities see that kids are wired at home before getting the public schools wired?

24. Thomas J. Watson Jr. of IBM warned that the most important people any organization could have around are "those sharp, scratchy, harsh, almost unpleasant individuals who see and tell you about things as they really are."[130] Do you have any such "important people" in your church? If not, why not? If so, do you treat such people as important, or as nuisances?

25. Ithaca, New York, prints its own currency—called "Ithaca Hours."

Why not the church? "Church Hours" would be backed by real capital—skills, time, tools—and could be accepted among participating stores, service providers, members' businesses, and so on. One Church Hour could be redeemable for $10 or for one hour of basic work such as housecleaning, child care, tutoring, music lessons, carpentry, and such. (By the way, as long as sales tax is paid in US currency, and the currency is declared for the purpose of federal income tax, there is nothing legally stopping church groups from issuing paper currency. Private coinage, yes, but paper currency, no.) The advantage of Church Hours is multiple: It connects believers, it stimulates business, it recycles the wealth among those who give the most.

now what? See the Net Notes in http://www.soultsunami.com

NOTES

1. Christian de Duve, *Vital Dust: Life as a Cosmic Imperative* (New York: Basic Books, 1995), 273.

2. De Duve, *Vital Dust,* 274.

3. See Vaclav Havel's speech "Faith in the World" in the magazine of the Library of Congress, *Civilization* (Apr-May 1998): 52.

4. As quoted in Barbara Kingsolver, "Homeland," in her *Homeland and Other Stories* (London: Faber, 1996), 11.

5. Don E. Eberly, *Building a Community of Citizens: Civil Society in the 21st Century* (Lanham, MD: University Press of America, 1994), xvii–xlviii.

6. Richard Monastersky, "Health in the Hot Zone: How Would Global Warming Affect Humans?" *Science News* (6 Apr 1996): 218.

7. Michael E. Mann, Raymond S. Bradley, and Malcolm K. Hughes, "Global-scale Temperature Patterns and Climate Forcing over the Past Six Centuries," *Nature* (23 Apr 1998): 779–87.

8. See S. S. Morse, ed., *Emerging Viruses* (New York: Oxford Univ. Press, 1993).

9. Richard Preston, *The Hot Zone* (New York: Random House, 1994). Also available on two audiocassettes from New York: Simon & Schuster Audio, 1994.

10. Stephen Mills, "The Rhyming Whale," review of Roger Payne, *Among Whales* (1996), in *TLS, Times Literary Supplement* (6 Sept 1996): 36.

11. Stephen Mills, "Pocket Tigers," *TLS, Times Literary Supplement* (21 Feb 97): 6.

12. David Quammen, *The Song of the Dodo: Island Biogeography in an Age of Extinction* (New York: Scribner, 1996), 262.

13. Richard Leakey and Roger Lewin, *The Sixth Extinction: Biodiversity and Its Survival* (New York: Doubleday, 1995); Peter Ward, *The End of Evolution: Dinosaurs, Mass Extinction and Biodiversity* (New York: Bantam Books, 1994).

14. For a devastating critique of the growth philosophy, see David C. Korten, *When Corporations Rule the World* (San Francisco: Barrett-Koehler, 1995), 39–40.

15. See, for example, Karl J. Niklas, *The Evolutionary Biology of Plants* (Chicago: Univ. of Chicago Press, 1997).

16. As cited in *Science News* (25 Oct 1997): 260.

17. John Tuxil and Chris Bright, "Protecting Nature's Diversity: Mending Strands in the Web of Life," *The Futurist* (June-July 1998): 46–50.

18. Timothy F. Flannery, "The Dodo and the Kestrel," review of *The Song of the Dodo*, by David Quammen, *TLS, Times Literary Supplement* (21 Feb 97): 9.

19. De Duve, *Vital Dust,* 275.

20. As quoted in Edward Luttwak, "Best of All Worlds: The Good News on the Human Condition and Why We Should Distrust It," *TLS, Times Literary Supplement* (29 Mar 1996): 4.

21. Alan Durning, *How Much Is Enough? The Consumer Society and the Future of the Earth* (New York: Norton, 1992), 26–28.

22. The most recent statistics come from the Center on Budget and Policy Priorities, which published its report in December 1997. It has found that families in the top fifth average $117,499 a year, almost 13 times the $9,254 average among the bottom fifth (cited in *USA Today* [17 Dec 1997]: 4B).

23. Part of the problem is that there are 30% more people sharing wealth in the top quintile than in the bottom. Also, while the average income of those in the bottom fifth was $6,748 in 1994, the average consumption of the same group was $14,066. For more, see Bruce Bartlett, "The Ominous Income Gap," *World & I* (Sept 1997): 106–11.

24. Hal Kane, "Gap in Income Distribution Widening," in *Vital Signs 1997: The Environmental Trends That Are Shaping Our Future,* ed. Linda Starke (New York: Norton, 1997), 116.

25. Sam Roberts, *Who We Are: A Portrait of America Based on the Latest U.S. Census* (New York: Times Books, 1994), 174–75.

26. Brad Edmondson, "Wealth and Poverty," *American Demographics* (May 1998): 20–21.

27. Roberts, *Who We Are,* 166.

28. Charles Handy, *Beyond Certainty* (Boston: Harvard Business School Press, 1996), 205.

29. "Guess Who's Behind Record Affluence?" *Boomer Report* (Jan 1998): 4.

30. See *Population and Environment in Arid Regions,* ed. John I. Clarke and Daniel Noin, Papers from a Conference Held in Amman, Jordan, 24–27 October 1994 (Pearl River, NY: Parthenon Publ. Group, 1998).

31. Lester Thurow, *The Future of Capitalism* (New York: Morrow, 1996), 42. The author leaves us with the haunting question, "How far can inequality rise before the system cracks?" (2).

32. For this thesis, see Frances Cairncross, *The Death of Distance: How the Communications Revolution Will Change Our Lives* (Cambridge, MA: Harvard Univ. Press, 1998).

33. C. J. Peters and Mark Olshaker, *Virus Hunter: Thirty Years of Battling Hot Viruses Around the World* (New York: Doubleday, 1997).

34. Jeffrey Fisher, *The Plague Makers* (New York: Simon & Schuster, 1994).

35. See Steve Kroll-Smith and H. Hugh Floyd, *Bodies in Protest: Environmental Illness and the Struggle over Medical Knowledge* (New York: New York Univ. Press, 1997).

36. Richard Rhodes, *Deadly Feasts: Tracking the Secrets of a Terrifying New Plague* (New York: Simon & Schuster, 1997).

37. Helen Epstein, "An Infectious Sense of Danger," *TLS, Times Literary Supplement* (15 Aug 1997): 25.

38. Epstein, "An Infectious Sense of Danger," 25.

39. For the best analysis of rap music and car customizing as a means of countering the prevailing definitions of property and propriety by providing opportunities "for people defamed by others to tell their own stories," see George Lipsitz in *Microphone Fiends: Youth Music and Youth Culture,* ed. Andrew Ross and Tricia Rose (New York: Routledge, 1994), 22.

40. Korten, *When Corporations Rule the World,* 20.

41. Marilyn Elias, "Girls Emulate Aggression Seen in TV Heroines," *USA Today* (30 Jan 1996): D1.

42. Martin Amis, "Blown Away," as reprinted in *Screen Violence,* ed. Karl French (New York: Bloomsbury, 1996), 12; see 12–17. *Bonnie and Clyde* was released in 1967.

43. According to the Department of Justice, between 1985 and 1995 the rate of murders by teens aged 14 to 17 rose by 165%.

44. As quoted in Korten, *When Corporations Rule the World,* 257.

45. Pierrepoint estimated he had hanged "some hundreds" of convicted murderers. At his retirement in 1956, he concluded that execution was nothing more than a primal urge for revenge. See Howard Engel, *Lord High Executioner: An Unashamed Look at Hangmen, Headsmen and Their Kind* (Toronto: Key Porter Books, 1996), 85, 247.

46. De Duve, *Vital Dust,* 280.

47. Peter Drucker is alarmed at the West's low birthrate. See Peter F. Drucker, "The Future Has Already Happened," *Harvard Business Review* (Sept-Oct 1997): 20. For a more positive view, see Joan Smith, *Different for Girls: How Culture Creates Women* (London: Chatto and Windus, 1997), 79–92.

48. There is no text to date that addresses the problem of overconsumption from a Christian perspective. The best general text I have found is *Beyond the Numbers: A Reader on Population, Consumption and the Environment,* ed. Laurie Ann Mazur (Washington, DC: Island Press, 1995).

49. Lester R. Brown, *Tough Choices: Facing the Challenge of Food Security* (New York: Norton, 1996). See also the excellent collection of essays *Food Ethics,* ed. Ben Mepham (New York: Routledge, 1996).

50. Barbara Albert, "And Room for Us All: The Myth of Overpopulation," *Mission America* (Winter 1997): 4–6.

51. "Pope John Paul II Addresses Over Consumption," *Green Cross* (Summer 1996): 4.

52. Liggett-Stashower Public Relations (1 Nov 1995).

53. "From Fred Krueger, Green Cross Director," *Green Cross* (Fall 1995): 2.

54. As quoted in "Consume, Consume, Consume . . . Can We Go On Like This?" *Green Cross* (Fall 1995): 9.

55. "Pope John Paul II," 5.

56. Edward Wenk Jr., *Making Waves: Engineering, Politics, and the Social Management of Technology* (Urbana: Univ. of Illinois Press, 1996), xi.

57. Frank Darvall, *Popular Disturbances and Public Order in Regency England* (London: Oxford Univ. Press, 1934; reprint New York: Augustus M. Kelley, 1969), 1–2.

58. For one of the best collections of critiques, see Ziauddin Sardar and Jerome R. Ravetz, eds., *Cyberfutures: Culture and Politics on the Information Highway* (Washington Square, NY: New York Univ. Press, 1996).

59. See Bill McKibben, *The End of Nature* (New York: Anchor Books, 1990) and *The Age of Missing Information* (New York: Random House, 1992).

60. James Patterson and Peter Kim, *The Day America Told the Truth: What People Really Believe About Everything That Really Matters* (New York: Prentice Hall, 1991).

61. As quoted in Anna Muoio, "Mihaly Csikszentmihalhyi," *Fast Company* (Aug-Sept 1997): 73.

62. Bryan W. Mattimore, *99% Inspiration: Tips, Tales and Techniques for Liberating Your Business Creativity* (New York: AMACOM, 1994), 162.

63. See Paul Oppenheimer's study of the movie industry, *Evil and the Demonic: A New Theory of Monstrous Behaviour* (New York: New York Univ. Press, 1996).

64. Alexander Pope, *An Essay on Man,* A Scholar Press Facsimile (Menston, Eng.: Scholar Press, 1969.

65. Elizabeth Newson's "Video Violence and the Protection of Children" was prepared for the British Parliament in 1994. See www.cultsock.ndirect.co.uk/MUHome/cshtml/newson.html. For a review by Larisa Washburn, see www.comm.cornell.edu/PUB/COMM626/Reports/lw32112207.html.

66. Wendell Berry, *Another Turn of the Crank: Essays* (Washington, DC: Counterpoint, 1995), 90.

67. Arthur Kroker, *Technology and the Canadian Mind: Innis/McLuhan/Grant* (New York: St. Martin's Press, 1985), 117.

68. For the changes in the business world regarding "office space," see Ronald A. Gunn and Marilyn S. Burroughs, "Work Spaces That Work: Designing High-Performance Offices," *The Futurist* (Mar-Apr 1996): 24.

69. With thanks to Tim Dearborn for this insight. See his *Taste and See: Awakening Our Spiritual Senses (*Downers Grove, IL: InterVarsity Press, 1996), 83.

70. Steve Perry, "An Interview with James Hillman," from *City Pages,* as reprinted in "Waking Up with the House on Fire," *Utne Reader* (Jan-Feb 1997): 55.

71. Interview with Richard G. Young, "A Foretaste of the World to Come," *Pathways* 7 (Summer 1998): 14. Rabbi Rami M. Shapiro is rabbi/storyteller of Temple Beth Or in Miami, FL, and the author of *Minyan: Ten Principles for Living a Life of Integrity* (New York: Random House, 1997).

72. *YOUTHviews* (Apr 1997).

73. "Power Week Mission Trip," *The Profile* 18 (26 Mar 1997): 3–4.

74. As quoted in Thomas A. Stewart, "Gray Flannel Suit?" *Forbes* (16 Mar 1998): 78.

75. Charles Handy, "The Citizen Corporation," *Harvard Business Review* (Sept-Oct 1997): 26, 28.

76. For example, see John Dalla Costa, *The Ethical Imperative: Why Moral Leadership Is Good Business* (Reading, MA: Addison-Wesley, 1998).

77. "Can Churches Save America?" *U. S. News & World Report* (9 Sept 1996): 46–53. The article provides excellent examples of some hands-on-missions of America's congregations.

78. John James Dilulio Jr., *Pennsylvania Gazette* (Oct 1997): 28.

79. See the work of Peter N. Miller, *Defining the Common Good: Empire, Religion, and Philosophy in Eighteenth-Century Britain* (New York: Cambridge Univ. Press, 1994).

80. As quoted in *Current Thoughts and Trends* (July 1997): 14.

81. This is the suggestion of Charles Siegel in "A New Declaration of Independence," *Utne Reader* (July-Aug 1996): 51–54.

82. As cited in David Ramsbotham, "Towards Zero Tolerance," *TLS, Times Literary Supplement* (11 July 1997): 25.

83. For the edited version of this challenge, see the *New York Times* (21 Aug 1996). The unedited version can be found in issue 38 of *Wellness Associates Journal*, 123 Wildwood Trail, Afton, VA 22920.

84. As quoted in Susan Page, *Now That I'm Married, Why Isn't Everything Perfect* (Boston: Little, Brown, 1994), 78.

85. Rodney Clapp, "Family Values Are Destroying the Family," *Perspectives* 10 (Jan 1995): 11.

86. William B. Rouse, *Best Laid Plans* (Englewood Cliffs, NJ: Prentice Hall, 1994), 63–74.

87. See Henry Mintzberg, *The Rise and Fall of Strategic Planning* (New York: Free Press, 1994).

88. Peter Schwartz, *The Art of the Long View* (New York: Currency Doubleday, 1995).

89. This comes from Liam Fahey and Robert M. Randall, eds., *Learning from the Future: Competitive Foresight Scenarios* (New York: John Wiley, 1998), 18.

90. Tom Brown, "On the Edge: Peter Schwartz," *Industry Week* (18 Nov 1991): 14. Why is Goodyear the lone remaining US tire company, with General Tire, BF Goodrich, Firestone, and Universal being taken over by companies from other nations? Because in the early 1980s Goodyear used some techniques pioneered in the '70s by Royal Dutch Shell and they envisioned a whole host of alternative futures for the company. They encouraged outside-the-box thinking and did not punish even the wildest ideas, and some of the notions that emerged from this process became business ventures. See Tibett L. Speer, "How Goodyear Forecast a Great Decade," *American Demographics* (Mar 1995): 39.

91. Peter Schwartz, James Ogilvy, and Paul Hawken, *Seven Tomorrows* (New York: Bantam Books, 1982).

92. The full title of the book by Ira Flatow, the host of NPR's science talk show, is *They All Laughed—From Light Bulbs to Lasers: The Fascinating Stories Behind the Great Inventions That Have Changed Our Lives* (New York: HarperCollins, 1992).

93. The best primer on scenario planning is Schwartz, *The Art of the Long View.*

94. Clients have included the South African government, the Pentagon and the Joint Chiefs of Staff, and Genetech. When asked to determine what might be the most challenging threats to the armed forces for the next 30 years, GBN presented their case for decades of peace as the greatest threat. For more on GBN, see Joel Garreau, "Conspiracy of Heretics," *Wired* (Nov 1994): 98–106, 153–58, and esp. "GBN," 154.

95. The actual log entry for Saturday, 13 October 1492, reads, "*Y yo estava atento y trabajava de saber si avia oro,*" which roughly translated says, "And I took great care and effort to find out if there was gold."

96. As quoted in James Buchan, *Frozen Desire: The Meaning of Money* (New York: Farrar, Straus & Giroux, 1997), 79–80.

97. In 1842 Russian novelist Nikolai Gogol published his classic satire *Mërtvye Dushi* (*Dead Souls*), the story of the schemer Chichikov, who devised a plan to finance a life of comfort and luxury by buying lists of dead serfs from landowners and mortgaging them as property.

98. *National Gaming Report,* 1995.

99. Garcia Canclini, Nestor, *Consumidores y Ciudadanos: Conflictos Multiculturales de la Globalizacion* (Mexico: Editorial Grijalbo, 1995).

100. Korten, *When Corporations Rule the World,* 280.

101. This interesting statistic is the discovery of Juliet B. Schor in *The Overspent American: Upscaling, Downshifting, and the New Consumer* (New York: Basic Books, 1998), 78.

102. Jacques Cousteau, *Calypso Log* (Aug 1991): 3.

103. Joel E. Cohen, *How Many People Can the Earth Support?* (New York: Norton, 1996).

104. Faith Popcorn and Lys Marigold, *Clicking: 16 Trends to Future Fit Your Life, Your Work and Your Business* (New York: HarperBusiness, 1996), 317.

105. Pope John Paul II, *The Ecological Crisis: A Common Responsibility* (Washington, DC: United States Catholic Conference, 1990).

106. In that year these organizations were founded, among others: Greenpeace, Friends of the Earth, and the International Fund for Animal Welfare.

107. Boston registers 14%, Pittsburgh 12.6%, Washington, DC, 11.8%, New York City 10.7%, Philadelphia 10.4%.

108. For more on cycle-friendly churches, see Leonard Sweet, *The Jesus Prescription for a Healthy Life* (Nashville: Abingdon Press, 1996), 76–77.

109. John Young, "The New Materialism," *World Watch* (Sept 1994): 30.

110. As reported by the National Gardening Association.

111. Maltbie D. Babcock, "This Is My Father's World," *The United Methodist Hymnal: Book of United Methodist Worship* (Nashville: The United Methodist Publishing House, 1989), 144.

112. The address of the Christian Society of the Green Cross is 10 E. Lancaster Ave., Wynnewood, PA 19096-3495. (www.esa-online.org/greencross//) For more on the work of Wes Jackson and the Land Institute in preserving the prairie and retrobioengineering perennial corn, see *Meeting the Expectations of the Land: Essays in Sustainable Agriculture and Stewardship,* ed. Wes Jackson, Wendell Berry, and Bruce Colman (San Francisco: North Point Press, 1984).

113. Janet Raloff, "Drugged Waters," *Science News* (21 Mar 1998): 187.

114. As mentioned in John H. Wigger, *Taking Heaven by Storm* (New York: Oxford Univ. Press, 1998), 175.

115. Richard D. Ryder, *Animal Revolution: Changing Attitudes Towards Speciesism* (Cambridge, MA: B. Blackwell, 1989).

116. Don Cupitt, *Radicals and the Future of the Church* (London: SCM Press, 1989), 52.

117. William Shakespeare, *Measure for Measure,* Act 1, Scene 1, in *The Works of William Shakespeare Gathered into One Volume* (New York: Oxford Univ. Press, n.d.), 786.

118. Jacques Attali as quoted in "Ideés Fortes," *Wired* (July 1997): 110.

119. See Frye Gaillard, *If I Were a Carpenter: Twenty Years of Habitat for Humanity* (Winston-Salem, NC: J. F. Blair, 1996), and Millard Fuller, *A Simple Decent Place to Live: The Building Realization of Habitat for Humanity* (Dallas: Word, 1995).

120. *Affluenza* (Oley, PA: Bullfrog Films, 1997) or (Seattle: KCTS Television, 1997).

121. George W. S. Trow, *Within the Context of No Context* (New York: Atlantic Monthly Press, 1997), 88.

122. Jonathan Kramer and Diane Dunaway Kramer, *Losing the Weight of the World: A Spiritual Diet to Nourish the Soul* (New York: Doubleday, 1997), 236.

123. Jim Goldberg, *Raised by Wolves: Photographs and Documents of Runaways* (New York: Corcoran Gallery of Art, 1995), no pagination, but the quote appears about two-thirds of the way through.

124. Alan Wolfe, *One Nation, After All* (New York: Viking, 1998). His actual quote is: "It's hard enough to decide what to do for yourself, which means that passing judgment on what others should do is beyond most people's horizon" (115).

125. See also the foundation's *Locked in the Poorhouse: Cities, Race, and Poverty in the Untied States* (Lanham, MD: Rowan & Littlefield, 1998).

126. The ratio figures come from "Harper's Index," *Harper's* (Jan 1998): 13; the bankruptcy figures come from the American Banking Institute statistics: www.abiworld.org/stats/newstatsfront.html.

127. Interview with Robert Morales, "Toni Morison: The Vibe Q," *VIBE* (May 1998): 98.

128. The Internet address of the Au Sable Institute of Environmental Studies, Mancelona, MI, is www.messiah.edu/acdept/EPICENTR/programs/ausable.htm or www.ausable.org/.

129. The full study of 6,000 US homes can be found in Donna L. Hoffman and Thomas P. Novak, "Bridging the Racial Divide on the Internet," *Science* (17 Apr 1998): 390–92.

130. As quoted in James C. Collins and William C. Lazier, *Beyond Entreprenuership: Turning Your Business into an Enduring Great Company* (Englewood Cliffs, NJ: Prentice Hall, 1992), 107.

IS THIS A GREAT TIME, OR WHAT?

Get Morphed

THE MULTIVERSE

or what? Things are not as black and white as they used to be.
People are not as black and white as they used to be.
The church needs leaders who can see the world in color, not simply in black and white.

The postmodern terrain is not solid ground but undulating waters. Waves are constantly breaking across the *tabula rasa* of postmodernity—waves that are disarmingly hypnotic, alarmingly seductive, armingly dangerous. Everything and everyone is in motion. Everything and everyone ebbing and flowing is morphing.

MY OTHER LIVES ～ Matter is moving and morphing—changing. In fact, matter is less "matter" than energy that is continually becoming. All life-forms are in motion, mutating and migrating to different spaces and places. All life-forms are becoming "multicultural," at least the ones that will survive. Plants, animals, insects, and people are learning how to adjust to new, less monoglot digs and environments. The dilation and contraction of migration, not stability, is the norm for this "new world disorder."

Some say we are in the midst of the greatest migration of all time, as populations migrate and morph. People are in motion all the time: tourists, business executives, refugees, immigrants (legal and illegal), believers. The Barna Research Group estimates that 9% of all USAmericans are intimately involved with more than one local church on a regular basis, and another 30% are less regularly so. Scholar Brenda E. Brasher is a member of both the Christian Church (Disciples of Christ) and the United Church of Christ. She describes her religious faith on her Web site as "bi-denominational."[1]

There is no longer *one* community to which postmoderns can only belong. A second home is to postmoderns what a second car was to our parents. And that is not because of increased economic expectations, but because postmoderns yearn for multiple homes for their multiple lives.

Morphing comes in many forms: economic, political, biological, social, literary, even physical. Morphing was introduced to a wide public in 1993 through a cover of *Time* magazine that featured "The New Face of America" as reflected in the "new Eve,"[2] and in Michael Jackson's "Black or White" music video, which Fox channel broadcast to some 27 countries. Jackson is himself a poster boy for body morphing as he takes the body as far as it can go through plastic surgery, body amendment, and body alteration. What is body modification—aerobics, gym culture, tattooing, piercing, cutting, third-sexing—but a means of reshaping the self? The phenomenon of MUDS and RuPaul suggests a mutative future filled with physical enhancement, gender-bending, and role-playing.[3]

This has enormous implications for the construction of the self and self-identity, which has shifted from a fixed-fate "point of view" to a "point of being."[4] Identity is now something constructed, not given by color or class or clan. The postmodern self is more multidimensional, morphable, and decentered than ever. Each of us has multiple centers—a spiritual center, an intellectual center, an emotional center.

Personal identity is something that emerges from the choices one makes in life, and life's spectrum of choices is ever-expanding: mixed identities, virtual identities, collective identities, and so on. MIT sociologist Sherry Turkle observes that we are encouraged to think of ourselves as "fluid," "emergent," "decentralized," "multiplicitous," "flexible," and "ever in *process*."[5]

It has always been thus to some degree. The "Len Sweet" that goes to bed deciding to jog the next morning can morph into another "Len Sweet" at the sound of an alarm clock at 5 a.m. But postmoderns have the power to redefine themselves at deeper and more subtle levels in ever more complex ways. If the secret of Mardi Gras is the freedom of anybody to become anybody for one day, postmodern society is a perpetual Mardi Gras. If the secret of Las Vegas is that it is the place people go when they aren't happy with who they are and become someone else, postmodern society is a perpetual Las Vegas. The challenge of postmodernity is how to stay true to who you are while changing who you are.

> The future is mestizo.
>
> Virgil Elizondo

USAMERICA'S NEW FACE ~ Hybrid is cool. One of the key issues of postmodern life is the hybridity of cultural identity. The face of USAmerica is changing. Take a look at the Brooklyn Tabernacle Choir. It is the face of the future.

Of course, the face of the USAmerica has always been morphed and mongrelized. Diversity is nothing new. Diversity has always been a part of US identity, albeit in a theoretical way.

What has made USAmerica great? The interfacing and intermixing of diverse cultures. A country without a name,[6] the United States of America depends on an influx of diverse populations to name it. Only the rich mix of disparate cultures has kept this country with no name one of the most creative places on the globe, able to continually reinvent itself and produce dynamic markets. Lawrence Fuchs writes,

> No nation before had ever made diversity itself a source of national identity and unity. . . . No nation in history had proven as successful as the United States in managing ethnic diversity. . . . No nation in history had so eroded the distinction between naturalized and native-born citizens or had made it so easy for aliens from vastly different cultures to become citizens.[7]

For more than 200 years the American experience has produced, according to Mexican-American theologian Virgil Elizondo, a *mestizo* culture—the mixing and intermingling of different cultures until something new is produced.[8] The *mestizo* stock for being an American is changing, however, from European to Asian and Latin and African.

Never again will the US be dominated by one ethnic group (Euro-American). The scale of global borrowing has crossed a threshold. Online technology connects people to multiple cultures they would not otherwise ever contact, much less experience, and this is creating a new cultural hybridity we have only begun to acknowledge.

The *mestizo* culture of the US is getting more diverse, more spicy in its tastes, especially more salsa. Some 9.3% of the USAmerican population (24.6 million people) were born in another country, the highest share since 1940.[9] What is more, the extent of culture bending, class bending, and ethnic bending is now of global as well as gargantuan generational proportions.

- Over 40% of the new students at New York University in 1996–1997 did not have English as their first language.
- 50% of the Ph.D.s granted in engineering and science in the United States are to "foreign nationals," disproportionately to Asians.[10]
- 13% of USAmericans speak another language at home besides English (mainly Spanish, French, German, and Italian).
- Counting "illegals," demographers say that USAmerica has absorbed more immigrants in the past 15 years than at any time in its history.
- The digital generations (Gen-X and Net-Gens) are not only largely color-blind, taking pluralism and diversity for granted, but also the first generations in history to look for friends among people *different* from them.[11]
- USAmerica receives more immigrants in a year's time than all the other nations of the world combined.
- The population of more than 50 of the 100 largest US cities will be predominantly immigrants and ethnic minorities by 2000.[12]

USAmerica is becoming a colorful place. Anyone listening for a uniform voice or looking for a single color will be disappointed. Wild *mestizo* is the name of the game, as postmodern culture is a dizzying kaleidoscope of combinations and colors and chords. One could even argue that USAmerica is now a better United Nations than the United Nations itself.

In this new world, everyone is a few clicks away from everyone else. Electronic media are compressing the world into one spot, forcing us to come to terms with a global civilization. For the first time in history, diverse people are having global experiences and developing a global consciousness. The famous broadcast of 27 September 1938, in which Neville Chamberlain spoke of "a quarrel in a far away country between people of whom we know nothing," seems to come almost from a different planet.

There are two images that historians may use to mark this historic passage into a global world. First is the photograph of a blue-white marble planet Earth shimmering in the blackness of space that was broadcast from Apollo 17 in December 1972. The second is the funeral cortege that left Westminster Abbey in September 1997 with a casket garlanded with a ring of white roses into which was inserted a handwritten card, "MUMMY," to commemorate the death of a global celebrity the whole world loved to death, literally.

Postmodern culture is more than multiplex cinemas; it is a multiplex cosmos, or what Iain M. Banks and others are calling "multiplex multicultures." Some are even suggesting that we don't live in a "universe," but in a "multiverse," a multitude of other universes that run parallel with our own and collectively constitute the Universe (with a capital "U").[13]

Here is the multiplex, morphed world in which we live: Temple United Methodist Church in San Francisco befriended a Ukranian refugee woman who works in San Francisco's most traditional German restaurant, which is owned by an Arab who is married to a Chinese woman who runs a pizza restaurant managed by a Russian.[14] In a Big Mac sold overseas in one of the 100 countries where McDonald's has a restaurant, the onions are from the US, but everything else is from everywhere else. In a Ukranian Big Mac, the beef patties come from Hungary, the lettuce from Ukraine, the bun from Russia, the pickles and special sauce from Germany, the sesame seeds from Mexico, and the cheese from Poland.[15]

> Has He then used up all His skill on the globe of the Earth so that He could not, or all His goodness, so that He would not wish to adorn with suitable creatures other globes also?
>
> Johannes Kepler

With the discovery of life on Mars and the terraforming of the Red Planet into a habitable human environment,[16] our children may be coming to terms with a polyglobal world. The globalization of economic and cultural life has meant the loss of Western hegemony and a lessening of the leverage of Western authority over the rest of the planet.

Postmodern kids process the world as artists do—all at once, not one step at a time as the Industrial Age taught us to do. This helps to explain one of the key stylistic features of postmodern culture: its playfulness, its multimindedness, its multicentricity, its multivoices, its love of disguise and antisynthetic fusion of different modes of human experience.

A *mestizo* mentality not only accepts growing diversity and multiplicity, but also celebrates the mosaic of multimindedness. There is now more interest in those who won rather than lost the battles at the Alamo and the Little Big Horn.

I am a big fan of sentence literature, and my favorite sentence literature is Proverbs. Proverbs presents several different perspectives—it is not written out of one voice.

Perhaps we need to take a fresh look at Isaiah Berlin's notion of pluralism that invokes the multiplicity of desires and dreams that humans can consistently embrace. Or why not look more closely into the thinking of the postmodern Jewish philosopher Emmanuel Levinas? For him, pluralism "does not signify a regrettable fragmentation of a totality, but that multiplicity of modes of transcendence called persons."[17]

AND/ALSO CULTURE ~ As we said in Life Ring #7, postmodern culture is obdurately oxymoronic: both/and, or better yet and/also, not either-or. Poet W. N. Herbert has a line in a poem that serves as an aphorism of the postmodern world: *"And not Or."*[18] And Cyril Connolly gave credit for his success as an editor to his belief in "god the Either, god the Or, and god the Holy Both."[19]

Michael New learned the hard way what it means to be a part of an "and/also culture." A specialist in the US army, New was formally charged in Wurzburg, Germany, in 1995 for disobeying an order. The order was to put on the uniform of the United Nations. New contended that the US government, to which he had already pledged his allegiance, could not force him to swear loyalty to a "foreign power," which is what he considers the UN to be.

Salman Rushdie's collection of stories entitled *East, West* revolves around the conflicts and choices that come from the hybridization of global cultures. One of Rushdie's Indian characters, after receiving a British passport, tells how his newfound freedom created new-felt anxiety.

> But I, too, have ropes around my neck, I have them to this day, pulling me this way and that, East and West, the nooses tightening, commanding, *choose, choose.*
>
> I buck, I snort, I whinny, I kick. Ropes, I do not choose between you. Lassoes, lariats, I choose neither of you, and both. Do you hear? I refuse to choose.[20]

As the global phenomenon of singer Madonna in the '80s and '90s revealed, issues and values are now articulated more through culture than through politics. Postpolitical ideology morphs right/left, liberal/conservative, Democrat/Republican, creating an amalgam of odd mixes and matches. Postmodernity revels in the double ring of exotic and unexpected combinations. It loves mixed metaphors—whether it's Moo Goo tacos, Bill Maher doing "Politically Incorrect" seminars where unlikely people are thrown together to discuss the same issue, or "alterna-fiddling"—a grafting of traditional and Maritime folk, step-dance, and fiddle tunes with grunge rock pioneered by a young fiddler from Cape Breton Island.[21] Cuisine fusion is blending styles like never before: Japanese-French, Mexitalian foods, Chinese-Cuban.

Collage is the archetypal postmodern art form. Global culture is mixing and matching its music, clothing, food, art, and games from a variety of cultures, until culture itself is becoming a "primordial ethnic soup" of art, entertainment, learning, and spirituality. People in the postmodern pot aren't melting, but melding and morphing into one another. They are splicing together multiple stars, multiple perspectives, and multiple styles, with the end result something greater and more beguiling than the sum of its parts.

MoTown, known for its soul sound, has signed on an Asian-American. Already, almost all the music played at European clubs and parties is multicultural—a Spanish song first, then an Italian song, then a French song, then an English song, and so on. On British Rail's first-class Pullman service, a traveler could enjoy food "from India, the Middle East, China, Greece, Italy, Scandinavia and France." One suggested menu starts with Dim Sum with Hoisin Sauce from China, then follows with Duck and Mixed Berry Sauce from southwest France, and ends with the desert Tiramisu from Italy, which is all the rage in Japan.[22] Across the British Isles, Indian takeouts outnumber fish-and-chip shops, with Chinese food and pizza standard fare everywhere.

SALSA-FLAVORED SOCIETY ~ Postmodern culture has a distinctive salsa flavor. "As Hispanics go, so goes Catholicism," says Alan Figuerora Deck, a Jesuit and coordinator of Hispanic Pastoral Programs at Loyola University in Chicago.[23] US Census Bureau projections for the year 2020 are that 48% of the under-20 population will be other than "white Anglos." Hispanics will be the second-largest group, followed by African-Americans and Asian-Americans. Already nearly 28 million Hispanics live in the US—a population equal in size to Canada—making the US the fifth largest Hispanic country in the world.

> It is pride to think that a thing looks ill because it does not look like something characteristic of oneself.
>
> Journalist/artist/writer
> G. K. Chesterton

Latino spiciness to American pop culture is more than the fad sparked by "Macarena," a flamenco-based, internationalized pop song written and first recorded by Spain's Los Del Rio. The Hispanic market now stands at more than 30 million and will leap to 42 million by 2010. (The market of Spanish speakers worldwide is more than 300 million.) By 2030, California is expected to become the first state with a Hispanic majority.

THE WILD, WILD EAST ~ If the 20th century was "the American Century," the 21st century will be "the Asian Century," or at least "the Pacific Century." In fact, the Far West is better seen as the Far East.

The first event shown live on coast-to-coast American television inaugurated "the Pacific Age." One hot Saturday morning in September 1951, 40 million Americans watched the Japanese peace treaty being signed at the ornate Italianate opera house in San Francisco. This parchment document was purported to have held more signatures than any other treaty in world history.

USAmerica has cultural, economic, even familial ties with some of the fastest-growing economies of the world, such as Latin America and Asia. More than 50% of the new wealth created in the world over the next decade will be created in Asia, the wild, wild East of capitalism. Some suggest that East Asia, adjusted for purchasing power, could account for half of the world's economy in 20 years, up from about 25% today. The "world's reigning strategy guru," Gary Hamel, believes that "over the next 10-to-20 years, 40% of the new purchasing power in the world is going to be created in Asia."[24]

THE CAFÉ AU LAIT SOCIETY ~ Postmodern culture is signing the death warrant of a single "hyphenism" and singing the birth of a new "blending," a "diversification of diversity"[25] that goes beyond multiculturalism. "Postethnic" some call it.[26] I prefer "cosmopolitanism," or the "café au lait society." Cultures are becoming colorfully colorless.

> Changes in latitudes, changes in attitudes.
>
> Jimmy Buffet

The world is becoming a single place. It is inherent in the medium of cyberspace to break down barriers. Postmodern children are playing in cyber-neighborhoods and forming friendships that have nothing to do with ethnography or ethnicity. Their world is global, interconnected, 24/7/365 (24 hours a day, 7 days a week, 365 days a year), with new concepts of space and time and neighborhood. The children of cyberspace are pioneering a global youth culture that blurs racial boundaries, a blurring that Benetton, Nike, Calvin Klein, and others are exploiting as an exchange of commerce.

Old ethnic categories no longer work, as new "body canons," new ideal forms of the human body, are emerging. One only has to name the movie *A Family Thing* (1996) or to name the names of the hero hyphenates[27] on the lips of kids to comprehend the varieties of racial morphing going on and the complex ethnic heritages of postmoderns: wheat-colored actor Keanu Reeves (Hawaiian, Chinese, white), caramel-colored singer Mariah Carey (black, Venezuelan, white), and almond-colored actor Johnny Depp (Cherokee, white).

> On planet Reebok there are no boundaries.
>
> Slogan of Reebok International, Ltd.

Mannequin Naomi Campbell, golfer Tiger Woods, and rocker Lenny Kravitz are more representative of the future than Kate Moss or Greg Norman or Sting. Campbell's beauty is the product of a Jamaican mother and an Asian father. Woods calls himself, not "African-American," but "Cablinasian," a combination of Caucasian, black, American Indian, and Asian. To separate out one or two parts of his past and claim only that, he claims, would be to deny the rest, the whole of who he is.

Kravitz is the son of famous parents of mixed cultures—Bahamian actress Roxie Roker and Jewish television producer Sy Kravitz. He testified to his deepening faith in *Rolling Stone* magazine in 1996 (gazing out from the cover with rings in his left nostril and left nipple): "Whether you believe or not, I know that you and I are created from the same energy, from the same God, from the same source."[28] Kravitz also testifies to the lingering power of race to define part-black Americans: "Accept the blessing of having the advantage of two cultures, but understand that you are Black. In this world, if you have one spot of Black blood, you are Black. So get over it."[29]

For the first time since Gallup began asking the question, a majority of whites in the United States approved of black-white marriages. In 1958, only 4% approved; in 1997, 61%.[31] Interracial marriages numbered 150,000 in 1970 but more than 1 million in 1990 and 1,392,000 in 1995. Mixed-race births increased 834% from 1960 to 1995, with the number of racially mixed children now at roughly two million.

In a culture in which one in four Boomers is a member of a racial or ethnic minority,[32] are these figures surprising? Until 1967, interracial marriage was illegal in 29 states.[33] By 1993, 12.1% of all new marriages involving an African-American were interracial (compared with 2.6% in 1970 and 6.6% in 1980).[34] By

> The absurdity of the biological reading of the one-drop rule is obvious.... How reasonable is it to say that a white woman can give birth to a Black baby, but a Black woman can't give birth to a white baby?
>
> Professor of anthropology and psychology Lawrence Hirschfeld[30]

1991, nearly half of first- and second-generation Hispanics in New York City were marrying someone of a different national origin from their own.[35] To take the issue of diversity into other arenas, in the past decade the vast majority of Jews who married took a gentile spouse. About half of Japanese-American women marry outside the Japanese-American community.

Amid vigorous discussion, the Office of Management and Budget, whose director Franklin Raines was in an interracial marriage and is the parent of racially mixed children, recommended to President Clinton that in the year 2000 census form, people be able to check however many racial boxes fit their ancestry. Between the 1970 and 1990 census, the number of hyphenated people choosing the "Other" box, the closest thing to specifying a multiracial identity, grew from less than a million to 9.8 million. In 1980, 250,000 multiracials checked "Other" and then itemized their multiple ethnic origins.[36]

In many ways the armed services (which are based on rank, not race) are doing better than the church in pioneering a multiracial society. Whitney Elaine Johnson, a mixed-race newborn, died on March 19, 1996, and was buried in the family plot of the Barnetts Creek Baptist Church graveyard in rural south Georgia. But the church directed the family to remove the body from the all-white cemetery. Pastor Leon VanLandingham proclaimed that in the church's action, "We were trying to do what God wanted us to do."

Hello?! Even while *Christianity Today* was editorializing against racial mixing and intermarriage in the '50s and '60s, evangelist Billy Graham always insisted that interracial marriages, if culturally problematic, are nevertheless a biblical option. We see familiar examples in the Bible: Zipporah, Moses' wife, was from the Cushites, who were black; Ruth, the Moabite woman who married Boaz, was also black.[37]

In the Detroit suburb of Oak Park, affluent African-Americans live alongside Jews and Anglos and Indians and Chinese. There is little mingling among the adults; the ethnic groups tend to stick with their own people. But their children (one-third of whom under age 18 in 1998 were minorities) go to school together, play together, and party together. In 1998, one-third of the children under 18 were minorities. The children have grown up watching the animated feature *Pocahontas,* with its expression of interracial marriage. They have seen the interracial remake of *Cinderella* (with pop singer Brandy-Cinderella rescued by a Philippine-born Prince Charming), which won for ABC-TV its highest rating for the time slot during the entire '90s. And as the children grow up, they are marrying one another in significant numbers.

> A culture is the equal inheritance of anyone who can appropriate and apply.
>
> Sociologist Kelly Miller[38]

These Net-generation, Nickelodeon children are the first residents of a new global world—a diverse world where ethnicity is something to be both celebrated and taken for granted. Postmodern children are leading a revolution in racial attitudes. For our children, the dream is both color blindness and color brilliance.

A 1997 story in *USA Today* announced that 57% of teenagers who date say they have been out with someone of another race or ethnic group.[39] The deracialization of USAmerican society does not mean that race will not continue to play a role in many black and brown and red and yellow and white lives. But the prevalence of interracial dating among the Net Generation, and the refusal of many teens to see "interracial dating" as anything other than "dating," means that race will be a declining factor in the lives of future generations and not the "central fact" it once was. Race is proving less and less foundational as a way of making sense of the world and is already being purged from Net-Gen thinking as a pernicious illusion.

Arthur Miller's play *All My Sons* (1947) tells the story of a man who makes airplane equipment during World War II. As the war intensifies, he falls behind schedule and cuts corners to meet deadlines and increase profits. Young pilots die because of the faulty airplane parts he ships to the Pacific front. His son, who is a pilot in the Pacific, realizes what his father has done and kills himself by crashing his plane.

The play is about the family's attempt to come to terms with the loss of this son. Toward the end, the father is trying to explain himself to his other son. He says that he did what he did for his sons, that he wanted them to have a house and security. Then he pauses and says, "I guess I didn't realize they were all my sons."

Do you remember the very last words of the movie *A Time to Kill*? Matthew McConnaughey, who received MTV's Breakthrough Performance award for his role, speaks them to Samuel L. Jackson: "I thought our children could play together."

THE GREAT CLASS DIVIDER ~ The major trope of difference for our children and grandchildren will not be race or gender, but class.[40] Their great temptation will be to find the essence of their identity, not in race or gender, but in class and culture. Class is becoming the chief determinant of our life-chances and experience, unrivaled in its structuring power.

The success of the movie *Titanic* can partly be explained by its baring of past class differences between "first class" and "steerage." The church's great challenge will be to find ways to defuse intense class consciousness, class antagonisms, and class tensions, some of which could escalate into Cold War II.[41] Lower-class USAmericans of all races will unite against the oppression of information capitalism's economic and intellectual elite. The biggest fights of the future will not revolve around political ideology, as in the modern era, but around economics, especially the "theoeconomic" doctrine that the economy is God and finance its philosophy.

USAmericans are increasingly segregating themselves by income and economic opportunity. Far more than ethnicity, educational attainment, and access to jobs will be the "great class divider of the 21st century," says Gregory Schmid, one of the directors at the Institute for the Future in Menlo Park, California.[42] Peter Drucker makes a case for the basic gap as not being between "rich and poor," but between "people with advanced education and people without." He writes, "The difference in income for an Afro-American with a college degree is statistically insignificant (if you adjust for age and length of service) from the income of a white, Latino, or Asian with a college degree."[43] In third-grade classrooms one can begin to see the parting of the waters between tomorrow's haves and have-nots, the knows and the know-nots; some march full speed ahead into the Information Age, while the information-disenfranchised form an electronic underclass, falling by the wayside because of wayward literacy and graphicacy skills.[44] African-Americans, whose income as a group is the fastest growing in the US (up 13% in 1996 to $367 billion),[45] have doubled their spending on computer hardware and software in recent years and are now responsible for 25% of online spending.[46] Ironically, impoverished blacks now show as much "upward contempt"[47] toward those affluent black consumers as they do toward white suburbanites.

THE GLOCAL DOUBLE RING ~ Boundaries are both collapsing and expanding at the same time. Our connections are to multiple places—shrinking to tribal locales, expanding to planetary boundaries. As the funeral of Princess Diana made evident, for the first time in human history people are having global experiences. We are living in the whole world.[48] But the more we know the same things and share the same experiences at the same moment, the more we experience them differently according to our particularized customs and circumstances.

A "global" world has been defined as "that matrix of transnational economic, political, and cultural forces that are circulating throughout the globe and producing universal, global conditions, often transversing and even erasing previously formed national and regional boundaries."[49] Yet paradoxically, globalism engenders localism. Contrary to what is widely believed, globalization is not synonymous with Americanization. The more globalized our world and globalized our identity, the more prized our particularities and the more celebrated our otherness.[50] Far from birthing a single world religion, all over the globe our religions seem more combatively at odds than ever before.

Take as an example the English language. English is currently used as a first or second language by some 600 million people. Michael Barber writes, "60% of the world's radio broadcasts are in English, 70% of the world's mail is addressed in English, 85% of all international telephone conversations are in English and 80% of the data in the world's computers is in English."[51] Moreover, 83% of the European Union's high school students learn English as their second language, while 32% are learning French, 16% German.[52]

English is now the global language of diplomacy. English is the closest thing we have to a global lingua franca.[53] Global computer networks are underscoring English as the dominant international language. (Despite all this, the number of English-speaking people dropped from 9.8% of the world's population in 1958 to 7.6% in 1992.)

Yet the worldwide dominance of English is a vehicle for negotiating the maze of cultural differences, not doing away with them. In the words of Samuel P. Huntington, resorting to "English for intercultural communication thus helps maintain and, indeed, reinforces people's separate cultural identities. Precisely because people want to preserve their own culture, they use English to communicate with people of other cultures."[54]

I love English. It is my mother tongue. But there are some things you can't say in English that you can say better in other languages. That's why we need to study and learn other languages. For example, there is the Yiddish word *nakhes* (NOKH-ess)—"a special kind of pleasure, a feeling of love infused with sensations of pride and joy." Postmoderns get a lot of *nakhes* from both their native tongue and their learned language. But note that there is no English equivalent for *nakhes*.

Hear the double ring: A few yards from Chairman Mao's mausoleum in Beijing, China, you can buy a burger at McDonald's. But fast-food homogeneity has not produced homogenized identities. From China to Istanbul, Western fast-food chains have increased, not decreased, interest in local culinary traditions.[55] Thus global food has often resulted in both sameness and difference, and reinforced local identities within a global context.

Global models are deconstructed and then recontextualized around local priorities, whether they be national or regional, traditional or tribal. MTV Latino, for example, combines Spanish and English to become something quite different. The more global we become, the more uniform our experiences. The more important our tribal identities, the more valuable are scarcity and each new strangeness. The scarcest of all is difference, which becomes the most valuable thing in the world.[56] The spectral, alluring strangeness of difference steals the postmodern show, if not quite saves it.

> I have a dream ... where little black boys and black girls will be able to join hands with little white boys and white girls and walk together as brothers and sisters.
>
> Martin Luther King Jr.

God is the creator of the cosmos, the ruler of the universe. Yet God calls *you* by name, knows the numbers of hairs on *your* head, and feels the pain of every bird that falls.

THE LAW OF CLEOPATRA'S NOSE ~ The Law of Cleopatra's Nose[57] is a double imperative requiring us to move from the provincial to the general, the particular to the universal, the common and everyday to the mysterious and sublime.

Singularizing at the same time it universalizes, New Delhi McDonald's serves Maharaja Macs, which are made with mutton. In Tokyo's Roppongi district, McDonald's "Bigu Maku" is topped with shredded cabbage. McDonald's coffee in parts of Washington State are roasted by "Seattle's Best Coffee," but they serve only decaf coffee at Idaho and Utah McDonald's. There is rice for breakfast at Hawaii McDonald's. The Canadian film industry has stopped trying to out-Hollywood Hollywood and is developing its own distinctive brand of offbeat, out-of-the-ordinary films. All these demonstrate that the more global our lifestyles become, the more prized cultural uniqueness becomes.

Diversity of all kinds is disappearing. In the past 500 years, more than half of the world's 15,000 known languages have disappeared. Philologists expect only 5% to 10% of the remaining 7000 languages to survive another 50 years. That is why I am an unrepentant cryptocentrist in my use of Appalachian phrases and vocabulary. (Cryptocentrism is the use of language to maintain group identity.) Hence I say "Willow Creek" (sounded "crik") defiantly, as I stubbornly take down the wash (sounded "worsh") to the "worshing machines."

The crash of the smash hit song "Macarena" tells us a lot: It wasn't nearly "authentic" enough in its "otherness" for devotees of "world music." Baaba Maal of Senegal puts it precisely: People in his country "want to have a music in which they can see themselves as Africans, but also as people who belong to the rest of the world."[58]

Nineteenth-century French philosopher Pierre-Joseph Proudhon, who fought for a decentralized model of economic development called "mutualism" in the face of Karl Marx's centralized vision, said that if all of us were brothers, then he had no brothers. But I say if my brother has a name, if my sister has a face—that is, if I am tied inextricably to people in the rain forests I have never met but on whom I depend for every breath (the oxygen the forests produce)—then I have said something profound and significant.

The motto of the biologist René Dubos—"Act locally, think globally"—is old-fashioned. One must do both at the same time. In fact, one can't do anything that is either simply local or simply global. The motto must become "Think globally and locally, act globally and locally." In shorthand: Think and act glocally.

All this multiculturalism doesn't mean that USAmericans aren't returning to traditional values, one of which is racism. If the evidence from college campuses and high schools is indicative, outcroppings of racial hostility will become more blatant and more violent. The potential for racial and ethnic strife is at its highest in the next few decades.

A strong double ring is this: At the same time culture is becoming more multicultural, there is a growing anti-multiculturalism going on in all sectors of society. Some on the right see "diversity" as a negative gift, not a positive one, and resent the glamorizing of minority cultures.[59] Some on the left argue that multiculturalism represents "a tacit renunciation of the struggle for socio-economic justice" in that it "demands not a preferential option for the poor but a much less threatening openness to otherness." Roberto S. Goizueta calls multiculturalism "the middle-aged yuppie's attempt to recover his or her long-forgotten political commitment without having to surrender the economic gains he or she has made in the interim."[60] Some in the middle, like Samuel P. Huntington, see multiculturalism as the death-knell of American civilization as we know it. Huntington coined the phrase "civilization of civilizations" to capture a future in which all the world's civilizations exist side by side and thrive.[61]

so what?   **A THEOLOGY OF PENTECOST** ~ If the church cannot come to terms with the profound changes wrought by globalization and unprecedented intercultural contact, then what right do we have to claim that word *church?*[62] Isn't the story of Pentecost (Acts 2:1–12), not the rolling back of multiplicity, but the ability of singularity to emerge out of multiplicity and the ability of any and all human languages to communicate the divine?

The spiritual and social implications of Pentecost, which defines the relationship of the human spirit to the Holy Spirit, have yet to be explored for the age in which we live. Just as the Spirit, brooding over creation, breathed the world out of nothing, so the Spirit at Pentecost breathed the church out of nothing.

Chaos theory has taught us that complexity and symmetry replace the order and linearity of the modern era. When things are allowed to interact, what will emerge is variety and surprise. God loves variety. When God lets a thousand flowers bloom and a thousand dialects be heard, why are we afraid around genuine diversity—whether it be ethnic or intellectual or spiritual?

Pentecost reversed Babel, not through the creation of one language, but through the ability to acknowledge and affirm difference. When barriers come down and a profusion of voices is allowed to sound, the result is harmonious difference. Variety is more than the spice of life that salts and peppers our existence; variety is the very stuff of life itself.

> Variety is the very spice of life
> That gives it all its flavour.
>
> William Cowper

To make a difference, you not only need to be different, but need to understand and attend to difference. A bird is not the best authority on air. A fish is not the best authority on water. A worm is not the best authority on earth. We need each other to be each other. To "rejoice in the truth," as the Bible instructs (1 Cor. 13:6), is to rejoice in diversity. As one postmodern put it, "A non-Christian friend can see Jesus in me, but not in a complete way. The more Christians I introduce him to, the more completely he can see Christ."[63]

You and I are different versions of the same thing: the image of God.

ONE ANOTHERING ~ Beatrice Bruteau of Fordham University asks the postmodern question, "How big is your *we*?" Or, as Jim Wallis puts it, "Can we expand our vision of community beyond our own skin, family, race, tribe, culture, country, and species? Spiritual life is more than what we believe, it also includes how we relate."[64] The question for us is, "Are we big enough to relate to our brothers and sisters, not by beggaring, but by one-anothering?"

In Mark 4:35 Jesus said, "Let us go across to the other side." The "other side" in the first-century culture around the Sea of Galilee meant Decapolis, the Gentile side of the lake. In other words, the "other side" is in contrast with "our side."[65] When Jesus first said he wanted to go to "the other side"—that is, the place where Gentiles lived and idols were worshiped and that Jews were supposed to stay away from—he was looking for an escape, a place to rest away from the pressing crowds on the shore. At this point Jesus still spoke of his ministry in terms of the Messiah of the Jewish people, not for anyone else. But after his second trip to the "other side," his second journey to the Decapolis, Jesus shifted from an exclusively Jewish ministry to an inclusive ministry that accepted Gentiles. The "other" in "one anothering" took on new meaning.

> The similarities between me and my father are different.
>
> Dale Berra,
> Yogi Berra's son

"One anothering" wasn't easy for Jesus, and it will not be easy for us. Prejudice has a history of winning out over evidence. Albert Einstein liked to note that a prejudice is harder to break down than the atom. Even for a church that likes to be on the side of the "other," there are good Others and bad Others. Or as George Orwell first put it, "some Others are more Other than other Others."[66]

It is the job of the church to cut across all boundaries, whether of biology or sociology, and to see people the way Jesus saw them rather than the way culture sees them. Diana Garland, a Southern Baptist scholar, writes that Jesus defined "family" neither as the first century defined it nor as the 21st century will define it. "The New Testament model is not the nuclear family. It is the adopted family. In God's kingdom, nobody has to be alone. Family transcends kinship for us."[67]

What keeps diversity from turning into division is the church's ability to provide with people a plenitude of ways to encounter the ultimate Other, the transcendent Other. Can we disagree with each other without reaching for the stun guns and adopting a scorched-earth policy toward those with whom we disagree? It is interesting to see how the business world is introducing customers to competition: General Motors' Buick division is placing Honda Accords, Toyota Camrys, and Ford Tauruses in their own showroom because they are confident that their own Buick Regal will outshine its competition.

> Always allow God the privilege of working in another's life differently from the way God has in your own.
>
> Actress/model/pastor's wife/mother Susan Yates

Would that the church could respond to those with somewhat strange ideas the way that physicist Robert Oppenheimer used to respond to ideas that seemed rather *outré:* "I am glad that there are people thinking along those lines." The notion that what pleases me may not please you exercises a kind of Sinai-esque presence and power in postmodern ministries.

How many languages does the Holy Spirit speak? "One anothering" is best expressed in the following adage: God likes a lot of things I don't.

TRUTH ON THE MARGINS ~ Postmoderns are truth-seekers first, truth-makers second. Whereas modern seekers sought the knowledge of truth, postmodern seekers want to *know* the truth in the biblical sense of that word "know"—that is, *experience* the truth.

The church of Jesus Christ doesn't open its mouth unless it can begin as Jesus did: "Verily, verily" (KJV) or "Truly, truly" (RSV and NASB) or, best of all, "I tell you the truth" (NIV).[68] "The truth is . . ." a show-and-tell Truth. To be anything other than true—to God, to oneself, to others—is to live a lie. A life in which "the truth is not in us" damages the body and soul. Postmodern truth is prediction before predication.

The Holy Spirit is the Spirit of Truth. Showing-and-telling the Truth is the church's principle weapon against the powers and principalities of evil. The gospel is nothing if it is not "full of grace and truth" (John 1:14). Sam Williams is a seminary professor and a church planter. His staff motto is "In-your-face/With-God's-grace." The more grace you show, he contends, the more truth you can tell.

But the question of truth is, as Oscar Wilde once put it, rarely pure and never simple. It certainly isn't for postmoderns, who love to flirt with truth more than commit to truth. The stern truth is that truth has gone to either tabloid or theory. Postmoderns are more likely to know the chaff, not the grain, of truth; to mistake loudmouths for truth-tellers. They are always learning and never coming to a knowledge of the truth.

Postmoderns have a preference for partial truths over "false totalities," in part because of temperament, but also in part because certain "literacies of power," as Donaldo Macedo calls them, keep us from knowing the whole truth (about ourselves, about our history of "white privilege," our treatment of others, etc.).[69] We can expect postmodern culture to be a heyday of "heresy," as John Henry Newman defined the word. Something was characteristic of Christian heresy, he argued, not because it was untrue, but because it was partial, that it was a truth taken out of the context of other truths.

Stock-in-trade postmoderns take truth to the edge, eschewing the conventional in favor of more difficult truths that bring together the central and the eccentric, the center and the margins. This should not set Christians' teeth on edge, for gospel truth itself is on the margins. For Jesus, the question was not to be on the top or on the bottom, but on the margins. Truth comes less through top-down or bottom-up than at-the-edges. Harvard theologian Harvey Cox unveils this truth-on-the-margins methodology quite clearly:

> A viable postmodern theology will be created neither by those who have completely withdrawn from the modern world nor by those who have affirmed it unconditionally. It will come from those who have lived within it but have never been fully part of it, like the women in Adrienne Rich's poem who, though they dived into the wreck, have not found their names inscribed within it. It will be created by those who, like black American Christians, have refused to accept the slave-master's gospel ... but have also refused to jettison the Gospel altogether. What is needed ... is not some measured middle ground ... but a theology forged by those who have been both inspired and abused, both touched and trampled on by the religion of the modern age.[70]

The postmodern tendency will be to celebrate the Many and forget the One. The church must hold the One and the Many together: the oneness and manyness of our one-in-three/three-in-one God; the oneness and manyness of truth; the oneness of heaven's throne and the manyness of heaven's mansions. The essence of the Trinity is this: The truth that is one in God becomes multiple outside God.

Ultimately, there is only One truth to tell, and that truth is untellable without the person of Jesus.

How does truth look? How does truth act? What does truth look like?

The Christian says, "Look at Jesus." Especially Jesus on the cross.

Jesus didn't just say, "I tell the truth." Jesus said, "I *am* the truth."

Jesus is the door—that opens to 21-C.

Jesus is the truth—that leads to the future.

Jesus is the key—that unlocks all prisons and opens all secrets.

Jesus is the bread—that feeds all hungers of postmoderns.

Jesus is the true vine—that fills our gardens and enables us to bear much fruit.

Jesus is the light—that shines upon this blue-marble planet.

Jesus is the good shepherd—that lays down life itself for the sheep.

Jesus is the teacher—that instructs us in his ministry.

Jesus is the way—that leads us into all truth.

Jesus is the life—the resurrection and the life—of the postmodern party.

Jesus is THE-ology. Truth is an Image. At the heart of biblical faith is an image: Jesus, the image of God. Christian Truth is not Torah ("the Teaching") or Doctrine or Representation. Truth is a Person and a Participation in the divine mission in the world. The founder of Methodism, John Wesley, said that "orthodoxy or right opinions is at best a slender part of religion."[71] What distinguishes the Methodist, Wesley said elsewhere, are not "opinions of any sort. . . . [These] are all quite wide of the point."[72]

> I love truth wherever I find it.
>
> John Wesley[77]

So what is the point? For Wesley, the point was the double ring of truth: "A Methodist is a person who has 'the love of God' . . . in his heart."[73] And again: "The truth is, neither this opinion nor that, but the love of God, humbles man, and that only."[74] About everything else, "We think and let think."[75] Or, as Wesley wrote to Richard Tompson on 28 June 1755, "I seek two things in this world, truth and love. Whoever assists me in this search is a friend indeed, whether personally known or unknown."[76] The truth does not need defending; the truth will defend itself.

BREATHE FREELY BUT BREATHE TOGETHER ~ Church is the place where people ought to breathe most freely and most together. Church is the place where people ought to feel most free to be themselves and most accountable to one another.

In her book *Walking on Water,* Madeleine L'Engle quotes Hawaiian Christian Alice Kaholusuna:

Before the missionaries came [to Hawaii], my people used to sit outside their temples for a long time meditating and preparing themselves before entering. Then they would virtually creep to the altar to offer their petitions and afterwards would again sit a long time outside, this time to "breathe life" into their prayers. The Christians, when they came, just got up, uttered a few sentences, said AMEN and were done. For that reason my people called them "haoles [people] without breath," or those who failed to breathe life into their prayers.[78]

The church can help postmoderns learn to "breathe together" (to use a concept from Latino culture). The church can lead the way in getting Christians from various backgrounds together and inhabiting each other's space so intimately that you "breathe together." When you breathe together, a simple melody is replaced by hard-won harmony.

Native Americans of the Southwest don't talk about "tolerating" one another. Toleration is not the issue. They talk about "honoring" each other. They gather in talking circles, in which everyone contributes his or her perspective about situations and events. When you "honor someone," you first hear them, affirm them, and understand them. Then you yourself expect to be heard, affirmed, and understood.

The church must find ways of setting up "breathing" dates between diverse theologies and tribes. Bill Maher's success with the TV program *Politically Incorrect* is putting in a circle the most diverse group he can gather to talk about current issues. Bill Moyers's success with the PBS television series *Genesis* was getting seven people from different backgrounds, faiths, professions, ages, and genders to sit in a circle and discuss the 10 best stories from the first book of the Bible.[79] (He received more response from this series than from anything else he has done on TV in 25 years.)

In a world of mutual incomprehension, where people exchange views with one another but don't have conversations with one another, can the Postmodern Reformation church be a place where people with contrasting approaches to God and life are made to sit down and have dinner together? Sometimes there will be awkwardness—but at other times there will be love at first sight.[80] Can the Postmodern Reformation church be a place that teaches us how to hear others, and overhear ourselves?[81] Can worship be a place where diverse ethnic and cultural identities come together to shape one-of-a-kind worship experiences?

In the modern world, Christians had problems breathing the air that other Christians inhaled and exhaled. In the postmodern world, the air has become even more exotic. We can no longer breathe air that only comes from Protestant, Catholic, and Jewish camps. By the second decade of 21-C, Islam is expected to replace Judaism as USAmerica's second-largest religious group.

There are already more Buddhists in America than Episcopalians or Presbyterians. This is not our parents' world.

The 18th-century English philosopher John Locke said that the search for innate principles of practical reason was ridiculous to "any who have been but moderately conversant in the History of Mankind and look'd beyond the Smoak of their own Chimneys." To understand one's own culture, one must first leave it and dive headfirst into another. To achieve equilibrium within our own heritage, we must first foster disequilibrium and promote paradox—"look beyond the smoak of our own chimneys."

> If you can't have humility to be in balance with others, you won't be as good a jazz musician as you might be.
>
> Wynton Marsalis[82]

The church facilitates this looking beyond. When it comes right down to it, the practice of postmodern ministry is inherently a cross-cultural exercise. Think about it: What do ministers do that isn't a transcultural experience? When you reach out to a lawyer or communicate with a physicist or pray with a machine operator, it's nowadays a cross-cultural experience.

N

The Good W E

S

This symbol used to be placed at the head of certain periodicals to indicate that the contents were drawn from the four corners of the earth. This is how we got the word *news-paper.*

Perhaps it's time for a local church to put a similar symbol on all its publications to indicate that it is involved in breathe-together cross-cultural missions around the world.

N

W E

S

BUT DON'T BREATHE IN ~ Truth may be shoved to the margins, but we must be careful not to take truth on margin. A grand gallimaufry of gospels out there demands to be heard and taken both seriously and equally. "Dogmatic neutrality"[83] is a cardinal tenet of New Age spirituality: All truths are equal, except that some truths are more equal than others. I heard about a church that refuses to speak against hell; they call it an "alternative lifestyle."

In a world struggling to live without transcendentals, disciples of Jesus proclaim transcendentals of faith. The relativist doctrine and pluralist ideology of "true for me" yields louche living. To say that "2 + 2 = 4, *for me*" is as ridiculous as saying that "killing is wrong, *for us*"[84] or "human sacrifice is wrong, *for me*" or "ethnic cleansing is wrong, *for us*" or "slavery is wrong, *for me*." Postmodernism's "absolutophobia" does not seem to extend to environmentalism or animal rights or female genital mutilation. In fact, some have suggested that the feminist revulsion toward the last is what killed cultural relativism as a philosophy in the West.[85]

But postmodernism does make the claim that all roads lead up the same mountain, where it is level at the peaks. Postmoderns are deeply suspicious about any and all metanarratives that provide all-encompassing authority for everyone everywhere. Jean François Lyotard, who popularized the term *post-modern* through his book *The Postmodern Condition: A Report on Knowledge*, even defined the term as "incredulity toward metanarrative."[86] The fact is, postmoderns have abandoned the unitary text, glory in the fragmentary and dissonant, and are deeply suspicious of all grand narratives and the central self.

For all these reasons and more, postmodern Christians (who refuse to relinquish metanarratives of God, Creation, the Fall, Redemption, or Eschatology) will be dealers in love more than dealers in dogma. But in classic double-ring fashion, postmodern culture needs more truth, not less. The difference is that Truth is not a principle or a proposition but a Person. Truth is not rules and regulations but a relationship. God did not send us a statement but a Savior. God did not send us a principle but a Presence. Surrendering to Jesus is not subscription to some "article of faith" but merging one's personal story into the story of the Son of God and the Savior of the world.

> This is my Story, This is my Song.
>
> Fanny Crosby,
> "Blessed Assurance"

The postmodern metanarrative is not a philosophical bent or theological construct but an all-encompassing, all-inclusive Story and all-embracing Song.

Postmodern Christians, who acknowledge the various degrees of truth, will protect the rights and rituals of people of other faiths while at the same time presenting Jesus as God Incarnate. It's not just that not all religions are equally true; many religions are mutually exclusive. If Hinduism is right, Buddhism is wrong. If Christianity is right, there are many religions that are wrong. Not all religions are born equal. Difference unmoderated by shared dreams and visions produces some horrifying results. There is such a thing as *bad faith*. There are such things as *bad-faith* beliefs (clitorectomies? human sacrifices? temple prostitution?). Every truth must be judged in the light of faithfulness to the total witness of Scripture.

We can embrace other people legally and socially without embracing them intellectually. The twin ideals of postmodern faith are (1) tolerance of all believers, however controversial, and (2) a confession of belief, however uncomfortable.

In the modern world there was an implied threat at the end of "Jesus is the Way, the Truth, and the Life"—Or Else. In the postmodern world there is something else at the end of the declaration: "Jesus is the Way, the Truth, and the Life"—But God Will Be God.

In an Or-Else Evangelism,[88] the Christian witness ends in judgment: "Go straight to hell. Do not pass Go" Or-Else Evangelism pours bile on those who muck about in other religions, and sneers and jeers at the septic sensibilities of other faith traditions and their hell-bent ways. The splenetic point-scoring of Or-Else Evangelism disfigured too much of modern missions.

In a But-God Evangelism,[89] the Christian witness ends in a Judge: God will be God, a God who is, in John Milton's words in *Lycidas,* "All-judging Jove."[90] God can do whatever God wants to do. Jesus is not *one* way or *a* way. Jesus is *the* way, *the* truth, *the* life. Yet, at the same time we proclaim with all that is within us that Jesus is the "human face of God," we also trust that God's Word will not return void (Acts 20:32), that God cannot do wrong (Job 34:10), that we cannot outlove the Lord. In John Wesley's words, "If you cannot *reason* or *persuade* a man into the truth, never attempt to *force* him into it. If love will not compel him to come in, leave him to God, the Judge of all."[91]

> "I must say that," one thinks, "and yet how, in this day and Age, can I? It is me, but only part of me. A part, but still essential. It will be false if I write it as I."
>
> Fernando Pessoa[87]

CALM, COOL, AND COLLECTED ~ The psychological challenge of post-modern culture is to keep our multiple selves integrated and "together." The modern era did not want to admit that a person is composed of different parts, of multiple selves. In postmodern culture people are mingled in a fugue of split identities and drifting story lines.

Portuguese poet Fernando Pessoa (1888–1935) accepted his multiplicity and wrote under four names ("heteronyms," he called them) that were more than pseudonyms. They were real imaginary poets with distinct characters and distinct styles: Alberto Caeiro, the soul with the greatest soul, wrote in free verse; Ricardo Reis composed metrical but unrhymed poetry; Pessoa was metrical and tightly rhymed; Álvaro de Campos wrote in free verse.[92]

As proto-postmodern Pessoa discovered, the different *parts* of us sometimes take over or stray, leaving postmoderns fragmented, scattered, torn apart, and needing collectedness, wholeness, and completeness. The inability to admit our multiplicity of "I's" leaves us feeling "crazy," a feeling that can prophesy us forward into true craziness. No wonder that what used to be called "multiple personality disorder" (but is now called "disassociative identity disorder" by the *Diagnostic and Statistical Manual of Mental Disorders*) is to the postmodern soul what ulcers and addictions were to the last two generations of advanced psychiatric society (Boosters and Boomers). J. L. Borges's parable on Shakespeare, "Everything and Nothing," ends with this acknowledgment of both our oneness and manyness:

History adds that before or after dying he [Shakespeare] found himself in the presence of God and told Him: "I who have been so many men in vain want to be one and myself." The voice of the Lord answered from a whirl-wind: "Neither am I anyone; I have dreamt the world as you dreamt your work, my Shakespeare, and among the forms in my dream are you, who like myself are many and no one."[93]

In the modern era we knew and were known only as one; in the post-modern era we know and are known only in parts. The challenge of the church is to help people stay true to who they are while changing who they are. The church will summon divided selves into an undivided love, a love for God with an undivided heart: "You shall love the LORD your God with all your heart, and with all your soul, and with all your might" (Deut. 6:5). The church will help people develop a calm, cool, and integral spirituality and will work for that day when we know ourselves and are known by others, not only in parts, but fully, even face-to-face.

FROM DENOMINATION TO TRIBE ~ From nation-state to mega-state and micro-tribe, from national to uniglobal and Multi-Tribal/Pan-Denominational: A wired world blows bureaucratic circuits. Bureaucracies can't keep up. The unionism of denominational bureaucracies is devolving downward into tribal identities and revolving upward into global connections.

People are already unlinking themselves from centralized institutions, most of which are tottering if not already toppled. There is little loyalty to anything that doesn't promote oneself and one's interests. The future is one of "the sovereign individual," where every person thinks and acts as states did in the past, in the midst of sovereign multinational and multilateral agreements.[94]

Take, for example, the collapse of sovereign nation-states and welfare states around the world. Beginning in the 15th century, cultures, politics, and ethnic entities coagulated into national states. The 300-year dominance of this modern entity of the nation-state is coming to an end, as reflected in the rising membership of the United Nations to 185 countries as of 1995.

With one refrain, even with the same words, this is being said over and over again. "The nation-state is becoming too small for the big problems of life and too big for the small problems of life," says sociologist Daniel Bell.[95] "The nation-state, the tribe writ large," says *Time* columnist Henry Grunwald, "today is often too big to cope with local problems and yet too small to func-tion adequately in the global marketplace."[96]

In a digital world there is little reason for middle structures like nation-states or denominations. Denominational religion is declining in significance in America, and denominations continue to decline if they do not become less a noun and more a verb. Denominations began as the middle way between local communities and whole religious traditions. (Methodism began, for example, as a middle position between the Church of England and Nonconformity.) The model of denominational church is middle brow, middle class, middle income, and middle age—a bourgeois style befitting the old industrial, modern age.

Denominations will continue to ride their depreciative curves so long as they insist on being regulatory agencies more than resource bodies. They could have a great future if they served as resources to bring together multiplicity and bridges between ethnic groups. For example, postmodern culture experiences profound cultural fragmentation; we are huddling together in ever-tighter ethnic, cultural, and professional tribes. What if the church worked harder than ever to overcome these overwhelming forces of cultural fragmentation and disintegration? Why are government agencies and political groups sponsoring culture festivals, and not churches? In Fort Wayne, Indiana, a group of pastors, priests, and rabbis gathers parishioners to conduct "healing the land" rituals after every racial crime or anti-Semitic incident. They go to the spot where the incident took place to succor and suffer the censorship of human decency.

The postdenominational church is taking various forms: independent churches (many Pentecostal and charismatic, but increasing numbers of independent Presbyterians, Lutherans, etc.), associations (Association of Evangelical Churches, Evangelical Presbyterian Association), megachurches (many of whom are functioning more and more as denominations used to, such as the Willow Creek Assocation), and what Kent R. Hunter calls "P.D.W.'s" (Post-Denominational Wanna-bes), which refers to those within denominations who have either divorced themselves from denominational concerns, are disinterested in denominational affairs, or are leading their individual churches toward new structures.[97]

DON'T DO NORMAL ~ One of the worst insults you can hurl at postmoderns is to accuse them of being "normal." Postmoderns don't "do normal." They try *not* to be part of the crowd. Mr. and Mrs. Normal have no place here.

Postmoderns "do ab-normal." Postmoderns "do morph." Postmodern culture has declared war on *Reader's Digest* blandness and *Main Street* averages. Why else are our foods showing higher spice levels? Americans use 68% more spices today than a decade ago; red pepper alone rose 105%, basil 190%, over the last 10 years.[98]

This is one of the greatest problems the church—"the bland leading the bland"—is facing. Too many sermons fall easily into the broad brackets of the nauseatingly normal. Too many churches are filled with pastors and people doing formula church—this in a culture where travel has become a quest for the quaint, a searching for that pot of gold at the end of the rainbow, of the quixotic.

A scientific study of eccentrics found that a little peculiarity is good for your mind, body, and soul. Normality is less healthful. The scientists also found that there are more eccentrics per capita in the Minneapolis–St. Paul region than anywhere else in the United States. Really? Not Montana—the Last Best Place to Hide, the Great Escape State, where the new state motto is "At least our cows are sane" or "Welcome to Montana: It's Where You're Wanted"?

> Nobody goes there anymore—it's too crowded.
>
> Yogi Berra

"ALL LABELS ARE LIBELS" ~ Do you remember how the TV program *Crossfire* begins? "The one on the left is . . . the one on the right is. . . ." There are more choices to life than left and right. The only way this kind of left-versus-right works is if the show is more amusement—shouts, insults, homilies—than informative.

Postmoderns are labelphobic. They resent being drawn into positions and perspectives that don't make left-right sense. Marketing-savvy and weary from ads that are everywhere, even on their textbook covers (classrooms news broadcasts are wrapped around commercials), their bull detectors are highly refined and always on. When they hear themselves tagged, they hear it as "Duck, you're in the crosshairs!" Take Andrew Sullivan, former senior editor at the *New Republic* magazine: an English-born, working-class, Harvard-educated, pro-life, devout-Catholic, gay, intellectual Republican. It *is* getting harder and harder to slot people into neat categories.

And there's a reason. The ideologies of modernity are either exhausted (conservatism) or expired (liberalism/socialism). The right and the left are coming to look more and more alike. US Senator Daniel Patrick Moynihan's "Iron Law of Emulation" has taken effect: Institutions or ideologies in conflict over periods of time come to resemble one another.

> All of a sudden you're like a trunk going through an airport, covered in stickers. I think I've spent most of my life pulling off stickers.
>
> Actress/Pairpont lamp collector
> Kim Basinger[99]

Postmodern discipleship is fuzzy. It blurs sharp distinctions; it entails mess and contradictions. In terms of liberal and conservative, theologically speaking, the moment has come to move on. To acquiesce in either is to get trapped in mazes of bureaucracy and brutality.

The church is a place where the theologically unclassifiable can feel at home. Postmoderns are temperamentally allergic to "fitting in." They want to "fit together," but not fit neatly into any envelope. In fact, it is a badge of postmodernity to do things the way you're *not* supposed to do them.[100]

The irrelevancies of putting fences and signs around our theologies is more apparent with each new study. Nancy Ammerman, for example, has found that theological categories have very little to do with how well people are dealing with changing demographics and economics. More important than whether a congregation is liberal or conservative theologically, she learned, is "its willingness to use the resources of its theological tradition to help it interpret the situation. Among the 23 churches we studied, the best example of a congregation that was able to become interracial in response to community changes was a theologically conservative church."[101]

The modern church's proliferation of ideological caucuses shows its death grip on the old categories, which helps explain why heresy-hunting has once again become the church's favorite indoor sport. Those who continue juggling old labels in the 21st century, however, will end up with hands as bloody and useless as those who juggle chain saws.

> I will go on adventuring, changing, opening my mind and my eyes, refusing to be stamped or stereotyped.
>
> Writer Virginia Woolf
> at age 52

Some churches are already holding services of repentance and reconciliation: repentance for labeling others, and reconciliation attempts to "accept one another, then, just as Christ accepted you" (Rom. 15:7 NIV). For example, Boomers and Busters face off at each other and repent of false labels and tags (such as "slackers" for Busters, "selfish" for Boomers).

Pre-screenings of *The Truman Show* revealed that two kinds of people came out of the theaters: those that got it, and those that didn't. The basic division in the church of Jesus Christ today is between those who get it and those who don't. These are about as close to genuine labels as anyone can get.

Until a few years ago, it gnawed away at me that I didn't fit in anywhere theologically. The left doesn't want me, since I critique liberal theology as sheer ideology. But the right doesn't want me either, since I critique conservative faith as religiosity more than piety. One day I realized that "right" and "left" are the static, sedentary categories of an establishment. Only an establishment mind-set thinks in terms of left and right. But they are not the only categories. A movement mentality is not "Are you left or right?" but rather "Are you at the front, or at the rear?"

INDIGENOUS WORSHIP ~ The church of Jesus Christ is now a non-Western church in terms of where the energy, new life, creativity, and growth exist. In 1960, 30% of evangelical churches were in non-Western nations; by 1997 that figure became 70%. The evangelical wing of the Protestant movement is a global phenomenon.[102]

How well do we really know our non-Western sisters and brothers? It is up to the non-Western church to learn new and indigenous languages, liturgies, music, and learn *from* them.

I use the phrase "indigenous worship" over "contemporary worship" intentionally. Contemporary worship basically means either "Boomer worship" or "what's-happening-now" worship. When worship is indigenous, it swells from the waters in which it is brought to life. Indigenous worship is incarnation, not imitation or replication. It is ministry by embodiment, not ministry by mimicry.

The problem with both "contemporary worship" and liturgical fundamentalism (which is to worship exactly the way our ancestors worshiped at some frozen moment of time) is that both are really displacement activities, a way of avoiding the real issues, the real problems, the real world.

When Jesus prayed, he didn't pray "in general." He prayed specifically about historical and personal issues relevant to his time and day. When he taught, he did not communicate in general, but in particular. Can we do the same?

INCREASE YOUR DIVERSITY IQ ~ A key measure of our ability to minister in the future will be this: Can we function among people of great difference? Can we foster contrarian thinking? Difference is not deviance. An ethic of alterity regards difference as positive, not negative. The global church of Jesus Christ needs more, not fewer, "body parts."

God must love diversity. God made an infinite variety of everything. C. S. Lewis once said that the one prayer God does not answer is "encore." God does not like copies.

"Different from" does not mean "better than" or "inferior to." Postmoderns celebrate uniqueness. Is your church celebrating the differentness of your heritage? Do your people know what it means that you're Reformed, or Roman Catholic, or Wesleyan, or free church? A loss of tradition means the impossibility of transformation. Churches of the Postmodern Reformation can find new imaginative worlds to claim inside the old ones, Chinese-box style, if only we learn to leverage our heritage.

Here is a little diversity IQ quiz:

1. How high is your theological diversity IQ? A mother once described how her three children responded to a big spiderweb in the garden:

- The first child examined the web and expressed wonder at how the spider wove it.
- The second child worried about where the spider was hiding.
- The third child exclaimed, "Oh, look! A trampoline!"

When those first Pentecost Christians were swept up in "the drunkenness of things being various"—to use the marvelous phrasing of poet Louis Mac-Neice—was not the church founded with a high diversity IQ?

2. How high is your economic-class diversity IQ? Can your church bring together for common experiences people high on the hog and people who have never even seen a hog? Is your church a microcosm of the economic macrocosm around you? Church growth (or what is better called "kingdom growth") in postmodern culture is not based on the "homogenous principle" but the "heterogenous principle."

3. How high is your geographic diversity IQ? Test it out with this: "You might be a Yankee if . . ."

- You don't know what a moon pie is.
- You've never, ever eaten Okra.
- You think grits are picked from trees.
- You think barbecue is a verb meaning "to cook outside."
- You don't have doilies, and you certainly don't know how to make one.
- You can't spit out the car window without pulling over to the side of the road and stopping.
- You don't know anyone with two first names (JoeBob, KayBob, Billy-Bob, BobBob).
- You think "Remington Action Scrubber" is an oven cleaner.

4. How high is your sociological diversity IQ? Postmoderns come from unconventional family lives. The average middle-aged adult today has more parents than children. At Father's Day, about half the kids make cards for uncles, grandfathers, or "special friends."

For your church to be "family friendly" means something different from nuclear-family friendly. There are many different kinds of families today: child-less-couple families (one of the fastest-growing trends in demography), single-person households, blended families, one-parent families, families headed by women (which now stand at an unparalleled 29% of all households).

Is your church reaching these people? What do you think it is like for singles to worship/meet/exercise/play in a space called the "Family Life Center"? Can the church stress the importance of multiple parenting of children while not making an idol of the nuclear family?

The 21st century will witness more and more female-headed families and people who live alone. The Trends Institute says that by 2005, single adults will account for more than half the adult population. Already singles are becoming one of the dominant baby-boom household types. One in five householders aged 45 to 54 lives alone—making the singles segment of the church's ministry one of the most important missions in postmodern culture. Catholics and Jews have the highest percentages of never-marrieds (25%); Pentecostals have the highest percentages of divorced or separated church attenders (14%).[103]

Yet the church in North America is aging, its missing components being young, single adults and younger-to-middle-aged childless couples. The church is made up of disproportionate numbers of empty-nesters and widowed persons. Is your church discovering new ways of "making family" and discovering how rich the niche of singles ministry can be? Or is your church nostalgic for the family of the '50s?[104] Within a few years there will be more step-families than birth families. How open is your church to these people? Couples without children already make up nearly a third of all adults—how many do you have? How involved is your church in the co-parenting movement (childless relatives and friends picking up the slack for working moms and dads)?

It is not just lay leadership that has lost one or two generations. Ordained leadership in mainline denominations is similarly homogenous. Only 2% of ordained leadership in the Episcopal Church is 35 or under. Only 8% of active clergy in the Lutheran churches is 35 or under. Only 9% of Presbyterian clergy appears to be under 40.[105]

5. How high is your ethnic identity IQ? Are you taking ethnic identity for granted and at the same time making much of it? Making much of ethnic identity, either negative or positive, without the double ring of taking it for granted can lead to "identity politics," which is another name for racism. Showing the way ethnic identity can lead us astray is cultural historian Walter Benn Michaels, whose book exploring "identitarianism" warns against trying to explain "what we do" and "what we mean" in terms of "who we are."[106]

TEAM OPPOSITES ~ Gerald Hirshberg, the president of Nissan Design International, hires people in pairs—not pairs of likes, but pairs of opposites. Management guru Tom Peters offers his personal hiring principle: "I seek out the best, slightly offbeat talent I can find, then I give them the best tools in the world and tell them to go play/explore in the markets. What else can I do?"[107]

Physicist Henry Margenau uses the term *onta* to describe individual elements that merge with one another to become something more than the sum of the two. When matter and energy join as a powerful new One, the resulting onta entities "defy ordinary intuition." This is also what happens when opposites are teamed together to work on a problem or project. Isn't this what Jesus did when choosing his disciples? His TeamNet was comprised of a motley mix of individuals who didn't "fit in," but who "fit together."

When scholars study the inner workings of "creativity," what stands out over and over again is the ability to put together outlandish, even opposing ideas and inventions, technologies, and thoughts. When 58 of the world's most creative geniuses were studied—including Einstein, Picasso, and Mozart—there emerged one common denominator: *All* breakthroughs occurred when "two or more opposites were conceived simultaneously, existing side by side—as equally valid, operative and true." In the face of accusations of illogic, insanity, or impossibility, creative people consciously embraced "antithetical elements and developed these into integrated entities and creations."[108]

PLANT GLOCAL CHURCHES ~ If you live in major urban centers such as New York, Los Angeles, Miami, Chicago, San Francisco, or Seattle, you are already living in a morphed USAmerica. The majority of preschoolers in Hawaii, New Mexico, and Texas—and soon in Arizona, Louisiana, Maryland, Mississippi, and New York—are minorities.[109] When the Boy Scouts of America discovered that 70% of youth growth from 1996 to 2000 is among minorities and urban families, this traditionally white and middle-class group decided to aggressively recruit minorities and urban kids.

Can we begin planting intentional glocal churches that reflect diverse, urban cultures of the 21st century? This does not mean an end to monocultural congregations. But it does mean that we must plant glocal congregations faster than we have been doing. In postmodern culture, racial diversity is the norm. Isn't it time racial diversity became the norm in the church as well? The fact of exclusivity in the church and inclusivity in the culture suggests something is awry. Isn't exclusivity as out of place in the Postmodern Reformation church as it is out of place in heaven?

> When everyone agrees, somebody is not thinking.
>
> Gen. George S. Patton

Some glocal churches are already here. There are many examples in the Southern Baptist Convention (SBC) alone, according to Charles L. Chaney, vice president of the North American Mission Board. Among them are Northwest Baptist Church in Miami, which Pastor Jim Summer calls an "international church," and Armitage Avenue Baptist Church in Chicago, where Charles Lyons is pastor. Chaney says that well over 6,000 SBC congregations worship in any of 106 languages other than English.[110]

SYNTHESIZE, DON'T SYNCRETIZE ~ One Sunday in December, the minister focused his "Children's Time" on the meaning of Advent. Speaking to the assembled kids sitting in a circle, he asked, "So, before we light this candle, can anyone tell me why we are lighting it?"

A child raised her hand and said, "Because it's the last day of Advent?"

"No, that's not it," the pastor replied. "Does anyone else know?"

The children were quiet for a moment. Then one boy blurted out, "Because it's Chanukah!"[111]

Postmoderns attend schools that celebrate Hanukkah, Kwanza (an African-American festival), and St. Lucia's Day (a Swedish festival) as well as Christmas.

Swiss theologian Hans Küng argues that the two greatest threats to the church are sectarianism and syncretism. A key temptation of the future is designer spirituality: cooking up your own religion to taste. Examples already exist in the form of New Age spirituality, which morphs different faith traditions into one giant stew (or spew, depending on who does the mixing). Morphing can easily move from synthesis to syncretism.

As Western dominance wanes and Islam swells around the world, there will be a tendency to splice Christ onto a diced Hinduism or sliced Buddhism or minced whatever. (It is perhaps easier to do this with Buddhism than with any other religion because Buddhism is not technically a theistic faith, but a wisdom system.) "Zen Buddhist Christians" are not only numerous, but have become a veritable publishing industry in their own right.[112] Fran Peavey, president of Friends of the Ganges, confesses to being "a Buddhist-Jewish-Protestant-Hindu-Muslim."[113]

There are now "Muslim-Christians" and "Adventist-Islamicists" who profess to be able to graft Jesus onto their bodies of belief.[114] Civil rights activist Benjamin Chavis protested the removal of his clergy credentials after he converted to the Nation of Islam: "My foundation is Christian. I am not turning against the church. I'm not turning against Jesus. I still have Jesus in my heart. Islam has given me a context to live Jesus."[115]

It is one thing to include Native American rites within Christian celebrations. It is quite another to commandeer Native American practices and use them as part of the Christian faith. Can one establish links without unifying the differences? Can we learn to live out our mutual ministries within a world of differences?

> Diversity without unity makes about as much sense as dishing up flour, sugar, water, eggs, shortening, and baking-powder on a plate and calling it a cake.
>
> Author/chairman of ServiceMaster
> C. William Pollard[116]

My religious home is Christianity, particularly Wesleyan Christianity. But a religious home need not be a religious prison. My tribe no longer offers Sunday night services, so I often find myself worshiping at Pentecostal churches on Sunday evening (and getting called a "Methecostal"). I don't trust my Christmas Eve to anyone but the Episcopalians, Romans, and Greek Orthodox, because at that time my soul craves the high pageantry of the eucharistic liturgy, not the low pageantry of the parading children's circus. What would it be like for the church to guide postmoderns in their religious morphing, to multiple-track people's faith journeys and faith communities with an emphasis more on the fulfilling than on the fulfillment?

MAKE PALS ~ The creation of PALS may point the way home. Harvard's Rosabeth Moss Kanter has coined the phrase "PALs" to describe how companies around the world are "pooling, allying, and linking." Elsewhere they are called "networks" or "joint ventures" or "strategic partnerships" or "R&D consortia." But economic entities understand that they need protectors, alliances, liaisons, and strategic partnerships (PALS again) if they are to fulfill their mission.[117] The greatest achievements of the future will be accomplished through the art of creative collaboration.[118]

The church needs to make PALs—with other denominations, with other faith traditions, and even with some unexpected entities, some of whom might have been adversaries in the past. One such entity could be a Global PAL along the lines of the United Nations in which, as two futurists have envisioned it, "a computerized 'World Heart'" would "monitor outbreaks of conflict and human suffering and recommend actions of the world's religious leaders to take."[119]

Ironically, one of the best PALS religious institutions can have is with the government—especially state and local welfare departments. Thanks to a provision in the 1996 welfare reform law called "charitable choice," the 260,000 church congregations in the United States can now solicit government funds directly without having to set up charitable subsidiaries. Churches can now receive government funding directly—without having to take down their crosses or remove their literature from the waiting room. It is so difficult to believe this is possible that I am still shaking my head: it had just become legal for US business corporations to make philanthropic gifts.[120]

Black churches are leading the way in making PALS with Uncle Sam. Buster Soares's First Baptist Community Development Corporation of Somerset, New Jersey, knows how to use partners in the formation of CDCs (community development corporations). In his 900-acre urban neighborhood that is enlarging all the time, Soares has a staff person paid for by the governor of New Jersey, an FBCDC Credit Union (with Summit Bank as partner), a $150,000 distance learning center (with Bell Atlantic as partner), an employment training center (with Johnson & Johnson as partner), a real estate venture (with another bank as partner), an inmate assimilation and training program (with the State of New Jersey as partner), and on and on.[121]

Global corporations make as good a partner as governments sometimes. The Community of Joy, North America's largest Lutheran church, is now building a 200-acre, $300 million campus in Glendale, Arizona. According to pastor Walt Kallestad, it will have in addition to the church a water theme park, two schools, a college, a hotel, senior housing development, a memorial garden and mortuary, and a conference center. But it is being achieved through corporate donations and partnerships with Shasta Pools, Shamrock Foods, McDonald's Corporation, Eldorado Holdings, US West, Baptist Health Systems, and Aid Association for Lutherans Insurance.

Are you right now forging strategic partnerships between your church and indigenous churches and ministries around the world for a specific mission project? Are you right now involving your people directly in alliances and liaisons with other partners? Pastors who are good PALS and teach others how to be PALS will be the most successful leaders of this emerging world.

My favorite PALS story comes from the Second World War, as told by David G. Myers.

> With Nazi submarines sinking ships faster than the Allied forces could replace them, the troop ship SS *Dorchester* steamed out of New York harbor with 904 men headed for Greenland. Among those leaving anxious

families behind were four chaplains, Methodist preacher George Fox, Rabbi Alexander Goode, Catholic priest John Washington, and Reformed Church minister Clark Poling. Some 150 miles from their destination, U-456 caught the *Dorchester* in its crosshairs. Within moments of a torpedo's impact, reports Lawrence Elliott, stunned men were pouring out from their bunks as the ship began listing. With power cut off, the escort vessels, unaware of the unfolding tragedy, pushed on in the darkness. On board, chaos reigned as panicky men came up from the hold without life jackets and leaped into overcrowded lifeboats.

When the four chaplains made it up to the steeply sloping deck, they began guiding the men to their boat stations. They opened a storage locker, distributed life jackets, and coaxed the men over the side. In the icy, oil-smeared water, Private William Bednar heard the chaplains preaching courage and found the strength to swim until he reached a life raft. Still on board, Grady Lark watched in awe as the chaplains handed out the last life jacket, and then, with ultimate selflessness, gave away their own. As Lark slipped into the waters he saw the chaplains standing—their arms linked—praying, in Latin, Hebrew, and English. Other men, now serene, joined them in a huddle as the *Dorchester* slid beneath the sea.[122]

THE KILLING FUTURIBLE ~ Blood is going to be shed over the events outlined in this chapter. If the fault lines of culture become the front lines of ministry, as we have argued, this front line will need to become a DMZ—demilitarized zone. Neo-Nazis, radical constitutional reformers, maverick militias, and pseudo-Christian supremacists—a loose network involving some 5 to 12 million people—will oppose with all they have much of what has been described here.[123] People in Rwanda, Afghanistan, and the former Yugoslavia are already fighting ethnic wars to the death.[124]

We must be careful not to overstate the morphing going on. Interracial marriages may be up dramatically, but they still make up less than 3% of all married couples. Entrenched patterns of housing segregation persist, an ugly demonstration of the cold-shouldering sympathy extended to this futurible, even among "liberals." Signs of an emerging multicultural society can easily be exaggerated, especially if the music venue is the only one considered. Discontinuities and dividedness will be with us for a long time.

The power of hate is what leads Protestant Ian Paisley to call Catholic mothers "incubators for Rome." If anyone still doubts the power of first-hate, remember this: Mixed race marriages were still illegal in some states in 1968. Diminishments of vigilance about how we treat the "other" are chased off in the tightening crosshairs of hate-at-first-sight groups.

say what? 1. Create a culturegram: full name/full ethnic background/full faith background/languages spoken/favorite pastimes and hobbies/most important book read/place you most like to be/current position/family. What would you add or subtract from a culturegram?

2. Discuss Mel Kernahan's belief that "Paradise is in the eye of the beholder with a return ticket."[125]

3. If respect needs to be expressed at every point in the church's life, if everyone deserves respect regardless of who or what they are, what are the implications for the church of the 21st century?

4. Listen to some global music and discuss the world-beat sound that blends various ethnic sounds with diverse musical genres. Find out if anyone in your group owns some old Santana albums—the trailblazing band that pioneered world-beat music.

5. Discuss the claim by Samuel P. Huntington that "the next world war, if there is one, will be a war between civilizations."[126] To help the discussion, you may wish to have someone review his book *The Clash of Civilizations and the Remaking of World Order* (New York: Simon & Schuster, 1997) or read his abbreviated argument in *Foreign Affairs* (Summer 1993) that the biggest conflicts of the new world will be cultural—not economic or political. Here is his position in a nutshell:

> Civilization-consciousness is increasing; conflict between civilizations will supplant ideological and other forms of conflict as the dominant global form of conflict; international relations, historically a game played out within Western civilization, will increasingly be de-Westernized and become a game in which non-Western civilizations are actors and not simply objects; successful political, security and economic international institutions are more likely to develop within civilizations than across civilizations; conflicts between groups in different civilizations will be more frequent, more sustained and more violent than conflicts between groups in the same civilization.[127]

6. There are times to celebrate difference and times to celebrate commonness. Have we gone too far in acknowledging gender difference, as if the sexes were from different planets (e.g., John Gray's *Men Are from Mars, Women Are from Venus*)? Novelist Dorothy L. Sayers once wrote, "The first thing that strikes the careless observer is that women are unlike men. They are 'the opposite sex' (though why 'opposite' I do not know; what is the 'neighboring sex'?). But the fundamental thing is that women are more like men than anything else in the world."[128] Discuss the two approaches to male-female relationships.

7. For an example of literary morphing, read the collaboration of Dave Barry and 12 other million-selling authors called *Naked Came the Manatee*.[129] Barry wrote the first chapter, then passed it to the next author, and so on down the line.

8. The tradition of the "talking circle," mentioned earlier, is part of the Hopi culture in the US Southwest. When there are problems with relationships, the elders separate the men from the women. The groups meet separately and talk about the issues that are bruising and dividing them. Then, when the timing is right, the men and women come together and affirm each other. The men ask apologies and state their issues; vice versa, the women. The evening can be very emotional and cathartic. Why not try a "talking circle" in your church?

9. Scientists tell us that there is less genetic difference between all the races of the human species than there is in *one* social group of Upland gorillas. What does it mean that we humans are the same and yet we are very different?

10. Julius Lester observed in the *Washington Post* (May 1995) that "America has never had an open and honest discussion about its racial dilemma. We—blacks and whites—argue, accuse, attack, mistrust, disparage, but we do not often make the effort to see with the other's eyes. We do not make ourselves available for the grace that would allow us to modify or even discard ideas and opinions that no longer work and may even be hurtful."

Would you agree or disagree with this observation?

11. Have a member of your group read and review *40 Ways to Raise a Nonracist Child* by Barbara Mathias and Mary Ann French (New York: Harper-Collins, 1997).

12. Listen to the song "A Picture Perfect World" by the gospel singing group Avalon. How can your church concretely make the world more "picture perfect"?

13. Have someone read and review Chinese novelist Gish Jen's *Mona in the Promised Land* (New York: Knopf, 1996), in which she explores how inhabiting that word *American* requires continual self-reinvention.

14. Review and reflect on Michael Jackson's *Black or White* music video, which used the same Morph 2.0 computer program as the editors of *Time* employed.

15. Assign for review and discussion Susan Gubar's book *Racechanges: White Skin, Black Face in American Culture* (New York: Oxford Univ. Press, 1997).

16. Explore Frank den Oudsten's video sculpture "Floating Identities" (1995), as found in the book and CD-ROM by Hans-Peter Schwarz, *Media-Art-History* (New York: Prestel/Biblios, 1997).

17. What do you think of the "Team Harmony Pledge," which begins, "I pledge from this day onward to do my best to interrupt prejudice and to stop

those who, because of hate, would hurt, harass, or violate the civil rights of anyone."

18. Study Luke's account of the day of Pentecost (Acts 2). In what sense is Pentecost a reversal of Babel, and in what sense is it not? What is the significance in the fact that the apostles speak in the vernacular of the people rather than the people speaking the one language the apostles speak?

19. Tom Sine, a consultant in futures research and planning, argues that we must come to "view the church less as a building we attend once a week or an institution we maintain . . . and more as an intergenerational, multicultural, organic community where we also happen to worship and celebrate our Christian faith, . . . praying that God's kingdom will come and God's will be done on earth as it is in heaven."[130] Do you agree? How far along is your church?

20. You can find 25 of the "amen, amen" sayings of Jesus in John's gospel. Have each member of your group read a different "amen, amen" saying, and discuss why Jesus may have begun his statements this way. John 1:51; 3:3, 5, 11; 5:19, 24, 25; 6:26, 32, 47, 53; 8:34, 51, 58; 10:1, 7; 12:24; 13:16, 20, 21, 38; 14:12; 16:20, 23; 21:18.

21. Former President Jimmy Carter has stated that "most church members—including me—rarely reach out to people who are different from us or less fortunate. Quite often my Sunday school class will say, 'Why don't we take up a collection and give a nice Thanksgiving meal to a poor family?' The next question is: 'Who knows a poor family?' Nobody does. We have to call the welfare office."[131]

Has President Carter accurately described your church?

22. If possible, have everyone purchase a copy of *Interrace* magazine, published in Atlanta, and discuss its presentation of interracial and multiracial couples, families, and singles.

23. Assign different members of your group an in-language cable offering to experience and explain: for example, the Filipino Channel, Native American Nations, TV Asia, World African Network. If you are in Los Angeles, watch the #1 station for viewers aged 18 to 34 during the 6 p.m. time slot: Univision-owned KMEX-TV, channel 34, which broadcasts exclusively in Spanish.

24. Get from your local library the book by Peggy Gillespie, with photographs by Gigi Kaeser, *Of Many Colours: Portraits of Multiracial Families* (Amherst: Univ. of Massachusetts Press, 1998), and pass it around during one of your discussions for people to put faces on the people they are talking about.

25. Watch the video of the Brooklyn Tabernacle Choir's Madison Square Garden concert. What does it tell you about the 21st-century church? Order it from Warner Alliance (615-214-1460).

26. Have someone bring to the group the Eurythmics song "This City Never Sleeps." Discuss what these musicians mean when they sing, "You know there's so many people living in this house/And I don't even know their names."

27. Look in your closet. Count how many countries are on the labels hanging in your closet and report back. Did anyone have less than a dozen?[132]

28. Celebrate ethnic cuisine in your church. Give people as many taste plunges as you can as you travel around the world where your church is investing in missions and ministry. Take them through *sanaan, dundicut, tien tsin, ancho, chipolte,* and *jalapeno peppers.*

now what? See the Net Notes in http://www.soultsunami.com

NOTES

1. Professor Basher is also an active scholar in the field of religion and cyberspace. See her http://www.muc.edu/~brashebe/.

2. The composite image was produced by morphing features of Anglo-Saxon, Middle Eastern, African, Asian, southern European, and Hispanic. See *Time*, Special Issue (Fall 1993).

3. Janine Lopiano-Misdom and Joanne De Luca, *Street Trends: How Today's Alternative Youth Cultures Are Creating Tomorrow's Mainstream Markets* (New York: HarperBusiness, 1997).

4. See Kevin Kelly, "What Would McLuhan Say?" an interview with Derrick de Kerckhove, Canadian humanities scholar/Marshall McLuhan successor at University of Toronto's St. Michael's College, *Wired* (Oct 1996): 149. For an excellent look at how concepts of "self" are changing, see Walter Truett Anderson, *The Future of the Self: Inventing the Postmodern Person* (New York: Jeremy P. Tarcher/Putnam, 1997). Anderson is especially good at probing how online identities in cyberspace are altering our concepts of what is "real."

5. See Sherry Turkle, *Life on the Screen: Identity in the Age of the Internet* (New York: Simon & Schuster, 1995).

6. The word *America* is a proper noun, but it is the name of a continent, not a country. There are many "Americas" out there—Latin America, South America, Canadian America—just as there are many "United States" out there—the United States of Brazil, the United States of Mexico, the United States of Argentina. It is for this reason that "USAmerica" is used throughout this book. For a fuller discussion of these issues and more, see Sebastian de Grazia, *A Country with No Name: Tales from the Constitution* (New York: Pantheon, 1997).

7. Lawrence H. Fuchs, *The American Kaleidoscope: Race, Ethnicity and the Civic Culture* (Hanover, NH: Wesleyan Univ. Press, 1990), 492.

8. With thanks to Kenneth L. Woodward for pointing me to this reference. See his "A Streetcar Named Diversity," *Speaking of Values* 7 (Summer 1997): 1, 4, 7. Also Ada Maria Isasi-Diaz, *Mujerista Theology: A Theology for the Twenty-First Century* (Maryknoll, NY: Orbis Books, 1996).

9. The 1996 Current Population Survey, as reported in Berna Miller, "Foreign-Born Diversify," *American Demographics* (July 1997): 33.

10. Ian Morrison, *The Second Curve: Managing the Velocity of Change* (New York: Ballantine Books, 1996), 16.

11. Watch one segment of *The Real World* on MTV and you will see this in action.

12. *Stimulus* (Spring 1997): 3.

13. See David Deutsch, *The Fabric of Reality* (New York: Viking/Penguin, 1997), and Lee Smolin, *The Life of the Cosmos* (New York: Oxford Univ. Press, 1997), who prefers the term "multi-universe."

14. With thanks to pastor Paul Sweet of the California/Nevada Annual Conference (United Methodist) for this reference.

15. *Details* (Aug 1997): 39.

16. Engineers have already proposed designs to make Mars into a place with breathable air and drinkable water within the 21st century at a reasonable cost.

17. Emmanuel Levinas, "Jean Wahl: Neither Having Nor Being," in his *Outside the Subject* (Stanford, CA: Stanford Univ. Press, 1994), 77.

18. W. N. Herbert, *Forked Tongue* (Newcastle upon Tyne: Bloodaxe, 1994), 93.

19. The new physics is the primary intellectual underpinning of and/also culture. The science of Albert Einstein, as interpreted by Sir Arthur Eddington's 1927 Gifford Lectures and the literary modernism of William Empson, pioneered both/and thinking among the intelligentsia. See Jonathan Bate, "Words in a Quantum World," *TLS, Times Literary Supplement* (25 July 1997): 14–15.

20. Salman Rushdie, *East, West: Stories* (London: Jonathan Cape, 1994), 211.

21. The evening I watched, Maher got actress Sarah Bernhardt, actor George Hamilton, former Governor Jerry Brown, and a fundamentalist Christian together. For "alterna-fiddling," see the CD by Ashley MacIsaac, *How Are You Today?* (Hollywood, CA: A&M Records, 1995).

22. Allison James, "Cooking the Books: Global or Local Identities in Contemporary British Food Cultures?" in *Cross-Cultural Consumption: Global Markets, Local Realities*, ed. David Howes (New York: Routledge, 1996), 77.

23. "The movement of people to the Pentecostal Church has to do with this crisis, in our families, our country, our world. Churches that respond to the pain, agony and confusion this brings about will grow. Churches that do not, that continue as if it was business as usual, will diminish" (*Los Angeles Times* [1 Aug 1996]: E10).

24. Gary Hamel, "Reinventing the Basis for Competition," in *Rethinking the Future: Rethinking Business Principles, Competition, Control and Complexity, Leadership, Markets and the World*, ed. Rowan Gibson (Sonoma, CA: Nicholas Brealey, 1997), 89.

25. John Naisbitt, "From Nation States to Networks," in *Rethinking the Future*, 216–17.

26. David Hollinger, *Postethnic America: Beyond Multiculturalism* (New York: Basic Books, 1995). See also Michael Lind, *The Next American Nation* (Monroe, LA: Free Press, 1995).

27. A hyphenate is someone who lives two or more ethnic identities at once. There are also triple hyphenates, quadruple hyphenates, quintuple hyphenates, etc.

28. As quoted by Leah Lin, "The Church of Lenny Kravitz," *Axcess* 3, no. 6 (1995): 72–73.

29. Lynn Norment, "Am I Black, White or In Between? Is There a Plot to Create a 'Colored' Buffer Race in America?" *Ebony* (Aug 1995): 112.

30. See ch. 7, "The Cultural Biology of Race," in Lawrence Hirschfeld, *Race in the Making* (Cambridge, MA: MIT Press, 1996), 159–85.

31. Haya El Nasser, "Poll: Whites Increasingly Accept Blacks," *USA Today* (11 June 1997): 1A. The General Social Survey from the University of Chicago's National Opinion Research Center reveals that whites who believe that interracial marriage should be outlawed fell from 59% to 13% between 1963 and 1996. For the movement of the middle class toward the left on issues of race, see Alan Wolfe, *One Nation, After All* (New York: Viking, 1998). For a sampling of African-American attitudes, see the responses to Sherman Miller's "A Black History Month Interracial Love Tale," at www.afrinet.net/~hallh/afrotalk/afrofeb95/0521.html.

32. "One in Four Is a Minority," *Boomer Report* (Jan 1998): 3.

33. A 1991 study showed that 64% of people ages 18–20 approved of interracial marriages. The figure would very likely be much higher now.

34. "Relaxing an Old Taboo," *Newsweek* (15 July 1996): 51.

35. A Fordham University study found that intermarriage rates among New York City Hispanics increased from 36% in 1975 to 48% in 1991: as reported by Kevin Heubusch, "Meet the New Hispanic Family," *American Demographics* (Oct 1996): 29.

36. Joseph Lowery and Amitai Etzioni, "The Place of Race in the Census," *Washington Post Weekly* 14 (16 June 1997): 21; *U.S. News & World Report* (14 July 1997): 22. The most probing and incisive reflection on the census proposal is chapter 1 in Ellis Cose, *Color-Blind: Seeing Beyond Race in a Race-Obsessed World* (New York: HarperCollins, 1997), 1–26. Cose concludes the chapter with the affirmation that "asking whether we should have a new racial category is a trivial question. The infinitely more important question is whether it is possible to divorce any system of racial classification from the practice of racial discrimination" (26).

37. Fred Prinzing, *Mixed Marriages: Responding to Interracial Marriage* (Chicago: Moody Press, 1991).

38. Quoted in Philip Rieff, *The Feeling Intellect: Selected Writings* (Chicago: Univ. of Chicago Press, 1990), 227.

39. Karen S. Peterson, "For Today's Teens, Race 'Not an Issue Anymore,'" *USA Today* (3 Nov 1997): 1–2A.

40. And perhaps even generation. I suspect that some of the biggest battles of the future will be between aging Baby Boomers and coming-of-age Net-Gens. For a contrasting view, see Daniel P. McMurrer and Isabel V. Sawhill, "The Declining Importance of Class," *Opportunity in America* 4 (Apr 1997):1–3. The Web site is www.urban.org.

41. At least this is the forecast of the Trends Research Institute. See "Cold War II: Challenge to Capitalism," *Trends Journal* 7 (Spring 1998): 4–5.

42. See also William Julius Wilson, *When Work Disappears* (New York: Knopf, 1996).

43. See "Wealth Is Overrated and Other Heresies as Pronounced by Peter Drucker," an interview by Kevin Kelly, *Wired* (Mar 1998): 161.

44. Ellen Graham, "Generation Y: When Terrible Twos Become Terrible Teens," *Wall Street Journal* (5 Feb 1997): B1.

45. "What's Race Got to Do with It? Less and Less," *John Naisbitt's Trend Letter* (15 Feb 1996): 4.

46. "U.S. PC Growth," *Trend Letter* (2 Oct 1997): 8.

47. The concept of "upward contempt" is that of William Ian Miller, *The Anatomy of Disgust* (Cambridge: Harvard Univ. Press, 1997).

48. Walter Truett Anderson, *Evolution Isn't What It Used to Be* (New York: W. H. Freeman, 1996), 38.

49. See the introduction, "Thinking Global and Local," in *Articulating the Global and the Local*, ed. Ann Cvetkovich and Douglas Kellner (Boulder, CO: Westview, 1997), 14.

50. This is the argument of Roland Axtmann in Cvetkovich and Kellner, *Articulating the Global and the Local*, 33–54.

51. Michael Barber, *The Learning Game: Arguments for an Education Revolution* (London: Victor Gollancz, 1996), 173.

52. John Andrews, "Culture Wars," *Wired* (May 1995): 136.

53. For the growing influence of English, see Frances Cairncross, *The Death of Distance* (Boston: Harvard Business School, 1997).

54. Samuel P. Huntington, *The Clash of Civilizations and the Remaking of World Order* (New York: Simon & Schuster, 1997), 61–62.

55. H. Chase, "The *Mayhane* or McDonald's—Change in Eating Habits and the Evolution of Fast Food in Istanbul," in S. Zubaida, ed., *Culinary Cultures of the Middle East* (London: Center of Near and Middle Eastern Studies, 1992), 68.

56. Anthropologist Gregory Bateson gave information its classic definition as "any difference that makes a difference." In the Information Age, difference is anyone's #1 asset.

57. This phrase comes from an observation by French mathematician/philosopher Blaise Pascal: "Cleopatra's nose, had it been shorter, the whole face of the world would have been changed."

58. Quoted in Will Hermes, "Pop Goes the Planet," *Utne Reader* (Jan-Feb 1997): 94.

59. For an example, see sociologist Alvin Schmidt, *The Menace of Multiculturalism: Trojan Horse in America* (Westport, CT: Praeger, 1997).

60. Roberto S. Goizueta, "Response to Peter C. Phan," in William Cenkner, ed., *The Multicultural Church: A New Landscape in U.S. Theologies* (New York: Paulist Press, 1996), 135.

61. See Peter Schwartz and Peter Leyden, "The History of the Future, 1980–2020," *Wired* (July 1997): 171. For more on Huntington's views, see also his *The Clash of Civilizations*.

62. Paul R. Spickard, "Christians in Multicultural America," *Christian Scholars Review* (June 1996): 479.

63. As quoted in Win Arn, *The Master's Plan for Making Disciples*: *Every Christian an Effective Witness Through an Enabling Church* (Grand Rapids: Baker Books, 1998).

64. Jim Wallis, *Who Speaks for God?* (New York: Delacorte Press, 1996), 86.

65. Charles R. Page II, *Jesus and the Land* (Nashville: Abingdon Press, 1995), 86.

66. See also Eleanor Heartney, *Critical Condition: American Culture at the Crossroads* (New York: Cambridge Univ. Press, 1997), 55.

67. *Baptist Message* (5 Sept 1996): 6. See also Janet Fishburn, *Confronting the Idolatry of Family: A New Vision for the Household of God* (Nashville: Abingdon Press, 1991), and Leonard I. Sweet, "The Family Ideal, Not Idol," *Homiletics* (Jan-Mar 1996): 35–38.

68. Todd D. Catteau, "Studying the 'Amen, Amen' Sayings of Jesus," *Discipleship Journal* 104 (1998): 20–21.

69. Donaldo Macedo, *Literacies of Power: What Americans Are Not Allowed to Know* (Boulder, CO: Westview, 1994).

70. Harvey Cox, *Religion in the Secular City: Toward a Postmodern Theology* (New York: Simon & Schuster, 1984), 204.

71. John Wesley, "A Plain Account of the People Called Methodist in a Letter to the Rev. Mr. Perronet, Vicar of Shoreham in Kent," in *The Methodist Societies, History, Nature, and Design,* ed. Rupert E. Davis, *The Works of John Wesley* (Nashville: Abingdon Press, 1989), 9:254–55.

72. John Wesley, "The Character of a Methodist," in *The Methodist Societies,* 33.

73. Wesley, "The Character of a Methodist," 35.

74. John Wesley, "Predestination Calmly Considered," in *The Works of John Wesley* (London: Wesleyan Conference Office, 1872; reprint, Grand Rapids: Zondervan, 1958), 10:256.

75. Wesley, "The Character of a Methodist," 34.

76. John Wesley, "Letter to Richard Tompson, 28 June 1755," in *Letters, 1740–1755, The Works of John Wesley* (Oxford: Clarendon Press, 1982), 26:567.

77. John Wesley, "Letter to Samuel Furly, 13 October 1762," in *The Letters of the Rev. John Wesley* (London: Epworth Press, 1931), 4:191.

78. Madeleine L'Engle, *Walking on Water: Reflections on Faith and Art* (Wheaton, IL: Shaw Publishers, 1980).

79. Bill Moyers, *Genesis: A Living Conversation* (New York: Doubleday, 1996); also available in five videocassettes (New York: BDD Audio, 1996).

80. Dean Timothy George of Beeson Divinity School insists that "we do not risk the loss of conviction when we enter into dialogue with those with whom we differ so long as our confidence is not in ourselves but in the God of the gospel who alone makes us 'sufficient' for such a task." See his excellent article "A Theology to Die For" in *Christianity Today* (9 Feb 1998): 49–50.

81. Nelle Morton, *The Journey Is Home* (Boston: Beacon Press, 1985), 202.

82. As quoted in Washington National Cathedral, *Cathedral Age* (Summer 1997): 14–17: With thanks to James A. Harnish of Tampa, FL, for pointing me to this reference.

83. The phrase is that of psychologist Vladimir de Lissovoy.

84. The best denial of the "true for me" doctrine is in Thomas Nagel, *The Last Word* (New York: Oxford Univ. Press, 1997).

85. Kenneth Anderson, "Where No Man Has Gone Before," *TLS, Times Literary Supplement* (3 Jan 1997): 18.

86. Jean François Lyotard, *The Postmodern Condition: A Report on Knowledge* (Minneapolis: Univ. of Minnesota Press, 1984), xxiv.

87. Fernando Pessoa, *Selected Poems*, 2d ed., trans. Jonathan Griffin (New York: Penguin Books, 1982), 15.

88. For those still arguing the exclusivism of the "Or Else," see Harold Netland, *Dissonant Voices: Religious Pluralism and the Question of Truth* (Grand Rapids: Eerdmans, 1991), and D. A. Carson, *The Gagging of God* (Grand Rapids: Zondervan, 1996).

89. For those arguing the inclusivist position, see Clark Pinnock, *A Wideness in God's Mercy: The Finality of Jesus Christ in a World of Religions* (Grand Rapids: Zondervan, 1992), and John Sanders, *No Other Name: An Investigation into the Destiny of the Unevangelized* (Grand Rapids: Eerdmans, 1992). The best short treatment of the difference between pluralism, exclusivism, and inclusivism is Daniel B. Clendenin, "The Only Way," *Christianity Today* (12 Jan 1998): 35–40.

90. John Milton, "Lycidas," in *Complete Poetry and Selected Prose of John Milton* (New York: Modern Library, 1950), 71.

91. John Wesley, "Advice to the People Called Methodists" (1745), in *The Methodist Societies*, 130.

92. See Jonathan Griffin, "Four Poets in One Man," Introduction to Pessoa, *Selected Poems*, 9–23.

93. Jorge Luis Borges, *Labyrinths: Selected Stories and Other Writings*, ed. D. A. Yates and J. E. Irby (New York: Random House, 1984), 285.

94. So argue James Dale Davidson and Lord William Rees-Mogg in *The Sovereign Individual* (New York: Simon & Schuster, 1997).

95. As quoted by David Morris, "The Return of the City-State," *Utne Reader* (Sept-Oct 1994): 80.

96. Henry Grunwald, "Memorandum to Woodrow Wilson," *Time* (14 Nov 1994): 104.

97. Kent R. Hunter, "The Coming of the Post-Denominational Age," *The Church Doctor Report* (Winter 1997): 1, 5.

98. Marvin J. Cetron, Fred J. DeMicco, and John A. Williams, "Restaurant Renaissance: Current and Future Trends in Food Service," *The Futurist* 30 (Jan-Feb 1996): 9.

99. As quoted in *Utne Reader* (July-Aug 1998): 41.

100. See the story on Jim Gross, a 40-year-old developer and entrepreneur in Charlotte, NC, in Irwin Speizer, "The Gross Effect," *Business North Carolina* (Nov 1997): 52ff.: With thanks to Superior Court Judge Jesse B. Caldwell III for alerting me to this article.

101. "Congregations in the Midst of Change: An Interview with Nancy Ammerman," *Christian Century* (15 Jan 1997): 50.

102. These figures come from the World Evangelical Fellowship.

103. Julia Duin, "Singles Have Economic Clout, But Many Remain Unsatisfied," *Insight* 12 (18 Mar 1996): 36.

104. An excellent resource for cross-generational ministries is Diana Garland and Diane Pancoast, *The Church's Ministry with Families* (Dallas: Word Books, 1990).

105. These figures come from Jacqueline Schmitt, "Editorial," *Plumbline* 25 (Winter 1998): 2.

106. Walter Benn Michaels, *Our America: Nativism, Modernism, and Pluralism* (Durham, NC: Duke Univ. Press, 1997).

107. Tom Peters, "Let Chaos Reign," *Forbes ASAP* (26 Aug 1996): 113.

108. Richard Pascale, *Managing on the Edge* (New York: Simon & Schuster, 1990), 110, fn. 87.

109. "Ethnic Marketing," *Boomer Report* (Apr 1998): 2.

110. Charles L. Chaney, "Two Key Words for the 21st Century," *Net Results* 16 (Oct 1996): 24–25.

111. "Cleopas" e-mail (24 Dec 96) at Cleopas55@aol.com.

112. Phyllis Tickle says that "not only do I know a few of them personally, but at least seven or eight whom I don't know published books on the subject in 1994 alone." See Phyllis A. Tickle, *Re-Discovering the Sacred: Spirituality in America* (New York: Crossroad, 1995), 45.

113. "An Interview with Fran Peavey," *EarthLight* 8 (Spring 1998): 12.

114. For more on this, see "Missionaries 'Going Native' in More Ways Than One," *Religion Watch* 12 (Oct 1997): 1–2.

115. As quoted in *Current Thoughts and Trends* 14 (Feb 1998): 3.

116. C. William Pollard, *The Soul of the Firm* (Grand Rapids: Zondervan, 1996), 35–36.

117. Rosabeth Moss Kanter first outlined "PALs" in *When Giants Learn to Dance: Mastering the Challenge of Strategy, Management, and Careers in the 1990s* (New York: Simon & Schuster, 1989), 117–40. More recently see her *World Class: Thriving Locally in the Global Economy* (New York: Simon & Schuster, 1995).

118. An excellent introduction to this subject can be found in Robert Hargrove, *Mastering the Art of Creative Collaboration* (New York: McGraw-Hill, 1998).

119. Richard Kirby and Earl D. C. Brewer, "Temples of Tomorrow: Toward a United Religions Organization," *The Futurist* (Sept-Oct 1994): 27–28.

120. Charitable gifts did not become possible for corporations until 1950.

121. For more information, write Buster Soares for a copy of his prospectus, *First Baptist Church CDC: Renaissance 2000. Building a Community One Family at a Time* (Somerset, NJ: FBCDC, 1997) at 630 Franklin Blvd., Suite 102, Somerset, NJ 08873.

122. David G. Myers, *The Pursuit of Happiness: Who Is Happy and Why* (New York: Morrow, 1992), 196.

123. Neil Earle, "The Christian Identity Crisis," *Plain Truth* 62 (Sept-Oct 1997): 53–57.

124. See most especially Michael Ignatieff, *The Warrior's Honor* (New York: Metropolitan Books, 1998).

125. Kernahan is writing on Polynesia in *White Savages in the South Seas* (London: Verso Books, 1995).

126. Samuel P. Huntington, "The Clash of Civilizations," *Foreign Affairs* 72 (Summer 1993): 39.

127. Huntington, "The Clash of Civilizations," 48.

128. As quoted in Joan Smith, *Different for Girls: How Culture Creates Women* (London: Chatto & Windus, 1997), 166.

129. Carl Hiassen et al., *Naked Came the Manatee, A Novel* (New York: G. P. Putnam's Sons, 1997).

130. Tom Sine, "A New Call for Community for a New Millennium," *Green Cross* 2 (Fall 1996): 25.

131. Jimmy Carter is quoted in *Christian Reader* (July-Aug 1997): 29.

132. The question arises from an observation of missions consultant Paul Borthwick in "The Future of Missions," *Vital Ministry* (July-Aug 1998): 26.

 ife ring #1

IS THIS A GREAT TIME, OR WHAT?

Get Souled Out

THE GOD RUSH

or what?

Come, all you who are thirsty, come to the waters.

—Isaiah 55:1 NIV

COME TO THE WATERS ~ The wind of spiritual awakening is blowing across the waters. Ever try to stop the wind? Spiritual awakening is the cascading of a people with "the knowledge of the glory of the LORD, as the waters cover the sea" (Hab. 2:14).

There is a wind-like quality to the Spirit. It sur-prises us; it takes us where we don't want to go; it is unpredictable; it drives us toward stillness, toward wholeness, toward shelter and safety. Will we trust the wind?

The Holy Spirit is working in a grand way on a global scale in the postmodern waters. Will we come to the waters? Or will we stay on dry ground? Or will we hug harbors?

> I ran aground in a harbor town,
> lost the taste for being free.
> Thank God He sent some gull-chased ship
> to carry me to sea.
>
> Bruce Cockburn[1]

Choose God—and God honors that choice. And one is glorified by one's choice. The Bible uses the language of heaven, the haven of God's influence.

Do not choose God—and God honors that choice. But one is horrified by one's choice. The Bible uses the language of hell, the haven from God's influence.

ON THE SOUL TRAIN ~ Two political philosophers recently introduced their reference volume by arguing that theism plays only a marginal role in the contemporary world.[2]

Hello?! What planet are they living on? What lead-lined cave have they just crawled out of? Have they never heard of Bosnia, or Lebanon, or the West Bank, or Tagorno-Karabakh, or . . .

We are only now realizing how dead wrong scientists like Carl Sagan or secularization theorists like Max Weber or science-fiction writers like Isaac Asimov and Gene Roddenberry actually were. Far from the future being reli-gion-free, the future is more filled with soulprints than ever before.

USAmerica is one of the most religious nations in the developed world. It is also one of the most secular.[3] Al Winseman, a pastor in Omaha, Nebraska, told his congregation, "We are living in a secular society but a spiritual cul-ture." Postmoderns prefer a nonreligious spirituality—a spirituality that is not associated with organized religion.

The double ring can be confusing. On the same day on the same page of the same journal, one headline read "Spiritual Renewal Flourishes" and the companion headline bannered "Religion's Influence May Be Fading."[4] Market researcher and futurist Ron Sellers ranks "Increasing Clashes Between

Science and Religion" as the #2 global trend in religion; third is "Increased Cooperation Between Science and Religion."[5]

Postmodern culture is entheogenic—it continually births the divine within itself. In the aftermath of the soullessness and sullenness of modern life, there is a massive soul search going on, a gusty circulation of spiritual energy throughout the culture. In fact, the entire culture seems to be "On the Soul Train."[6]

> Revival is when God gets tired of being misrepresented and shows up to represent Himself.
>
> Karen Bacon[7]

Sociologists testify to a "widespread turning inward across the land."[8] The Roof Report calls the generation raised during the '50s—one of the most religious periods in American history—a "generation of seekers." Jessica Lipnack and Jeffrey Stamps predict the already-come-to-pass: "The search for soul will accelerate and move from the individual and family to organizations of all sorts and sizes."[9]

The real truth, as journalist Phyllis Tickle points out, is that "first and foremost, we are believers."[10] This culture is one of the most God-besotted cultures in the history of the planet. The waters of superstition rise as high in postmodern culture as anyone could wish. People believe in everything and anything—mind reading, channeling, witches, ESP, crystals, spells, UFOlogy, palmistry, the Tarot deck. In the US, seven persons in 10 believe in angels, five in 10 in UFOs, three in 10 in reincarnation and communication with the dead.[11]

Stephen Carter's widely quoted book *The Culture of Disbelief*[12] has it backward. Postmodern culture is not so much a "culture of disbelief" as a culture of spiritual hungerings and hucksterings. What appears to be a "culture of disbelief" is actually a rejection of traditional religious reasoning in ethical and intellectual and political debate. There is a huge spiritual hunger and at the same time a rejection of Christianity as the kind of spirituality that can slake the spiritual hunger.

> The unsecularization of the world is one of the dominant social facts of life in the late twentieth century.
>
> George Weigel

It is not as if we have not been there before. In his missionary efforts Paul acknowledged that the Athenians were "extremely religious . . . in every way" (Acts 17:22).

Our believers' status is underscored by futurist Faith Popcorn. In an online interview someone asked her this question: "Do you see any icons that have not been toppled, or aren't likely to be?"

Popcorn: "God."

Questioner: "That's it?"

Popcorn: "That is it."[13]

Popcorn goes even further. She argues that "we're at the start of a Great Awakening. A time of spiritual upheaval and religious revival." The difference this time, she contends, is that "there's very little agreement on who or what God is, what constitutes worship, and what this ritualistic outpouring means for the future direction of our civilization."[14] Other writers see us at the headwaters of a great religious revival, a worldwide awakening that will transform everything in its path.[15] The Russian novelist Aleksandr Solzhenitsyn writes that

> If the world has not approached its end, it has reached a major watershed in history, equal in history to the turn from the Middle Ages to the Renaissance. It will demand from us a spiritual blaze. . . . This ascension is similar to climbing onto the next anthropological stage. No one on earth has any other way left but—upward.[16]

William Van Dusen Wishard, president of World Trends Research, contends that the US is "in the midst of the most significant spiritual search our country has ever known." He said,

> This search is seen in the resurgent fundamentalism, in New Age spirituality, in the interest in Eastern thought and religions, and in the rise of cults such as Heaven's Gate. It's seen in TV shows such as "The X-Files." . . . It's seen in those who look to technology such as artificial intelligence for some higher state of being.[17]

For the first time in US history, however, we are in the midst of a massive spiritual awakening that the Christian church is not leading. USAmericans are exhibiting the highest interest in spiritual matters in 50 years, and Christianity is registering the least amount of interest and energy in 50 years.

The percentage of USAmerican adults attending church has remained about the same during the '80s and '90s, with Protestant church membership actually declining. Forty-nine percent of USAmericans attended traditional religious services in 1991, compared with 37% in 1996.[18] Eighty percent of the growth through church-growth principles is through transfer, not conversion. There is *not one* county in the US that has a higher percentage of churched people than a decade ago.

But numbers tell the least of the story. During the 69th General Convention of the Episcopal Church, a waitress at one of the Detroit hotels was comparing the world and national events of the week and all that she had read in the *Detroit Free Press* about the church convention. She commented to a delegate as she served breakfast one morning, "There is something odd going on around here."[19]

Things simply don't add up. Postmoderns are turning their backs on traditional religious expressions and creating new spiritual traditions and do-it-yourself spiritualities.

GREAT SOUL ~ "Great Soul" is the Holy Grail of postmodern culture. Experiences of "good sex" now take a backseat to "good soul" experiences. Postmoderns are hungry, spiritually malnourished. People want to grow spiritually above all else.[20]

The healing and harmonizing of the powers of the soul are what is called "spirituality."[21] In a day when our intellectual and technological intelligence is skyrocketing, but our emotional and spiritual intelligence is flat, the soulful and spiritual become the culture's most sought-after commodity.

> Our current intellectual predicament springs not, as it has been fashionable to say, from the death of God, but from the demise of 19th-century God substitutes.
>
> Philosopher/anthropologist Ernest Gellner[22]

The way the apostle Paul began a sermon, in another deeply "spiritual" time, applies equally as well to Beacon Hill and Silicon Valley as to Mars Hill: "Men of Athens! I see that in every way you are very religious" (Acts 17:22 NIV). The personal is no longer political. The personal is now spiritual. The new soul perspective turns us back to moderation and self-discipline, meditation, mindedness, and wisdom—the training of mind and body and spirit over material accumulation.

But the search for an ever-expanding soul can also be seen as a new acquisitiveness—spiritual growth and creative development for the sake of a better self, friends, family, community, and health. People can want God—but why? To bliss out.

Faith Popcorn summarizes well the core of this awakening: "We're looking for the essence of ourselves—our lost souls."[23] The modern world sucked soul out of life; postmoderns are putting soul back into it. It is not clear whether what is "lost" is the divine or the self, whether "spirituality" is nothing more, or less, than loving God, or loving self; whether the soul's journey is the knowledge of God, or *nosce te ipsum* ("know thyself"). Is the soul to be found in the depths of God, or the depths of the self? Are we looking for God through the wrong end of the telescope?

> The most interesting story of our time ... is emerging in the intersection between the secular and the sacred.
>
> TV journalist Bill Moyers[24]

Princeton sociologist Robert Wuthnow confesses to being "pessimistic about the future of the local congregation," partly because "much of the searching for spirituality is quite shallow and self-interested. It's focused on the by-products of spirituality, not on really having a relationship with God."[25]

Similarly, Craig Dykstra of the Lilly Endowment wonders whether our "spirituality craze" is "really an inchoate yearning for a kind of life that dives down beneath the surface into richer, truer levels of meaning and reality" (which is what he suspects is going on), or whether it is really a craving for "a community of confirmation, one that acknowledges neither the necessity of discipline nor the power of sins confessed and sufferings shared." If the latter is what is happening, then "our search is not for salvation, it is for cosmic affirmation."[26]

Whatever the answer to these questions, the great untold story of the '90s is not the great Internet land rush. It is the great global God rush. How serious are we to put bells and whistles on the soul? Four out of 10 of us meet in some kind of small group on a regular basis for purposes of experiencing God and deepening our spiritual life.

As with any gold rush, there is a lot of fool's gold out there. In his chapter on "Religion and Spirituality," talk-radio host Art Bell ("America's voice in the night") has the hokum and hysterical as coequal subheadings with the historical: "Are You Spiritual?" "Cults and the Occult," "Scientific Religion," "One World Religion," "Modern Psychology and Mind Technologies," six pages on "Religions of the World," seven pages on "The New Age Movement," seven pages on "The Paranormal and the Supernatural," and a whopping 13 pages on "UFOs and Extra-Terrestials" (including "The UFO Quickening," "Aliens," "The Roswell Case," "Alien Autopsy," "Alien Abductions and Encounters," "Crop Circles and Animal Mutilations," "Monuments on Mars?" etc.).[27] There are some 3000 "new" religious groups in the United States today, many with beliefs even more bizarre than Heaven's Gate. How does one distinguish the pure gold from the counterfeit, the spiritual jewels from the psychic junkshops, the authentic witness from the wacky exotica and pseudo-spirituality that are everywhere to be picked up?

1. GOD IS "HOT" WITH HOLLYWOOD ~ *USA Today* featured an article on "Hollywood Immersed in a Spiritual Rebirth" with the announcement that "as movie makers are being bashed more than ever for glorifying wrong-doing at its lowest levels, new films are reaching more blatantly than ever into religious imagery to harvest heavenly heroes."[28] Throughout the '90s Hollywood was fascinated, even fixated, on haloed heroes, who showed up everywhere. Denzel Washington was an angel and Whitney Houston a preacher's wife in the Disney movie *The Preacher's Wife*. Greg Kinnear was a post office angel in *Dear God*. John Travolta was an angel who fornicates and drinks beer in *Michael*.

In contrast to the '80s, when *Dallas* was the most popular network program, *Touched by an Angel* proved to be one of the most popular prime-time shows of the '90s. It was also the first explicitly religious drama to break into the Nielsen Top 10 in the ratings service's 46-year history.

The year 1997 seemed to be a turning point. The networks' fall lineup that year included an unprecedented eight shows with religious and spiritual themes.[29] The fall offerings on PBS alone included five religious specials. A 1997 Parents Television Council study reported a fourfold increase in religious depictions on network prime time since 1993.

The first big movie of DreamWorks SKG—the Hollywood studio run by the powerhouse trinity of Steven Spielberg, Jeffrey Katzenberg, and David Geffen—was a biblical animated telling of the story of Moses called *The Prince of Egypt*. Katzenberg claims that his greatest hope for the movie is that "people will have a spiritual experience watching it."[30]

With our cultural and spiritual pivot moving increasingly toward the East, one could almost predict the making of *Kundun*, a Martin Scorsese film about the Dalai Lama's life. Brad Pitt's film *Seven Years in Tibet* tells the story of the spiritual changes that came after climbing the Himalayas and meeting the Dalai Lama. It is wonderfully symbolic that America's leading Buddhist authority, Robert Thurman, is the father of movie star Uma Thurman. Actors are turning to God (or Allah or Kali or Shiva or Whoever) for help. "God is coming back. People don't know where else to go," testifies director Garry Marshall.

> [Movies] fulfill a spiritual need that people have to share a common memory.
>
> Director Martin Scorsese[31]

But is Hollywood where the church wants them to go? Is *City of Angels, Contact, The Butcher Boy, The Devil's Advocate, Phenomenon, A Price Above Rubies, Wide Awake, Touch, Fallen,* and *The Apostle* the best we can do?

2. GOD IS "HOT" WITH THE RICH AND FAMOUS ~

The top high-fashion magazine in the world, *W*, featured among its models an article on Hollywood's fascination with spirituality, noting that it has come to the point where "nobody of note can leave home these days without having a spiritual guide to accompany their bodyguard, driver, lawyer and accountant."[32] Gothic revival furniture is now all the rage, partly because it connects the wealthy who buy antiques with a more spiritual past.

The actor Matthew McConaughey says unabashedly, "God has helped a lot, honestly. My relationship with Him is up at the top right now." Marla Maples Trump attributes her problems with her former husband, billionaire Donald Trump, to the fact that she couldn't teach him "spirituality."

3. GOD IS "HOT" WITH MUSICIANS ~

It used to be that rockers like XTC's Andy Partridge sang such songs as "Dear God" (1986):

I won't believe in heaven and hell
No saints, no sinners, no devil as well
No pearly gates, no thorny crown
You're always letting us humans down.[33]

Now Uncle Tupelo is singing "Satan, Your Kingdom Must Come Down."

Technoartist Moby is confessing his faith to club hoppers. Joan Osborne asks, "What if God was one of us?" Bono of U2 constantly zings spirituality at his listeners. Sixteen Horsepower's debut album *Sackcloth'n'Ashes* featured

David Eugene Edwards singing "There is won-
der-working power in the blood of the Lamb."
Jim White has a CD *Wrong-Eyed Jesus*. Nick
Cave and the Bad Seeds' album *The Boatman's
Call* includes this song:

What time's church?

Singer Madonna to Ray Kybartas,
her personal trainer, asking for
her workout schedule[34]

> There is a kingdom
> There is a king
> And He lives without, and He lives within.[35]

Moreover, Jars of Clay and Kirk Franklin were named Top Billboard 200
Album Artists in 1996. Franklin's single "Stomp" ("You can't take my joy,
Devil") was the first gospel video ever to appear on MTV. Christian music
sales alone topped $550 million in 1996, and Christian books and music
together are a $3-billion-a-year business.

**Spiritual writing is not about
God.... it is about the human
longing for all that God can
mean.**

Patricia Hampl[36]

The say-no-more/says-it-all clincher is
that Madonna has repudiated "the Material
Girl" image and has now morphed into "the
Spiritual Girl."

4. GOD IS "HOT" WITH PUBLISHERS ~
Phyllis Tickle, editor-at-large for *Publisher's
Weekly,* reveals that spirituality has been "the
fastest-growing segment in adult publishing the
last two years."[37] Slurp your way through one of the easy-to-sip *Chicken Soup
for the Soul* books, and lick your lips at the fortunes being made in this literary
franchise. Sales of religious publishers topped $1 billion in 1996, with more than
150 million book units sold. Sale of New Age books went from an astonishing
5.6 million copies in 1992 to an unbelievable 9.7 million three years later.

In the spring of 1994, the top book on the fiction best-selling list was *The
Celestine Prophecy* by James Redfield.[38] Since 1995, nearly 1000 books with
the word *soul* in the title or subtitle have been published.[39] Seven of the top
10 books on the *New York Times* bestseller list in the spring of 1998 were
about spirituality and personal growth. A check of one book supplier just
before this book went to press demonstrates how hot spirituality still is with
publishers. On amazon.com's bestsellers page for November 3, 1998, the
"New on the Bestseller List" featured *Something More: Excavating Your
Authentic Self* by Sarah Ban Breathnach, author of the bestseller *Simple Abundance,* and the "Destined for Greatness" category listed *The Best Spiritual
Writing 1998,* the first-ever anthology of the kind, edited by Philip Zaleski,
senior editor of *Parabola* magazine.[40]

No wonder Wal-Mart, Target, Borders, and Barnes and Noble all expanded
their religious inventory. Syndicated evangelical columnist Cal Thomas appears

now in 450 newspapers, second only to George Will. The fastest-growing club in the history of the nine specialty clubs of the Book of the Month Club is One Spirit. The nation's largest book wholesaler, Ingram Books, saw a 249% growth in the spirituality market since 1994. The explosive growth has settled into extraordinary growth of 27% annually.[41]

Capital Publishing Company has inaugurated a new magazine on philanthropy called *American Benefactor*. The magazine, according to CEO Randall Jones, is designed to appeal to Boomers, whose coffers will supposedly be full from inheriting trillions from their parents. The theme and thrust of the magazine, says Jones, are "all about having soul."[42]

God is even hot with Hallmark Cards, whose Crown division has trouble keeping up with the increasing demand for cards with explicitly spiritual messages.[43]

5. GOD IS "HOT" WITH POLLSTERS ~ Two-thirds of USAmericans, according to a Gallup Poll, believe religion can answer all or most of the problems people face in life.[44] Similarly, in 1987, 53% said religion is very important, and by 1997 that figure was 61%.

Of course, all the while these same people think the influence of religion in American society is declining.[45]

When USAmericans were asked in early 1997 who is most likely to go to heaven, the winners were Mother Teresa (at 79%), Oprah Winfrey (66%), and Michael Jordan (65%). More people thought that Bill Clinton would go to heaven (52%) than Pat Robertson (47%).[46] *Utne Reader*, in its selection of "America's 10 Most Enlightened Towns," make one of the criteria "diverse spiritual opportunities."[47] One *Newsweek* poll found that 58% of Americans feel the need to experience spiritual growth.

6. GOD IS "HOT" EVEN WITH ATHEISTS ~ Have you noticed that atheists either have disappeared (à la Madalyn Murray O'Hair, who disappeared in August 1996 along with her son Jon and granddaughter Robin) or else are practicing spiritual one-upmanship? Psychologist Gregory Bateson, raised in a dogmatically atheistic household, came to believe at the end of his life (1904–1980) that only through the *sacred* could one make comprehensible and communicate the wonder of creation.[48] Historian E. R. Dodds, whose study of Nietzsche as a young man led to his rejection of Christianity, came to believe at the end of his life that his "liberation" from faith was a diminishment, not enhancement, of human existence: "At 17 I saw it as a liberation. At 83 I am more inclined to see it as an impoverishment, the inevitable drying-up of one of the deeper springs from which the human imagination has in time past been nourished."[49]

Peter Lamborn Wilson, writing in the technology-and-culture magazine *21C*, insists that "while I am not atheist in the strict sense of the word, I don't think you have to believe in God to understand that there can be an experience of the Divine Becoming Within."[50] Another atheist/agnostic claims to be on a spiritual search, defining spirituality as "like heaven naked, but with an attitude."[51] One of Britain's finest novelists, Jim Crace, calls himself a "scientific atheist," yet he wrote a fictional biography of Jesus that won the Whitbread Novel of the Year award and is a finalist for the Booker Prize.[52]

> We love all the incense, the stained glass windows, the organ music, the vestments, and all of that. It's drama. It's aesthetics. It's the ritual. That's neat stuff. I don't want to give all that up just because I don't believe in God.
>
> Episcopalian atheist James Kelly[55]

Atheism is such a "virtually extinct social type"[53] that German philosopher Christoph Turcke is forced to begin his radical critique of religion by admitting that "today avowed atheists seem like a survival of a past era."[54] Woody Allen, who admitted once in an interview that the two characteristics he wishes he had were "courage" and "religious faith," says in one classic scene: "To you, I'm an atheist. To God, I'm the loyal opposition."[56] Missionary of unbelief Luis Bunuel said he was an "atheist by the grace of God."

Of course, in classic double-ring fashion, atheism is growing statistically: Close to 1 million US adults now say they "don't believe in God"—nearly five times the number 30 years ago. But a lot of these "atheists" don't so much believe in the nonexistence of God as in the absence of God or in the nonavailability of God. Many of these postmodern "atheists" are in the pews, forming a new kind of hybrid religion in which atheism is integrated into their faith. According to former Jesuit scholar Jack Miles, who first identified this hybrid faith while on tour for his book *God: A Biography* (1997), "If I may doubt the practice of medicine from the operating table, if I may doubt the political system from the voting booth, if I may doubt the institution of marriage from the conjugal bed, why may I not doubt religion from the pew?"[57]

7. GOD IS "HOT" WITH POLITICIANS ～ First Ladies Hillary Rodham Clinton and Nancy Reagan got caught consulting New Age gurus. Actress Demi Moore and financier Michael Milken look to physician and endocrinologist Deepak Chopra, who is the "Billy Graham" of this current spiritual awakening but who touts gurus as fallible mentors.[58] One of the quaternion of power gurus (Terence McKenna, Tony Robbins, and Marianne Williamson are the others), Chopra is negotiating with TCI Communications' John Malone to develop his own consciousness channel.

8. GOD IS "HOT" ON THE INTERNET ～ By early 1997, when there were by several estimates more than a half-million Web sites on the Net, almost 15% of these (71,200) were Christian Web sites—28,600 of them Roman

Catholic, 11,800 Methodist, and 11,000 Baptist. There were also 27,100 Muslim/Islam sites.

In 1997 Christianity Online was named one of the most popular sites on America Online. But this is no time for gloating. The Internet now boasts 9000 Web sites devoted to psychic and spiritual phenomena, including such exotica as "the First Presleyterian Church of Elvis the Divine," a church founded for those who worship Elvis (chelsea.ios.com/~hkarlin1/welcome.html). Tarot Web sites and chat rooms attest to the power of this form of "spiritual solitaire."[59]

9. GOD IS "HOT" ON THE LECTURE CIRCUIT ~ I shall never forget a meeting at Opryland Hotel with the Home Mission Board of the Southern Baptist Convention.

I had just finished lecturing on the "God Rush" and stepped outside the lecture hall to greet some friends. Right outside our room another convention was meeting—the 43rd annual meeting of the American Society on Aging. The plenary session was on "The Idea of Aging as Spiritual Journey." Some of the workshops included "Spiritual Assessment," "Spiritual Growth: A Developmental Task of the Second Half of Life," "Healing Connections: Ethnic Perspectives on Spirituality and Mental Health," "A Spirituality of Giftedness," "It's a Wonderful Life: Life Review as Spiritual Affirmation," "Spiritual Well-Being in Congregations and Continuing Care Retirement Communities," "Aging—The Mind, Body, and Spirit Connection: The Whole Is Greater Than the Sum of Its Parts," "Rituals: The Magic and Mystery for Our Elder Years/Using Scripture to Reflect on Aging," "Faith Stories: The Heart of the Intergenerational Community," "Affirming a 'Caring' Contract: Exploring Ethical and Spiritual Dilemmas in Caregiving for People with Dementia."

> We're not in the business of filling bellies. We want to fill souls. Good coffee provides gratification at many levels.
>
> Howard Schultz, chair and CEO, Starbucks Coffee Co.[60]

The existence of a widespread awakening is seen in the human-potential movement.[61] The largest-drawing lecturer since I have been at Drew University was not a presidential candidate, not an academic dignitary, not a head of state, not even former head of the Joint Chiefs of Staff Colin Powell. It was Deepak Chopra, with tickets starting at $40.

10. GOD IS "HOT" ON MADISON AVENUE ~ as well as on the fashion catwalks of Paris, New York, and Milan. Spiritual search sells even more now than sex, as Nissan, IBM, Gatorade, Chevrolet, even the American Dairy Association have discovered in some of their successful '90s TV ads.[62]

Look at the range of what is being sold by soul: cars, sports teams, beverages, watches, fragrances. Tierry Mugler calls his popular scent "Angel"; Karl Lagerfeld names his fragrance "Sun, Moon, Stars." The Gap introduced a unisex fragrance OM and presented it to Gap executives on the Buddha's birthday: "I wanted to do fragrance about simplicity, sensuality and spirituality." Clarins introduces a new "heaven-on-earth" perfume, "Elysium," with the line "Stir the senses, rejuvenate the soul."

The new ad campaign by Kentucky Fried Chicken features a girl on her bed in a yoga position doing her mantra. Aveda is doing a line of products for Deepak Chopra's wellness center. There is the 1997 Infiniti Q45 ad, with the motto "Everything changes but the soul" and the challenge to "Take one out for a Guest Drive and see why the soul is eternal."

Count on it: Primary colors will not be the colors of the future. The colors of early 21-C will be celestial hues (shades of purples and greens) and shimmery heavenly natural colors, especially platinum, gold, silver, bronze, jasper, the metallic natural hues reflecting this larger cultural shift toward the spiritual and supernatural.

11. GOD IS "HOT" WITH CORPORATE AMERICA AND THE WORK-PLACE ~ A 1998 issue of *Sales and Marketing Management* began a cover story in this way: "Spirituality, folks, is taking hold of the workplace." Consultant David B. Wolfe tells his clients that the current "passion for spirituality" is here to stay and will transform the workplace.[63] Boeing Corporation uses the services of poet David Whyte to help managers get in touch with their souls. Lotus Development boasts a "soul" committee for self-scrutiny. Even the World Bank has weekly soul seminars.[64]

The servant leadership movement is a major manifestation of the melding of spirituality and economics. A Harvard psychiatrist/musician/business professor wrote a book on leadership in which he argues that leadership "requires a strategy of deploying and restoring one's own spiritual resources."[65]

Postmoderns expect their business ventures to be spiritually based. Success is reached, not through "reengineering," but through reawakening. "Downsizing" is not "rightsizing" but "dumbsizing" (Gerald Celente), "reengineered to the point where the spirit has gone," according to the latest IFTF (Institute for the Future) research report. "In Good Company" warns about the spiritual vacuum and meaninglessness felt by many reengineered organizations.[66]

12. GOD IS "HOT" WITH BROADCASTERS ~ NBC's soap opera *Another World* is 30 years old. For its first 29 years its characters were without any religious identity or affiliation; their lives were devoid of any spirituality. Within the past couple of years the characters all developed spiritual sides until spirituality is now part of the warp and woof of their lives.

In 1996, Fox News Channel initiated the program "Fox on Religion." In 1997, two news shows opened dealing exclusively with religion. One started at 5:30 p.m. on the interfaith-oriented Odyssey cable network, set in Nashville. The other started on July 17 on PBS. These two half-hour news shows are not related, but they are doing the same thing—looking at religion in America.

13. GOD IS "HOT" WITH SCIENTISTS ~ The three "aristoscientists"[67]—E. O. Wilson, Stephen Jay Gould, and the late Carl Sagan, each of whom had rejected religious interpretations of the cosmos—all linked hands with faith communities because they believed the ecological movement needs the support and strength of religious faith if it is to win the hearts and minds of postmoderns.[68] Frank Tipler, one of the top scientists of the day, is now offering nothing less than a "testable physical theory for an omnipresent, omniscient, omnipotent God who will one day in the far future resurrect every single one of us to live forever in an abode which is in all essentials the Judeo-Christian heaven."[69] Tipler borrows from Teilhard de Chardin the concept of an Omega Point, a singularity in time of infinite density and temperature toward which the universe will collapse in a backward Big Bang he calls the Big Crunch. The energy of such an implosion, he believes, could bring back to virtual life every creature that ever lived.

Unlike the modern era, when science and theology declared war on each other, the superforces of science and spirituality are coming together in the postmodern world. Paul Davies's book *The Mind of God: The Scientific Basis for a Rational World* demonstrates that even those who don't call themselves "religious" can interpret the cosmos to be a smile.[70] Chet Raymo has a book on how to experience science spiritually called *The Virgin and the Mousetrap.*[72]

> The more I examine the universe and study the details of its architecture, the more evidence I find that the universe in some sense must have known that we were coming. There are some striking examples in the laws of nuclear physics of numerical accidents that seem to conspire to make the universe inhabitable.
>
> Physicist Freeman Dyson[71]

Biologist Christian de Duve debates for 300 pages whether to agree with Macbeth—life is "a tale told by an idiot, full of sound and fury, signifying nothing"—or with Hamlet—"There are more things in heaven and earth, Horatio, than are dreamt of in your philosophy." De Duve ends by declaring for Hamlet. The universe is meaningful, he concludes, "not because I want it to be so, but because that is how I read the available scientific evidence. . . . To Monod's famous sentence 'The universe was not pregnant with life, nor the biosphere with man,' I reply: 'You are wrong. They were.'"[73] His last words are, "We must bow to the mystery."

The list goes on and on: God is "hot" in environmentalism. People are searching for spirituality in nature; discovering God in creation; peering into the heavens for the divine (*Glamour* magazine replaced its political column with horoscopes due to reader demand); finding God in the workplace. *Wired* magazine (August 1998) invested a feature article exploring the "growth stock" of spirituality in the workplace. The *New York Times* put on its front page the crumbling walls between religion and the workplace—there is a Koran study at Boeing, Torah classes at Microsoft, Islamic theology at Intel. Management consultant Richard Barrett puts on conferences that offer sessions on "Emotional Intelligence and Spiritual Leadership," panel discussions on "The Entrepreneur Walking Through the Dark Night of the Soul," and one prayer meeting.

SPIRITUAL TSUNAMI ~ A spiritual tsunami has hit postmodern culture. This wave will build without breaking for decades to come. The wave is this: People want to *know God*. They want less to *know about God* or *know about religion* than to *know God*. People want to experience the "Beyond" in the "Within."

Postmoderns want something more than new products; they want new experiences, especially new experiences of the divine.[74] As one marketing expert writes, "If the '80s were the decade when nothing was sacred, then this is the one when everything is."[75]

This spiritual tsunami has hit the postmodern generations especially hard. To get a pulse on the quest for a personal spirituality among Gen-X and Net-Gens, I examined plays produced by young British playwrights under the age of 25. In particular, I studied those plays that won the right to be professionally produced at London's Royal Court Theatre. To my amazement, the winning plays literally teemed with issues of spirituality.[76]

The first postmodern generations (Gen-Xers, Net-Gens) are deeply spiritual. "WWJD" (What Would Jesus Do), Veggie Tales, and prayer clubs in schools are only early signs of this spiritual tsunami. In 1998, teens cited religion as the second-strongest influence in their lives, beating out teachers, peers, the media, and friends; only parents registered higher.[77] In the class of 2001, nine in 10 believe in God, 75% believe in life after death, 57% attend religious services, and 45% say that religion will become even more important to them in the future than today.[78]

This huge spiritual hunger does not automatically bode well for organized religion or translate into an interest in the church. Try to find a magazine for teenagers that does not have something on spirituality: How much of what you find is church-oriented? One out of six teens told the Barna Research Group in 1998 that they expect to use the Internet as a substitute for their current church-based religious experience. Already, 25 million adults rely on the Internet for religious experience and expression at least monthly. By the way, African-American teens are four times more likely than white teens to expect to rely on the Internet for their future religious experience.

Ironically, younger postmoderns can be more churchgoing than their elders. They understand that every soul needs an address and can be more prone than Boomers to trust the teachings of their tradition to help them make decisions. A 1998 Gallup Poll revealed that 45% of USAmericans go to church weekly, but the figure is 55% for teens. Another study found that 40% of people born between 1963 and 1976 who named a religious preference said they attend worship services twice a month or more. That's almost the same number as the Boomers reported on the same question (43%).[79] What younger postmoderns seem able to do is bring together the institutional and noninstitutional aspects of their spiritual life better than their modern parents.

This does not mean there is not often a rebellion against the church's record of handling spiritual experiences across all generations. Asian theologian C. S. Song writes, "It is sad to say but it is often the case that one comes across Jesus in the Spirit of love more outside the church than inside it."[80] For Jeff Woods, that helps explain why "society is not disinterested in God; society is disinterested in the institutionalized church."[81]

> The world in which we live is the most technological there ever was, but spiritually also the most empty.
>
> Spanish philosopher
> José Ortega y Gasset

Just about every newspaper has a daily astrology column. How many newspapers have even a *weekly* church column?

FAILURE OF MATERIALISM ~ Materialism has replaced socialism as the world's #1 totalitarianism. Postmoderns are awakening to the fact that material goods do not feed the soul. There has been a 47% increase in US consumption per capita since 1970, yet there has been a 51% decline in the quality of life during that same period.[82] The bottom line bottoms out.

Since 1960, US population increased by 41%, the gross domestic product nearly tripled, and total social spending by all levels of government rose from $142 billion to $787 billion, more than a fivefold increase. During the same time, there was a 560% increase in violent crime, more than a 400% increase in illegitimate births, a quadrupling of divorces, a tripling of the percentage of children living in single-parent households, a 200% increase in teen suicides, and since 1967, a drop of 38 points in the average SAT verbal scores.

The verdict is in, and it is fatal to materialism: Increased consumption does not lead to increased fulfillment. We may know how to live well materially, but we do not know how to live well. The highest quality of life comes through spiritual sources, not economic ones. More than any other reason, Communism collapsed around the world because its materialistic philosophy had no room for transcendence, for the spirit.[83]

The future of malls and all monuments to consumerism is bleak.[84] Tired of materialistic treadmills, postmoderns are choosing spiritual enrichment over material embellishments, homefronts over storefronts. The new postmodern motto is "The legacy you leave is the life you lead." The Trends Research Institute of Rhinebeck, New York, selected Voluntary Simplicity as one of the top 10 trends of the 1990s. Shop-till-you-drop consumers have started to drop shopping, opting to purchase things they need, not things they want. Even Boomers are not interested in neo-anything, but eternal everything.

so what? MARVELLISM/MIRACULISM ~ In 1987 only 47% of USAmericans agreed with the statement, "Even today miracles are performed by the power of God." Ten years later the figure had skyrocketed to 61%.[85] At the same time, scientific achievement and scientific sophistication are at an all-time high, yet we are as much "miracle mongers" as our forebears in the Middle Ages.

The 15th edition of the *Encyclopaedia Britannica* (1973) declared in no uncertain terms that superstition "being irrational, should recede before education and especially science." The 1998 online edition of the *Encyclopaedia Britannica* left this prediction completely out.

Postmodern culture is deeply superstitious. Some 73% of US pedestrians step into the street to avoid walking under a ladder.[86] Gallup has found that one in four of us believes in ghosts; one in six claims to communicate with the deceased; one in four claims to have communicated "telepathically" with another person; one in 10 claims to have seen a ghost or felt its presence; one in seven claims to have seen a UFO; one in two believes in ESP; and one in four follows astrology.[87] Ad infinitum; ad nauseum.

Jesuit Carols Maria Staehlin calls our current infatuation with miracles "marvellism." Some examples of miracle mania? We rush to see icons that weep, paintings that bleed, Virgin Mary sightings in Texas and Yugoslavia, rosaries turned to gold, angel visitations. Even when they're obvious hoaxes, we aren't deterred.

The church must not sweep mysticism under the rug. The paranormal is normal. Extrasensory perception (ESP) is real, not imagined or schizophrenic. Mystical experiences happen. Could it be that Dan Johnson, a pastor in Gainesville, Florida, is right in his conviction that "the world does a better job of helping people be spiritual than the church"? If the church isn't helping one to get mystified, better misty-fied than nothing.

But at the same time . . .

There is room for a new religious specialty/profession one might call "spook busters." A new role for leadership is as anti-brainwashing specialists who can help people navigate through the kooks, charlatans, crackpots, cranks, and cults.

SPIRITUAL SEX ~ What is the first thing that is taught about sex in the public schools? Its sacredness, right? Hello?! AIDS awareness is many of our kids' introduction to sex. "Sex" and "scared" go together more than "sex" and "sacred."

Physical sex is no longer enough. Sex is more about joy, depth, intimacy, trust—at least spiritual sex is. Postmoderns want to be bonded to their partners through spiritual orgasms more than sexual orgasms,[88] soul-stirring sexuality that lasts 24 hours, not just 24 seconds.

> We are all the result of sexual events, and their faded heat still warms us.
>
> Novelist John Updike[89]

It's long overdue for the church to connect spirituality and sexuality. Show how to make sex spiritual. Do not let Eastern practices like yoga and Tantra define the connections. Show how the Bible brings together mind, body, and spirit into a heightened awareness of our senses. Sex is more about modes of discourse than forms of intercourse.

Ask anyone having sex: Did their problems start to go away the moment they started bedding someone? Many people need less a sexual partner than a creative presence and a loving touch; they need affection, not sex; they need an emotionally costive bedding, not a playmate to bed. Fill the pit of emptiness with the sex pill, and the hole only gets bigger, the pit only gets deeper.

You can have a sensual relationship with life in celibacy—and no, you don't need to masturbate three times a day to do it. The issue here is a passionate affair with life. Sexual energies can be expended on flowers, trees, books, ideas, and so on.

Postmodern culture is desperate for models of a healthy sexuality. The church can help married couples to go to bed with each other, not Mommy and Daddy. Couples don't have to curl up with "husband-Daddy" or "wife-Mommy." Can the church help postmoderns see the development of sex in terms of cultivating an art? Fidelity is an artistic discipline that leads to the masterpiece of lifetime love.[90]

When was the last time you knelt by the bed before having sex with your spouse and prayed, thanking God for each other and for the feast of which you will partake? Read Tobit 8 from the Apocrypha or read the Song of Songs if you want some biblical precedents and examples. Thread sex into a densely woven pattern of religious life, social existence, and spiritual being.

EVERY CHILD'S FOUR MOST MAGICAL WORDS ~ Every kid in the world knows these four words: "*Erzahl mir eine Geshichte*" (German); "*Raconte-moi une histoire*" (French); "*Nanika hanashite*" (Japanese); "*Gao su wo i ge gushi*" (Chinese). Or in English, "Tell Me a Story."

The religious and social life of the Cree Indians, a cluster of three tribes (the "Swampy People," the "Woods People," and the "Prairie People") situated between the Hudson Bay and Lake Winnipeg in Canada, revolves around what they call the "shaking tent." One tent is reserved for ceremony and storytelling, the two things that Crees believe can truly "shake" the foundations of the universe.

> Never trust the teller, trust the tale.
>
> D. H. Lawrence

The 300-mile-wide island known as Iceland is celebrated on every front. Icelanders are said to be among the tallest and largest of human beings. The women of Iceland are alleged to be the most beautiful in the world (two Miss Worlds in the last two decades). Reykjavik's nightlife is the best anywhere. Iceland sports more chess grandmasters per capita than anywhere else, more bridge champions, more poets and authors, more readers, and more bookstores. Iceland even ties with four other nations in the number of fourth-graders with computers at home (75%).[91] It is home to some of the best Internet companies in the world, as well as the queen of electronica, Bjork Gudmundsdottir. Iceland has one of the longest-living citizenry and one of the lowest infant mortality rates.

Why is Iceland celebrated as the most perfect society on earth—at least the consummate nation-state? Its 268,000 Icelanders know the stories of every building, every bridge, every museum, every monument, every hill ridge of lava, every river and rock and rill.[92]

In the modern world, *story* became a negative word. One of the worst things you could call anyone was a "storyteller." In the postmodern world, the future belongs to the "storytellers"—those who can tell their stories in all the basic media forms: print, software, audio, and video.

The *con* in the icon is the notion that image can carry the day without story. No film has ever won a best-film Oscar that only won in the category of "Best Cinematography." Storytelling is as important to postmodern culture as storytelling was to a premodern world where, in the words of Jared Diamond, "the knowledge possessed by even one person over the age of 70 could spell the difference between survival and starvation for a whole clan."[94]

> This is my story. I lay it before you.
>
> Opening words to the novel *Pity* by James Buxton[93]

The heart, the gift, of storytelling is the exchange of experience and the "experience of other." Life experiences are rinsed and renewed and reproduced in the waters of storytelling. Telling stories gives meaning to the suffering of our lives and the seeming randomness of existence. Telling stories builds bridges across generational divides.

The importance of story can be seen in the way science increasingly discards the language of laws in favor of story. What science finds in nature is story. Physicist Brian Swimme says that at base, the universe is not matter, not energy, not information, but story. (I argue that it is really song, but that's another book.)

Similarly, historians are less inclined to see history as a set of laws and more prone to view it as an unfolding, never-ending story. Even literary figures have discovered the ancient art of storytelling. Why is 25-year-old Irish writer Conor McPherson hard for critics to place? His funny "play" *St. Nicholas* is not really a play at all, but traditional storytelling.

Postmodern culture needs more stories, or—more accurately—we need better stories, or what a Plains friend of Kathleen Norris calls "good telling stories."[95] Why are multinational corporations like Disney, Nike, and Pepsi the only ones telling stories to our children?

Jesus' life was not an essay. Jesus' life was not a doctrine. Jesus' life was not a sermon. Jesus' life was a story. People don't live essays or doctrines or sermons. They live stories. People are not pulled from the edge of the pit by essays or doctrines or sermons. They are rescued by stories. They are healed by stories.

The Christian message is not a timeless set of moral principles or a code of metaphysics. The Christian message is a story, the greatest story ever told, of love come down from heaven to earth, a love so vast and victorious that even hatred could not keep it down. In other words, the Christian message is not "synchronic" like a photograph, but "diachronic" like a film. Diachronic narrative is at the heart of the Christian message—it is story enfolded within story.

> The oldest pathway for which the brain is hardwired is the narrative.
>
> Chief scientist/vice president of Xerox Corp. John Seely Brown

My favorite definition of preachers is "story doctors." People come to worship with problem stories, with painful stories, with jostling narratives and "narrative dysfunctions," a condition and process "by which we lose track of the story of ourselves, the story that tells us who we are supposed to be and how we are supposed to act."[96] Preachers help heal people's narrative dysfunctions and help them live out of new, whole stories. Bad stories hurt and impair; good stories heal and help. In worship we learn that some stories we should keep; some stories we should create; and some stories we should abandon, especially the excuse stories—the abuse story, the codependency story, the inner-child story.

The major requirement for getting out of seminary, in my mind, is singular: Know the stories of the Bible. Master the biblical narratives. If Muslims studying to become a mullah or teacher have a requirement of memorizing the Koran (about the same length as the New Testament) *before* they can obtain entrance into Cairo's Al Azhar University, why can't preachers be expected to at least know the stories of the Scriptures *before* they graduate?[97]

Storytelling is a performance ritual, the primary art form of the future. The three founders of DreamWorks SKG think of themselves primarily as "storytellers": Stephen Spielberg's storytelling medium is film, Jeffrey Katzenberg's storytelling medium is animation, and David Geffen's storytelling medium is music.

Like every good yarn spinner, the preacher plays off the audience—spinning around to encourage someone's laugh, seeking out a likely looking candidate for the delivery of a knockout punch line, serving as a straight person to hand off to another the best quote. If anyone needs to be master and manipulator of cultural codes, it is the storytelling preacher, who combines the science of audience reaction with traditional storytelling skills and brings the audience to an unforgettable emotional plane.

> Storytellers will be the most valued workers in the twenty-first century.
>
> Editors of *The Futurist*[98]

The American Film Institute conducted a "Storytelling for the New Millennium Conference" in the spring of 1996. Its featured workshops were on Web storytelling, nonlinear editing, and animations.

Holographic simulations will enable emotional involvements in storytelling never before even imagined.[99]

Every village used to have its resident storyteller. Who are your church's storytellers?

THIS IS YOUR STORY, THIS IS YOUR SONG ~ Most importantly, preaching helps people see themselves as an extension of the biblical story. The Hebrews do not refer to their ancestors as "they," but as "we." In the Ritual of the Feast there is this text: "In each generation, each one must consider himself or herself as having come out of Egypt personally. . . . It is not just our ancestors whom the Holy-One-Blessed-Be-He brought out of Egypt, but ourselves; he delivered us with them."

Pastor Jack Graham's motto for the 6000-member Prestonwood Baptist Church in Dallas is "Underpromise: Overdeliver." The church gave up its weekly information-based newsletter for a very slick monthly magazine that features people from the parish. Prestonwood Baptist produces the stories of its members and helps them to see their lives as continuations of the biblical drama.

The teachings of Jesus begin in story and end in symbol—they begin in parable and end in us. These are not Bible stories that we learn; these are *our* stories.

SOUL-MINING ~ The gold is in you. Are you willing to go digging in the mines? Every story of every human being is there in story.

A French narratologist once said that there were three basic stories: a story in which a contract is made and then broken; a story in which a goal has to be reached or a task performed; and a story of departure and return—you make a journey, you undertake a quest, and you come back a different person.

Church is dead unless God is alive. Postmodern worship creates live encounters. It conducts itself the way a vital presence behaves. Preachers are storytellers who are experience intensifiers: stories that make you more firmly, deeply you; stories that make things more

> The word myself is not in the Gospel.
>
> William Tyndale[100]

firmly, deeply themselves; tellers of stories that make feelings for God, once dead, become real and alive; stories that help you discover in your own life the One who bore evil and bore it away; stories that help you hear God's heartbeat within you.

TELL ME THE STORIES OF JESUS ~ Charles Arn's studies of growing churches reveal that they spend about 10% of their total budget on local evangelism and outreach (excluding staff salaries). Arn argues that half this amount, or 5% of the total budget, should be spent on local community advertising: "A man doesn't go to the hardware store to buy a -1/2" drill bit. He is buying a -1/2" hole. A mother doesn't go to the store to buy baby food, she is buying a healthy child. Take the same approach to promoting your church. Identify and highlight the desired outcome."[101]

> One person with a belief is equal to a force of ninety-nine who only have interest.
>
> John Stuart Mill

I agree with everything Arn says except for that word *advertising*. Replace it with *storytelling*. It's storytelling that uses direct mail, brochures, newspaper ads, radio spots, whatever, but storytelling nonetheless.

Eva Schmatz is president of Summus, a research firm that specializes in something called "ValueStructuring." She warns the business clients she works with that when you deal with the "hows" and the "whys," you have to go deep; but when you deal with the "whens" and the "wheres," you have to go wide, go broad.

Storytelling evangelism must go both deep and wide. There are four stages to postmodern storytelling evangelism: (1) reckoning, (2) drafting, (3) piloting, and (4) sailing.[102] In the reckoning phase there is listening, observing, learning, identifying, and interpreting the stories that are already being told. What stories are important to your audience? Perhaps even use interviews and questionnaires to find what issues they take seriously. In the drafting stage, one puts forward some biblical stories that connect with their own context and models stories that match with their experience. Get people to respond to a variety of approaches. In the piloting phase, one builds on what one has garnered from the first two stages to implement a storytelling strategy and test its validity and reliability. In the sailing stage, one continues to refine and refocus what one is doing, trusting the Spirit to lead and guide and bring the person home.

SOUL OUT, CHURCH ~ Organized religion is over, as are all "organized" organizations.[103] Order your church around self-organizing structure and skills, not procedures and policies. Forgo order for ardor. Organizations need soul.

Everybody is out looking for people and places with "soul." People can't define it, but they know it when they see it and feel it. And they respond to soul powerfully, more than rational discourse as the exclusive basis for the pursuit of truth.

Postmoderns wants to live radically. They want to be "souled out" for God. "Soul out," church! Live out of your passion points.

Not one of the 200 "DreamWorkers" who worked for four years on the DreamWorks animation film *The Prince of Egypt* had a "job description." Not one of them had a title, either. What they did have was an employment interviewer who "hires the heart." The "heart" that the Spielberg-Katzenberg-Geffen team is hiring has three chambers: (1) passion and enthusiasm, (2) creative adventuring, and (3) risk taking.

Passion alone can bring forth the very greatest art or spirituality. Passion is the "zest test" of life. If you fail the "zest test," you will fail at anything. The first item in the Spirit Description of the Postmodern Reformation church is this: Are you on fire for God? Do you have fire in your belly? Do you have a "hot center"? Is your heart's engine of desire for goods, for goodies, or for God? Postmoderns fight fire with fire.

A recent study of business hiring practices revealed that the #1 and #2 requirements for a new employee were (1) attitude and (2) experience. The new mantra of human resources is "Hire the Heart." Lt. Col. Dennis Kremble, who has selected the pilots for the US Air Force "Top Gun" program, says he looks for passion in a pilot above all else. "More than talent, I want the person with desire who is willing to go that extra measure."[104]

There is an old mountain saying: "There's a heaven, there's a hell, and there's a hurry."

What's *your* hurry, church?

WE CAN DO IT, CHURCH ~ Christians are walk-on-water types. Physicist Lawrence Krauss tells his students at Case Western Reserve University to remember this maxim: "That which is not explicitly forbidden is guaranteed to occur." He tells them to remember what Data said about the laws of quantum mechanics in the "Parallels" episode of *Star Trek:* "All things which can occur, do occur."

> Twenty years from now you will be more disappointed by the things you didn't do than by the ones you did do. So throw off the bowlines. Sail away from the safe harbor. Catch the trade winds in your sails. Explore. Dream. Discover.
>
> Mark Twain

When God's Spirit lives in us, and we live in God, all things are possible. Nothing is impossible. Perfect love is possible. Perfect joy is possible. Perfect peace is possible. All can be everywhere.

If we can do 320,000 church meetings per day, we can do it, church. If our church facilities alone are worth $180 billion, double the combined assets of the top Fortune 500 companies, we can do it, church.

God's answers are as big as our problems. That's why I don't sit down and cry "Maranatha" out of despair, but out of desire.

KISS IT, CHURCH ~ One of my favorite West Virginia stories is of a boy and girl at the conclusion of their first date. Standing under the porch light of the girl's front door, the boy looked at her and said, "Can I kiss you?"

The girl smiled demurely and said nothing. The boy tried again. "I mean *may* I kiss you?"

Again the girl smiled and said nothing.

"Are you deaf?" the boy added.

"Are you paralyzed?"

> We are condemned to live out what we cannot imagine.
>
> Sir Thomas More

Are you paralyzed, church? Why can't you show this world how much God loves it? Even though you think this world is ugly and froggish, why can't we kiss it with the love of Christ?

Ultimate reality is not a thing or a thought or principle or set of laws. Ultimate reality is a set of relationships. What if the church were to help others see the world in terms of relationships and patterns, not laws and regulations? Paul says not, "I know *what* I have believed," but "I know *whom* I have believed" (2 Tim. 1:12 NIV). Jesus didn't come to build churches; he didn't come to found a new religion; he came to be born in you and me.

The German theologian Jürgen Moltmann has written that "the church's first word is not church, but Christ."[105] Are our churches making room for Jesus? In the high modern church there is room for many things—for order, for opinions, for resolutions, for programs. But is there room for Jesus?

To fall in love is to fall out of loneliness. In Michael Curtin's bitter, comic novel *The League Against Christmas,* London Irishman Percy Bateman cries out, "O Sweet Jesus, Christmas was the tap of a mallet on the stake in the heart of the lonely."[106] When one is in love and in relationship, the whole world appears differently. The colors are brighter, the air is fresher, the moments are richer, the world is alive.

Or reflect on these words of novelist Jostein Gaarder, "You don't think about the law of cause and effect or about modes of perception when you are in the middle of your first kiss."[107]

One of the key influences on my thinking has been that of the missiologist Bishop Lesslie Newbigin. His commentary on John was one of the books that brought me out of my deconversion. In the memorial address at the funeral service for Newbigin, who died at age 89 on 30 January 1998, the Reverend Dan Beeby mentioned that the bishop knew everybody. He rubbed shoulders with kings, with queens, with prime ministers and presidents. But "when he dropped a name, it was always the name of Jesus."[108]

Like the apostle Paul, postmodern Christians know one thing: "Jesus Christ and him crucified."

MAKE WAVES ~ No one is an island. But every one makes a wave. In physics, light is both a particle and wave (sometimes called a "wavicle").

Light makes waves. No greater wave has ever been made than the Morning Star of Jesus Christ, whose death and resurrection created a tidal wave that has not crested even yet. In the words of Fanny Crosby's hymn,

Near the cross, a trembling soul,
Love and mercy found me;
There the bright and Morning Star
Shed its beams around me.[109]

The Bible is filled with stories of women and men of faith, morning stars who made waves for God.

Abraham made a wave. In the midst of the darkness, he set off for places he knew not where . . . and his descendants became as numerous as the stars.

Jacob made a wave. In the midst of the darkness, he wrestled with an angel . . . and the nation of Israel was born.

Jochebed made a wave. In the midst of the darkness, she set her infant son adrift in a reed basket on the Nile River . . . and the Pharaoh let God's people go.

Moses made a wave. In the midst of the darkness, he led the Hebrews into the desert . . . and they found the Promised Land.

Deborah made a wave. In the midst of the darkness, she accompanied the army into battle . . . and the Canaanites were defeated.

Gideon made a wave. In the midst of the darkness, he took 300 men to battle armed only with trumpets, torches, pitchers, and faith . . . and the Midian army ran.

Rahab made a wave. In the midst of the darkness, she befriended Israelite spies . . . and Jericho's tumbling walls missed her and her household.

Esther made a wave. In the midst of the darkness, she stood up to her husband the King . . . and saved the Jews from annihilation.

Hannah made a wave. In the midst of the darkness, she surrendered her young son Samuel to the priests . . . and the Israelite monarchy was anointed.

Naaman made a wave. In the midst of the darkness, he bathed in a muddy stream . . . and his leprosy was healed.

Peter made a wave. In the midst of the darkness, he ignored Jewish law and traveled to another land to visit Cornelius . . . and the "Holy Spirit [was] poured out even on the Gentiles."

Barnabas made a wave. In the midst of the darkness, he brought a new convert to the apostles in Jerusalem . . . and the gospel was spread to the uttermost parts of the world.

Onesimus made a wave. In the midst of the darkness, he fell from slavery to Rome . . . and the apostle Paul found a "son" (Philem. 10 NIV).

Anna made a wave. In the midst of the darkness, she placed her young daughter Mary in the temple . . . and Jesus the Savior was born.

You made a wave. In the midst of your darkness, you _____ . . . and _____.

In the modern world, we had to "get your feet on the ground."
In the postmodern world, we must "put your feet in the water."
Sail as close to the wind as possible, and . . .
Make a wave.

say what? 1. Every time you read the Bible, hear these words: "This text is being fulfilled today even while you are listening" (see Luke 4:21 NJB).

2. Astrologist Rob Brezsny's "Real Astrology" column (www.realastrology.com) took a strange turn in January 1997. Brezsny—who studied religion at Duke University as an undergraduate and describes himself as "a tantric poet, storyteller, and teacher in disguise"—challenged his readers, "Find or create a symbol of your greatest pain. Mail it to me. I will then conduct a sacred ritual of purification during which I will burn that symbol to ash."

Several months later, Brezsny reported in his column the results of this request. He took more than 900 artifacts to a beach in Marin County, California, and there created a bonfire, during which "I begged the Goddess to release you from the karma that brought you the pain."

What is the appeal of astrology to postmodern culture?

3. Have a team visit one of the 75 airports worldwide that have chapels or meditation rooms. Have another team attend one of the 150 prayer services offered by our 2000 truck stops.

4. What is in the way for a healthy approach to sexuality in your life, church, and community? According to Mariana Caplan, "Demi Moore and Arnold Schwarzenegger are in the way. Books that tell her how to increase (or flatten) her breast size in thirty days are in the way. *The Enquirer* is in the way. Nutrasweet is in the way. Cellulite treatments are in the way. Child pornography is in the way. Internet sex is in the way. Advertisements that use larger-than-life-size men and anorexic women to sell phallic-shaped cars are in the way. Miss Manners is in the way."[110] Do you agree? What else is "in the way"?

5. More than 40 companies are producing electronic products relating to a Bible concordance. Have different members of the group compare and review *Bible Windows*, *Bible Works for Windows*, and *Accordance* (Mac), to name but a few of many.

6. Invite each member of your cell/class to bring to the group some cultural artifact that symbolizes the beliefs of both moderns and postmoderns. Forbid the obvious, such as crystals, crosses, or madonnas.

7. Is there any mainline church that is poised to be a significant player in the spiritual life of the next century? Is there any mainline church that has expressed a *desire* to be a significant player in the next century?

8. Reggie McNeal argues that the wrong question is, "How do we do church work better?" and the right question is, "How do we partner with God in His redemptive work in the world beyond the church's institutional concerns?" Do you agree with Dr. McNeal? How is your church making the transition from one question to the other?

9. Labyrinth walking is an ancient way of praying. Read Lauren Artress's book *Walking A Sacred Path: Rediscovering the Labyrinth as a Spiritual Tool* (New York: Riverhead Books, 1995). Take an "audio tour" of the labyrinth or go on one of the "pilgrimages" at Grace Cathedral's "Veriditas: The World-Wide Labyrinth Project." You can rent the audio tour through the Grace Cathedral gift shop or walk the labyrinth, which is open 24 hours every day. A subscription to their newsletter *SOURCE* is available by writing to Veriditas at 1100 California Street, San Francisco, CA 94108, or www.gracecom.org. To order by phone, call 415-749-6356. To order by e-mail: veriditas@gracecathedral.org. To order by fax call 415-749-6357.

10. George E. Hunter and Elmer Towns have independently studied cutting-edge, "new apostolic" churches. For their lists, see *Church for the Unchurched* (Nashville: Abingdon, 1996) and *Ten of Today's Most Innovative Churches* (Ventura, CA: Regal Books, 1990).

11. More USAmericans believe in God, in miracles, and in prayer than ever before. Yet more of us are in a moral crisis than ever before. Radio talk-show host Dr. Laura Schlessinger asserted on NBC's *Meet the Press* that one of the reasons why is because of the clergy. "I yell at the clergy all the time," she admitted. "I think the clergy—with all due respect—have become more like camp counselors than leaders. What they're doing is saying, 'I want the people to come back next week. You can't challenge them too much, can't ask too much, can't tell them that religion demands something of them.' God demands something of you."

Do you agree with "Dr. Laura"?

12. In an article in the *New York Times Book Review* called "Write Till You Drop," Annie Dillard challenges us to live as if we were dying: "Write as if you were dying. At the same time, assume you write for an audience consisting solely of terminal patients. That is, after all, the case. What would you begin writing if you knew you would die soon? What could you say to a dying person that would not enrage by its triviality."[111]

What would you say to someone if you knew they had only three months to live? What would you say to someone if you knew *you* had only three months to live?

13. George Barna rates the effectiveness of a church according to the "six pillars of ministry"—education, evangelism, stewardship, worship, relationshipbuilding, and community service. Rate your church from 1 to 10 (with 10 being highest) for each of these pillars. What is your composite rating?

14. Exercise: Take a sheet of paper and draw a line down the middle. On the left side write down the six most important features of your church. On the right side, for each feature write what you would say if a prospective member said to you, "So what?"

15. When was the last time you visited other churches in your community?

16. What do you think would happen if for one week all of the USA— by all, I mean *everyone* from criminals to children—went off cigarettes, coffee, alcohol, sugar, antidepressants, and stimulants? Up the ante: What if all television, movies, video games, and computers were unplugged for one week? What would this nation turn into?

17. Mainline denominations (such as my own United Methodist Church) are like the former Soviet Union—fiendishly difficult to reform. Why? Are the difficulties encountered by both analogous? Need their fates be the same?

18. Discuss the essayist Susan Sontag's contention that "human sexuality is, quite apart from Christian repressions, a highly questionable phenomenon, and belongs, at least potentially, among the extreme rather than the ordinary experiences of humanity. Tamed as it may be, sexuality remains one of the demonic forces in human consciousness—pushing us at intervals close to taboo and dangerous desires, which range from the impulse to commit sudden arbitrary violence upon another person to the voluptuous yearning for the extinction of one's consciousness, for death itself."[112]

19. Here are some sample slogans from churches across the country:[113]

"Come and see then grow to go"
"Where people matter"
"A fresh experience of God's love"
"Where the flock likes to rock"
"Where neighbors become friends in Christ"
"A place to belong . . . A place to become"
"Building relationships that last"
"Healing hurts and building dreams"

Which ones do you like best? How long could one of these remain useful without getting trite and needing to be changed? What might be a good slogan for your church?

now what? See the Net Notes in http://www.soultsunami.com

NOTES

1. Bruce Cockburn, "All the Diamonds in the World," *Salt, Sun and Time* (New York: Columbia, 1995), CD.

2. Robert E. Goodin and Philip Pettit, eds., *A Companion to Contemporary Political Philosophy* (Cambridge, MA: Blackwell, 1993), 3.

3. Thomas Reeves, "Not So Christian America," *First Things* (Oct 1996): 16–21.

4. "God Is in the Details," *The New Republic* (12 Sept 1994).

5. Ron Sellers, "Nine Global Trends in Religion," *The Futurist* 32 (Jan-Feb 1998): 21–22.

6. "On the Soul Train," *Boomer Report* (Apr 1997): 4–5. Also see my treatment of this "God Rush" phenomenon in Leonard I. Sweet and K. Elizabeth Rennie, "Soul Train," *Homiletics* (Oct-Dec 1997): 44.

7. Quoted by Karin Bacon in a personal letter, without attribution.

8. Wade Clark Roof, "God Is in the Details: Reflections on Religion's Public Presence in the United States in the Mid-1990s," *Sociology of Religion* 57 (1996): 153.

9. Jessica Lipnack and Jeffrey Stamps, *The Age of the Network: Organizing Principles for the 21st Century* (Essex Junction, VT: Omneo, 1994), 232.

10. Phyllis A. Tickle, *Re-Discovering the Sacred: Spirituality in America* (New York: Crossroad, 1995), 35.

11. For more on this, see Michael F. Brown, *The Channeling Zone: American Spirituality in an Anxious Age* (Cambridge, MA: Harvard Univ. Press, 1997).

12. Stephen Carter, *The Culture of Disbelief* (New York: Anchor Books, 1994).

13. Faith Popcorn, "Interview," *Business Week Online* (1 May 1996), (bwarchive.businessweek.com/).

14. Faith Popcorn and Lys Marigold, *Clicking: 16 Trends to Future Fit Your Life, Your Work, and Your Business* (New York: HarperCollins, 1996), 143.

15. See, for example, Neil T. Anderson and Elmer L. Towns, *Rivers of Revival* (Ventura, CA: Regal Books, 1997).

16. *Solzhenitsyn at Harvard: The Address, Twelve Early Responses, and Six Later Reflections,* ed. Ronald Berman (Washington, DC: Ethics and Public Policy Center, 1980), 20.

17. William Van Dusen Wishard's speech "Economic Man and Environmental Man" was delivered to the International Fund for Animal Welfare at its strategic planning retreat in Brewster, MA (9 Apr 1997), and reprinted in *Vital Speeches of the Day* 63 (15 May 1997): 459. Wishard's speech continues:

> For almost two millennia, Christianity served as the core expression of the inner wholeness of the Western psyche. But in the past two centuries, and especially in the twentieth century, our knowledge, awareness and technological capability have radically expanded.
>
> These advances have altered the ability of the historic world religions to transmit loving meaning. Religious symbols and rituals developed centuries ago may not resonate in the soul of many people today with the same force as when they first evolved. Yet people cannot live without meaning, and if we're not given to some creative meaning, we'll find a perverse meaning in destruction.
>
> In such circumstances, some people have been left without vital symbols of spiritual or psychological wholeness. Technological society offers no transcendent meaning that sustains people at the deepest level of their being; it offers no conviction about the ultimate matters of human worth and destiny. The result is a psychological disorientation we see revealing itself in emptiness, violence, and belief in anything from science fiction to the paranormal.

18. *The Trends Journal* (Spring 1997): 7.

19. As quoted in Anne Rowthorn, *Caring for Creation* (Wilton, CT: Morehouse, 1989), 80.

20. George Barna, *The Index of Leading Spiritual Indicators* (Dallas: Word Books, 1996); Alan J. Toxburgh, *Reaching a New Generation: Strategies for Tomorrow's Church* (Downer's Grove, IL: InterVarsity Press, 1993).

21. Sandra Schneiders, professor of New Testament at the Jesuit School of Theology in Berkeley, CA, defines spirituality as "the experience of consciously striving to integrate one's life in terms not of isolation and self-absorption but of self-transcendence toward the ultimate value one perceives. If the ultimate concern is God revealed in Jesus Christ and experienced through the gift of the Holy Spirit within the life of the Church, one is dealing with Christian spirituality." See the "Introduction" in Bradley C. Hanson, ed., *Modern Christian Spirituality* (Atlanta: Scholars Press, 1990), 23.

22. Ernest Gellner, "What Do We Need Now: Social Anthropology and Its Global Context," *TLS, Times Literary Supplement* (16 July 1993): 3.

23. Popcorn and Marigold, *Clicking: 16 Trends.*

24. Bill Moyers's lecture was part of the 1997–98 Year of Religion in American Life at Wake Forest University, as quoted in *North Carolina Biblical Recorder* 163 (27 Dec 1997): 1, 3.

25. Interview in *Lutheran* (Sept 1994): as quoted in *Context* (1 Nov 1994): 5.

26. Craig Dykstra, "Religion and Spirituality," *Initiatives in Religion* 5 (Summer 1996): 1–2.

27. Art Bell, *The Quickening: Today's Trends, Tomorrow's World* (New Orleans: Paper Chase Press, 1997), 149–202.

28. Ann Oldenburg, "Hollywood Immersed in a Spiritual Rebirth" *USA Today* (1 Nov 1996): 1–D.

29. Joel Stein, "The God Squad" *Time* (22 Sept 1997): 95–98. Three shows in addition to CBS's *Touched by an Angel* returned from the previous year: *7th Heaven* (Warner Brothers), *Soul Man* (ABC), and *Promised Land* (CBS). The four new shows were *Good News* (UPN), *Teen Angel* (ABC), *The Visitor* (Fox), and the serious drama *Nothing Sacred* (ABC).

30. Personal conversation with Jeffrey Katzenberg.

31. Martin Scorsese and Michael Henry Wilson, *A Personal Journey with Martin Scorsese Through American Movies* (New York: Hyperion, 1997), 166.

32. Anne Slowey and Merle Ginsbert, "The God Rush," *W* 25 (Sept 1996): 278–88.

33. Ray Kybartas, *Fitness Is Religion: Keep the Faith* (New York: Simon & Schuster, 1997), 19.

34. The full text of XTC's 1986 song "Dear God" can be found on home./ican.net/~dougan/lyrics/deargod.html.

35. Nick Cave and The Bad Seeds, "There Is a Kingdom," in *The Boatman's Call* (Brubank, CA: Reprise Records, 1997).

36. Patricia Hampl, Introduction to Sarah Ban Breathnach, *Something More: Excavating Your Authentic Self* (New York: Warner Books, 1998).

37. The two years in question are 1996 and 1997, as quoted in "Spiritual Reality," *Forbes* (27 Jan 1997): 70. See also Lynn Garret, "Notes from the Marketplace: Booksellers Continue to See Steady Growth in the Sale of Religion and Spirituality Titles and Look Forward to More of the Same," *Publishers Weekly* (10 Nov 1997): 32–37.

38. James Redfield, *The Celestine Prophecy* (New York: Warner Books, 1994).

39. Kenneth L. Woodward, "More Chicken Soup for Barnes and Noble," *Newsweek* (13 Jan 1997): 64.

40. *The Best Spiritual Writing 1998,* ed. Philip Zaleski (San Francisco: HarperCollins, 1998).

41. Jennifer Harrison, "Advertising Joins the Journey of the Soul," *American Demographics* (June 1997): 25.

42. *Boomer Report* (Dec 1996): 8.

43. Kevin Heubusch, "Cards for Life's Bummers," *American Demographics* (Oct 1997): 32.

44. A 1997 Gallup Poll, as reported in *Emerging Trends* (Oct 1997): 1.

45. "Religious Fervor Strengthens," *Boomer Report* (May 1998): 6.

46. Douglas Stanglin, "Oprah: A Heavenly Body?" *U.S. News & World Report* (31 Mar 1997): 18.

47. Jay Walliasper, "America's 10 Most Enlightened Towns," *Utne Reader* (May-June 1997): 43.

48. Gregory Bateson and Mary Catherine Bateson, *Angels Fear: Towards an Epistemology of the Sacred* (New York: Macmillan, 1987). The coauthor, anthropologist Mary Catherine Bateson, is the daughter of Gregory Bateson and anthropologist Margaret Mead.

49. E. R. Dodds, *Missing Persons* (Oxford: Clarendon Press, 1977), 194.

50. Peter Lamborn Wilson, "Neurospace," *21C* 3 (1996): 28. See also some of the selections in Sarah Anderson, ed., *The Virago Book of Spirituality* (London: Virago, 1996), especially where Simone Weil says that "not to believe in God, but to love the universe, always, even in the throes of anguish, as a home—there lies the road toward faith by way of atheism" (270).

51. As quoted in Tickle, *Re-Discovering the Sacred,* 100.

52. Jim Crace, *Quarantine* (New York: Farrar, Straus & Giroux, 1998).

53. Michael Kinsley, "Martyr Complex," *The New Republic* (13 Sept 1993): 4. "Believers predominate and non-believers either pretend otherwise or keep quiet about it. There is a vast unacknowledged Church composed of those who believe in religion rather than (or at least more than) believing in God."

54. Turcke ends his book by conceding to both camps: "Theism today is itself deeply permeated with unbelief, and atheism is far from being as unbelieving as it pretends to be" (*What Price Religion?* [London: SCM Press, 1997], 100).

55. As quoted in *Current Thoughts and Trends* 14 (Apr 1998): 20.

56. Mark Berkey-Gerard, "Woody Allen and the Sacred Conversation," *The Other Side* (Jan-Feb 1997): 62.

57. Interview with Jack Miles in the *Los Angeles Times,* as reprinted in the *Arizona Republican* (4 July 1998).

58. "Heaven's Gate," *W* 25 (Sept 1996): 64.

59. For an attempt to give Tarot a more respectable face, see Paul LaViolette, *Beyond the Big Bang: Ancient Cosmology and the Science of Continuous Creation* (Rochester, VT: Inner Traditions International, 1995).

60. As quoted in *Parade* (16 Nov 1997): 4.

61. Barbara Marx Hubbard, *Conscious Evolution: Awakening the Power of Our Social Potential* (Novato, CA: New World Library, 1998).

62. Harrison, "Advertising Joins the Journey of the Soul," 22–28.

63. David B. Wolfe, "The Psychological Center of Gravity," *American Demographics* 20 (Apr 1998): 16.

64. Michele Galan, "Companies Hit the Road Less Traveled," *Business Week* (5 June 1995).

65. Ronald A. Heifetz, *Leadership Without Easy Answers* (Cambridge, MA: Harvard Univ. Press, 1995), 274.

66. See the report by Bob Johansen and Rob Swigart, as discussed in Ian Morrison, *The Second Curve: Managing the Velocity of Change* (New York: Ballantine, 1996), 23.

67. Arthur Peacocke identifies a class of people he calls "aristoscientists" whose influence and authority can only be compared to that of medieval theologians. See Arthur Peacocke, *Theology for a Scientific Age* (Minneapolis: Fortress Press, 1993), 8.

68. The "Joint Appeal by Religion and for the Environment" was signed by Carl Sagan, E. O. Wilson, Stephen Jay Gould, and other scientists and religious leaders at the Global Forum of Spiritual and Parliamentary Leaders, held in Moscow, 15–19 January 1990. See Carl Sagan, "Preserving and Cherishing the Earth: An Appeal for Joint Commitment in Science and Religion," *American Journal of Physics* 58 (1990): 615, 617.

69. Frank Tipler, *Physics of Immortality: Modern Cosmology, God and the Resurrection of the Dead* (New York: Doubleday, 1994), 1. See also the version on four cassettes (New York: Bantam Doubleday Dell Audio, 1994).

70. Paul Davies, *The Mind of God* (New York: Simon & Schuster, 1992), 231–32.

71. Freeman Dyson, *Disturbing the Universe* (New York: Harper & Row, 1979), 250.

72. Chet Raymo, *The Virgin and the Mousetrap* (New York: Viking, 1991).

73. Christian de Duve, *Vital Dust: Life as a Cosmic Imperative* (New York: Basic Books, 1995), 300. "If the universe is not meaningless, what is its meaning? For me, this meaning is

to be found in the structure of the universe, which happens to be such as to produce thought by way of life and mind. Thought, in turn, is a faculty whereby the universe can reflect upon itself, discover its own structure, and apprehend such immanent entities as truth, beauty, goodness, and love. Such is the meaning of the universe, as I see it" (301).

74. Roper Starch Worldwide, 1996.

75. Cyndee Miller, "People Want to Believe in Something," *Marketing News* 28 (5 Dec 1994): 1.

76. Elyse Dodgson, ed., *First Lines* (London: Hodder & Stoughton, 1990).

77. *USA Weekend* survey on "Teens and Self-Image," as reported in *USA Weekend* (1–3 May 1998): 12.

78. "Generation 2001: A Survey of the First College Graduating Class of the New Millennium" can be found at http://www.Northwesternmutual.com/2001.

79. A 1998 General Social Survey released by the National Opinion Research Center at the University of Chicago.

80. C. S. Song, *Jesus in the Power of the Spirit* (Minneapolis: Fortress Press, 1994), 301.

81. C. Jeff Woods, *Congregational Megatrends* (Bethesda, MD: Albans Institute, 1996), 88.

82. *The 1996 Index of Social Health: Monitoring the Social Well-being of the Nation* (Tarrytown, NY: Fordham Institute for Innovation in Social Policy, 1996), 10.

83. This is the argument of David Satter, *Age of Delirium: The Decline and Fall of the Soviet Union* (New York: Knopf, 1996).

84. Tim Cavanaugh, "Mall Crawl Palls," *American Demographics* (Sept 1996): 14–16.

85. Pew Research Center for the People and the Press.

86. The study was done in 1993. See Adrian Berry, *The Next 500 Years: Life in the Coming Millennium* (New York: W. H. Freeman, 1996), 257.

87. As reported in "Believe It or Not," *Science News* (9 Mar 1991): 159. For a detailed account of the survey, see George H. Gallup Jr. and Frank Newport, "Belief in Paranormal Phenomena Among Adult Americans," *Skeptical Inquirer* 15 (Winter 1991): 137–46.

88. For the first nationwide survey on how women are integrating spirituality and sexuality, see Gina Ogden, "Spiritual Sex," *New Woman* (July 1998): 105–9.

89. The quote is from Nicholas Clee, "Old Timer's Reunion," *TLS, Times Literary Supplement* (27 Jan 1995): 21, a review of John Updike, *The Afterlife and Other Stories* (New York: Knopf, 1994).

90. This is the thesis of Catherine Wallace, *For Fidelity: How Intimacy and Commitment Enrich Our Lives* (New York: Knopf, 1998).

91. In England, Scotland, Ireland, and the Netherlands also, 75% of fourth-graders have computers at home. The United States trails with 56%.

92. See Horlygur Hbalfdanarson, ed., *The Visitor's Key to Iceland: Its Saga and Scenery* (Reykjavik: Icelandic Publishing House, 1996).

93. James Buxton, *Pity* (New York: Orion, 1997).

94. Scott Russell Sanders, "The Most Human Art," *Utne Reader* (Sept-Oct 1997): 56.

95. Kathleen Norris, *Dakota: A Spiritual Geography* (New York: Ticknor & Fields, 1993), 6.

96. Charles Baxter in *Burning Down the House* (St. Paul: Graywolf Press, 1997) borrows the phrase "narrative dysfunction" from poet C. K. Williams.

97. So argues Harry N. Wendt, president of Crossways International, in an address delivered to the Chicago Synod Assembly of the Evangelical Lutheran Church of America (14 June 1997).

98. *The Futurist* (Nov-Dec 1996): 27. The quote is based on Rolf Jensen, "The Dream Society," *The Futurist* (May-June 1996): 9–13.

99. For more of this, see Janet H. Murray, *Hamlet on the Holodeck: The Future of Narrative in Cyberspace* (New York: Free Press, 1997).

100. Quoted in Patrick Collinson, "The Martyred Ghost: Tyndale's Bible and Its Contribution to the English Language," *TLS, Times Literary Supplement* (21 Oct 1994): 4.

101. Charles Arn, "The Growth Report," *Ministry Advantage* 5 (July-Aug 1994): 9.

102. Planning consultant William B. Rouse, in *Best Laid Plans* (Englewood Cliffs, NJ: Prentice Hall, 1994), proposes the four stages of planning: naturalist, engineering, marketing, and sales.

103. Gareth Morgan's *Imaginization: The Art of Creative Management* (Newbury Park, CA: Sage Publications, 1993).

104. Quoted in Barry J. Farber, "Success Stories for Salespeople," *Sales and Marketing Management* (May-June 1995): 30.

105. Jürgen Moltmann, *The Church in the Power of the Spirit: A Contribution to Messianic Ecclesiology* (Minneapolis: Fortress Press, 1993), 19.

106. Michael Curtin, *The League Against Christmas* (London: Fourth Estate, 1997).

107. Jostein Gaarder, *Sophie's World: A Novel About the History of Philosophy,* trans. Paulette Moller (New York: Farrar, Straus & Giroux, 1994), 381.

108. The exact quote is, "He knew everybody and talked easily with the great but easiest with the humble, poor and lost. When he dropped a name, it was always the name of Jesus" (unpublished eulogy by Rev. Dan Beeby at Dulwich Grove United Reformed Church [8 Feb 1998]. With thanks to Donald Barber Jr. for showing me this material.

109. Fanny J. Crosby, "Jesus, Keep Me Near the Cross," in *The United Methodist Hymnal: Book of United Methodist Worship* (Nashville: United Methodist Publishing House, 1989), 301.

110. Mariana Caplan, *Untouched: The Need for Genuine Affection in an Impersonal World* (Prescott, AZ: Hohm Press, 1998), 233.

111. Annie Dillard, "Write Till You Drop," *New York Times Book Review* (28 May 1989): 1.

112. Susan Sontag, "The Pornographic Imagination," reprinted as an introduction to Georges Bataille, *Story of the Eye* (London: Penguin Books, 1982), 103.

113. As printed in *Ministry Advantage* (July-Aug 1994): 5.

appendix 1

Edge-Churches

Here is my off-the-top-of-the-head list of churches that are struggling with some of the over-the-top issues discussed in this book.

For edge-churches that are working with high moderns in transitioning them to postmodern culture, see especially the following:

- Saddleback Valley Community Church in Mission Viejo, California. See Rick Warren, *Purpose-Driven Church* (Grand Rapids: Zondervan, 1997), and the audiocassette by Rick Warren and Leonard Sweet, *Tides of Change* (Nashville: Abingdon Press, 1996). www.pastors.net/svcc.html

- Prince of Peace Lutheran Church in Burnsville, Minnesota, with pastor Michael Foss. For information on Mike's Weekly Thematic Programming, which he does with musician/composer Handt Hanson, see www.changingchurch.org.

- Community Church of Joy in Glendale, Arizona, with Walt Kallestad. See his *Entertainment Evangelism* (Nashville: Abingdon Press, 1996). www.joyonline.org

- Casas Adobes Baptist Church in Tucson, Arizona. Visit www.az*net. com/%abc or see Roger Barrier's new book *Listening to the Voice of God* (Minneapolis: Bethany House, 1999).

- Cokesbury United Methodist Church, Knoxville, Tennessee. You can e-mail senior pastor Steve Sallee at Jabbok51@aol.com. Expect to hear a lot more about this church's ministry (including "Sacred Grounds") in the future.

- Noroton Presbyterian Church, Darien, Connecticut, with George Claddis. Preacher33@aol.com. The first volume in the Religion in Practice series Jossey-Bass is doing in partnership with Leadership Network: *Leading the Team-Based Church* (San Francisco: Jossey-Bass, 1999).

- Christ Church, Fort Lauderdale, Florida. www.christchurchum.org/. For Dick Wills's transitioning of a traditional church, see the article by Bill Easum, "What Churches Are Teaching Me About Permission-giving Churches," www.easum.com/netresul/97-06.htm.

- Wooddale Church, Eden Prairie, Minnesota. See the audiocassette with pastor Leith Anderson and church consultant Lyle E. Schaller, *The Best Is Yet to Come: For Churches Ready to Change* (Nashville: Abingdon Press, 1994) and *Dying for Change* (Minneapolis: Bethany House, 1998). www.wooddale.org

- Jubilee! in Asheville, North Carolina. For subscriptions to Howard Hanger's *Visions,* contact 828-252-5335.

- First Presbyterian Church, Orlando, Florida. wwwfpco.org. For Howard Edington's ministry, see his book *Downtown Church: The Heart of the City* (Nashville: Abingdon Press, 1996).

- Windsor Village United Methodist Church, Houston, Texas. Kirbyjon Caldwell's newest book is entitled *The Gospel of Good Success: A Road Map to Spiritual, Emotional and Financial Success* (New York: Simon & Schuster, 1999).

- First Baptist Church of Lincoln Gardens, New Jersey. www.fbclg.com. Buster Soares is now Secretary of State of New Jersey, but continues to preach on Sunday.

- NorthWood, a Church for the Communities, Keller, Texas, the base of Bob Roberts's ministry and global missionary outreach. For more see www.northwoodchurch.org.

- Community Presbyterian Church, Celebration, Florida. Patrick Wrisley's cyberspace "Refrigerator Door" contains some of my favorite reading. For more see www.celebration.church@celebration.sl.us.

- First Church of the Nazarene, Portland, Oregon. Jeff Crosno is pastor. jtcrosno@worldstar.com

- Dawson Memorial Baptist Church, Birmingham, Alabama, where Gary Fenton is pastor. www.dawsonmemorial.org

For edge-churches that have placed both feet in the postmodern waters, see most especially:

- Hillvue Heights Church, Bowling Green, Kentucky, where Steve Ayers is lead pastor. For more information about this fast-paced, multi-dimensional, multiethnic, interactive church that has grown from 30 to 5000 in seven years, see their Web site www.hillvue.com.

- Ginghamsburg Church in Tipp City, Ohio. See Michael Slaughter's books *Living on the Edge* (Nashville: Abingdon Press, 1998) and *Spiritual Entrepreneurs* (Nashville: Abingdon Press, 1996). Minister of media Len Wilson has a book forthcoming from Abingdon Press in 1999.

- Vineyard Community Church in Cincinnati. See Steve Sjogren, *Servant Warfare* (Ann Arbor, MI: Servant, 1996) and *Conspiracy of Kindness* (Ann Arbor, MI: Vine Books, 1993).

- Mosaic Church in Los Angeles, with lead pastor Erwin McManus. For more information on one of the largest multicultural churches in North America, see http://member.aol.com/lamosaic/home.htm.

- Crystal Evangelical Free Church in Minneapolis, where Steve Goold is pioneering creative forms of multigenerational worship.

- Harambee Center, Pasdadena, California, a multicultural community headed up by the biracial team of Rudy Carrasco and Derek Perkins. For articles by them and about them, see the church home page at www.harambee.org.

- Calvary Church, Costa Mesa, California. For more on Tim Celek's ministry, see Tim Celek and Dieter Zander, *Inside the Soul of a New Generation* (Grand Rapids: Zondervan, 1996). tcelek@sayyes.org

- MarsHill Fellowship, Seattle, Washington, with pastor Mark Driscoll. See the video *Postmodern Pilgrims,* produced by a member of this church. (VHS copies can be ordered by calling 206-570-9467 or visiting www.marshillchurch.org.)

- Faith Lutheran Church, Mundelein, Illinois, with pastor Bruce Cole. Web site is www.members@aol.com/faithweb.

- Pathways Church on the Denver University campus, Denver, Colorado. Sally Morgenthaler, author of *Worship Evangelism* (Grand Rapids: Zondervan, 1995), is working with this church.

- University Baptist Church, Waco, Texas. For Chris Seay's ministry, see "Pastor X" in *Christianity Today* (11 November 1996): 40–43, or listen to the church's two fantastic worship CDs, *Pour Over Me* (1996) and *Robbie Seay* (1998).

- Parallel Universe, a ministry of Cityside Baptist Church, Penrose, Auckland, New Zealand. Mark Pierson is pastor. See Mike Riddell's altspirit@metro.m3: *Alternative Spirituality for the Third Millennium* (Oxford: Lion Publishing, 1997), or e-mail cityside@xtra.co.nz.

- Warehouse, a ministry of St. Michael's Church, York, England. Worship services are called "Visions" and are held at St. Cuthbert's Church Sunday evenings at 8 o'clock. For a narrative of what Warehouse is, download www.abbess.demon.co.uk/paradox/docs/fag.txt or contact Sue Wallace at sue@abbess.demon.co.uk.

- Hills Christian Life Center in Sydney's northwest corridor, better known as Hillsongs, in Australia. The story of Hillsongs can be gleaned from senior pastor Brian Houston's *Get a Life,* worship pastor Darlene Zschech's *Worship,* and composer/keyboardist Russell Fragar's *The Art of the Chart,* all of which can be ordered from www.hillsclc.org. Their latest live recording is available on CD as *Touching Heaven Changing Earth.*

- Bay Marin Community Church in San Rafael, California. Pastor Sam Williams is also on the faculty of Golden Gate Theological Seminary. www.baymarin.org

- All God's Children United Methodist Church in North Carolina. Pastor Laura Early has made this church a vestibule for the community, a place where, as she puts it, "the unchurched are churching the churched." For more about the church's ministry and a video about it's children's ministry, call 252-345-1077.

appendix 2

Selected Bibliography on
Church-based Urban Ministry

(Compiled by Carl E. Savage, Ph.D. candidate, Drew University)

Ammerman, Nancy, with Arthur E. Farnsley II et al. *Congregation and Community.* New Brunswick, NJ: Rutgers University Press, 1997.

Bakke, Ray. *A Theology as Big as the City.* Downers Grove, IL: InterVarsity Press, 1997.

_____. with Jim Hart. *The Urban Christian: Effective Ministry in Today's Urban World.* Downers Grove, IL: InterVarsity Press, 1987.

Bradbury, Nicholas. *City of God?: Pastoral Care in the Inner City.* London: SPCK, 1989.

Carle, Robert D., and Louis A. DeCarlo Jr. *Signs of Hope in the City: Ministries of Community Renewal.* Valley Forge, PA: Judson Press, 1997.

Christensen, Michael J. *City Streets City People.* Nashville: Abingdon, 1988.

Claerbaut, David. *Urban Ministry.* Grand Rapids: Zondervan, 1983.

Conn, Harvie M. *The American City and the Evangelical Church: An Historical Overview.* Grand Rapids: Baker Book House, 1994.

_____. *A Clarified Vision for Urban Mission: Dispelling the Urban Stereotypes.* Grand Rapids: Zondervan, 1987.

_____, ed. *Planting and Growing Urban Churches: From Dream to Reality.* Grand Rapids: Baker Book House, 1997.

Dudley, Carl S. *Basic Steps Toward Community Ministry.* Washington, DC: Alban Institute, 1991.

_____. *Energizing the Congregation: Images that Shape Your Church's Ministry.* Louisville: Westminster/John Knox Press, 1993.

_____. *Next Steps in Community Ministry: Hands-on Leadership.* Washington, DC: Alban Institute, 1996.

Edington, Howard. *Downtown Church: The Heart of the City.* Nashville: Abingdon Press, 1996.

Elliot, John Hall. *A Home for the Homeless: A Sociological Exegesis of I Peter, Its Situation and Strategy.* Philadelphia: Fortress Press, 1981.

Ellison, Craig W., and Edward S. Maynard. *Healing for the City: Counseling for the Urban Setting.* Grand Rapids: Zondervan, 1992.

Elliston, Edgar J., and J. Timothy Kauffman, *Developing Leaders for Urban Ministries.* New York: Peter Lang, 1993.

Fischer, Claude S. *The Urban Experience*. New York: Harcourt, Brace, & Jovanovich, 1984.

Gager, John G. *Kingdom and Community: The Social World of Early Christianity*. Englewood, NJ: Prentice Hall, 1975.

Goings, Kenneth W., and Raymond A. Mohl, eds. *The New African American Urban History*. Thousand Oaks, CA: Sage Publications, 1996.

Green, Clifford J., ed. *Churches, Cities, and Human Community: Urban Ministry in the United States, 1945–1985*. Grand Rapids: Wm. B. Eerdmans, 1996.

Greenway, Roger S. *Cities: Mission's New Frontier*. Grand Rapids: Baker Book House, 1989.

_____, ed. *Discipling the City: A Comprehensive Approach to Urban Mission*. Grand Rapids: Baker Book House, 1992.

Harris, Forrest E. *Ministry for Social Crisis: Theology and Praxis in the Black Church Tradition*. Macon, GA: Mercer University Press, 1993.

Hartley, Loyde H. *Cities and Churches: An International Bibliography*. Metuchen, NJ: ATLA and Scarecrow Press, 1992.

Holmes, Urban T. III. *The Future Shape of Ministry: A Theological Projection*. New York: Seabury Press, 1971.

Jacobs, Allen R. *Looking at Cities*. Cambridge, MA: Harvard University Press, 1985.

Kretzmann, John P., and John L. McKnight. *Building Communities from Inside Out: A Path Towards Finding and Mobilizing a Community's Assets*. Evanston, IL: Northwestern University Press, 1993.

Linthicum, Robert. C. *City of God, City of Satan: A Biblical Theology of the Urban Church*. Grand Rapids: Zondervan, 1991.

Lupton, Robert D. *Return Flight: Community Development Through Reneighboring Our Cities*. Atlanta: FCS Urban Ministries, 1993.

_____. *Theirs Is The Kingdom: Celebrating the Gospel in Urban America*. San Francisco: Harper & Row, 1989.

McGreevey, John T. *Parish Boundaries: The Catholic Encounter with Race in the Twentieth-Century Urban North*. Chicago: University of Chicago Press, 1996.

McKnight, John. *The Careless Society: Community and its Counterfeits* New York: Basic Books, 1995.

McNamee, John P. *Endurance: The Rhythm of Faith*. Kansas City, MO: Sheed & Ward, 1996.

Meeks, Wayne. *The First Urban Christians*. New Haven, CT: Yale University, 1983.

Meyers, Eleanor Scott, ed. *Envisioning the New City: A Reader on Urban Ministry*. Louisville: Westminster/John Knox Press, 1992.

Miller, Kenneth R., and Mary Elizabeth Wilson. *The Church That Cares: Identifying and Responding to Needs in Your Community*. Valley Forge, PA: Judson Press, 1985.

Neyrey, Jerome H., ed. *The Social World of Luke–Acts: Models for Interpretation*. Peabody, MA: Hendrickson Publishers, 1991.

Niebuhr, H. Richard. *Christ and Culture.* New York: Harper & Row, 1951.

Ortiz, Manuel. *One New People: Models for Developing a Multiethnic Church.* Downers Grove, IL: InterVarsity Press, 1996.

Overman, J. Andrew. *Church and Community in Crisis: The Gospel According to Matthew.* Valley Forge, PA: Trinity Press International, 1996.

Pasquariello, Ronald D., Donald W. Shriver Jr., and Alan Geyer. *Redeeming the City: Theology, Politics, and Urban Policy.* New York: Pilgrim Press, 1982.

Perkins, John M. *Beyond Charity: The Call to Christian Community Development.* Grand Rapids: Baker Book House, 1993.

_____. *Restoring At-Risk Communities: Doing It Together and Doing It Right.* Grand Rapids: Baker Book House, 1995.

Pierce, Gregory F. *Activism That Makes Sense: Congregations and Community Organizing.* New York: Paulist Press, 1984.

Recinos, Harold J., ed. *Jesus Weeps: Global Encounters on Our Doorstep.* Nashville: Abingdon Press, 1992.

Reed, Gregory I. *Economic Empowerment Through the Church.* Grand Rapids: Zondervan, 1994.

Ronsvall, John, and Sylvia Ronsvall. *The Poor Have Faces.* Grand Rapids: Baker Book House, 1992.

Roseman, Curtis C., Hans Dieter Laux, and Günter Thieme, eds. *EthniCity: Geographic Perspectives on Ethnic Change in Modern Cities.* Lanham, MD: Rowman & Littlefield, 1996.

Sample, Tex. *Hard Living People & Mainstream Christians.* Nashville: Abingdon Press, 1993.

Sassen, Saskia. *The Global City: New York, London, Tokyo.* Princeton, NJ: Princeton University Press, 1991.

Schaller, Lyle E. *Center City Churches: The New Urban Frontier.* Nashville: Abingdon Press, 1993.

_____. *The Seven-Day-a-Week Church.* Nashville: Abingdon Press, 1992.

Schottroff, Luise. *Jesus and the Hope of the Poor.* Maryknoll, NY: Orbis Books, 1986.

Sedgwick, P. H., ed. *God in the City: Essays and Reflections from the Archbishop's Urban Theology Group.* London: Mowbray, 1995.

Sherman, Amy. *Restorers of Hope: Reaching the Poor in Your Community.* New York: Crossway Books, 1997.

Short, John Rennie. *The Urban Order: An Introduction to Cities, Culture and Powers.* Cambridge: Blackwell, 1996.

Smith, Michael Peter, and Joe R. Feagin, eds., *The Bubbling Cauldron: Race, Ethnicity, and the Urban Crisis.* Minneapolis: University of Minnesota Press, 1995.

Stark, Rodney. *The Rise of Christianity: A Sociologist Reconsiders History.* Princeton, NJ: Princeton University Press, 1996.

Stewart, Carlyle Fielding. *African American Church Growth: 12 Principles of Prophetic Ministry.* Nashville: Abingdon Press, 1994.

_____. *Street Corner Theology.* Nashville: J. C. Winston, 1996.

Stumme, Wayne. *The Experience of Hope: Mission and Ministry in Changing Urban Communities.* Minneapolis: Augsburg, 1991.

Taylor, Clarence. *The Black Churches of Brooklyn.* New York: Columbia University Press, 1994.

Teaford, John C. *The Rough Road to Renaissance: Urban Revitalization in America, 1940–1985.* Baltimore: Johns Hopkins University Press, 1990.

Tonna, Benjamin. *A Gospel for the Cities: A Socio-Theology of Urban Ministry.* Maryknoll, NY: Orbis Books, 1985.

Van Engen, Charles, and Jude Tiersma, eds., *God So Loves the City: Seeking a Theology for Urban Mission.* Monrovia, CA: MARC, 1994.

Villafañe, Eldin. *Seek the Peace of the City: Reflections on Urban Ministry.* Grand Rapids: Wm. B. Eerdmans, 1995.

Washington, Preston Robert. *God's Transforming Spirit: Black Church Renewal.* Valley Forge, PA: Judson Press, 1989.

Webber, George W. *Today's Church: A Community of Exiles and Pilgrims.* Nashville: Abingdon Press, 1979.

West, Cornel. *Race Matters.* Boston: Beacon Press, 1993.